Collaboration with Justice in the Netherlands, Germany, Italy and Canada

Collaboration with Justice in the Netherlands, Germany, Italy and Canada

A Comparative Study on the Provision of Undertakings to Offenders Who Are Willing to Give Evidence in the Prosecution of Others

J.H. Crijns, M.J. Dubelaar and K.M. Pitcher

eleven

international publishing

Published, sold and distributed by Eleven International Publishing
P.O. Box 85576
2508 CG The Hague
The Netherlands
Tel.: +31 70 33 070 33
Fax: +31 70 33 070 30
e-mail: sales@elevenpub.nl
www.elevenpub.com

Sold and distributed in USA and Canada
International Specialized Book Services
920 NE 58th Avenue, Suite 300
Portland, OR 97213-3786, USA
Tel.: 1-800-944-6190 (toll-free)
Fax: +1 503 280-8832
orders@isbs.com
www.isbs.com

Eleven International Publishing is an imprint of Boom uitgevers Den Haag.

ISBN 978-94-6236-867-5
ISBN 978-94-6274-912-2 (E-book)

© 2018 J.H. Crijns, M.J. Dubelaar and K.M. Pitcher | Eleven International Publishing
Afbeelding omslag: Loïs Boomsma, "Muurschildering" olieverf over acryl/doek, 100×120 cm.

Printed in the Netherlands

TABLE OF CONTENTS

PREFACE

This is a comparative law study on the provision of undertakings to offenders who are willing to give evidence in the prosecution of others, conducted by staff members of the Institute of Criminal Law and Criminology of Leiden University and commissioned by the Research and Documentation Centre of the Dutch Ministry of Justice and Security. It was carried out in cooperation with a number of external partners. In this regard we thank Professor M. Lindemann and Dr. D.A.G. van Toor (authors of the German country report); Dr. M.L. Ferioli and Professor M. Caianiello (authors of the Italian country report) and Dr. N. Kovalev (author of the Canadian country report).

For this study interviews were conducted with various practitioners within the Public Prosecution Service, the judiciary, the police and the criminal defence bar. We thank all of the interviewees for their time, hospitality and frankness in answering the questions put to them. In particular we thank the secretary of the Internal Review Committee on the use of special investigative measures of the Public Prosecution Service (*Centrale Toetsingscommissie*) who at our request conducted further research into the use of the Dutch instrument of undertakings to witnesses, on the basis of the Committee's archives.

We also wish to thank the focus group members for sharing their thoughts on the topic. On behalf of our external partners also we wish to thank all those who participated in the empirical research in Germany, Italy and Canada.

We also express gratitude to the members of the advisory committee for their valuable remarks at the various committee meetings and for putting us into contact with key figures within the organisations mentioned above. The committee was composed as follows: prof. mr. G.P.M.F. Mols (Chair of the committee, Maastricht University), mr. drs. J. Dobbelaar (Ministry of Justice and Security, Department of Organised Crime) and mr. H.L.M. Obispo – van Rooijen (Ministry of Justice and Security, Legal Administrative and Operational Affairs), mr. A.M. van Hoorn (Bureau for Criminal Law Studies of the Netherlands Public Prosecution Service), mr. dr. S. Brinkhoff (Radboud University Nijmegen), prof. dr. E. Giebels (University of Twente), mr. dr. J.M.W. Lindeman (Utrecht University) and dr. F.W. Beijaard (Research and Documentation Centre, Ministry of Justice and Security).

Finally, we thank our former student assistants Kiki Twisk and Linda Harmsen, who assisted us with the desk research, and Ybo Buruma jr. who assisted us with the interviews. His critical questions were much appreciated.

Jan Crijns, Marieke Dubelaar, Kelly Pitcher
December 2017

1 INTRODUCTION

J.H. Crijns, M.J. Dubelaar & K.M. Pitcher

1.1 BACKGROUND, PURPOSE AND RESEARCH QUESTIONS

One of the more far-reaching investigative tools in criminal cases is the instrument of collaboration with justice, the measure by which undertakings are made to otherwise unwilling 'offender witnesses', i.e. witnesses who themselves are suspected or who have been found guilty of committing a criminal offence, in order to persuade them to cooperate with the authorities, by giving (incriminating) evidence in the prosecution of others.[1] While the instrument is generally viewed as a useful tool for penetrating the higher echelons of a criminal organization, it is not uncontroversial, entailing as it does the promise of 'benefits' to persons who themselves are suspected of, or who have been found guilty of, committing a criminal offence, thereby posing a risk to the reliability of the testimony as well as to the integrity of the proceedings and the criminal justice system more generally. This study aims to gain insight into the legal avenues available for making undertakings to witnesses in exchange for their evidence in several countries – the Netherlands, Germany, Italy and Canada[2] –, ultimately with a view to drawing lessons from the comparative exercise for the Netherlands in particular.

The Netherlands has had a statutory provision since 2006 on collaboration with justice.[3] However, since its introduction into the Code of Criminal Procedure, it has been applied in only a handful of cases, while one of those cases in particular – *Passage* – has raised important and sometimes difficult questions concerning the nature and applicability of the statutory provision. In July 2013 – six months after passing judgment in the first instance in the *Passage* case[4] – the then (Dutch) Minister of Security and Justice[5] sent a letter to the Lower House of Parliament[6] in which he indicated that in

---

1 More is said about the term 'collaboration with justice' and the corresponding term 'collaborator of justice' below and in the following chapter, in further defining the subject of the research.
2 More is said about the selection of the countries in § 1.4.
3 Undertakings to Witnesses in Criminal Cases Act of 12 May 2005, Bulletin of Acts and Decrees 2005, 254 and the Act of 12 May 2005 on amending the Code of Criminal Procedure in connection with failing to make a witness statement after making undertakings to that effect, Bulletin of Acts and Decrees 2005 255.
4 See Amsterdam District Court 29 January 2013, ECLI:NL:RBAMS:2013:BZ0392. In June 2017, the judgment on appeal was delivered (see Amsterdam Court of Appeal 29 June 2017, ECLI:NL: GHAMS:2017:2496). See for an in-depth examination of the two judgments Chapter 3.
5 As the title was then; it is now the Minister (and Ministry) of Justice and Security.
6 Letter from the Minister of Security and Justice dated 5 July 2013 about the civilian in criminal investigations, Parliamentary Papers II 2012/13, 29911 no. 83, p. 7.

the context of effectively combatting organized crime, he considered it necessary 'to widen the scope for working with members of the civilian population who themselves are – or have been – active in groups which are subject to investigation, or who are in some way closely related to members of such groups'. The statutory framework which currently applies to the instrument of collaboration with justice was felt to be too restrictive, in the minister's view. For these reasons he announced that a bill would be prepared 'that provides for a widening of the Public Prosecution Service's [...] room to negotiate in order, in exceptional situations, to be able to make greater undertakings than are now possible.' As an example the minister referred to undertakings to reduce sentences by *more* than half, i.e. more than may currently be granted, without this amounting to an undertaking of complete immunity from prosecution, or providing financial compensation, which is currently forbidden. The minister also indicated that he wanted to make the instrument of collaboration with justice available for more offences than is currently possible under the statutory provisions, and for economic and financial crime and corruption, in particular. As part of the current legislative process for modernising the Dutch Code of Criminal Procedure,[7] this topic is once again up for consideration by the Dutch legislator. In drawing lessons from the comparative exercise for the Netherlands, then, the more specific aim of this study is to provide input for the purpose of the determination of whether or not to introduce a new statutory provision on collaboration with justice or to refine the existing one.

In examining each of the four countries, it will be considered how the instrument has been legally framed, along with how it is applied in practice, and what kinds of problems and public debate that has engendered. Accordingly, this study is not only concerned with 'the law in the books', but also 'the law in action',[8] and this is reflected in the research questions (as well as the more general aim of the study, as set out above). Thus, the main questions to be answered in this study are as follows.

a. How is the instrument of collaboration with justice (hereafter: 'the instrument') regulated in each of the countries under examination?
b. How is the instrument applied in practice in each of the countries under examination, and what are the experiences and results achieved in this regard?
c. How does the relevant law and practice in Germany, Italy and Canada compare to that in the Netherlands?

The above list can be subdivided into the following research questions, which fall into three main categories, reflecting the aforementioned 'law and practice' approach.

---

7   See for more details the website of the government: https://www.government.nl/topics/modernisation-code-of-criminalprocedure.
8   More is said about the comparative law and 'law and practice' approach in § 1.3.

Legal Framework

1. What types of undertakings are provided for?
2. In respect of which offences is it possible to use the instrument?
3. What is the legal basis for (using) the instrument?
4. How did the rules on collaboration with justice come about?
5. Who holds authority to make use of the instrument and where does the responsibility lie in this regard?
6. How does the instrument relate to other measures whereby private individuals provide information for the purposes of criminal investigation and/or prosecution?
7. How does the instrument relate to the phenomenon of witness protection?

Practice

8. What types of undertaking are used in practice?
9. How often and on the basis of which considerations is the instrument used or not used?
10. What have the positive and negative experiences been in practice with the instrument and the legal framework in this regard?
11. What results have been achieved by use of the instrument in individual cases?
12. Which factors contribute to the successful use of the instrument and which form obstacles in this regard?
13. In general, do the rules on collaboration with justice achieve their objective?

Scrutiny, Transparency and Debate

14. To what extent is the use of the instrument subject to scrutiny by a judicial or other authority?
15. In how far is the instrument itself and the use thereof in individual cases publicly transparent?
16. To what extent is there debate or discussion regarding the use of the instrument? On which aspects of the instrument is the debate focused?
17. In how far and in what regard has scrutiny, transparency and debate led to changes in the regulation of the instrument?

Conclusion

18. In which respects do the law and practice in Germany, Italy and Canada correspond to that in the Netherlands, and in which respects do they differ?

19. Which lessons can be drawn from the comparative exercise for the Dutch regulation of, and practice with respect to, the instrument?

More is said about the structure of the report below, but for now it may be noted that sub-questions 1 to 17 form the basis for each of the country reports, as set out in Chapters 3 to 6, while sub-questions 18 and 19 form the basis for Chapters 7 and 8, respectively.

1.2   SCOPE

As stated above, this study is concerned with the instrument of collaboration with justice, i.e. of providing undertakings to individuals who themselves are suspected or who have been found guilty of committing a criminal offence, in exchange for their (incriminating) evidence in the prosecution of others.[9] This instrument should be distinguished from *other* instruments whereby private individuals provide information for the purposes of criminal investigation and prosecution, examples of which are the informer and the infiltrator. While this study is not concerned with the latter instruments as such, given their close relationship with the instrument under consideration and, correspondingly, the potential for 'overlap' in practice, they are considered in this study, if only in order to further delineate the instrument of collaboration with justice and/or problematize its definition. More is said about the relationship between the instrument of collaboration with justice and the other instruments referred to above in Chapter 2, in further defining the subject of the research.

Nor is this a study about the protective measures afforded to persons who cooperate with the authorities in the investigation and/or prosecution of others as such, an issue that is clearly related to the instrument under consideration. Nevertheless, precisely due to this (close) relationship and the potentially problematic nature thereof (about which more will be said in the country report for the Netherlands in particular, as well as in the comparative analysis), the issue of witness protection cannot be excluded from this study.

Also important to note here is that while this study adopts a 'law and practice' approach to the topic under consideration, and in it, consideration is given to whether or not the rules on collaboration with justice achieve their objective(s), this study is not (nor is it meant to be) an evaluation of the legislation for any of the countries compared, in the sense of an evidence-based assessment made by the researchers themselves of how well the legislation in the different countries is achieving its objective(s). The answers to the aforementioned questions on frequency, results and success are based on desk research (into pre-existing sources in the different countries) and interviews only.[10]

---

9   This definition largely corresponds with the definition given by Janssen in his thesis on this subject, but has been slightly more broadly formulated for the purpose of the comparative law study. See Janssen 2013, p. 17.

10   More is said about the research methods in § 1.3.

1.3   RESEARCH METHODS

As stated above, this is a comparative law study in which the law *and* practice of several countries are examined and compared with one another. Before describing the more specific research methods adopted in order to implement this approach, it is worth saying something about the nature and importance of comparative law analysis, and of a 'law and practice' approach, more generally.

Comparative law has long been an important instrument for proposed amendments to the legislation; it provides examples which could be followed or rather which should not be followed, an overview of alternatives and heuristic arguments which can be used later by the legislature for developing a sound legislative bill.[11] More generally, it should be noted that comparative criminal procedure is a widely recognized metric or parameter in the Dutch scholarship,[12] as it is in many other countries. While states are not bound by the law and practice of another state as such and comparative analysis should not result in 'strong value judgements', it does provide a tool by which to establish whether certain rules and practices adopted in a given state 'make sense', in terms of cogency, coherence and consistency.[13] Correspondingly, the law and practice of another state may provide inspiration and guidance to the state in question, in the application of its own law.[14] In light of the purpose of the tool – establishing whether certain rules and practices 'make sense' – it is important, in embarking on a comparative exercise, to be mindful of the fundamental and idiosyncratic features of each of the jurisdictions under consideration, including legal tradition, and also of the stage of development of the law and practice in each jurisdiction at the time of comparison. In this regard it bears observing that what is problematic in one jurisdiction need not be problematic (to the same extent) in another; this may be due to the fundamental features of, or the state of development of the law and practice in, the jurisdiction(s) in question, and this warrants caution in seeking to draw lessons from the law and practice of other jurisdictions.

Regarding the 'law and practice' approach, it should be noted that, before amending legislation, it is useful to gain insight into potential problems and pitfalls in practice. Such problems may be due to lacunae, shortcomings or limitations in the existing statutory provisions, i.e. the law, but could equally well be related to other factors (such as available capacity, knowledge of the instrument among practitioners and the crime rate in the jurisdiction in question). Accordingly, in studying the practice and considering such questions as how the rules on collaboration with justice are applied in practice, how often the instrument on collaboration with justice is used, and also what factors contribute to the successful use of the instrument and what factors form obstacles in this regard, the

---

11 Nijboer 1994, p. 11.
12 Van Boom en Van Gestel 2015.
13 Vasiliev et al. 2013, p. 28.
14 Siems 2014, p. 3.

aim is to provide input for the purpose of the determination of whether or not to introduce a new statutory provision or amend the current one. In this regard it is especially useful to know how other jurisdictions deal (or have dealt) with certain problems and what is being done to achieve optimal results.

The approach outlined above was implemented in the form of a number of specific research methods, which are set out below.

1.3.1 Desk Research

To determine the legal framework and how it was arrived at, an analysis was carried out in the form of desk research of the relevant legislation and regulations, the literature on the topic and the policy documents and parliamentary documentation available for each of the countries included in the study. Case law research was also carried out to determine where there may be any problems in the statutory provisions and to what extent the jurisprudence further regulates the instrument of collaboration with justice. The case law research was also aimed at identifying any problems in practice with the use of the instrument in the countries compared. It was also attempted – insofar as possible – to gain insight into how often the instrument is used and what variations there may be in the undertakings given. A complication in this regard was that not all the relevant jurisprudence is published in all the countries concerned.

1.3.2 Interviews

For the purpose of this study interviews were also conducted in all the countries concerned. These interviews focused on: 1) determining the common methods in practice insofar as these are not clearly described in public or other documents; 2) providing insight into how often the instrument is used; 3) highlighting the problems encountered and successes achieved, and; 4) creating an inventory of the views held and perceived needs in the practice with regard to the use of the instrument. Semi-structured interviews were conducted with various practitioners in the field including public prosecutors, police officers, judges and defence lawyers. A questionnaire drawn up by the Dutch researchers was used for the interviews in all the countries compared, with some modifications tailored to the situation in that country. There was consultation between all the partners about the set up of the empirical study as well as the benefits and drawbacks of such an approach. It was attempted as far as possible in the method to take a uniform approach in terms of conducting the interviews and reporting on them. All the interviews were carried out by experienced researchers. The various country reports provide further details about how the study was carried out and the people spoken to for that purpose, although it may be noted here that in all countries, the interviews were conducted in the period between

September 2016 and March 2017. Also important to note here is that the empirical study in the Netherlands was the most comprehensive, because only a detailed and balanced picture of the situation in practice, along with the prevailing views and perceptions there, may provide the foundations on which the legislature can base its decisions, should it come to that.

1.3.3   Focus Group

For the Netherlands a focus group was also organized in which representatives of the various professional groups were brought together to reflect on the results of the study in the Netherlands and the countries compared. This offered an opportunity, on the one hand, to validate and probe more deeply into the perceptions surrounding the instrument of collaboration with justice in Dutch practice and, on the other hand, to examine how representatives of various professional groups view the legislation and the methods used in the countries compared. That focus group took place in March 2017.

1.4   SELECTION OF THE COUNTRIES AND PARTNERS

Given that the bill promised by the minister in 2013 aims to *widen* the scope for using the instrument of collaboration with justice, in selecting countries for the purpose of the comparative exercise, the logical solution was to consider countries where the possibility of making undertakings to witnesses appears at first glance to be greater than in the Netherlands. This is the case in all three of the countries selected.

In Germany, there is the option of imposing no sentence in certain cases, the instrument can be used for a wide range of offences and there are several '*Kronzeuge*' regulations specifically aimed at certain offences. In Canada the competence to make undertakings is not statutorily underpinned, but regulated by an internal guideline of the Public Prosecution Service, in which the availability of the instrument is not limited to certain offences and which provides for a broad range of undertakings, which, moreover, are not listed exhaustively. While in Italy the range of offences in respect of which benefits may be provided and the range of benefits on offer are comparable to those in the Netherlands, there, the process by which an individual becomes a collaborator of justice is less strictly regulated than in the Netherlands, and the instrument has been used more frequently.[15]

Regarding this selection criterion, it should be noted that only examining jurisdictions that adopt, or appear to adopt, a (more) liberal approach to the institution of collaboration with justice in exchange for their evidence may give rise to the perception

---

15 Admittedly, though, the primary reason for including Italy in the comparative exercise was its extensive experience with the instrument, as explained below.

that such an approach is the norm. It is beyond the scope of this research to provide an overview of which jurisdictions provide for an instrument of collaboration with justice (and, within this category, which provide for a (more) liberal approach thereto and which for a (more) restrictive approach) and which do not;[16] suffice to say that we accept that a (more) liberal approach to the institution is not necessarily the norm, and that we are well aware of the legal, moral and practical considerations that may lead a jurisdiction to reject the institution altogether, or to adopt a (more) restrictive approach thereto.[17] It is also worth emphasizing that although the research does not include jurisdictions that have rejected the institution of collaboration with justice altogether, or who have adopted, or purport to adopt, a (more) restrictive approach thereto, the comparison is nevertheless a worthwhile one, and one which is justified on the basis of the ability of the jurisdictions selected to 'teach us something'.[18] Indeed, the jurisdictions selected might tell us something about the successes and pitfalls of a (more) liberal approach to the institution, and about what is required by way of regulation in order to achieve successful results or to avoid pitfalls in this regard. In this regard it may be noted that the law and practice of such jurisdictions, and the theoretical accounts and critical discussions thereof in the scholarship, provide a rich source of reference material for the comparative exercise to be undertaken in Chapter 7.

The more liberal nature of the approach to the instrument of collaboration with justice was not the only criterion used to select jurisdictions for the purpose of the assessment of the Dutch law and practice in this regard. Thus, the decision to include Germany was also based on the similarities between the Dutch and German legal systems, the socio-economic context and (as far as is known) the nature and scale of crime, while Canada was also selected on the basis that it is comparable to the Netherlands in terms of the nature and scale of serious crime and policy. The decision to include Italy was also based on its extensive experience with the instrument of collaboration with justice, primarily in combatting the Mafia.

A further selection criterion relates to the character of Dutch criminal procedure. Although Dutch criminal procedural system is predominantly inquisitorial in nature (as apparent from, among other things, the emphasis that is placed on the pre-trial phase of criminal proceedings vis-à-vis the trial phase thereof, and the continued commitment to the notion of substantive truth-finding (*materiële waarheidsvinding*)), certain features thereof – for example, the ability of the accused to exercise certain procedural rights – are more reflective of the adversarial procedural model. In light of the character of Dutch criminal procedure, it would seem appropriate, in undertaking a comparative exercise for the purpose of drawing lessons for Dutch law and practice, to have reference to both

---

16 See for an overview of fifteen countries within the European Union Tak 2000, although this may be outdated in some respects.
17 See in this regard § 2.3 and § 2.4, where the benefits and risks of the instrument are set out.
18 See Oderkerk 2001, p. 313.

inquisitorial and adversarial procedural systems (bearing in mind, of course, that there is no such thing as a purely inquisitorial or a purely adversarial system, as Dutch criminal procedure itself demonstrates). With this in mind, Canada was selected on the basis that it is representative of the adversarial procedural model, while Germany and Italy were selected on the basis that they are representative of the inquisitorial procedural model.[19]

As to the individual country reports, the report for Germany was drawn up by Professor Michael Lindemann, professor of criminal law, criminal procedure and criminology at the University of Bielefeld and Dr. Dave van Toor, researcher at the same university. The Italian country report was written by Dr. Maria Laura Ferioli who, at the time of writing, was connected with the University of Bologna as a researcher and Professor Michele Caianiello who works at the same university as professor of criminal law and European and international criminal procedure. The country report for Canada was drawn up by Dr. Nikolai Kovalev, associate professor at Wilfrid Laurier University in Brantford, Ontario.

1.5   STRUCTURE OF THE REPORT

The report comprises an introduction, a more detailed consideration of the instrument of collaboration with justice as such (Chapter 2), four country reports (Chapters 3 to 6), a comparative law analysis (Chapter 7) and a concluding analysis in which the findings from the Dutch practice and the comparative law analysis are brought together, in an attempt to provide input for the determination of whether or not to introduce a new statutory provision or to refine the existing framework in the Netherlands (Chapter 8).

In the chapter following the introduction, the instrument of collaboration with justice – the subject of the research – is more fully defined and the benefits and risks associated with the use of undertakings are further examined. In addition, the question of when the instrument may be considered to be a success is addressed (also in light of such benefits and risks), and consideration is given to the requirements set by the European Court of Human Rights (ECtHR) in relation to this type of evidence. The country reports then cover the requirements that apply in the national legal systems.

The country reports are largely structured in the same way although the emphasis may be placed in different areas and the problems which arise in practice may differ. Each of the country reports first considers the development of the statutory provisions for the scheme. Various aspects of the scheme are then further examined, followed by an examination of the practice.

The individual country reports make no comparison with the Netherlands. In other words, the law and practice in the various countries were described entirely indepen-

---

19 However, as explained in the Italian country report in Chapter 5, Italian criminal procedure contains some distinctly adversarial elements.

dently, without reference to the Dutch situation. In Chapter 7, the law and practice of the various jurisdictions are compared, while in Chapter 8 lessons are drawn from the comparative exercise for the Netherlands in particular.

2 PRELIMINARY OBSERVATIONS

J.H. Crijns, M.J. Dubelaar & K.M. Pitcher

2.1 INTRODUCTION

Before describing the law and practice in the various countries included in this study, this chapter will first consider the instrument of undertakings to witnesses as such, to make clear what the use of this instrument essentially boils down to and to enable the reader to consider the law and practice set out in the various country reports against the backdrop of the benefits and risks generally associated with the instrument. First a definition of what is meant by the instrument in the context of this study will be provided, followed by a description of the purpose for which it may be used and the risks and objections associated with that use. The definition of the instrument as set out in this chapter was also the starting point for the comparative law analysis, in the sense that it was used in the various comparison countries to further delineate the boundaries of the subject and scope of this study.[1] It was also decided to discuss the goals, risks and objections associated with the use of the instrument together in this chapter (rather than separately in each country report), given that to a large extent these are similar, on the understanding that in any particular system some arguments may be given more weight or dominate the debate more than in another, but that will be apparent from the individual country reports and the final comparative law analysis. This chapter will also look at the question of when the use of the instrument of undertakings to witnesses may be deemed a success and the viewpoints from which this question may be addressed. Finally, brief consideration is given to the matter of how use of the instrument stands in relation to the relevant jurisprudence of the ECtHR in terms of the right to a fair trial (Article 6 ECHR), bearing in mind that the focus of this study is on Dutch law and the role of the Dutch authorities in the use of this instrument.

2.2 THE SUBJECT OF THE RESEARCH FURTHER DEFINED

This research focuses on the instrument of providing undertakings to offenders who are willing to give evidence in the prosecution of others. Put differently, it is concerned with persons suspected of committing a criminal offence or who have been convicted of one,

---

1   The definition in § 2.2 was provided to the researchers in the various comparison countries in advance of the study.

who are willing to give evidence against another person, in exchange for certain benefits, such as sentence reduction.

In certain systems such persons are referred to as 'crown witnesses' (*kroongetuigen* or *Kronzeugen*). Although the information provided by such persons consists of testimonial evidence, we chose not to use the term 'witness' as the *key* term in this research. The first reason for this is that such persons are not 'regular' witnesses, in light of the undertaking provided by the authorities to such persons in exchange for their testimony (about which more will be said below). Accordingly, in employing the term 'witness', there will always be a need for some adjective or qualification in this regard, whereby it is not immediately clear what that should be. The term 'crown' witness is problematic from a comparative perspective, since in many systems, this term simply denotes a witness who is being called by the prosecution. The second reason for not employing the term 'witness' is that the persons we are focussing on may appear as co-accused in the same proceedings as the person against whom they are willing to give evidence, or may have been involved in the crimes they are testifying about in some way (although this need not be the case, as is the case in the Netherlands). As will be seen in Chapter 5, in Italy a distinction is drawn between persons who bear knowledge of the offence in question because they were somehow involved (as an accomplice) and provide testimony in that regard, and persons who bear knowledge of a criminal offence simply because they had the misfortune to be present at the time or be the victim; there, the term 'witness' is employed in relation to the latter category only. The third and final reason for not employing 'witness' as the key term is that in certain jurisdictions the term 'witness' implies that evidence is given at trial, and that only when evidence is given at trial, the information-provider will be considered to be a witness. Although in most countries 'collaborators of justice' – the persons under examination in this report, about which more is said below – will be required to testify at trial before their statement can be used as evidence, this may not always be the case. Therefore this – the giving of evidence *at trial* – is not a central feature of the definition of collaboration with justice in this report.

For comparative reasons and for the sake of convenience we prefer the term 'collaborators of justice'. In our view, the term 'collaborator of justice' captures the 'two-way' or bilateral nature of the relationship between such persons on the one hand and the authorities on the other: the person concerned undertakes to make a formal witness statement in the prosecution of another which can, if need be, tested at trial (in exchange for benefits), while the authorities undertake to provide certain benefits to that person (in exchange for the evidence). Put differently, there are two 'parties' involved, both of whom 'undertake' or promise to do something (subject to what is said below, at the end of this section). Nevertheless, it is the undertaking provided by the authorities that makes a person willing to give evidence in the prosecution of others more than 'merely' a witness, and which justifies this phenomenon's treatment as an autonomous subject of study; indeed, it is the undertaking by the authorities that makes such a person – the witness – a 'collaborator of justice'. Moreover, the term 'collaborator of justice', and,

by extension, the verb 'collaboration (with justice)', capture the witness's (ultimate) submission to the authorities. The terms 'collaborator of justice' and (correspondingly) 'collaboration (with justice)', then, are convenient terms in the context of the current
research, and, accordingly, will be employed throughout (alongside the term 'providing
undertakings', which will be used to refer to that which the authorities undertake to do in
the context of the collaboration in particular). It bears observing here that in the Italian
criminal justice system, the term 'collaborator of justice' has a slightly different –
seemingly narrower – meaning (as will be explained below, in further defining the subject
of the research, as well as in the Italian country report itself). To avoid any confusion in
this regard, where it is the Italian measure that is being referred to, the Italian term –
collaborator di giustizia – will be employed.

The subject of the current study, then, is the collaborator of justice: a person suspected
of committing a criminal offence or who has been convicted of one, who is willing to
make a formal witness statement in the prosecution of another person (which can, if need
be, be tested at trial), in exchange for certain benefits. For the purpose of further defining
the subject of this study, this definition may be broken down into three elements (which
serves to further delineate the scope of the research). The first element concerns the
'capacity' of the person willing to make a formal witness statement (in the prosecution
of another person in exchange for benefits). This study is only concerned with persons
suspected of a criminal offence, or who have been convicted of one. For the purposes of
this research, the criminal offence in question (of which the person willing to make a
formal witness statement is suspected or of which he or she has been convicted) need not
be connected to the criminal offence of which the other person now being prosecuted is
suspected. The second element concerns the undertaking provided by the person seeking
benefits. That person must be willing to make a formal witness statement in the
prosecution of another person, which can, if need be, be tested at trial. It is this element
of the definition of the subject of this study that sets the collaborator of justice apart from
other information-providers, such as the civilian informer or infiltrator. The purpose of
the use of the latter category of information-provider is to obtain, on a confidential and/
or anonymous basis, 'lead' information, i.e. information to further the investigation,
rather than to obtain evidence for use at trial. The third element concerns the
undertaking provided by the authorities, i.e. the 'benefits' on offer. As stated, it is this
element that makes a person willing to make a formal witness statement in the
prosecution of others more than 'merely' a witness, and which justifies this phenomenon's treatment as an autonomous subject of study. As to what this may entail, for the
purposes of this research, 'benefits' is to be defined broadly, to encompass not only 'trial'
benefits, such as sentence reduction, but also – for instance – measures of a more protective nature, and for which a different authority may be responsible.

Finally, it bears emphasizing that to depict the relationship between the collaborator
of justice and the authorities as 'two-way' or bilateral in nature is not to suggest that that

relationship – the collaboration – involves negotiation. Put differently, while a feature of this relationship is that the two parties both undertake to do something, what is undertaken will not necessarily be the result of a process of negotiation.

2.3   Purposes and Benefits of the Measure

As implied by the foregoing, the essence of the instrument of collaboration with justice lies in the fact that it offers an opportunity to obtain for the investigation and for use as evidence witness statements which otherwise could not be obtained, or could only be obtained at great difficulty. While in most legal systems witnesses are in principle required to make a statement if they are called upon to do so, this only works if in a particular case the authorities are aware of the fact that the witness has useful information. Moreover, even where the authorities are indeed aware that such is the case, the obligation to make a statement cannot always simply be enforced, particularly in situations where the witness himself is also active in criminal circles. For example, there may be legal barriers, particularly in the various rights by which a witness may refuse to give evidence, the most important of which in this context is the right not to have to incriminate oneself. More objective reasons, for example, an acute fear of reprisals, may also stand in the way of being able to enforce the obligation upon the witness to make a statement.[2] In such cases – which mainly occur in the context of the investigation and prosecution of organised crime – the instrument of collaboration with justice may offer a solution, as a way of persuading the witness to make a statement by offering one or more undertakings (and where applicable to relinquish his right to refuse to give evidence).

At the same time the fact that a price must be paid for these statements in terms of consideration means that use of the instrument will only be appropriate in cases where the statement would meet a particular need, i.e. in cases where criminal offences would either not be cleared up or it would be difficult to obtain a conviction without these statements. This too means that the instrument of collaboration with justice is usually associated with cases of organised crime in which it is often difficult to obtain evidence against suspects who move in the upper echelons of criminal organisations. It is also said that special investigation techniques which go beyond systematic surveillance and telephone tapping are often inadequate (these days) in these types of cases, not least because professional criminal organisations often make use of advanced technology and counter strategies to protect themselves. If in such cases the authorities can find a person who themselves is a member of the criminal organisation and who, in exchange for certain benefits in his own criminal case, is willing to make a statement incriminating certain key figures within the same organisation that are reliable and can be used as evidence, the

---

2   See § 3.2.2.1 for further details of the relationship between the duty to testify and the instrument of undertakings to witnesses.

instrument of collaboration with justice can provide an effective means of combatting organised crime.

This does not mean however that the scope of the instrument has to remain limited to this; potentially it could also be used as a tool in the investigation and prosecution of other, less serious types of criminal offences. As the individual country reports show, the scope of application of the instrument in the different countries also ranges widely. Nevertheless, it appears that in most of the countries included in this study the instrument is mainly used in more serious criminal cases, not least because it is a far-reaching investigation method and it is generally assumed that its use should be in reasonable proportion to the purpose that it is intended to serve.

2.4   OBJECTIONS AND RISKS

As mentioned in the introduction to this report, while the instrument has its purposes (as set out above), there are also a number of objections and risks associated with it. Whereas the objections touch on the legitimacy of the instrument itself, the risks relate to the instrument's use, particularly its rash use, although it bears observing that these categories are interrelated and therefore can only be separated to a certain degree. These risks and objections will be briefly set out below without further discussion or evaluation here;[3] the various country reports give further consideration to these risks and objections, as well as the matter of the extent to which they have presented themselves in the jurisdiction concerned, and how they are perceived and addressed in those jurisdictions. In this regard it should be noted that these risks and objections were not considered to be so compelling in any of the countries concerned to abandon the introduction or use of the instrument.[4] No sweeping conclusions may be drawn from this fact however, given that the selection of the comparison countries included in this study was specifically based on jurisdictions which at first sight appeared to offer greater opportunities for the use of the instrument than currently exists in the Netherlands. The fact that none of the countries included in this study has halted the introduction and use of the instrument of collaboration with justice in view of the attendant risks and objections in itself says little about how these risks and objections are perceived in other jurisdictions.[5] It will also be apparent from the various country reports that – notwithstanding the decision to adopt the instrument – the risks associated with and objections to the use of the instrument

---

3   The following overview of risks and objections is based mainly on the academic literature on the instrument of collaboration with justice. For an overview of the risks and objections to the instrument based on the Dutch literature, see Crijns 2010, pp. 119-124. For the risks and objections to the instrument found in the international literature, see also Tak 1997, Menza 1999 and Fyfe & Sheptycki 2005, p. 29-32.

4   In this context see also § 1.4.

5   The Scandinavian countries in particular, appear to be relatively more reluctant about the instrument of collaboration with justice. See with regard to Denmark, Finland and Sweden Tak 2000, p. 106-107, p. 328-329 and p. 804, although this may be outdated in some respects.

outlined below do or have certainly played a role (at the time of its introduction) in the jurisdictions included in this study.

The objections to the instrument itself are fairly fundamental in nature. It is argued, for example, that as a result of making agreements with criminal or other witnesses the authorities are lowering themselves to the same level as those they aim to combat. In that sense the instrument of collaboration with justice is argued to put the integrity of the authorities directly at stake. In the literature reference is also made to the conflict with the proportionality principle and by extension, the equality principle, which could arise when – in the context of his own criminal case – a suspect receives a lighter sentence as a result of having made a statement while acting in the capacity of witness in someone else's case: does the accused then receive the sentence he deserves based on the seriousness of the criminal offence?[6] In this context reference is also made to the position of the victim of the crime which the witness himself is guilty of, when the victim then sees that a lower (or much lower) sentence is handed down than would normally be the case given the seriousness of the offence.

In the literature also reference is made to the main risks involved, which may be expected to become more acute as the instrument is used more widely. The most significant risk associated with the instrument of collaboration with justice – as will be clear from the legislative history, literature and jurisprudence in the various jurisdictions concerned and which also receives the most attention – relates to the issue of reliability; the undertakings which may be offered could have an adverse impact on the truthfulness of the statements made by the witness. This is because the witness has an interest in satisfying the authorities by making an incriminating statement in order to claim the undertakings offered to him. He may also have a certain interest in minimizing his own share in the criminal offences on which he is making a statement, in order to (or continue to) present himself as an attractive partner for the authorities.

It is also pointed out in the literature that by making undertakings to a witness the authorities risk becoming far too dependent on that witness, with all the attendant consequences in terms of being able to control the criminal proceedings. This objection was specifically highlighted in the Dutch context, partly owing to the events which took place during the *Passage* case which suffered serious delays in the first instance proceedings due to the uncooperative attitude of the witness to whom undertakings had been made.[7] In addition, reference is often made to the risks to the witness himself: he cannot expect any sympathy from the criminal circles against whom he will be testifying not only because he is collaborating with the authorities but also because he will generally be obtaining certain advantages for himself. As repeatedly came to the fore in this study, the use of the instrument of collaboration with justice therefore is almost always associated with the need to take protection measures for the witness, which – quite apart from the constant

---

6   See § 4.4, for example, in the German country report.
7   See § 3.5.5.2 for further details.

threat itself – can have a major impact on the wellbeing of the witness. On the other hand, by entering into an agreement with the witness the authorities are accepting a long-term responsibility for his safety, which requires maintaining a witness protection system that operates flawlessly. This creates a situation which demands a lot of both the witness and the authorities. Finally, in line with the foregoing, it has also been pointed out that the use of undertakings to witnesses could lead to turmoil in criminal circles which in turn could lead to a hardening of that world. To put it another way: there is concern that if it is made too attractive for those involved in criminal organisations to talk to the authorities then those organisations will do whatever it takes to prevent current and former members from talking to the authorities, through the use of lethal force if necessary. In that sense a system of undertakings to witnesses which is too generous could incite violence in the underworld.[8]

When the various legal frameworks concerning the instrument of undertakings to witnesses in the separate jurisdictions are looked at more closely, there are other risks and objections that can be identified in addition to those mentioned here. However these are more closely related to the way in which the instrument is regulated in a particular jurisdiction than the instrument itself and for that reason have not been discussed here. These and the specific risks and objections pertaining to a particular jurisdiction are discussed in the individual country reports.

2.5 SUCCESS IN THE USE OF THE INSTRUMENT

Although the purpose of the present study was not to evaluate the legal framework in place or the use of undertakings to witnesses in the jurisdictions included in this study by undertaking an independent investigation of the efficacy of the instrument and its associated regulations, the research questions posed did lead to a certain degree of reflection in each of the countries concerned on how successful the use of undertakings to witnesses has been.[9] In view of the purpose of this study – drawing lessons for the Netherlands from the way in which various other jurisdictions deal with undertakings to witnesses – it was only natural to consider whether and to what extent the legislation and the use of undertakings to witnesses works in practice in each of the various countries. The following section provides an overall reflection on the question of success, which is then further built upon in the various country reports, the comparative law analysis and the concluding observations.

Based on the idea that collaboration with justice can be viewed as an instrument which serves a specific purpose, i.e. helping to combat organised and other forms of crime,[10] when considering the success of the instrument and its underlying legal frame-

---

8 This objection was specifically raised by a number of respondents in the empirical study conducted in the Netherlands. See Chapter 3 for further details.
9 See § 1.1, research questions 11, 12 and 13.
10 For further details of this aim, see § 2.3. For a further examination of the question of whether and to what extent undertakings to witnesses can actually be considered to be an instrument, see § 7.2.

work the first logical step is to consider the extent to which the intended goal has actually been achieved or whether a significant contribution has been made towards achieving that goal. Has the use of undertakings to witnesses actually resulted in convictions of those involved in organised crime that would otherwise not have been achieved? And is it even possible to penetrate the upper echelons of criminal organisations with the aid of undertakings to witnesses? It will be clear that the use of undertakings to witnesses and the legal framework itself will more readily be deemed a success to the degree that these and other such questions can be answered in the affirmative.

At the same time in any consideration of the success of the instrument and the underlying legal framework, it is necessary to guard against simply reducing the question to whether or not it has achieved its goal(s), given that the price paid to achieve this also has to be taken into account. In this context, the risks and objections relating to the instrument of collaboration with justice identified in the foregoing will first be examined.[11] Although the aforementioned fundamental objections to the instrument are not shared by everyone (and were considered by the legislature or the prosecutorial authorities in any event to be too minor for the introduction or use of the scheme as a whole to be abandoned), the successful use of the instrument could to a certain extent be undermined if support for these objections were to widen. In other words: the more the legitimacy of the instrument is questioned, the less inclined people will be to view the instrument as successful – irrespective of its results. With regard to the risks associated with the instrument of collaboration with justice it will be clear that the more these risks become apparent and grow in seriousness in practice, the more they could undermine the success of the instrument. In particular when the use of undertakings leads to a witness making untruthful statements that (in some cases) could lead to wrongful convictions, this will be significantly detrimental to the success of instrument.

In addition, the investment made in terms of time, money and the human resources required to make the instrument operational also has to be taken into account in any evaluation of the success of the instrument of undertakings to witnesses. If these capacity investments are not in reasonable proportion to the results achieved, it is hardly possible to speak of the successful application of the instrument, especially where better results could have been achieved if this time, money and human resources had been put into other investigation methods.

Based on the foregoing the success of the instrument and its underlying legal framework could be defined as the degree to which the legislature and the prosecutorial authorities responsible are able to achieve the objectives of the instrument as fully as possible on the one hand, and to minimise the risks associated with and objections to the use of the instrument as far as possible, while the capacity invested is at least in reasonable proportion to the results achieved, on the other hand.

---

11 See § 2.4.

At the same time it should be noted that this does not entail a clear-cut benchmark by which to measure the degree of success of the instrument and the legal framework on which it is based in the jurisdictions included in this study (particularly given that in those jurisdictions generally no clear statements are or have been made by the legislature or the relevant authorities concerning the matter of when and under what circumstances the use of the instrument may be considered to be a success). Moreover – even if it were possible to turn this fairly general definition of success into a suitable benchmark – as it turned out the data necessary to answer this question is hardly, if at all, available in the countries included in this study. Generally there were no clear figures concerning the matter of how often the instrument is used in practice and what the results of this use were.[12] Insofar as it is possible to provide a rough overview of this in the following chapters, this was mainly based on the impressions of the respondents (insofar as these were substantiated). These complicating factors, in part at least, mean that nothing concrete can be said in the present study about the matter of whether the instrument of undertakings to witnesses or the underlying legal framework in the various jurisdictions may be described as successful or otherwise. Based on the available literature, jurisprudence and the empirical study, the main factors which may well contribute to or diminish the success of the instrument and the legal framework on which it is based are identified in the various country reports. These factors were then included in the comparative law analysis and the concluding observations thereafter.

Further – and as to some extent implied by the foregoing – it should be noted that the question of success can also be divided into the success of the instrument in individual cases, on the one hand, and the overall success of the legal framework on which the instrument is based, on the other. Although both of these matters are essentially interrelated, they do not overlap entirely. For example, the instrument may be successful in an individual criminal case because its use helped to clear up the case and the accused were convicted which would not otherwise have happened, while at the same time the legal framework underpinning the instrument is inadequate in certain respects. Conversely, a situation could arise in which the legal framework itself is adequate while in practice the instrument hardly ever achieves its goal (e.g. more because of the practical obstacles which stand in the way of its successful use). This also has to do with the fact that when examined more closely the legal framework regulating undertakings to witnesses has a wider remit than the instrument itself. While the instrument itself may be viewed as something which is primarily intended to help combat organised crime, the purpose of the legal framework is also to minimise the aforementioned risks and objections associated with the use of the instrument and to be able to select the right candidates for the application thereof. For example, if it were to be applied to witnesses who make untruthful statements, it could not be said that a success has been achieved if convictions

---

12 This was to a certain extent possible in the Netherlands. For further details, see § 3.5.2.

were nevertheless obtained on the basis of these statements. Nor can the legal framework be deemed successful if the integrity of the investigation is constantly questioned or the position of the witness is insufficiently safeguarded. For this reason also it should be borne in mind that the matter of the success of the legal framework in particular has been more broadly interpreted below than simply considering whether and to what extent convictions are being obtained with the aid of the framework.

Finally, it is self-evident that the term 'success' should not be confused with the term 'frequency', certainly in the context of comparative law. The fact that the instrument is clearly utilised on a much greater scale in one jurisdiction than another, provides no more than an initial indication of success. It should be noted in this context that the frequency with which the instrument is used will also be determined by the purpose and thus the scope of the legal framework on which it is based. As will be apparent from the country reports, there are significant differences between the countries included in this study. In some jurisdictions (Italy and the Netherlands) the instrument is reserved for combatting serious and organised crime, while in other jurisdictions (Germany and Canada) the instrument can be applied in considerably more cases. In addition it should be noted that the use of the instrument may be linked to a subsidiarity requirement in the sense that it may only be used when other special investigation techniques fall short. Therefore, the more conditions are included in the legal framework which limit the use of the instrument, the less frequently it will be applied. But this too should not be equated with a lack of success.

2.6   Relationship to Article 6 ECHR

As stated in Chapter 1, this is essentially a comparative law study, in the sense that several countries – the Netherlands, Germany, Italy and Canada – are compared with one another. With the focus of this study being on the Dutch law and practice with respect to the institution of collaboration with justice, in that the ultimate purpose of the comparative exercise is to draw lessons for the *Dutch* law and practice (in an attempt to determine whether modification of the Dutch rules could contribute to their success and to the resolution of problems encountered in practice), it would seem appropriate to briefly consider the case law of the European Court of Human Rights (hereafter 'the ECtHR') in this regard (although it bears emphasizing that an evaluation of the Dutch law and practice in light of the human rights law is beyond the scope of this research). In this regard it should be noted that Article 6 of the European Convention on Human Rights (hereafter 'the ECHR') has direct effect in the Dutch legal order.

According to the ECtHR, while the use at trial of statements made by collaborators of justice has the potential to negatively impact on the fairness of the proceedings (since, 'by their very nature, such statements are open to manipulation and may be made purely in order to obtain advantages or for personal revenge'[13]), on its own, such use will not suffice to render the proceedings unfair under Article 6 of the ECHR.[14] In determining whether the use of such statements has rendered the proceedings unfair, the ECtHR adopts a holistic approach (as it generally does in respect of complaints regarding the fairness of the use of evidence[15]), whereby the question is whether the proceedings *as a whole* were fair, which depends on the particular circumstances of the case.[16] In particular, the ECtHR has in cases involving the use of the instrument of collaboration with justice attached importance to whether the defence was provided with a fair and effective opportunity to challenge the statements made by the collaborator, the degree of scrutiny to which the statement was subjected at trial, and how the statement was used. Regarding the first factor, what matters is that the defence was provided enough information to be able to challenge the credibility of the collaborator and the reliability of the statement made.[17] Thus, the defence should be made aware of the identity of the collaborator,[18] but not necessarily of all parts of the agreement, provided this non-disclosure is counterbalanced by adversarial proceedings.[19] Regarding the second factor, what matters is that the trier of fact was (made) aware of the 'dangers, difficulties and pitfalls surrounding agreements with criminal witnesses', and exercised due caution in using the statements made by a collaborator[20] or otherwise was in a position to assess the risk that such use might

---

13 See e.g. ECtHR 27 January 2004, appl. no. 44484/98 (Lorse v. the Netherlands), p. 13; ECtHR 27 January 2004, appl. no. 54445/00 (Verhoek v. the Netherlands), p. 10; ECtHR 25 May 2004, appl. no. 994/03 (Cornelis v. the Netherlands), p. 15; ECtHR 2 June 2015, appl. no. 12512/07 (Shiman v. Romania), para. 33; and ECtHR 17 January 2017, appl. no. 43000/11 and 49380/11 (Habran and Dalem v. Belgium), para. 100.

14 See e.g. ECtHR 27 January 2004, appl. no. 44484/98 (Lorse v. the Netherlands), p. 13; ECtHR 27 January 2004, appl. no. 54445/00 (Verhoek v. the Netherlands), p. 10; ECtHR 25 May 2004, appl. no. 994/03 (Cornelis v. the Netherlands), p. 15; ECtHR 2 June 2015, appl. no. 12512/07 (Shiman v. Romania), para. 34; and ECtHR 17 January 2017, appl. no. 43000/11 and 49380/11 (Habran and Dalem v. Belgium), para. 102.

15 See in this regard ECtHR 12 July 1988, appl. no. 10862/84 (Schenk v. Switzerland), para. 46 and ECtHR 12 May 2000, appl. no. 35394/97 (Khan v. UK), para. 34.

16 See e.g. ECtHR 27 January 2004, appl. no. 44484/98 (Lorse v. the Netherlands), p. 12-14; and ECtHR 27 January 2004, appl. no. 54445/00 (Verhoek v. the Netherlands), p. 9-11.

17 See in this regard ECtHR 27 January 2004, appl. no. 44484/98 (Lorse v. the Netherlands), p. 14; ECtHR 27 January 2004, appl. no. 54445/00 (Verhoek v. the Netherlands), p. 11; ECtHR 25 May 2004, appl. no. 994/03 (Cornelis v. the Netherlands), p. 15; and ECtHR 17 January 2017, appl. no. 43000/11 and 49380/11 (Habran and Dalem v. Belgium), para. 113.

18 See ECtHR 27 January 2004, appl. no. 44484/98 (Lorse v. the Netherlands), p. 14; ECtHR 27 January 2004, appl. no. 54445/00 (Verhoek v. the Netherlands), p. 11; and ECtHR 17 January 2017, appl. no. 43000/11 and 49380/11 (Habran and Dalem v. Belgium), para. 104.

19 See ECtHR 17 January 2017, appl. no. 43000/11 and 49380/11 (Habran and Dalem v. Belgium), paras. 112-116. See however ECtHR 27 January 2004, appl. no. 44484/98 (Lorse v. the Netherlands), p. 14; ECtHR 27 January 2004, appl. no. 54445/00 (Verhoek v. the Netherlands), p. 11; ECtHR 25 May 2004, appl. no. 994/03 (Cornelis v. the Netherlands), p. 15.

20 See ECtHR 27 January 2004, appl. no. 44484/98 (Lorse v. the Netherlands), p. 14-15; ECtHR 27 January 2004, appl. no. 54445/00 (Verhoek v. the Netherlands), p. 11-12; ECtHR 25 May 2004, appl. no. 994/03 (Cornelis v. the Netherlands), p. 15.

pose risks to the fairness of the trial.[21] Regarding the third factor, the ECtHR has attached importance to the fact that the statement was not the sole or decisive evidence against the defendant,[22] and in later decisions to the fact that even if the statement was the main evidence, there were sufficient counterbalancing measures in place such that the statement could be said to be sufficiently reliable.[23]

Accordingly, while the ECtHR acknowledges the risks surrounding the use of statements made by persons in exchange for benefits,[24] in particular the (epistemic) danger of false statements, it is not opposed to the institution of collaboration with justice as such. In this regard it should be noted that, in a number of cases, the ECtHR has expressly acknowledged the importance of the instrument in combatting serious crime.[25]

2.7   Final Remarks

This chapter looked more closely in general terms at the main subject of this comparative law study by describing in more detail the instrument of collaboration with justice and its aims. The risks and objections associated with the use of this instrument were also discussed and the question of when the use of the instrument may be deemed a success was also considered, along with the perspectives which need to be taken into account when answering this question. This then paves the way for the country reports in which the law and practice on the instrument of collaboration with justice are described in the four countries included in this study. The country reports also build on this introductory chapter by looking more closely at the objectives of the instrument of collaboration with justice and the results that have been achieved with it, as well as how the attendant risks and objections are dealt with or minimised.

---

21 See ECtHR 17 January 2017, appl. no. 43000/11 and 49380/11 (Habran and Dalem v. Belgium), para. 115.

22 See e.g. ECtHR 27 January 2004, appl. no. 44484/98 (Lorse v. the Netherlands), p. 15; and ECtHR 25 May 2004, appl. no. 994/03 (Cornelis v. the Netherlands), p. 15-16.

23 See e.g. ECtHR 17 January 2017, appl. no. 43000/11 and 49380/11 (Habran and Dalem v. Belgium), para. 109-110.

24 For an overview of such risks, see § 2.4.

25 See e.g. ECtHR 25 May 2004, appl. no. 994/03 (Cornelis v. the Netherlands), p. 15; and ECtHR 2 June 2015, appl. no. 12512/07 (Shiman v. Romania), para. 33.

3 COLLABORATION WITH JUSTICE IN THE NETHERLANDS

J.H. Crijns, M.J. Dubelaar & K.M. Pitcher

3.1 INTRODUCTION

This chapter is concerned with the Dutch law and practice on collaboration with justice. The purpose of this chapter is therefore twofold: firstly, to provide a description of the legal framework for providing undertakings to witnesses (the basis of which is the Provision of Undertakings to Witnesses in Criminal Cases Act dating from 2005 and the Instructions on Undertakings to Witnesses in Criminal Cases which sets out this statutory framework in more detail); and secondly, based on findings obtained from empirical research, to provide insight into how often and in what way the legal framework is applied in practice, along with the positive and negative experiences of those directly involved and their views concerning possible changes to the existing framework.

In this chapter the focus will first be on defining the instrument of undertakings to witnesses (§ 3.2). What is meant by this under Dutch law and what is the relationship between this instrument and other more generally associated instruments for the purpose of furthering the investigation, such as the use of informants, civilian infiltrators (criminal or otherwise) and threatened witnesses? This section will also briefly touch upon the relationship between the instrument of undertakings to witnesses and the phenomenon of witness protection, which will be examined in more detail later on in this chapter.

The development of the present legal framework will be considered in § 3.3. As indicated, this is based on the Provision of Undertakings to Witnesses in Criminal Cases Act from 2005, which entered into forced on 1 April 2006, together with the associated Instructions on Undertakings to Witnesses in Criminal Cases which further sets out the statutory provision in more detail. However, the period prior to the entry into force of the present legal framework is also worth discussing, given that – as the following will show – the present statutory provision was to a large degree influenced by the experience with and views on the legal practice surrounding the provision of undertakings to witnesses prior to 2006. The long parliamentary history of the Provision of Undertakings to Witnesses in Criminal Cases Act as well as the jurisprudence of the Supreme Court of the Netherlands dating from the 1990s concerning this instrument also provide useful starting points for the elucidation of the present framework.

The present legal framework will then be discussed in § 3.4 in which, for the purpose of the comparative exercise to be undertaken in Chapter 7, the same structure will be adhered to as that used in the other country reports. Thereafter the questions are examined of who is responsible for the deployment of the instrument of undertakings to witnesses; for which criminal offences this instrument may be used; what undertakings may be made to the witness; the procedure to be followed concerning the provision of undertakings to witnesses as well as the external scrutiny of the use of this instrument; and – finally – how it is related to taking measures to protect the witness.

The second part of this chapter – mainly comprising § 3.5 – is devoted to the practice of and experience gained with providing undertakings to witnesses. This section is based on the empirical study that was carried out.[1] Here too, for the purposes of comparison, the same structure has been observed as in the other country reports. Thereafter the questions are examined of how often undertakings to witnesses are used in practice and the results that this achieves; how potential witnesses to whom undertakings are later made come into contact with the police or the Public Prosecution Service and what the process for entering into an agreement entails; how the internal and external scrutiny of any (provisional) agreement arrived at takes place and how the agreement is implemented; how this relates to protection of the witness in practice; and – finally – the consequences that the various judges then attach to the fact that a witness has made their statements in exchange for certain undertakings: how does this affect the use of these statements as evidence and how does this affect the sentencing of the witness in their own case?

§ 3.6 Thereafter sets out some findings with respect to the successes and difficulties with the present statutory provision, as revealed by the empirical study. This section also sets out the respondents' views concerning possible changes to the present legal framework and the need for such changes. Finally, in § 3.7, the most important findings to emerge from this chapter with respect to the law and practice on undertakings to witnesses are set out, and the question of the extent to which such law and practice may be considered successful is reflected upon.

3.2   Definition of Terms and Comparison with Other Information Providers

3.2.1   Definition of Terms and a First Reading

This study is concerned with undertakings made to persons who are accused of having committed an offence or who have already been convicted of such and who are willing to make a statement which may be used as evidence in the criminal proceedings of one or more persons in exchange for certain benefits such as a sentence reduction, and for that

---

1   For a description of the methodology of the empirical study, see § 3.5.1.

purpose enter into an agreement (formal or otherwise) with the Public Prosecution Service.[2] In this context, the Code of Criminal Procedure refers to undertakings to witnesses or witnesses to whom undertakings are made (cf. the headings of Divisions 4B and 4C of Title II of the Second Book). In the public and legal debate, the jurisprudence and the literature, the term 'crown witnesses' or 'witnesses with whom a deal has been made' is also sometimes used, but as a result of the heated debate in the 1990s surrounding this instrument (and its legitimacy), these terms have to some extent become charged or obtained a more specific meaning.[3] In this chapter, therefore, the statutory terminology has been observed by making use of the terms 'undertakings to witnesses' to designate the instrument itself, and 'witnesses to whom undertakings will or have been made' to designate those individuals with whom the Public Prosecution Service makes agreements about providing a witness statement in exchange for some consideration on the part of the Public Prosecution Service. As already indicated in chapter two, three elements are necessary before we can speak of a witness within the meaning of this study.

1. The capacity of the individual who is offering their knowledge, i.e. that of an accused or convicted person.
2. The type of information that the individual is offering; there must be willingness to make a statement (on a non-anonymous basis) which can be used as evidence in proceedings against another person (and therefore serves not simply as 'lead' information, i.e. information to further an investigation).
3. The statement is made in exchange for some consideration on the part of the authorities.

Based on these elements the instrument of making undertakings to witnesses implies that the witness – in addition to this capacity – also has another particular capacity, i.e. that of accused or convicted person (cf. again the headings of the Divisions 4B and 4C: 'Undertakings to witnesses who are also accused' and 'Undertakings to witnesses who have already been convicted'). It is precisely in this double capacity that the essence of the instrument lies: acting as a witness benefits the individual's other capacity, i.e. that of an accused or convicted person. This also means that the instrument of making undertakings to witnesses always involves two sets of criminal proceedings: 1) those in which the witness to whom undertakings are made is making statements which can be used for the criminal investigation into and/or as evidence against the accused in that criminal case; and 2) those in which the witness him or herself is being tried or has been convicted, in which context the

---

2   For a description of the subject of this research, see also § 2.2.
3   See § 3.3.2 for further details.

undertakings made by the Public Prosecution Service are usually implemented (e.g. a mitigated sentencing demand or a positive pardon recommendation).

The two sets of proceedings may be strongly connected, because the witness is or was a co-accused in the same proceedings as the person against whom he or she is making a statement, and/or because the witness was directly involved in the criminal offences he or she is testifying about, but this need not be the case. Although this will often be the case, strictly speaking, such a connection is not a requirement under the statutory provision on undertakings to witnesses.[4] It may be therefore that the offences for which the witness is being (or has been) prosecuted, are entirely separate from the offences on which he or she is making a statement as a witness. Therefore it is also not a requirement that the witness should in any way be involved in the offences on which s/he is making a statement. The witness to whom undertakings are made could, for example, also have gained knowledge of the crime in some other way (e.g. because while in detention s/he obtained information from another detainee about criminal offences committed by someone else).

3.2.2   *Compared with Other Information Providers*

In essence the witness to whom undertakings are made is an information provider for the purpose of establishing the truth in criminal cases. There are however many of these in the Code of Criminal Procedure and in practice. In particular, the question arises as to the relationship between the witness to whom undertakings are made on the one hand, and the 'ordinary' witness, the threatened witness, the protected witness, the informant and the criminal civilian infiltrator on the other hand, who could all be considered as individuals providing information for the purpose of establishing the truth. In what way does the witness to whom undertakings are made differ from such other information providers? As discussed above, this distinction lies not so much – or rather, not solely – in the fact that the witness to whom undertakings are made is (or was) a co-accused along with the other accused in whose case s/he is making statements and/or was personally involved in the criminal offences about which s/he is testifying. This may be so, but it does not have to be.

---

4   This can be derived *a contrario* from the wording of Section 226g CCP which does not require there to be such a connection. This question was also specifically raised during the parliamentary consideration of the Bill on undertakings to witnesses in criminal cases, but the minister considered that there was insufficient reason to stipulate the existence of a connection as a requirement in the statutory provision, e.g. in the sense that the witness is also a member of the criminal organisation on which s/he is making a statement. See also Parliamentary Papers II 1999/2000, 26 294, no. 6, p. 11-12 and Parliamentary Papers II 1999/2000, 26 294, no. 15, p. 6.

3.2.2.1   Compared with 'Ordinary' Witnesses

In principle, members of the public are required – if called upon to do so – to make a witness statement. The question which arises therefore is why some witnesses can only be enticed to do so by making undertakings to them. In this context the double capacity of the witness to whom undertakings are made is important: s/he is not only a witness, but also themselves accused of one or more criminal offences. This means that under certain circumstances s/he can also invoke their right to refuse to give evidence (*verschoningsrecht*) as referred to in Section 219 CCP and for that reason is not obliged to lend their cooperation in the form of making a statement. However this applies only where such persons would incriminate either themselves or their immediate relatives, which will generally be the case if the witness was also involved in the criminal offences on which s/he is making a statement in some way. In which event providing one or more undertakings to the witness may help to persuade him/her not to invoke their right to refuse to give evidence and to nevertheless make a statement. Although s/he may also incriminate him/herself by doing so, the idea is that s/he will receive compensation for this in their own criminal case.

As previously indicated, witnesses as defined in this study could also make statements about offences in which they had no part. In such cases there is no need to override the right to refuse to give evidence under Section 219 CCP by making undertakings, given that, strictly speaking, the obligation to make a witness statement still fully applies in such cases, with all the coercive measures that are available to further enforce this obligation. Nevertheless, in such cases there may also be legitimate reasons for not simply observing the obligation to make a statement, for example, because it would result in disproportionate prejudice for the witness, most particularly in the form of a serious threat to his or her own safety or that of family members. In these sorts of cases the provisions applicable to the anonymous threatened witness as meant in Section 226a CCP may well offer a solution, but the legal framework does not appear to exclude that in these sorts of cases[5] the witness could instead be persuaded to make a statement by providing undertakings to them within the meaning of Section 226g CCP, together with the implementation of protective measures pursuant to Section 226l CCP. This option however blurs the distinction with the ordinary witness making a statement in his/her own name who may or may not have an own criminal case or confiscation order outstanding. This is even more so given that protection measures for 'ordinary' witnesses may also be instituted under Section 226l CCP. This will be the case where an urgent need for it arises as a result of the witness's cooperation and government action in the same context (Article 3 Witness Protection Decree).[6] If the threat is serious

---

5   The legislation makes it impossible to apply both arrangements at the same time. Section 226j paragraph 2 CCP specifically states that witnesses to whom undertaking are made within the meaning of Section 226g CCP may not be questioned as a threatened witness within the meaning of Section 226a CCP. See § 3.2.2.2 for further details.

6   See the Witness Protection Decree of 21 December 2005. Bulletin of Acts and Decrees (*Stb.*) 2006 (last amended on 30 November 2012, Bulletin of Acts and Decrees 2012, 615 which entered into force on 1 January 2013).

enough, this could lead to inclusion in a witness protection programme. However, protection measures should not be seen as 'consideration' or an 'undertaking' given that these arise out of the government's duty to ensure the safety of witnesses.[7] The difference between an 'ordinary' witness and a witness to whom undertakings have been made therefore lies in the fact that the latter gets something (or something different) in return for making a statement which s/he would not otherwise be entitled to, for example, a sentence reduction, and agreements are made on this before the statement is made. An agreement with the authorities about witness protection is not something to which the witness would not otherwise be entitled. Formally, therefore, 'ordinary' witness statements are not made in exchange for consideration. Under certain circumstances, however, an 'ordinary' witness can claim a reward under the Ministerial Circular on Special Payments for Investigation Purposes.[8] This must have been offered beforehand and therefore is not something which the witness can stipulate or negotiate with the authorities.

3.2.2.2 Compared with the Anonymous Threatened Witness and the Protected Witness

The law differentiates between the witness to whom undertakings are made and the 'threatened witness' (*bedreigde getuige*) within the meaning of Section 226a CCP. The latter is a witness who makes an incriminating statement and whose identity is kept hidden from the accused in whose criminal case s/he makes a statement, for fear of reprisals by the accused or those acting on his/her behalf. For this purpose there is a special procedure by which the investigating judge can grant the witness the status of 'threatened witness' within the meaning of Section 136c CCP. For the sake of completeness it should be added that the provision of Section 226a ff. CCP is solely concerned with witnesses that the accused – about whom they will be making a statement – does not yet know about (in their specific capacity as witnesses, that is) and who can therefore be protected by offering complete anonymity.[9] Accordingly, anonymous threatened witnesses within the meaning of Section 226a CCP will not generally be placed in a witness protection programme, if, and as long as, the witnesses' identity remains successfully hidden.

The legal framework assumes that an accused to whom undertakings are made cannot also be a threatened witness within the meaning of Section 226a CCP, seeing that Section 226j paragraph 2 CCP explicitly states that the witness to whom undertakings are made cannot be heard as envisaged under Sections 226a ff. CCP.[10] Their identity must therefore

---

7   See § 3.4.5 for further details.
8   See § 3.2.2.3 for further details.
9   For an overview of the possibilities under the provision of Section 226a ff., see Van Hoorn 1996.
10   See Parliamentary Papers II 1998/99, 26 294, no.3, p. 28 for the rationales underlying this provision: "Because the trial judge must have the opportunity to question the witness, and the defence must also have the same opportunity, this rules out the procedure for the threatened witness. This is because the essence of this procedure is that the threatened witness no longer has to appear at the public trial and that his/her identity

be made known and they therefore make their statement in their own name.[11] Conversely, both the system and purpose of the law suggest that it is not permitted to make certain undertakings or offer benefits to witnesses who are interviewed as a threatened witness within the meaning of Section 226a ff. CCP in exchange for his/her statement, other than guaranteeing their anonymity.

Finally, for the sake of completeness it should be added that Dutch law also recognizes the figure of the protected witness (*afgeschermde getuige*) whose position is laid down in Section 226m ff. CCP. As a rule this will concern individuals working in the criminal intelligence and security services who are questioned for the purpose of verifying official reports sent by these services to the Public Prosecution Service. These people can be interviewed by the investigating judge using a special protection procedure 'if it may reasonably be assumed that this is necessary in the interests of State security' (Section 226m paragraph 1 CCP). Little or no use is made of this provision however[12] and in terms of its purpose there is little to connect it with the provisions for the anonymous threatened witness within the meaning of Section 226a CCP or the witness to whom undertakings are made, as referred to in Section 226g CCP.

3.2.2.3 Compared with the Informant

A distinction also needs to be made between witnesses to whom undertakings are made and 'informants'. Informants are persons who provide the police with covert information – sometimes at a danger to themselves or others – and who are included in a 'register of informants'[13] but who make no official witness statements in the above sense.[14] These informants are 'run' by the Criminal Intelligence Team (*Team Criminele Inlichtingen*; hereafter TCI) which as part of the police force gathers intelligence about serious offences. Every regional police unit as well as the National Unit has its own TCI.[15] There is no specific statutory basis for the use of informants but it is generally assumed that it is covered by the general mandate of the police force as laid down in Section 3 of the Police Act 2012. The identity of informants is protected by the TCIs. The personal details of

---

remains concealed from the defence." In this regard see also Parliamentary Papers I 2004/05, 26 294, and 28 017, C, p. 8.

11 The statutory provision does provide for the possibility of temporarily hiding from the accused the identity of the witness to whom undertakings have been made (cf. Section 226j paragraph 4 CCP).

12 See Bokhorst 2012.

13 Inclusion in the register takes place only with the consent of the public prosecutor responsible for the gathering and use of criminal intelligence by the police. See Brinkhoff 2014, p. 99.

14 For a (comparable) definition of the term 'informant' see also Section 12 paragraph 7 of the Police Data Act (Wpol) and Article 1 under j of the Ministerial Circular on Special Payments for Investigation Purposes.

15 In addition, the National Police Internal Investigations Department, the Royal Netherlands Military Constabulary and the four special investigative services each have their own TCI. See Brinkhoff 2014, p. 91 and Van der Bel, Van Hoorn and Pieters 2013, p. 182.

informants are known only within the TCI and for security reasons this information is not shared with others inside or outside the police force.[16]

The distinction between informants and witnesses to whom undertakings are made lies mainly in the purpose for which the information is requested or given. An informant provides the investigation with information which in principle will not be used as evidence but only to start and/or steer the criminal investigation in the right direction. By contrast, a witness to whom undertakings are made provides an official witness statement (in his/her own name) which can be used as evidence. A second distinction lies in the nature of the consideration. While numerous undertakings can be made to a witness, apart from financial compensation,[17] money is the principal reward for an informant. Under the Ministerial Circular on Special Payments for Investigation Purposes[18] an informant can claim financial compensation (referred to as tip-off money) in exchange for information provided. This will be the case if the information provided helped to clear up an offence, led to the arrest of a wanted suspect or person convicted of a serious crime, or to the tracing of goods of (almost) irreplaceable value.

Finally, an informant may not provide information regarding criminal offences in which s/he is personally involved. This is also laid down in Article 1 (under j) of the Ministerial Circular on Special Payments for Investigation Purposes, which defines an informant as 'a person who provides covert information to an investigating officer concerning criminal offences or serious violations of public order, which have been or are being committed or carried out by others, the provision of which results in a threat to this person or third parties'. Article 4 of this Circular also explicitly states that no tip-off money will be paid if it turns out 'that the person who provided the information may be deemed as a suspect with respect to the criminal offences on which he provided information'. By contrast, witnesses to whom undertakings are made may make statements about offences in which they themselves were involved (although that does not have to be the case).

3.2.2.4   Compared with the Criminal Civilian Infiltrator

Terms such as undertakings to witnesses, witnesses with whom a deal has been made (*dealgetuigen*) or crown witnesses (*kroongetuigen*) are often mentioned in the same breath as the instrument of the civilian infiltrator (criminal or otherwise), whose use is based on Sections 126w and 126x CCP. This in itself can be explained, given that both phenomena were expressly called into question for the first time during the Par-

---

16 For further details about TCI information, see Brinkhoff 2014, p. 91-138.

17 See the Instructions on Undertakings to Witnesses in Criminal Cases, Government Gazette (*Stcrt.*) 2012, 26860 (which entered into force on 1 January 2013), § 5. See § 3.4.3 for further details of what undertakings may be made to witnesses.

18 Ministerial Circular on Special Payments for Investigation Purposes dated 17 December 2014, Government Gazette 2014, 37536 (which entered into force on 1 January 2015).

liamentary Enquiry of the Van Traa Commission further to the IRT scandal[19] and that both entail a civilian being deployed on the basis of specific agreements with the Public Prosecution Service for the purpose of establishing the truth, on the understanding that this deployment should or could generate information that may be used as evidence. But that is where the similarities end. While the use of civilian infiltrators focuses on membership of a criminal organisation and its future activities for the purpose of gathering evidence in this way (through the reporting of findings in official police reports), the use of undertakings to witnesses is aimed at obtaining witness statements concerned with past events which can, if need be, tested at trial. Other than is the case with undertakings to witnesses, the identity of a civilian infiltrator is in principle not made known in court, even if s/he makes a court statement.[20] The most important distinction however concerns the issue of supervision. Criminal civilian infiltrators are actively deployed for the purpose of the criminal investigation to gather evidence (or additional evidence). This is done under the supervision of the Public Prosecution Service in which agreements are made with the infiltrator beforehand about his/her deployment. By contrast, the witness to whom undertakings are made 'does not take part in a criminal group *under the supervision* of the PPS and only makes a statement on matters about which he has information after the fact'.[21]

3.2.2.5   Flexibility in the Preliminary Phase

Based on the foregoing it will be clear that, in theoretical terms, the witness to whom undertakings are made or have been provided can easily be distinguished from other information providers in criminal proceedings. In practice, however, the picture may become more blurred, particularly during the early phase in which a person is identified by the police or Public Prosecution Service as a potential information provider but where it is not yet clear whether this person is actually willing to do that or can be made to do so and in what capacity s/he will then provide that information. In other words: it must first be established in what capacity this person could act before *deciding* how a person will be deployed for the purpose of establishing the truth, which depends not only on the legal criteria for the various capacities, but also the tactical and strategic considerations on the part of both the police and the Public Prosecution Service, as well as those of the potential information provider. As a result, it may well be easy to establish *afterwards* in what capacity a person has been operating in the criminal proceedings, but the status of this person *during* (in the early phase of) the criminal proceedings may still be vague. This will be examined in more detail in § 3.5.3 based on the findings from the empirical study.

---

19 See § 3.3.2 for further details.
20 For further information about the criminal civilian infiltrator see Pluimer 2015.
21 See the Letter from the Minister of Security and Justice dated 5 July 2013 about the civilian in criminal investigations, Parliamentary Papers II 2012/13, 29 911, no. 83, p. 7.

3.3   Development of the Legal Framework

The present legal framework for undertakings to witnesses in criminal cases has had a long and, in certain respects, tumultuous history. Given that this history has influenced the set up of the present framework and is still important for its interpretation, the legislative history of the present statutory provision will be considered in general terms below.[22]

3.3.1   *The 1983 Model Letter for Deals with Criminals*

The lawfulness and legitimacy of making undertakings to witnesses as such was only first discussed in the 1990s. Before then there was little or no debate in the jurisprudence or literature about the use of this instrument, insofar it was used. Nevertheless, there were already some (internal) regulations in the 1980s covering this area in the form of the 1983 Model Letter from the procurators general to the Heads of the various District PPSs concerning 'deals' with criminals.[23] This Model Letter however did not provide a detailed legal framework for the use of undertakings to witnesses. The document merely set out in fairly general terms that this instrument should be used with caution. Concepts such as proportionality and subsidiarity were also included in the Model Letter, as well as the procedure to be followed when considering the use of this instrument. In this regard the Model Letter stated the following:

> "Making special agreements with criminals may only be considered in exceptional circumstances in which the interests of the investigation, or the cessation or prevention of criminal offences, weighs more heavily than the drawbacks associated with making such a deal. It must therefore be a matter of life and death, or a matter that may be deemed to be of equal gravity, such as a serious threat to State security or public health.
>
> Concluding a deal should be a means of last resort: it must be unlikely that the intended goal can be achieved in any other way. Moreover, the criminal intelli-

---

22 For further details about the legislative history of the present statutory provision see Crijns 2010, p. 62-70 and Janssen 2013, p. 45-117. This section is largely based on these sources.

23 Model Letter from the procurators general to the Heads of the various District PPSs dated 1 July 1983. The Model Letter was intended only as an internal instruction to the public prosecutors and Heads of the various District PPSs, but its contents were also known outside the PPS (inter alia, as a result of its publication in the Sdu-volume 'Criminal law. PPS Guidelines and Circulars' ('*Strafrecht. Richtlijnen & Circulaires Openbaar Ministerie*')). Indeed, the early jurisprudence contained regular references to and comparisons with the Model Letter. Given the limited availability of the contents of the Model Letter, its essence will be set out below. Currently the full text of the Model Letter can be found in the appendices to the final report of the Van Traa Commission (Parliamentary Papers II 1995/96, 24 072 no. 12, p. 402). For further information about this commission, see § 3.3.2.

gence to be obtained must be able to make a vital contribution to achieving that goal. Finally, it must be such that the consideration requested in exchange can only be provided after the information provided has been shown to be reliable. Under these circumstances it may be acceptable for the consideration also to lie outside standard criminal justice policy.

In order to keep the objections and risks associated with an agreement with a criminal within acceptable bounds, the assembly of procurators general decided on 15 July 1983 that the following procedure should be followed with written reports provided at all stages of the procedure. On the basis of the information provided by senior police officers, the handling public prosecutor should consult you or a designated member of the management of the District Public Prosecution Service. In all cases which, in your initial judgement, meet the essential aspects described in the foregoing, you are kindly requested to contact me."

The Model Letter provided no answer to the not-unimportant question of what undertakings could or could not be made to criminals in exchange for the information they provided. Nor did the Model Letter provide any clarification concerning the issue of in what capacity the person with whom the Public Prosecution Service entered into an agreement is acting, or what type of information this person would be expected to provide: is it about agreements with informants who provide lead information or is it (also) about witnesses who provide official statements that can be used as evidence? The Model Letter therefore left important questions unanswered. Nonetheless, the existence and the wording of the Model Letter show that even in the early 1980s it was recognised in the Public Prosecution Service that – in view of the objections and risks associated with the use of 'deals' – it is a delicate instrument which should only be used with due restraint.[24]

3.3.2   The Van Traa Commission and the Guidelines on Agreements with Criminals

An important next step towards the realisation of the present statutory framework on making undertakings to witnesses was the Parliamentary Enquiry led by the Van Traa Commission further to the so called IRT scandal (concerning *inter alia* drug trafficking by the police as an investigation method). The Commission's task was to "investigate: 1) the nature, seriousness and scale of serious organised crime; 2) the practical application, lawfulness, accountability and effectiveness of the investigation methods; and 3) the organisation, functioning and supervision of the investigation".[25] In its 1996 report

---

24 See Crijns 2010, p. 62.
25 Parliamentary Committee of Enquiry into Investigation Methods 1996, p. 11.

'*Inzake opsporing*' ('Concerning investigation'), the Commission also considered the phenomenon of 'agreements with informants'.[26] The Commission first observed that in the
past, the then Regulation on tip-off money (*Regeling tip-, toon en voorkoopgelden*) dating
from 1985 provided for financial remuneration to be paid to informants in connection
with the information they provided. The Commission also noted that this remuneration
could sometimes run to very large sums of money.[27] More important in the context of the
present theme of undertakings to witnesses, however, is that the Commission also noted
that besides financial recompense other agreements were also made with informants. For
example, during its investigation the Commission came across – in the words of the
Commission itself – "deals with informants" in which the Public Prosecution Service
promised, among other things, not to begin actively investigating, to drop charges, to
reduce the sentencing demand, to arrange for a milder detention regime, to release the
detained informant or to suspend the sentence of the convicted informant. The
Commission also observed in this context that the instructions in the Model Letter that
was already in force at the time on making deals with criminals form 1 July 1983 were
"often not" followed. According to the Commission there were also examples where –
contrary to the instructions in the Model Letter, neither the Head of the District PPS nor
the procurator general were notified of the deal. The Commission also reported an
example in which there had also been no consultation with a public prosecutor and the
police had therefore made agreements outside the Public Prosecution Service.[28] In addition, the Commission came across an intended agreement between the prosecutorial
authorities and an informant (who had also been arrested as a suspect) entailing that in
exchange for the information he provided on a drugs ring, he would be released as a
result of a procedural violation in his own case deliberately committed by the
authorities for this purpose. The Commission decided to inform the Minister of Justice
of the intended agreement following which the minister obstructed the agreement in this
form by taking steps which prevented the procedural violation from taking place. The
agreement was then changed such that the anonymity of the informant was still safeguarded but the intended immunity from further prosecution no longer applied.[29] In
another – at that moment still ongoing – criminal case, the Commission discovered an
agreement with an informant in which the Public Prosecution Service – with the consent
of the Minister of Justice – had promised immunity from prosecution and protection of
the informant and his family in exchange for information about a criminal

---

26 Parliamentary Committee of Enquiry into Investigation Methods 1996, p. 215-219. The terminology from
    the Commission's investigative report will be used in this paragraph because the Commission did not make
    a clear distinction in this context between agreements with informants in the foregoing sense and agree-
    ments with witnesses.
27 Parliamentary Committee of Enquiry into Investigation Methods 1996, p. 215-217.
28 Parliamentary Committee of Enquiry into Investigation Methods 1996, p. 217-218.
29 Parliamentary Committee of Enquiry into Investigation Methods 1996, p. 218.

organisation.[30] The Commission also came across a case in which an informant who had reached an agreement with the Public Prosecution Service was liquidated before he could finish making all his statements. Finally, the Commission reported that in practice agreements had also been considered with informants who had already been sentenced in exchange for a sentence reduction, but that no agreements with such individuals had yet ever been made.[31]

On the basis of its findings the Commission came to a number of clear conclusions and made several recommendations. It is important to note in this context that the Commission made a distinction between the notions of 'deals with criminals' and so called 'crown witnesses' (*kroongetuigen*). In the latter category were included witnesses who had been promised immunity from prosecution in exchange for their statements. In the Dutch situation at the time the Commission considered use of the crown witness in this sense to be going too far:

> "The introduction of the institution of the crown witness creates a situation in which the penalty, or even the lack of any penalty, is no longer in proportion to the seriousness of the offences committed. This has to be offset against the possible conviction of people who would otherwise evade the law. In Italy the institution of the collaborator of justice has led to a number of successes in combatting the Mafia and reducing the influence of organised crime on the democratic institutions. Particularly with that last goal in mind, it is justifiable to use *pentiti*. In the Netherlands organised crime does not seem to have a major influence on the functioning of the democratic institutions. Therefore, it is the Commission's view that the figure of the crown witness should not be introduced into Dutch criminal law. In the Commission's view the options listed under deals with criminals [see below], possibly linked to a witness protection programme, currently constitute the maximum to which the Netherlands should go as a democratic state under the rule of law."[32]

What is interesting about this finding is that despite its acknowledged objections to such, the Van Traa Commission does not categorically reject the institution of the 'crown witness' (in the above sense). Instead the Commission bases its conclusion on the degree of influence which organised crime has on the functioning of the democratic institutions in the Netherlands which at the time were thought to be rather less than would have been the case in Italy in the 1990s. The argumentation adopted by the Commission therefore does not appear to entail a wholesale rejection of the phenomenon of crown witnesses in the above sense, as also apparent from the Commission's finding that the options for

---

30 Parliamentary Committee of Enquiry into Investigation Methods 1996, p. 219.
31 Parliamentary Committee of Enquiry into Investigation Methods 1996, p. 218-219.
32 Parliamentary Committee of Enquiry into Investigation Methods 1996, p. 466.

making deals with criminals 'currently' constitute the maximum to which the Netherlands should go, as a democratic state under the rule of law.

Thus the Van Traa Commission ruled against the introduction of the phenomenon of the crown witness, but was in favour of the use of deals with criminals, which unlike crown witnesses could not be promised complete immunity from prosecution. By 'deals' was meant: "an agreement between a criminal and the Public Prosecution Service for the purpose of obtaining an witness statement that can be tested at trial in exchange for some consideration on the part of the Public Prosecution Service".[33] Although the Commission did not disallow the use of this instrument, it did state that deals with criminals reached "the limits of acceptable investigation methods". Firstly, "the purpose of criminal law" would be undermined if "on a systematic basis one criminal was allowed to walk free in exchange for incriminating evidence against another criminal who had been involved in the same criminal acts".[34] Secondly, the Commission warned against the risk that by entering into negotiations with criminal witnesses the authorities would lose control of the situation: simply accepting deals with criminals could lead to "an undesirable relationship of dependency between the prosecutorial authorities and the criminal".[35] Partly for these reasons the Commission stated in no uncertain terms that the use of deals with criminals needed a statutory basis. The Commission also advocated great caution in the use of deals with criminals as well as transparency: it must be possible for deals to be put before the judge. However, the Van Traa Commission said nothing about the matter of what role precisely the judge should play in the conclusion and scrutiny of the deal. The Van Traa Commission did formulate the following concrete criteria for concluding deals with criminals, reproduced here in light of their importance for the later statutory framework:

- "They are only permissible as a means of last resort in cases of organised crime or cases of life and death.
- The information to be obtained should be essential for the investigation and evidence in these cases. A deal must produce witness statements which can be assessed by the judge. It is not sufficient for a deal to provide information only for the Criminal Intelligence Service (CID).[36]

---

33 Parliamentary Committee of Enquiry into Investigation Methods 1996, p. 465.
34 Parliamentary Committee of Enquiry into Investigation Methods 1996, p. 465. This sentence fragment is interesting in that in the distinction made by the Commission the key difference between the instrument of deals with criminals and the phenomenon of the crown witness specifically lies in the fact that only in the latter case the witness walks free.
35 Parliamentary Committee of Enquiry into Investigation Methods 1996, p. 465.
36 The CID (Criminal Intelligence Service) is now known as the TCI (Criminal Intelligence Team). In the intervening period these police units were also called CIE (Criminal Intelligence Units). For further details about this development see Brinkhoff 2014, p. 92-98 as well as Van der Bel, Van Hoorn and Pieters 2013, p. 25-30.

- Immunity from prosecution cannot be promised in return. Criminal prosecution may only be ruled out if without the deal it would be decided not to proceed with a prosecution or there would only be a transaction.
- The return consideration could be:
  a. a financial recompense in accordance with the national tip-off rules (similar to informants);
  b. demanding a lower sentence than would normally be the case on the basis of the charge, in which the public prosecutor states this in his/her sentencing demand;
  c. some mitigation of the execution of the sentence. This may not contravene the Pardons Act (*Gratiewet*).
- The consent of the Board of Procurators General is required to enter into a deal. The Head of the District PPS responsible shall make the request."[37]

With hindsight it can be seen that with these conditions the Van Traa Commission set out important markers for the later Provision of Undertakings to Witnesses in Criminal Cases Act in terms of the cases in which the instrument may be used (serious and/or organised crime and also only as a means of last resort), the purpose of the instrument (obtaining testable evidence), the nature of the undertakings (no complete immunity from prosecution, although sentence reduction is possible) and the setup of the procedure (internal consent procedure in the Public Prosecution Service, followed by judicial scrutiny).

The report of the Van Traa Commission was endorsed in the Lower House of Parliament which fully subscribed to the conclusions regarding the instrument of undertakings to witnesses, including the need to create a statutory basis for this instrument and a ban on undertaking to grant complete immunity from prosecution (the crown witness in the above meaning).[38] In addition to this, during the parliamentary debate of the Van Traa Commission's recommendations and on the initiative of Kalsbeek MP the Lower House indicated that it was in favour of requiring judicial scrutiny of the proposed agreement before it was actually entered into.[39] In retrospect it may be said that this motion was very important to the way in which the process of entering into agreements was laid down in the later Provision of Undertakings to Witnesses in Criminal Cases Act.

In anticipation of the bill that would further regulate this matter, the Public Prosecution Service drew up the Guidelines on Agreements with Criminals to replace the Model Letter of 1983 which had applied up until that time.[40] These Guidelines from 1997 fully reflected the

---

37 Parliamentary Committee of Enquiry into Investigation Methods 1996, p. 465.
38 See Parliamentary Papers II 1995/96, 24 072 no. 25.
39 See Parliamentary Papers II 1995/96, 24 072 no. 51.
40 Guidelines on Agreements with Criminals dated 13 March 1997, Government Gazette 1997, 61, which entered into force on 1 April 1997.

recommendations of the Van Traa Commission that had been adopted by the Lower House of Parliament and further set out a fairly detailed procedure for within the Public Prosecution Service when the use of undertakings to witnesses was being considered. The Guidelines however did not provide for prior judicial scrutiny of the proposed agreement as specified by the Lower House of Parliament, because such a procedure could not be laid down in a Public Prosecution Service Guideline.

3.3.3 Developments in the Jurisprudence Prior to the Statutory Provision

Faced with the various cases in which the Public Prosecution Service had made undertakings to witnesses, in the 1990s the courts, including the Supreme Court, were also forced to say something about the admissibility of this instrument. This often concerned large cases of organised crime which also often attracted considerable media attention. The first rulings of the Supreme Court in which the phenomenon of undertakings to witnesses played a role (albeit a modest one) arose around the time the Van Traa Commission's report was published.[41] However, the matter only really started to gain momentum in the jurisprudence (and the literature[42]) from the time of the judgments of the Amsterdam District Court in 1997 in the cases of Johan V. (alias de Hakkelaar) and his co-accused Koos R. In these cases (that are also known as the Octopus case) the Public Prosecution Service had made extensive undertakings to the two witnesses (Karman and Abbas), on which cases the Supreme Court ruled in 1999.[43] The year before the Supreme Court had already issued a comprehensive ruling in the Lorsé case[44] and shortly after the judgments in the Octopus case in June 1999, the Supreme Court handed down two interesting rulings in the Juliët case.[45] The following discussion is limited to a brief description of the parameters set by the Supreme Court during this period concerning the use of undertakings to witnesses in criminal cases.[46]

As mentioned above, in the 1990s the matter of providing undertakings to witnesses was only minimally regulated. The courts were therefore forced to set out a legal framework themselves for the use of this instrument (whereby the Supreme Court was able, in the aforementioned rulings in the late 1990s, to use the findings and recommendations of the Van Traa Commission). At the same time – partly in view of the legislative developments[47] –

---

41 See SC 15 February 1994, NJ 1994, 322 with commentary by AHJS; SC 23 May 1995, NJ 1995, 683 with commentary by Sch and SC 19 March 1996, NJ 1997, 59 with commentary by Kn.
42 For a brief discussion of the (mainly critical) literature from this period, see Crijns 2010, p. 119-124.
43 See SC 6 April 1999, NJ 1999/565 and 566 with commentary by Sch (Koos R. and Johan V.) and SC 1 June 1999, NJ 1999, 567 with commentary by Sch (Karman). The witness Abbas was himself never prosecuted in the Netherlands.
44 See SC 30 June 1998, NJ 1998, 799 with commentary by Sch (Lorsé).
45 See SC 8 June 1999, NJ 1999, 772 and 773 (Juliët).
46 See also Crijns 2010, p. 67-69. For a more detailed discussion of this jurisprudence, see Janssen 2013, p. 50-65.
47 The Undertakings to Witnesses in Criminal Cases Bill (Parliamentary Papers II 1998/99, 26 294 nos. 1-2) was put before the Lower House on 17 November 1998.

the Supreme Court did this only to a certain extent. The Supreme Court limited itself to examining the lawfulness of the use of undertakings to witnesses in the case at hand, stopping short of formulating general rules concerning the admissibility of undertakings to witnesses. The Supreme Court repeatedly emphasised that this went beyond the scope of judicial decision-making and was a matter for the legislature.[48] On the basis of the rules in place at the time, however, the Supreme Court gradually set some important parameters in this regard which most certainly influenced the later statutory framework.[49]

In its jurisprudence dating from the 1990s, the Supreme Court never categorically rejected the use of undertakings to witnesses. While at the time an explicit statutory basis may have been lacking, the Supreme Court took the view that providing undertakings to witnesses could be based on the principle of prosecutorial discretion (Section 167 paragraph 2 and Section 242 paragraph 2 CCP) and therefore had an implicit statutory basis.[50] In response to the question of whether providing undertakings to witnesses in the particular case before the court was permissible, the Supreme Court consistently adopted the general assessment framework applicable under Article 6 ECHR and the principles of due process of law (*beginselen van een goede procesorde*). More specifically in this regard the Supreme Court looked at whether the requirements of proportionality and subsidiarity had been met, as well as the principles of due care and whether the accused had adequate facilities for the preparation of his defence.[51] In this way the Supreme Court adopted the assessment framework used by the European Court of Human Rights concerning the use of undertakings to witnesses in criminal cases, in which, among other things, a key consideration is whether the defence was aware of the identity of the witness and was given sufficient opportunity to question the witness.[52]

With regard to the nature, content and extent of the undertakings made by the Public Prosecution Service, in its jurisprudence the Supreme Court on the whole took a generous approach, which is not really surprising given the lack of a statutory framework setting out clear guidelines concerning the admissibility of the various possible undertakings. For example, the Supreme Court repeatedly deemed undertakings which essentially either directly or indirectly boiled down to immunity from prosecution to be admissible.[53] In addition, undertakings relating to sentence reduction, where the Public Prosecution Service made a positive recommendation concerning a future request for a pardon, reduction of the confiscation of unlawfully obtained advantage and taking measures to

---

48 See e.g. SC 19 March 1996, NJ 1997, 59 with commentary by Kn and SC 30 June 1998, NJ 1998, 799 with commentary by Sch (Lorsé).

49 See SC 30 June 1998, NJ 1998, 799, with commentary by Sch (Lorsé); SC 6 April 1999, NJ 1999, 565 and 566 with commentary by Sch (Koos R. and Johan V.); SC 1 June 1999, NJ 1999, 567 with commentary by Sch (Karman); SC 8 June 1999, NJ 1999, 772 and 773 (Juliët).

50 See also SC 30 June 1998, NJ 1998, 799 with commentary by Sch (Lorsé).

51 See Janssen 2013, p. 64-65.

52 See § 2.6 for a description of this assessment framework. See e.g. Crijns 2010, p. 68-69.

53 See also SC 30 June 1998, NJ 1998/799 with commentary by Sch (Lorsé) and SC 6 April 1999, NJ 1999/565 and 566 with commentary by Sch (Koos R. and Johan V.)

provide the witness with physical protection, were repeatedly approved by the Supreme Court.[54] More 'minor' undertakings such as placing someone under a different or milder detention regime were also deemed permissible. Only once did the Supreme Court draw a boundary in this regard and that was in the Karman-case, in which the Public Prosecution Service had promised that any custodial sentence that the court might impose on Karman would not be implemented. The Supreme Court deemed this undertaking to be categorically unlawful given that this would be in contravention of the statutory system which imposes on the Public Prosecution Service a duty to execute decisions taken by the court (cf. Section 553 CCP).[55]

3.3.4   *Legislative Bill and Temporary Instructions on Undertakings to Witnesses in Criminal Cases*

The Provision of Undertakings to Witnesses in Criminal Cases Act has a long history. The underlying bill was put before the Lower House of Parliament on 17 November 1998,[56] but it was not until 1 April 2006 that the legislation entered into force. Besides general political factors which are not directly related to the subject matter here, such as a rapid succession of governments, etc., this long history can be ascribed to a number of more specific factors which will be examined in more detail below.[57]

The parliamentary consideration in the Lower House initially proceeded fairly smoothly. Most of the political parties adopted an essentially positive stance on the bill. Later, however, doubts started to creep in, partly due to the media reporting of various cases in which the Public Prosecution Service has made far-reaching undertakings to witnesses in exchange for information. These undertakings were considered not to meet the rules in force at that time, nor the terms of the proposed legislation. In the words of Abels, this provided "fodder to undermine faith in the Public Prosecution Service's ability to observe any rules and thus doubt the usefulness of a statutory provision".[58] The parliamentary debate on the bill, in particular, was therefore also laborious, but ultimately the bill could count on a majority and on 5 July 2001 it was adopted by the Lower House. The consideration of the bill in the Upper House however was delayed because it was necessary to wait for a separate rectification bill that provided for the penalisation of the witness who at a later stage, after the agreement with the Public Prosecution Service has been concluded, then refuses to make their promised statement (Section 192 paragraph 2 CC). While this provision already formed part of the original Bill on Undertakings to

---

54 See Crijns 2010, p. 69.
55 See SC 1 June 1999, NJ 1999, 567 with commentary by Sch (Karman). See also Janssen 2013, p. 54-61.
56 See Parliamentary Papers II 1998/99, 26 294, nos. 1-2.
57 For an overview of the legislative history e.g. Abels 2005 and Crijns 2010, p. 62-67. For a detailed examination of the parliamentary consideration of the Bill, see Janssen 2013, p. 45-117.
58 See Abels 2005, p. 862.

Witnesses in Criminal Cases, due to an error during the voting this part of the bill was accidentally rejected, despite there being a majority in support of this provision in the Lower House.[59] This made it necessary to submit this tailpiece of the framework on undertakings to witnesses to the Lower House as a separate bill.[60] The consideration of the Bill on Undertakings to Witnesses in Criminal Cases was then suspended in the Upper House to await the consideration of the rectification bill in the Lower House, so that at a later date the Upper House could handle both bills at the same time. At the same time however the Guidelines on Agreements with Criminals dating from 1997 that was in force at the time was replaced by the Temporary Instructions on Undertakings to Witnesses in Criminal Cases[61] in anticipation of the statutory framework that would further regulate this matter, once again with the exception of the prior judicial scrutiny of the intended agreement by the investigating judge, given that this could not be laid down as an instruction.

Secondly – and perhaps more importantly – the thinking with respect to the instrument of undertakings to witnesses continued to evolve pending the legislative procedure. In 2004, for example, a memorandum published by an internal working group within the Public Prosecution Service made it clear that the statutory provision as presented at that time in the Upper House would be too restrictive, which in practice would mean that it would only be possible to make an agreement with a witness in a limited number of cases.[62] The working group of the Public Prosecution Service instead argued for a more generous scheme whereby the question of which undertakings are permissible would as far as possible be left to practice and the jurisprudence. In the working group's view, the general principles of proportionality and subsidiarity would provide an adequate basis on which to determine the permissibility of a particular undertaking in a concrete case. Although the then minister was sympathetic to this argument for creating more scope for the Public Prosecution Service when it comes to providing undertakings to witnesses, he remained (along with the Board of Procurators General) committed to the need for a statutory provision for undertakings to witnesses in criminal cases. He did agree with the working group that it should be possible to make undertakings concerning the amount of the unlawfully obtained gains to be confiscated as well as having an issued request for extradition withdrawn. However, he was not willing to accept other proposals for widening the scope of the provision – such as granting a financial reward to a witness.[63]

---

59 See Janssen 2013, p. 85-86.
60 For the bill in question see Parliamentary Papers II 2001/02, 28 017, nos. 1-2.
61 Temporary Instructions on Undertakings to Witnesses in Criminal Cases dated 13 July 2001, Government Gazette 2001, 138, entered into force on 1 August 2001.
62 For the memorandum see the annex to the letter of the Minister of Justice dated 1 July 2004, Parliamentary Papers II 2003/04, 28 017 and 26 294, no. 6. Concerning the memorandum see e.g. Crijns 2010, p. 65-66 and Janssen 2013, p. 86-92. See in this regard also Plooy 2004, Buruma 2004 and Crijns 2004.
63 Parliamentary Papers II 2003/04, 28 017 and 26 294, no. 6.

Partly as a result of the arguments put forward by the working group of the Public Prosecution Service and the minister's response in this regard another interesting and (as it would turn out later in practice) important debate arose during the consideration of the bill in the Upper House about the matter of whether the proposed legislation on undertakings to witnesses was not intended as a closed system for making undertakings and about the question of whether and to what extent therefore there was still room to make other undertakings than those explicitly mentioned in the legislation.[64] This was because the bill only provided for agreements with witnesses to whom sentence reduction had been promised (Section 226g paragraph 1 CCP) as well as a lighter regime for promising a so called 'inducement' (small courtesies; *gunstbetoon*) (Section 226g paragraph 4 CCP).[65] Did this now mean that other undertakings were impermissible or could other types of undertakings still be made, for example, concerning the amount of the unlawfully obtained gains to be confiscated? The latter stance was supported mainly through invoking the principle of prosecutorial discretion that even before the enactment of the statutory provision had already been recognised by the Supreme Court as providing sufficient basis for the instrument of agreements with witnesses.[66]

Ultimately, however, the proposals of the working group of the Public Prosecution Service and the debate surrounding the relationship between the proposed statutory provision and the principle of prosecutorial discretion did not lead to any change in the bill. The minister did promise to the Upper and Lower Houses however that Instructions would be provided alongside the statutory provision which would also deal with the matter of which undertakings may or may not be deemed permissible, taking into account what had been said about this matter during the parliamentary consideration of the bill.[67] In this context the minister distinguished three categories: 1) permissible undertakings for which a statutory provision was necessary (in particular undertakings relating to sentence reduction); 2) permissible undertakings for which this was not necessary (in particular an inducement); and 3) undertakings which are not permissible (in particular undertakings entailing immunity from prosecution).[68] A little while later the minister fleshed out these three categories in a letter to the Lower House in which, among other things, he indicated that in his view – despite the lack of an explicit statutory basis in this regard – undertakings concerning the amount of the unlawfully obtained gains to be confiscated as well as concerning the withdrawal of an issued request for extradition or a European arrest warrant should also be considered permissible undertakings.[69]

---

64 In particular see Parliamentary Papers I 2004/05, 26 294 and 28 017, B, C and E.

65 See further § 3.4.3.2.

66 See § 3.3.3. Cf. in this regard also the arguments put forward by the working group of the Public Prosecution Service, as set out above.

67 For a detailed discussion of the debate between the minister and the Upper House, see Janssen 2013, p. 96-117.

68 See Parliamentary Papers I 2004/05, 26 294 and 28 017, E.

69 See Parliamentary Papers II 2004/05, 28 017 no. 8, p. 4-6.

However, with hindsight it can be said that this still had not provided the legal profession with a sufficiently clear answer concerning the matter of whether or not the legislation should be considered a closed system for providing undertakings to witnesses, and what that means in terms of the lawfulness of undertakings for which there is no explicit statutory basis (such as undertakings concerning the confiscation of unlawfully obtained gains) and the procedure to be followed in respect thereof.[70]

Ultimately, both bills were passed by the Upper House on 12 May 2005 and entered into force on 1 April 2006.[71] At the same time the Instructions on Undertakings to Witnesses in Criminal Cases entered into force, which anticipated the new statutory framework – and which, as stated, had been promised by the minister partly as a result of the aforementioned debate in the Upper House about the open or closed nature of the proposed statutory framework – together with the Witness Protection Decree.[72] The latter amounts to a further specification of Section 226l CCP that provides for the physical protection of witnesses.

3.4   Legal Framework

This section will look at a number of aspects of the present legal framework concerning undertakings to witnesses. As described in the foregoing section, the statutory framework concerning undertakings to witnesses in Section 226g ff. CCP, the legislative history of this provision, the Instructions on Undertakings to Witnesses in Criminal Cases[73] and the jurisprudence relating to undertakings to witnesses constitute the most important elements of this legal framework.

---

70 See the complications in the Passage case in which this question was one of the most important issues of contention between the defence and the Public Prosecution Service. See in this regard Amsterdam Court of Appeal 29 June 2017, ECLI:NL:GHAMS:2017:2496 (Dino S.), § 2.2.2.6. See also § 3.4.3.3.

71 See Provision of Undertakings to Witnesses in Criminal Cases Act of 12 May 2005, Bulletin of Acts and Decrees 2005, 254 and the Act of 12 May 2005 on amending the Code of Criminal Procedure in connection with failing to make a witness statement after making undertakings to that effect, Bulletin of Acts and Decrees 2005, 255.

72 See Instructions on Undertakings to Witnesses in Criminal Cases dated 13 March 2006, Government Gazette 2006, 56 and the Witness Protection Decree of 21 December 2005, Bulletin of Acts and Decrees 2006, 21 (most recently amended on 30 November 2012, Bulletin of Acts and Decrees 2012, 615, entered into force on 1 January 2013). The current version of the document is the Instructions on Undertakings to Witnesses in Criminal Cases, Government Gazette 2012, 26860 (entered into force on 1 January 2013); this is largely the same as the original version dating from 2006.

73 See Instructions on Undertakings to Witnesses in Criminal Cases, Government Gazette 2012, 26860 (entered into force on 1 January 2013).

3.4.1 Responsibility for Making Agreements

Responsibility for making agreements with witnesses rests with the Public Prosecution Service. Given the institutional structures in the Netherlands, this is only natural, given that the Public Prosecution Service is responsible for the investigation of criminal offences and in that context potentially for the collection of material that may be used as evidence. Making agreements with witnesses also has a bearing on the Public Prosecution Service's role in bringing prosecutions. In the context of the agreement the Public Prosecution Service commits itself to the way in which the witness will be prosecuted in their own criminal case and the sentencing demand that the witness may expect. This has direct implications for the exercise of judgment under the principle of prosecutorial discretion, which makes it all the more clear that making agreements must be considered the responsibility of the Public Prosecution Service.

This does not mean, however, that the Public Prosecution Service acts or should act fully independently in such matters. Given that prior to making an agreement a witness will have been thoroughly interrogated concerning their own involvement in criminal offences, as well as offences about which they can make a statement as a witness, from which it should also become clear what their own share in that was, the police also play an important role in reaching agreements with witnesses, although the legal framework says little about that aspect. This naturally all takes place under the responsibility and in close consultation with the Public Prosecution Service but does not alter the fact that in practice the police also play a significant part in reaching the agreement. This however does not mean that the police is able to make undertakings to the witness; this is the exclusive domain of the Public Prosecution Service.[74] The actual division of roles between the police and the Public Prosecution Service, as well as the actual procedure followed in the Public Prosecution Service itself, will be discussed below in this country report, in examining the practice surrounding the use of undertakings to witnesses.[75]

The investigating judge is another important actor in the framing of the agreement, given that the agreement with the witness can only actually be implemented after the investigating judge has deemed the intended agreement to be lawful and found the witness to be reliable (Section 226h paragraph 3 CCP).[76] This does not mean, however, that the investigating judge becomes a party to the agreement; only the witness and the Public Prosecution Service agree with one another to commit to meet certain obligations.

During the phase in which the agreement with the witness is implemented the trial judge then also enters into the picture.[77] This is because in the case in which the witness to whom

---

74 As is evident from the law and the Instructions on Undertakings to Witnesses in Criminal Cases, Government Gazette 2012, 26860 (entered into force on 1 January 2013), § 7.1.

75 See § 3.5.2.

76 See § 3.4.4.3.

77 See § 3.4.4.4.

undertakings have been made is making their statements, the trial judge will have to determine whether the statements made by the witness will be used as evidence, in which context the judge will not only have to make his own assessment of the lawfulness of the agreement but also of the reliability of the witness and their statements and their value for the purposes of the evidence. In the case in which the witness stands trial as the accused, the trial judge will have to consider whether or not a milder sentence may be imposed further to the witness' cooperation in the other case. In this way the final judgment of the trial judge is vital to the question of whether the agreement actually produces the results which the Public Prosecution Service and the witness intended when making the agreement. However, this does not make the trial judge a party to the agreement; no obligations upon him/her arise out of the agreement which – strictly speaking – means that s/he is free to ignore the agreement, even in the event that he/she does use the statements given by the witness as evidence. In the legislative history, the jurisprudence and the literature however the assumption is that in passing sentence the judge will and should take into account the fact that the Public Prosecution Service and the witness have entered into an agreement (even if only due to the fact that – if s/he were to set aside the promised sentence reduction either, fully or partially, by imposing a much higher penalty than that demanded by the Public Prosecution Service – this would by default make the future use of the instrument of undertakings to witnesses essentially illusory),[78] but the fact remains that from a strictly legal point of view the trial judge holds no responsibility for the formation and/or implementation of the agreement.

The weighty interests involved in making agreements with witnesses – both the individual interests of the witness who puts themselves in a vulnerable position by cooperating with the investigation and prosecution of serious criminal offences and the public interest – and the particular responsibility of the Public Prosecution Service in the context of making agreements with witnesses, are reflected in a strict internal procedure within the Public Prosecution Service as set out in the Instructions on Undertakings to Witnesses in Criminal Cases.[79] Before an agreement can be placed before the investigating judge for scrutiny, the draft agreement is reviewed (in this order) by the State Advocate and the Internal Review Committee of the PPS on the use of special investigative measures (*Centrale Toetsingscommissie*; hereafter CTC), following which the Board of Procurators

---

78 During the Parliamentary debate the Minister adopted this position also. See e.g. Parliamentary Papers II 1998/99, 26 294 no. 3, p. 7 and p. 16-17; and also Parliamentary Papers II 1999/2000, 26 294, no. 6, p. 9-10 and p. 27 and p. 37. See also Amsterdam Court of Appeal 29 June 2017, ECLI:NL:GHAMS:2017:2494 (Peter la S.), § 6.2 and Amsterdam Court of Appeal 29 June 2017, ECLI:NL:GHAMS:2017:2495 (Fred R.), § 7.2, where the Court of Appeal ruled that the Public Prosecution Service's account of why it should be accepted that witness has made a significant contribution to the investigation and prosecution of criminal offences (cf. the criterion laid down in Section 44a CC for sentence mitigation) in principle serves as a guideline for the judge in the determination of the punishment to be imposed on the witness in his or her own case. See also Crijns 2010, p. 104-105. See § 3.4.4.4 for further details.

79 See Instructions on Undertakings to Witnesses in Criminal Cases, Government Gazette 2012, 26860 (entered into force on 1 January 2013), § 7.

General takes a decision, while in some cases the Minister of Justice and Security will also be informed about the agreement to be made with the witness.[80]

3.4.2   With Regard to What Offences?

The statutory provision concerning undertakings to witnesses primarily came into being in light of the perceived need for an effective means to combat organised crime.[81] As evident from the statutory provision, the instrument's scope of application, however, is much wider than that. Pursuant to Section 226g paragraph 1 CCP undertakings to witnesses may be made in the context of a criminal investigation into: 1. offences in respect of which pre-trial detention may be lawfully ordered, which were committed in the context of organised crime and which give rise to severe public disorder on account of their nature or connection to other criminal offences; or 2. offences punishable by eight years' imprisonment or more. In the event of investigations into serious criminal offences where no organised element is involved, the use of undertakings to witnesses is therefore also possible. Nevertheless, the instrument of undertakings to witnesses is mainly associated – also by the legislature – with combatting organised crime and in that context is considered a useful instrument for penetrating the higher echelons of a criminal organisation.[82]

Further to the statutory criteria, the Instructions on Undertakings to Witnesses in Criminal Cases stipulates that providing undertakings to witnesses should be reserved only for exceptional cases. In that context the Instructions expressly states that when providing undertakings to witnesses the requirements of proportionality and subsidiarity must also be taken into account.[83] Under the subsidiarity requirement, according to the Instructions the public prosecutor may only decide to make an agreement with a witness if this agreement is urgently needed "for the investigation, which also includes the prevention or cessation of criminal offences and/or the consequences of such".[84] In other words, before actually providing undertakings to witnesses the public prosecutor must first ensure that the matters about which the witness wishes to make a statement cannot be investigated, prevented, ceased and/or prosecuted with the aid of other investigative powers, or not in time. It must also be likely that the witness's statement could not have been obtained without making an undertaking.[85]

---

80 See further § 3.4.4.3.

81 See Parliamentary Papers II 1998/99, 26 294 no. 3, p. 3: "It cannot be denied that the growth and impact of organised crime is such that special measures are warranted".

82 See e.g. Parliamentary Papers II 1998/99, 26 294 no. 3, p. 3-4.

83 Instructions on Undertakings to Witnesses in Criminal Cases, Government Gazette 2012, 26860 (entered into force on 1 January 2013), § 2.2.

84 Instructions on Undertakings to Witnesses in Criminal Cases, Government Gazette 2012, 26860 (entered into force on 1 January 2013), § 3.2.

85 Instructions on Undertakings to Witnesses in Criminal Cases, Government Gazette 2012, 26860 (entered into force on 1 January 2013), § 3.2 with reference to SC 6 April 1999, NJ 1999, 565, para. 2.4.

In this context an interesting question is whether there are limits with regard to the number of witnesses to whom undertakings can be made in one and the same set of facts. It is clear that the legislation sets no absolute limits regarding this matter and that there are known cases in the jurisprudence in which undertakings were made in any event to two witnesses, which was deemed permissible by the Supreme Court (although it should be noted that these were to some extent also cases dating from before the entry into force of the present statutory framework).[86] This question is related to the requirement of subsidiarity, as discussed above, of course: the assessment with respect to the requirement of urgent necessity will need to be more rigorous as more witnesses are presented to whom undertakings have been made. The question of whether and to what extent there are limits to the number of witnesses to whom undertakings may be made in a single case cannot therefore be answered in general terms, but will greatly depend on the specific circumstances of the case.[87]

In the context of assessing the proportionality of the proposed agreement, according to the Instructions the public prosecutor needs to take into account the relationship between: 1) the importance of the statement on the one hand and the weight of the undertaking made on the other; and 2) the nature of the criminal offence on which the witness is providing a statement and the nature of the criminal offence for which the witness himself is being prosecuted.[88] The first relates mainly to the question of whether the agreement is in balance (i.e. will the Public Prosecution Service be getting 'value for its money'?); the second is related more to the question of whether an agreement may be made in this criminal case (given its seriousness) and with this witness (given their criminal background). The latter consideration clearly reflects the 'large fish, small fish' argument that was raised repeatedly during the parliamentary consideration of the bill as justification for the legitimacy of using the instrument of undertakings to witnesses.[89] However neither the legislation nor the Instructions set any limitations in absolute terms with regard to the matter of what offences the witness is accused of. The present framework therefore in no way precludes undertakings from being made to witnesses who themselves are accused of (relatively) serious criminal offences.[90]

---

86 See for such older cases SC 30 June 1998, NJ 1998, 799 (Lorsé); SC 6 April 1999, NJ 1999, 565 and 566 (Koos R. and Johan V.).

87 In the Passage case the Amsterdam Court of Appeal ruled – further to a defence argument (to the effect) that the use of two witnesses to whom undertakings had been made in one and the same criminal case must be deemed contrary to the principle of proportionality – that this was more a matter of effectiveness (a prerogative of the Public Prosecution Service) than a question of lawfulness, which is why the Court of Appeal adopted a cautious approach to the examination of this fact to then conclude that in this particular case the principle of proportionality had not been contravened. See Amsterdam Court of Appeal 29 June 2017, ECLI: NL:GHAMS:2017:2496 (Dino S.), § 2.2.2.3.

88 Instructions on Undertakings to Witnesses in Criminal Cases, Government Gazette 2012, 26860 (entered into force on 1 January 2013), § 3.2.

89 See e.g. Parliamentary Papers II 1999/2000, 26 294, no. 6, p. 12.

90 See once more the rulings of the Amsterdam Court of Appeal in the Passage case in which the Court of Appeal deemed as lawful the use of two witnesses to whom undertakings had been made and who them-

The legislator drew only one boundary in this regard and that is the prohibition on making agreements with witnesses accused of such serious offences that they run the genuine risk of being sentenced to life imprisonment. This prohibition found expression in the legislation also, in Section 44a CC, which refers to the possibility of reducing a *determinate* sentence of imprisonment only. The Minister's considerations on this matter are worth reproducing here:

> "The second paragraph [of Section 44a CC] lists the modalities by which sentence reduction may be granted. Under a, the possibility of granting sentence reduction is limited to determinate sentences of imprisonment; I assume that the judge considering the imposition of life imprisonment will only do so in exceptional cases, where the legal order has been very seriously shaken [by the offence(s)]. It would not be acceptable to take into account the cooperation of a person accused of such offences by appearing as a witness in another case in the sentence to be imposed."[91]

However, the question arises as to whether this prohibition on making the undertakings envisaged by the law – entailing sentence reduction – where there is a genuine prospect that the witness will in his or her own case be sentenced to life imprisonment precludes agreements from being made on the basis of Section 226k CCP, with witnesses who in their own cases have definitively been sentenced to life imprisonment. The answer to this question is not entirely clear, given that the ground for sentence reduction in Section 44a CC is by nature limited to agreements within the meaning of Section 226g CCP, and that Section 226k itself does not restrict the undertaking envisaged therein (about which more is said below) to determinate sentences of imprisonment. Nor does the legislative history shed any light on this issue. In light of the considerations set out above, it is fair to assume that the Minister considered making agreements with witnesses who have definitively been sentenced to life imprisonment equally unacceptable. Twenty years on, however, it

---

selves were also accused (and convicted) for their involvement in various homicides. See e.g. Amsterdam Court of Appeal 29 June 2017, ECLI:NL:GHAMS:2017:2496 (Dino S.). One of the witnesses had been sentenced to thirty years' imprisonment in the first instance proceedings, but owing to his later willingness to act as a witness, on appeal his sentence was reduced by half (see Amsterdam Court of Appeal 29 June 2017, ECLI:NL:GHAMS:2017:2495 (Fred R.)).

91 See Parliamentary Papers II 2008/09, 26 294 no. 3, p. 26. It bears observing here that this prohibition does not go so far as to preclude the making of undertakings to witnesses suspected of an offence punishable by life imprisonment (among other forms of punishment). It does preclude making undertakings to witnesses where, in light of the particular circumstances of the case, there is a genuine prospect that a sentence of life imprisonment actually will be imposed.

is questionable whether this would still be the position, given, among other things, that since the turn of the century the number of life sentences has increased considerably.[92]

In addition, the question arises as to how strict the aforementioned prohibition is. In this regard it bears observing that the quote above predates the discussion in the Upper House of Parliament as to whether or not the proposed statutory scheme was to be considered a closed system for providing undertakings to witnesses, i.e. whether and to what extent there would still be room to provide other undertakings than those explicitly mentioned therein.[93] In light of the outcome of this discussion, the question is whether there is nevertheless some room to make agreements with witnesses accused of such serious offences that they run the genuine risk of being sentenced to life imprisonment, for example with respect to the confiscation of unlawfully obtained advantage or to an inducement envisaged under Section 226g paragraph 4 CCP. The fact remains that the restriction set by Section 44a CC pertains to imprisonment only; strictly speaking, therefore, the authorities are not precluded from making such other undertakings to the aforementioned category of witnesses.

3.4.3   Nature of the Undertakings

The statutory provision and the Instructions on Undertakings to Witnesses in Criminal Cases[94] both shed light on the question of which undertakings are permissible and which are not in the context of an agreement with a witness, while the parliamentary history of the statutory framework also offer useful starting points in this context.[95] We will look at this more closely below. It should be noted, however, that the question in this regard is whether or not a certain undertaking is generally permissible. The determination of whether or not a certain individual undertaking or a particular combination of undertakings in a specific case is permissible is among other things dependent on the proportionality and subsidiarity thereof (as discussed above), and is moreover a matter for the investigating judge and the trial judge.[96]

3.4.3.1   The Term 'Undertaking'

Before addressing the question of what undertakings may be made to witnesses, it is first necessary to consider the question of what is an undertaking. In this context the Instructions on Undertakings to Witnesses in Criminal Cases states that: "In making an

---

92 See e.g. Forum Levenslang 2011.
93 See further § 3.3.4 and § 3.4.3.3.
94 Instructions on Undertakings to Witnesses in Criminal Cases, Government Gazette 2012, 26860 (entered into force on 1 January 2013), § 4, 5 and 8.
95 See § 3.3.4.
96 See § 3.4.4.3 and 3.4.4.4.

undertaking to a witness, the benefit on offer must be a real one. An undertaking which comprises no more than what the public prosecutor would have decided under normal circumstances based on existing policy (e.g. a decision not to prosecute a minor offence) is not an undertaking in the meaning of these instructions."[97] The summary in the Instructions on Undertakings to Witnesses in Criminal Cases adds the following: "It is important that there is a direct link between that which is provided by the one party and the consideration given by the other party." Thus there needs to be a certain degree of reciprocity for an undertaking to be relevant in criminal law: the consideration to be granted by the Public Prosecution Service should be in proportion to that which the witness provides (in exchange). That which the Public Prosecution Service would have provided anyway, does not qualify as an undertaking under criminal law.[98] It also appears from the summary in the Instructions on Undertakings to Witnesses in Criminal Cases that only where the undertaking has been made in writing will it be considered an undertaking within the meaning of the Instructions.

The jurisprudence also has something to say about the matter of when a undertaking may actually be said to have been made. According to the Supreme Court it should be a "reasonably well defined and concrete undertaking, from which the individual concerned may derive certain expectations".[99] By this interpretation simply offering the vague prospect that a cooperative attitude will be taken into account when reaching the sentencing demand, does not qualify as an undertaking in the meaning of the statutory provision. Nevertheless, it clearly shows that there is no sharp dividing line which can be drawn in these situations and the answer to the question of whether in a specific case an undertaking has been made is therefore open to discussion. That there is a written record of the fact that in the future the Public Prosecution Service will provide consideration will relatively quickly lead to the conclusion that an undertaking has been made; conversely, the lack of a written record does not necessarily warrant the conclusion that no undertaking has been made. The aforementioned requirement in the Instructions that undertakings should be made in writing could therefore be seen as a formal requirement for making lawful undertakings within the meaning of Section 226g ff. CCP, but the lack of such does not mean that it may not be concluded that materially an undertaking within the meaning of the law has been made.[100] At the same time, in practice it will be difficult to ascertain whether and to what extent material undertakings have been made if these have not be made in writing.

---

97 Instructions on Undertakings to Witnesses in Criminal Cases, Government Gazette 2012, 26860 (entered into force on 1 January 2013), § 2.3.
98 See Crijns 2010, p. 75.
99 See SC 2 April 2002, NJ 2002, 357. Although this judgment dates from before the entry into force of the present statutory provision in 2006, it nevertheless still appears relevant with regard to whether an undertaking has been made or not.
100 See SC 2 April 2002, NJ 2002, 357.

3.4.3.2   Permissible Undertakings

The statutory framework concerning undertakings to witnesses is relatively concise when it comes to the nature of the undertakings which may be made in exchange for making formal statements. Section 44a of the Criminal Code provides a summary of permissible undertakings, which essentially all boil down to sentence reduction. More specifically, Section 44a paragraph 2 CC states that the sentence reduction may comprise of: a) a maximum of half for an unconditional determinate custodial sentence, community service order or fine, or b) converting a maximum of the half of the unconditional part of a custodial sentence, community service or fine into a conditional part, or c) replacing a maximum of a third of a custodial sentence by community service order or an unconditional fine.[101] Important in this context is that Section 44a CC – the only article in Title IIIA headed 'Grounds for reducing sentence' – is framed as a set of sentencing instructions for the judge. Presented with an agreement between the Public Prosecution Service and the witness, the judge *may* in the witness' own case (upon application by the public prosecutor) reduce the sentence "that s/he was considering imposing" in line with the provisions of the aforementioned paragraph 2. The second complete sentence of Section 44a paragraph 1 CC is rather less neutrally formulated: "In considering sentence reduction the judge shall take into account the fact that, by making a witness statement, an important contribution has or can be made to the investigation or prosecution of serious offences." In this way the legislature sought to convey that the judge cannot simply set aside agreements entered into between the Public Prosecution Service and the witness.[102]

Section 226g paragraph 4 CCP further states that in exchange for witness statements the public prosecutor may provide an 'inducement'. According to the Instructions on Undertakings to Witnesses in Criminal Cases this may be taken to mean: "performing actions which fall within the normal competences of the public prosecutor, which have a relatively small impact and which do not bear upon the answers to the questions of Sections 348 and 350 CCP, but which could influence willingness to make a witness statement in some way".[103] More specifically the Instructions offer as examples "cooperating with or not opposing a request to suspend remand, the more speedy return of seized goods, insofar as this is not incompatible with the interests of the prosecution, arranging for a milder detention regime for

---

101 In the original version of the Undertakings to Witnesses in Criminal Cases Bill (Parliamentary Papers II 1998/99, 26 294, no. 2) as it was submitted to the Lower House of Parliament in 1998, the maximum sentence reduction was a third. At a later stage, during the course of the Parliamentary debate of the rectification bill referred to in § 3.3.4, further to an amendment adopted by the Lower House of Parliament concerning parts a and b, this was increased to a half (Parliamentary Papers II 2004/05, 28 017, no. 7). For further details, see Janssen 2013, p. 92-96.

102 For further details, see § 3.4.1 and § 3.4.4.4.

103 Instructions on Undertakings to Witnesses in Criminal Cases, Government Gazette 2012, 26860 (entered into force on 1 January 2013), § 8.1. In this context, see also the parliamentary history as described in § 3.3.4, more specifically Parliamentary Papers I 2004/05, 26 294 and 28 017, E, p. 3 and Parliamentary Papers II 2004/05, 28 017 and 26 294, no. 8, p. 5.

a convicted person serving a custodial sentence, arranging for the suspect's remand sentence to be served in a prison closer to their social environment, urging that a sentence imposed abroad can continue to be served in the Netherlands under the Enforcement of Criminal Judgments (Transfer) Act (WOTS) and providing intercession before governing bodies such as the Immigration and Naturalisation Service (IND) and the Tax and Customs Administration".[104] Because a number of these favours require the permission or cooperation of third parties (such as foreign authorities, the Minister of Justice and Security or the State Secretary for Justice and Security), the public prosecutor has to make it clear to the witness that no guarantees can be given about the envisaged result. In such cases therefore only a commitment to do their best can be made.[105] To be able to offer this inducement under Section 226g paragraph 4 CCP and the Instructions, a different, more straightforward procedure applies than for undertakings entailing sentence reduction. While the latter is subject to a detailed internal procedure of the Public Prosecution Service followed by prior scrutiny by the investigating judge,[106] for an inducement it is sufficient to draw up a police report in which it is noted that one or more favours have been granted in exchange for formal statements. This police report should then be added "as soon as possible" to the case file in both the criminal case of the witness, as well as the case of the accused in which an incriminating statement has been made.[107]

Finally, Section 226k paragraph 1 CCP states that agreements may also be made with witnesses who themselves have already been convicted. In this context the undertaking made by the public prosecutor will be that when a request for a pardon is submitted a positive recommendation will be made to reduce the sentence imposed by up to half. The provisions of Section 226g ff. CCP similarly apply with regard to the conclusion of this agreement. These types of agreements are therefore also subject to an internal procedure at the Public Prosecution Service and to prior scrutiny by the investigating judge.[108]

3.4.3.3   Grey Areas

In addition to undertakings which are explicitly deemed as permissible under the law there are, as previously discussed, also undertakings in respect of which it is assumed in the legislative history that they are permissible. More specifically this relates to an undertaking to reduce the amount of unlawfully gained advantage to be confiscated and undertakings concerning the withdrawal of an request for extradition or a European arrest warrant issued

---

104 Instructions on Undertakings to Witnesses in Criminal Cases, Government Gazette 2012, 26860 (entered into force on 1 January 2013), § 8.4.
105 Instructions on Undertakings to Witnesses in Criminal Cases, Government Gazette 2012, 26860 (entered into force on 1 January 2013), § 8.3.
106 For further details, see § 3.4.4.3.
107 According to the Instructions this procedure only applies if there is a "clear and causal connection" between granting the favour and the witness making a statement. See Instructions on Undertakings to Witnesses in Criminal Cases, Government Gazette 2012, 26860 (entered into force on 1 January 2013), § 8.2.
108 For further details, see § 3.4.4.3.

for the purpose of prosecution.[109] Both these undertakings are included in the Instructions on Undertakings to Witnesses in Criminal Cases as specifically permissible, where it is stated with regard to the measure of confiscation of unlawfully obtained gains that the amount to be ordered may be reduced by no more than half, also in the context of the settlement pursuant to Section 511c CCP.[110] That such undertakings should be considered permissible under the present legal framework has however also been challenged.[111] For example, the defence in the Passage case (in the proceedings before both the district court and the court of appeal) adopted the position that in the absence of a sound statutory basis for such, undertakings relating to the reduction of the confiscation of unlawfully obtained advantage are unlawful, and that in this regard, the Instructions are contrary to the statutory provision. The defence also argued that the actual undertaking made in the Passage case – that the public prosecutor would refrain from seeking to confiscate the unlawfully obtained advantage altogether – was contrary to the Instructions, which provides for a maximum reduction of fifty per cent. The Amsterdam district court rejected both arguments. Regarding the first argument, it held that, viewed as a whole, the statutory framework does allow for undertakings relating to the reduction of the confiscation of unlawfully obtained advantage to be made, basing its decision on, inter alia, the parliamentary history in which this question expressly was addressed when the Undertakings to Witnesses in Criminal Cases Bill was considered by the Upper House and in which the Minister adopted the position that such undertakings could lawfully be made within the limits of the proposed legal framework.[112] Regarding the second argument, the district court held that the lack of a confiscation order could not be regarded as an undertaking in exchange for a statement, and therefore that the argument put forward by the defence lacked a factual basis. The Amsterdam Court of Appeal concurred with the district court's findings.[113]

This discussion is related to the aforementioned debate during the parliamentary consideration of the Bill on Undertakings to Witnesses in Criminal Cases concerning the question of and to what extent the statutory system of Sections 226g ff. should be considered as a closed system for making undertakings to witnesses, or is only intended as the framework within which undertakings to witnesses relating to sentence reduction are arranged and that in introducing this framework for making undertakings the principle of prosecutorial discretion as a general basis for using the instrument was not abandoned.[114] In the first analysis – apart from the inducement referred to in Section 226g paragraph 4 –

---

109 See Parliamentary Papers I 2004/05, 26 294 and 28 017, E, p. 5 and Parliamentary Papers II 2004/05, 28 017 and 26 294, no. 8, p. 4-6. See further § 3.3.4.
110 Instructions on Undertakings to Witnesses in Criminal Cases, Government Gazette 2012, 26860 (entered into force on 1 January 2013), § 4.
111 See specifically in this context Janssen 2013, p. 242-255.
112 See Amsterdam District Court 29 January 2013 ECLI:NL:RBAMS:2013:BZ0392. See further § 3.3.4.
113 See Amsterdam Court of Appeal 29 June 2017, ECLI:NL:GHAMS:2017:2497 (Jesse R.), § 2.1.2.2.6.2.6.
114 According to the Amsterdam Court of Appeal – partly as a result of its long-drawn out parliamentary consideration and the evolving ideas about the legitimacy of the instrument of undertakings to witnesses – the legislative history provides openings for both views, which is what led the Court of Appeal to take a

there is little or no room for making undertakings other than those relating to sentence reduction. In the second interpretation, there is room for this, although it is open to question what the precise relationship is with the procedure laid down in Section 226g ff. CCP. Are such undertakings – insofar as they cannot be characterised as an inducement to which a lighter regime applies pursuant to paragraph 4 – subject to the same procedure as undertakings pertaining to sentence reduction within the meaning of Section 226g paragraph 1 CCP or does a different procedure apply which in terms of stringency lies somewhere in between the extensive procedure for undertakings related to sentence reduction and the lighter regime as that applies for an inducement?

3.4.3.4   Impermissible Undertakings

The Instructions on Undertakings to Witnesses in Criminal Cases also makes clear what types of undertakings are not permitted.[115] The Instructions summarise eight situations in this respect (each of which is set out below), which largely arise from the legislative history of the Provision of Undertakings to Witnesses in Criminal Cases Act and the jurisprudence on this subject matter dating from before this act entered into force.[116] This partly relates to undertakings which – given the limitations on the competence or relationship with other criminal law actors – the public prosecutor is not authorised to make; and partly to undertakings which the public prosecutor is in principle competent to make but which nevertheless were or are generally considered to be undesirable.[117]

1   *Changing the Legal Qualification of the Charged Facts and Omitting*
         Provable Facts

It is not permitted to change the legal qualification (*juridische kwalificatie*) of the charged facts in exchange for making formal statements in the sense that the individual is charged with a less serious offence than they would have been on the basis of the case file. Nor is it permitted to omit provable facts from the indictment in exchange for making formal state-

---

cautious stance concerning the intention of the legislature. See Amsterdam Court of Appeal 29 June 2017, ECLI:NL:GHAMS:2017:2497 (Jesse R.), § 2.1.2.2.6.2.

115 Instructions on Undertakings to Witnesses in Criminal Cases, Government Gazette 2012, 26860 (entered into force on 1 January 2013), § 5.

116 With regard to the parliamentary history, see also Parliamentary Papers I 2004/05, 26 294 and 28 017, E, p. 4-5 and Parliamentary Papers II 2004/05, 28 017 and 26 294, no. 8, p. 6-8; and with regard to the jurisprudence also SC 1 June 1999, NJ 1999, 567 with commentary by Sch (Karman). For further details see § 3.3.3 and § 3.3.4.

117 In this context, see also Amsterdam Court of Appeal 29 June 2017, ECLI:NL:GHAMS:2017:2497 (Jesse R.), § 2.1.2.2.6.2 where the Court of Appeal states that – regardless of the previously mentioned discussion about the open or closed nature of the statutory provision – what may be derived from the parliamentary history in any event is that the following three undertakings must be considered impermissible: 1) undertakings extending to complete immunity from prosecution; 2) undertakings relating to the contents and scope of the indictment, and 3) financial remuneration.

ments. Thus the Public Prosecution Service may neither make undertakings about the number of facts to be included in the indictment nor about their legal qualification (also known as charge bargaining). This is because this could result in sentence reduction for the information-provider, without the means by which such sentence reduction was achieved having been subject of scrutiny by the trial judge, bound as it is to the indictment.[118] In itself this ban does not prevent the normal application of the principle of prosecutorial discretion in the context of the decision to prosecute in the case of the witness. The omission of certain facts in the indictment based on 'normal' considerations under the principle of prosecutorial discretion – for example, pursuant to the Public Prosecution Service's guidelines – is therefore possible, provided and as long as this does not happen in exchange for making formal statements. Nevertheless it will be clear that there is only a thin dividing line between overstepping this ban, on the one hand, and the normal application of the principle of prosecutorial discretion, on the other.

2 Offering Immunity from Prosecution

In line with the aforementioned ban on changing the legal qualification of the charged facts and omitting provable facts, it is not permitted to abandon an active investigation or prosecution of criminal offences which the witness may have committed in exchange for statements, if and to the extent that this would be contrary to prevailing investigative and prosecutorial policy. Offering immunity from prosecution in exchange for making a witness statement is therefore out of the question.[119] As discussed above, the Van Traa Commission held the view that offering completely immunity would be going too far in the Dutch context at that time.[120] As well as the previously mentioned ban on undertakings relating to the content of the indictment, this ban is not without its problems in light of the principle of prosecutorial discretion. It is clear from the addition of "if and to the extent that this would be contrary to prevailing investigative and prosecutorial policy" that this

---

118 See Crijns 2010, p. 92. As far as is known the Supreme Court has not explicitly said anything about the permissibility of making undertakings concerning the content of the indictment. The Supreme Court has previously ruled however that the use of statements as evidence in a Dutch criminal case which were obtained abroad as a result of plea bargaining were not as such inadmissible, although the judge will have to expressly address any consequences the plea bargain may have had on the reliability of the statements. See SC 23 May 1995, NJ 1995, 683 with commentary by Sch. It should be noted however that this relates to jurisprudence dating from before the present legal framework on undertakings to witnesses. See also Parliamentary Papers II 2004/05, 28 017 and 26 294 no. 8, p. 6 where the minister makes reference to his position rejecting the introduction of a system in the Netherlands similar to plea bargaining (Parliamentary Papers II 2003/04, 29 200 VI, no. 31). The Amsterdam Court of Appeal recently emphasized in the Passage case that under the present regime, undertakings concerning the content and scope of the indictment were out of the question. See Amsterdam Court of Appeal 29 June 2017, ECLI:NL:GHAMS:2017:2497 (Jesse R.), § 2.1.2.2.6.2.

119 See Parliamentary Papers II 2004/05, 28 017 and 26 294, no. 8, p. 6 where the minister commented that the undesirability of making an undertaking not to prosecute was never seriously in question during the parliamentary debate. In line with this, see Amsterdam Court of Appeal 29 June 2017, ECLI:NL:GHAMS:2017:2497 (Jesse R.), § 2.1.2.2.6.2.

120 See § 3.3.2. and Parliamentary Committee of Enquiry into Investigation Methods 1996, p. 466.

ban also does not preclude the normal application of the principle of prosecutorial discretion. At the same time, here too there is a thin dividing line between overstepping this ban by dropping charges in exchange for a statement, on the one hand, and dropping one or more facts in the case against the witness in line with normal prosecutorial policy or based on 'normal' considerations of prosecutorial discretion, on the other. A ban on granting immunity from prosecution can also lead to other sorts of questions. Is the Public Prosecution Service infringing this ban, for example, if it makes an agreement with a witness who in their own criminal case was acquitted in first instance, in which it promises that the previously lodged appeal against that acquittal will be withdrawn? Materially this leads to immunity, albeit that in such a situation the witness' case will already have been put before the court. For precisely this last reason the Supreme Court therefore also deemed that such an undertaking was not contrary to the ban on immunity from prosecution under the previous Guidelines on Agreements with Criminals.[121]

3   *Promising That a Custodial Sentence Imposed Abroad May Be Served in the Netherlands*

In the context of the Enforcement of Criminal Judgments (Transfer) Act (WOTS), the public prosecutor is not permitted to make the undertaking that a custodial sentence imposed on the witness abroad can be served in the Netherlands.[122] This is only natural, given that the public prosecutor himself cannot enforce such an undertaking because the authorities in the country where the custodial sentence was imposed must give their consent for that.[123] The public prosecutor can therefore make no further undertaking than to urge that a WOTS procedure be followed. According to the Instructions, such an undertaking can be made in the context of an inducement as referred to in Section 226g paragraph 4 CCP.[124]

4   *Financial Reward*

This next forbidden undertaking concerns providing a financial reward in exchange for statements. Although this was not discussed in any detail during the parliamentary debate, it was considered by the legislature to be going too far.[125] In older jurisprudence dating from

---

121 See SC 15 June 2004, NJ 2004, 479 with commentary by JR.
122 In this context the Instructions only make reference to the Enforcement of Criminal Judgments (Transfer) Act (WOTS). However, the Measures Involving Deprivation of Liberty and Conditional Penalties (Mutual Recognition and Enforcement) Act (WETS) also entered into force on 1 November 2012, which regulates the transfer of criminal sentences within the European Union. It may be assumed that the intended ban in the Instructions is also partly in connection with the transfer of sentences under the WETS legislation.
123 See Parliamentary Papers II 2004/05, 28 017 and 26 294, no. 8, p. 7.
124 Instructions on Undertakings to Witnesses in Criminal Cases, Government Gazette 2012, 26860 (entered into force on 1 January 2013), § 8.4. See also § 3.4.3.2.
125 See e.g. Parliamentary Papers II 2004/05, 28 017 and 26 294, no. 8, p. 6-7, where the minister also indicated that this ban is not inconsistent with the permissible undertaking to reduce a monetary fine (Section 44a paragraph 2 CC), given that this concerns a sentence reduction awarded by the court.

before the entry into force of the present legal framework, the courts regularly approved agreements which also included a financial benefit for the witness, although it should be noted that in each case these were payments which were promised for a specific purpose, for example, for the witness to organise their own protective measures.[126] The Guidelines on Agreements with Criminals dating from 1997 also still included granting a financial reward among the permissible undertakings. With the entry into force of the Temporary Instructions on Undertakings to Witnesses in Criminal Cases in 2001 however such an undertaking became banned.[127]

5   *Undertakings Relating to Additional Penalties and Measures*

It is not permitted to make undertakings relating to additional penalties and measures (*bijkomende straffen en maatregelen*) (or abandoning any demand for such), other than the measure of confiscation of the unlawfully obtained gains where the assumption is that this could become part of any undertaking made. It is therefore not permitted to make undertakings relating to forfeiture or confiscation of seized goods. The reasoning for this ban appears to lie in the notion that Section 44a CC contains a limitative list of sentence reduction options which may be granted.[128] In light of the later reconsideration of the closed nature of the scheme of undertakings to witnesses and deemed permissibility of undertakings relating to the confiscation of unlawfully obtained gains, this reasoning however seems to be rather out of step.[129] Another possible justification for this ban could lie in the fact that undertakings entailing partial or no confiscation or seizure of confiscated goods essentially amounts to a disguised financial reward which – as stated – is not permitted. At the same time, to a certain extent, this will also be the case when a monetary fine is reduced or the amount in unlawfully obtained gains to be confiscated is reduced, which are included among the undertakings that are deemed permissible.[130]

6   *Non-Implementation of Court Decisions*

It is strictly forbidden to make an undertaking that any future court decision will not be implemented (or only implemented in part) by the Public Prosecution Service. This ban – which is only natural given the institutional structure of the criminal justice system (cf. Section 553 CCP) – arises directly from the Karman case dating from the 1990s in which the Public Prosecution Service had made such an undertaking and was severely reprimanded

---

126 See Crijns 2010, p. 94, where a number of other examples are also referred to.
127 See Guidelines on Agreements with Criminals of 13 March 1997, Government Gazette 1997, 61, which entered into force on 1 April 1997 and Temporary Instructions on Undertakings to Witnesses in Criminal Cases of 13 July 2001, Government Gazette 2001, 138 which entered into force on 1 August 2001.
128 See Parliamentary Papers II 2004/05, 28 017 and 26 294, no. 8, p. 7.
129 See § 3.3.4 and § 3.4.3.3.
130 As previously noted, in the minister's view, it is incorrect to compare a financial reward with reducing a monetary fine given that the latter is only possible through the intervention of a court. See Parliamentary Papers II 2004/05, 28 017 and 26 294, no. 8, p. 6-7.

for this by the District Court, the Court of Appeal and the Supreme Court.[131] This ban however does not prevent undertakings from being made concerning the way in which court decisions will be executed, for example, regarding the place where or the regime under which the witness will be detained; generally such undertakings will be made in the form of an inducement within the meaning of Section 226g paragraph 4 CCP.[132]

7   Benefits to Third Parties

An undertaking may not be made which benefits anyone other than the witness, for example a life partner. It must expressly be the witness in person who benefits from the undertaking, given that he or she is also the person making the official statements. However in this context it should be noted that this ban does not impinge upon the issue of witness protection. In that context, if there is cause for such, proper protection measures can also be provided to people other than the witness.[133]

8   Witness Protection Measures

It is not permitted to make undertakings concerning the physical protection of the witness, other than the undertaking that the public prosecutor will urge that such measures upon instruction of the Board of Procurators General will be provided if necessary. The public prosecutor with whom the witness negotiates on the intended agreement, is therefore not the person responsible for the protection measures to be arranged for the witness. Accordingly, two separate agreements are entered into.[134]

3.4.4   The Procedure to Be Followed and (Interim) Scrutiny

As we have seen from the foregoing, the public prosecutor is responsible for making agreements with potential witnesses. This does not mean, however, that they can do

---

131 See § 3.3.3 and SC 1 June 1999, NJ 1999, 567 (Karman). Among the considerations of the Amsterdam Court of Appeal was: "The Public Prosecution Service is not free to take upon itself the authority to not execute the prison sentence that the judge imposed on Karman. This unlawful undertaking by the Public Prosecution Service shows contempt for the decision of the court. Under our system of criminal law there is no room for the court to be bound by an undertaking made by the Public Prosecution Service concerning the sentence. The judge should be able to freely determine any sentence to be handed down within the limits set by the law."

132 See § 3.4.3.2 and Instructions on Undertakings to Witnesses in Criminal Cases, Government Gazette 2012, 26860 (which entered into force on 1 January 2013), § 8.4, which gives various examples of permissible inducements with regard to the execution of sentences. In between impermissible undertakings to not execute a sentence and permissible undertakings relating to the way in which a sentence is served lie undertakings concerning the matter of when the sentence will be served. The jurisprudence has not so far said anything about the permissibility of such undertakings. Although SC 2 July 2002, NJ 2003, 2 with commentary by Kn (Mink K.) does include an example of such a situation. See also in this context Crijns 2010, p. 93.

133 See § 3.4.5 for further details.

134 See § 3.4.5 for further details.

this independently. Before an agreement can actually be entered into, an extensive internal scrutiny procedure must be followed. This procedure is described in some detail in the Instructions on Undertakings to Witnesses in Criminal Cases.[135] The statutory provision further provides for an external procedure for scrutiny by the investigating judge (Section 226h cf. CCP).

3.4.4.1 The Orientation Phase

The Instructions are somewhat vague about the very initial stages of the process of concluding an agreement, but given the nature of the matter this can hardly be otherwise. This is because it will not be clear in advance how the Public Prosecution Service and the potential witness[136] will come into contact with one another, or who will take the initiative to make an agreement. The Instructions state in this regard that the intention to make an agreement can come from either the public prosecutor or the witness. If the witness makes such an intention known to the police, the police should inform the public prosecutor of this immediately. Further to this, the Instructions make it absolutely clear that any undertakings may only be made by the public prosecutor (and therefore not by the police).[137] The Instructions also state that the public prosecutor may only start the discussion with the witness after having first obtained permission from the Head of the District PPS. The purpose of the exploratory talks between the public prosecutor and the witness is to determine whether and to what extent there is a worthwhile basis on which to begin the negotiation process. To be able to determine this, it is, of course, necessary for the witness to provide insight into what statements they can make. The general substance and scope of the statement will be set down in writing by the public prosecutor, and the witness should also be informed of this. If the public prosecutor comes to the conclusion that this statement offers insufficient basis to start negotiations, the discussions will end there. If the public prosecutor is of the opinion that there is a sufficient basis for this, the negotiation process can begin.[138] Accordingly, it is the public prosecutor who is responsible for the negotiations with the witness. Pursuant to the Instructions the police cannot do this independently, which is to be expected based on the normal division of responsibilities between the police and the Public Prosecution Service as laid down in the Code of Criminal Procedure.

---

135 Instructions on Undertakings to Witnesses in Criminal Cases, Government Gazette 2012, 26860 (entered into force on 1 January 2013), § 7. See also Crijns 2010, p. 98-102.
136 Although, strictly speaking, during the period up until the agreement is concluded it would be more correct to speak of the 'potential witness', for the sake of readability and to be consistent with the Instructions from here on the term 'witness' has been used.
137 Instructions on Undertakings to Witnesses in Criminal Cases, Government Gazette 2012, 26860 (entered into force on 1 January 2013), § 7.1.
138 Instructions on Undertakings to Witnesses in Criminal Cases, Government Gazette 2012, 26860 (entered into force on 1 January 2013), § 7.2.

3.4.4.2 The Negotiation Phase and the Intended Agreement

If in the view of the public prosecutor the initial statements made by the witness offer sufficient basis to start the negotiation process, then this process may be initiated. The Instructions state in this context that during the negotiations the witness may be supported by a defence lawyer. A defence lawyer will be assigned to a witness who does not yet have one (Section 226h paragraph 1 CCP). The Instructions state in this regard that the public prosecutor will do their utmost to urge the witness to allow themselves to be assisted by a chosen or allocated defence lawyer. The public prosecutor must also keep a written record in a journal of the course of the negotiations and during it ascertain "the validity of the witness' statement and their reliability". If the negotiations do not produce a result, the statements previously made by the witness may not be used. These statements therefore may only be included in the case file is after the agreement has been concluded (cf. Section 226g paragraph 4 CCP).[139]

If the negotiations do produce a result, the intended agreement will be drawn up in writing. Under Section 226g paragraph 2 CCP and the Instructions on Undertakings to Witnesses in Criminal Cases the written agreement should as accurately as possible describe: "a) the crimes and (insofar as possible) the suspect(s) against whom the witness is willing to make a statement; b) the criminal offences in the case in which the witness is a suspect, for which he is being prosecuted or has been convicted and to which of these the undertaking relates; c) the conditions which the witness will be subject to and which they are willing to abide by; d) the nature of the undertaking".[140] With regard to the conditions which the witness will be subject to, the Instructions state that in any event this will include that the witness is willing to make a statement to the court during the public trial, and – where the witness is also a co-accused – to give full details and complete disclosure of the state of affairs concerning the witness' own share in the criminal offences to which their statement relates. In addition, based on the Instructions, agreements can be made "about the extent to which the witness will rely on the right to refuse to give evidence which may be available to him in various situations" which means that "it is reasonable to assume that it will be agreed that the witness will not invoke Section 217 CCP".[141]

3.4.4.3 Scrutiny of the Intended Agreement

After the public prosecutor and the witness have set down the intended agreement in writing, the internal scrutiny procedure begins. First of all, the intended agreement is

---

139 Instructions on Undertakings to Witnesses in Criminal Cases, Government Gazette 2012, 26860 (entered into force on 1 January 2013), § 7.3.
140 Instructions on Undertakings to Witnesses in Criminal Cases, Government Gazette 2012, 26860 (entered into force on 1 January 2013), § 7.4.
141 Instructions on Undertakings to Witnesses in Criminal Cases, Government Gazette 2012, 26860 (entered into force on 1 January 2013), § 6 and 7.4. It may be assumed that the Instructions are also referring to the right to refuse to give evidence under Sections 218 and 219 CCP, given that the Instructions speak of 'the right to refuse to give evidence that is conferred on him in various capacities'.

submitted to the State Advocate for advice. The Internal Review Committee of the PPS on the use of special investigative measures (CTC) then makes its recommendations, following which the Board of Procurators General review the intended agreement. "If there is cause to" the chairman of the Board of Procurators General consults the Minister of Justice and Security on the proposed agreement. According to the Instructions such cause exists in any event if there are politically-sensitive aspects associated with the agreement. What this may refer to however is not further specified in the Instructions.[142]

If the Board of Procurators General makes a positive recommendation concerning the intended agreement, the investigating judge becomes involved in the case when the public prosecutor requests that the lawfulness of the intended agreement be examined by the investigating judge (Section 226g paragraph 3 CCP). This scrutiny by the investigating judge arises directly from the view expressed by the Lower House of Parliament in a motion that agreements with witnesses should be made subject to prior judicial review.[143] In scrutinising the intended agreement the investigating judge must take into account "the urgent need and the importance of obtaining the statement to be made by the witness" (Section 226h paragraph 3 CCP). In other words, the investigating judge must specifically check that the intended agreement meets the requirements of subsidiarity and proportionality.[144] If the investigating judge is of the opinion that these requirements have been met and the agreement otherwise meets the statutory conditions, then it may be deemed lawful. The investigating judge also has to assess the reliability of the witness and their statements. Among other things, this assessment must also be based on the questioning of the witness as laid down in Section 226h paragraph 2 CCP. The investigating judge is then required to set out his or her assessment of the lawfulness of the intended agreement and the reliability of the witness and his/her statements in a reasoned decision (Section 226i paragraph 1 CCP). If the investigating judge deems the agreement to be lawful, this will then (as a result) take effect (Section 226h paragraph 3 CCP).[145] In the event that investigating judge reaches a negative conclusion, the public prosecutor can institute an appeal against this with the district court (Section 226i paragraph 2 CCP); however the law does not provide for a similar option for the witness. Should the district court also reach a negative conclusion, there is no further appeal available (Section 226i paragraph 3 CCP).

---

142 Instructions on Undertakings to Witnesses in Criminal Cases, Government Gazette 2012, 26860 (entered into force on 1 January 2013), § 7.5. The Rules of Procedure of the Board of Procurators General (Government Gazette 1999, 106) also includes no specific instructions on when the minister must be informed of an intention to make an agreement with a witness. This is different where the intention is to use a criminal civilian infiltrator; in such situations Section 11 paragraph 2 of the aforementioned rules specifically states that the minister must be informed of this.
143 See Parliamentary Papers II 1995/96, 24 072 no. 51. See § 3.3.2 for further details.
144 For further details, see § 3.4.2.
145 However this does still have to signed by the public prosecutor and the witness, after which it is referred to in the Instructions as an agreement ('*overeenkomst*'). See Instructions on Undertakings to Witnesses in Criminal Cases, Government Gazette 2012, 26860 (entered into force on 1 January 2013), § 7.7.

3.4.4.4   Implementation of the Agreement

After the Board of Procurators General has given its consent for the agreement to be made and it has also been found to be lawful by the investigating judge, the public prosecutor and the witness sign the written agreement. From this moment on the Instructions refer to it as an agreement ('*overeenkomst*').[146] The public prosecutor encloses a copy of the agreement in the case file of the suspect or suspects to whom the witness statement relates as well as in the witness' own case file.[147] From this point onwards the agreement is "ready to use". The Instructions provide relatively little information, however, about how the obligations arising from the agreement should be implemented. To a certain extent, this is also to be expected, not least because of the fact that it also depends on what the precise nature of the agreement is. Furthermore, the agreement will be implemented in the context of the examination conducted by the investigating judge in the pre-trial phase of the proceedings and of the subsequent trial phase thereof, meaning that the question of how the obligations should be implemented is not appropriately addressed in a set of instructions by the Public Prosecution Service, given that both phases fall under the remit of the investigating judge and the trial judge, respectively.

In essence the agreement will always include the obligation to make one or more verifiable witness statements in the witness' own name in the presence of the investigating judge and during trial in exchange for the undertakings which the Public Prosecution Service has made to the witness (usually also including a mitigated sentencing demand). This means that such an agreement will always be used in the context of two or more different criminal cases: the criminal case or cases in which the witness makes their statements and the criminal proceedings in which the witness himself is prosecuted as an accused.[148] When the witness is a co-accused in the same set of facts as the accused against whom he has made a statement, generally these cases will be handled at the same time and by the same trial judge, but this is not a requirement. The statutory provision does not rule out that the criminal cases concerned will be handled one after another and/or by a different trial judge; where this involves co-accused however this will generally not be preferable, not least for practical reasons. Conversely, in the (less common) cases in which the witness cannot be considered as a co-accused in the same set of facts, a simultaneous hearing would not be very likely. It is not possible to say in general whether in such circumstances it would be preferable for both cases to be heard by the same trial judge. All in all the determination of the most suitable approach to the two cases is a matter for practice. The Instructions in this respect state only that the public prosecutor should try to arrange for the criminal case against the accused, in which an incriminating statement is made by the witness, to be held earlier than the criminal

---

146 Instructions on Undertakings to Witnesses in Criminal Cases, Government Gazette 2012, 26860 (entered into force on 1 January 2013), § 7.7.
147 Instructions on Undertakings to Witnesses in Criminal Cases, Government Gazette 2012, 26860 (entered into force on 1 January 2013), § 7.8.
148 For further details, see § 3.2.1.

proceedings against the witness.[149] The reason for this instruction is self-evident because if the sequence were to be reversed, the public prosecutor would no longer have any leverage in the event that the witness should refuse to provide further cooperation in the case in which they had agreed to make their statements,[150] while in the context of the sentencing in the criminal case against the witness, the judge would not be able to properly determine whether and to what extent the witness has actually met their obligations arising from the agreement and therefore whether they are entitled to the promised sentence reduction pursuant to Section 44a CC. At the same time this instruction should not be read such that handling both cases simultaneously would be out of the question, as long as the case against the witness does not take place *sooner* than the case or cases against the (one or more) accused against whom the witness is testifying. For the purposes of clarity the following sections of the analysis will take a separate look at the implementation of the agreement in the criminal case in which the witness makes their statements[151] and thereafter the criminal proceedings in which the witness himself is being prosecuted. In connection with the foregoing it should also be noted that both criminal cases could in fact be handled in parallel and/or by the same trial judge.

In the first criminal case the witness is expected to meet their obligations arising from the agreement, i.e. by making one or more (incriminating) statements in their own name. Usually the witness will do so in the pre-trial phase in the presence of the investigating judge (Section 226j paragraph 1 CCP) and at a later date once again in the trial proceedings. As previously noted, the witness who is also a co-accused should give full details and complete disclosure of the state of affairs concerning the witness' own share in the criminal offences to which the witness statement relates.[152] The public prosecutor is expected to provide full disclosure during the court hearing "concerning the facts and circumstances which were important in reaching the agreement".[153] It is then up to the trial judge to determine whether or not the statements made by the witness can be used as evidence. As with the scrutiny by the investigating judge, this involves an assessment of the lawfulness of all aspects of the agreement, as well as an assessment of the reliability of the statements made by the witness. The trial judge is not bound in this by the previous judgment of the investigating judge.[154] In

---

149 Instructions on Undertakings to Witnesses in Criminal Cases, Government Gazette 2012, 26860 (entered into force on 1 January 2013), § 7.8.

150 In the event of a refusal to provide further cooperation, Section 192 paragraph 2 CC allows for the prosecution of the witness to whom undertakings have been made for refusing to make the statement previously promised. See in this regard § 3.4.4.5.

151 In the event of multiple accused this may, of course, also affect several criminal cases.

152 Instructions on Undertakings to Witnesses in Criminal Cases, Government Gazette 2012, 26860 (entered into force on 1 January 2013), § 6.

153 Instructions on Undertakings to Witnesses in Criminal Cases, Government Gazette 2012, 26860 (entered into force on 1 January 2013), § 7.8.

154 See Parliamentary Papers II 1998/99, 26 294 no. 3, p. 17. By ruling that the responsibility for assessing the lawfulness of the agreement lies primarily with the investigating judge and that the trial judge should mainly be concerned with assessing the reliability of the witness and their statements, the Court of Appeal in its judgments in the Passage case, while making reference to the parliamentary history, appears to see its role

particular the trial judge should assess whether the fact that the witness statements obtained from the witness in exchange for undertakings on the part of the Public Prosecution Service has any negative consequences in terms of the reliability of these statements. If the judge reaches the conclusion that the statements were lawfully obtained (i.e. the underlying agreement is lawful) and are (sufficiently) reliable, they may be used as evidence. In doing this, the judge has to take into account a number of special rules concerning proof and reasoning. In this context, Section 344a paragraph 4 CCP prescribes a minimum evidence requirement, entailing that a declaration that the charges have been proven may not rest exclusively on statements obtained as a result of an undertaking within the meaning of Section 226g or 226k CCP.[155] Furthermore, in connection with the potentially greater risk that the statements made are unreliable, the judge should provide specific reasons for their use in accordance with Section 360 paragraph 2 CCP.[156]

The trial judge in the case in which the witness is standing trial as an accused, will also have to make an assessment of the agreement.[157] This is because it is in the context of this criminal case that the undertakings made to the witness will be redeemed.[158] This judge too will therefore have to make an assessment of the lawfulness of the agreement.[159] This judge will also have to reach a conclusion about the matter of whether or not the witness has met all the obligations arising from the agreement and thus to what extent they are entitled to claim the undertakings made to them in exchange for that, in particular the undertakings concerning sentence reduction. The views of the Public Prosecution Service will, of course, be important in answering these questions. In this regard the Instructions on Undertakings to Witnesses in Criminal Cases states that the public prosecutor's demand in the criminal case against the witness should state the sentence that they would have argued for on the basis of the offence as charged in the indictment if no agreement had been concluded (i.e. the basic sentencing demand), as well as the contribution made by the witness to the investigation and prosecution,

---

with regard to the scrutiny of the agreement as rather more limited. While there may be questions about the lawfulness of the agreement underlying the statements, these should be evaluated in the light of Section 359a CCP and Article 6 ECHR. See e.g. Amsterdam Court of Appeal 29 June 2017, ECLI:NL:GHAMS:2017:2496 (Dino S.), § 1.6.2.

155 For further details of this particular minimum evidence requirement and its added value, see Dubelaar 2014, p. 314-315.
156 See Parliamentary Papers II 1998/99, 26294, no. 3, p. 17-18 for further details on the rationales of these provisions.
157 It bears repeating here that in practice it may also be – and often will be – the same trial judge who has to consider whether these statements can be used as evidence in the context of the criminal case in which the witness makes their statements.
158 Although it should also be noted that not all undertakings depend on the judge when it comes to their delivery. While accomplishing a sentence reduction that was agreed to depends on the cooperation of the judge, some other undertakings can also be made independently by the public prosecutor – mainly in the context of an inducement as referred to in Section 226g paragraph 4 CCP (and in the event of agreements with convicted persons, based on Section 226k CCP).
159 See Crijns 2010, p. 104.

how the witness has met their obligations and the amount of sentence reduction which on the basis of these circumstances should be granted to the witness in their own criminal case.[160] If the public prosecutor reaches the conclusion that the witness has met their obligations and for this reason seeks the sentence reduction pledged to him, it is up to the judge to decide whether or not to concur with that.[161] The judge is not required to defer to the public prosecutor's judgement, given that the agreement between the Public Prosecution Service and the witness is not binding upon the judge. For these reasons the witness does not receive an undertaking of sentence reduction but more one of a mitigated sentencing demand. Nevertheless it is assumed in the literature that there is relatively little room for the judge to not or only partially honour the sentence reduction claimed.[162] Firstly, it would appear that Section 44a paragraph 1 CC – the statutory basis for granting a sentence reduction in exchange for a witness state-ment – sets out more or less binding sentencing instructions: "In considering sentence reduction the judge shall take into account that by making a witness statement an important contribution is or could be made to the investigation or prosecution of criminal offences".[163] While the judge may not be bound by the agreement, this statutory provision would appear to suggest that it cannot simply be set aside.[164] If the judge nevertheless decides not to honour the undertaking concerning sentence reduction (or only partially) which results in a higher sentence being imposed than was advocated by the public prosecutor, then pursuant to Section 359 paragraph 2 CCP, the reasons for this must be given in view of the fact that s/he is deviating from a 'position expressly substantiated' by the Public Prosecution Service (*uit-drukkelijk onderbouwd standpunt*). Perhaps the most compelling justification for the afore-mentioned stance is the political legal argument that the judge who sets aside agreements between the Public Prosecution Service and the witness deals a heavy blow to the instrument of undertakings to witnesses as a whole, with the possible consequence that in the future there would be few witnesses willing to enter into an agreement with the Public Prosecution Service knowing that they run a real risk of being left empty handed. Although from a legal point of view therefore the judge is not bound by an agreement between the Public Prosecution Service and the witness, it would appear that in practice the room to

---

160 Instructions on Undertakings to Witnesses in Criminal Cases, Government Gazette 2012, 26860 (entered into force on 1 January 2013), § 7.8.

161 If the judge decides on sentence reduction and therefore applies the provisions of Section 44a CC, then pursuant to Section 359 paragraph 4 CCP, the specific reasons for this should be given.

162 See e.g. De Roos 2006, p. 10; Schuyt 2009, p. 128-129; and Crijns 2010, p. 104-105. See also § 3.4.1 and 3.4.3.2.

163 In the Explanatory Memorandum too it is assumed that, in principle, the judge should adopt the mitigated sentencing demand put forward by the public prosecutor. See Parliamentary Papers II 1998/99, 26 294, no. 3, p. 7 and pp. 16-17. See also Parliamentary Papers II 1999/2000, 26 294, no. 6, pp. 9-10, p. 27 and p. 37.

164 In its rulings in the Passage case, the Amsterdam Court of Appeal made a similar judgment with reference to the criterion provided in Section 44a paragraph 1 CC (see Amsterdam Court of Appeal 29 June 2017, ECLI:NL:GHAMS:2017:2496 (Dino S.), § 1.6.2 as well as in the cases against the two witnesses to whom undertakings had been made, see Amsterdam Court of Appeal 29 June 2017, ECLI:NL:GHAMS:2017:2494 (Peter la S.), § 6.2 and ECLI:NL:GHAMS::2017:2495 (Fred R.), § 7.2).

manoeuvre is fairly limited in cases where the Public Prosecution Service is of the view that the witness has fulfilled the terms of the agreement.

3.4.4.5   The Uncooperative Witness

While the question of what happens in the event that contrary to the agreements made the witness refuses to make the statements as promised (or to make them again) has already been touched upon above, it is worth fleshing out the issue further. The legislation tries to prevent this in two ways: firstly by providing that the public prosecutor should do the utmost to ensure that the criminal case in which the witness is required to make their statements is completed earlier than the criminal proceedings against that witness,[165] so that the Public Prosecution Service can maintain pressure on the witness and the witness cannot benefit from the undertakings made before first meeting their own obligations.[166] Secondly, through the introduction of a separate offence (Section 192 paragraph 2 CC): the witness who in defiance of an agreement under Section 226h or Section 226k CCP, deliberately refuses to make a statement risks a prison sentence of up to one year or a monetary fine in the fifth category.[167] Although this is not expressed as such in the wording of the provision, the legislature specifically intended this penalisation for cases in which the witness – contrary to the preferred sequence – has already obtained their sentence reduction. The older Section 192 paragraph 1 CC – that provides for penalisation of an 'ordinary' witness who refuses to make a statement – and the possibility of committal for failure to comply with a court order were not considered by the legislature to be sufficiently effective in the case of an uncooperative witness to whom undertakings have been made.[168] In the literature however it is argued that one should not expect too much from this new qualified (*gekwalificeerde*) offence, at least insofar as this can actually deter the witness from withdrawing their cooperation. Not least because the threatened punishment is small, certainly when seen in light of the fact that this provision is primarily intended for cases in which the witness has already

---

165 Instructions on Undertakings to Witnesses in Criminal Cases, Government Gazette 2012, 26860 (entered into force on 1 January 2013), § 7.8.
166 It is worth noting here that this will also have consequences in the appeal phase. If the Public Prosecution Service wishes to continue to motivate the witness to whom undertakings have been made to cooperate in this phase too, then for this reason alone the Public Prosecution Service will always have to lodge an appeal in the criminal proceedings against the witness. See in this regard Amsterdam Court of Appeal 27 September 2013, ECLI:NL:GHAMS:2013:3125 (interlocutory decision Peter la S.), in which the court held that, on its own, the purpose of maintaining pressure on the witness provides a sufficient basis on which to lodge an appeal.
167 This refers to a qualified version of the older Section 192 paragraph 1 CC, introduced by the Act of 12 May 2005 amending the Criminal Code in connection with failing to make a witness statement after an undertaking to that effect had been made, Bulletin of Acts and Decrees 2005, 255 (entered into force on 1 April 2006), at the same time as the Provision of Undertakings to Witnesses in Criminal Cases Act.
168 See Parliamentary Papers II 2001/02, 28 017 no. 3 and Parliamentary Papers II 1998/99, 26 294, no. 3, p. 26.

obtained their sentence reduction further to the agreement.[169] Added to which this provision appears to be somewhat at odds with Article 6 ECHR and the privilege against self-
incrimination arising therefrom, given that by making their statements the witness will
often also incriminate themselves. Although the counterargument to this is that the
witness has already made a contractual agreement to do so, in the light of Article 6
ECHR it is open to question whether they can be held to this under the threat of penalisation, particularly in light of the prison sentence that may be imposed.[170] To which
may be added finally that over the course of time a change in the witness' circumstances
(including the safety situation) may render the wholesale fulfilment of the terms of the
agreement unreasonably burdensome.[171]

3.4.5   Relationship with Witness Protection

Making a witness statement may necessitate the adoption of protective measures for the
witness. This may be the case with 'ordinary' witnesses who have made a statement and
then suffer adverse consequences as a result. However this is particularly so for witnesses
to whom undertakings are made, given that this instrument can only be used for the
purpose of combatting serious criminal offences – as discussed above – which may or
may not have been committed in the context of organised crime and that the witness in
question will have to make a statement in their own name, thereby making them even
more vulnerable to any repercussion on the part of the accused or the organisation in
which they operate.[172] The authorities have a general duty to protect such witnesses. This
duty arises out of Articles 2 and 8 ECHR,[173] and elsewhere, and is quite separate from any
undertakings made by the public prosecutor and the question of whether or not an agreement has been entered into in that context.[174] For this reason also, the agreements on
undertakings to witnesses in exchange for statements and those about witness protection
are kept strictly separate from one another, in that the procedure to be followed in respect

---

169 See Crijns 2010, p. 105-108 which also looks at the matter of whether and to what extent it would be
    possible in certain cases to apply both sanctions (i.e. withdrawing the undertakings made as well as
    prosecuting under Section 192 paragraph 2 CC).
170 See in this context Parliamentary Papers II 1998/99, 26 294, A, p. 6, where the Council of State indicates that
    the use of witness statements which were made under the threat of a criminal prosecution could contravene
    Article 6 ECHR. These and similar objections were also among the reasons why this part of the Bill on
    Undertakings to Witnesses in Criminal Cases was initially rejected by the Lower House, following which
    this provision was introduced later in a separate legislative bill. In this context see also § 3.3.4.
171 See Crijns 2010, p. 106.
172 See § 3.2.1, § 3.2.2.1 and § 3.4.2 for further details.
173 See with regard to Article 2 ECHR also ECtHR 28 October 1998, 23452/94, NJ 2000, 134, § 115-116
    (*Osman/United Kingdom*). See also Korten 2015, p. 41-112 for a comprehensive overview of the (scope of
    the) duty of care. See regarding the relationship between the contractual obligation to protect the witness on
    the one hand and the general duty of care on the other Bleichrodt and Korten 2012 as well as § 3.5.5.4.
174 With the proviso that if no agreement is reached and the identity of the witness is not made public, there
    will be no reason to provide protection measures.

of each is separate. In these procedures responsibility for the witness protection process (and its implementation) rests with the Witness Protection Team of the national unit of the police force and the public prosecutor responsible for that at the National Public Prosecutors' Office (hereafter the WPT public prosecutor), while, in principle, the undertakings process falls under the auspices of the Criminal Intelligence Team and the public prosecutor responsible for the gathering and use of criminal intelligence by the police.[175] If an agreement with the witness about making statements in exchange for undertakings is actually entered into and there is also cause for measures to be taken to protect the witness, two separate agreements will be concluded.[176] In other words, the witness protection programme therefore forms no part of the agreement on undertakings to the witness in exchange for their statements. As previously mentioned, it is possible however to include in the agreement on the undertakings that the public prosecutor will urge that measures to protect the witness are put in place.[177] It is the Board of Procurators General however that decides on this.[178]

The criminal procedure basis for specific measures to be taken to protect the witness is provided in the aforementioned Section 226l CCP and the Witness Protection Decree.[179] This sets out when physical measures to protect the witness can be instituted and what the procedure is in this regard. Based on the Decree and its Explanatory Memorandum, witnesses "will only be eligible for protection measures when there is a real and serious threat which is directly related to (a) the cooperation given or to be given to the police and the Public Prosecution Service, and (b) action on the part of the authorities in this context. In which event there will generally be an urgent need for the authorities to take protective measures."[180] Not unimportant is that the threat must have arisen due to action on the part of the authorities. The Explanatory Memorandum to the Decree states that if the threat is caused by the witness him/herself then in principle there is no duty of care on the part of the authorities.[181]

---

175 See also § 3.5.2.1 for the organisational aspects of the undertakings process.

176 For full details of the legal character of these agreements and their relationship to one another, see Crijns 2010 and Janssen 2013.

177 See the Instructions on Undertakings to Witnesses in Criminal Cases, Government Gazette 2012, 26860 (which entered into force on 1 January 2013), § 5. For further details, see § 3.4.3.4.

178 The public prosecutor responsible for witness protection acts as the intermediary between the Board of Procurators General and the Witness Protection Team and can give the team instructions. See Explanatory Memorandum to the Witness Protection Decree of 21 December 2006, p. 4 (Bulletin of Acts and Decrees 2006, 21, last amended on 30 November 2012, Bulletin of Acts and Decrees 2012, 615 which entered into force on 1 January 2013).

179 See the Witness Protection Decree of 21 December 2006 (Bulletin of Acts and Decrees 2006, 21 last amended on 30 November 2012, Bulletin of Acts and Decrees 2012, 615, which entered into force on 1 January 2013) and the associated Explanatory Memorandum (published in Bulletin of Acts and Decrees 2006, 21).

180 See Explanatory Memorandum to the Witness Protection Decree, Bulletin of Acts and Decrees 2006, 21, p. 5.

181 See Explanatory Memorandum to the Witness Protection Decree, Bulletin of Acts and Decrees 2006, 21, p. 5.

The procedure for taking measures to protect the witness is as follows. Under Section 4 Witness Protection Decree, the Board of Procurators General can ask the Witness Protection Team to carry out a threat analysis with regard to the witness and where necessary those close to him/her and on the basis of this analysis give advice on the measures to be taken and their practical feasibility.[182] If it appears from the threat analysis that there is an urgent need to take protection measures and these are also feasible to implement, under Section 5 Witness Protection Decree, the Board of Procurators General can then give the order for these measures to be taken following which the WPT public prosecutor will conclude a written agreement with the individual concerned "which in any event shall include provisions concerning the obligations of the person to be protected and of the witness protection unit as well as the consequences of non-observance" (Section 7 paragraph 1 Witness Protection Decree).[183] In principle the protection measures will only take effect after the agreement with the individual concerned has been concluded (Section 7 paragraph 2 Witness Protection Decree).[184] Under Section 5 paragraph 2 Witness Protection Decree the agreement must also include a duration period, which pursuant to Section 8 paragraph 1 Witness Protection Decree may be extended further to a renewed threat analysis by the Board of Procurators General. The Explanatory Memorandum states the following concerning this.

> "Under this Decree protection measures may be taken for the duration of a threat against a person. These measures therefore do not have a permanent nature. Nor are these measures aimed at providing for the entire livelihood of the individual concerned. This means that the person to be protected continues to be responsible for organising their own life. The protection measures will only contribute to the protection of that individual during the period that he/she is seriously threatened as a result of their actions for the purpose of or in the context of criminal proceedings. As soon as that threat has passed, the duty of care on the part of the authorities ceases, the measures will end and the individual concerned should be capable of resuming his life fully independently."[185]

---

182 According to the Explanatory Memorandum a recommendation on feasibility is necessary in each specific case because of the serious impact which certain measures could have for the person to be protected and their immediate family. If it is thought that some people would not be able to deal with the consequences, then other solutions must be sought (Explanatory Memorandum, p. 6). For details of the psycho-social effects of witness protection upon the individuals concerned, see Beune and Giebels 2012.

183 This agreement is considered to be one of civil law. See Explanatory Memorandum to the Witness Protection Decree, p. 7. For a critique of this, see Janssen 2013, p. 170-172.

184 Section 6 Witness Protection Decree also provides for a 'fast-track procedure' under which emergency measures can be taken temporarily.

185 See Explanatory Memorandum to the Witness Protection Decree, Bulletin of Acts and Decrees 2006, 21, p. 4.

What measures will be taken will depend on the nature and seriousness of the threat as made apparent by the threat analysis. The measures will be tailored to "the specific needs in the given case" and therefore may vary in duration and intensity.[186] The package of protection measures may include that a witness – possibly with their immediate family – is moved abroad and (perhaps temporarily) receives a new identity. If a witness is given a new identity, the law also offers the possibility of keeping this new identity hidden in the criminal proceedings. For example, under Section 190 paragraph 3 CCP and Section 187d paragraph 1 under a CCP[187] the investigating judge, and under Section 290 paragraph 3 CCP and Section 293 paragraph 1 CCP the trial judge, can obstruct certain questions from the defence to prevent the new identity or place of residence of the witness from being revealed. The district court can also take other measures to prevent such information from being revealed, for example, by permitting the witness to disguise him/herself.

When a witness is included in a witness protection programme and enters into an agreement with the Public Prosecution Service, this then gives rise to an obligation of means on the part of the State when it comes to taking appropriate protection measures. The individual to be protected in turn accepts the obligations necessary to allow the Witness Protection Team to implement the protection measures as effectively and safely as possible. If the individual fails to observe the agreements this can "undermine the proper implementation of the measures such that they are essentially made impossible" which could lead to a change in the measures or their cessation.[188] Ultimately it is the Board of Procurators General which decides on this, based on the recommendations of the Witness Protection Team. It may also however be that the witness is not satisfied with the way in which the agreement or previous agreements are implemented. Given that the agreement is one of civil law, in the event of a dispute, the witness will, according to the Explanatory Memorandum, have to turn to an arbitrator, provided that an arbitration clause is included in the agreement, or to a civil law court.[189] Moreover, in the Passage case both the Amsterdam District Court and the Amsterdam Appeal Court ruled that disputes arising from the agreement relating to the witness protection is the sole preserve of the civil courts and thus may not be heard by a criminal court.[190] However this does

---

186 See Explanatory Memorandum to the Witness Protection Decree, Bulletin of Acts and Decrees 2006, 21, p. 6.
187 Section 187d paragraph 1 concerns obstructing the answers to questions on a particular matter from being made public where it may be expected that the witness would suffer serious harm as a result. The scope of this provision is wider than that of Section 190 paragraph 3 CCP which only provides for obstructing questions on matters which relate to establishing identity as referred to in Section 27a paragraph 1, first sentence, CCP.
188 See Explanatory Memorandum to the Witness Protection Decree, Bulletin of Acts and Decrees 2006, 21, p. 7.
189 See Explanatory Memorandum to the Witness Protection Decree, Bulletin of Acts and Decrees 2006, 21, p. 7.
190 See Amsterdam District Court 27 April 2010, ECLI:NL:RBAMS:2010:BM2493 (interlocutory order) and Amsterdam District Court 29 January 2013 ECLI:NL:RBAMS:2013:BZ0392 (final judgment). See also Amsterdam Court of Appeal 29 June 2017, ECLI:NL:GHAMS:2017:2496 (Dino S.), § 2.2.2.4.

not alter the fact that disputes concerning witness protection may have a direct impact on the willingness of the accused to make a statement and could lead to complications in the context of the criminal case.[191]

The relationship between witness protection and agreements concerning undertakings is, for other reasons also, not without its problems, as is clear from the literature.[192] For example, those taking part in the proceedings i.e. the defence, the judge and the public prosecutor responsible for the case, will have no idea what the protection agreement contains, which means that they cannot determine whether and to what extent agreements (financial or otherwise) have been made in that context which would be deemed inadmissible on the basis of the Instructions on Undertakings to Witnesses in Criminal Cases.[193] Moreover, unlike the agreements made concerning undertakings, the protection agreement is not subject to external scrutiny. The only external party involved in drawing up an agreement on witness protection is the State Advocate, whose role is only to "assist" the public prosecutor.[194] In this context it is therefore interesting that in its rulings on the Passage case the Amsterdam Court of Appeal appeared to see scope, albeit very limited, for the trial judge to express an opinion about the protection agreement, namely in circumstances:

> "[…] in which, based on the facts and circumstances, there are such compelling indications of unlawful action on the part of the Public Prosecution Service that it must be considered that – in the guise of witness protection – agreements or undertakings have been made which cannot reasonably be considered to be related to providing adequate protection but which nevertheless extend to simply or largely providing financial remuneration for the witness' willingness to give a statement in the context of criminal proceedings. That implies an unlawful situation which is the result either of deception on the part of the State or the complete failure of the administrative scrutiny laid down in the Witness Protection Decree."[195]

In the opinion of the Court of Appeal in the Passage case however no such situation had taken place and on the basis of the wording used by the Court of Appeal it should be clear that this concerns only a very minor exception to the basic tenet also subscribed to by the Court of Appeal that, in principle, the implementation and substance of the protection agreement is in no way subject to the scrutiny of the criminal court.[196]

---

191 See § 3.5.5.2. for further details.
192 See also Bleichrodt 2010, p. 20; Bleichrodt and Korten 2012; and Janssen 2013, p. 255-264.
193 Instructions on Undertakings to Witnesses in Criminal Cases, Government Gazette 2012, 26860 (entered into force on 1 January 2013), § 5. For further details, see § 3.4.3.4.
194 See Explanatory Memorandum to the Witness Protection Decree, Bulletin of Acts and Decrees 2006, 21, p. 7.
195 See e.g. Amsterdam Court of Appeal 29 June 2017, ECLI:NL:GHAMS:2017:2496 (Dino S.), § 2.2.2.5.2.
196 See e.g. Amsterdam Court of Appeal 29 June 2017, ECLI:NL:GHAMS:2017:2496 (Dino S.), § 2.2.2.4.

3.5   Legal Practice

This section looks at the legal practice surrounding the use of the instrument of collaboration with justice in criminal cases in the Netherlands, against the backdrop of the intention expressed by the Minister of Security and Justice in 2013 to, insofar as necessary, amend the legal framework relating to this instrument which – as previously discussed in the introduction – in part was the reason for this study.[197] In order to determine whether or not to introduce a new statutory provision on collaboration with justice or to refine the existing one it is necessary to gain an understanding of what the practical experience has been with providing undertakings to witnesses, where difficulties arise in practice and what practitioners think and would like to see in terms of the statutory provision and its application.

3.5.1   *Method*

As also apparent from the introduction to this chapter, the description and analysis in this section of the methods adopted, problems encountered and views held in practice are based on empirical research conducted mainly in the form of interviews. A focus group was also held and a file search (*dossieronderzoek*) was conducted through the Internal Review Committee of the PPS on the use of special investigative measures (*Centrale Toetsingscommissie*, hereafter CTC). Further details of the structure of that empirical study follow below, together with the choices made in that context.

3.5.1.1   Respondents

In the Netherlands key figures were spoken to in the Public Prosecution Service (PPS) (i.e. public prosecutors, members of the CTC and a member of the Board of Procurators General), members of the police, judges, defence lawyers and a lawyer with the State Advocate's Office. In principle, these were all people who have been directly involved with the legislation concerning undertakings to witnesses and/or its application.[198] It should be noted, however, that the pool of people with direct experience with the scheme is limited. The explanation for this lies in the fact that it is a 'closed' world and the scheme is not often used in the Netherlands.[199] The numbers were thin on the ground, particularly among lawyers and judges. It was also difficult to ascertain who was involved in a case in

---

197 See the letter from the Minister of Security and Justice to the Lower House dated 5 July 2013 (Parliamentary Papers II 2012/13, 29 911 no. 83, p. 6 ff.). See further § 1.1.

198 Some interviewees only had experience with other types of special witnesses, such as the threatened witness, and not with the witness to whom undertakings are made. These respondents could nevertheless provide useful information given that the methods and problems to a certain extent are similar. This was the case for three of the 19 interviewees. See for a list of the respondents Annex 2.

199 See further § 3.5.2.

which a witness within the meaning of this study appeared or in which the use of such a witness was seriously considered although that did not ultimately happen. In the end, most of the respondents from the PPS and the police were found with the assistance of contacts of members of the supervisory committee. It was mostly their networks that were drawn upon. The judges were nominated by the Council for the Judiciary (*Raad voor de rechtspraak*) in consultation with the researchers. In terms of the criminal defence bar, it was easiest to approach the lawyers who had been involved in the more often mentioned Passage case. Almost everyone approached was willing to take part in the interviews.

Altogether 19 interviews were conducted in the Netherlands: seven with members of the Public Prosecution Service, three with members of the judiciary, three with the criminal defence bar, a lawyer with the State Advocate's Office, plus five interviews with members of the police. Sometimes the person initially approached for the interview was accompanied by someone else. Whether that person was then included in the list of respondents attached as an annex to this report was dependent on their contribution to the interview. The annex includes all the interviewees together with their position. Because some of the respondents work undercover the report does not include the respondents' names; instead a number has been used to indicate each respondent.[200]

It should be noted at the outset that the Public Prosecution Service and the police are overrepresented in the selection of respondents. This is because the PPS and the police have the most data available on the use of the instrument and together, they have the broadest view of the various aspects of the procedure surrounding the use of the instrument of undertakings to witnesses. Such overrepresentation is also justifiable given that members of the PPS and police are uniquely placed to shed light on the very initial stages of the process of concluding an agreement, which is otherwise unregulated and regarding which the literature and jurisprudence say little, while a clear picture of this is vital in relation to any decisions that have to be made by the legislature. At the PPS, only those public prosecutors with experience with special witness procedures and undertakings to witnesses in particular were approached. As for the police, interviews were held with officers who are on the Special Witnesses Teams in Amsterdam and with the National Unit, who are responsible for conducting the exploratory talks with potential witnesses and for the verification and falsification of the information provided. Members of the Witness Protection Team were also spoken to, who are involved with the screening of witnesses and the protection of special witnesses.

Among the defence lawyers who were interviewed, there were both lawyers who had represented clients in whose cases use had been made of undertakings to witnesses for the investigation and prosecution, as well as one lawyer who had represented a client to whom such undertakings had been made. Among the judges interviewed, there were three who had been involved as an investigating judge (either directly or more

---

200 To preserve the anonymity of the respondents they have all been referred to with a male pronoun.

indirectly) in a case in which the instrument of undertakings to witnesses had been used, and one who had served as a trial judge in a major case involving the use of a witness as referred to in Section 226g CCP.

3.5.1.2 Questionnaires

The respondents were sent a questionnaire in advance so that they could prepare for the interview if they so wished, and, if necessary, obtain further information in their own organisation for that purpose. The questionnaire they were sent was tailored to the respondent's background (e.g. judge, public prosecutor, etc.). Separate questionnaires were drawn up for the different professional groups.[201] The focus for the police was mainly on the early phase (how do potential witnesses present themselves, where do the procedures run aground, etc.?). The public prosecutors were asked about the entire procedure from start to finish. For the judges the emphasis lay on assessing the lawfulness and reliability of the agreement made with the witness. The defence lawyers were mainly asked about their experience of the procedure after the formal statement has been made, and the treatment and scrutiny of the agreement by the judge. All the respondents were asked for their views regarding the performance of the existing scheme.

3.5.1.3 The Course of the Interviews

In the Netherlands, the semi-structured interviews were conducted by experienced researchers[202] in the presence of a student assistant.[203] The interviews all took place face-to-face and as a rule lasted between an hour and 90 minutes. At the start of the interview further information was provided about the purpose and set-up of the study, some instructions were given and arrangements were made about the reporting, following which the background and experience of the interviewee were established. This last step also marked the start of the interview itself. The order of the questions was largely determined by the course of the interview. The researchers particularly wanted to provide the respondents with the opportunity to tell their side of the story and say what, in their view, needs to be said. Because in certain cases the individuals involved only had insight into a particular part of the procedure and the time was limited, sometimes not all the questions included in the standard questionnaire were actually put to them or answered in equal detail. The interviews mainly focused on those aspects of the procedure or its implementation in practice with which the respondent concerned had had the most experience. In this context, questions were also asked which were not included in the

---

201 The general questionnaire, in which the questions were divided by professional group, is included as annex 3 to this report. It should be noted that the questionnaire included in the annex was not sent to all the respondents in this form. Additional questions were often included which were more tailored to that part of the procedure in which that particular interviewee is specifically involved.
202 In almost all cases this was M.J. Dubelaar; occasionally the interview was conducted by K.M. Pitcher.
203 This was Ybo Buruma Jr.

questionnaire sent in advance. The interviews took place in the period from September 2016 to the end of March 2017. This provided an opportunity to build on information from previous interviews to examine certain themes in more depth. In the early stages more attention was focused on gaining an impression of the actual course of events and, in particular, how the procedure is set up, in later interviews there was more detailed probing of obstacles and perceptions, as well as the moral and legal dilemmas involved. The time frame also provided the opportunity to verify certain information and ask for responses to problems mentioned or opinions expressed in previous interviews. Finally, it should be noted that the interviews were conducted during a period in which the appeal in the (often mentioned) Passage case was still ongoing. The Amsterdam Court of Appeal issued its ruling on this case at the end of June 2017.[204] When respondents referred to this case, it must therefore also be borne in mind that they did so at a time when the proceedings were still pending on appeal.

3.5.1.4   Reporting Procedure

To maintain confidentiality arrangements were made at the start of the interviews about the way in which the information would be handled. This was because operational information might be mentioned during the interviews which is not suitable for inclusion in a public report. This could relate to information which might make it possible to identify certain individuals from the examples given, or reveal procedures which have thus far remained secret. From the interviews it was also apparent that people were cautious about sharing information which relates to the way in which the witness protection procedure is set up in order not to endanger witnesses in protection programmes. In accordance with the arrangement made prior to the interview, all the respondents received a report afterwards which gave them the opportunity to designate certain passages as confidential. The purpose of this was to enable the respondents to speak freely during the interview. The reports were drawn up by the student assistant who was present during the interviews, in consultation with the researcher in question. Sound recordings were used for this, provided that the respondent had given their consent for the interview to be recorded.[205] In addition to the reports of the interviews, the passages in the current report that make direct reference to a certain interview were also submitted to the respondents separately.

3.5.1.5   Processing the Results

The information from the interviews was analysed on the basis of a number of preselected themes which also provided the basis for the standard questionnaire. In doing so, the

---

204 See also Amsterdam Court of Appeal 29 June 2017, ECLI:NL:GHAMS:2017:2496 (Dino S.).
205 This was the case in 17 of the 19 interviews.

information related to that theme was as far as possible compared and validated based on the interviews with other key figures. In the discussion of these themes below, an attempt has been made to present an overall picture based on all the interviews, highlighting as far as possible the various approaches and considerations of the different parties. Where respondents' opinions differed widely, or no consistent view of a certain aspect of the practice emerged, this has been expressly noted. The same applies to other striking matters. The fact that a certain piece of information is mentioned by just one person, was in itself insufficient reason to leave this information unreported given that only a small number of respondents was approached and that often someone has an overview of only part of the process. For this reason too, no attempt was made to quantify the information (e.g. by stating that 12 respondents think this, while the other respondents think that). When respondents were in agreement or something was often mentioned as a problem, explanation or argument, this has been stated. Where a finding has been made which is contradicted by other respondents, this is always mentioned.

3.5.1.6   Focus Group

The results of the interviews were also validated with the aid of a focus group in which the most important and most striking findings from the empirical study were presented to a panel of seven individuals from the various relevant professional groups and academia.[206] This focus group – which met at the end of March 2017 – was also attended by two of the three researchers and a student assistant who took written notes during the meeting. One of the researchers acted as a moderator and in that capacity was responsible for steering the exchange of ideas and monitoring the speaking time of the various participants.

In preparation for the meeting, the focus group members had read the answers to the research questions in the other comparison countries. This essentially amounted to a summary of the (then provisional) findings per comparison country. The participants were also sent a list of topics.[207] This topic list provided a guideline for the discussion. The participants were each given an opportunity at the start of the meeting to give an initial reaction and to contribute whatever they thought necessary – whether in connection with the presented findings or not.

In particular, the focus group looked at whether and to what extent the picture of the practice surrounding undertakings to witnesses as revealed in the interviews corresponded with their own impressions and experiences, and whether and to what extent in that context the various professional groups involved hold differing views. At the same time the opportunity was taken to ask the participants for their views on certain specific proposals to change the scheme, and to reflect on certain aspects of the legislation on undertakings to witnesses in the various comparison countries. However, the primary

---

206 See Annex 4 for a list of the roles of the focus group members.
207 See Annex 5 for the list of topics used in the focus group.

purpose of the meeting was to validate the findings relating to the practice in the Netherlands. In consultation with the researchers the student assistant drew up a report on the meeting which lasted more than two and a half hours.[208]

3.5.1.7   File Search via the Internal Review Committee of the PPS (CTC)

At the request of the researchers a file search was carried out at the CTC. The aim of this search was to gain an impression of how often the instrument of undertakings to witnesses is used and the type of cases in which this occurs. It was natural to approach the CTC for this because requests to provide undertakings to witnesses as referred to in Section 226g paragraph 1 and Section 226k CCP must be submitted to the CTC, following which the Board of Procurators General advises on the use of this instrument.[209] The Secretary of the CTC – referred to in this report as respondent [2] – looked at all the cases in which the CTC was asked to give advice during the period from 1 April 2006 to 15 December 2016. At the request of the researchers respondent [2] answered the following questions: 1) how often is advice sought from the CTC; 2) what offence was the (potential) witness accused of; 3) in which cases was use of the statement sought; 4) what type of undertaking was made; 5) what advice was given by the CTC (positive or negative); 6) what had happened to the case where the advice given by the CTC was negative; and 7) was the witness taken into a protection programme or not? The last question turned out to be difficult to answer, given that, in principle, as the respondents indicated, the CTC has no insight into what happens after the CTC has issued its advice and a decision had been taken by the Board of Procurators General. For reasons of confidentiality, the respondents did not report per case but provided clustered answers to the questions (i.e. for all cases taken together). This means that it is only possible to report on this in general terms as it was not possible for the researchers to make any connection between the type of undertaking and a particular offence, or to gain insight into the reasons for issuing advice in an individual case, whether positive or negative.

3.5.1.8   Results of the Empirical Study

The interviews provided a clear picture of the working methods adopted in practice in seeking to use undertakings, the problems which may arise in that context, and the views held in practice on the instrument of making undertakings to witnesses. Where the views of the respondents differed, these mainly concerned opinions about the desirability of using such an instrument and the need to widen the existing scheme. The impression of current practice regarding the use of undertakings to witnesses as expressed in the interviews, was confirmed by the focus group. The members of the focus group did, however,

---

208 The student assistant used recordings for this that were made during the focus group meeting.
209 For further details see § 3.4.4.3 and § 3.5.4.1.

mention a few more points which in their view merited attention in this report. However, this almost always concerned issues which had already been raised by the respondents but which had not yet been included in the provisional findings presented to the focus group.

Based on a number of themes the results of the empirical study will be examined more closely below. It should be noted however that it was not always possible to describe in detail the examples given by the respondents, given the need to ensure that it would not be possible to determine to which specific case they related and thus endanger the informant or witness in question.

3.5.2   *Frequency and Results of Using the Instrument of Undertakings to Witnesses*

This section will look at the matter of how often since its entry into force the statutory provision on undertakings to witnesses has been applied in practice and the results of the efforts made in that context. First, however, the motives for using this instrument will be briefly considered.

3.5.2.1   Motives

According to the interviewees, the Public Prosecution Service and the police want to be able to make undertakings mainly because certain information about serious criminal offences would not be provided without making such undertakings. In this context respondent [1] made reference to the liquidations in the Amsterdam underworld which would not have been cleared up without the witnesses to whom undertakings had been made. In this regard the respondents from the Public Prosecution Service also referred to the failure of other special investigation methods. Respondent [5] stated the following.

> "The present investigative practice shows that the tool of collaborator of justice is increasingly necessary to be able to solve serious crime. There is a growing segment of the criminal world which we simply cannot catch with all the other inventive investigative methods, because they no longer leave any trace. This means that those who do know something, by definition, are close to the source and that we must be able to offer something attractive to this small group to get them to talk."

There is also a desire to cash in on certain information already in the hands of the authorities and the TCI more specifically. The catch however with TCI information is that it can only be used as information to start or steer the criminal proceedings (e.g. to use certain powers) and not as evidentiary material. This type of information comes to the case team (*zaaksteam*) through an anonymous TCI report which provides a brief summary of the information.[210]

---

210 This is referred to as TCI-type information.

The ability to verify such information as a case team (and later as a judge), said respondent [17], is therefore much more limited than with a witness statement where the identity of the individual who made the statement is known.[211] According to respondent [6] the police are likely to have a goldmine of information to hand which cannot be used as evidence in specific criminal cases (or in police jargon: "which cannot be made tactically operational"). In this regard, one of the focus group members observed that for the police the inability to use the information as evidence is not so much due to the difficulties involved in verifying or falsifying the information as the need to protect the source of the information (the informant) and ensure their safety. The aforementioned issues arise not only in respect of information provided by existing TCI informants, but also in exploring new information sources. In this context respondent [6], who is a TCI public prosecutor, stated the following:

> "If colleagues have a case in which a person says that they have certain information but don't want to have that put down on paper, then they often end up coming to me. [...] But TCI information is no panacea, because it is not evidence. Ideally you want to get people down on paper. I will take Willem Endstra as an example. He was in the back seat, at the TCI, while actually he should have been in the front seat, as a witness. Then we would have had much more tactical information and more insight into the financial dealings of the criminal world that could then have been used as evidence."

3.5.2.2   Frequency of Use

The first thing to stand out is that the instrument of undertakings to witnesses is not very often used at the moment. All the respondents said that they had not often come across it in legal practice. To obtain a better impression of how often undertakings to witnesses are used, as previously mentioned, further inquiries were made with the Internal Review Committee of the PPS on the use of special investigative measures (CTC).[212] The information obtained from the CTC shows that during the period from 1 April 2006, when the Provision of Undertakings to Witnesses in Criminal Cases Act entered into force, to 15 December 2016 advice has been sought from the CTC for a total of twelve cases, in which the Committee's advice was positive nine times, which was then also adopted by the Board of Procurators General.[213] The other three cases were rejected, which in two cases resulted in the applicant withdrawing the plan to make use of the instrument and in the third case in the Board of Procurators General rejecting the request in accordance with the advice of the CTC.

---

211 It bears noting here that the identity of informants will be known to the relevant TCI, where informants' statements can, to a certain extent, be verified or falsified.
212 See § 3.5.1.7.
213 In one case an application was made for the use of two witnesses as referred to in Section 226g CCP, where the advice issued by the CTC was positive.

The actual use of the instrument turned out to be even less than that. Only three cases are known in which statements from witnesses as referred to in Section 226g CCP were actually submitted in court as evidence. The first was the Passage case concerning liquidations (and attempted liquidations) among the Amsterdam underworld, where in the first instance proceedings a witness as referred to in Section 226g CCP was introduced by the Public Prosecution Service, following which on appeal a second witness to whom undertakings had been made was also introduced.[214] In the second instance proceedings there were ten accused involved[215] and, according to the Court of Appeal in its introduction to the various judgments, seven murders. The second one concerns the Yellowstone case in which statements from a witness as referred to in Section 226g CCP were also used.[216] And the third case involved, among other things, the attempted murder of Cor van Hout in which two witnesses as referred to in Section 226g CCP made statements at the same time.[217] Altogether, therefore, there were five witnesses to whom undertakings were made in three different cases. In the other six cases in which the advice issued by the CTC was positive, the CTC stated that (so far) the witness in question has not been used. The CTC indicated in general terms what the reasons may be for the fact that despite a positive recommendation it was nevertheless decided not to use the instrument, for example, because the witness later decided to withdraw or the evidence could be provided in another way which made it no longer necessary to use statements from the witness concerned.

The above relates only to the use of witnesses in the context of Section 226g paragraph 1 and Section 226k CCP. It should be noted that a different procedure applies in relation to an 'inducement' (small courtesies; *gunstbetoon*) in the sense of Section 226g paragraph 4. As explained above, the agreements made in this context are not submitted to the CTC. The public prosecutor can make an independent decision on this.[218] Interviewees from the Public Prosecution Service indicated that the inducement is applied more often than sentence reduction within the meaning of Section 226g CCP, but that it is nevertheless not used very often. The various case law search engines were also used to search for the term 'inducement' (*gunstbetoon*) and the associated statutory provision, but that produced few hits thereby confirming the impression that such small courtesies are hardly if at all used in legal practice.[219]

---

214 See also Amsterdam District Court 29 January 2013, ECLI:NL:RBAMS:2013: BZ0392 and Amsterdam Court of Appeal 29 June 2017, ECLI:NL:GHAMS:2017:2496 (Dino S.). For further details see § 3.4.2.

215 Originally there were 12 accused but two of them died during the criminal proceedings.

216 The statements made by the witness were used against several of the accused. The same considerations concerning the lawfulness of the agreement are found in all of the various judgments. See also Amsterdam District Court 3 May 2013, ECLI:NL:RBAMS:2013: CA1739 and Amsterdam Court of Appeal 17 August 2015, ECLI:NL:GHAMS:2015:3345.

217 See Haarlem District Court 20 June 2008, ECLI:NL:RBHAA:2008:BD4909/BD4924 and Amsterdam Court of Appeal 21 March 2011, ECLI:NL:GHAMS:2011:BP9113/BP9115.

218 See § 3.4.3.2 for further details.

219 This search was performed in the case law search engine Rechtspraak.nl, the case law reports *Nederlandse Jurisprudentie Feitenrechtspraak Strafzaken (NJFS)* and *Nieuwsbrief Strafrecht*. See for a case in which inducements were used: Amsterdam Court of Appeal 13 April 2010, ECLI:NL:GHMAS:2010:BP2459.

3.5.2.3   Results

From the foregoing it appears that undertakings to witnesses in the meaning of Section 226g paragraph 1 CCP have been used in only a relatively small number of cases, in which regard it should be noted that the statement made by the witness to whom undertakings have been made, need not be the critical statement necessary in order to conclude that the charges have been proved. The witness' statement could also be used to direct the course of the investigation, as a result of which more evidence is gathered. It is known that of the twelve cases on which the CTC advised, most concerned homicides. The following criminal offences were also involved, sometimes in combination with a homicide: a robbery with fatal consequences, extortion, money laundering, membership of a criminal organisation, forgery of documents, intentional arson/causing an explosion, threatening behaviour and fraud. In terms of the type of undertakings, in eight cases this involved an intended undertaking to make a reduced sentencing demand (Section 226g paragraph 1 CCP). In three cases the undertaking made involved a positive recommendation concerning an application for a pardon (Section 226k CCP). In one case it involved reducing the confiscation order that was to be submitted or reducing the proposed settlement that would be made under Section 511c CCP. As already mentioned, there are three cases where it is clear that the instrument was also actually used. These will be discussed below, following which an attempt will be made to piece together a picture of the processes which did not come to fruition.

a   *Cases in Which the Instrument Was Actually Used*

The first time that the instrument of undertakings to witnesses under the present provision was actually used related to the case previously referred to which, among other things, concerned the attempted murder of Cor van Hout, in which two witnesses made statements in exchange for undertakings. These statements were made by two brothers. The accused in whose case the statements were introduced had at a previous stage already been told that the Public Prosecution Service had decided to take no further action. Further to the statements of the aforementioned witnesses the Public Prosecution Service decided that it would prosecute him after all. In assessing whether there were so-called 'new objections' (*nieuwe bezwaren*) within the meaning of Section 255 CCP which would justify a new prosecution, the district court had ruled that the statements introduced were insufficiently reliable and further that the other new information provided was not sufficient to indicate new objections which would warrant a new prosecution, further to which the district court declared the prosecution inadmissible. The reasons for this were that the information provided by the main witness was deemed unreliable and unsound and the statement of the other witness did not relate to the failed attack and had come to him mainly from his own brother.[220] On appeal the Court of

---

220 See Haarlem District Court 20 June 2008, ECLI:NL:RBHAA:2008:BD4909/BD4924.

Appeal referred the case back to the district court, because in its view the district court had wrongly declared the prosecution inadmissible given that the fact that a statement will only be found to be insufficiently reliable in the context of the trial proceedings did not mean that there were no new objections within the meaning of Section 255 CCP.[221] This case was referred back to the Noord-Holland District Court in 2011 and at the time of completing this report had not yet been disposed of.

The Yellowstone case concerned, among other things, an attempted murder and arson attack.[222] This is an example of a case in which the use of the instrument appears to have taken place without too many obstacles. This case was also described by the focus group as a success. No interviewees spoken to for the purposes of this study were directly involved with this case, but there are no indications to suggest the contrary. Based on the decisions and rulings handed down in this case it would indeed appear that no particular problems arose with respect to the use of the instrument.[223] In the end, various accused were convicted on the basis of the statements of the witness to whom undertakings had been made. The Court of Appeal's decision was as follows.

> "The Court of Appeal has established that the criminal offences about which the witness has stated he is willing and able to make a statement also concern: an attempted murder, causing an explosion with a general danger to property and arson attacks with general danger to property. This therefore concerns serious offences as referred to in Section 226g CCP.
>
> The Court of Appeal has also established that, in consideration of the importance, on the one hand, of the nature and seriousness of the offences about which the witness could make a statement and the importance of obtaining that statement and, on the other hand, the nature of the undertaking made to the witness, the agreement met the requirements of proportionality. It is also likely that the offences on which the witness was able to make a statement could not have been investigated or prosecuted by any other means.
>
> The public prosecutor therefore could have reached the opinion that the agreement was necessary for the investigation. The public prosecutor could also have

---

221 See Amsterdam Court of Appeal 29 June 2017, ECLI:NL:GHAMS:2011:BP9113/BP9115.

222 See also Amsterdam District Court 3 May 2013, ECLI:NL:RBAMS:2013: CA1739 and Amsterdam Court of Appeal 17 August 2015, ECLI:NL:GHAMS:2015:3345.

223 This can also be deduced from the fact that on appeal the lawfulness of the agreements made with the witness was no longer contested by the defence. See Amsterdam Court of Appeal 17 August 2015, ECLI: GHAMS:2015:3345.

made the judgement that the witness statement could not have been obtained without the undertaking.

Based also on the requirements as laid down in the Instructions on Undertakings to Witnesses in Criminal Cases, the public prosecutor could have reached the agreement on a sound basis.

The Court of Appeal deems the agreement to be lawful."[224]

In the debate surrounding the instrument of undertakings to witnesses it has been the Passage case in particular – that has been in progress for almost ten years now and both in the first instance proceedings and on appeal, led to several of convictions (and partial acquittals) – that has received the most attention.[225] The criminal proceedings began in 2008 and concern a series of liquidations and attempted liquidations in the Amsterdam underworld and even at the appeals stage, there were ten accused. In the first instance proceedings a witness as referred to in Section 226g CCP was introduced, who himself was accused and convicted for two homicides, these being murder and attempted murder. On 29 January 2013 the Amsterdam District Court ruled that the agreement with this witness was (for the most part) lawful and his statements sufficiently reliable for them to be used as evidence.[226] In addition the district court applied the sentence reduction claimed by the Public Prosecution Service in the criminal proceedings against the witness himself.[227] Respondent [1] from the Board of Procurators General indicated that without this witness the cases could not have been concluded and there would have been no convictions. In the second instance proceedings the Public Prosecution Service introduced a second witness within the meaning of Section 226g CCP. This witness, referred to in the press as the 'murder broker', was sentenced to thirty years' imprisonment in the first instance proceedings for his involvement in multiple homicides but later decided that he was willing to serve as a witness in exchange for undertakings by the Public Prosecution Service. On 29 June 2017 the Court of Appeal passed judgment in the cases against the various defendants in which the agreements with both witnesses were ruled to be lawful and their statements sufficiently reliable for them to be used as evidence.[228] In addition the Court of Appeal applied the sentence reduction claimed by

---

224 See Amsterdam Court of Appeal 17 August 2015, ECLI:GHAMS:2015:3345.
225 See also Janssen 2013 for further details of the Passage case (up to the first judgments in the court of the first instance).
226 See e.g. Amsterdam District Court 29 January 2013, ECLI:NL:RBAMS:2013:BZ0392. One aspect of the agreement – referred to as the 'omission agreement' in which the witness would not have to make a statement on a particular person – was ruled to be unlawful, but this did not lead to the conclusion that the entire agreement with the witness should be deemed unlawful. See § 3.5.4.3 for further details.
227 See Amsterdam District Court 29 January 2013, ECLI:NL:RBAMS:2013:1291 (Peter la S.).
228 See also Amsterdam Court of Appeal 29 June 2017, ECLI:NL:GHAMS:2017:2496 (Dino S.).

the Public Prosecution Service in the criminal proceedings against the witnesses them-selves.[229] Now it is a matter of waiting for the outcome of the proceedings in cassation. According to interviewees from the Public Prosecution Service and the judiciary involved in these cases, there was a great deal of innovation involved.[230] The judgments handed down in these cases raise many questions which those directly involved are facing in practice. These will be touched upon below – as they were also referred to in the legal framework section of this chapter.

b   *Processes Which Ran Aground*

When examining the results it is necessary to look not only at those cases in which the instrument as referred to in this study was actually used, but also cases in which such processes ran aground. As previously mentioned, in not all cases where the CTC was asked for advice was the instrument actually used in the end. There are however also processes which ran aground even before the CTC was asked to give its advice. In the interviews it was revealed that there had been many more instances in which exploratory talks or negotiations were conducted with potential witnesses which were then broken off before there was any scrutiny on the part of the CTC. This raises the question of how often this happened.

In the context of this study no insight was gained into how often potential witnesses within the meaning of this study presented themselves. There is also no central record of this kept.[231] The Special Witnesses Team of the National Unit does keep a record of how often one or more exploratory talks take place with potential 'deal witnesses'.[232] On the basis of this record, Respondent [16] from the Special Witnesses Team of the National Unit concluded that since 2010, there have 91 such cases. However, these only concerned cases which fall under the remit of the investigators in the National Unit. This figure cannot simply be extrapolated to the regional units, given that the National Unit mainly investigates more serious cases and has a special team dedicated to dealing with special witnesses. In the end only one case was actually used by the National Unit (this related to the previously mentioned Yellowstone dossier).

Such numbers should be treated with caution, however, given that the question of what conclusions may be drawn in this regard depends on when a 'procedure' may be said to have been started. The above figures could give the impression that the 'success

---

229 See Amsterdam Court of Appeal 29 June 2017, ECLI:NL:GHAMS:2017:2494 (Peter la S.) and ECLI:NL:GHAMS:2017:2495 (Fred R.).

230 It should again be noted that at the time of the interviews the respondents did not yet know the outcome of the appellate proceedings, given that the Court of Appeal only issued its judgment later.

231 There is however a national database held by the National intelligence team (*Team Nationale Inlichtingen; TNI*) of the police, known as the Informants Coding System (*Informanten Coderingssysteem*) in which every informant and special witness is assigned a unique code to prevent several TCIs all speaking to the same person.

232 This also includes cases where the potential witness decided not to lend any further cooperation after the first talks.

rate' is extremely low (1 in 91). This is because the exploratory talks are taken as a starting point. Respondent [16] also indicated however that it is often the case that an exploratory discussion is also the exit meeting. If the discussion on conditions were to be taken as the starting point, this could well result in a different picture. Respondent [18a] from the Special Witnesses Team in the Amsterdam regional unit said the following about this.

> "Let's say we give notification that we have someone and after the first intake meeting it is clear that they are not all that interesting after all. You could then say that it is a stranded process, and in a year of a hundred such meetings you might have one that is successful. If you start counting only when it really starts to get serious, then there will perhaps be just ten. If there is then just one left over, the picture will be quite different. It depends on where you draw the line."

The reason why the National Unit takes the exploratory talks as its starting point to see how 'procedures' develop is that they are interested not only in the instrument of undertakings to witnesses but also consider it a success if a person can be passed on to the TCI to act as an informant or is willing to make a statement in their own name without any undertakings as referred to in Section 226g CCP being made in exchange for such.

Although it is necessary to place some reservations against the above numbers, it is clear that the discussions held often do not lead to the instrument of undertakings to witnesses actually being used and thus producing a result in that sense. This was also confirmed in the interviews. Respondent [3] from the National Public Prosecutors' Office, the body responsible for witness protection and a centre of expertise on the use of special witnesses, said the following in this context:

> "The majority of cases where there are exploratory talks or vault statements are taken, ultimately lead nowhere."[233]

When asked how often the National Public Prosecutors' Office is approached by public prosecutors elsewhere in the country with questions, they indicated that nationally this was "a few dozen times a year".

In the interviews various explanations were given for the low frequency with which this instrument is used, all of which impact upon one another. This will be examined in more detail in § 3.5.3.5 after first looking at the way in which the potential 'deal witnesses' are selected and agreements are entered into.

---

233 See also § 3.4.4.2 for an explanation of the term 'vault statements'.

3.5.2.4   Scope of the Scheme

Based on the foregoing it is clear that the provisions of Section 226g paragraph 1 and Section 226k CCP are used in only a small number of cases.[234] In this context it may be asked whether and to what extent some 'agreements' made with witnesses remain off the radar.

The study showed that in practice the various different types of people providing information were not always clearly distinguishable from one another and questions can arise regarding the scope of the legislation. Respondent [9], a member of the judiciary, compared the scheme with a wooden mould into which only a small proportion of the witnesses will fit, while a large proportion will not. In his view, this did not mean however that the information that they have to offer would not be used. The respondents from the police said that as soon as someone comes into view as an individual who could potentially provide information, it is often a matter of searching for the capacity (special or otherwise) which will best fit the given situation: informant, threatened witness, witness as referred to in Section 226g CCP or 'ordinary' witness.[235] Under certain circumstances even 'ordinary' witnesses can claim witness protection if making a statement would put them at serious risk.[236] In the Instructions on Undertakings to Witnesses in Criminal Cases, however, witness protection is not viewed as a form of consideration.[237] However, a number of respondents in the judiciary and the criminal defence bar appear to see that differently, in the sense that they do consider the opportunity to begin a new life to be part of the 'undertakings package'.[238]

Moreover, based on the principle of prosecutorial discretion the public prosecutor also has a degree of flexibility not to prosecute a witness who themselves are accused of an offence and to introduce the statements of this person as ordinary witness statements, if and insofar as dropping the case against the witness falls within the normal prosecution policy pursued.[239] From the interviews with the respondents from the Public Prosecution Service it also appeared that this option is also used in practice. There is, however, no overview of how often that takes place. An example is the Briard case in which the witness was, according to the defence, a "co-accused", but who was not deemed as such by the Public Prosecution Service and who had already been admitted to the witness protection programme.[240] The respondents involved in this case considered this situation to be very

---

234 In which – as previously mentioned – the procedure in Section 226g paragraph 1 ff. CCP does not have to be followed to provide the 'inducement' as referred to in Section 226g paragraph 4 CCP.

235 See § 3.5.3.4 for the factors which are taken into account when making this assessment.

236 For further details see § 3.2.2.1.

237 For further details see § 3.4.3.4.

238 For further details see § 3.5.5.

239 If it would be decided not to prosecute anyway, i.e. on the basis of said policy, no consideration will have been made. If the decision not to prosecute is not based on such policy, a benefit will have been provided to the accused that is forbidden by the Instructions on Undertakings to Witnesses in Criminal Cases. It is however open to question whether it is as easy as that to draw the line in practice. See § 3.4.3.4 for further details.

240 With regard to the matter of whether and to what extent the witness himself could be considered a suspect, see Rotterdam District Court 2 June 2014, ECLI:NL:RBROT:2014:4399 (Briard).

close to the figure of the witness to whom undertakings are made within the meaning of Section 226g CCP. The Public Prosecution Service however does not consider a decision not to prosecute that falls within the scope of the normal criminal law framework to constitute an undertaking within the meaning of that provision, with all that this entails; in such circumstances, the procedure laid down in Section 226g et seq. CCP does not apply. The problems which may arise in such circumstances, however, are similar. For example, the witness in the Briard case refused to make (any further) statements due to his dissatisfaction with the way in which the witness protection was being provided which ultimately led to the defence not being able to exercise its right to confrontation pursuant to Article 6 paragraph 3 under d ECHR. A recurring question throughout the proceedings was whether this witness should (materially) be deemed a witness to whom undertakings had been made.[241] The district court deemed that there was no evidence that other agreements than a witness protection agreement had been made. The district court then considered the matter of whether owing to his place on the witness protection programme the witness should not materially be considered as a witness to whom undertakings had been made. In this context the defence had argued that owing to his forced departure as a result of his admission to that programme the witness had evaded prosecution for several criminal offences and also avoided his many creditors. However, the district court considered that it was not really possible and would also be going too far in the judgment to observe that with his departure the witness had intended to avoid prosecution and his creditors. This would insufficiently take into account the witness' primary reason for leaving, that of his safety. Nevertheless, in the district court's view it could be established with sufficient certainty that other, secondary interests were also served by his departure. This then led the district court to argue that also for these reasons – the other being that at the trial hearing the witness turned out to be not entirely reliable – the statements made by the witness should be used with due caution. Ultimately the district court acquitted the accused of the primary charge of extortion due to doubts surrounding the reliability of the witness and the fact that there was insufficient supporting evidence to compensate for not being able to exercise the right to confrontation. Respondent [9], a member of the judiciary and involved with this case at the time, commented that it is not always easy to place witnesses in a particular category and that mixed variants are often used in practice. What may also be added here – further to the case law research – is that analogous to the provisions of Section 44a CC, it is also possible to take into account a cooperative attitude towards the proceedings in the form of moderating the sentencing demand or the sentencing itself without making prior undertakings to that effect.[242]

---

241 See Rotterdam District Court 2 June 2014, ECLI:NL:RBROT:2014:4399 (Briard). A similar defence was also made in Den Bosch Court of Appeal 22 April 2016, ECLI:NL:GHSHE:2016:1596 (Chemie-Pack), where the argument was also rejected by the court.
242 See, for example, The Hague Court of Appeal 11 November 2009, ECLI:NL:GHSGR:2009:BK2957.

Nor is the dividing line with informants and those providing information on a more incidental basis (tipsters) always clear in practice. Such persons in principle provide information which can be used as lead information to further an investigation, but may only be rewarded for such on the basis of the Ministerial Circular on Special Payments for Investigation Purposes.[243] Other forms of considerations do not appear to be possible because, in principle, informants do not provide information on cases in which they are personally involved. However, in this regard the question arises as to what the legal options are if an accused or convicted person presents themselves who has valuable information about a criminal case that has already been closed and who wants something in return for his/her own case (sentence reduction or assistance with a pardon application). In other words, can agreements also be made with accused and convicted persons about something other than making a verifiable witness statement in an ongoing criminal case? For example the recovery of a valuable painting while the thief has already been convicted for that and in that sense the case is already closed? These are the types of questions which arise in practice, as apparent from the interviews. According to the CTC at least an agreement as referred to in Section 226g or 226k CCP cannot be made if the agreement is not entered into in the investigation or prosecution phase of proceedings. However, this is not to say that the information could not be used in some other way and that the witness could not still get what he or she has asked for.

To summarise, although it is clear that the instrument of undertakings to witnesses in criminal cases is not extensively used, this may also to some extent be due to the limited scope of the provision and how it is interpreted. Although the interviews gave no cause to assume that anything is happening in practice which is overtly contrary to the statutory provision[244], on the basis of those same interviews it may be said, however, that there is a grey area.

3.5.3   Procedure for Making the Agreement

The Instructions on Undertakings to Witnesses in Criminal Cases describes in some detail the procedure to be followed when entering into an agreement with the witness as referred to in Section 226g paragraph 1 and Section 226k CCP.[245] Certain aspects concerning the process of making such an agreement however remain largely neglected in the Instructions,[246] even though these may well be relevant to the question of whether the present legal framework needs to be changed. These aspects relate mainly to the very initial stages up to the negotiation phase (which in the foregoing was referred to as the

---

243 For further details see § 3.2.2.3.
244 Certainly in view of the Van Traa debacle that was mentioned by many of the respondents.
245 For further details see § 3.4.4.
246 This is partly due to the fact that the Instructions provide further details of the statutory provision that are primarily intended for the Public Prosecution Service and the court.

exploratory phase).[247] What is the precise role of the police in the entire procedure, and in the very initial stages in particular? What does this phase entail? How do the witnesses present themselves and what motivates them to collaborate with justice? How is an individual's suitability assessed and what factors will or could lead to the procedures that have been initiated running aground prematurely? And how is the procedure as a whole viewed by legal practitioners?[248] These matters will be further examined below, first looking at how the internal process is set up in the police and the Public Prosecution Service. It should be noted however that the role of the police with regard to the protection of witnesses and the tasks of the national Witness Protection Team in particular will only be considered in § 3.5.5.1, where the process by which protective measures are adopted will also be considered. This is because this process is essentially separate in a strictly legal sense.[249] The Witness Protection Team (*Team Getuigen-bescherming*; hereafter TGB) which is responsible for the protection process is therefore separate from the Special Witnesses Team (*Team Bijzondere Getuigen*; hereafter TBG) which is responsible for the process of obtaining a witness statement in exchange for an undertaking by the Public Prosecution Service as referred to in Section 226g ff. CCP.

3.5.3.1   Allocation of Tasks Within the Police and the Public Prosecution Service

As shown above, the police play an important role in the initial contact with witnesses with whom agreements may possibly be made. From the interviews it appeared that, among other things, it is the police who conduct the exploratory talks with and questioning of the witness, and examine the reliability of the person concerned and their statements. However the Instructions on Undertakings to Witnesses in Criminal Cases does not say anything about the role of the police. It mainly focuses on the role of the public prosecutor but does not as such consider the investigation carried out by the police. According to the Instructions it is the public prosecutor who discusses the conditions with the witness under which procedures such as this can be initiated and who ultimately decides whether or not there is sufficient basis to begin the negotiations and who then conducts them.[250] Everything else is actually done by the police under the auspices of the public prosecutor.

In most of the regional units the work process concerning the use of special witnesses is handled by the Criminal Intelligence Team (TCI) whose primary task is to gather criminal intelligence and run informants.[251] The reason why this task is allocated to the

---

247 For further details see § 3.4.4.1.
248 The various aspects of the internal and external scrutiny of the intended agreement will be considered below in § 3.5.4.
249 For further details see § 3.4.5.
250 For further details see § 3.4.4.1 and § 3.4.4.2.
251 For further details see § 3.2.2.3.

TCI and not to the case team is that the TCI has experience of working with confidential information and the information provided by the witness may not be made tactically operational as long as no agreement has been concluded.[252] This also leaves open the avenue – if for whatever reason a procedure has to be ended prematurely – of using the information as TCI-type information.[253] To do that however the witness' consent must be obtained, stated respondent [17], who works in the Special Witnesses Team of the National Unit.

At the National Investigation Service of the National Unit and at the Amsterdam unit there are two special teams charged with handling 'special witnesses', which also includes witnesses to whom undertakings are made. Both teams are referred to as the 'Special Witnesses Team'. In Amsterdam organisationally this team comes under the TCI, but it is in fact a separate branch (of the Information Gathering Department (*Dienst Inwinning*)) alongside the TCI. At the National Unit, however, it is a separate 'department' with its own budget. The respondents from the police and the Public Prosecution Service also said that these two teams hold the most expertise concerning the use of special witnesses. The procedures referred to in the previous section that did come to fruition were also all arranged in Amsterdam and by the National Unit. If a potential witness as referred to in Sections 226g and 226k CCP should present themselves, then this should be handled in the region concerned. This is the route that was decided upon when the national police force was set up. Final responsibility therefore lies with the regional public prosecutor's office. However those involved are increasingly working together.[254] This cooperation however has not been formally laid down and takes place mainly on the basis of personal contacts, said respondent [17]. Although other police units do not have a dedicated team for special witnesses, this does not mean that other regions have not developed any initiatives for this, as apparent from the interviews with respondents [6] and [7].

Responsibility for these sorts of special witness procedures in the initial phase lies primarily with the public prosecutor responsible for the gathering and use of criminal intelligence by the police (*CI-officier van justitie*; hereafter CIPP). The CIPP has to give permission if someone wants to approach a witness with a view to making undertakings and is also the person who conducts the interview with the potential witness about the conditions under which the talks will take place and who later conducts the negotiations. This is all done in consultation with the public prosecutor responsible for the quality of the investigation and prosecution (*rechercheofficier van justitie*) and the Head of the District PPS. In the National Public Prosecutors' Office there is a 'special witnesses

---

252 For further details see § 3.4.4.2.
253 This is described in the internal working procedures.
254 In addition, a procedure that has already been initiated may, in proper consultation, be taken over by another unit, since not every unit possesses sufficient knowledge and/or capacity in this regard.

procedure' public prosecutor who is responsible for these types of procedures and who steers the Special Witnesses Team.[255]

The police has internal working arrangements on how to deal with special witnesses. These are mainly concerned with the organisational structure and the matter of what steps must be taken as soon as a witness appears who may be eligible for a special procedure. Finally, the safety of the witness is considered. These internal working arrangements are mainly in addition to the procedure as described in the Instructions on Undertakings to Witnesses in Criminal Cases[256] which, as indicated, says very little regarding the phase prior to the actual negotiations. The interviews showed that a lot happens in this phase and that this phase of the procedure also takes up a lot of time within the overall process for making agreements. The procedure will be outlined below based on the internal working arrangements and information provided in the interviews, together with further details on the various aspects involved, up to the point of the negotiations with the public prosecutor.

3.5.3.2   How Witnesses Are Identified

There are various ways in which witnesses come into view who may be willing to make statements in exchange for benefits. The potential witness may come into view via the TCI or the case team, for example because during police questioning the individual indicated that they would like to be considered for protection or some form of consideration.[257] If a potential witness has been identified by a case team, then according to the internal working procedure he/she should be transferred as soon as possible to the TCI to prevent that the tactical reporting officer and public prosecutor(s) handling the case becoming aware of the contents of the statement and that it is included in the case file and/or that further investigative activities are being carried out on the basis of that statement.[258] A potential

---

255 In addition, another public prosecutor is solely responsible for witness protection.

256 See § 3.4.4 for further details.

257 It is also possible that someone contacts the community police officer or appears at the front desk of the police station, said a member of the focus group.

258 If during questioning a witness/accused states that they are willing to make a statement in exchange for consideration, this must be reported to the tactical team leader immediately, but is not shared with the rest of the team. The internal working procedures state that further to consultation with the public prosecutor responsible for the case, the team leader must make contact with the Head of the TCI. The Head of the TCI in turn must immediately contact the public prosecutor responsible for the gathering and use of criminal intelligence by the police (CIPP) who then reports the matter to the public prosecutor responsible for the quality of the investigation and prosecution. If a witness makes him/herself known to a tactical team, then this information must immediately be kept separate and recorded in a separate police report (which can later be added to any vault statement – regarding this term, see § 3.5.3.3 – that may be made).

witness may also be actively approached. This can only be done in consultation with and with the consent of the CIPP, who ultimately is the person who must grant confidentiality. Finally, a potential witness can present him/herself to the public prosecutor handling the case, either directly or through their defence lawyer. Various respondents from the Public Prosecution Service and the police stated that most potential witnesses within the meaning of Section 226g and 226k CCP fall into the last category. In other words, the witnesses usually present themselves to the public prosecutor directly, indicating that they are willing to make a statement in exchange for undertakings. However, in important investigations certain teams, such as in Amsterdam, also actively look to see where there may be opportunities to use special witnesses.

The respondents indicated that there may be various reasons why a potential witness would be willing to collaborate with the authorities within the meaning of this study. One reason for being willing to make a statement may be that the person concerned wants to escape the criminal world, has while alone in their cell started to reconsider their life choices, or finds themselves in detention abroad and would like to get back to the Netherlands. The respondents stated that as a rule the reasons why accused and convicted individuals are willing to share some information[259] are opportunistic and not based on any moral grounds, which in itself need not be an obstacle to working with them. Respondent [3] who works at the National Public Prosecutors' Office, said that it is easier to make agreements with someone who is clear about their motives for doing so.

Respondents from the Public Prosecution Service and the police stated that the option of actively approaching people is hardly used (or not used enough). In an ongoing investigation the police may come across someone and ask this person to provide information anonymously, but such information cannot be used as evidence. If they do want to use that information as evidence then they have to see if that person is willing to make a witness statement which can then be used as evidence, either in the capacity of a threatened witness as referred to in Section 226a CCP, or as a witness whom undertakings have been made as referred to in Section 226g ff. CCP. Respondents from the Public Prosecution Service and the police believe that this should be more actively pursued. Actual recruitment in the sense of actively approaching people who have not yet been considered as an informant, in any event hardly ever happens at present.[260] The

---

259 In this context see also the considerations of the Amsterdam Court of Appeal in the case against Peter la S., a witness in the Passage case (Amsterdam Court of Appeal 29 June 2017, ECLI:NL:GHAMS:2017:2494, § 6.1):

"The Court of Appeal observes that it may be noted with a certain degree of cynicism that his motives for taking this step are probably driven more by opportunistic self-interest and hardly, if at all, by an actual desire to change for the better. Whatever the case, the fact remains that his successful contribution to the investigation, prosecution and conviction of himself and others as a result of that step has ultimately turned out to be in his favour."

260 Internal working arrangements stipulate that a potential special witness will only be actively approached in consultation with and with the consent of the CIPP.

respondents stated that the success rate of such an approach is also very small.[261] The Public Prosecution Service would rather that the police focus more on so-called 'facilitators' to see if such individuals can be persuaded to make a statement in any given capacity. Respondents from the Public Prosecution Service and the police indicated that this all ties in with the wider strategy of involving members of the public more in investigations.

3.5.3.3   Internal Working Arrangements and the Procedure to Be Followed

As soon as a potential witness as referred to in Section 226g CCP is identified, the internal working arrangements specify the steps to be taken by the police.[262] The first step consists of the initial exploratory talks. The purpose of these discussions is to gain an overall impression of what the witness can make a statement about, as well as to inform the witness of the various options available and the consequences of making a witness statement. A written report on these discussions is drawn up, as stipulated in the internal working procedures. However, the information obtained from the witness will not be made public at a later stage either.[263] Further to the exploratory talks the Head of the TCI and the public prosecutor responsible for the gathering and use of criminal intelligence by the police (CIPP) in consultation with the public prosecutor responsible for the quality of the investigation and prosecution, will decide whether or not the meetings should continue. If it is decided to proceed, the Head of the TCI and the CIPP can conduct a 'conditions discussion' with the witness. This may only be done with the consent of the Head of the District PPS. During that discussion the general substance and scope of the statement to be made by the witness are discussed and the conditions under which an agreement can be reached. It is up to the CIPP to determine whether this statement offers a sufficient basis on which to begin the negotiation process. If the witness is still willing to cooperate after the discussion on conditions, s/he is then expected to make a full statement in the presence of the police officers designated to take such a statement.[264] The internal working procedures state that preferably this should not be done by members of the TCI but by detectives with interrogation experience. The reasons given for this in the interviews was that not all TCI-members have the necessary interrogation experience and the wish to avoid them later being called

---

261 A question which could be asked here, raised by a member of the focus group from the police, is on the basis of what arguments should an individual be considered potentially suitable. In other words: are the authorities actually encountering the people with whom the procedure is most likely to succeed and if not, could this then be an explanation for the poor success rate?

262 The working arrangements apply to all special witnesses however, while this study is concerned only with witnesses to whom undertakings are (or could be) made. This point was specifically addressed in the interviews with police officers. This will also be referred to below.

263 This will be different with the 'vault statements' which in principle must be added to the court documents if an agreement is made between the witness and the Public Prosecution Service (that is also approved by the Board of Procurators General and the investigating judge). In this context, see also Amsterdam District Court 29 January 2013, ECLI:NL:RBAMS:2013:BZ0392 (Passage).

264 For further details of the extent of the witness' obligation to make a statement, see § 3.5.4.3.

as witnesses in order to protect their identity. From the interviews it is apparent that such persons – detectives with interrogation experience – can be obtained from other teams further to signing a confidentiality agreement. The involvement of other detectives is intended to prevent that the information provided by the witness is leaked and nevertheless made tactically operational. The Special Witnesses Teams with the National Unit and in Amsterdam generally conduct these interviews themselves.[265] The detectives who record the statement however do this under the authority of the Head of the TCI and the public prosecutor responsible for the gathering and use of criminal intelligence by the police (i.e. the CIPP). The statements made at this stage are known as 'vault statements' (*kluisverklaringen*) on account of their highly confidential status; such statements may in no way be used until the agreement has been reached and approved by the investigating judge.[266] These therefore remain in the vault until the agreement has been concluded, although the witness can later give permission for their vault statements to be used even if, in the end, no agreement is reached.[267] As soon as these statements have been made they have to be assessed in terms of their value as evidence. A full verification investigation is carried out to check what is true and what is false. This investigation is carried out by the Special Witnesses Team or, failing that, by members of the TCI. If the statement has sufficient evidentiary value the witness is then screened in terms of his/her psychological suitability for such a process and any associated protection measures.[268] After this the 'negotiations' about the content of the agreement can begin with the CIPP.[269] In principle, the police are not involved with this. In any event, they have no formal role but are sometimes present, stated one respondent from the Amsterdam Special Witnesses Team. The reason for this, respondent [18b] said, is that a relationship of trust has already been built up with the witness and the police also want to know who they are dealing with.

The respondents indicated that the steps as stated are followed in practice, but not necessarily in the given order. For example, the psychological assessment takes place at an earlier stage in the National Unit, i.e. following the conditions discussion, and the Witness Protection Team may also be involved in the procedure at an earlier stage to give the witness an idea of what such protection entails.[270] The interviews also indicated that activities to verify the statement of the witness are also conducted earlier in practice. The starting point is always that the vault statements are taken down and the verification process is completed before the public prosecutor begins the negotiations, said respondent [17] from the Special Witnesses Team with the National Unit.

---

265 The teams comprise a mixture of TCI staff running informants and people with a tactical background.
266 For further details, see § 3.4.4.2.
267 See SC 13 April 2009, NJ 2009, 61.
268 For further details of the verification process and the psychological assessment, see § 3.5.3.4.
269 For further details of the negotiation process, see § 3.5.3.5.
270 For further details about the Witness Protection Team, see § 3.5.5.1.

3.5.3.4   Selection of Witnesses

As apparent from the foregoing, it will not always be clear in advance to which procedural capacity the potential witness to have presented him/herself will be assigned. For this purpose, consideration is given to how the information can best be utilised and which capacity would be most suitable in that given context. A person may act as an informant, but in certain cases also as a threatened witness within the meaning of Section 226a CCP, as a witness to whom undertakings have been made as referred to in Section 226g CCP, or as an 'ordinary' witness. The respondents indicated that various factors are involved when weighing-up the options, such as the capacity in which the person wanting to make a statement does so (whether or not they themselves are accused of a possibly related criminal offence), the seriousness of the offence, the value of their statement in relation to other evidentiary material, the importance of someone making a statement in their own name and the available options for protecting that individual afterwards.[271] The character of the potential witness is also considered, in particular, in terms of whether it would be possible to make an agreement with him or her. If the intention is to start a procedure as referred to in Section 226g ff. CCP, the potential witness must be willing to give full disclosure and not give the impression that they are withholding all sorts of relevant information.[272] The respondents indicated that the statement of the potential witness must, in any event, be sufficiently reliable. Faith that the individual will hold their own for the remainder of the procedure and during questioning at trial is also essential in this regard. That is why both a psychological assessment and a thorough process of verification are carried out. This will be discussed in more detail below.

a   Psychological Assessment

As previously mentioned, a psychological assessment is also carried out in the context of selecting witnesses to whom undertakings will be made. This is generally an initial psychological screening. Based on the internal working procedures this takes place after taking down the vault statements and the verification process. In the National Unit, however, this takes place immediately after the discussion on conditions and, in principle, before the vault statements are taken. There is a psychologist at the National Unit who spends much of his time on undertaking psychological assessments of special witnesses. He does this not only for the National Unit but also for regional units when requested to do so. During the intake the witness is asked to complete a standard questionnaire and interviewed. The psychologist performing the assessment also looks at the motives of the

---

271 It is fair to assume that consideration is also given to the matter of whether and to what extent the anonymity of the person concerned can be successfully guaranteed in view of the content of their statement. Often enough the contents of the statement will be sufficient to reveal from what source it came.

272 The matter of how far the obligation upon the witness to give full disclosure extends is discussed in more detail in § 3.5.4.3.

potential witness in making a statement and the individual's impression of what such a procedure actually involves (i.e. realism). The character of the witness is also looked at as well as the structure of his/her life (i.e. their social environment). Finally, consideration is given to how deeply rooted the witness is in the criminal world.

In principle, the psychologist does not look at the reliability of the statements already made or the value of these statements to the investigation, but mainly at the witness' profile. Information about the character of the witness may serve as background information for the interrogating officers who take down the vault statements. Respondent [16], who performs these psychological assessments, said that the personal profile of the witness is also an important factor in deciding whether or not to continue with someone. Because if a witness exhibits paranoid or psychopathological traits or is highly unstable, then this can lead to various complications later on in the procedure. Consideration is also given to whether, further down the road, someone could be kept in a witness protection programme at a later stage. In this context it is important that an individual is stable, can accept rules and has a realistic view of what this involves. It is also assessed whether the 'cooperativeness' of the witness is something consistent, or whether it is purely dictated by recent events. Respondent [16] explained that an attempt is made to estimate how someone will behave when the pressure is off, because the witness could then exhibit entirely different behaviour. The same respondent also indicated however that the personal profile is not always the deciding factor. The psychological assessment provides only an indication of the risks associated with the individual concerned. If the information involved is important, in certain cases the Public Prosecution Service may still be willing to continue with the witness. In which event and if protection measures have to be taken (which will generally be the case), the Witness Protection Team is then also brought in. This team then has its own psychological assessment carried out, which respondent [19b] said, takes into account the information from the earlier phase.[273]

b   *Verification Process*
In addition to an assessment of the character of the witness, an investigation is of course also carried out into the reliability of their statement. A statement may appear at first sight to be very useful, but it also has to be reliable. To gain an impression of this, the police conduct a thorough verification process. Respondent [5], a public prosecutor responsible for the gathering and use of criminal intelligence by the police (CIPP), had the following to say about this:

> "We want to prevent that we end up being misled as a result of witnesses glossing over their own role. [...] I have certainly had experience of dealing with people who try to do that, so you need to be aware of that. To some extent it

---

273 See § 3.5.5 for further details.

also attracts such cases, when you consider the amount of publicity generated by the collaborators of justice that we have had. As a result many more have come to us with the idea of "I want what he had, too". They may have good intentions about wanting to tell the truth, but it could also be with the intention of wanting to gain something with a story that is completely made up."

As indicated, the verification process generally takes place after taking down the vault statements, but in practice certain matters have already been verified at an earlier stages. Respondent [17] from the Special Witnesses Team of the National Unit explained that right from the initial stages an attempt is made to assess the feasibility and reliability of the statements. The reliability of the statements made is also considered while the vault statements are being taken down. Respondent [17] said that the motivation of the witness is also constantly monitored.

The verification process takes place on the basis of information that is available in the various police systems and other information already available, such as traffic data, camera footage and tracking data. The case team may not be involved in this process and because the identity of the witness must continue to be protected as long as their statements remain 'in the vault' and no agreement has yet been concluded, by their own account the police are also cautious about approaching other people for information. In principle, this process must be completed before a final agreement with the witness can be concluded.

Respondent [5] mentioned as an example of a case in which the verification process was very important, a procedure which had been started with a potential witness who had been convicted and unconditionally sentenced and who wanted a pardon. During the exploratory talks it was already clear that he was glossing over his own role entirely and pointing the finger of blame at people who were already dead. In the end the police, in agreement with the CIPP, allowed him to make a vault statement in order to be able to hear the whole story. This story turned out not to be based in fact. On the contrary, in the end it could be established with reasonable certainty that the witness himself had committed the offence on which he had made the statement. The problem, however, is that if the Public Prosecution Service does not reach an agreement with a witness, these vault statements cannot be used (except in the situation previously mentioned, where the witness gives permission for this), not for a prosecution, and also not as a starting point for further investigation. About this the respondent concerned said the following:

"You can find yourself in the terrible situation that you (as public prosecutor) are sitting with someone who makes a confession that you then cannot use. [...] In the meantime we have reached the point where if you want to achieve some success with this (and then we are often talking about murder or other very serious offences), you have to give people the assurance that their vault statements will remain such (unless you both agree that the statement no long-er has to be deemed highly confidential). If you don't do that, then they will never tell you the whole story. Therefore you have to accept that it may be the case that someone confesses to the most dreadful crimes, but we cannot prosecute him on the basis of those statements. If you agree that the statement someone makes is highly confidential (and will remain in the vault), then you cannot use that statement unless both parties agree to that."

The results of the verification process are provided in a report that the CIPP uses in support of the application to the CTC to make undertakings to a witness. This report itself is also sent with the application to the CTC but is not included in the final case file. This also applies to the reports of the exploratory talks, due to the confidential nature of the discussions (which is maintained even after any agreement is concluded).

3.5.3.5   The Negotiations

As soon as it becomes clear that the statement has value and the verification process has been completed, according to the internal working arrangements, the negotiation process with the witness can then be started. According to the internal working arrangements, in this context it should be established "in which investigations the statements can be used and what consideration it would be reasonable to give in exchange for that". During the discussion on conditions the potential witness will have already been told what would and would not be possible. The respondents were asked about what witnesses ask for during the negotiations. The requests related not only to sentence reduction, but also anonymity, for example. In this context respondent [15] said the following:

"What most witnesses want is anonymity. I understand that entirely. Take a situation like that in Zaandam, for example, where if someone talks to the police (because they are standing on their doorstep), their windows are smashed right after that. In Schilderswijk [in The Hague] too, we see that if we have spoken to someone, we haven't even left the street before there is already a crowd of people who come to ask them what they said to the police. We can also disguise that. [...] But we as the authorities also sometimes leave the witness out in the cold ("just call 112 if you need to"). This applies mainly to people other than witnesses with whom a deal has been made, of course, because they do get real protection. In such cases it is often impossible to main-tain anonymity, while that's what is asked for. The accused has often only told one person, which means that he knows immediately who betrayed him."

As noted above,[274] it is impossible to grant anonymity in an undertakings procedure, just as it is also impossible to pay someone for making a statement.[275] As the respondents observed, however, this last thing is something that witnesses do ask for. A member of the focus group from the police stated that not being able to offer financial compensation presents a serious obstacle to the willingness of potential witnesses to cooperate.

With regard to sentence reduction the respondents indicated that at the moment the standard practice is to give either a 50% reduction in the sentencing demand, or nothing at all. Currently, no real negotiation takes place about the amount of the sentence reduction (within the margins set by the law). Respondent [4] said the following about this:

> "At the moment it appears that either 50% sentence reduction is given or noth-
> ing at all, while a 10% or 20% reduction is never agreed. It would be a good idea
> to introduce more variation in this, i.e. sometimes more (80% or even 100%
> where this is statutorily possible) as well as less (10%, 20% or 30%). Not least
> because the criminals who come to us as witnesses have their own reasons for
> doing so and having taken the step, they are not simply going to turn back. We
> make too little use of our own negotiating position."

Respondent [5] stated that 'negotiation' is not really the correct term in this context because, as the respondent indicated, it is up to the public prosecutor to decide what is a suitable basic sentencing demand and the amount of the sentence reduction.

> "This should never become a haggling matter. The Public Prosecution Service (PPS)
> is required to make a decision based on the standard rules pertaining to the prin-
> ciple of prosecutorial discretion about what would be a reasonable sentencing
> demand in a normal situation and what should be granted in terms of a sentence
> reduction. And that decision is than presented to the witness. It is a matter of 'take
> it or leave it'. The PPS generally applies the 50% reduction as a standard because
> that is already not very much."

Questions were also raised by the focus group about the nature of the negotiations and in particular the framework in which they take place. Here the risk of conflicts of interest was also pointed out and it was also asked whether the public prosecutor responsible for the gathering and use of criminal intelligence by the police (CIPP) is sufficiently equipped to be able to conduct such negotiations and is able take sufficient distance. A member of the focus group from the police sees, in any event, sufficient cause to make this role more professional and asked why the decision had been made that it should be the CIPP who

---

274 See also § 3.2.2.2.
275 See § 3.4.3.4.

does this. In his view, negotiation is not a competence held only by those in a particular position. He also stated that a 'take it or leave it' approach requires "a strong mandate" and "robust back up".

3.5.3.6   When Processes Run Aground

In the majority of the cases where there are exploratory talks with potential witnesses, these come to nothing. The process can run aground at various stages of the procedure, on both sides. Negotiations also run aground because the witness does not find the offer made attractive enough (many respondents stated that the fact that the undertaking on sentence reduction is set at a maximum of 50%, in particular, is a stumbling block).[276] But a witness may also withdraw because his situation has improved (e.g. he is no longer subject to restrictions in the context of his pre-trial detention) or has found another way to escape the criminal environment. Here it bears observing that the procedure which follows after agreements have been made involves a degree of uncertainty, given that it cannot be established in advance whether or not the court will accept the reduced sentencing demand, the procedure can take a very long time and in many cases the witness with whom a deal has been made may end up in witness protection. The Public Prosecution Service, for its part, also indicated that in some cases the individual in question may not be found to be reliable or 'solid' enough. A witness with whom a deal has been made must be able to hold up in court. The Passage case showed that this can have a significant impact on a witness within the meaning of this study who are questioned repeatedly at various stages of the proceedings (which, as mentioned, is why in the psychological assessment in the early stage consideration is given to the matter of whether the witness is capable of dealing with this). In the exploratory phase, in consultation with the Witness Protection Team, it is also considered whether it is actually possible to protect someone. If an individual is tied to the Netherlands (e.g. to care for a sick parent or for any other reason), this may be sufficient reason not to initiate this procedure with that person.[277] It is also sometimes the case that the Board of Procurators General does not give permission to go ahead with the person concerned.

Respondent [16], a psychologist and operational specialist with the Special Witnesses Team of the National Unit, using police journals has made an overview of the primary motivations of those considering collaborating with the authorities within the meaning of this study. This inventory shows that in approximately 30% of cases this was related to matters of safety. People feel threatened and fear for their lives and see a unique partner in the police. In roughly 20% of cases it cannot be properly determined what people's motives are or were. This may be because they do not entirely know why themselves, or

---

276 In this context, see § 3.6.2.1 for further details.

277 The consideration in this regard is whether the required measures are sufficient to counter the threat and whether the witness can stick to the agreements made.

they do not wish to reveal that, or because they were approached by the police and it was thought that they want to talk, although that was not yet entirely clear. Sentence reduction is the primary motivation in about 15% of cases. Roughly 10% of cases are driven mainly by emotional reasons, such as seeking revenge or holding a grudge. Less than 10% is primarily looking for financial gain for themselves and think that they can earn money by making a statement. Among an even smaller percentage the motivation is primarily an inducement as referred to in Section 226g paragraph 4 CCP, such as a different detention regime or suspension of the pre-trial detention. Just 3% consider collaborating with justice for moral reasons. The above percentages are linked to the exploratory talks, where it should be noted that a certain motive may be the reason for entering into talks with the authorities, but those involved may have the wrong impression about what is possible under such a procedure. A witness, for example, may find safety to be the most important thing, but at the same time expects not to be prosecuted or to receive a large financial reward for making a statement.

In the context of the aforementioned overview, it was also examined why cases run aground at an early stage. More than 30% of the potential witnesses are rejected due to the content of the statement. They simply do not have enough to offer, either because the information is not good enough or because this information is already available to the authorities, or the charges can be proved without that information. Approximately 45% fail due to a lack of motivation or realism. As soon as it becomes clear what such a procedure involves and what can be offered in this context, some potential witnesses withdraw. About 12% run aground due to the witness' character and their complex profile. Roughly 5% decide not to lend any further cooperation because of their own criminal involvement. The people who fall into this category are those about whom the authorities do not yet know that much and who still have a relatively clean sheet but who would – if they had to make a statement after entering into an agreement – incriminate themselves to such an extent that they could face a heavy sentencing demand. An even smaller percentage withdraw because of their social environment and close connections with the Netherlands.

Taking everything together, it may be observed that roughly half the procedures run aground because the authorities see no benefit, while the remaining half run aground because after weighing up the pros and cons, the potential witness sees no benefit. When all the cases which are aborted for substantive reasons are left aside, then about 70% of the procedures run aground due to a lack of motivation/realism on the part of the potential witness. These witnesses did not have a realistic idea about what would be possible when they entered into talks with the authorities, or they cannot be persuaded to cooperate on the basis of the offer made.

3.5.3.7 Views on the Procedure as a Whole

All the respondents were asked how they view the prescribed procedure and the cooperation with the other professional parties involved.[278] In general they were reasonably satisfied; those in the police indicated that the cooperation with the Public Prosecution Service runs smoothly, and vice versa. The respondents were also positive about the various steps which have to be taken in order to reach a final agreement, in the sense that they consider it important that decisions are taken carefully. None of the respondents proposed eliminating certain steps. This point was also specifically addressed in the focus group. The focus group members also did not consider the present procedure to be too stringent.[279] Only one member, from the police, was critical in this regard. He stated that there are too many actors involved in making decisions through the procedure, the decision-making process has not been properly set up and too much redundancy has been built into the system. A member from the judiciary responded that it may appear on paper to be stringent, but in practice that is a good thing:

> "These are complex cases, but the procedure itself is not."

Although the respondents generally appeared to be positive about the procedure, several of them had reservations about the length of the internal procedure. Some respondents saw this as a bottleneck, because it could reduce the impact of the instrument and there is a greater risk that potential witnesses could withdraw as a result, as well as the danger for witnesses with whom the discussions are still in progress but who are not yet protected. Respondent [7] pointed out that potential witnesses start to lose confidence when the procedure takes too long. However the respondents could not say how long a procedure takes on average, because this very much depends on the nature of the case in question. The respondents stated that the reason why the procedure generally takes the time it does, is mainly because of the investigation carried out in the initial phase. Performing a threat analysis, in particular, takes a lot of time. While in the later stages with the CTC and the Board of Procurators General, it can go very quickly. Respondent [2] from the CTC stated the following in this context:

> "It is an old misconception that the CTC procedure takes a long time. In the past it did indeed take much longer. The delay is not so much because of us, because we can make a recommendation relatively quickly, but the procedure before us takes a lot of time."[280]

---

278 It should be noted that a number of aspects of the procedure – specifically the internal and external scrutiny of the intended agreement – will be examined in more detail in the section below. See § 3.5.4 for further details.

279 However certain reservations were expressed about scrutiny by the investigating judge. See § 3.5.4.2 for further details.

280 The Board of Procurators General also indicated that a decision can be made within a week, unless the case is politically sensitive.

Respondent [6], who works as a public prosecutor, however stated that the Public Prosecution Service is also slow in taking decisions.

> "I cannot give an indication of how long an average procedure takes, but the more critical it is the more people want to take a closer look, as they say. And 'a closer look' in this context may sometimes be synonymous with concern, which means it takes even longer."

Respondent [10b], an investigating judge, mentioned that the Public Prosecution Service and the Board of Procurators General, in particular – fearful of problems arising – are extremely cautious and perhaps less willing to give their approval than an investigating judge would. The respondent indicated that this mainly concerned the very big cases which draw administrative or political attention.

With regard to the initial stages, respondent [17] from the Special Witnesses Team of the National Unit mentioned that in certain cases time can be gained by involving the Witness Protection Team in the procedure at an earlier stage, so that the Witness Protection Team is ready at the same time as the Special Witnesses Team (or in some cases the TCI) is also ready. But the respondent noted that there could be some difficulties with this given that most procedures run aground prematurely:

> "Starting a threat analysis at the same time places a huge load on the Witness Protection Team, while the return is low."

3.5.4   Scrutiny and Implementation of the Agreement

The foregoing looked at the procedure up until the negotiations. This is not where it ends, however. As soon as the CIPP and the witness reach agreement, the proposed agreements are set down on paper. The draft agreement then first has to be approved internally within the Public Prosecution Service by the Board of Procurators General that receives advice from the CTC (which in turn obtains advice from the State Advocate's Office, hereafter also the State Advocate). If the Board of Procurators General gives its approval, the draft agreement is then submitted to the investigating judge for approval. Only after that approval has been given, does the agreement take effect and the statements can be introduced into the criminal proceedings and used tactically.[281] The internal scrutiny within the Public Prosecution Service (and the State Advocate's role in this) will be considered below, along with the external scrutiny of the investigating judge.

---

281 For further details of the legal framework for the internal and external scrutiny of the intended agreement, see § 3.4.4.3.

Following which some experiences and problems surrounding the implementation of the agreement will be discussed.

3.5.4.1 Internal Scrutiny Within the Public Prosecution Service

As outlined above, there are various moments of scrutiny in the internal procedure of the Public Prosecution Service. The CIPP cannot make undertakings as referred to in Section 226g CCP independently. There must always be consultation with the public prosecutor responsible for the quality of the investigation and prosecution, and the Head of the District PPS. The interviews show that these parties mainly provide a sounding board for the CIPP. Not least because the CIPP has a duty of confidentiality concerning special witnesses and criminal intelligence matters and may not discuss such with colleagues. The public prosecutor responsible for the quality of the investigation and prosecution is the functional manager of the CIPP and also has a clear overview of the various investigations that are in progress. The respondents indicated that this means that s/he has a better overview of the interests involved and on that basis can advise on whether or not to make use of a special witness. Final responsibility rests with the Head of the District PPS. Respondent [5] stated that in practice only with the consent of the Head of the District PPS will the CIPP say to a witness that his statements will be treated as vault statements. Applications to the State Advocate, the CTC and the Board of Procurators General also formally go via the Head of the District PPS, who is also the person who must give permission for the lawyer's fees to be paid, said respondent [5].[282]

The proposed agreement is submitted to the State Advocate by the Head of the District PPS. In his own words – respondent [14] – stated that he looks at the scope of the law, the nature of the offences, the extent of the undertaking, the need for the investigation, the proportionality and the question of whether its use could lead to difficulties with the implementation. In the respondent's own words, this is essentially an arm's length assessment, because the State Advocate does not have access to the underlying case file. The State Advocate, the respondent said, is more closely involved in the witness protection agreement.[283] The State Advocate therefore looks at the draft agreement and checks that it is contractually in order and whether the agreements made remain within the limits of the law. The State Advocate can comment on the draft agreement, and the public prosecutor involved can decide whether or not to make use of those comments. The comments could relate to the undertakings made, but equally well to the text or underlying substantiation of parts of the draft agreement. The State Advocate's advice is provided in writing and sent together with the draft agreement to the CTC

---

282 This is not handled through the Legal Aid Board (*Raad voor Rechtsbijstand*), given that the use of the defence lawyer is still secret during the preliminary phase.

283 See § 3.5.5 for further details.

which then reaches at its own conclusion in the form of a recommendation to the Board of Procurators General.

The scrutiny by the CTC is carried out by the Fourth Chamber (as it is known) which consists of members of the Public Prosecution Service (both primary and secondary tiers) and the police, plus a psychologist, as well as an external member from academia. In addition to the draft agreement and an explanation by the public prosecutor making the application, in principle, a memo concerning the verification process will also be attached, together with the results of the psychological screening, a threat analysis and the vault statements. The CTC looks at a number of factors. Firstly, the value of the witness statement: is the statement of vital importance in furnishing proof or to be able to 'break open' the investigation of the case? It is also considered whether the information could be used by way of a TCI report. The reason for not just using TCI reports is that a statement in the witness' own name is much more valuable. Such a statement can always be used as evidence and also makes a positive contribution to the transparency of the criminal proceedings. Respondent [2] from the CTC also added in this context that:

> "[…] a statement which the witness makes in their own name offers room for more detail to be added. You will have a full statement from a witness with whom a deal has been made in which – if it is truthful – he tells everything he knows, which provides more clues for the investigation. This detailed information cannot be included in a TCI report because of the need to protect an informant."

The CTC also looks at whether the consideration to be given is in proportion to what the statement provides (what it adds to existing knowledge). Also considered in this context are the basic sentencing demand (is it realistic) and the promised sentence reduction (is it reasonable)? If the CTC takes the view that the basic sentencing demand is either on the high or the low side, then generally a comment will be made about this in the recommendation to the Board of Procurators General. The CTC also takes the advice of the State Advocate into account in arriving at its opinion. If a comment made by the State Advocate is not adopted, consideration is also given to whether or not that is justified. The CTC can ask the public prosecutor responsible for the case for further information, whether or not in the form of further investigation, which it has also done in the past. The CTC has also been asked a few times (less than five times) for collegial advice. Respondent [1] indicated that this concerned cases where the public prosecutor was considering starting a 'deal' process and wanted to know in advance whether or not the CTC would be in favour of this.

Of the 12 cases concerning potential witnesses within the meaning of this report that were submitted to the CTC, the advice given was negative in three cases.[284] Reasons for

---

284 See also § 3.5.2.1 for further details.

making a negative recommendation could include the value of the information (insufficient), the fact that it could be obtained in another way (subsidiarity), the fact that the witness in question is unwilling to give full disclosure, or the fact that the proposed consideration is not in proportion to the information on offer. In those cases where the advice given was negative, this related mainly to the value of the evidence. There has to be a reasonable expectation that the statement given by the witness will make a real contribution to the criminal proceedings. Respondent [16] from the Special Witnesses Team with the National Unit, mentioned the example of a statement which was largely based on the statements of others (hearsay evidence). If it is believed that using this instrument will not clear up the case or will not result in a successful prosecution, this would be another reason for making a negative recommendation. In one of the cases in which the CTC's negative advice was accepted, there were also many risks surrounding the use of protection measures. Respondent [2] explained that this made entering into an agreement disproportionate relative to the quality and value of the information offered.

Partly on the basis of the advice of the CTC, the Board of Procurators General then decides whether or not consent will be given to enter into an agreement with the witness. Respondent [1], a member of the Board of Procurators General, stated that the advice given by the CTC is usually assessed by two or more members of the Board. The decision is generally based on the information provided in the CTC's advice, but the Board can also see the underlying case file. He said that they rarely do that. The interview with respondent [1] indicated that the Board also looks at the political implications of the case and its impact on society. In so doing the Board bears in mind that a 50% sentence reduction will not always be welcomed by 'the man in the street', "but is sometimes necessary", said respondent [1]. The use of this tool also has a major impact on the trial proceedings which then follow. Respondent [1] emphasised that the instrument of undertakings to witnesses has far-reaching consequences and is not something which should be undertaken lightly. The general public may have a very different view of the proportionality and subsidiarity of the instrument, which may lead to questions being asked. The safety of the witness is another risk. The minister is the person ultimately responsible for this. For this reason also, said respondent [1], the instrument of providing undertakings to witnesses is politically sensitive.

3.5.4.2 External Scrutiny of the Agreement by the Judiciary

After the Board of Procurators General has given its consent, the public prosecutor in whose case the witness will be used submits the agreement to the investigating judge for scrutiny (Section 226g paragraph 3 CCP). The investigating judge looks at both the lawfulness of the intended agreement and the reliability of the witness.[285] After the investigating judge has found the agreement to be lawful, the witness is interviewed again

---

285 See § 3.4.4.3 for further details.

(Section 226j paragraph 1 CCP), this time to take a full statement which will provide the basis for the examination at trial. The investigating judge has the option to, in the interests of the investigation, order that the identity of the witness should remain concealed for a certain period of time (Section 226j paragraph 4 CCP).[286]

The respondents stated that in cases where the intended agreement as referred to in Section 226g CCP is submitted to the investigating judge for scrutiny, it will thus far have been deemed lawful. Respondent [8] from the judicial authorities stated that the scrutiny of the lawfulness of the intended agreement entails an assessment of reasonableness. In this sense, there is little room for the investigating judge to perform his own assessment.[287] With regard to the reliability of the witness, respondent [9], an investigating judge, indicated that there is more room for the investigating judge to exercise his own judgement in this regard. The respondent considers it the task of the investigating judge to check whether the statements made by the witness are actually based on truth. This is done by questioning the witness in person, as well as studying the available documents. When asked how much room he has to investigate that, the respondent stated that he takes as much room as he needs and he also gets that from the organisation. A member of the focus group who as an investigating judge had examined an intended agreement stated however that it is very difficult to assess the reliability of the witness and their statements, because there is insufficient time for the investigating judge to familiarise himself thoroughly with the underlying case file and gain an impression of the witness' position and the associated risks in terms of reliability. It emerged from the focus group that the Public Prosecution Service has a major advantage in that respect. The same focus group member mentioned that the investigating judge is actually brought into in the procedure too late.

> "I am involved in the procedure at a time when ideally it should all start next week. The way things are now, the pressure of time and the knowledge gap that you have as an investigating judge means that the scrutiny is necessarily marginal [in the sense that it entails an assessment of the reasonableness of the agreement only, as opposed to a de novo review thereof]. I think that the legislature failed to make a clear decision on this point."

---

286 Section 226j paragraph 4 CCP states that the investigating judge should revoke such an order upon conclusion of his investigation at the latest.

287 Cf. in this context the rulings of the Amsterdam Court of Appeal in the Passage case in which the Court of Appeal indicated that scrutiny of the lawfulness of the agreement is primarily the task of the investigating judge, while the task of the trial judge lies more in examining the reliability of the statements (where applicable preceded by consideration of matters related to the lawfulness of the agreement in light of Section 359a CCP and Article 6 ECHR). See also Amsterdam Court of Appeal 29 June 2017, ECLI:NL:GHAMS: 2017:2496 (Dino S.), § 1.6.2. See also § 3.4.4.4 for further details.

Regarding the pressure of time, the same focus group member added that this alludes not so much to the ability to study the documents attached to the application for scrutiny of the agreement,[288] but the impossibility in that phase to, in a short time, gain an impression of all the ongoing or future proceedings in which the Public Prosecution Service intends to use the statements. This point was also raised by respondent [13] from the criminal defence bar.

> "The investigating judge has to assess its lawfulness, but only gets to see the statements presented to him, with the message from the Public Prosecution Service that otherwise they would not be able to make the case and that these statements are supported by objective facts. At that moment there is not one investigating judge who can make a proper assessment of lawfulness, which means that his scrutiny is actually worthless. [...] He should be involved right from the outset, rather than being called *ad hoc* together with the entire case file."

The opinion that the investigating judge should be involved at an earlier stage in the investigation was not shared by everyone. The defence lawyer in the focus group pointed out that the impartiality of the investigating judge could be endangered if he were to be too closely involved in the investigation. He would prefer to have someone who has sufficient distance when looking at the case.

Another complication concerns the safety of the witness. In some districts there is not always an investigating judge available who has experience of dealing with special witness procedures, let alone the use of witnesses as referred to in Section 226g and Section 226k CCP. The respondents indicated that this has inherent risks because of the importance of protecting the identity of the witness (which will only be made known after the investigating judge has ruled that the agreement is lawful). Lack of experience can mean that mistakes are made which could endanger the safety of the witness. One respondent mentioned the example of an investigating judge who had drawn up a police report containing an anonymous witness statement but which included the witness' citizen service number (*BSN*). The fact that the investigating judge is not aware of the agreements made about witness protection was also mentioned as a problem by respondents from the judiciary. At present the investigating judge only examines the intended agreement with regard to making a statement and the consideration to be given in exchange for that by the Public Prosecution Service. The agreements made in the context of witness protection fall beyond the scope of that and he will not be aware of them. According to the respondents from the judiciary this makes it difficult for the investigating judge to determine whether or not the witness should answer certain ques-

---

288 Although the same focus group member said that here also there is pressure of time.

tions and to take a position when a conflict arises between the witness and the Witness Protection Team, and the witness therefore no longer wishes to make a statement.

Another point that touches upon the role and the scrutiny of the investigating judge relates to the procedure on appeal. The Explanatory Memorandum assumed that – in the event that a witness willing to collaborate with the authorities within the meaning of this study presents himself at the appeals stage of the proceedings – the trial judge would then refer the case back to the investigating judge to begin the procedure as referred to in Section 226g ff. CCP.[289] In the Passage case in second instance proceedings the Public Prosecution Service introduced a new witness to whom undertakings had been made, while the hearing was already at an advanced stage. The Public Prosecution Service decided to introduce the vault statements directly after the lawfulness and reliability of the intended agreement was examined by the investigating judge and to omit the further questioning by the investigating judge on the content of the statement as referred to in Section 226j CCP. This latter step was based on the idea that it would be better to examine the witness during the trial proceedings because the defence would also have more room there to question the witness. Respondent [11] from the criminal defence bar stated that examination by both the investigating judge and in court would also be a replication. The problem with the present framework, said the same respondent, is that it is silent on the procedure surrounding undertakings to witnesses in appeal proceedings. A referral back by the Court of Appeal, as was assumed by the legislature, leads to many complications in practice in which the need to keep an intended agreement confidential could end up being compromised. This is because if the agreement is not concluded, the statements may not be included in the case file, but have to remain in the vault. Simply making it known that an intended agreement has to be submitted to the investigating judge can already lead to speculation about or even revelation of the identity of the potential witness. Even after the Public Prosecution Service had introduced the vault statements in the Passage case the Court of Appeal did not refer the case back to the district court.[290]

The question may arise as to whether it is useful to maintain the role of the investigating judge in this part of the procedure,[291] particularly given that ultimately the judge has to make a final decision about the lawfulness of the agreement and the value of the statement made.[292] This question as such was not put to the interviewees

---

289 See Parliamentary Papers II 1998/99, 26 294 no. 3, p. 12.

290 Amsterdam Court of Appeal 30 September 2014, ECLI:NL:GHAMS:2014:4008 (interlocutory order Passage case).

291 As discussed in § 3.3.2, it was the express wish of the Lower House of Parliament at the time that the prior judicial scrutiny of the intended agreement with the witness should be made part of the procedure. In this context it should also be noted that of all the legal systems included in this study only the Dutch system requires prior judicial scrutiny of the intended agreement.

292 As previously noted in this section, in the Passage case the Amsterdam Court of Appeal saw only a limited role for the trial judge when it comes to scrutiny of the lawfulness of the agreement with the witness. See also

but interestingly enough, when responding to the question of whether the present scheme needs to be changed, no one suggested omitting the assessment made by the investigating judge from the procedure. Clearly the scrutiny of the investigating judge in the preliminary phase is seen as having value (or at least is not seen as an obstacle). Respondents [10a and 10b], both investigating judges, remarked that the role of the investigating judge really is different from that of the trial judges, particularly in relation to the defence:

"You can still do business with an investigating judge, who safeguards the proceedings in relation to the accused, the witness and the defence. The role of a hearing judge is quite different, they arrive at a judgment based on what has been presented to them."

3.5.4.3 Implementation of the Agreement

As soon as agreement has been reached about the undertakings and an agreement has been made which has been approved by the Board of Procurators General and the investigating judge, the witness is then expected to make a statement (in principle both to the investigating judge at the pre-trial stage as well as during the trial proceedings).[293] However problems may also arise after the agreement has been finalised, in the implementation of the agreement. There may also be a dispute about the agreements made. A number of these problems will be discussed below as they were revealed during the various interviews and in the focus group discussion.

One of the main problems encountered in practice is dissatisfaction on the part of the witness about the protection offered. Respondents from the judiciary and the Public Prosecution Service reported situations where witnesses suspended or ended their collaboration because they felt that the authorities were failing to meet their agreements concerning protection. Even though under the present scheme the two agreements are seen as separate from one another in the legal sense,[294] witnesses do not appear to see it that way, respondents stated. For the witnesses, ceasing or suspending their cooperation is the only means by which can exert pressure to have their wishes granted. This problem also occurred in the Passage case previously referred to. This problem will be discussed in more detail in § 3.5.5 on the subject of witness protection in practice.

At trial also, discussion may arise regarding the agreements made with a witness, whether or not pursuant to information which only later came to light, after the agreement was concluded. In the Passage case, for example, agreements were made with a

---

Amsterdam Court of Appeal 29 June 2017, ECLI:NL:GHAMS:2017:2496 (Dino S.), § 1.6.2. See also § 3.4.4.4 for further details.

293 See Parliamentary Papers II 1999/2000, 26 294, no. 6, p. 6 and pp. 22-23.

294 See § 3.4.5 for further details.

witness during the pre-trial phase that statements about a certain person, i.e. Holleeder, would not be brought to light.[295] In the vault statements, that were attached to the agreement providing a summary of the witness's statements, certain passages had been omitted against a certain number.[296] According to the Public Prosecution Service the omitted passages did not contain any exonerating information, or evidence against any of the accused in the Passage case.[297] The district court in the first instance proceedings however ruled that the agreement to make these omissions was unlawful,[298] because they related to one of the offences included in the deal and, in the district court's view, the Public Prosecution Service is obliged to provide the defence and the district court with complete transparency concerning the agreement and how it has been entered into. In doing so the district court essentially adopted the position that vault statements form part of the court documents (*processtukken*) from which no information may be omitted, unless the passages concerned are not relevant to the case and for compelling reasons are not suitable for inclusion in the case file (such as the safety of a witness or de *modus operandi* of the Public Prosecution Service) and this course of action can also be accounted for. In the Passage case the district court reached the conclusion that if "a potential crown witness cannot or will not provide a full statement about a certain offence, this offence may not be included in the deal".[299]

A further question is how much information the Public Prosecution Service should provide about the past of a certain witness insofar as this concerns whether s/he has ever collaborated with justice. This is an issue not only where undertakings are made but also with respect to ordinary witnesses. In practice, for example, questions occasionally arise concerning the 'informant history' of a certain witness. The basic principle is that the

---

295 This part of the agreement has since become known as the 'omissions agreement' or named after the person about whom the statements were made – the 'Holleeder omissions'. See Amsterdam District Court 29 January 2013, ECLI:NL:RBAMS:2013:BZ0392 (Passage).

296 This also applied to the verbatim transcriptions of the interviews that were later introduced into the proceedings. Where it was indicated that certain passages were missing.

297 According to the Public Prosecution Service these were "passages relating to the negotiation process and/or other (present or future) investigations which could be damaged as a result, and/or passages which could endanger the safety of the witness, his family or third parties, and/or the tactics of the investigation and/or the CIE and/or the WPT". See Amsterdam District Court 29 January 2013, ECLI:NL:RBAMS:2013:BZ0392 (Passage).

298 See Amsterdam District Court 29 January 2013, ECLI:NL:RBAMS:2013:BZ0392 (Passage). In one of the cases (Dino S.) this led to the exclusion from evidence of the statements made by the witness with whom a deal had been made, resulting in partial acquittal for the most serious offences in the case (See Amsterdam District Court 29 January 2013 ECLI:NL:RBAMS:2013:BY9841). In the other cases in the Passage proceedings, the district court ruled that this unlawfulness did not have to have any further consequences given that the interests of the accused concerned were not damaged by this unlawfulness. On appeal the Amsterdam Court of Appeal in the Dino S. case ruled that the omissions agreement was indeed unlawful, but that in the meantime there had been sufficient compensation for the subsequent damage to the accused, which meant that the statements could be used as evidence (see Amsterdam Court of Appeal 29 June 2017, ECLI:NL: GHAMS:2017:2496, § 2.2.2.6.2.8).

299 See Amsterdam District Court 29 January 2013, ECLI:NL:RBAMS:2013:BZ0392 (Passage).

identity of informants will always be preserved, but this can sometimes lead to friction when the same person then appears as a witness. Respondent [5], a public prosecutor responsible for the gathering and use of criminal intelligence by the police (CIPP), out-lined the dilemma in a case in which this occurred and the consequences that it had. This concerned a witness to whom undertakings had been made, but who was already detained when the talks with him began. Initially it was decided not to make it known that this individual had also been an informant, because it was feared that this could create a precedent. That the identity of an informant should never be revealed is, after all, considered to be sacrosanct. Later the informant's background was revealed and there was a request by the defence – and later an order by the court – to see what he had stated about the case in question as an informant. When it appeared however that there were discrepancies between what he had previously said as an informant and his statement as a witness, the district court deemed the statement to be insufficiently reliable. The result of this was that the authorities were then burdened with a heavy and long-lasting duty of care with regard to the safety of the witness involving a full set of protection measures without achieving the desired result in the case in question. The respondent stated that this shows the importance of taking a close look at the veracity of statements at an early stage. If they turn out to be untrue then that's the end of the matter, but it also provides the opportunity to point out and clarify any differences in the vault statements, to avoid unpleasant surprises later on at trial.

Respondent [13] from the criminal defence bar reported how difficult it is to obtain certain information about the preliminary phases of the procedure, thereby alluding to the omission agreement referred to above, among other things. The respondent had the following to say about this:

> "In 95% of cases there are no problems with establishing the truth and we should be proud of our police force. But in the large cases they start haggling with the truth. Here in such a way that they tried to camouflage Holleeder's omissions by saying that it was for safety reasons, or because it was illegible. It took a huge effort to bring this to light. Initially the judge said that we must assume the integrity of the investigation, but later it appeared that this had been seriously compromised. In this case it turned out that what the Public Prosecution Service did was to the detriment of the truth. And this is not because of corruption, because they are all people of integrity, but because of the major interests at stake and the fact that they then overlook things and then in panic start to say things which are not true. The courts need to crack down on that; there really needs to be consequences attached."

In this context respondent [8] from the judiciary indicated that the law does not provide a clear yardstick by which to evaluate requests for further investigation. According to the respondent it is the 'magisterial role' (*magistratelijkheid*) of the Public Prosecution Service that provides the starting point in this regard. In the Passage case the district court then ruled that there must be some plausibility (*een begin van aannemelijkheid*) before further investigation will be ordered, a criterion which is commonly applied when assessing defence arguments that attempt to bring to light any unlawfulness in the investigative phase of proceedings. The aim here is to prevent 'fishing expeditions', but also the idea that the defence has sufficient room to probe certain matters. The district court in the Passage case took the view however, that with regard to matters which touch upon the witness protection procedure a stricter criterion should apply, given the nature of that procedure. The district court ruled at the time that to further explore that territory there needed to be 'strong indications' (*sterke aanwijzingen*) and not just some plausibility.[300] The question, however, is whether the Court of Appeal will also adopt this measure in its findings, said respondent [8].[301]

Another potential problem concerns the scope of the statement made by the witness in terms of his own criminal past. How much disclosure must a witness give about this in advance? If no clear agreements are made about this, problems can arise in the implementation phase. The Instructions on Undertakings to Witnesses in Criminal Cases states that the witness who is an accused (or co-accused) must provide full disclosure of the situation concerning his share in the criminal offences to which his witness statement relate.[302] Other than that, the respondents indicated, it is a grey area. However, it is important for the Public Prosecution Service to know who they are dealing with. If the potential witness already has such an extensive criminal record that in the end the proceedings will be only about that, then this may be a reason not to continue with him. If matters later come to light which the Public Prosecution Service was not aware of, this can put the PPS in a difficult position, stated the respondents from the PPS and the police. Conversely, suspects cannot be expected to reveal their entire past and provide a full statement about offences which are not yet known to the authorities. If these are offences which are entirely separate from the set of facts and the person about whom the statement is being made, then most respondents from the PPS and the police take the position that the witness can invoke his right to silence in respect thereof. Respondent [5] who is a CIPP, stated that it is therefore possible to conclude a deal:

---

300 See Amsterdam District Court 29 January 2013, ECLI:NL:RBAMS:2013:BZ0392 (Passage).

301 It has since transpired in this context that the Amsterdam Court of Appeal did indeed adopt a similar criterion to that of the district court. See Amsterdam Court of Appeal 29 June 2017, ECLI:NL: GHAMS:2017:2496 (Dino S.), § 2.2.2.2.5.2. See § 3.4.5 for further details.

302 Instructions on Undertakings to Witnesses in Criminal Cases, Government Gazette 2012, 26860 (entered into force on 1 January 2013), § 6.

> "[…] on just a slice of someone's criminal activities. The rule is that although they do not have to tell everything, everything they do tell must be complete and entirely truthful."

The same respondent also said that the risks of not providing a complete statement about his own criminal history are pointed out to the witness.

> "We say to the witness: you don't have to make a statement about everything, but you do need to remember that the people against whom you are testifying and who may have a bone to pick with you, may perhaps present evidence in other cases. Cases in which you do not have a deal."

Sometimes it is beneficial for the witness to make a statement about other offences also. The defence lawyer of the witness also plays an important part in terms of advising him on this, said respondent [5].

Respondent [11], defence counsel for one of the witnesses to whom undertakings were made in the Passage case, also drew attention to the psychological pressure and the exceptional position of the witness and his defence lawyer. Such a procedure can be very stressful for the witness, because it can take a very long time,[303] he often has to appear in court and spend long days in the witness box (a secure cabin),[304] but not least because there is little more that he can say. The respondent indicated that the legal position of the witness is currently poorly provided for. He stated for example that the witness has almost no means of legal recourse for himself.

> "Let's say that the witness finds himself in conflict with the authorities about something simple (for example, where he will live), then he has to go to great lengths to institute proceedings in this regard, as set out in the agreement. If he is then only partially successful or he loses the case, then he has to bear the cost of that himself."

According to the respondent, this should be arranged differently. The legal position of the witness could also be improved, in his view, by making arrangements for the pre-trial detention.[305] The respondent also stated that there needs to be more psychological support for the witness.

---

303 Respondent [11] in this context pointed to the risk of losing face in personal relationships if it all takes too long: "People withdraw if they think it is taking too long and they say: 'You would have been free by then. I am not going to do it anymore'." This all undermines the resilience of the crown witness. Because a witness, after all, is only human."

304 In the Passage case the examination of the witness with whom a deal had been made went on for weeks in the first instance proceedings. But that does not always have to be the case.

305 See § 3.5.6.2 for further details of the sentencing in the case pertaining to the witness himself.

"I am continually having to coach. It now all ends up on the defence lawyer's plate. It is a criminal or former criminal, of course. But the police, the PPS and the Witness Protection Team need to see more clearly that the goal is one and the same, which is to bring the criminal proceedings to a successful conclusion. It is important to make sure that the witness does not cave in. It is in everyone's interest to keep him going mentally. Besides which, he is entitled to have a good position in the criminal procedure. I do see room for real improvements to be made there."

Such a procedure also demands a lot of the criminal defence lawyer who sometimes has to spend days at a time with the witness in the secure cabin but who otherwise has no protection. A situation which is quite different for the civil lawyer involved in the witness protection agreement, who operates in the slipstream and whose identity is not revealed. Respondent [11] stated that more attention could be given to the safety of the criminal defence lawyer representing the witness. This applies also to a number of practical matters. The respondent had the following to say about this.

"It should be easier to make contact with him. At the moment he can always call me, but I cannot call him. That has to go via the Witness Protection Team. I should also be able to e-mail him; the dossier already amounted to 700 lever arch files with something being added to them every day. If I want him to see that, I have to bring it to him. It would be easier if I could simply e-mail it to him. Facilities like that. … Hearings take place in the Schiphol Judicial Complex. I do not sit in the courtroom, of course, but in the secure cabin. We sit in there together for days on end. I go in there really early and only get to leave when everyone else has left. So that means you are shut up in there together from 8.30 in the morning to 6 or 7 in the evening. You cannot leave before that, not even for a breather. We are shut up in there for long periods of time and it's just me and him. Fortunately we get along just fine, but what if you find yourself stuck with someone with whom there is no click. Little thought has been given to such matters."

3.5.5   Relationship with Witness Protection

As discussed above, the Instructions on Undertakings to Witnesses in Criminal Cases states that instituting measures to protect the witness and the agreements about that should be seen as separate from the agreement as referred to in Section 226g CCP and that, in the context of the latter agreement, the only thing that may be promised is that the public prosecutor will urge that such measures, insofar as necessary, be taken, by order of the Board of Procurators General.[306] Separate agreements are made about protection that are laid down in a contractual agreement (sometimes referred to as a covenant), which is in no way connected with the agreement made concerning the undertakings provided in exchange for the statements to be made by the witness. The procedures are also separate. The undertakings in the meaning of Section 226g are made by the public prosecutor responsible for the gathering and use of criminal intelligence by the police (CIPP), while the WPT public prosecutor is responsible for witness protection. Both procedures – as previously stated – are also handled by a different police teams. Essentially, the Criminal Intelligence Team (TCI) or Special Witnesses Team is concerned with the process of reaching an agreement about the undertakings (the criminal law agreement), while the Witness Protection Team is involved with protection measures and the agreements made concerning that (the civil law agreement).[307] However, as was also observed in the literature and discussed in the foregoing, it is difficult to keep these matters separate from one another.[308] Among other things, this has to do with the fact that these procedures partly overlap in time and it is very important for the witness to know how the witness protection will be arranged before they are willing to cooperate with the authorities.

The literature study showed that the relationship with witness protection is problematic for a number of reasons, which was also confirmed by the empirical study. Dissatisfaction on the part of the witness can lead to him becoming less willing to make a statement or even withholding or suspending all further cooperation with the undertakings procedure. Some witnesses are also not inclined to accept the rules imposed by the authorities, as shown in the foregoing, which raises the question of whether the duty of care also allows other agreements to be made than inclusion in a witness protection programme. Similarly scrutiny of the witness protection, or the lack thereof, is seen as a problem in practice. The question is therefore raised in the literature whether the procedures should remain separate or whether in the future there should not be some form of (internal or external) scrutiny of the witness protection measures.[309] These points will be examined in more detail below, but first consideration will be given to how the protection agreement is arrived at and what it covers.

3.5.5.1 Drafting and Content of the Protection Agreement

Previously in this chapter reference was made to the Witness Protection Decree which lays down the conditions under which protection measures may be implemented and

---

306 See § 3.4.3.4 and § 3.4.5 for further details.
307 See § 3.5.3. For further details about the qualification of the agreement as a criminal law or a civil law agreement, see § 3.4.5 and the literature referred to there concerning this point.
308 For further details, see also § 3.4.5 and the literature referred to there concerning this point.
309 See also Bleichrodt 2010, Bleichrodt and Korten 2012, Janssen 2013 and Korten 2015.

how the procedure is set up in general terms.[310] The internal working procedures state that as soon as the statement made by the witness has sufficient value as evidence and those concerned wish to begin the negotiations, the CIPP should make contact with the Witness Protection Team of the National Unit.

Although witnesses to whom undertakings are made will generally be subject to protective measures, that is not always the case. The matter of whether the witness is included in a protection programme is primarily dependent on the seriousness of the threat. In addition, the information which the witness has to offer must be important enough to justify inclusion in a witness protection programme and the individual in question must be capable of operating within the limits of such a programme. If that is not the case or the witness does not wish to be included in a programme, then he could be covered by the general Surveillance and Protection System (*Stelsel bewaken en beveiligen*).[311] As respondent [19a], who works with the Witness Protection Team of the National Unit, however indicated, it is a grey area.

> "It depends on the degree of threat (seriousness and probability), but also how someone can be managed in a programme. Some people have such complex personalities that they are not capable of sticking to the rules of conduct intended to preserve their safety."

It appeared from the interviews that another psychological assessment is carried out at this stage. At the same time respondent [19b], who also works with the Witness Protection Team of the National Unit, reported that an estimate is made of the challenges and risks in terms of the character of the witness. This is done by an external psychologist who, in consultation with the psychologist who made the first assessment of the witness, makes a recommendation. This recommendation forms part of the threat analysis drawn up by Witness Protection Team's own analyst. Respondent [19b] explained that this threat analysis together with the recommendation of the public prosecutor responsible for witness protection is sent to the Board of Procurators General and includes all available information about the seriousness and probability of the threat.

For the witness protection procedure the witness is allocated a civil lawyer who supports the witness during the negotiations about the protection agreement. This civil law agreement is drawn up by the State Advocate and, as noted, from the legal perspective is entirely separate from the criminal law agreement relating to the undertakings made. Respondent [14], who works in the State Advocate's Office, reported that this agreement sets out the nature and duration of the protection measures. Obligations are also placed

---

310 See the Witness Protection Decree of 21 December 2006, Bulletin of Acts and Decrees 2006, 21 (last amended on 30 November 2012, Bulletin of Acts and Decrees 2012, 615, which entered into force on 1 January 2013). See § 3.4.5 for further details.
311 For further details about the Surveillance and Protection System, see Janssen 2013, p. 119-146.

upon the witness, for example, the obligation to remain silent about the protection measures and the requirement to take steps to provide for his own living expenses. Inclusion in a protection programme, said the respondents from the Witness Protection Team, always involves moving house and being given a new identity, but other than that it is mostly a matter of tailoring the agreement to the situation such that the aim is for the individual to become independent. Witnesses are assisted with this as far as possible, for example, with finding a job.

The impression that by being included in a witness protection programme the witness can expunge his debts and his criminal past, appears to be wrong. Respondent [19a] stated that the agreement is based on the principle of a life for a life. The income that someone earned in a legal manner before he entered witness protection is also the starting point for life under protection.[312] It is not the case that debts are cancelled. These are taken into account in the witness protection programme and in such an event a payment scheme is arranged with the witness. The agreement lasts for a set period and is regularly evaluated.[313] Respondent [19a] stated that the ultimate aim is for the witness to be able to live and function independently and to be financially self-supporting again.

> "That is the moment when the witness protection ties can be cut. Based on the assumption that the threat is no longer there in the new situation."

It cannot be ascertained from the agreement where the witness will go, but mutual agreements are laid down (rights and duties) about the protection measures to be taken concerning the personal situation or circumstances of the witness in question, and other matters. Revelation of that information, respondent [19a] noted, could endanger the witness (should such an agreement inadvertently reach the public domain).

Respondent [14] from the State Advocate's Office, considers it a problem that there are no rules in place regulating the content of the witness protection agreement. Section 226l CCP may provide a statutory basis for taking protection measures and in terms of the procedure to be followed there is the previously mentioned Witness Protection Decree, but other than that there is no framework within which the agreements are to be made. This provides room in the negotiations which potential witnesses can exploit. The respondent said this in this context:

> "I can imagine that if a witness is negotiating a deal, he will want to know something about what will happen in terms of the witness protection. Anyone would want to know that, because it is just a black hole. [...] So I think that it would be more helpful to have a clear-cut framework: 'these are the measures

---

312 See also Korten 2015, p. 290-291 and p. 295-297.
313 See also Korten 2015, p. 301-308.

we can take', or you could consider scrutiny by a judge who then says 'this is what it is'."

In response to the question of which aspects should be given more attention, respondent [14] also mentioned how long the protection is provided for and the amount of the allowance paid. With regard to the second matter the question is: to what extent should this depend on the socio-economic position of the witness before the protection or should it be a standard amount? At the moment this is decided on a case-by-case basis. The duty of care can also be widely interpreted.[314] The respondent said the following about this.

> "It is not possible to say that the duty of care leads to certain measures or an allowance of so much per month as a minimum, the duty of care is not as strictly regulated as that. The witness may well have an interest in ensuring that it is as much as possible and continues for as long as possible. Particularly if the negotiations surrounding the deal are taking place at the same time, the witness will be inclined to try to get as much out of it as possible, I think, while the public prosecutor responsible for witness protection must not interpret the duty of care as being wider than it is because then you start to border on the area of giving a reward."

The impression that the procedure leaves room open for negotiation was also confirmed by the interview with respondents [19a and 19b] from the Witness Protection Team, who mentioned that it would be helpful if there was more clarity and consistency concerning the amounts to be paid to the witness.

> "There are guidelines, but these provide a wide margin, which the accused and his defence lawyer can then sometimes cleverly make use of."

In this context respondents [19a and 19b] also mentioned that the type of witness you are dealing with also makes a difference, in particular whether it a 'push' or a 'pull' witness (i.e. a witness whose motives are either push or pull driven).[315] The biggest motivation of a push witness is to get out of the situation. While a pull witness make his own cost/benefit analysis.

---

314 For further details about the duty of care, see § 3.4.5 and the literature and jurisprudence referred to there.
315 With regard to this distinction, see also Beune and Giebels 2012, p. 25. Pull witnesses may be described as those who are not yet known to their possible attackers or the police and who voluntarily decide to approach the police with information; push witnesses can be described as those who are already being threatened or blackmailed, or who are approached by the police to act as a witness because they have been encountered during an investigation.

"From moral point of view you could say that there should be a clear framework … but a crime fighter will say that the pull factor has to be big enough.
[…] Independent scrutiny would be helpful in these situations."

Respondents [19a and 19b] emphasised that the pull factor also should not be too great.

"You should not pull out all the stops to get people in, because in the long term
that will be to your detriment. They really have to make up their minds for
themselves. It is, after all, a very hard path. You cannot possibly know in advance what the real impact will be. You can't show people what it means. People with many pull motives have most difficulty with the restriction on their
autonomy, that they have to abide by the rules, have little control over the
situation and that their freedom of movement is curtailed."

3.5.5.2 How This Affects Willingness to Make a Statement

In practice it is already considered fairly early on whether or not it will be possible to
provide adequate protection to a potential witness with whom a deal is to be made. If that
is not so, then the procedure will founder for this reason alone. The agreements made
about protection are also very important to the witness. For these reasons alone the two
procedures cannot be seen as separate from one another, as several respondents pointed
out. Respondent [16] who for the Special Witnesses Team performs intake interviews
with potential witnesses in the context of the undertakings procedure, said the following:

"What is difficult in the process, I think, is that when you are talking about
deals, you cannot see this as entirely separate from the entire protection
process. This is certainly a bottleneck. The problem is that when you enter
into a discussion about the conditions for a deal there are immediately questions
about safety, while the person concerned sees the police as a single entity and
then has to negotiate with various different units. It would be much better if a
case manager were to be appointed, in the same way as they do in hospitals."

Respondent [14] from the State Advocate's Office mentioned in this context:

"I don't know if the witness now sees (or even wants to see) the difference
between the deal and the witness protection. That is also not his concern."

As previously mentioned, it may be that a witness decides that he does not want to
collaborate with justice, because the package of protection measures are not acceptable
to him. In the event that the agreement as referred to in Section 226g CCP has been

concluded and problems arise with regard to the witness protection while the agreement about the witness protection has not yet been finalised, this can then lead to awkward situations if as a result the witness decides to withdraw or suspend further cooperation further to the agreement in the sense of Section 226g CCP, as occurred in the Passage trial. Respondent [4] who has long worked as a WPT public prosecutor, said the following about this:

> "The witness could direct the entire course of the criminal proceedings because, he stated, he was not satisfied with the safety measures taken, and adopted the position that for this reason he could not meet his obligation to make a statement under the terms of the deal that had been concluded."

The lesson learned by the Public Prosecution Service from this was – wherever possible – only to bring to trial cases in which witnesses figure to whom undertakings have been made if the negotiations about the witness protection have already been completed, said respondent [4]. Respondents [19a and 19b] from the Witness Protection Team also indicated that the aim is to ensure that the signature is placed on the agreement about the undertakings in the sense of Section 226g CCP on the same day as the agreement on the witness protection is also signed.

Problems arise not only with concluding the protection agreement but also its implementation. In this phase it can again occur that dissatisfaction on the part of the witness about how the witness protection is carried out can influence his willingness to make a statement. This occurred in the previously mentioned Briard case, as well as the Passage case. In the Briard case the district court held the following in this regard.

> "Without having a complete picture of the relationship in this case between [key witness 1] and [key witness 2] on the one hand and the WPT public prosecutor or the Witness Protection Team on the other hand, at a certain point in this case it looked as though the witness protection process to some extent had started to overshadow the interests of the criminal proceedings. This had very serious consequences for the course of the criminal proceedings. The conclusion that must be drawn is that this was caused in the first place by the present allocation of roles in which the WPT public prosecutor takes a leading role, alongside the public prosecutor responsible for the case who is responsible for the criminal proceedings. In this context it was remarkable that [key witness 1] and later [key witness 2] also appeared at the hearing only after the district court had instructed the investigating judge to organise the hearing of the witnesses during the examination in court at the hearing in May 2013. Secondly, it appears that the overshadowing of the interests of the criminal proceedings by the witness protection procedure was caused by the way in

which the dispute resolution between the witness and his protectors had been arranged through arbitration. The arbitration procedure that was a constant background factor in this case, often constituted a barrier to the criminal proceedings and – to a large extent, at least – was incompatible with completing the original task, i.e. fulfilling the role of witness."[316]

Respondent [14] from the State Advocate's Office explained what the problem may be in this context:

"What may be an issue is that a lot is arranged verbally, and therefore discussion can arise later about what was said and what was agreed. Particularly when someone is removed from their familiar surroundings, completely cut off from everything and his freedom of movement is curtailed, then I can easily imagine that the witness does not hear everything that is said to him. If agreements are made in this situation and only verbally and the witness later says that he heard something different, then you are in a difficult position, because nothing has been written down. And this can create difficulties in any dispute about how the agreements are implemented."

Respondent [14] indicated that it is therefore sensible to include more in the agreement, whether or not in an annex. In response to this respondent [19a] from the Witness Protection Team stated that indeed nowadays more is put down. It is worth noting in this context however that, according to respondent [14], it is not often that a lawsuit is brought about the witness protection or that an arbitrator is used if an arbitration clause is included in the agreement.[317]

3.5.5.3   Scrutiny and Further Regulation of the Protection Agreement

Problems also occur in connection with the type of agreements made in the context of the witness protection. The Instructions on Undertakings to Witnesses in Criminal Cases states that within the framework of the criminal law agreement, i.e. the undertakings, no agreements may be made on providing a financial reward.[318] In this context, reference is sometimes made to a ban on 'buying' a statement. However, when asked whether offering the prospect of a sum of money also automatically meant that the statements had been bought, respondents differed in their opinions. In the Passage case the media had reported that in the context of the witness protection € 1.4 million had been paid to witness Peter La S. with whom a deal had been made, a report that has also never been

---

316 See Rotterdam District Court 2 June 2014, ECLI:NL:RBROT:2014:4399 (Briard).
317 See § 3.4.5 for further details.
318 See § 3.4.3.4 for further details.

confirmed by the Public Prosecution Service. This was, in any event, grist to the mill for the defence, who argued that this was actually a camouflaged reward given in exchange for statements, in contravention of the Instructions. The fact that the witness protection procedure is secret, can create a difficult situation in this respect. The Public Prosecution Service, for example, stated that it was not fully able to provide information on that point in connection with the safety of the witness, while the defence lawyers indicated that this part of the agreement cannot be examined by the defence,[319] while that may well be relevant to determining its lawfulness (to check whether any of the agreements made are not permitted under the Instructions). Thus judicial scrutiny of the agreements made about the witness protection is largely lacking. Both the Amsterdam District Court and the Amsterdam Court of Appeal in the Passage case considered that, in principle, it is not for the trial judge to express an opinion about the protection agreement, except in very exceptional circumstances, i.e. where there are such strong indications for unlawful action by the Public Prosecution Service that it must be ruled that, in the guise of witness protection, undertakings have been made which cannot reasonably be connected with witness protection, but which may be entirely or largely ascribed to providing a financial reward to the witness for his willingness to collaborate with justice.[320] According to the district court and the court of appeal, that was not so in the Passage case. This does not obviate the fact that in the Passage case the district court saw reason in its judgment to recommend that a more concrete set of standards should be introduced for witness protection, along with a separate scrutiny procedure to be carried out by a (partially) judicial body with expertise in this area.[321] That body can then look at whether or not undertakings were made in the protection procedure which, in fact, are not permitted and thus do not indirectly constitute a reward.

On the whole, the respondents were positive about some type of judicial scrutiny of this kind with regard to the protection agreement. This also applied to respondents [19a and 19b] who both work with the Witness Protection Team. They also thought that making the agreements about protection subject to scrutiny by a judge would benefit both the transparency and the care taken. The judge can therefore also check whether any financial agreements concerning safety have been set at the right level.

---

319 For further details, see also Janssen 2013, p. 255-264.
320 See Amsterdam Court of Appeal 29 June 2017, ECLI:NL:GHAMS:2017:2496 (Dino S.), § 2.2.2. See § 3.4.5 for further details. For the precise wording of the district court in this context, see Amsterdam District Court 13 December 2011, ECLI:NL:RBAMS:2011:BW1461 (interlocutory order Passage case).
321 See Amsterdam District Court 29 January 2013, ECLI:NL:RBAMS:2013:BZ0392 (Passage). For a similar argument, see Rotterdam District Court 2 June 2014, ECLI:NL:RBROT:2014:4399 (Briard). In the literature also, calls have repeatedly been made for the introduction of a form of judicial scrutiny in this regard. See also Bleichrodt 2010, Bleichrodt and Korten 2012, Janssen 2013 and Korten 2015. See also § 3.4.5 regarding this point. In its rulings in the Passage case the Amsterdam Court of Appeal made no statement about the recommendation of the district court to introduce a separate (judicial) scrutiny procedure.

"In this way a counterbalance can be provided to the defence accusation that the statements have been bought."

When asked whether this would also satisfy the defence, respondent [12], a defence lawyer himself, said that the defence would likely think that it was not enough, but that it would be a definite improvement compared to the present situation. In this context he said the following:

"The most honest approach would be to offer no negotiation whatsoever on the witness protection, but that would not be realistic because people want to know at least where they will be sent to and will often have their own wishes or even demands when it comes to that. This form of reward will therefore continue to exist and there will have to be some form of transparency about the witness protection. It can never be fully transparent, of course, because that would be too dangerous, but some form of judicial scrutiny, by the investigating judge for example, who can made a judgment about the matter of whether or not it is lawful, would seem to me to be logical. We do that with anonymous threatened witnesses as well. That judgment can then be set down on paper and brought into the hearing."

A point raised in the focus group was that if judicial scrutiny were to be introduced, it is also important that the judge should have tools by which to undertake his scrutiny. The focus group members said that the involvement of a judge would not be of much use if it is not clear what the assessment criteria are or if there are no means by which to do this.[322]

3.5.5.4   Relationship with the Duty of Care
A final point connected with financial compensation is that certain witnesses want to arrange their protection for themselves and therefore would rather receive a sum of money to spend as they see fit rather than having it all arranged by the Witness Protection Team. This is complicated in view of the duty of care that rests upon the state to safeguard the safety of witnesses, said respondent [4] who has long worked as a WPT public prosecutor. The Public Prosecution Service has argued that the scope of the state's duty of care should be fixed, given that at the moment it remains unclear how far this extends.[323] A number of interviewees from the Public Prosecution Service and the police

---

322 In its judgments in the Passage case the Amsterdam Court of Appeal gave some consideration to the reasons for the lack of an assessment framework for the institution of protection measures. See also Amsterdam Court of Appeal 29 June 2017, ECLI:NL:GHAMS:2017:2496 (Dino S.), § 2.2.2.4. See in this regard Korten 2015, p. 320-322.

323 See Korten 2015 for further information of the (scope of the) duty of care, p. 41-112.

indicated that in practice much (or too much) is expected in this context. Respondent [18a] said the following about this:

> "At present if the state enters into a contract, then the state bears full responsibility for the safety of the witness. Other agreements could be made about this. To put it another way: if a Polish man with a Polish family presents himself who has something to say about a criminal organisation which may well pose a threat, but who does not wish to have witness protection because he can have a reasonable standard of living in Poland, he only needs a bit of money for that, then perhaps his safety will not be fully guaranteed but I would not consider it a problem to arrange that if everyone (i.e. witness, government, etc.) agrees to that."

In this context it was pointed out that the people involved in such cases are often already at risk. The interview with respondent [1] and others revealed that in this context senior figures at the Public Prosecution Service would therefore like to make it possible to offer financial compensation for that duty of care. Some witnesses want to arrange their own protection instead of being included in a witness protection programme. These witnesses could be given a sum of money for that purpose. According to respondents [19a and 19b] from the Witness Protection Team, this already happens, but only when someone cannot be fully included in a programme (i.e. with a full package of measures).

There is a certain risk, said respondent [4], that the witness will quickly get through all the money. The respondent referred to the example of 'Haagse Kees' who in the late 1990s received a large sum of money to provide for his own security but in no time had spent all the money on a luxury villa and cocaine parties, among other things. The problem is that on the basis of its duty of care the state still has to offer protection in such a situation, said respondent [4]. The question is then what form that duty of care should then take. Respondent [14] from the State Advocate's Office said that the state always retains a basic duty of care. The state cannot entirely buy off its duty of care, but the respondent did see room for certain agreements to be made to the effect that in principle a witness would arrange for his own safety.[324] To prevent situations such as occurred with 'Haagse Kees', any sum of money could always be 'earmarked', for example, by including provisions in the covenant to ensure that as far as possible the money will only be spent on creating a safe environment in which to live and work, said respondent [4].

Another point that touches on the duty of care is the protection of the witness during the period until the agreement is finalised. The Witness Protection Team is responsible for the protection of the witness only from the moment that the agreement is concluded. Before that time the regional units are responsible for the safety of the witness. From the

---

324 See for a similar stance Korten 2015, p. 323.

interviews it appears that particular care is taken not to remove the witness from his environment too soon. This is because no one wants to take on the burden of a duty of care before it is sufficiently clear whether the witness concerned also has enough useful information. In certain exceptional cases however it is not possible to leave someone in their own environment pending the proceedings because the threat is already too great. Respondents [18a and 18b] from the Special Witnesses Team in Amsterdam indicated that they would then take a witness into their care. They reported that in the last six years they had done this only once.[325] However, self-reliance on the part of the witness appears to be the point of departure in this context. This is also the stance adopted by the Special Witnesses Team with the National Unit. Respondent [17] said the following about this:

> "We say that the accused has got into difficulties not because of us, and there-
> fore in principle they have to sort it out for themselves until we have the state-
> ment and have verified that it provides valuable information which can be
> made tactically operational. Only then is there a duty of care. That means
> that the first six to nine months they are on their own. At first we took a
> different approach. In the beginning we also rented a house, because there
> was nowhere that the witness could go and we wanted to keep him on board,
> but then you are already taking on a duty of care. There are people who have
> instituted proceedings against us, because we have said 'perhaps it would be
> better for you to go abroad for a while'. They then say: 'the judicial authorities
> thought that we were not safe and we had to go abroad, so that duty of care has
> already begun'. If someone wants to go abroad, they may do so, and we will go
> and see them there."

A respondent from the police mentioned that the Witness Protection Team is only brought into the process at a late stage.

> "At the moment the Witness Protection Team only gets involved if the Board
> of Procurators General has made a positive decision regarding the undertaking
> to be made. The process of deciding whether someone is useful or not, etc. has
> already been completed by then. Actually that is too late. As a result, during the
> phase before that, these witnesses come under the police (Surveillance and
> Protection System under the responsibility of the Head of the District PPS)
> and the TCI has taken this upon itself [in Amsterdam], although I do not think
> it belongs there. After all, they do not have the competences of a Witness
> Protection Team when it comes to protection. The TCI is the right partner

---

325 In these sorts of cases it is possible to fall back on the general Surveillance and Protection System, but the respondents from the Special Witnesses Team in Amsterdam mentioned that this is not always ideal given that sometimes more information has to be shared than might be considered desirable.

for probing, but not for protection. We prefer doing business with someone who is already detained, because then he is already safe at least, and we run the least risks."

Respondents [19a and 19b] from the Witness Protection Team indicated that they would be willing to get involved at the start and have an initial meeting with the witness to explain what he can expect in general terms. They believe that this would save time, because people can start collecting information, but at that point in time they do not themselves provide the protection.

> "Once someone is with us, everyone thinks: now they will take care of it. You don't want to have that duty of care already if there is still a risk that the procedure will run aground, for example, because it is not accepted by the CTC."

Respondent [11], a member of the criminal defence bar, pointed out the risks to the witness when the procedure takes too long to complete. Because eventually the people around him can start to get suspicious. The longer it takes, the more dangerous it becomes for the witness. In this context the respondent said the following:

> "As soon as it becomes clear what a person can talk about, then you as the Public Prosecution Service actually know enough and need to act quickly. Now it takes months and months. Because what I hear now from other criminals when I visit them, is that there are guards who talk with other detainees, etc. And then my alarm bells started to ring. Because it is also seen as odd if as a major criminal you no longer turn to the outside world (if you no longer contact anyone or avoid contact with other detainees), while you have perhaps agreed with the judicial authorities that you will no longer do that. It would be better if you could simply continue to maintain your criminal contacts and with the entire scene, in order to raise less suspicion. The Public Prosecution Service has been lucky [so far] that it hasn't gone wrong. There have been various situations where we thought: now it is getting very dangerous. Particularly for a witness who has family outside who could suffer as a result."

3.5.5.5   Whether to Maintain Separate Procedures?
Given that the agreement as referred to in Section 226g CCP and the protection agreement are difficult to separate in practice, it has been proposed that they should be merged into one agreement. Respondents from the criminal defence bar in particular stated that the distinction between the two agreements is essentially an artificial one. Respondent [12], a criminal defence lawyer, said the following about this:

> "My main criticism of the legal framework on crown witnesses is that a separation was applied – a separation between the statement agreement and the witness protection agreement – which only exists in theory, and which does not exist in practice, neither according to the Public Prosecution Service nor according to the witness himself, who sees the two agreements as a package deal."

Respondents from the judiciary reported that it is difficult for the witness to see the distinction between the two procedures. In the words of respondent [10b]:

> "We don't know what the agreement is between the Witness Protection Team and the witness, but I think that it is a misconception to think that you can always keep them separate, and I think too that this is not what we should be aiming for. Because for the witness it is a matter of his own safety: where will I be, how will I get food, how can I see my family, how can I let my parents safely meet their grandchildren, etc? All these sorts of things are closely connected with their position as a witness and that which they can and will provide a statement on. You may well think that there is a watertight partition between the two, but for the people involved it feels very different."

However there were other respondents and members of the focus group who were not in favour of merging the two procedures and agreements. Respondents who are aware of the content of such agreements indicated that knowing certain details of the agreement could endanger the safety of the witness in a witness protection programme. Another argument that was put forward is that it is a good thing to keep the responsibilities separate. The benefit of separate procedures is that the public prosecutor responsible for the case does not come under too much pressure to make far-reaching promises about the protection of the witness in order to help the criminal case along, said respondent [19a] from the Witness Protection Team.

3.5.6 Use of Evidence and Sentencing

As previously described in the first part of this chapter,[326] ultimately it is up to the criminal court to decide what the value is of the statements made by the witness to whom undertakings have been made and whether the undertaking made will be honoured in terms of the sentence reduction that has been promised. These two aspects will be considered in more detail below, firstly by considering how the reliability of the statements made by witnesses to whom undertakings have been made are viewed in practice and the

---

326 See § 3.4.1 and § 3.4.4.4.

evaluation thereof by the court. Next the sentencing will be considered, in which the degree of freedom available to the court when it comes to the promised sentence reduction will be examined along with the complications that may arise as a result.

3.5.6.1   Use of Evidence

Before the judge can arrive at a ruling on the evidence (*bewijsbeslissing*), it is necessary to determine the value of the evidentiary material that has been presented by the Public Prosecution Service. Besides reaching a conclusion about the lawfulness of the agreement, under Section 226h paragraph 3 CCP the investigating judge is always expected to rule on the reliability of the witness. These are provisional judgments however, in the sense that the court is not bound by them.[327] In this context respondent [8], who is a judge, stated the following:

> "The investigating judge looks at whether there is enough to go ahead, but the trial judge has to make the final judgment. It is a good thing that there is an investigating judge in the middle. But it is important not to put too much reliance on that. There is a lot that can happen after that. The investigating judge provides more of a provisional judgment and that is useful in the sense that there is scrutiny and matters can be streamlined. If the investigating judge were to make a final judgment, as the trial judge you could feel that your role had been diminished."

Ultimately the trial judge therefore has to arrive at his own judgment based on the information presented later on in the proceedings and what the Public Prosecution Service and the defence put forward in that context. In its judgments in the Passage case the Amsterdam Court of Appeal appeared to take a slightly different view about the (scope of) the role of the trial judge in relation to assessing the lawfulness of the agreement, by stating that the scrutiny of the lawfulness of the agreement is primarily the task of the investigating judge, while the task of the trial judge lies more in assessing the reliability of the statements (where applicable prior to considering questions relating to the lawfulness of the agreement in light of Section 359a CCP and Article 6 ECHR).[328]

If the judge is to arrive at a positive ruling on the evidence then the statutory minimum evidence requirement must also be met. As previously mentioned, for these witnesses a special minimum evidence requirement has been laid down in Section 344a paragraph 4 CCP, which provides that the court may not allow its decision to be based solely on statements made by witnesses to whom undertakings have been made.[329]

---

327 See § 3.4.1 and § 3.4.4.4.
328 See e.g. Amsterdam Court of Appeal 29 June 2017, ECLI:NL:GHAMS:2017:2496 (Dino S.), § 1.6.2. For further details see also § 3.4.4.4 and § 3.5.4.2 of this report.
329 See § 3.4.4.4.

Pursuant to Section 342 paragraph 2 CCP and the Supreme Court's interpretation of this provision, the statement made by the witness should find sufficient support (*voldoende steun*) in the other evidentiary material. Finally, under Section 360 paragraph 2 CCP the judge should provide specific reasons for using the statements made by a witness to whom undertakings have been made.

As indicated, the judge must arrive at his own judgment regarding the reliability of the witness and the value of the statements made by the witness as evidence. In the Instructions on Undertakings to Witnesses in Criminal Cases a distinction is made between the reliability of the witness and the soundness (*deugdelijkheid*) of the statements.[330] The judge will have to form an opinion on both these aspects. With regard to the 'soundness' of the statements[331] it may be assumed that the judge will mainly look at the extent to which they are truthful or accurate. Determining the reliability of the witness and the soundness of his/her statements is difficult, particularly because the witness stands to gain some benefit from making a statement. This is also why the judge, upon use of such statements, is required to provide 'further reasoning' (*nadere motivering*) in this regard (Section 360 paragraph 2 CCP).[332]

This study has nevertheless shown that in practice the reliability of witnesses to whom undertakings are made and their statements are viewed in different ways. Respondent [1], a member of the Board of Procurators General in the Public Prosecution Service stated that defence lawyers incorrectly make a link between the reliability of the statement and the consideration given. He emphasised the fact that just because the witness receives a benefit this does not mean that what he says in his statement is untrue. The judge needs to be aware that consideration has been provided, said respondent [1], but in his judgment about the value of the statement the judge looks for confirmation from the other evidence and from the questioning of the witness at trial. Some respondents from the Public Prosecution Service and the judiciary also noted in this context that the problem of reliability also exists in ordinary cases. The fact that something has been given in exchange for the statement is seen only as an added complication. However, respondents from the criminal defence bar noted that it is very difficult for the judge to determine whether or not someone is lying. Respondent [12] said the following in this context:

---

330 See Instructions on Undertakings to Witnesses in Criminal Cases, Government Gazette 2012, 26860 (entered into force on 1 January 2013), § 7.

331 To make it more complicated: the term 'reliability' is also often used in relation the value of the statements (for further details see Dubelaar 2014, p. 50 ff.). However this is generally about the extent to which the witness' statements provide a sound basis on which to draw conclusions about 'what actually happened'. The reliability of the statement is crucial to this.

332 Cf. in this context also Amsterdam Court of Appeal 29 June 2017, ECLI:NL:GHAMS:2017:2496 (Dino S.), § 3.1: "these witnesses are anything but choir boys and the judge will therefore have to be extra alert to the risk of false statements".

> "If someone can present a well-put-together story, particularly about matters which happened years ago, it is difficult to check that. The legislature therefore needs to remove any incentive to make a false statement. [...] The Public Prosecution Service stated that the reasons for someone to make a statement have nothing to do with the reliability of that statement. It is true that someone with a wrong motive can still make a reliable statement. However, if you assume that criminals are only concerned with serving their own interests, and then you give them the opportunity to do that by making incriminating statements about other people, then you are asking for false statements to be made. This is also why the legislation bans financial rewards."

Respondent [9] from the judiciary also expressed the view that there is a risk of unreliability with witnesses to whom undertakings have been made.

> "The problem is that you have rewarded someone to repeat what he has previously said, and not to tell the truth specifically. In other words, he receives an undertaking in exchange for repeating what he has already said. As a judge you need to check carefully whether that is correct."

Respondent [1] however argued that the motive for making the statement and the reliability of the statement should be seen as separate from one another, on the one hand because every witness has their own reasons for making a statement, and on the other hand because a great deal of time is spent during the initial phase on checking the reliability of the statement with a verification process and because the judge cannot conclude that the charges have been proven on the basis of just one statement.

It is clear from the interviews that the respondents take differing views on the relationship between reliability and the consideration given, as well as on the judge's ability to distinguish satisfactorily between accurate and inaccurate statements. This view to some extent also determines how the respondents see the proposal to widen the scheme in terms of the nature of the undertakings.[333] It should be noted in this context, however, that neither the legislation nor the jurisprudence provide a clear framework against which the statements of those to whom undertaking have been made can be evaluated. The legislation does provide for a number of minimum requirements given that a declaration that the charges have been proved may not rest solely upon the statement of witnesses to whom undertakings have been made and must be sufficiently supported by other evidentiary material, but according to respondent [8] this can be a problem, because it is not clear how much evidence there needs to be in addition to the statements in order to reach the conclusion that the charges have been proven. This

---

333 For further details about the wish to widen the scope for making undertakings to witnesses, see § 3.6.2.1.

respondent indicated that the minimum evidence rules as they now stand in the legislation are currently open to various interpretations given that it is not clear to what extent the evidence minimum as laid down in Section 344a paragraph 4 CCP requires all aspects of the statement pertaining to the accused's participation in the offence (*daderschap*) to be corroborated by an independent source. This requirement of 'double coverage' does not apply in relation to ordinary witness' statements; such statements need only find sufficient support (*voldoende steun*) in the other evidentiary material. The hearing judges in the Passage case in the first instance proceedings however did require double coverage with regard to the participation in certain offences.[334] However, according to respondent [8] this was specific to that case and lay in the (potential) unreliability of the particular witness in question. This respondent was not in favour of a general requirement that all aspects of the statement of a witness to whom undertakings have been made pertaining to the accused's participation in the offence should be corroborated by an independent source. What this respondent would like to see, however, is that in any widening of the scheme the minimum evidence requirement should be tightened up, based on the idea that it would become more attractive to make incriminating statements and therefore stricter requirements must be set with regard to the other available evidence. Quite apart from any widening of the scheme, respondent [13] from the criminal defence bar also argued that stricter standards should be applied with regard to the minimum evidence requirements and the duty to provide reasons under Section 360 paragraph 2 CCP.

> "There has to be full evidence in addition to the collaborator of justice. The [Amsterdam] district court [in the Passage case] believed this too with witness La S. because it had been established that he had lied. Thereafter they classified his statement as supporting evidence. I think that should be the case with all collaborators of justice, even if there are no obvious untruths to be found. Because our entire system is based on the principle that witnesses are required to make a statement."

3.5.6.2   Sentencing

It is up to the trial judge to decide what the value is of the statements that have been made by the witness to whom undertakings have been made and then to decide whether or not these can be used as evidence. This also has its impact on judge's scrutiny of the undertaking that have been made. Unlike the Public Prosecution Service itself, strictly speaking, the judge is not bound by the undertaking made by the Public Prosecution Service concerning the sentence.[335] This means that for the witness it remains

---

334 See Amsterdam District Court 29 January 2013, ECLI:NL:RBAMS:2013:BZ0392 (Passage).
335 See § 3.4.1 and § 3.4.4.4 for further details.

uncertain right up until the last moment whether or not the promised sentence reduction will also be applied by the court. This can be very hard on the witness in cases where the proceedings go on for a long time, said respondent [11], who had supported a witness to whom undertakings had been made.

Although the judge is not bound by the undertaking made by the Public Prosecution Service, it can result in him being faced with awkward questions, for example in relation to the decision of whether to extend the pre-trial detention. Thus, in the Passage case the Court of Appeal ruled that the witness should remain in pre-trial detention throughout the second instance proceedings despite the fact that he had already been detained longer than he would have had to have done pursuant to the agreement with the Public Prosecution Service. For this reason both the defence and the Advocate General asked for the pre-trial detention to be lifted on the basis of the anticipation requirement under Section 67a paragraph 3 CCP, but the Court of Appeal did not wish to prejudge the final decision to be taken and rejected the request to lift the pre-trial detention, as well as the alternative request for the detention to be suspended.[336] Some respondents indicated that the uncertainty surrounding the final sentencing and the risk of ultimately having to serve a longer sentence than was initially promised by the Public Prosecution Service, also constitutes a barrier for certain potential witnesses with whom a deal could be made to collaborate with the authorities. It should be noted in this context however that for the most part the courts have thus far always followed the Public Prosecution Service in terms of the sentence reduction promised, at least that was what one of the respondents from the Public Prosecution Service said, who worked for many years in the National Public Prosecutors' Office. The researchers are not aware of any examples where this was not the case, with the exception of the above case in which the witness to whom undertakings were made remained on pre-trial detention for longer than the sentence which the public prosecutor responsible for the case had demanded on the basis of the agreement.[337] Respondent [8] from the judiciary, indicated that in cases such as these he feels more bound by the demand of the public prosecutor than in normal criminal cases. The agreement serves as the primary starting point and the sentence reduction promised by the Public Prosecution Service is the guiding principle, because otherwise the instrument would be rendered worthless. In practice, respondent [8] said, the scrutiny lies somewhere in the middle between a de novo assessment and an assessment of the reasonableness.

---

336 See Amsterdam Court of Appeal 9 December 2016, ECLI:NL:GHAMS:2016:5211 (interlocutory order Fred R.).

337 In the final judgment in the criminal proceedings against the witness himself, the Court of Appeal also followed the Public Prosecution Service concerning the matter of the promised sentence reduction. See Amsterdam Court of Appeal 29 June 2017, ECLI:NL:GHAMS:2017:2497 (Fred R.).

3.6   Whether to Amend the Present Scheme?

The foregoing looked at the experiences with the instrument of undertakings to witnesses in practice. The next question is whether it is also seen as a useful instrument and whether the present scheme is practicable or in need of adjustments. The respondents had differing opinions on these matters. This section will look more closely at the success of the existing scheme (or the lack thereof) and the changes suggested, and how the different professional groups view them.

3.6.1   *Success of the Instrument and Its Associated provisions*

3.6.1.1   Further Reflection on the Low Frequency

From the foregoing it appears that the instrument is used only modestly in the Netherlands, while at the National Unit and in Amsterdam, at least, exploratory talks are taking place with potentially suitable candidates.[338] From which it appears that the offer made to witnesses is not always considered to be attractive to the witnesses in question and the procedure may run aground as a result. The respondents indicated that this related not only to the amount of the sentence reduction but the total package in which protection plays an important part. In this context the focus group pointed out that the sentencing regime in the Netherlands is relatively mild with respect to certain offences compared with Italy, for example. One member mentioned that it definitely makes a difference whether the witness finds himself confronted with a sentencing demand of thirty years and then has to serve half of that or whether four years is demanded of which only two are left over.

Another reason often mentioned in the interviews by respondents from the police and the Public Prosecution Service is the reluctance or caution shown by some public prosecutors in using the instrument. A number of respondents stated that the use of the instrument of undertakings to witnesses entails a stringent procedure and is therefore seen by some prosecutors in the field as 'a lot of hassle'. On top of which there is always the risk of something going wrong. Respondent [3] drew a parallel with a football match:

> "All the effort is put into preventing the other team from scoring, which is not always the best strategy to win a match."

This respondent also indicated that this approach requires a different mind-set on the part of the public prosecutor concerned. When a bookkeeper is arrested, the respondent said, he should be used to "tackle the big boys, not to put someone away for six months

---

338 See § 3.5.2.2.

for document forgery". Respondent [7] mentioned that the police tactical teams are also not particularly geared up for this.

> "Tactical teams often opt for the classical investigation methods (such as wiretapping, surveillance, recording confidential communications (OVC) and if you are lucky, undercover operations (WOD)), but generally do not consider making deals with witnesses. It is something that really has to come your way. For example, if you have arrested someone who says they have information but is only willing to provide it in exchange for something."[339]

The same respondent, however, also indicated that this is changing and that the police are increasingly on the lookout for opportunities in ongoing investigations.

In this regard reference was also often made in the interviews to the legacy of the Van Traa Commission as a result of which people are less inclined to test the limits of the law. Respondent [4] who works for the Public Prosecution Service, expressed this as follows.

> "To be able to offer something more [than just an inducement] many colleagues have to cross a certain threshold: because of the time-consuming nature of the instrument one the one hand, and the repercussions of the Van Traa fiasco which still resonate, on the other, even though that was quite some time ago now. The Public Prosecution Service is also very cautious about serious breaches of privacy, for example, through the use of a criminal civilian infiltrator or the systematic gathering of information by a member of the public. The prosecutors sometimes consider the use of such to be going too far, while they are often willing to give consent for wiretapping, which constitutes a far greater breach of privacy (because then everything is recorded about matters which have little to do with the suspected offence)."

Respondent [15], who was head of a Criminal Intelligence Team for many years, also confirmed this impression.

> "Before Van Traa we went to extremes and did anything, unless it was actually forbidden. Now we find ourselves at the other extreme and we don't even use the instruments which the law provides."

Further to this, it was also mentioned in the interviews that not all police regions and district court public prosecutor's offices have sufficient expertise in the area of special

---

339 OVC stands for *opnemen van vertrouwelijke communicatie* (recording confidential communications) and WOD for *werken onder dekmantel* (undercover operations).

witnesses, or the capacity to properly make a go of it. In Amsterdam and in the National Unit there are special teams dealing with such witnesses, but such teams are not yet available in other regions.[340] Respondent [6] stated that there should be a special witness team in every regional unit.

> "The police say that they consider it important, but they don't make any capacity available for that. This is also because it is difficult to decide how much personnel time should be made available when you don't know how much time will be needed for that. You don't want to reserve personnel time which is then not used and people end up sitting around twiddling their thumbs."

The foregoing does not mean to say that nothing is being done about this in other districts and regional police units. As the interviews also showed, various initiatives are being developed at least to draw this instrument more to the attention of public prosecutors and the police. The National Public Prosecutors' Office has also set up a working group for this purpose.[341] The aim is also to bring together the available knowledge and expertise in order to draw on the experience gained by the National Unit and in Amsterdam. In this context forming 'satellite groups' is being considered in which various units work together and provide support to one another, also in terms of personnel and capacity. When asked whether it would not be wiser to manage these sorts of procedures centrally, respondent [17] stated that it had been decided not to do this.[342] The Special Witnesses Team in Amsterdam is also not in favour of this.

> "We are known for this in this unit and have been involved with it for some time. We also attend the weekly briefings. Once people know what you do, then they know where to find you."

The public prosecutor responsible for the gathering and use of criminal intelligence by the police (CIPP) involved also mentioned this as one of the explanations for the success of Amsterdam, besides the fact that they have their own team. The Public Prosecution Service wants to involve the general public more in investigative work, but then money/

---

340 Respondent [17] stated that they do not have sufficient budget or personnel: "Since the re-organisation most of the criminal intelligence groups have been downsized which makes it difficult to take on additional tasks."

341 In principle the working group is concerned with all aspects of using the general public in investigations. The working group therefore is concerned not only with special witnesses.

342 By contrast, one focus group member from the police said that management of the procedure relating to undertakings should be centrally organized, within both the police and the Public Prosecution Service. This would have a number benefits, such as combined expertise and overview of the various procedures; sufficient professional distance from the investigation; and better opportunities to develop and maintain negotiating skills.

personnel must be made available to actively recruit people, several respondents stated. Respondents differed in their views about whether capacity really constitutes an obstacle to starting procedures with witnesses within the meaning of this study. A member of the focus group indicated that if a potential witness who has important information were to present himself then this capacity would definitely be made available.

A final explanation for the low frequency lies in the fact that it is a far-reaching method of investigation subject to certain restrictions. Respondent [1] from the Board of Procurators General emphasised in this context that it is an instrument which should not be used lightly and which they would prefer to use only exceptionally.

> "We don't want to make undertakings in every case. It will always be an exception to what we normally do."

In this context it should be noted that the requirement of subsidiarity is a condition that must be met before undertakings to witnesses may be used, which means that this instrument can only be used if it can be demonstrated that using other investigation methods will not lead to the desired result.[343]

3.6.1.2   Success of the Scheme and the Need to Widen It

Another important question to consider in determining whether to amend the statutory provision is whether and to what extent the existing regulation has achieved its goal. This question will be answered below primarily in the words of the respondents.[344] In this context it is important to look at: 1) cases where the instrument has actually been used to answer the question of whether this led to the desired result; and 2) cases where exploratory talks took place but where ultimately this did not lead to use of the instrument.[345]

From the foregoing it appears that in individual cases results have indeed been achieved with the use of the instrument in the sense that in two out of three cases it led to convictions. Respondent [1], a member of the Board of Procurators General, was asked when the Board would consider use of the instrument to be successful. His response was that if with the aid of undertakings to witnesses criminal offences of a particularly distressing nature, such as liquidations, could be solved which would otherwise not be solved, the instrument can been considered a success. He made reference to the Passage case in which without the said witness, no convictions would have resulted in the first instance.[346] In this respondent's view, this was a criminal sector which the authorities would not otherwise be able to touch.

---

343 See § 3.4.2 for further details.
344 For further reflection on this question see § 3.7 and Chapter 8.
345 See in this regard § 3.5.2.3.
346 It bears recalling that, at the time of the interviews, the respondents were not aware of the outcome of the appeal proceedings in which the court of appeal handed down convictions partly on the basis of the statements of a second witnesses to whom undertakings had been made. See further § 3.5.2.3.

However, it is not just about the outcome of the criminal case, but more the impact on society that it has, as well as the redress obtained for victims as a result, the respondent said. However, respondents in the criminal defence bar were critical (even highly critical) as regards the 'successes' achieved in the Passage case, and pointed to the many problems that arose during that case. Respondent [13] said the following in this context:

> "There are already plans to widen the scope for making undertakings to witnesses, while it is has been used in only a handful of cases. This is all the more remarkable given that it went very wrong with La S. [in the Passage proceedings], and indeed the present legal framework only came about after decades of debate. I am trying to understand why this widening would be necessary. I understand that you want to catch the top criminals but then you should not give them the idea that this cannot be done without resorting to such a drastic remedy. The crown witness in its present form is already such a remedy, and if you widen it, then it will only get worse. What I am wondering is what does not work now, and how it will work better if the Public Prosecution Service can offer even more money or even less detention."

The judge in the focus group who was involved in the Passage case as an investigating judge also had reservations about the success of the Passage proceedings. He stated:

> "The Passage case is taking so long that it almost doesn't matter anymore what the final result will be. We are all completely powerless to bring such a case to a positive conclusion."

The Yellowstone case however was – as already mentioned[347] – considered by members of the focus group to be a success.

It was also said in the focus group that the instrument may well have proved its usefulness in individual cases, but it is very difficult to say whether it is now being used too little. Its modest use thus far would tend to suggest so, given that plenty of exploratory talks with potential witnesses do take place. Some thought that the key to the success of the legal framework and whether it should be changed or not lies in the explanations for the low frequency of its use.

> "The question is whether the instrument is not being used because it is not necessary, or because the legal framework presents obstacles that need to be removed."

---

347 See § 3.5.2.3.

Members of the focus group recognised however that there is a complex set of factors involved. Respondents [18a and 18b] with the Special Witnesses Team in Amsterdam said the following in this regard.

> "Along the path between the first step and the final agreement there are dozens of possible reasons why a procedure might run aground. There are so many circumstances which could affect the success or otherwise of the instrument in an individual case. These are often major obstacles which you, as the witness, are completely unaware of in the beginning (upon the initiation of such a process)."

Respondent [1] further emphasised that it is an exceptional instrument which should be reserved for exceptional cases. For this reason the respondent also could not conclude that the nine instances in which approval was given by CTC and the Board of Procurators General for the instrument to be used (ultimately resulting it being used five times, i.e. undertakings were made to five witnesses in three different cases),[348] was too few, given that each of those cases could have had a major impact on society. Respondent [16] who works for the police, also stated that the term success may be applied not only where this leads to an agreement and a conviction as a result, but also if the scheme filters out people who have no intention of making a truthful statement or who are entirely unsuitable for such a procedure.

> "Success could also be: given the problems with this individual, you shouldn't do it, because later in the process this could cause a great many more problems."[349]

It is clear that at the moment the instrument is not used often, that before it actually can be applied certain obstacles need to be overcome and that witnesses do not always find the offer made to be attractive enough to actually agree to collaborate with the authorities. However, this does not, in itself, mean that there is a need to widen the scope for making undertakings to witnesses. Respondents from the Public Prosecution Service suggested in this context that this need lies more in the failure of more traditional investigation methods, such as wiretapping and systematic surveillance.[350] Respondent [7] said:

> "What I see every time is that you do not get where you want to be with the classical methods. The classical methods require a great deal of time and money and are used all the time, but they do not work as well as we would like them to."

---

348 See further § 3.5.2.2.
349 For the various perspectives on the notion of success, see further § 2.5.
350 See also the letter from the Minister of Security and Justice dated 5 July 2013, Parliamentary Papers II 2012/13, 29 911 no. 83, p. 1 and 2.

The Public Prosecution Service also mentioned that criminals are becoming increasingly smart and leave fewer traces.[351] That the nature of crime in that sense has changed was however disputed by some members of the focus group.

3.6.2 Proposed Changes

As is clear from the foregoing, according to the practitioners interviewed for the purposes of this study, several matters could be better or more carefully arranged. Some of the suggestions related to widening the scope for making undertakings to witnesses so that the instrument can be used more readily, other suggestions related to strengthening and streamlining the procedure itself. These included taking measures which provide for the use of the instrument on appeal, improving the legal position of the witness and providing the investigating judge with more room to manoeuvre when it comes to providing adequate scrutiny of the lawfulness of the agreement and the reliability of the witness, for example. These and other issues were raised above, in setting out the findings from the interviews.

The two main points that were proposed and which almost all the respondents were expressly asked about, however, concerned the widening of the scope for using the instrument in terms of the undertakings that may be made and the offences in respect of which this instrument could be used, and the scrutiny of the agreements made in the context of the witness protection. These two proposed changes will be considered in more detail below.

3.6.2.1 Widening in Terms of the Undertakings on Offer or the Types of Offences in Respect of Which the Instrument is Available

In 2013, the Minister of Security and Justice in 2013 expressed the intention of widening the scope for using the instrument in terms of the offer which may be made to the witness in exchange for his statements.[352] As previously mentioned, the respondents stated that presently no real negotiation actually takes place given that, according to them, the statutory maximum of a 50% sentence reduction is applied as the *de facto* standard.[353] There also appeared to be a wide level of acceptance among the respondents from the Public Prosecution Service and the police for widening the scope for using the instrument by increasing the amount of sentence reduction, even though not everyone thought that this would actually help to persuade witnesses and despite some misgivings about where the boundary should lie. Respondent [18a] expressed his objections as follows.

---

351 See § 3.5.2.1.
352 See the letter from the Minister of Security and Justice dated 5 July 2013, Parliamentary Papers II 2012/13, 29 911, no. 83. p. 6 ff.
353 See § 3.5.3.5.

"To put it this way: I know of no examples of anyone who said: '50% is too little, but for 75% I would have done it'. But that is not to say that people don't think about it in those terms. There's nothing you can really say about that. It is more of a gut feeling. And there may be someone who thinks: you are going to offer them more, so you will have more chances. But you also have a responsibility to society and as a public authority you also have to be able to say: 'this is it, we go no further'. And then you simply have to accept that you cannot use that statement."

Some respondents also argued in favour of dropping all the charges or reducing the sentencing demand in full (by 100%).[354] Both options essentially amount to the same (no punishment for the witness), with the proviso that in the latter case an independent judge would have to consider the case against the witness and his share in the events on which he has made a statement. In that respect this differs from a decision not to prosecute, where no judge is involved. It was mentioned by someone from the Board of Procurators General that in case of a decision not to prosecute, the judge ruling on the case in which the statement is used does need to be aware of the agreements made and the intention or decision not to prosecute the witness for his share in the case in question (or another). It is then up to the judge to decide whether or not to use the statement, but the witness in question will know where he stands. Respondent [1]:

"Complete (100%) sentence reduction combined with prosecution, leads to more uncertainty for the accused. [...] If it is decided not to prosecute then for the judge that is a *fait accompli*, but he could weigh the decision not to prosecute against the statement made by the witness."

Respondents thought that a full (100%) sentence reduction or a decision not to prosecute may be permissible in cases where the sentencing demand is already low, because it entails a less serious offence or in cases where the witness had not yet been considered at all as a suspect by the authorities and is only prepared to make a statement if he does not have to go to prison.

Another suggestion related to granting a reward or 'financial compensation', as respondent [1] preferred to call it. At the moment the Instructions on Undertakings to Witnesses in Criminal Cases does not permit that,[355] while this is something that witnesses do actually ask for, said respondents from the police and the Public Prosecution Service. As an argument for deviating from the position so far adopted in the legislative history that providing a financial reward in exchange for statements is out

---

354 The term 'immunity' is also used in this context in the parliamentary history and the literature, although this term is more fitting in the context of dropping charges than full sentence reduction.
355 See § 3.4.3.4 for further details.

of the question, it was mentioned that agreeing to collaborate has far-reaching consequences affecting the witness' life and social position from that point on. It would not
be a matter of buying a statement, given that the consideration should be in proportion to
the damage suffered by the witness as a result of making his statement.[356] Respondent [1]
said about this:

> "Every witness who sticks his neck out, suffers financially as a result. That is the
> reality: either he loses his job or he has to spend the rest of his life looking over
> his shoulder, or he loses his position in society, etc. He may want to have
> money to compensate for that hardship, and I can well imagine that."

The wish to be able to offer compensation is separate from the agreements made about
protection of the witness to which there are also costs attached. This respondent further
referred to the fact that tipsters are also paid and that no one sees that as a problem.
Respondent [17] from the police also mentioned this.

> "If you look at the value of the information: as an informer you are rewarded
> for good information. If you provide a good statement as a threatened or anon-
> ymous witness, you enter into the same system, but you get nothing. People
> then think: I would be better off telling my story to the people next door (the
> TCI), at least I will get money for it there."

This was also mentioned by respondent [7] from the Public Prosecution Service as a
stumbling block in the present scheme. A TCI (Criminal Intelligence Team) source
receives money and remains anonymous while in the context of the instrument of making undertakings to witnesses no money is paid and the source has to reveal his identity.
For this reason, TCI sources are less likely to collaborate with the authorities within the
specific meaning of this study, unless they really have something to lose because there is a
long sentence hanging over their head.

Finally, senior officials in the Public Prosecution Service have called for the scope of the
instrument to be widened in terms of the offences in respect of which it may be applied.
When asked, respondents from the public prosecutor's offices did not see an immediate
need for that, now that the so-called 'pre-trial detention criterion' and the supplementary
requirement that the offences in respect of which pre-trial detention may be lawfully
ordered must have been committed in the context of organised crime are generally satisfied. In practice then, these requirements do not really constitute an obstacle, also given
that it is an exceptional instrument. Similarly, respondent [4] observed that while the

---

356 See also the Letter from the Minister of Security and Justice dated 5 July 2013, Parliamentary Papers II
2012/13, 29911 no. 83, p. 6.

instrument is hardly used in major fraud cases and other white collar crime, this is not so much because of the requirements set by the law (as just set out), but more due to the fact that the National Public Prosecutor's Office for Financial, Economic and Environmental Offences ('*Functioneel parket*') still hardly looks at the available opportunities in this area. The respondent had the following to say in this context:

> "You could easily conclude a deal with someone who has a conflict in the work-place or ethical objections, provided that he or she has good information about subversive fraud. People still think very much in classical terms, i.e. seizure (paper is an means of proof), wiretapping and surveillance."

Respondent [1] from the Board of Procurators General mentioned, however, the example of the theft of a Rembrandt painting. If this does not take place in an organised context, then according to him the provisions of Section 226g CCP cannot be used.

Objections were raised by members of the criminal defence bar about any widening of the scope for making undertakings to witnesses along these lines. They were concerned that a more generous provision could have an attractant effect, which could lead to unreliable statements. In this regard, respondent [5] from the Public Prosecution Service explained that the publicity surrounding the Passage case and the undertakings made to the witnesses in that case led to others presenting themselves to the authorities with an attitude of 'whatever he had, I want too'. They also have experience of people trying to take the Public Prosecution Service for a ride by glossing over their own role, with complete fabrications, or by grassing on others. This respondent pointed out the importance of a thorough verification process in this context. Further, one respondent from the criminal defence bar fears that crime as such could increase if the scope for using the instrument were to be widened, based on the thinking of the calculating accused that – if he should be caught – he can always count on making an agreement with the authorities by incriminating the person who commissioned the crime or some other random individual.

More generally, respondents pointed to the moral aspects of widening the scope for using the instrument in terms of the undertakings on offer and the offences in respect of which the instrument is available. Some respondents indicated that they felt that a decision not to prosecute or a complete (100%) sentence reduction would be going too far with homicides or offences which are subject to life imprisonment. Others stated that there is also a proportionality consideration involved (if the interest is big enough then this can still be justified). In this context reference was also often made in the interviews to the so-called big fish/small fish discussion and the question of whether there is a dividing line in this regard and, if so, where it lies. Respondent [12] noted, as did a number of other respondents, that the amount of the sentence reduction could also be linked to the seriousness of the offence (e.g. no undertaking to dismiss a case for offences punishable by 12 years' imprisonment or more).

> "But this is first and foremost a decision which the legislature has to make, after having debated the matter and under all the guarantees surrounding the legislative process."

A member of the focus group mentioned that making the determination of how much sentence reduction to grant dependent on the seriousness of the offence could also help to land the 'smaller fish'.

Outside of the Public Prosecution Service there is also support for calls to widen the scope for making undertakings to witnesses. Respondent [8] from the judiciary, for example, thinks it is quite understandable that the Public Prosecution Service wants to have more room to manoeuvre, but stated that this should be accompanied by stricter demands on the supporting evidence.

> "It should also not be made too attractive. For example, if plea bargaining were to be introduced and the Public Prosecution Service were to decide not to prosecute, a deal would be arrived at more quickly. At the moment prison is still an obstacle. It is matter of finding a balance. But the witness still has to appear in public, testify against his friends, and enter a [witness protection] programme. … But if someone is simply released after making a statement, there may still be reasons to apply stricter standards to the evidence. There has to be some degree of balance."

3.6.2.2 Scrutiny and Further Regulation of the Protection Agreement

Given that the agreement concerning the undertakings provided in exchange for the statements to be made by the witness and the witness protection agreement are difficult to separate in practice, in the literature it has been proposed that they should be merged into one agreement. As previously indicated, however, among the respondents there was little support for this.[357] What this study did show, however, is that there is broad consensus on the need to increase the oversight of the agreements made about witness protection. In the Public Prosecution Service, the police and the judiciary, there is support for some form of judicial scrutiny of the witness protection agreement. Members of the criminal defence bar hold differing opinions about this. Respondent [13] is concerned about the potentially secret nature of any such procedure, while other respondents from the bar saw it as an improvement relative to the present situation.[358]

---

357 See § 3.5.5.5 for further details.
358 See § 3.5.5.3 for further details.

Opinions differed about the way in which this judicial scrutiny should take place. The hearing judges in the first instance proceedings of the Passage case argued for scrutiny by a body which includes judges. There were also respondents who were more in favour of involving an investigating judge for this purpose. In this context it was argued that there should be a specialist investigating judge for this, in view of the fact that such scrutiny demands a lot of an investigating judge and there is a danger that errors could affect the safety of the witness. The respondents asked about this all thought that a specialist investigating judge would be a good idea because of the expertise that this person would then develop. It was emphasised in the focus group that this investigating judge should then have a clear framework by which to perform the scrutiny. The focus group members did not think it should be one particular investigating judge, but that there should be a pool of investigating judges with experience of this.[359] A complex question to arise in this regard is what consequences should be attached to a negative ruling by the investigating judge on the protective measures proposed. However, this point was not discussed with the respondents as such.

Another question is whether the investigating judge who scrutinises the witness protection agreement – should the legislature opt for that – should be the same investigating judge who also looks at the lawfulness of the intended agreement and has to make a judgment about the reliability of the witness. This question was raised during the interview with respondents [10a and 10b], who both work as investigating judges and have experience of special witness procedures (although not with undertakings as referred to in Sections 226g and 226k CCP). They were positive about this, mostly because now the investigating judge is not aware of the agreements about witness protection in the present undertakings procedure, as referred to in Section 226g ff., which can lead to complications.[360] This makes it difficult for the investigating judge to decide whether the witness should or should not answer certain questions. Similarly, when there is a conflict between the witness and the Witness Protection Team, it is useful to know what agreements have been made. Respondent [10a] said the following in this context:

"It would be nice if there was just one person to oversee all aspects of the matter, and who can then rule on its lawfulness and decide who is in the right."

The respondents thought that it should be someone who has an overview of both the civil law and criminal law sides and who can give a judicial opinion to the hearing judges ultimately determining the value of the witness statement. They pointed out that at the

---

359 In an altogether different context, the question has arisen as to whether the designation of a (pool of) specialist investigating judge(s) should be organized at the legislative level or rather within the judiciary itself, in consultation with the Public Prosecution Service. In the end, the latter option was chosen. See Parliamentary Papers II 2016/17, 34 720, no. 3, p. 2-3.
360 See § 3.5.4.2.

moment it is very easy for the defence to challenge the witness' reliability when the witness does not want to answer a particular question. That problem could be surmounted if the investigating judge is aware of the agreements regarding witness protection and can arrive at his own judgment about that. Respondent [10a] said the following about this:

> "It works the other way round for the lawyers too, because this person could also say which questions really do have to be answered. So it would also be positive for the defence if there was an informed person who says: 'we are going to do this and not that' and can explain that where necessary."

3.7   To Conclude

The first part of this chapter looked in some depth at the development and content of the legislation related to the use of the instrument of undertakings to witnesses in the Netherlands. The second part of this chapter gives an impression of the practical implementation of this instrument since the present legislation entered into force in 2006 and the experience of the various respondents in that context based on the results of the empirical study. On this basis the following picture emerged.

From the first part of the study it is apparent that the legislation on providing undertakings to witnesses has had a turbulent history, the roots of which lay in the IRT scandal of the 1990s.[361] The legal framework – which comprise the Provision of Undertakings to Witnesses in Criminal Cases Act and the associated Instructions on Undertakings to Witness in Criminal Cases – which entered into force in 2006 following eight years of parliamentary debate, could be described as relatively conservative in terms of the types of offences for which the instrument may be used and the nature of the undertakings that may be made to witnesses. For example, providing undertakings to witnesses is reserved for the most serious offences (i.e. offences in respect of which pre-trial detention may be lawfully ordered and which were committed in the context of organised crime; and offences which are subject to a prison sentence of eight or more years). Moreover, in connection with the subsidiarity principle, they may only be made when other investigation methods will not produce the desired result or not in time, and it is unlikely that a statement will be obtained from the witness without such an undertaking.[362] In addition, apart from including a general requirement of proportionality, the legislation sets certain limits on the nature and extent of the undertakings, in which offering a sentence reduction of up to 50% or a small inducement are considered permissible, but offering complete immunity or a financial reward are ruled out. At the

---

361 See § 3.3.2.
362 See § 3.4.2.

same time, the legal framework appears to be not entirely conclusive in terms of the nature of the undertakings, given that even today there is still discussion in the legal practice and in the literature about the matter of what undertakings may and may not deemed permissible under the present legislation. In that respect a grey area may be said to exist.[363] Finally, the legal framework provides for a fairly extensive procedure which has to be completed before the instrument may be used. The advance scrutiny of the intended agreement by the investigating judge, which was incorporated into the framework at the express request of the Lower House of Parliament due to the controversial nature of the topic, constitutes an important aspect of that procedure.[364]

The study of the practice confirms the prior impression that the instrument has thus far been used only to a modest extent. Since its entry into force on 1 April 2006, the instrument has been used only five times. This was for five witnesses to whom undertakings were made in three different criminal cases against multiple suspects.[365] These mainly related to homicides and the individuals concerned had presented themselves to the authorities with the wish of reaching an agreement with them in exchange for making a statement. In that respect the experience gained with the legislation introduced in 2006 is still limited. Among the reasons for the modest use of the instrument thus far many respondents pointed to the repercussions of the aforementioned IRT scandal and the caution that this has led to among the police and the prosecutorial authorities and which to a certain extent still exists. From the empirical study however it appears that both the Public Prosecution Service and the police are doing more to bring this instrument to the attention of people in the field in order to be able to apply it on a wider scale.[366]

The study of the situation in practice also showed that although the procedure to implement the instrument may have only been fully completed a few times, talks with potential witnesses have taken place much more often in recent years to determine whether or not an agreement could be reached. The majority of the talks conducted however produced no result, where in approximately half the cases the potential witness for his own reasons decided to withdraw from further cooperation and in the other half the police and the prosecutorial authorities saw no benefit from continuing the talks.[367] The interviews show that it is mostly people who are not yet known to the authorities but who do have a criminal history, who will not be readily inclined to collaborate with the authorities. After all, entering into an agreement means that the witness will be faced with a criminal prosecution which might not otherwise happen, while the sentence reduction that can be offered is limited to fifty percent, which, moreover, cannot be promised with

---

363 See § 3.4.3.
364 See § 3.4.4.
365 See § 3.5.2.2.
366 See § 3.6.1.1.
367 See § 3.5.3.6.

any certainty given that the court could still deviate from that. The offer that may be made by the prosecutorial authorities therefore also appears to be an obstacle in persuading potential witnesses to come forward.[368] Added to this – to the extent that witnesses do collaborate with the authorities – the limited application thus far appears to show that it is mainly witnesses who themselves are accused of serious crimes who 'make use' of the framework currently in place.[369] There may well be an explanation for this too. Because it is only when an accused or convicted person finds himself faced with a long prison sentence that a sentence reduction of fifty percent really becomes attractive, not least in view of the other difficulties which the witness will be faced with as a result of his collaboration with the authorities.[370] In that sense the effect of the present scheme has been somewhat paradoxical: while the scheme was original intended to catch the 'smaller fish'[371], in practice it has so far mainly attracted the 'bigger fish'.

The findings from the empirical study also show that whether a witness is willing to cooperate is dependent not only the amount of any sentence reduction to be granted, but also the agreements about the protection of the witness. Legally speaking, the agreements relating to witness protection fall outside the scope of the legislation as laid down in Section 226g ff. CCP, but for the witness concerned this may be so important that re-strictions or problems in this context may be a reason to cease any (further) cooperation with the authorities. If the Public Prosecution Service and the witness do reach an agree-ment pursuant to Section 226g CCP, it appears from the study that what has been agreed with the witness concerning his protection can lead to certain questions being raised during the criminal proceedings. The confidentiality of the procedure for putting protec-tive measures in place means however that these questions are either difficult to answer or remain unanswered even though this (to some extent) may obstruct the course of the criminal proceedings.[372]

Finally, the findings of the empirical study show that there are certain questions con-cerning the application of the current legal framework which continue to occupy the legal profession. These include the question of the scope of the scrutiny of the intended agree-ment by the investigating judge and the possibilities and limitations in this context;[373] the

---

368 Although given the wide range of reasons for potential witnesses to enter into discussions with the judicial authorities it is not really possible to make any firm statements about the percentage of cases where the breaking point for the witness lay in the offer (or the perceived limitations thereof) made by the authorities. For a cautious estimate see also § 3.5.3.6.
369 Almost all the witnesses to whom undertakings have been made so far were facing a substantial criminal penalty.
370 See § 3.6.1.1.
371 See § 3.4.2. It should be noted here that statements about the intentions of the legislature concerning this legislation may only be made with due caution, not least because the long duration of the parliamentary treatment also meant that the positions adopted sometimes tended to change and it then becomes hazar-dous in this context to make statements about *the* intentions of the legislature. In this context see also Amsterdam Court of Appeal 29 June 2017, ECLI:NL:GHAMS:2017:2497 (Jesse R.), § 2.1.2.2.6.2.
372 See § 3.4.5 and § 3.5.5.
373 See § 3.5.4.2.

question as to what exactly is the scope of the witness's obligation to make a statement;[374] the question as to what exactly the minimum evidence requirement stated in Section 344a paragraph 4 CCP entails;[375] and the question of how to deal with the pre-trial detention of the witness in relation to the anticipation requirement under Section 67a paragraph 3 CCP.[376] In addition, the need to take into account the enormous pressure on the witness (and his defence lawyer) after an agreement has been entered into with the authorities was mentioned, which is not always reflected in appropriate facilities.[377]

Having set out very generally the findings that arose from this chapter concerning the legislation and the practical implementation of undertakings to witnesses, the next question to be considered concerns the extent to which this legislation and its practical implementation may be described as successful. The respondents were given the opportunity to answer this question in the empirical study.[378] It should be noted however that the question of the success of the Dutch legislation and its practical implementation can only be fully answered after the findings from the comparative law analysis carried out below have also been taken into account.[379] This is not to say that nothing can be said about the success of the present legislation and its implementation in practice on the basis of the foregoing. However, in the paragraphs below, no reflection is provided on the suggestions for amending the present legislation, as put forward by the respondents above.[380] This will only be done in Chapter 8, when these and other suggestions will be looked at, also in the light of the comparative law analysis.

The modest use of the instrument would, at first sight, tend to suggest a lack of success. However, the simple observation that the instrument has not often been used, does not justify the conclusion that the legal framework is failing. While to date there has been only a handful of witnesses to whom undertakings have been made, their statement were used – often with the desired result for the Public Prosecution Service – in the investigation and prosecution of several accused. For example, in the largest and most renowned case, the Passage case, the use of the instrument led to the conviction of ten accused in an extensive investigation into liquidations in the Amsterdam underworld.[381] Moreover, the modest use is also partly because of the same legislation, in which the use of this instrument is strictly limited in that – as previously mentioned – it may only be used in cases of serious crime (whether or not organised) and only if it is absolutely necessary in the sense that other investigation methods have not provided or cannot

---

374 See § 3.5.4.3.
375 See § 3.5.6.1.
376 See § 3.5.6.2.
377 See § 3.5.4.3.
378 See § 3.6.1.
379 See Chapter 8 for further details.
380 See § 3.6.2.
381 See § 3.5.2.3.

provide a solution. As the respondents also indicated, it is an exceptional tool which is reserved for exceptional cases. In that sense the legislation is being used as the legislature intended when it was drafted.[382]

The modest use of the instrument stands in contrast with the number of exploratory talks that take place behind the scenes. Based on what respondents from the police and the Public Prosecution Service have said about it, initiatives that have been developed to persuade witnesses to step forward appear thus far to have had little effect. It could be argued that the results in terms of the recruitment of potential witnesses have been poor and in that context the legislation and its implementation have not been successful. However, as mentioned, in roughly half the cases talks were not continued because the authorities saw no benefit in doing so.[383] Other factors also contributed to the limited use of the instrument which cannot be ascribed to the legislation, but more to the prevailing culture and the budget available within the organisations concerned. It is not apparent from the study, however, to what extent this is the case. Respondents were nevertheless aware that the existing opportunities were not yet being fully utilised and that there is still room for more extensive use of the instrument of undertakings to witnesses under the present legislation.[384]

It is also difficult to determine the degree of success in those cases where use was made of the instrument as referred to in Section 226g ff. This is primarily due to the fact that the legislator provided no clear prior indicators by which the success or efficacy of the legislation could be measured.[385] It is fair to assume that to describe the deployment of the instrument in a specific criminal case as successful will also depend on whether the witness made a real contribution to the successful resolution of the case and the conviction arising therefrom, and the undertaking made to the witness by the Public Prosecution Service is also honoured by the court. In that sense, the use of the instrument in the Yellowstone and Passage cases may also be deemed successful.[386] However, it can only be qualified as a success if the conviction is based on truthful statements and thus the real perpetrators are convicted. However, given that the 'ground truth' cannot be known it is impossible to make any firm statements about this. The degree to which the legislation or procedure enables the relevant parties to identify statements which are not truthful, will to some extent also determine the degree of success of the scheme.[387] Here it should be noted that the procedure does in fact provide safety nets in this regard. Indeed both the investigating judge and the trial judge are

---

382 Cf. the above comment concerning the intentions of the legislature in n. 175.

383 For example, because the information is already known or it has insufficient value or because the profile of the witness is too complex. See § 3.5.3.6 for further details.

384 See § 3.6.1.

385 See § 2.5 for further details of the various ways in which the notion of success can be viewed.

386 In the third case in which the instrument was used – the attempt to liquidate Cor van Hout – the court deemed the statement made to be insufficiently reliable in its entirety and for that reason it was not used. See § 3.5.2.3.

387 For further details, see § 2.5.

expected to form an independent opinion about the reliability of the witness, while a comprehensive verification process is carried out before such statements are used.[388] In addition to the matter of whether the witness has contributed to clearing up one or more cases and the conviction of the (real) perpetrators, respondents also mentioned other factors relevant to the evaluation of the success of the legal framework, such as the course of the criminal proceedings (referring to the delays and the problems in the Passage case) and the safety of the witness to whom undertakings are made. Although strictly speaking, this last aspect is a separate matter, the two themes are so closely related that problems in the context of the witness protection will have an impact on the success of the legal framework on undertakings to witnesses. Little is known about what happens to those witnesses who are included in a witness protection programme.[389] As far as is known, thus far there have been no witnesses to whom undertakings were made pursuant to Section 226g ff. CCP who as a result of their cooperation with the authorities have suffered (lethal) violence and thus it may be assumed that in this respect that protection has been successfully achieved.

Although no hard and fast statements can therefore be made about the success of the scheme as a whole, is it clear that with the aid of this instrument a number of satisfactory results appear to have been achieved in individual cases. At the same time, it became apparent that both the legal as well as the more practical obstacles to the use of the instrument are relatively high. It appears also that the scheme is most favourable to those accused of more serious crimes who find themselves facing a long (or very long) prison sentence, while it was originally mainly intended for witnesses who were accused of relatively less serious crimes. Finally, it appears that the questions and problems which arise across the board in practice cannot be adequately addressed on the basis of the legislation. Examples of this include the ongoing discussion regarding the permissibility of certain undertakings, the sometimes unclear relationship in practice with the agreements concerning witness protection, and the lack of clarity concerning the scope of the scrutiny of the proposed agreement by the investigating judge. The following chapters will look closely at the legislation and the practical application of the instrument of undertakings to witnesses in the three other countries, and thereafter the concluding remarks will reflect on the analysis carried out in Chapter 7 in which these countries are compared with the findings concerning the Dutch legislation and practical implementation of the instrument. Changes which could be made to the present legislation will also be considered in this context.

---

388 Strictly speaking, the process referred to here is not part of the procedure because the Instructions say nothing about it. The internal working procedures however state that this investigation must be carried out before an agreement may be entered into. For reservations concerning the scope of the investigating judge's scrutiny of the reliability [of the statement] and the possibilities and obstacles in this context, see § 3.5.4.2.

389 See Beune and Giebels 2012 for further information.

Appendix 1
Answers to the Research Questions

Legal Framework

1   *What types of undertakings are provided for?*

The statutory provision provides for sentence reduction (Section 226g paragraph 1 CCP in conjunction with Section 44a CC), assistance with a pardon application (Section 226k paragraph 1 CCP in conjunction with Section 44a CC) and what is referred to as an 'inducement' (Section 226g paragraph 4 CCP). Examples of such inducements referred to in the Instructions on Undertakings to Witnesses in Criminal Cases include cooperation with or not opposing a request to suspend pre-trial detention, arranging for a milder detention regime for a convicted person who is serving a custodial sentence, and urging that the remainder of a sentence imposed abroad be served in the Netherlands.

   A question repeatedly raised in the context of the enactment of the statutory provision, as well as the jurisprudence, is whether or not the statutory provision on undertakings to witnesses is exclusive, in light of the fact that Dutch criminal procedure is governed by the principle of prosecutorial discretion. In other words, is it also possible to make other undertakings that have not been specifically laid down in the legislation, such as the undertaking that the demand for confiscation of unlawfully obtained gains will be reduced? In the Instructions on Undertakings to Witnesses in Criminal Cases the confiscation order may be reduced by up to a half and the withdrawal of an extradition request or a European arrest warrant are specifically deemed to constitute permissible undertakings (in addition to those undertakings already specifically laid down in the legislation). The Instructions also state what types of undertakings are not permissible. These include granting a financial reward or making an undertaking that a criminal prosecution will not be pursued in exchange for making a statement.

2   *In respect of which offences is it possible to use the instrument?*

Under Section 226g subsection 1 CCP undertakings to witnesses may be made in the context of a criminal investigation into: 1. offences in respect of which pre-trial detention may be lawfully ordered, which were committed in the context of organised crime and which give rise to severe public disorder on account of their nature or connection to other criminal offences; or 2. offences punishable by eight years' imprisonment or more. It is therefore also possible to use undertakings to witnesses in the investigation of serious criminal offences which were not committed in the context of organised crime. It is clear from the legislation that providing undertakings may only be considered in exceptional situations, where it is urgently required in the interests of the investigation. When considering whether and how to use the instrument, the public prosecutor therefore always has to take into account the requirements of proportionality and subsidiarity.

3   What is the legal basis for (using) the instrument?

The legal basis for providing undertakings to witnesses is laid down in the Code of Criminal Procedure (Sections 226g to 226k CCP) and the Criminal Code (Section 44a CC). These provisions were incorporated into both Codes pursuant to the Provision of Undertakings to Witnesses in Criminal Cases Act of 12 May 2005, Bulletin of Acts and Decrees 2005, 254 that entered into force on 1 April 2006. Alongside the statutory framework, the Instructions on Undertakings to Witnesses in Criminal Cases – that entered into force on the same date – also provide for further regulation of the instrument, specifically with regard to the internal procedure that must be followed in order to make an agreement.

4   How did the rules on collaboration with justice come about?

The present legal framework for making undertakings to witnesses in criminal cases has had a long and, in certain respects, tumultuous history. The findings of the Van Traa Parliamentary Committee of Inquiry provided a major impetus for the development of this legislation. The Van Traa Commission noted a crisis in criminal investigation in the mid-1990s and criticised the various malpractices surrounding providing undertakings to witnesses, not least in granting generous rewards and immunity while there was no statutory basis for this and without adequate scrutiny. The Commission therefore reached the conclusion that these matters should be more closely regulated by law. The findings and recommendations of the Van Traa Commission to a large degree shaped the legislation that followed. However it was a long time before the statutory provision was actually enacted. The undertakings to witnesses bill was submitted to the Lower House of Parliament on 17 November 1998 but only entered into force on 1 April 2006, partly due to the media interest in incidents from the past which cast the instrument of undertakings to witnesses in a poor light, as well as the long-drawn-out parliamentary debate concerning the appropriate scope for the instrument. The result was a fairly cautious provision which included quite some restrictions on the possible undertakings that may be made. The statutory provision also provided for an extensive internal scrutiny procedure, followed by prior external judicial scrutiny of the intended agreement. The statutory provision entered into force at the same time as the Instructions on Undertakings to Witnesses in

Criminal Cases (that had been amended line with the new statutory provisions) and the Witness Protection Decree. This decree provides for the implementation of Section 226l CCP which lays down the statutory basis for instituting measures to protect a witness.

5   *Who holds authority to make use of the instrument and where does the responsibility lie in this regard?*

The Public Prosecution Service is legally responsible for providing undertakings to witnesses. The actual negotiations are conducted by the public prosecutor appointed to do that, but the final intended agreement must be approved by the Board of Procurators General further to an internal procedure in which both the State Advocate and the Internal Review Committee of the PPS on the use of special investigative measures (CTC) issue an opinion. The instrument may however only actually be used once the investigating judge has given approval for the intended agreement by judging it to be lawful. In this sense the Public Prosecution Service does not operate entirely independently (which is different for what is known as an 'inducement' in the meaning of Section 226g paragraph 4 CCP, in respect of which moreover the aforementioned procedure does not apply), but is still responsible. Final (political) responsibility rests with the Minister of Justice and Security who, if the need arises, must also be informed of the intended agreement.

   From a practical point of view, the police also play an important role in the use of the instrument. On the instructions of the public prosecutor concerned, for example, the police conduct the preliminary interviews with the witness and – if the procedure is further pursued – take down 'vault statements' (*kluisverklaringen*; such statements may in no way be used until the agreement has been reached and approved by the investigating judge). The verification and falsification process which then follows is also carried out by the police, as is the first psychological assessment. These activities are of great practical importance to the successful application of the instrument.

6   *How does the instrument relate to other measures whereby private individuals provide information for the purposes of criminal investigation and/or prosecution?*

This question cannot readily be answered in just a few sentences, not least because the various instruments used in practice to some extent overlap and often it is not clear in advance in which capacity the individual who presents himself with certain information will act. There is no statutory definition of the instrument of undertakings to witnesses but in this study witnesses to whom undertakings are made are understood to be: witnesses who are also suspected of having committed a criminal offence or who have been convicted of one, and who agree with the prosecutorial authorities that in exchange for some consideration they will make an incriminating witness statement (in their own name, i.e. on a non-anonymous basis) against one or more other suspects. In this study, such persons are referred to as 'collaborators of justice'.

Witnesses to whom undertakings are made should in any event been seen as separate from 'informants' and those providing information on a more incidental basis (tipsters). The instrument of providing undertakings to witnesses is primarily aimed at obtaining in a transparent manner evidence in the form of a personal witness statement which can be tested at trial, while the phenomenon of informants and tipsters is more aimed at obtaining on an anonymous and confidential basis lead information for the purposes of the investigation (generally in exchange for some financial recompense). Witnesses to whom undertakings are made should be distinguished criminal civilian infiltrators who are actively used by the authorities to gather evidence, which they do under the control of the Public Prosecution Service. Finally, the witness to whom undertakings are made also needs to be distinguished from the (anonymous) 'threatened witness' in the meaning of Section 226a CCP. These are witnesses who make an incriminating statement but whose identity is kept hidden from the accused in whose criminal proceedings they make an official statement, for fear of reprisals on the part of the accused. Like the collaborator of justice, such witnesses may require protection measures. Unlike the threatened witness however the collaborator of justice is expected to reveal their identity and make their statements in their own name, as is apparent from Section 226j paragraph 2 CCP.

7   *How does the instrument relate to the phenomenon of witness protection?*

A witness to whom undertakings are made may be included in a protection programme if it is believed that there is a serious threat to their physical safety. Given that the instrument can only be used for serious offences and generally in the context of organised crime, the need to take protection measures will often be considered. Strictly speaking however, witness protection measures fall outside the scope of the legislation on undertakings to witnesses. These are separate procedures involving different divisions of the police and which fall under the responsibility of different public prosecutors. Accordingly, two separate agreements are concluded. The legal basis for taking protective measures are laid down in Section 226l CCP and in the Witness Protection Decree.

Despite the fact that the procedures are separate, in practice the undertakings procedure and the witness protection procedure are closely connected with one another. In practice it is already considered at a fairly early stage whether it will be possible to provide adequate protection to a potential witness with whom an agreement is to be made. If it is not possible, then the procedure may run aground for this reason alone. It may also be the case that the witness himself does not want to be included in such a programme and for this reason decides not to make a statement. In addition, the practice shows that dissatisfaction with the witness protection can lead a witness to decide to cease or suspend all further cooperation. This can lead to complex situations in which the proceedings are 'hijacked' by the witness. Finally, there is some discussion about the transparency of the agreements made concerning witness protection, given that these agreements are neither made public nor subject to any form of external scrutiny.

PRACTICE

8   *What types of undertaking are used in practice?*

In the present study, which focused on the situation in practice since the entry into force of the present statutory provision in 2006, the researchers came across undertakings in the form of sentence reduction, reductions in the order to confiscate unlawfully obtained gains, and 'inducements' as referred to in Section 226g paragraph 4 CCP. The researchers did not come across undertakings in the form of the withdrawal of an extradition request or a European arrest warrant.

9   *How often and on the basis of which considerations is the instrument used*
         or not used?

From the study it appears that during the period from 1 April 2006 to 15 December 2016 undertakings were provided to five witnesses in three different criminal cases. Several accused were tried in those criminal proceedings (in the biggest case – the Passage case – there were ten accused before the court of the second instance). There are no figures available on how often an 'inducement' within the meaning of Section 226g paragraph 4 CCP is used, given that the procedure as laid down in Section 226g ff. CCP does not have to be followed. Respondents indicated, however, that such inducements are not often used. They are also hardly encountered in the published jurisprudence.

Among the reasons for considering using the instrument is that it would not be possible to clear up certain very serious criminal offences without providing undertakings. These are cases where accused or convicted persons are only willing to provide information for some form of consideration. Besides this, there are situations where the authorities possess certain information concerning serious criminal offences but this cannot be used. Wanting to present this information as evidence in a criminal case may be another a reason for making undertakings.

The reliability or the value of the statement may be among the reasons for deciding not to use the instrument. It is also considered whether the information could be used in another manner, for instance via an anonymous TCI report. The character of the witness and the protection options may also be reasons for deciding not to use the instrument. In addition, there are cases where the authorities would like to use the instrument, but the witness does not wish to cooperate (or lend any further cooperation), because the offer is considered not to be attractive enough.

10   *What have the positive and negative experiences been in practice with the instrument and the legal framework in this regard?*

Only very limited practical experience has been gained with the use of this instrument in the Netherlands. The use of this instrument has resulted in convictions a number of times in cases which otherwise may well have been difficult to clear up. Respondents from the police and the Public Prosecution Service however feel that the legislation is too restrictive. Exploratory talks take place on a regular basis with witnesses, but in the majority of cases these amount to nothing. The respondents indicated that one of the reasons for this is that potential witnesses do not consider the offer to be sufficiently attractive. From data held by the National Unit of the police on exploratory talks with potential collaborators of justice that ultimately foundered, it is apparent that in roughly half these cases the talks ran aground because the authorities saw no benefit from it and in the other half this was due to insufficient motivation on the part of the witness.

In addition the relationship with witness protection appears to be problematic in practice. While strictly speaking witness protection measures fall outside the scope of the legislation on undertakings to witnesses, given that there are separate procedures involved resulting in separate agreements, the agreements concerning witness protection are of direct influence on the willingness of the witness to make a statement and therefore on the use of the instrument. If the protection is not arranged to his satisfaction, this may give cause for the witness not to cooperate or to withdraw his cooperation with the authorities. Moreover, discussion may arise during the trial proceedings about the way in which the protection has been arranged where the witness can use his statement as a means to exert pressure in order to get what he wants. The lack of transparency surrounding the witness protection procedure and the lack of independent judicial scrutiny thereof are also seen as problems, particularly in view of the fact that there are no clear guidelines governing the content of such a protection agreement.

There are also certain questions concerning the application of the current legal framework which continue to occupy the legal profession. This includes the question of the scope of the scrutiny of the intended agreement by the investigating judge and the possibilities and limitations in this context; the question as to what exactly is the scope of the witness's obligation to make a statement; the question as to what exactly the minimum evidence requirement stated in Section 344a paragraph 4 CCP entails; and the question of how to deal with the pre-trial detention of the witness in relation to the anticipation requirement under Section 67a paragraph 3 CCP. One of the respondents also requested that consideration be given to the enormous pressure on the witness (and his defence lawyer) after an agreement has been entered into with the authorities, which is not always reflected in suitable facilities.

11   *What results have been achieved by use of the instrument in individual cases?*

In terms of cases where the instrument was used it may be observed that this has been done successfully on a number of occasions in the sense that it led to convictions, while it may be assumed that these convictions would not have been secured without the statement that was provided. The Passage case (see also Amsterdam Court of Appeal 29 June 2017, ECLI:NL:HR:2017:GHAMS:2017:2496) is a clear example in this regard. The question as to results however cannot be viewed only from the perspective of convictions. Because only if the correct person is convicted will the instrument have achieved its intended result. In many cases however this cannot be irrefutably established (because the 'ground truth' in criminal cases is unknown). The degree to which the legislation enables the relevant parties to identify statements which are not truthful, will also determine its degree of success. The procedure does in fact provide safety nets for this purpose. This is because both the investigating judge and the trial judge are expected to come to their own conclusion about the reliability of the witness, while a comprehensive verification and falsification process is carried out before the agreement becomes final.

12   *Which factors contribute to the successful use of the instrument and which form obstacles in this regard?*

An important factor is the capacity that can be made available within the police force and the Public Prosecution Service for the use of this instrument, as is the attitude (or mind set) of those directly involved. The greater the willingness to invest in this instrument by making resources available to actively look for potential witnesses and bring such a process to a successful conclusion, the greater the success that may be expected as a result. At the moment only the National Unit and the unit in Amsterdam have a Special Witnesses Team that is specifically geared to be able to deal with this type of witness. That is also where the most expertise is at the moment. Respondents indicated that there is some reluctance among public prosecutors to use this instrument because of the complications it may bring in a case (although there are also public prosecutors who actively look for ways to make use of this instrument).

Another important factor is the offer that can be made to the witness by the authorities. It became apparent from the study that many procedures which initially appear to be promising, ultimately run aground because the witness considers that the offer made to him is not sufficiently attractive. This mostly relates to witnesses who have not previously come into contact with the authorities and who – should they make a statement – would be expected to provide full disclosure of the criminal offences in which they have been involved. The basic sentencing demand in his own criminal case could quickly mount as a result, while without his cooperation the witness could end up not being prosecuted at all (because without his permission the 'vault statements' that he has made cannot be used either for investigation purposes or to start a prosecution).

Respondents also indicated that the witness protection can present problems. Some witnesses are not suitable to be included in a witness protection programme or do not want to be. Inclusion in a protection programme not only means that a witness has to leave his old life behind him and cut all ties with his social network, but – certainly during the initial period – he also has to accept severe restrictions on his autonomy and freedom of movement.

Another aspect concerns the trustworthiness of the Public Prosecution Service as a partner with whom to enter into an agreement. From the interviews it was apparent that practitioners are also well aware of this. Should the Public Prosecution Service fail to meet its agreements, for example, by releasing certain information into the public domain without the consent of the witness or using it for investigative purposes, this could be detrimental to the success of the instrument in future cases. Respondents emphasised that it is extremely important that the witness can trust the Public Prosecution Service. It is clear that a lot is invested in developing such a relationship of trust. The judges who also find themselves faced with this instrument are aware that it they were to deviate (too much) from the sentencing demand of the Public Prosecution Service and thus the agreements made, this could affect the future willingness of witnesses to cooperate with the Public Prosecution Service. It is not clear to what extent processes run aground because the Public Prosecution Service is unable to offer any certainty about the severity of the final sentence. Respondents did mention it as a factor which witnesses take into consideration when deciding on whether or not to collaborate with the authorities.

13   *In general, do the rules on collaboration with justice achieve their objective?*

It is not easy to answer this questions, given that there has been no evaluation since the statutory provision entered into force. Nor were clear indicators established in advance on the basis of which the degree to which the legislation achieves its goal can now be properly assessed. In view of the legislative history and the substance of the statutory provision it may be assumed that the purpose of the legislation is not only for the application of the instrument to be successful, but also (and perhaps more importantly) to prevent the instrument from being used too lightly, the integrity of the authorities from being damaged and unreliable statements from being submitted as evidence.

It appears that the instrument has been successfully used in a number of cases (see also the comments under question 12), from which it may be concluded that in those cases the legislation served its purpose. Conversely, there are also the cases where ultimately it was not used. Some of the procedures in which exploratory talks took place, ran aground because the witness thought that the offer was not attractive enough. The fact that respondents perceive the legislation as too restrictive and witnesses are not easily persuaded to cooperate, may be an indication that the legislation does not always achieve its goal.

Scrutiny, Transparency and Debate

14   *To what extent is the use of the instrument subject to scrutiny by a judicial or other authority?*

The Dutch legislation on undertakings to witnesses provides for a detailed procedure in which judicial scrutiny takes place both when the agreement is drawn up in the pre-trial phase, as well as during the trial proceedings. The investigating judge looks at whether the intended agreement is lawful, as well as whether the witness and his statement may be deemed as reliable. If not, no agreement will be considered to have been made. If it is, the agreement made is then also examined by the trial judge who may come to his own conclusion on the lawfulness of the agreement and the reliability of the witness and his statements. In accordance with the Instructions on Undertakings to Witnesses in Criminal Cases the Public Prosecution Service also follows an extensive internal procedure which includes various forms of (semi-external) scrutiny. For example, before the intended agreement is submitted to the investigating judge, it is first examined by the State Advocate and the Internal Review Committee of the PPS on the use of special investigative measures (CTC), both of whom make a recommendation to the Board of Procurators General. The Board then has the last word on the matter. The study also showed that in most cases the Board adopts the recommendation of the CTC.

The procedure as described above applies to undertakings concerning sentence reduction (Section 226g paragraph 1 CCP) or providing assistance with a pardon application (Section 226k CCP). This procedure does not have to be followed in order to offer an inducement within the meaning of Section 226g paragraph 4 CCP. According to the Instructions on Undertaking to Witnesses in Criminal Cases however, this procedure does apply to undertakings related to the confiscation of unlawfully obtained gains or the withdrawal of an extradition request or a European arrest warrant.

15   *In how far is the instrument itself and the use thereof in individual cases publicly transparent?*

If undertakings are made to a witness and his statements are used as evidence in someone else's case, this is done in a transparent manner. The agreement is included in the case file and, in principle, the witness will have to make his statements at trial. The agreement will also be raised during the course of the trial in the witness's own case, in which context he will be eligible for the sentence reduction promised to him. This is different only where an undertaking has been made to a witness who has already been convicted in his own criminal case. However in such cases also the instrument of undertakings to witnesses is used in a transparent manner.

There are some reservations however about the (public) transparency of the statutory provision with regard to the nature of the undertakings which may made to witnesses. While 'afterwards' it will always be clear what undertaking was provided, prior to an agreement being made, the statutory framework provides only so much clarity as to the undertakings that may be made. This relates to the discussion referred to under question 1 about the exclusivity of the statutory provision.

It should also be noted that the phase prior to the internal and external scrutiny of the intended agreement referred to above, i.e. the exploratory and the negotiation phases, itself is not transparent, neither to those directly involved in the process nor to the outside world. There are internal working agreements which lay down the steps that the police and the public prosecutor responsible for the gathering and use of criminal intelligence by the police (CIPP) involved should take in these phases, but these are not public. Neither can the outside world ascertain at a later date what was discussed during these phases leading up to the framing of the intended agreement, for example, concerning the extent of witness's the obligation to make a statement in relation to his own criminal past. A related aspect is that the outside world is not aware of what activities the police and the Public Prosecution Service engage in to recruit potential witnesses. For obvious reasons, this takes place out of sight.

Finally, the agreements made concerning the witness protection and the actual implementation of this agreement are also not transparent. Nor can they ever be, because attempting to obtain more transparency in this area would jeopardize the safety of the witness. In the present study however, there was wide consensus among the respondents in favour of the introduction of some form of external (judicial) scrutiny of the witness protection agreement (see also question 10).

16   *To what extent is there debate or discussion regarding the use of the instrument? On which aspects of the instrument is the debate focused?*

There is a lively ongoing debate among lawyers about the use of this instrument. However there is currently no wider public or political debate about the use of this instrument (unlike in the 1990s further to the IRT scandal and Van Traa Parliamentary Committee of Inquiry). This may well be due to the scant use of the instrument. However, even the Passage case that received a considerable amount of media attention and in which far-reaching undertakings were made by the Public Prosecution Service to witnesses who themselves are suspected of very severe crimes such as homicide, did not prompt a wider public discussion about the instrument (and its legitimacy). The debate among lawyers is mainly focused on the reliability of the statements made, the matter of whether the statutory provision is exclusive, the relationship with and transparency of the witness protection agreement, and the matter of whether it is appropriate to conclude agreements with witnesses who themselves are suspected of very severe crimes.

17   *In how far and in what regard has scrutiny, transparency and debate led to changes in the regulation of the instrument?*

As previously discussed under question 4, the findings of the Van Traa Parliamentary Committee of Inquiry provided the basis for the further regulation of this instrument. The present statutory provision entered into force in 2006, along with the Instructions on Undertakings to Witnesses in Criminal Cases and the Witness Protection Decree. None of these regulations has been further amended since then (in either substance or content). From the interviews it is apparent that both police operating procedures and the internal work instructions have since been amended further to the experience gained. In 2013 the then Minister made clear his wish to widen the statutory provision (see letter from the Minister of Security and Justice dated 5 July 2013, Parliamentary Papers II 2012/13, 29911 no. 83).

Appendix 2
List of Respondents of the Interviews

1. Member of the Board of Procurators General
2. Secretary of the Internal Review Committee of the Public Prosecution Service
3. Public prosecutor with the National Public Prosecutors' Office
4. Public prosecutor with the National Public Prosecutor's Office for Financial, Economic and Environmental Offences
5. Public prosecutor responsible for the gathering and use of criminal intelligence by the police
6. Public prosecutor responsible for the gathering and use of criminal intelligence by the police
7. Public prosecutor responsible for the gathering and use of criminal intelligence by the police
8. Judge
9. Investigating judge
10. Investigating judge (10a) and investigating judge (10b)
11. Defence lawyer
12. Defence lawyer
13. Defence lawyer
14. Lawyer with the State Advocate's Office
15. Police officer seconded to the National Unit
16. Psychologist and operational specialist with the Special Witnesses Team of the National Unit
17. Police officer with the Special Witnesses Team of the National Unit
18. Head of operations within the Criminal Intelligence Team (18a) and coordinator of the Special Witnesses Team of the National Unit (18b)
19. Deputy coordinator (19a) and coordinating psychologist with the Witness Protection Team of the National Unit (19b).

The list above sets out the positions held by the respondents at the time of the interview.

Appendix 3

Basic Questionnaire Used for the Interviews

General

What is your full name, position and relationship to the theme of undertakings?

Questions for the Public Prosecution Service

- What experiences have you or your colleagues gained from the use of undertakings?
- How do persons to whom undertakings are subsequently provided enter the picture? Are they actively approached or do witnesses take the initiative? Which problems arise in this regard?
    - *Can you provide an indication of how often potential witnesses present themselves?*
    - *Can you indicate how often the Public Prosecution Service works with potential witnesses?*
- What types of undertaking are used/applied in practice? What types of undertaking (that are permitted by the relevant rules) are not used in practice?
- What types of undertaking do potential witnesses seek? What is the first thing they ask for? How do you view the undertakings sought by the potential witness in exchange for a statement?
- How often, in which situations and for what reasons are undertakings provided to witnesses/used?
- In your view, what are the main risks associated with the use of undertakings, and how often do they manifest?
- What can you tell us about the process?
    - *Can you describe the process in a concrete case?*
    - *How long does the process, including the negotiations, take?*
    - *How often does a process that has been initiated fail and why?*
    - *Which factors have the potential to interfere with the result or to impede success? Which solutions are found in this regard?*
    - *In how far is the process, including the negotiations, transparent for the defence and for the trial judge?*
- To what extent is there debate or discussion regarding the use of undertakings within your organization? And in how far has internal or public debate on the issue impacted on existing rules/agreements as regards the use of undertakings?

- How do you view the (judicial) supervisory mechanisms in place with respect to the use of undertakings; are they effective? In what way? What are your experiences in this regard?
- How do you view the way in which the trial judge handles the evidence tendered?
  - *What stands out in this regard?*
- Does the way in which the Public Prosecution Service is organized present any problems as regards the use of undertakings?
- How does the cooperation with the police work?
  - *What is expected of the police (should the police wait passively for a potential witness to present themselves, or should it actively approach potential witnesses?)*
  - *Does the Public Prosecution Service have a good picture of what the police has to offer?*
- What are your experiences regarding the interplay between the provision of undertakings and witness protection?
  - *Can you say something about how witnesses to whom undertakings have been provided (and who end up in witness protection) fare generally?*
- What are your experiences with certain features of the existing rules with respect to the use of undertakings, such as (insofar as applicable): the use of deadlines as regards the provision of information by potential witnesses; the use of undertakings with respect to a broad range of offences or with respect to certain offences only; and the use of a broad range of measures or the use of certain measures only (for example, the ability to seek sentence reduction)?

QUESTIONS FOR THE POLICE

- What experiences have you or your colleagues gained from the use of undertakings?
- What is the role of the police as regards the provision of undertakings to witnesses?
- How do persons to whom undertakings are subsequently provided come into the picture? Are they actively approached or do potential witnesses take the initiative? Which problems arise in this regard?
  - *Which strategies are adopted in order to induce persons to provide a statement?*
  - *Can you provide an indication of how often potential witnesses present themselves?*
- What types of undertaking do potential witnesses seek? What is the first thing they ask for? How do you view the undertakings sought by the potential witness in exchange for a statement?
- Does the way in which the police is organized present any problems as regards the use of undertakings?
  - *Are there sufficient expertise in this regard within the police organization?*
  - *Do colleagues know whom to approach within the organization when potential witnesses present themselves?*

- How is the communication with the Public Prosecution Service as regards the use of undertakings? And how do you view the role of the public prosecutor in this context, and the procedure that is to be followed?
  - *Is the Public Prosecution Service clued-up on the knowledge and expertise of the police?*
  - *And is the Public Prosecution Service of the view that the police should be proactive or reactive in this regard?*
  - *Do processes that have been initiated often fail? If so, why? If not, why not?*
- To what extent is there debate or discussion regarding the use of undertakings within your organization? And in how far has internal or public debate on the issue impacted on existing rules/agreements as regards the use of undertakings, or their execution?
- What are your experiences regarding the interplay between the provision of undertakings and witness protection?
- What are your experiences with certain features of the existing rules with respect to the use of undertakings, such as (insofar as applicable): the use of deadlines as regards the provision of information by potential witnesses; the use of undertakings with respect to a broad range of offences or with respect to certain offences only; and the use of a broad range of measures or the use of certain measures only (for example, the ability to seek sentence reduction)?

QUESTIONS FOR THE (TRIAL) JUDGE

- What experiences have you or your colleagues gained from the use of undertakings?
- Which types of undertakings have you encountered in practice?
- In your view, what are the main risks associated with the use of undertakings, and how often do they manifest?
- How do you evaluate the process (duration, transparency, stumbling blocks)?
- How do you view the (judicial) supervisory mechanisms in place with respect to the use of undertakings; are they effective? In what way? What are your experiences in this regard?
- How do you view your own role in the context of the use of undertakings in relation to other parties who exercise supervision over the process, including the lawfulness of the agreement and the reliability of the witness?
- How do you view your own role as regards the use of undertakings, in relation to the role of the public prosecutor, particularly in light of the ability of the public prosecutor to seek a reduced sentence for the witness in the criminal proceedings against them?
- Which problems arise as regards the use of the statement/admission of the statement? Which factors interfere with the use of the statement?
- In your view, are the possibilities currently provided for being fully exploited?

- *If so, can you provide an example? If not, why not?*
- What are your experiences regarding the interplay between the provision of undertakings and witness protection?
- What are your experiences with certain features of the existing rules with respect to the use of undertakings, such as (insofar as applicable): the use of deadlines as regards the provision of information by potential witnesses; the use of undertakings with respect to a broad range of offences or with respect to certain offences only; and the use of a broad range of measures or the use of certain measures only (for example, the ability to seek sentence reduction)?

QUESTIONS FOR MEMBERS OF THE BAR

- What experiences have you or your colleagues gained from the use of undertakings?
- In your view, what are the main risks associated with the use of undertakings, and how often do they manifest?
- How do you evaluate the process (duration, transparency, stumbling blocks)?
- How do you view the (judicial) supervisory mechanisms in place with respect to the use of undertakings; are they effective? In what way? What are your experiences in this regard?
- How do you view the manner in which the trial judge handles the agreement between the public prosecution service and the witness and the evidence obtained thereby? What stands out in this regard?
- What are your experiences regarding the interplay between the provision of undertakings and witness protection?
  - *Can you say something about how witness fare after entering an agreement?*
- What are your experiences with certain features of the existing rules with respect to the use of undertakings, such as (insofar as applicable): the use of deadlines as regards the provision of information by potential witnesses; the use of undertakings with respect to a broad range of offences or with respect to certain offences only; and the use of a broad range of measures or the use of certain measures only (for example, the ability to seek sentence reduction)?

Appendix 4

Focus Group Members

1. G. van der Zee, L.LM – Public prosecutor
2. S.F. van Merwijk LLM – Investigating judge
3. Prof. A.A. Franken – Defence lawyer and professor of criminal law and criminal procedure
4. F.A.W. Debije MPM – National Police, National Unit
5. Dr. C. van Putten – National Police, National Unit
6. Prof. F.W. Bleichrodt – Advocate General at the Supreme Court and professor of criminal law and criminal procedure
7. Dr. E.W. Kruisbergen – Researcher at the Research and Documentation Centre of the Ministry of Justice and Security

Appendix 5
List of Topics Used in the Focus Group

Validating Research Results

- Use/necessity/effectivity/success of the current legal provisions
- Grey area between the various measures whereby private individuals provide information for the purposes of criminal investigation and/or prosecution
- Closed or open system for providing undertakings to witnesses?
- Role of the investigating judge in approving the intended agreement between the witness and the public prosecutor
- The relationship between the instrument of undertakings to witnesses and the system of witness protection
- Various procedural aspects regarding the use of the instrument of undertakings to witnesses

Subject of Discussion with a View on the Future

- Is there reason to adapt the current legal provisions in the Netherlands?
- In which cases can undertakings be provided?
  - *Also possible in cases of financial or economic crime and corruption?*
  - *Also possible in cases in which the witness himself is accused of very severe crimes or has been/might be sentenced to life imprisonment?*
  - *Also possible for other purposes than the prosecution of others (for example to find the stolen loot)?*
  - *Introduction of the criterion of substantive connection between the offence on which the witness is making a statement and the offence he himself is accused of as in Germany?*
- Which undertakings may be provided?
  - *Adjustment of the maximum sentence reduction of fifty percent?*
  - *Immunity from prosecution or a full discount on the sentence?*
  - *Allowing the promise of financial reward in exchange for the statement of the witness?*
  - *Introduction of a fully 'open' system in which the public prosecutor has full discretion to determine the type and extent of the undertakings provided?*
- Introduction of a time limit within which witnesses must report themselves as collaborator of justice?

- Reconsideration of the relationship between the instrument of undertakings to witnesses and the system of witness protection?
  - *Both type of agreements in one and the same contract?*
  - *More transparency and/or judicial scrutiny of the agreements made in relation to witness protection?*
  - *Stricter rules on witness protection and the agreements made in this regard?*

4 COLLABORATION WITH JUSTICE IN GERMANY

M. Lindemann & D.A.G. van Toor

4.1 INTRODUCTION

To facilitate an understanding of the German legislation on those collaborating with justice, a brief introduction to a few general principles governing German criminal procedure seems appropriate.[1] One of these principles is the principle of indictment (*Anklagegrundsatz*), which is established in Section 151 of the Code of Criminal Procedure (*Strafprozessordnung*, StPO). Under this provision, the opening of a court investigation is conditional upon a request by the prosecuting authorities. This provision is complemented by Section 155 (1) StPO, under which the court's investigation and decision are limited to the offence specified and to the persons accused in the charges. Additionally, Section 264 (1) StPO states that the subject of adjudication shall be the offence specified in the charges and apparent in the light of the outcome of the hearing. With a few exceptions,[2] only the public prosecution office has the authority to prosecute and bring charges (*Offizialprinzip*).

Another important principle in the present context is the principle of mandatory prosecution (*Legalitätsgrundsatz*), which is laid down in Section 152 (2) StPO. This establishes an obligation for the public prosecutor's office to take action in relation to all prosecutable criminal offences, provided that there are sufficient factual indications that a crime has been committed and nothing to the contrary has been laid down in the law. It should be noted, however, that the law provides for a wide range of exceptions to this principle. Under certain circumstances as described in Sections 153 et seq. StPO, the prosecuting authorities and the courts may discontinue proceedings if they consider this to be appropriate (*Opportunitätsprinzip*).[3]

Furthermore, German criminal procedure is governed by the inquisitorial principle (*Ermittlungsgrundsatz*), which means that – within the limits set by the charges as outlined above – the court is required to extend the evidence taken to include all facts and means of proof relevant to the decision without being bound by any statements made by the prosecution or the defence (Sections 155 (2) and 244 (2) StPO). The view that the

---

1   For an extensive introduction in English, see Bohlander 2012. An introduction in German can be found at Beulke 2016, rn. 15 et seq.
2   In some cases the victim must request prosecution (*Antragsdelikte*) or even prosecute the offence him- or herself (*Privatklagedelikte*, Section 374 StPO) unless the public prosecution office prefers public charges (Section 376 StPO); see Bohlander 2012, p. 25.
3   The prerequisites are described at Bohlander 2012, p. 25 et seq. and p. 108 et seq.

German system is inquisitorial but not adversarial in nature[4] is supported by Section 160 (2) StPO which requires that the prosecution should ascertain not only the incriminating circumstances but also the exonerating circumstances.[5]

Another key feature of German criminal procedure – which to some extent arises from the interaction between the aforementioned general principles – is relevant to proceedings involving collaborators of justice: While the intermediate proceedings and main proceedings are controlled by the trial judge(s), the investigation procedure is governed by the public prosecutor (for this reason the public prosecutor is also known as 'Herrin des Ermittlungsverfahrens').[6] Under Section 162 (1) StPO, it is the public prosecutors office that is entitled to request information from all authorities and to conduct investigations of any kind (although the latter task is usually delegated to the police in cases involving minor or moderate offences). The role of the judges during the investigation is limited, insofar as a judge's decision is only required for certain intrusive measures during the investigation (e.g. search and seizure, the physical examination of the accused or telephone tapping) and usually requires a corresponding request from the public prosecutor (for an exception, see Section 165 StPO).[7] This clear separation of competences creates a serious problem for a suspect who is willing to cooperate with justice, because he or she is expected to make his or her statement during the investigation before the prosecutorial authorities, while a decision about sentence mitigation or a total exemption from punishment will be left to the discretion of the trial judge (s) who will not be involved in the prior negotiations and therefore may not feel bound by any commitments made by the prosecution.[8]

It would go beyond the scope of this report to analyze in detail all other principles and features of German criminal procedure that may potentially be relevant to cases of collaboration with justice. Therefore, we shall confine ourselves here to the consideration that the way in which principles of oral presentation of evidence (Mündlichkeitsgrundsatz), immediacy (Unmittelbarkeitsgrundsatz) and public hearings (Öffentlichkeitsgrundsatz) are implemented may create an atmosphere of threat for the collaborator with justice who has to deliver his or her witness statement in public. We will deal with this problem and the solutions envisaged by the law below.

This report is divided into five parts. The first part (§ 4.2) provides essential information about the concepts and terminology used in German law. Sections 4.3 and 4.4 give an over-

---

4   A critical analysis of this distinction can be found at Bohlander 2012, p. 6 et seq.
5   Another provision relevant in this context is section 296 (2) StPO which states that the prosecution may also make use of the appellate remedies for the benefit of the accused.
6   See Bohlander 2012, p. 56.
7   In urgent circumstances, the public prosecution office and the officials assisting it are usually entitled to decide on their own and are only obliged to apply for court confirmation afterwards (see for example Section 98 (1 and 2) StPO for the order of seizure).
8   Labs 2016, p. 249.

view of the development of German law on collaborators with justice and a detailed description of the elements of the relevant provisions. Section 4.5 presents the results of the interviews held with judges, public prosecutors, defence lawyers, a police officer and legal scholars. That section is – after a description of the methodology of the empirical research in § 4.5.1 – divided in five sections: how often the relevant provisions are applied in Germany (§ 4.5.2); the procedural aspects of becoming a collaborator of justice (§ 4.5.3); how the undertakings are fulfilled (§ 4.5.4); the collaborators' provisions in relation to the inclusion in a witness protection program (§ 4.5.5) and; peculiarities associated with the use of the evidence disclosed by collaborators (§ 4.5.6). In § 4.6 conclusions will be drawn on the basis of the results presented.

4.2   CONCEPTUALIZATION, TERMINOLOGY AND RELATIONSHIP WITH OTHER INFORMATION PROVIDERS

Witnesses who provide information about a crime committed by another person in exchange for a reduced sentence or exemption from punishment for their own crime are called *Kronzeugen* in the German literature.[9] The official legal term is *Aufklärungsge-hilfe*, which literally means 'clarification helper'.[10] This refers to the fact that the witness will help the justice department to get to the truth in criminal cases. The emphasis of the legislation is on the help that he or she offers to uncover the criminal offences of other persons. Therefore, the relevant provisions – which form part of the substantive criminal law – state precisely what information must be disclosed in order to make the provision applicable, but do not provide procedural rules (which will be discussed in more detail below). In order to make collaboration attractive, the legislator offers sentence mitigation in most cases and total exemption from punishment only in minor cases.

At the start of this in-depth study on collaboration legislation in Germany, we need to clarify some potentially confusing terms: On the one hand, collaborators of justice must be distinguished from informers. Informers are people who will provide the State with information regarding *a single* offence,[11] and usually they are not subject to a criminal investigation themselves. Nevertheless, informers and collaborators of justice have the position of *Aufklärungsgehilfe* in common. On the other hand, collaborators of justice should be distinguished from confidants. A confidant is a civilian who provides information in *several* cases[12] and usually gets paid for his or her work;[13] additionally, the law enforcement authorities tend to refrain from prosecuting the confidant for his or her involvement in the

---

9   For example Allgeier 2012, p. 73; Jeßberger 2015, p. 1153.
10   MüKoStGB/Maier, 2nd edition 2013, § 31 BtMG rn. 2.
11   Lorenz 2016, p. 316.
12   Lorenz 2016, p. 316.
13   See for example: BVerfG 18 December 2014, 2 BvR 209/14, 2 BvR 240/14 & 2 BvR 262/14, ECLI:DE: BVerfG:2014:rk20141218.2bvr020914, par. I.2.

crimes concerned. However, the reward for the information provided by the confidant will not be stated in a trial, as is the case for a collaborator of justice, but will usually be monetary in nature. Annex D of the guidelines on criminal and administrative proceedings (*Richtlinien für das Straf- und Bußgeldverfahren – RiStBV – Anlage D*)[14] provides some general principles concerning cooperation between the State authorities and informers and confidants.

Although what informers, confidants and collaborators of justice have in common is their role as possibly important witnesses, they are viewed as different legal 'entities'. The first major difference is that they will have different benefits. The second difference is that there are distinctions in their contact with and the guidance given by the authorities during the investigation of an offence. The authorities instruct and guide informers and confidants while they gather information. This is not the case for collaborators of justice, who are only put in touch with the authorities *after* the information has been gathered (and they are themselves questioned during a criminal investigation). When they are interrogated as a suspect, they can express their interest in offering information about other crimes in exchange for a milder sentencing. By contrast, the contact with informers and confidants is established earlier in the investigation phase.

Furthermore, a collaborator of justice will also be a suspect, which is not necessarily the case with informers and confidants. As will be explained below, when the interviews are analyzed, there is no proactive recruitment of collaborators of justice. Potential collaborators are not approached in advance, but – when they are interrogated as a suspect – the interrogating officer may mention the possibility of collaboration. A collaborator of justice can try to make a 'deal' after committing his or her own offence which is subject to an investigation. However, there is little room for negotiation. It is more or less a 'take it or leave it' situation (the same applies to inclusion in the witness protection program and measures related to the program).

4.3   Development of Legal and Other Rules

The precursors to today's collaborators of justice instrument (Sections 129 (6), 129a (7) StGB (*Strafgesetzbuch*, the German Criminal Code)) were enacted in 1976. The provisions were (and still are, see below) preventive in nature insofar as they aim to prevent the commissioning of (further) crimes by members of a terrorist organization.[15]

The first *Kronzeugen* legislation honoring the disclosure of information which allows the prosecution of offences that have already been committed, originated in the *Betäubungsmittelgesetz* (abbrev.: BtMG, the German Narcotics Act) that was enacted in 1982.[16]

---

14 Annex D of the RiStBV is printed on 2372-275, in: L. Meyer-Goßner & B. Schmitt, *StPO*, 59th edition 2016.
15 For a brief overview of the German *Kronzeugen* legislation, see Frahm 2014, p. 24 et seq.; Kneba 2011, p. 22 et seq.
16 Cf. for more details Labs 2016, p. 197 et seq.

The idea at that time was that the collaborator of justice could help with the investigation and prosecution of narcotics-related crimes committed by criminal organizations.[17] It was not widely discussed in the *Bundestag* at the time because the discussion was completely overshadowed by another topic, i.e. 'therapy instead of punishment'.[18] The text of Section 31 BtMG has been amended a number of times since the 1980s, most notably in 2013 when the requirement of 'connectivity' was incorporated into the law.[19] In short, this requirement entails that the collaborator of justice has to disclose information about crimes that are in some way connected to his or her own crimes in order to be eligible for the application of Section 31 BtMG. We will come back to this requirement in the next section where all the conditions of the general *Kronzeugenregelung* are discussed in detail.

In 1989 a similar provision concerning collaborators of justice in terrorism cases entered into force despite strong criticism by legal scholars and further to intense parliamentary debate.[20] The three main points of criticism were: (1) that a collaborator's deal would infringe the principle of mandatory prosecution (*Legalitätsgrundsatz*); (2) that the exemption from punishment (especially) would seriously challenge the legal order, because some offenders will walk free without punishment and; (3) that the information provided by the collaborator of justice could not be presumed to help improve the truth-finding, because statements made by collaborators of justice can be seen as unreliable due to their personal gain in collaborating.[21] Notwithstanding this criticism, Article 4 of the *Gesetz zur Änderung des Strafgesetzbuches, der Strafprozeßordnung und des Versammlungsgesetzes und zur Einführung einer Kronzeugenregelung bei terroristischen Straftaten* (KronzG)[22] provided for sentence mitigation or a total exemption from punishment for collaborators of justice in terrorism cases. In 1994 the aforementioned legislation was supplemented by a provision regarding organized crime (Article 5 KronzG).[23] Both Articles were temporary legislation and remained in force only until 1999.

Besides the aforementioned crime-specific *Kronzeugen* legislation in the BtMG and KronzG, German law had and still has more crime-specific *Kronzeugen* articles. One of which was Section 261 (10) StGB that applied only to money laundering. The court could refrain from imposing a penalty on the collaborator of justice or mitigate the sentence in cases of money laundering where the collaborator provided information on another

---

17   Fischer, StGB, 63rd edition 2016, § 46b, rn. 2.
18   Hoyer 1994, p. 234.
19   The last three changes can be seen here: <https://www.buzer.de/gesetz/631/al20531-0.htm>, last retrieved on 19 October 2016.
20   Hoyer 1994, p. 234.
21   Hoyer 1994, p. 234.
22   BGBl. I. p. 1059. Translation: The Law to change the Criminal Code, the Criminal Procedural Code and the Freedom to Demonstrate Law, and the introduction of a collaborators of justice provision in terrorism cases.
23   Article 5 KronzG was introduced by the Gesetz zur Änderung des Strafgesetzbuchs, der Strafprozessordnung und anderer Gesetze (Verbrechensbekämpfungsgesetz) of 28 October 1994, BGBl. I p. 3186. An evaluation of the practical implementation of article 5 KronzG can be found at Mehrens 2001, p. 123 et seq.

money launderer.[24] This Section was repealed when the general *Kronzeugen* legislation entered into force. However, two more crime-specific Sections are still in force: The afore-mentioned Section 129 (6) StGB offers sentence mitigation or exemption from punishment to a collaborator of justice who provides information that could be used to prevent the continued existence of a criminal organization or to prevent crimes being committed by the members of such an organization, and Section 129a (7) StGB declares this provision to be applicable to collaborators of justice who inform on a terrorist organization. These two Sections, which focus on criminal structures and networks, have different requirements than the general *Kronzeugen* legislation, so they are still relevant.

The first general *Kronzeugen* legislation stems from 2009.[25] Section 46b StGB combines preventive and repressive elements; it provides for sentence mitigation or exemption from punishment in exchange for information about crimes already committed (Section 46b (1) No. 1 StGB) or crimes to be prevented (Section 46b (1) sentence 1 No. 2 StGB). This provision is called the 'big *Kronzeugen* legislation' because it is not crime-specific in its application.[26] However, the implementation of the 'big *Kronzeugen* legislation' did not lead to a complete abandonment of the crime-specific legislation (as described above). Most criminal law practitioners (lawyers associations and the judges association) have expressed concerns about the government's plans to introduce a general *Kronzeugen* article.[27] The alleged conflict with the principle of mandatory prosecution was again one of the main points of criticism,[28] as was the risk of untruthful statements.[29] However, this lobby was unsuccessful.

On the 1st of August 2013, Section 46b StGB was amended and now only applies to cases where the collaborator of justice discloses information on a crime committed or provides information that can be used to prevent a crime as listed in Section 100a (2) StPO; a further requirement for both alternatives is that the crime to be prosecuted or prevented is in some way connected with the offence committed by the collaborator of justice. Before the amendment to the legislation was made, the collaborator's statement and the sentence mitigation could be used for any offence.

With the amendment made in August 2013, the scope of the provision was (at least in theory) severely reduced because the provision now only applied to cases that have a 'connection' with the offences committed by the collaborator (the precise meaning of 'connection' will be explained below),[30] proposed, strangely enough, by the same political

---

24 See <https://www.buzer.de/gesetz/6165/al11605-0.htm> for the old text, last retrieved on 19th October 2016.
25 StrÄndG, BGBl I 2009, 2288, <https://www.buzer.de/gesetz/6165/al11605-0.htm>, last retrieved on 8th February 2017.
26 Fischer, StGB, 63rd edition 2016, § 46b, rn. 2.
27 MüKoStGB/Maier, 3rd edition 2016, § 46b rn. 7; Fischer, StGB, 63rd edition 2016, § 46b, rn. 2.
28 MüKoStGB/Maier, 3rd edition 2016, § 46b rn. 7; an in-depth analysis of the conflict between section 46b StGB and the principle of legality can be found at Kneba 2011, p. 34 et seq.
29 König 2009, p. 2481.
30 BeckOK-StGB/von Heintschel-Heinegg, § 46b rn. 1. A critical analysis of this amendment can be found in Christoph 2014, p. 84-86; Peglau 2013, p. 1910; see also Labs 2016, p. 231 et seq.

parties that had suggested an unlimited provision in 2009.[31] The reason for this amendment was that the legislator considered a reduced sentence or exemption of punishment to be unsuitable for random offences,[32] although there was no evidence that the judiciary did mitigate sentences in an excessive manner. The legislator considered the existing scope for application at the time to be too broad.[33] Since statements on completely different offences cannot directly diminish the culpability of the collaborator, the regulation was intended to reduce the possibility of excessive mitigation, particularly from the point of view of the victim.[34] The second reason given by the legislator was that a collaborator is generally used because he or she is part of a criminal organization or structure, and that the State is particularly dependent on the reconnaissance and preventive involvement of collaborators to detect such.[35] The benefit that the collaborator of justice receives in his or her own case should, therefore, in some way be related to the solved offence. In the next section (§ 4.4) we will discuss this and the further requirements of Section 46b StGB in more detail. Towards the end of § 4.4 we will focus on the comparison/distinction between the different *Kronzeugen* provisions.

4.4 LEGAL FRAMEWORK

Section 46b StGB is the central provision providing the legal framework with regard to collaborators of justice in German criminal law. It reads as follows:

"Section 46b

Contributing to the discovery or prevention of serious offences

(1) If the perpetrator of an offence punishable by an increased minimum sentence of imprisonment or a sentence of life imprisonment,

1. *has substantially contributed to the discovery of an offence under section 100a(2) of the Code of Criminal Procedure which is related to his own offence by voluntarily disclosing his knowledge, or*

---

31 Peglau 2013, p. 1911.
32 Fischer, StGB, 63rd edition 2016, § 46b, rn. 9b. Critical about this change is: Peglau 2013.
33 BT-Drs. 17/9695, p. 1; <http://dip21.bundestag.de/dip21/btd/17/096/1709695.pdf>, last retrieved on 10th November 2016.
34 BT-Drs. 17/9695, p. 1; <http://dip21.bundestag.de/dip21/btd/17/096/1709695.pdf>, last retrieved on 10th November 2016.
35 BT-Drs. 17/9695, p. 1; <http://dip21.bundestag.de/dip21/btd/17/096/1709695.pdf>, last retrieved on 10th November 2016.

2. *voluntarily discloses his knowledge to an official authority in time for the completion of an offence under section 100a(2) of the Code of Criminal Procedure related to his own offence, the planning of which he is aware of, to be averted,*

the court may mitigate the sentence under section 49(1); a sentence of life imprisonment shall be replaced with a term of imprisonment of no less than ten years. In order to determine whether an offence is punishable by an increased minimum sentence of imprisonment, only aggravations for especially serious cases but no mitigations shall be taken into account. If the offender participated in the offence, his contribution to its discovery under the 1st sentence No. 1 above must exceed his own contribution. Instead of a reduction in sentence the court may order a discharge if the offence is punishable by a fixed-term sentence of imprisonment only and the offender would not be sentenced to a term exceeding three years.

(2) In arriving at its decision under subsection (1) above the court shall have particular regard to:

1. *the nature and scope of the disclosed facts and their relevance to the discovery or prevention of the offence, the time of disclosure, the degree of support given to the prosecuting authorities by the offender and the gravity of the offence to which his disclosure relates, as well as*

2. *the relationship of the circumstances mentioned in No. 1 above to the gravity of the offence committed by and the degree of guilt of the offender.*

(3) A mitigation of sentence or a discharge under subsection (1) above shall be excluded if the offender discloses his knowledge only after the indictment against him has been admitted by the trial court (section 207 of the Code of Criminal Procedure)."[36]

Section 46b is part of the second title of the StGB and, therefore, part of substantive criminal law. The second title of the StGB is called '*Strafbemessung*' (in Dutch: '*straftoemeting*', in English: sentencing (decision)). Due to the fact that Section 46b StGB is part of this sentencing title of the Criminal Code it contains more detailed rules about *inter alia* sentence mitigation, sentence deliberation and a deadline for the contribution by the collaborator of justice. However, there are no rules about the process of becoming a

---

36 Translation <www.gesetze-im-internet.de/englisch_stgb/>, last retrieved 28 July 2016.

collaborator of justice and procedural safeguards. For example, there is no previous legitimacy test of the deal done by an (investigative) judge. The position of Section 46b StGB in relation to the other sections regarding sentencing will be discussed in § 4.4.3 in the context of the precise benefits that a collaborator of justice can obtain.

Subsections (1) and (2) of Section 46b StGB describe the possible legal effects of the provision – sentence mitigation or exemption of punishment – and in respect to which offences the provision can take effect. Some other aspects of Section 46b StGB are important to consider; these are (a) the people who can become collaborators of justice (*Täter* as mentioned in section 1); (b) the offences which are eligible for Section 46b StGB to be applied; (c) the sort of information the collaborator of justice can provide in order to be eligible for sentence mitigation (*Aufklärung* or *Prävention* as mentioned in subsections (1) 1 and (1) 2); (d) the way the information has to be presented (*Freiwilligkeit* as mentioned in subsections (1) 1 and (1) 2); (e) the connection between his or her own criminal offence and the offence about which he or she provides information (*Zusammenhang* as mentioned in subsections (1) 1 and (1) 2); (f) the deadline by which a person must disclose his or her knowledge (subsection 3) and; (g) factors that influence the sentence mitigation (subsection 2). These topics will be discussed below.

a   **Offender**

Section 46b StGB is applicable only to an offender, in German a *Täter*. It is important to keep in mind that Section 46b StGB is substantive law, more precisely a part of the law regulating the sentencing decision. Therefore, it is only applicable when a person is convicted who offered information about another case before the trial phase started. The law uses the concept of offender, but that does not mean that the person has to be convicted before he or she makes his or her (verbal) agreement with the public prosecutor's office. On the contrary, the agreement is likely to be made at an earlier stage of the proceedings but becomes effective only when the suspect is convicted and the court applies the collaborators of justice instrument. Then the sentence can be mitigated or he or she can obtain exemption from punishment. So, the discussions about a possible collaboration with justice will usually take part in the investigation phase of the collaborator's own offence and he or she will be labeled a collaborator of justice as part of his or her own conviction/sentencing decision. Section 46b StGB therefore refers to offenders and not suspects.

In this context, the term *Täter* can be translated as offender which, for the purposes of the collaborators provision, not only includes the joint offender (*Mittäter*)[37] and the indirect perpetrator (*mittelbarer Täter*) but also the inciter (*Anstifter*)[38] and the accomplice (*Gehilfe*).[39]

---

37 Cf. the Dutch *medepleger*.
38 Cf. the Dutch *uitlokker*.
39 Cf. the Dutch *medeplichtige*. For the details see MüKoStGB/Maier, 3rd edition 2016, § 46b rn. 18-19. A divergent concept of the term *Täter* (excluding *Anstifter* und *Gehilfen*, but including *Mittäter* and *mittelbare*

b   The Offence Committed by the Collaborator

The *Kronzeugen* Section of the StGB has two different requirements regarding an offence: The perpetrator of an offence, i.e. the *Anlasstat*, can become a collaborator of justice, when he provides the State with information regarding a serious offence (the *Katalogtat*). The first requirement is discussed in this section, the second requirement is discussed in § 4.4.3. The categories *Anlasstat* and *Katalogtat* are not the same.

The offence committed by the collaborator of justice is called the *Anlasstat* and must be an offence that carries the threat of an increased minimum prison sentence or lifelong imprisonment.[40] The legislator deliberately did not opt for an enumerative list of certain offences, but for an abstract boundary.[41] This system opens up a wide scope of application with regard to offences committed by the collaborator of justice him- or herself. The prerequisite of an increased minimum sentence means that offences with the threat of (only) the standard minimum sentence of one month imprisonment (Section 38 (2) StGB) or a fine (Section 40 StGB) are ruled out as *Anlasstaten* as referred to in Section 46b StGB.[42]

In this context (as well as in relation to the sentence mitigation for collaborators of justice that will be dealt with below), it may be beneficial to provide some introductory notes about the German sentencing system with sentencing frameworks (*Strafrahmen*). The German Criminal Code works with a framework of minimum and maximum sentences. For example, the minimum sentence for manslaughter (*Totschlag*; Section 212 StGB) is five years imprisonment. Because Section 212 StGB mentions no maximum penalty, the general maximum of fifteen years laid down in Section 38 (2) StGB applies. As regards human trafficking (Section 232 StGB), the sentencing framework lies between a minimum of six months and a maximum of ten years imprisonment. Both examples could be an *Anlasstat*, because the increased minimum sentence is six months and five years, respectively. By contrast, the provision regarding causing bodily harm (*Körperverletzung*; Section 223 StGB) only states that the penalty should be a maximum prison sentence of five years or a fine. In this case, the standard minimum prison sentence of one month as laid down in Section 38 (2) StGB applies, and therefore the offence is not eligible for the application of Section 46b StGB.

As a result, all moderate and serious crimes fall within the scope of the collaborators instrument.[43] Under Section 46b (1) sentence 2 StGB, only aggravations for especially

---

Täter) can be found in Section 28 (1) StGB. This distinction is a key feature of German criminal law doctrine (see Roxin 2015), but the sentencing title of the StGB uses a different concept.

40 Other than the *Katalogtat*, it does not have to be listed in Section 100a (2) StPO; BGH, Beschl. v. 25. 4. 2013 – 2 StR 37/13, *NStZ-RR* 2013, 241.

41 MüKoStGB/Maier, 3rd edition 2016, § 46b rn. 12.

42 Fischer, StGB, 63rd edition 2016, § 46b, rn. 6 with critical remarks in rn. 6a.

43 Frahm 2014, p. 33; Schönke/Schöder/Kinzig, StGB, 29th edition 2014, § 46b rn. 4.

serious crimes with no mitigations shall be taken into account in order to determine whether an offence is punishable by an increased minimum prison sentence.[44]

c   **Disclosure About Offences Committed or to Prevent Offences**

Subsection 1 of Section 46b StGB determines that a collaborator of justice can produce two sorts of information. Based on Section 46b (1) sentence 1 No. 1 StGB, he or she can disclose information which enables the authorities to solve a crime referred to in Section 100a (2) StPO. The information provided by the collaborator of justice must create the conditions to enable a case to be built against another individual and for a prosecution to be started with a reasonable expectation of leading to a conviction.[45] Thus, it is not a requirement that the information actually leads to a conviction or is used as evidence (because the collaborator's statement can lead to further evidence being obtained, such as the drug laboratory or a weapon deposit), but the trial judge has to be persuaded that the statement provides a reliable *foundation* for a successful prosecution (this is called the *Aufklärungserfolg*[46]). Based on the case-law of the Federal Court of Justice (*Bundesgerichtshof*, abbrev. BGH), that is the case when the crime would not have been cleared up without the collaborator's statement or when the statement offers a crucial confirmation of already known information.[47]

If the offender participated in the offence he or she provides information about, his or her contribution must exceed his or her own contribution (see Section 46b (1) sentence 3 StGB). Based on the prevailing opinion, this does not mean that he or she also has to confess to the crime he or she committed (the *Anlasstat*).[48]

A further prerequisite is that the information is disclosed to a person working for the public prosecutor's office or the police (*Strafverfolgungsbehörde*). However, the information does not have to be delivered in person but can also be delivered indirectly.[49] A messenger, covert agent or a joint offender can also deliver it if they have both agreed to come clean, but it must be clear that the statement/information can be assigned to the potential collaborator of justice.[50] Therefore, the statement may not be made anonymously.

According to Section 46b (1) sentence 1 No. 2 StGB, the collaborator of justice can also disclose information about a planned offence. The requirement is that his or her information is disclosed in a timely manner, allowing the authorities to intervene and

---

44 Fischer, StGB, 63rd edition 2016, § 46b, rn. 6.
45 MüKoStGB/Maier, 3rd edition 2016, § 46b rn. 44.
46 Frahm 2014, p. 50; Streng in: Nomos Kommentar zum StGB, 4th edition 2013, § 46b rn. 9.
47 BGH 15 March 2016 – 5 StR 26/16, *NStZ* 2016, 720; see also Frahm 2014, p. 54.
48 BGH 27 March 2012 – 3 StR 83/12, *NStZ-RR* 2012, 201.
49 Schönke/Schöder/Kinzig, StGB, 29th edition 2014, § 46b rn. 10.
50 MüKoStGB/Maier, 3rd edition 2016, § 46b rn. 21-22.

prevent the offence from taking place. In contrast to the *Aufklärungshilfe*, the information provided to prevent a criminal offence does not have to be successful in doing so (a '*Verhinderungserfolg*' is not required).[51] The information only has to reach the authorities allowing them to intervene in a timely fashion. Furthermore, the information to prevent a crime may be disclosed to a State official, a Municipal official or a court employee.[52] The disclosure does not have to meet any formal conditions.[53] A written document directed to a qualified person will suffice.

d   **Prerequisites Regarding the Disclosure of Information**

The act of disclosing information is called the *Kronzeugenhandlung* (literally translated: collaborator's action) and is subject to several requirements.[54] Firstly, the collaborator of justice must declare his or her *own* knowledge. However, a *testimonium de auditu* is not prohibited.[55] Secondly, the information has to be *factual and concrete*: assumptions and suspicions,[56] as well as general knowledge[57] are not sufficient. Thirdly, the information must be disclosed on a *voluntary* basis. A person can only make an autonomous and voluntary decision when he or she, from his or her own perspective, has multiple options. This means that persuasion can be used and a person can be urged to come forward with the information (especially in light of the evidence already gathered).[58] The individual who has or thinks that he or she has only one option left, acts involuntarily.[59] The use of unlawful methods of coercion will make the admission involuntary[60] and the entire statement cannot be used in court (Section 136a StPO). Additionally, the court may not use the statement when the potential collaborator of justice was not given correct information about the conditions of the collaboration and the possible effects on his or her sentence.[61] Usually, the potential collaborator will receive detailed information on the conditions during the interrogation, the so-called *Belehrung* (instruction), allowing the collaborator to give his or her 'informed consent'. Fifthly, the information cannot be disclosed anonymously.[62] Lastly, it is important to note that these requirements only

---

51 Frahm 2014, p. 75; MüKoStGB/Maier, 3rd edition 2016, § 46b rn. 134.

52 Frahm 2014, p. 72; Streng in: Nomos Kommentar zum StGB, 4th edition 2013, § 46b rn. 10.

53 Eschelbach, in: Satzger/Schluckebier/Widmaier, StGB, 2nd edition 2014, § 46b rn. 24.

54 Eschelbach, in: Satzger/Schluckebier/Widmaier, StGB, 2nd edition 2014, § 46b rn. 24.

55 Eschelbach, in: Satzger/Schluckebier/Widmaier, StGB, 2nd edition 2014, § 46b rn. 24.

56 MüKoStGB/Maier, 3rd edition 2016, § 46b rn. 23.

57 Schönke/Schöder/Kinzig, StGB, 29th edition 2014, § 46b rn. 10.

58 MüKoStGB/Maier, 3rd edition 2016, § 46b rn. 26.

59 Schönke/Schöder/Kinzig, StGB, 29th edition 2014, § 46b rn. 11. Fear of imprisonment or punishment as such do not result in an assumption of involuntariness, BGH 18 March 1983 – 3 StR 49/83, *NStZ* 1983, 323. The same applies to the obligation to bring planned offences to the attention of the authorities (Section 138 StGB), BGH 19 May 2010 – 5 StR 182/10, *BGHSt* 55, 153, 155. Summarizing Frahm 2014, p. 43 et seq.

60 MüKoStGB/Maier, 3rd edition 2016, § 46b rn. 25

61 MüKoStGB/Maier, 3rd edition 2016, § 46b rn. 26.

62 Schönke/Schöder/Kinzig, StGB, 29th edition 2014, § 46b rn. 10.

apply to the information the collaborator of justice discloses about another case or other cases (and not his or her own case, the *Anlasstat*).

e   Connection

The scope of the *Kronzeugen* legislation is limited by the fact that a collaborator of justice can only disclose information about a criminal offence that has a 'connection' with the offence that he or she committed. This condition was added to Section 46b StGB in 2013 because the legislator found a reduced sentence or exemption from punishment unsuitable for random offences that have no connection with the collaborator's offences.[63] The law uses the word *Zusammenhang*, which literally means 'link' or 'connection'. Christoph uses the concept *Konnexität* to explain the requirement of connection,[64] which can be translated as 'related actions'. The legislator left the concept open, to be filled in by case-law.[65]

The connection required between the criminal act committed by the collaborator of justice and another act will, of course, be established when the collaborator of justice was the inciter, accomplice or joint perpetrator.[66] Furthermore, crimes committed by a group of criminals (or some members of such a group) are clear examples of connected offences, even if the collaborator did not take part in all the offences.[67] Thus, the criterion of *Zusammenhang* is broad. Fischer gives the following examples: independent preparatory offences and the principal offence (such as the purchase of weapons and an armed bank robbery); the principal offence and offences after the fact (robbery and money laundering); the principal offence and accompanying offences; the principal offence and offences to cover the principal offence (for example threatening a witness).[68] Peglau gives the following case as an example: the collaborator stole a getaway car knowing that it would be used for the perpetration of criminal acts but not knowing what crime – a murder, a robbery or making threats – would be committed.[69] In the absence of complicity, participation or a substantial connection, a link can also be established where there is temporal or local correlation between the offences.[70] A connection cannot readily be made when the collaborator gives information about a rival or a rival gang.[71]

---

63   Fischer, StGB, 63rd edition 2016, § 46b, rn. 9b. Critical about this change is: Peglau 2013.
64   Christoph 2014, p. 84-86. Also Schönke/Schöder/Kinzig, StGB, 29th edition 2014, § 46b rn. 7a.
65   Schönke/Schöder/Kinzig, StGB, 29th edition 2014, § 46b rn. 7b.
66   Eschelbach in: Satzger/Schluckebier/Widmaier, StGB, 2nd edition 2014, § 46b rn. 22.
67   Peglau 2013, p. 1912.
68   Fischer, StGB, 63rd edition 2016, § 46b, rn. 9b.
69   Peglau 2013, p. 1912.
70   Schönke/Schöder/Kinzig, StGB, 29th edition 2014, § 46b rn. 7b.
71   Peglau 2013, p. 1912.

f   Deadline

The *Kronzeugen* regulation in the StGB contains a deadline for coming forward with information about committed crimes. Under Section 46b (3) StGB, collaborators of justice must disclose their information before the start of the main proceedings (*Eröffnung des Hauptverfahrens*, Section 207 StPO). One of the reasons for this deadline is tactical.[72] The collaborator of justice cannot wait until he or she has assessed the strength of the case against him or her to arrange a deal. Furthermore, this deadline gives the authorities and the court the opportunity to evaluate the quality of the information (which is necessary because the deal can only take effect when the statement that has been made is strong enough to provide the conditions to be able to build a case against another individual with the likelihood of achieving a conviction).[73] Besides, the trial cannot be suspended and delayed because the collaborator of justice comes forward with a new *Aufklärungshilfe*.[74]

The suspect can, of course, also give information on another crime during the course of the trial, but then he or she will no longer be eligible for sentence mitigation or an exemption from punishment on the basis of the *Kronzeugen* legislation. However, this late disclosure can still be of benefit because the German Criminal Code also includes general mitigation grounds, so things are not as strict as Section 46b (3) StGB would lead you to believe at first glance. Even if the collaborator of justice does not disclose the information before the opening of the main proceedings, the court is still required to weigh all the circumstances for and against the offender in arriving at its sentencing judgment (Section 46 (2) StGB).[75] The fact that the collaborator came forward with knowledge that helped solve another crime can mitigate other aspects, even if he or she did not come forward with this information in a timely fashion.[76] However, the sentence mitigation in the *Kronzeugen* legislation is more specific (it states a precise minimum and maximum penalty) and even allows for mitigation in cases where a sentence of life imprisonment may be given.

g   Factors Influencing the Sentencing Decision

The court can mitigate the sentence according to Section 49 (1) StGB or (under certain additional conditions listed in Section 46b (1) sentence 4 StGB) decide not to impose a

---

72 MüKoStGB/Maier, 3rd edition 2016, § 46b rn. 32.
73 Schönke/Schöder/Kinzig, StGB, 29th edition 2014, § 46b rn. 20. Labs 2016, p. 245 et seq. is critical about the reasonableness of the deadline.
74 Fischer, StGB, 63rd edition 2016, § 46b, rn. 21.
75 (2) *When sentencing the court shall weigh the circumstances in favor of and against the offender. Considera-tion shall in particular be given to the motives and aims of the offender; the attitude reflected in the offence and the degree of force of will involved in its commission; the degree of the violation of the offender's duties; the modus operandi and the consequences caused by the offence to the extent that the offender is to blame for them; the offender's prior history, his personal and financial circumstances; his conduct after the offence, particularly his efforts to make restitution; for the harm caused as well as the offender's efforts at reconciliation with the victim.*" Translation <www.gesetze-im-internet.de/englisch_stgb/>, last retrieved on 28 July 2016.
76 BGH 15 March 2011 – 1 StR 75/11, *NStZ-RR* 2011, 321.

sentence at all. With cases of imprisonment for a fixed term, Section 49 StGB allows for the maximum penalty to be reduced by one quarter and additionally provides for reduced minimum sentences. As a result, the court has a wide margin in deciding on a precise sentence.[77] To help steer the sentence deliberations, Section 46b (2) StGB mentions some factors which the courts should take into account during the course of arriving at their sentencing decision. These include the nature and degree of the offences clarified, the quality of the information disclosed, the moment of disclosure and the degree of cooperation shown. All this has to be weighed against the collaborator's guilt and the nature and gravity of his or her offence. It is not permitted only to take into account factors related to the collaboration with justice and completely ignore, for example, the gravity of the *Anlasstat*.[78]

h   Other *Kronzeugen* Articles

As previously mentioned, the German legislator started introducing crime-specific *Kronzeugen* legislation in the 1970s. Some of this legislation still remain in force, even after the implementation of the general collaborators' provisions in Section 46b StGB, as discussed above. The most notable existing crime-specific provisions are Section 31 BtMG[79] (the Narcotics Act) and Section 129 (6) StGB[80] (criminal organizations; Section 129a (7) StGB states that Section 129 (6) StGB by analogy is applicable to terrorist organizations).

These provisions are crime-specific because they only apply to information regarding narcotic crimes and the dismantlement of an organization or planned offences by the organization, respectively. While Section 31 sentence 3 BtMG refers to the deadline for disclosure laid down in Section 46b (3) StGB, this is not the case in Section 129 (6) StGB which is partly based on the legal concept of contrition.[81] Additionally, the benefits granted

---

77 Schönke/Schöder/Kinzig, StGB, 29th edition 2014, § 46b rn. 23.
78 MüKoStGB/Maier, 3rd edition 2016, § 46b rn. 118.
79 (1) *Das Gericht kann die Strafe nach § 49 Abs. 1 des Strafgesetzbuches mildern oder, wenn der Täter keine Freiheitsstrafe von mehr als drei Jahren verwirkt hat, von Strafe absehen, wenn der Täter*
1. *durch freiwilliges Offenbaren seines Wissens wesentlich dazu beigetragen hat, daß eine Straftat nach den §§ 29 bis 30a, die mit seiner Tat im Zusammenhang steht, aufgedeckt werden konnte, oder*
2. *freiwillig sein Wissen so rechtzeitig einer Dienststelle offenbart, daß eine Straftat nach § 29 Abs. 3, § 29a Abs. 1, § 30 Abs. 1, § 30a Abs. 1, die mit seiner Tat im Zusammenhang steht und von deren Planung er weiß, noch verhindert werden kann.*
(2) *War der Täter an der Tat beteiligt, muss sich sein Beitrag zur Aufklärung nach Satz 1 Nummer 1 über den eigenen Tatbeitrag hinaus erstrecken. 3§ 46b Abs. 2 und 3 des Strafgesetzbuches gilt entsprechend.*
80 (6) *The court may in its discretion mitigate the sentence (section 49(2)) or order a discharge under these provisions if the offender 1. voluntarily and earnestly makes efforts to prevent the continued existence of the organisation or the commission of an offence consistent with its aims; or 2. voluntarily discloses his knowledge to a government authority in time so that offences the planning of which he is aware of may be prevented; if the offender succeeds in preventing the continued existence of the organisation or if this is achieved without his efforts he shall not incur criminal liability.*
Translation <www.gesetze-im-internet.de/englisch_stgb/>, last retrieved on 26 October 2016.
81 Schönke/Schöder/Sternberg-Lieben, StGB, 29th edition 2014, § 129 rn. 18a.

in Section 129 (6) StGB (which relates to Section 49 (2) StGB) are not completely in line with those granted in Sections 46b StGB and 31 BtMG; we will turn to that in § 4.4.3.

Furthermore, there is a specific provision for collaborators of justice in competition law (which is part of administrative law), mainly based on EU law.[82] The most important part in light of the *Kronzeugen* provisions is the *Bonusregelung*, which is to be applied by the National Cartel Agency (*Bundeskartellamt*, BKartA). Announcement no. 9/2006 regulates the mitigation of fines for collaborators of justice in competition law.[83] According to sections 3 and 4 of the Announcement, there will be a mandatory reduction of the fine by 100 percent for the first company revealing the cartel (but not for the initiator of the cartel or the company that forced other companies to join the cartel), and according to Section 5 the reduction will not exceed 50 percent for further companies that collaborate. Additionally, the BKartA uses a settlement procedure at the prosecutor's discretion with a 10 percent reduction in the fine when a company comes forward with a guilty plea. The settlement bonus can be combined with the 'cartel revelation' bonus.[84]

i   Discussion

There has been a lot of criticism of and debate surrounding the *Kronzeugen* provisions and practice. Lawyers describe that the collaborator of justice's double role – of suspect in one case and witness in another – is difficult to handle.[85] They have to find a balance between the requirement to make truthful statements, on the one hand, and his or her protection after the case is closed, on the other hand. As will be explained in more detail below, this criticism is not just theoretical. A defence lawyer and his or her client have to make a decision about collaboration before the start of the trial (and actually even earlier to provide the police with enough time to verify the information). This means making a commitment to a certain strategy early on, even when the consequences of the collaboration are not clear. Other points of discussion about the practice of the *Kronzeugenregelung* are the possibility of making false statements to downplay one's own role and exaggerate the role of other people, or simply to benefit from the option of sentence mitigation, for example.[86] Furthermore, some authors fear that the police could coerce offenders into delivering statements about other crimes, using sentence mitigation as bait.[87]

The scheme itself has also been criticized. The two main points of criticism are that the prosecution cannot make a binding agreement about the sentence during the preli-

---

82 Nowak, in: Loewenheim/Meessen/Riesenkampff/Nowak/Kersting/Meyer-Lindemann, Kartellrecht, 3rd edition 2016, Art. 23 VerfVO rn. 37-47.
83 See for a commentary on the Announcement: Dannecker 2015; Achenbach 2015.
84 Achenbach 2015, rn. 40.
85 Eisenberg 2008, p. 197; Malek 2010, p. 204.
86 Matt/Renzikowski *Strafgesetzbuch* 2013, rn. 2.
87 MüKoStGB/Maier, 3rd edition 2016, § 46b rn. 5.

minary proceedings (because the trial judge is the final authority and decides at the end of the trial)[88] and the prerequisite that collaboration with justice is limited to statements about crimes that have a 'connection' with the offence committed by the collaborator.[89] The first aspect makes the position of the defence considerable weaker. The collaborator of justice has to make a statement in the hope that the trial judge will use his or her discretion to mitigate the sentence. The second aspect results in the limited application of the *Kronzeugen* provision because a collaborator can only provide information on offences that have a connection with his or her own offence. Criticism of this limitation of the provision is expressed by judges[90] as well as scholars; it is thus shared by experts from different professions.[91]

Two further points of debate are the fact that German law contains several distinct and concurrent *Kronzeugen* provisions (Section 46b StGB) / Section 31 BtMG / Sections 129 (VI), 129a (VII) StGB, known as the *Milderungskonkurrenz*)[92] and that sentence mitigation in general violates two principles of German substantive criminal law, i.e. the principle of adequacy of the sentence in relation to the offender's guilt[93] and the obligation to treat like cases alike.[94] According to critics, both requirements are not met in cases of collaboration with justice because the sentence would normally be higher had the *Aufklärungshilfe* not been taken into account and offenders who committed the same offence without being eligible for the mitigation would not be treated alike.

Lastly, it has been criticized as being inconsistent that the provision regarding *Präventionshilfe* (Section 46b (1) sentence 1 No. 2 StGB) grants benefits to the collaborator who helps to prevent serious crimes, although in doing so he or she only fulfils his or her general obligation to bring planned (serious) offences to the attention of the authorities as specified in Section 138 StGB. The significance of this potential conflict is considerably attenuated by the fact that the applicability of Section 138 StGB is limited to offences planned by *others*[95] while Section 46b StGB only comes into play if there is a *connection* between the planned offences and the collaborator's *Anlasstat* (which will often be established by the collaborator's participation in both crimes).[96]

---

88   Fischer, StGB, 63rd edition 2016, § 46b, rn. 35; Labs 2016, p. 249; Malek 2010, p. 204.
89   Christoph 2014, p. 91.
90   Peglau 2013, p. 1910.
91   Christoph 2014, p. 91.
92   Streng in: Nomos Kommentar zum StGB, 4th edition 2013, § 46b rn. 14; see also Frahm 2014, p. 118 et seq.; Kneba 2011, p. 141 et seq.
93   MüKoStGB/Maier, 3rd edition 2016, § 46b rn. 5; Schönke/Schöder/Kinzig StGB, 29th edition 2014, § 46b rn. 2.
94   Mellinghoff 2014, p. 511.
95   MüKoStGB/Hohmann, 3rd edition 2016, § 46b rn. 132.
96   See Labs 2016, p. 245.

4.4.1   Responsibility for Providing Undertakings

There are three distinct moments with respect to the competent authority for managing the collaborator of justice and providing for the undertakings. Firstly, the collaborator of justice has to disclose his or her information regarding an offence committed to an employee of the prosecutor's office or to the police (*Strafvervolgungsbehörde*). Where this is information that is suitable to prevent a crime, the information can be disclosed to a larger group of public officials, namely those working at a *Dienststelle*. This encompasses State and municipal public officials.[97]

Secondly, when this information is disclosed to the competent authority and the case of the collaborator of justice goes to court, the trial judge becomes the competent authority. When he or she receives this information the public prosecutor cannot make binding agreements about the sentence.[98] The (verbal) 'agreement' between the public prosecutor and the collaborator of justice (usually also involving the defence counsel of the latter) is a 'gentlemen's agreement'. The public prosecutor commits him or herself during the course of the proceedings to emphasizing before the court the collaborator's involvement in helping to clear up other crimes and asking for a reduced penalty.

The public prosecutor can only promise not to prosecute some offence(s) as part of his or her discretionary prosecution decision (Sections 153 to 154 StPO)[99] and to encourage the police to include the collaborator of justice in the witness protection program.[100] The court has to assess several aspects before they can mitigate the sentence or, in some cases, allow the collaborator of justice to walk free. The court has to assess all the formal requirements (as described above, e.g. the criminal offence being part of the catalogue and the information having been disclosed voluntarily). In addition, the court has to anticipate what the judgment will be in the case against the third party (the person who is incriminated by the collaborator of justice).[101] In the *Aufklärungsvariante* (Section 46b (1) sentence 1 StGB), the court may only mitigate the sentence of the collaborator of justice if it is convinced that the information provided by the collaborator will make a significant contribution (*wesentlicher Beitrag*) to achieving a conviction of the third party.[102] In fact, this comes down to an assessment of the reliability of the collaborator's statement. If all requirements have been met the court *can* mitigate the sentence and has to take the factors determining the sentence (see above) into consideration. The use of sentence mitigation is fully managed by the trial court, because it alone has the authority to decide on the collaborator's deal.

---

97 MüKoStGB/Maier, 2nd edition 2012, § 138 rn. 22.
98 Malek 2010, p. 204.
99 Malek 2010, p. 204.
100 See Heubrock et al. 2013, p. 60.
101 Malek 2010, p. 205.
102 Fischer, StGB, 63rd edition 2016, § 46b, rn. 14.

Thirdly, other parts of the 'deal' – the witness protection program – are arranged and supervised by a special police unit (see Section 2 (1) of the *Zeugenschutz Harmonisierungsgesetz* (ZSHG) which will be discussed below in § 4.4.5).[103] All arrangements must be documented (Section 2 (3) ZSHG) and are drawn up by the police. The law explicitly states that these documents do not form part of the case file (Section 2 (3) ZSHG). The public prosecutor and the court play no role in this aspect and have no direct influence on it.

4.4.2   Catalogue of Offences Eligible for the Application of Section 46b StGB

Under Section 46b (1) sentence 1 StGB, the *Kronzeugen* provision applies only to crimes listed in Section 100a (2) StPO, which are referred to as "serious criminal offenses" (*schweren Straftaten*; see also Section 100a (1) No. 1 StPO). Section 100a StPO is the provision regarding telephone tapping. Therefore, offences where a telephone may be tapped are considered the same as those eligible for the *Kronzeugen* provision.[104] It is difficult to provide an overview of the catalogue because it mentions individual criminal offences from several statutes (such as the German Criminal Code, the Weapon Control Act, Tax Law, the Anti-Doping Law and the Asylum Law). Furthermore, Section 100a (2) StPO does not stipulate a minimum sentence, but is an exhaustive list of offences on which a collaborator of justice can offer information. It includes property crimes, such as fraud, money laundering and robbery, violent crimes, such as murder and manslaughter and tax crimes, such as tax evasion, and international crimes.[105] The complete catalogue can be found in Annex 1.

As stated above, there has to be a connection between the criminal act the collaborator discloses information about and his or her own offence (*Konnexitätserfordernis*).

4.4.3   Nature of the Undertakings

As mentioned above, the German *Kronzeugen* legislation forms part of the Criminal Code concerning the sentencing decision and the chosen undertaking to collaborators of justice is a mitigation of the sentence (and in some cases, exemption from punishment once convicted). Furthermore, to understand properly how the sentence mitigation that can be applied to collaborators of justice works, it is important to understand that the German Criminal Code works with mandatory minimum penalties and a fixed maximum penalty. Above, the examples of manslaughter and human trafficking

---

103 An overview of the organizational structure is provided by Mischkewitz 2014, p. 27 et seq.
104 Frahm 2014, p. 37 is critical about this general reference to a provision with a procedural background.
105 In the German literature on Criminal Procedure, the large scale of crimes listed in Section 100a (2) StPO (which has even been expanded several times) has been subject to reasonable criticism. See for example SK-StPO/Wolter/Greco, 5th edition 2016, § 100a rn. 48 et seq.

were used to explain the *Anlasstat*. These offences have, respectively, a minimum sentence of five years imprisonment and a maximum penalty of fifteen years, and a six months prison term and a maximum of ten years imprisonment.

Section 49 (1) StGB provides a sentence mitigation structure that also applies to the *Kronzeugen* provision (Section 46b (1) StGB). Section 49 (1) StGB reads:

> **"Special mitigating circumstances established by law**
>
> *(1) If the law requires or allows for mitigation under this provision, the following shall apply:*
>
> 1. *Imprisonment of not less than three years shall be substituted for imprisonment for life.*
>
> 2. *In cases of imprisonment for a fixed term, no more than three quarters of the statutory maximum term may be imposed. In case of a fine the same shall apply to the maximum number of daily units.*
>
> 3. *Any increased minimum statutory term of imprisonment shall be reduced as follows:*
>   *a minimum term of ten or five years, to two years;*
>   *a minimum term of three or two years, to six months;*
>   *a minimum term of one year, to three months;*
>   *in all other cases to the statutory minimum.*
>
> *(2) If the court may in its discretion mitigate the sentence pursuant to a law which refers to this provision, it may reduce the sentence to the statutory minimum or impose a fine instead of imprisonment."*[106]

This provision encompasses three rules for mitigation/sentencing decisions. Section 49 (1) No. 1 StGB states that when the law allows sentence mitigation under this provision (as is the case for with collaborators of justice) and penalty for the offence is life imprisonment, the court must order imprisonment for at least three years. However, the general *Kronzeugen* provision amends this rule. The provision determines that life

---

106 *Das Gericht kann die Strafe nach seinem Ermessen mildern (§ 49 Abs. 2) oder von einer Bestrafung nach diesen Vorschriften absehen, wenn der Täter 1. sich freiwillig und ernsthaft bemüht, das Fortbestehen der Vereinigung oder die Begehung einer ihren Zielen entsprechenden Straftat zu verhindern, oder 2. freiwillig sein Wissen so rechtzeitig einer Dienststelle offenbart, daß Straftaten, deren Planung er kennt, noch verhindert werden können; erreicht der Täter sein Ziel, das Fortbestehen der Vereinigung zu verhindern, oder wird es ohne sein Bemühen erreicht, so wird er nicht bestraft.*

imprisonment shall be replaced by a prison sentence of no less than ten years. This part of the sentence mitigation determines a *new mandatory minimum sentence of ten years* for offences that can be sentenced to life imprisonment.[107]

The second part (Section 49 (1) No. 2 StGB) states that in cases of imprisonment for a fixed term the sentence mitigation results in a 25 percent reduction in the maximum term. To use the same examples as before, the maximum penalty for manslaughter will be reduced from fifteen years to eleven years and three months and the maximum penalty for human trafficking will be reduced from a ten year term of imprisonment to a maximum of seven years and six months. It is important to note that Section 46b StGB is formulated as a 'can provision'.[108] The court can decide to use the 'three-quarters option' but is not required to do so. There is no *'Strafmilderungsautomatismus'*.[109] This part of the sentence mitigation sets *a new limit on the maximum sentences.*

The third part (Section 49 (1) No. 3 StGB) is bit more complicated to understand. For this part, you have to keep the German system of mandatory minimum sentences and maximum penalties in mind. The three possibilities are: (1) for crimes with a mandatory minimum sentence of five or ten years imprisonment, the sentence can be mitigated to a minimum of two years; (2) for crimes with a mandatory minimum sentence of two or three years imprisonment, the sentence can be mitigated to a minimum of six months and; (3) for crimes with a mandatory minimum sentence of one year, the sentence can be mitigated to a minimum of three months. So, manslaughter, for example, carries a minimum sentence of five years imprisonment. On the basis of Section 49 (1) StGB a manslaughter-collaborator of justice will be eligible for a minimum sentence of two years imprisonment. This part of the sentence mitigation sets *new limits on the mandatory minimum sentences.*

When the second and third parts are combined in the case of manslaughter (under a normal sentencing framework of five to fifteen years imprisonment) the court can penalize manslaughter-collaborators of justice with between two years imprisonment as a mandatory minimum and eleven years and three months imprisonment as a maximum.

Furthermore, the German courts can refrain from punishment entirely if the crime is punishable by a fixed-term sentence and the hypothetical sentence[110] for the collaborator of justice would not be more than three years of imprisonment based on the court's assessment (see Section 46b (1) sentence 4 StGB).[111]

The law does not offer any other benefits than sentence mitigation or exemption from punishment. However, as will be discussed below, other benefits – which the law does not

---

107 Schönke/Schöder/Kinzig StGB, 29th edition 2014, § 46b rn. 24.
108 MüKoStGB/Maier, 3rd edition 2016, § 46b rn. 118.
109 Jeßberger 2015, p. 1158.
110 Frahm 2014, p. 85; Malek 2010, p. 202.
111 Hardinghaus 2015, p. 143.

recognize as collaboration benefits – are granted in practice (e.g. benefits related to immigration law).

4.4.4 Procedure to Be Followed and (Interim) Scrutiny

As previously mentioned, it is the trial judge who plays a crucial role in the application of the German *Kronzeugen* provision because the provision is part of the sentencing decision. Owing to the fact that trials are, in principle, open to the public (Section 169 Courts Constitution Act (GVG)), most decisions regarding sentence mitigation are transparent. When all the criteria have been met, the court has a wide discretionary sentencing margin available to it.[112] The use of this margin is linked to the high demands placed on the motivation for the sentence, which makes the deliberation more transparent. The law demands that the court takes several factors into account when determining a sentence (see above § 4.4), e.g. factors relating to the quality of the information and factors relating to the collaborator's own offence.

However, it has to be borne in mind that the law provides for exceptions from the principle of a public hearing (see Sections 170 et seq. GVG)[113] and that there may be an abridged judgment if all parties entitled to an appellate remedy waive their right of an appellate remedy or if no appellate remedy is sought within the given time limit (see Section 267 (4) of the Code of Criminal Procedure, StPO).[114]

In addition, the German Code of Criminal Procedure provides for a special procedure (*Strafbefehlsverfahren*, laid down in Sections 407 et seq. StPO), which in cases of minor offences allows a prosecution without a public trial. Thus, if the parties involved in a deal want to avoid publicity, this written procedure could offer a suitable solution.

It goes without saying that the witness protection program is much less transparent than the criminal proceedings because the aim of this procedure is not compatible with transparency. The law explicitly states that the documents related to witness protection do not form part of the case file (see Section 2 (3) ZSHG).

4.4.5 Relationship to Witness Protection

The *Zeugenschutz-Harmonisierungsgesetz* (ZSHG) is the German law regulating the witness protection program. This program is available to all witnesses who are in danger because they made an admission to the justice department. It is not a program solely for

---

112 Fischer, StGB, 63rd edition 2016, § 46b, rn. 25.
113 For an overview see Beulke 2016, rn. 376 et seq.
114 Under Section 267 (4) StPO, in these cases only the proven facts establishing the statutory elements of the criminal offence and the penal norm must be indicated and the further content of the reasons for the judgment shall be determined by the court's discretion.

collaborators of justice. In practice, the police or the public prosecutor will suggest intake into the program.[115] However, under Section 2 ZSGH, the *Zeugenschutzdienststelle* (witness protection bureau) is the competent authority. Therefore, contact with the police and the public prosecutor's office is at a bare minimum. Intake into this program can be offered to a collaborator of justice, but it is not a mandatory part of the procedure for collaborators of justice.[116] Based on Section 1 ZSHG, the witness must agree to being taken into the program and the formal requirement is that his or her role as a witness and his or her statement will endanger the witness's life, body, health, freedom or bring substantial monetary disadvantages. The witness can obtain a new identity (Section 5), a new home and job, among other things.[117]

4.5   PRACTICE

The provision(s) on collaborating with justice in exchange for sentence mitigation or exemption from punishment are relatively clear. They explicitly state (1) who can inform the authorities (*Täter*) about a (2) committed or planned (3) listed crime in a (4) timely fashion (before admission of the indictment by the trial court) and (5) the requirements that the crime committed by the potential collaborator must meet. Although the provision(s) are reasonably clear, it remains open to question whether the law in action is in accordance with the written provision(s) and, furthermore, whether the practitioners find the provision(s) satisfactory.

4.5.1   *Methodology*

To gather information about the practical implementation of the collaborator of justice provision(s), we held eleven interviews, with two judges (a Federal Court of Justice judge and a court of appeals judge), two prosecutors (both specializing in organized crime in large German municipalities), three defence lawyers (one specializing in crimes against the State and terrorism and two in general practice), two legal scholars (both experts in the 'big *Kronzeugen* provision'), a leader of a witness protection team (member of the State Police (*Landeskriminalamt*)) and a member of the National Cartel Agency (*Bundeskartellamt*, BKartA).[118]

---

115 Eisenberg 2008, p. 197-198.
116 See Mischkewitz 2014, p. 70.
117 Eisenberg 2008, p. 200. For a critical analysis of the ZSHG see Mischkewitz 2014, p. 149 et seq.
118 In this section we will use numerous quotes from the interviewees. Therefore we have (loosely, not literally) translated the statements to the best of our ability. The German quotation will be included in a footnote. Abbreviations will be used to ascribe quotes to a specific interviewee. The Federal Court of Justice judge and the court of appeals judge are abbreviated to [2] and [1]. The two prosecutors are abbreviated to [6] and [7]. The defence lawyer specializing in crimes against the State and terrorism is abbreviated to [3]. The other two

Firstly, the court of appeal judge [1] was chosen, because of the presumed experience with the collaborators of justice provisions in their court, and because they are a prominent figure in the scholarly debate about the provision in the literature. The Federal Court of Justice judge [2] was invited for the interview because they, according to their position as a cassation judge, should have a broad overview of all the concurrent provisions on collaborators of justice. Secondly, the defence lawyer [3] is specialized in defending suspects charged with crimes against the state and terrorism, and we therefore presumed that they have acquired experience with the crime specific collaborators provision regarding terrorism. The other two defence lawyers ([4] & [5]) are working in a general practice, whereby both also have experience in Narcotics law and its crime specific collaborators provision. In our perspective, we covered the general and the crime specific collaborators provisions while interviewing this trinity. Thirdly, we assumed that prosecutors of large German municipalities would have more experience in prosecuting organized crime, and we further assumed that organized crime suspects would be more likely to collaborate, because the stakes are high and the collaborators of justice provisions require a connection between the offence committed by the collaborator and the offence(s) on which they collaborate. Therefore, we interviewed two prosecutors specialized in organized crime ([6] & [7]), both working in a district with about one million inhabitants in two different Federal States.

In addition to these seven interviewees from a 'general legal profession', we selected four other interviewees. The fourth chosen profession of an interviewee was a member of the National Cartel Agency [10]. They could provide insight on another crime specific collaborators provision, because cartel law has its own collaborators provision. Although cartel law is ruled by specific mechanisms different from criminal law, it was of interest for us whether the same problems and discussion arise in that field of law, especially because the cartel collaborators provision is used in a relatively high percentage of the cases. Furthermore, an interview with a member of the police was necessary, because the first contact of a (potential) collaborator is with the police. We interviewed a leader of a police's witness protection team [11] that is part of the State Police. Lastly, we interviewed two legal scholars ([8] & [9]), both active in the debate on collaborators of justice, to verify the information gathered in the other interviews.

The interviewees were contacted by e-mail or telephone, and in all but one case the invitation was immediately accepted. We had difficulty getting into contact with a member of the police, mainly because it is a closed organization and the closed character is necessary for the functioning of their work. However, after contacting the Federal State's

---

defence lawyers are recognizable as [4] and [5]. The abbreviations used for the legal scholars are [8] and [9]. The member of the National Cartel Agency is abbreviated to [10] and the leader of a witness protection team to [11].

Ministry of Justice, the head of the local police and the head of the Federal State's Police, all without success, we got into contact with a member of the witness protection team, who we were able to interview.

The interviews were conducted at the University of Bielefeld, with the exception of the interview of prosecutor [6], which took place in the prosecutor's office. The interviews were conducted via telephone, with the exception of the interviews with prosecutor [6], defence lawyer [4] and the member of the State's Police [11]. The interviews were recorded with a recording device. The interview protocol was semi-structured, with fixed questions for interviewees from the police, the prosecutor's office, defence lawyers and judges. The member of the National Cartel Agency [10], who is responsible for the investigation and sanctioning of cartels, was interviewed on the basis of the (slightly modified) interview protocol for prosecutors. The interview with the legal scholars was more openly structured, because the goal was to verify our findings with their knowledge of the collaborators provisions. A small deviation of the structure of the interviews took place in later interviews. When later interviewees had an opposing view with another interview, they were confronted with our conflicting information. Furthermore, later interviewees were asked if they could substantiate information we gathered in earlier interviews.

The interviews were conducted by prof. dr. Michael Lindemann, and dr. Dave van Toor was present during all interviews. After the interview, the digital file was transferred to a transcription office, who made a *verbatim* transcription of all interviews. The interviewees received the *verbatim* transcripts and could make adjustments, which all of the interviewees did.

The corrected *verbatim* transcripts formed the basis for the qualitative social legal analysis. The information from the interviews was used to gather insight in the law in action regarding collaborators of justice in Germany, which cannot be derived from the text of the law. The transcripts were not coded, but, in line with Mayring's method, analyzed in a categorical system, namely (1) experience with the provisions; (2) communication between the different authorities involved in the practice of collaborators and; (3) discussion about the legal provisions.[119]

To provide an insight into the law in action, quotes are used frequently throughout the report. In this way, the information is presented in (more or less) the same way as it was communicated during the interviews. Therefore we (loosely, not literally) translated the statements to the best of our abilities. The German quotation has been included in a footnote. Abbreviations have been used to ascribe quotes to a specific interviewee. In addition to the presentation of the quotes, the overall view of the practice and (part of) the law are summarized, and, where necessary, provided with implications and conclusions.

The results of the interviews are described and analyzed in this section, which has been divided into five parts: (1) application of the collaborators' provision(s); (2) the

---

119 Mayring 2015, p. 51.

process of becoming a collaborator of justice; (3) implementation and scrutiny of the undertakings; (4) witness protection in relationship with the law and; (5) the use of the statements made by collaborators and their punishment.

4.5.2 Application: Frequency and Results

The first question put to all interviewees was in how many cases a provision concerning the collaborator of justice is used and whether they had more general information about how often the collaborators instrument(s) were applied. As was to be expected, the interviewees did not have any information on the total frequency of the use of the provisions in question. It has further proved to be impossible to gather official information on the absolute frequency, mainly because most of the case-law of the lower courts is not published in an accessible way while use of the collaborators provisions is not separately registered by the Federal Statistical Office.[120] Nevertheless, some quantitative studies have been conducted in the past to establish the frequency with which the collaborator's provisions are applied. We will therefore include a brief overview of the results of these studies at the end of this section.

With the exception of the appellate judge,[121] everyone interviewed reported to have at least some experience with one of the collaborators provisions but only the provisions regarding information about crimes that have already been committed. It seems thus that the preventive use of collaborator's information has hardly any practical significance.

On the basis of the interviews, it appears that there are wide differences in the use of collaborators provisions in different areas of criminal law. The defence lawyer specializing in crimes against the State and terrorism estimated that the crime-specific collaborators provision is used in 20 to 25 percent of their cases. A similar assessment was made with regard to the crime-specific provision in competition law. A public prosecutor [6], formerly active in competition law, and the employee of the BKartA [10] stated that there are collaborators of justice in the majority of cases even in that field of law.[122]

A public prosecutor specializing in organized crime [7] stated that in their ten year career, they only knew of a handful of cases where a 'real' collaborator was involved,

---

120 Referring to information provided by the Federal Office of Justice (*Bundesamt für Justiz*), Kaspar & Christoph 2016a, p. 319 state that until 14 November 2014 240 cases were registered in the central penal register (*Bundeszentralregister*) but indicate that the size of the dark number cannot be guessed.

121 The appellate court's jurisdiction only covers cases with a maximum penalty of four years. Mostly, these cases are low or mid-level crimes, in all probability not committed in any organized sense and, therefore, the *Kronzeugen* provision does not play any practical role (although the *Täter* can theoretically become a collaborator when his offence is penalized with a minimum sentence of one month). The appellate judge, though, was able to provide us with an in-depth analysis of the collaborators' provisions from a theoretical point of view, which is why we included him or her in the sample.

122 "Wir machen Kartellverfolgungsfälle und es gibt heute fast keinen Fall, also ich glaube es gibt keinen Fall, wo die Regelung, d.h. unsere Bonusregelung, nicht irgendwann zur Anwendung kommt."

whereby they meant a 'big fish' used to catch other 'big or even larger fish'. The same public prosecutor stated that, in general, the application of the general provision (Section 46b StGB) and the crime-specific drugs provision (Section 31 BtMG) in conjunction with witness protection lay in the negligible range. The Federal judge stated that occasionally questions arise regarding the general provision (Section 46b StGB) and the crime-specific drugs provision (Section 31 BtMG). In contrast with the aforementioned defence lawyer, they stated that the crime-specific provisions for terrorism (Sections 129, 129a StGB) do not play any role in their daily practice. Their explanation for this finding is the following:

> "This connection, which one has as a group, as an association, when one entered the group, is probably stronger than in cases in which some people simply come together and commit crimes together for economic reasons."[123]

This seems to prevent group members from collaborating with the criminal justice authorities. However, another possibility is that public prosecutors or defence lawyers in such cases use legal remedies less often.

To sum up, it has proven difficult to obtain an overview of the use of collaborators of justice in German criminal procedure by means of the qualitative interviews we conducted. Most interviewees – judges, prosecutors and defence lawyers – have some experience with the different provisions, and the crime-specific provisions for competition law and terrorism seemed to be used more often than the general provision or the other crime-specific provisions.

Our (limited) findings are by and large consistent with the results of quantitative studies previously published by other researchers. In a study conducted in 2012, Frahm had the opportunity to interview 112 public prosecutors, 37 judges and 21 defence lawyers by means of a questionnaire about the use of the general collaborators provision (Section 46b StGB).[124] Although the interviews took place before the amendments of 2013 (see § 4.3), the results still offer a relevant indicator for current practice.[125] Frahm found that the application of Section 46b StGB tends to be the exception rather than the rule.[126] 87% of the interviewees stated that little or no (0-9%) use was made of the provision in cases with at least one offence eligible for the application of Section 46b StGB. It was only among the judges that a moderately higher frequency was estimated. When asked in

---

123 "[M]öglicherweise ebenso diese Verbindung, die man hat als Gruppe, als Vereinigung, die man da mal eingegangen ist, dass die halt doch vielleicht stärker trägt, als wenn jetzt irgendwelche Leute einfach zusammen irgendwelche, aus wirtschaftlichen Motiven irgendwelche Straftaten begehen."
124 Frahm 2014.
125 Unfortunately, this is not the case with the results of a thoroughly conducted study by Mühlhoff and Mehrens which concerned the practice of the (in the meantime repealed) Articles 4 and 5 KronzG. See Mehrens 2001, p. 123 et seq.; Mühlhoff & Mehrens 1999.
126 See Frahm 2014, p. 290 et seq.

which areas of crime they guessed the general collaborators provision was most often used, the judges, public prosecutors and defence lawyers mentioned organized crime (73.1%), drug offences (62.2%) and terrorism (26.9%), followed by economic crimes (23.1%) and corruption (19.2%). (Note that the first three offences all have a crime-specific collaborators provision.)

Kaspar and Christoph recently published the first results of an ongoing quantitative study which includes not only actors of the judiciary and defence lawyers but also police officers.[127] Just as Frahm, Kaspar and Christoph have found indications for the fairly restrained use of Section 46b StGB, which to some extent is in contrast with the finding that 63.4% of the interviewed public prosecutors and 69.6% of the interviewed police officers stated that the provision had proven to be effective in practice.[128] So far, only the results of the 106 interviews conducted with defence lawyers have been published in detail. Here, the assessment was much more skeptical: The majority (53.1%) of the interviewees who had at least some experience with the application of Section 46b StGB (n = 49) had reached the conclusion that the provision had proven to be ineffective. Kaspar and Christoph commented very cautiously on statements made concerning the number of cases in which the interviewees claimed to have experienced the application of the general collaborators provision because the figures given by some interviewees (45, 50 or even 100 cases) seemed quite unrealistic. Having made some adjustments, they established that the average number of cases in the group of defence lawyers with practical experience was 4.9.

It should be noted in this context that there has also been an empirical study regarding the practice of witness protection programs.[129] Mischkewitz has collected publicly available and unpublished data on the quantitative significance and characteristics of witness protection programs in Germany. It can be seen from the results he presented that intake into one of the programs he investigated is a fairly rare phenomenon. During the period between 1990 and 2009, the total number of witness protection cases never exceeded 481 (and was usually much lower).[130] The majority of cases (72%) were assigned to the area of organized crime, while crimes against the State (*Staatsschutzdelikte*) provided the background to only 6% of cases. About half the persons who were accepted into a program were witnesses (1,643 from 2004 to 2008) and the other half were relatives (1,677 in the same period). A substantial part (50.1% on the average) of the program participants were foreigners. The length of time that people spend in a witness protection program lasts from several months to up to more than five years.

---

127 Kaspar & Christoph 2016b, p. 487 et seq.; Kaspar & Christoph 2016a, p. 318 et seq.
128 Kaspar & Christoph 2016b, p. 490 et seq.
129 Mischkewitz 2014.
130 For this and the following see Mischkewitz 2014, p. 37 et seq.

4.5.3   *The Process of Becoming a Collaborator of Justice*

As previously indicated, the general provision on collaborators of justice forms part of the German Criminal Code, more specifically the section regarding the sentencing decision. Therefore, the procedural aspects of becoming a collaborator, among other things, are not regulated. This is why the recruitment procedure was of particular interest to us during the interviews. In this section we will present the results of the interviews concerning the procedural aspect, especially (1) the (timely) recruitment of collaborators; (2) what sort of information the authorities are looking for; (3) how the legal criterion of the connection (*Zusammenhang*) is dealt with and; (4) the binding nature of the agreement made between the collaborator and the justice department.

4.5.3.1   Timely Recruitment of Collaborators of Justice

One of the scholars interviewed [9] called the police 'the driving force' of collaborators recruitment. When the interrogation of a suspect by the police starts, he or she will be instructed on his or her rights. Important aspects of this instruction (*Belehrung*) are to make the suspect familiar with his or her procedural rights, such as the right to remain silent (see Sections 136 (1) sentence 2, 163a (IV) sentence 2 StPO). Although not formally regulated, according to the public prosecutors interviewed, in Germany the possibility of collaborating with the authorities in exchange for sentence mitigation is part of the instruction. A public prosecutor [6] stated that this is an integral part of the *Belehrung* in cases which at first glance seem suitable for the collaborators provision to be applied and that the specific mention of the *Kronzeugen* provisions is standardized with regard to these cases.[131] It could be that the practice of both public prosecutors, namely organized crime, has a major influence on the standardization of the instruction. In organized crime, there will always be the possibility of providing information on another person (otherwise it would not be organized crime). When it is clear that an offender acted alone, for example, for traffic offences or petty theft, it is pointless to instruct the suspect on the collaboration opportunities.

Both public prosecutors indicated that the police and the justice department do not actively recruit collaborators any other way than during the interrogation. The legal scholars interviewed confirmed this statement. A significant example was the case of

---

131 "Also, glücklicherweise bringen wir das in das Gespräch. Und zwar muss man sich das so vorstellen, in den allermeisten Fällen ist es so, dass eine Festnahme eines Verdächtigen erfolgt und schon mit dem Erstkontakt mit dem Verdächtigen eine ganze Reihe von Belehrungen abgearbeitet werden. Also man muss quasi in Deutschland einen halben Berg an Papier abarbeiten, bis dann die erste Frage zur Sache gestellt wird. Also, sprich, also man belehrt darüber, welche Rechte ein Festgenommener hat. Man belehrt darüber, das sind ja in aller Regel Leute, die auch ein ausländisches Dokument haben, Passdokument haben, man belehrt über konsularische Vertretungsbenachrichtigungsregelungen. Man belehrt schließlich über den 136 StPO, also die Rechte eines Beschuldigten und man belehrt DANN, nachdem der Belehrte halb ermüdet ist, schließlich auch über die Möglichkeit 46 b StGB und 31 BtMG. Das ist standardisiert, dieses Vorgehen."

the leader of a criminal organization who turned himself in and made detailed incriminating statements about the organization and its members. In this case, the defence lawyer of the gang member was called by the police with the announcement that their client was in custody and was already talking to the police in detail. As interviewed public prosecutor [6] reported, the police did not actively recruit this person and the person concerned made an informed decision to collaborate after the instruction (*Belehrung*) (even without their lawyer present).

One defence lawyer [5] declared that in their experience in promising cases the police will mention the possibility of collaboration, especially the crime-specific narcotics variant. They would also instruct their client during the first conversation on the possibility of collaborating because this can lead to a substantial mitigation of the sentence. The same lawyer stated that they had defended collaborators a few times and had also gained experience with collaborators *a charge*. Two defence lawyers interviewed ([3] and [4]) stressed however that not a lot is known about the recruitment from their perspective. One lawyer [4] stated that the process of recruitment is 'very opaque'. These two defence lawyers did not know how actively the authorities attempt to recruit collaborators, whether they mention the possibility of collaborating during the instruction for the interrogation or whether the possibility is only offered to suspects after they ask for it.

In addition, the legal scholars stated that it is unknown how the police behave during the instruction (and interrogation) because defence lawyers are not present during the initial interrogation and the interrogations are not transcripted *verbatim*. Furthermore, one defence lawyer [3] stated that in "most of the cases, it is impossible to find out during the trial phase exactly how the recruitment occurred".[132] A judge [1] confirmed this statement, especially with regard to the deadline to collaborate.

> "This has changed, of course, because everything has to happen before the trial phase. That means that the court, so to speak, can no longer actively act somehow, that everything is already been done by the public prosecutor's office and the police when the case comes to court."[133]

The two public prosecutors, a defence lawyer [5] and a judge [1] emphasized that the early identification of potential collaborators is important (and not just because it is a criterion for the application of the scheme). A public prosecutor [6] sees the benefit from

---

132 "Also das ist etwas, was ich teilweise gar nicht genau weiß. Ob die Initiative jetzt zum Beispiel von der Polizei ausgeht, die einen solchen Schutz anbietet oder ob das von den Zeugen ausgeht, die danach fragen. Das lässt sich häufig in der Hauptverhandlung auch gar nicht genau herausfiltern und herausfinden."

133 "Das hat sich natürlich geändert, dadurch, dass es jetzt alles schon vor der Hauptverhandlung passieren muss. Das heißt, es ist natürlich den Gerichten damit, also die können damit jetzt sozusagen nicht mehr aktiv irgendwie umgehen, sondern die haben ja, das ist ja alles schon gelaufen, wenn es zu Gericht kommt, ja. Das muss ja dann eigentlich die Staatsanwaltschaft und die Polizei im Wesentlichen schon irgendwie angehen und, ja."

an early disclosure of the information for the authorities in the shortening effect the disclosure has on the length of the proceedings (besides, of course, the necessity for collaborators as an instrument for some crimes, especially in organized crime). The confession of the collaborator will not only lead to a more efficient proceeding in his or her case, but will also accelerate the proceedings against the persons on whom the collaborator provided information. To shorten the proceedings as much as possible, it is essential to acquire the information as quickly as possible. This is one of the reasons why the possibility of becoming a collaborator forms part of the instruction at the beginning of the interrogation.

In addition, the public prosecutors and judges interviewed emphasized that the information provided by the collaborator has to be verified and that this is more easily done in the investigation phase. This verification consists of two parts. Firstly, the reliability of the information has to be assessed because there is always a danger of the collaborator providing false information for personal gain. Secondly, the investigation against the third party has to be pushed forward as far as possible because, in the *Aufklärungsvariante* the collaborator can only obtain a mitigation of his or her sentence or exemption from punishment if the information he or she provided has contributed to the clarification of an offence committed. Furthermore, one public prosecutor [6] and a member of the BKartA [10] stressed that early disclosure of the information puts pressure on other people. If other suspects learn that the authorities know significant and truthful information, this can create a domino-effect causing more people to collaborate with the authorities (which then adds to the shortening effect as more suspects collaborate).

For example, in a major case against a criminal organization that was involved in extortion, violent crime, possession of and traffic in weapons as well as drug trafficking, one of the gang members confessed to his involvement during the interrogation conducted after his arrest and, on top of that, made incriminating statements about other gang members, including about the import of three kilograms of amphetamine. The court explicitly considered in its judgment that this was an important step for the authorities because it confirmed facts that had remained uncertain until then. This statement, along with other information such as travel patterns via GPS, led three other members of the gang to 'turn' during the court hearing and make incriminatory statements about themselves and others, according to the interviewed public prosecutor [6], because the lawyers recognized that an acquittal was no longer possible.[134]

According to the interviewed BKartA employee [10] and the public prosecutor with prior experience in cartel cases [6], this domino-effect happens in most cartel cases

---

134 "Da hat letztlich der Umstand, dass der Erste ausgepackt hat und dann die Anwälte auch gesehen haben, okay, das wird jetzt schwierig, die haben Sachen sichergestellt, die haben die Telefonüberwachung, die haben die Aussagen eines Ersten, der umgefallen ist, das hat dann auch bei den anderen dazu geführt, dass es letztlich zu belastenden Aussagen gekommen ist."

"[b]ecause it is not an effective defence strategy to deny the allegations after several people or companies have disclosed information".[135]

A fourth reason for including a deadline on the disclosure of the information, and therefore the timely recruitment of collaborators also, is offered by a judge [1]:

"Otherwise the collaborators' procedure would be impractical. It would be practically impossible for the court to have, let's say, twenty, thirty, forty, or fifty trial days and then at some point, somewhere, the suspect discloses information regarding another person's crime(s) in his or her last words. Then the court has to decide, can we do something with that, do we need to adjourn to make further investigation possible to verify the information substantially. If the latter were to be the case, the trial phase would be dragged out for a long time".[136]

However, this deadline and timely recruitment puts the defence at a disadvantage according to the defence lawyers interviewed. For example, a defence lawyer interviewed [4] stated that the police will use this deadline to put pressure on suspects to disclose information early because that has substantial advantages compared to later disclosure. But the most important disadvantage is that the defence has to decide on a strategy at an early stage of the investigation [3].

"This deadline is absolutely problematic, because we have to advise our client and decide on a course at an early stage, but we cannot know how the whole process will turn out. When I find myself in such a position, I personally find it very unpleasant to commit myself to a certain course at such an early point from which I cannot deviate later on".[137]

One judge [1] and the legal scholars explained that the courts sometimes clearly indicate that the trial will start in, for example, two months. This indication will often be presented to the defence lawyer when the authorities think that the suspect has useful

---

135 "[W]eil dann eigentlich ab einer gewissen Anzahl von Leuten, die ein Kartell bestätigen, macht das Bestreiten wenig Sinn".

136 "Ja, das hat mit der Praktikabilität der Regelung zu tun. Es wäre praktisch für ein Gericht kaum handhabbar, wenn man sagt, man führt erst mal die Hauptverhandlung ganz normal über zwanzig, dreißig, vierzig, fünfzig Hauptverhandlungstage durch und dann irgendwann in seinem letzten Wort kommt dann der Angeklagte und macht bestimmte Angaben und dann muss das Gericht jetzt überlegen, ob es damit schon etwas anfangen oder ob es nach ermitteln muss. Das wird die Hauptverhandlung sehr in die Länge ziehen".

137 "Ja, also für die Verteidigung ist es natürlich äußerst problematisch, weil wir zu einem ganz frühen Zeitpunkt versuchen müssen jetzt, zu beraten und Weichen zu stellen, von denen wir nicht wissen, wie es dann hinterher ausgeht. Also ich persönlich finde das äußerst unangenehm, wenn ich in so einer Situation bin, zu diesem frühen Zeitpunkt praktisch die Strategie schon unveränderlich festlegen zu müssen."

information but has not yet been willing to collaborate. In such cases, the defence lawyers are given ample opportunity to decide on a (collaborating) strategy and are allowed sufficient time to actually collaborate. It seems that the courts can be flexible with regard to the deadline and timely recruitment.

In summary, both judges and lawyers stated that the recruitment of collaborators is not transparent. According to the two public prosecutors, collaborators are not actively recruited, but the possibility of collaborating is mentioned during the first interrogation. Lawyers seemingly are not present (most of the time) at the start of the interrogation when the suspect is instructed on his or her rights and options. In the trial phase it is difficult to find out how the recruitment went. Public prosecutors and judges stated that timely recruitment is essential for several reasons, *inter alia* the efficiency of the process and the possibility of verifying the information without delay. From the lawyers' perspective, the deadline is problematic because they have to commit themselves and their clients to collaborating at an early stage with no assurances about the outcome because the prosecutor can only pledge him or herself to the agreement, but it will be the court's decision in the end (this is discussed in more detail in § 4.5.3.4 en § 4.5.6.2).

4.5.3.2   The Information Sought by the Authorities

According to Section 46b StGB, a collaborator can provide the authorities with information about an offence already committed or information about a planned crime which can still be prevented. The provision does not specify if the collaborator should disclose information about all known offences or if he or she can reveal information selectively. Furthermore, the provision does not clarify whether the collaborator only has to disclose information about the offence in question or if he or she also is expected to disclose information, for example, about the structure of a criminal organization, personal knowledge of offenders, such as nicknames, whereabouts and telephone numbers. The criterion is that the information provided for by the collaborator should substantially contribute to a successful prosecution, but that can be achieved in many ways. In the interviews, we tried to discover what type of information is normally demanded of the collaborator by the police and the justice department.

The two interviewed public prosecutors were diametrically opposed concerning what information is valuable, although they both specialize in prosecuting organized crime. One of the public prosecutors [7] declared that:

> "Information about the structure or something like that is of no use to me. I do not need such information. The collaborator must give something on top of his

or her own confession so that we can prosecute other people.[138] For example, when we investigate a biker group, there are persons who want to provide us with background information. For example, nicknames, who are members, what role someone has and more. I have to make it clear to the potential collaborator that this is not the kind of information I am looking for".[139]

The other prosecutor [6] gave an example of a member of a foreign criminal organization and explicitly highlighted the importance of background information:

"They have someone, a collaborator from the mafia, and he or she can provide us with information about the language the organization uses, the code used. Information about the structure of the organization and information about capo regimes. Who plays what role in the organization? This is, as I would term it, soft data and it is invaluable".[140]

One reason why these prosecutors take opposing views about the value of background information may be that, as the second prosecutor mentioned, the practice and the courts do not really know how to value the information because most of the time it is only used as a starting point for further investigations and not as a foundation for a prosecution. Therefore, it may be problematic to get the court to apply the general *Kronzeugen* provision of Section 46b StGB because the value of the information for a successful prosecution is unclear. Nevertheless, as mentioned before, the court has several options for taking collaboration into account. As part of the sentencing decision, the court can mitigate the sentence when the person has provided information about other crimes (Section 46 StGB). However, the precise mitigation is unclear, while Section 46b StGB gives clear-cut information about the minimum and maximum sentences which apply.

Another reason why the prosecutors have opposing views may be related to how the provisions are applied to specific crimes. According to one public prosecutor [7] and the legal scholars, the general collaborators provision is mainly applied to moderate property crime (which is in a certain contradiction to the legislator's aim). One legal scholar [9]

---

138 "Also mit irgendwelchen strukturerhellenden Angaben oder ähnlichem mehr kann ich nichts anfangen, brauche ich nicht. Da muss Butter bei die Fische, das heißt, es müssen Angaben erfolgen, die zu Anklage für Urteile weiterer Personen führen können."

139 "Um ein Beispiel zu nennen, wenn Sie gegen eine Rockergruppierung ermitteln, werden Sie auch Personen treffen, die bereit sind, Hintergrundangaben zu einer Gruppierung zu machen. Also beispielsweise, wer welchen Spitznamen trägt, wer Mitglied ist, ob jemand in seiner Funktion sich noch befindet oder ähnliches mehr. Und dann muss man solchen Personen klar machen, darum geht es hier nicht."

140 "Sie haben jemanden, einen Kronzeugen aus einer Mafiaorganisation, der uns bestimmte An-gaben machen kann zum Thema, welche Sprache wird benutzt, weiß nicht, vielleicht Code-wörter. Wie sind bestimmte Strukturen. Also wie ist das organisiert im Sinne wirklich/ Also gibt es tatsächlich, wie man ja immer, also Mafia oder sonst was oder (unv.) strukturen oder Clanstrukturen. Wer spielt welche Rolle. Es gibt, sage ich mal, weiche Daten, die für uns unschätzbar wertvoll sind."

gave the following case as a typical example of collaboration: while drinking, three people form a plan to rob a gas station. After they succeed in stealing goods from a closed gas station, one of the three is arrested. He turns on his co-conspirators and is treated by the court as a collaborator. The public prosecutor [7] stated that the German practice, especially with regard to the general collaborators provision, has nothing to do with turning 'big fish' to catch even larger 'fish'.[141] An accused that turns on his or her co-perpetrators falls under the general provision, and that is the stereotypical application.

By contrast, in cases against large criminal organizations, such as the mafia or biker gangs, and in terrorism cases, the police and public prosecutor's office rely heavily on background information. According to the defence lawyer specializing in crimes against the State and terrorism [3], the police and the public prosecutor's office are mostly interested in background information.

> "Especially of interest is information by which structures can be recognized and on which, without further information and without any compulsory power, certain investigative methods can be applied such as a telephone tapping, search and seizure, maybe even pretrial detention. In short, information that can lead to further investigation".[142]

So, it seems that the diametrically opposed views of the public prosecutors interviewed are in some way related to a heterogeneous assessment of the question of which crimes should be prosecuted with the aid of a collaborator. The first public prosecutor [6] tended to focus on the help of collaborators in prosecuting serious and organized crime. The second public prosecutor [7] focuses on other crimes, such as the narcotics user turning on his or her dealer (and not on the organization which imports or processes the narcotics).

When the collaborator provides information about offences that have already been committed, it remains unclear whether he or she should disclose all known information. In principle, the public prosecutors and judges stated that they do not like to be surprised during the subsequent course of the proceedings with new and incriminating information that the collaborator had not already disclosed. However, in practice the idea that a collaborator should disclose all his or her information is – not least with respect to the

---

141 "Nein, also mit großen Fischen hat man es da nicht zu tun und da muss man auch ganz offen sagen, unsere Arbeit hat auch nicht mit großen Fischen zu tun. Also die deutschen Strafverfolgungsbehörden sind nicht so ausgestattet, weder personell noch technisch, dass sie mit großen Fischen in irgendeiner Weise konkurrieren KÖNNTEN. Also deutsche Bekämpfung organisierter Kriminalität bewegt sich am mittleren und unteren Spektrum der organisierten Kriminalität."

142 "Das ist ja das, was man am liebsten hätte. Also dass man Strukturen erkennt, ja, und weitergehende Hinweise auch auf Beteiligte und solche Informationen, die dann Grundlage sind, ohne Zwangsmaßnahmen durchgesetzt werden. Also TKÜ-Beschlüsse, Wohnungsdurchsuchungen, vielleicht auch Haftbefehle. [...] All das, was dann Grundlage für weitere Ermittlungsmaßnahmen sein kann."

danger that may ensue from the disclosure of all information – unlikely. As a public prosecutor [6] stated:

> "The agreement is that you will disclose all information – but of course, I know that you will not disclose information about some murder(s) – or leave it at that".[143]

Lastly, with regard to the information the authorities are looking for, both public prosecutors made it very clear that the collaborator first has to deliver. He or she has to disclose the information and only after full disclosure (more or less) will the authorities fulfill their promises.

> "You have to be very consistent, because the suspect may have the impression that two people are sitting at the table in an equal position. That is not the case, instead the suspect has to deliver first and subsequently we will deliver, we will keep to our agreement" [6].[144]

One of the defence lawyers mitigated these statements slightly. They declared that it mainly depends on the strength of the position of the collaborator. When we put the above quote before this lawyer [5], they responded:

> "It also depends on how important the collaborator is to the authorities. When the collaborator is a major narcotics trafficker who has extensive knowledge about the distribution network, smuggle routes and organizational structures, then the defence is in a strong position because the authorities will be very interested in that information. As far as I can remember, it was not an easy process. The suspect demanded undertakings, some were accepted but others were not. It was a constant back and forth between us and the authorities".[145]

---

143 "[W]eil der Deal ist eigentlich, entweder du sagst es jetzt vollständig, Klammer auf, die Morde werden sie uns nicht einräumen, das ist klar, aber entweder du sagst es vollständig oder lass es sein."

144 "Da muss man sehr, sehr konsequent auftreten, weil Beschuldigte teilweise den Eindruck gewinnen können, man würde da gleichberechtigt miteinander am Tisch sitzen. Das ist nicht der Fall, sondern es ist so, dass ein Beschuldigter liefern muss und wir dann anschließend liefern, alle Zusagen erfüllen."

145 "[W]eil das hat auch natürlich auch damit zu tun, wie wichtig ist der Zeuge für die Ermittlungsbehörden. Also wenn das ein, sagen wir mal, ein Dealer ist, der in großen Mengen Betäubungsmittel verkauft und der also in dessen Augen einen erheblichen Überblick hat über Distributionswege, auch über Lieferwege großer Mengen von Betäubungsmitteln oder andere Strukturen, was kann man? [...] [W]enn ein solcher Zeuge von großem Interesse für die Ermittlungsbehörden ist [...] Aber da ist nach meiner Erinnerung, der hat immer wieder Bedingungen gestellt der Angeklagte, denen dann zum Teil entsprochen, zum Teil auch nicht entsprochen wurde, ich weiß, es war ein langes Hin und Her mit vielen, auch Verärgerungen auf beiden Seiten, also es war nicht so einfach."

To sum up, in general – for middle-range crimes – the authorities are looking for detailed information about an offence committed but the collaborator is not required to disclose literally all the information known to him or her. Collaboration to prevent crimes almost never occurs in practice. In addition, when fighting organized crime the authorities also appear to look for background information, but it remains unclear how such information should be evaluated in the context of the *Kronzeugen* provision and/or the general sentencing decision. The public prosecutors were very clear on the point that the collaborator must make the first move and disclose the information, but one defence lawyer stated that this largely depends on the strength of the collaborator's position.

4.5.3.3   Connectivity (*Konnexität*)

The legislator reduced the scope of the *Kronzeugen* provision with the aforementioned legal reform of 2013 by determining that only offenders that can provide information about an offence that has a connection with their own offence can qualify for sentence mitigation, the requirement of connectivity (*Konnexitätserfordernis*). Because this criterion reduces the range of people qualifying for sentence mitigation, it potentially plays a (significant) role in the recruitment of potential collaborators and/or in the procedure of becoming a collaborator. Therefore, we asked the interviewees if and how the requirement of connectivity plays a role in the practice.

Some of the interviewees, the judges, scholars and public prosecutors, confirmed the view expressed in the literature that in theory the requirement of connectivity reduces the scope of the provision. However, all interviewees found that the requirement does not play a significant role in practice. The defence lawyer specializing in crimes against the State and terrorism [3] stated that although the requirement does not apply to the crime-specific provision of a criminal organization and terrorism, the requirement would not provide any difficulties in those cases in any event because such crimes are always committed by a group of people. Therefore, there would always be a connection. The second defence lawyer [4] interviewed responded to our question if and how the requirement of connection plays a role in practice bluntly: "No. Full stop!"[146] The appeals court judge [1] confirmed this: "In normal cases, in normal constellations, there will always be a connection."[147]

A point of criticism came from the same judge [1]. They could understand the need to reduce the scope for the use of collaborators because the use of this instrument is always problematic and invokes considerable discussion. What they could not understand is why the same requirement applies to the collaborators provision regarding the prevention of

---

146 "Nein. Punkt."
147 "Also die normalen Konstellationen, in den normalen Konstellationen wird es vermutlich immer einen Zusammenhang geben."

crimes. The prevention of serious crimes with the aid of a collaborator should always be of interest, whether or not *Konnexität* can be established.[148]

4.5.3.4   The 'Gentlemen's Agreement'

In the German Criminal Code, the judge is the competent authority to apply the collaborators provision and to reduce the sentence or to exempt the collaborator from punishment. This means that the police and the public prosecutor cannot make any binding promises. According to one public prosecutor [7], it is important to point out clearly that it is the judge who is the ultimate authority with regard to the determination of the sanctions, and that there are some judges who are stricter, while others are less strict.

> "I do not have any influence over the matter of who will judge a particular case. The only thing that I can do is to put forward the notion during the trial that the offender should be given a milder sentence because of his collaboration and, furthermore, I can promise to ask for a conditional punishment. But still, I have to make it clear that I cannot give any guarantees regarding the form and the duration of the penalty".[149]

Because they cannot make binding promises, the two public prosecutors explicitly stated that they explain the procedure very clearly to the collaborator in order to prevent further uncertainties and disputes. The main point for the authorities is to create a basis of trust (because that is their only option given that they cannot make binding agreements).

> "What we can do and what we cannot do must be made clear. Honesty, and that we try not to create any illusions regarding the undertakings, in my experience, provides the basis for a relationship of trust with the collaborator" [6].[150]

Trust is necessary not only for the case at hand, but for all later cases too. Both public prosecutors and the two defence lawyers ([3] and [4]) underlined the importance of honoring the 'gentlemen's agreement'. Both public prosecutors expressed that once they had a bad reputation because agreements were not honored, defence lawyers would ad-

---

148 Eschelbach, in: Satzger/Schluckebier/Widmaier, StGB, 3rd edition 2016, § 46b rn. 27 is also critical about the practicability of this prerequisite.

149 "[I]ch habe keinen Einfluss darauf, wer Richter im konkreten Fall wird. Das Einzige, was ich machen kann, ist, eine Aussage zu treffen, dass aus unserer Sicht einen milderen Antrag erzeugt und ich kann auch mal beispielsweise die Aussage treffen, wenn das ALLES ist, wenn das was hier geliefert ist und nicht mehr dazu kommt, was ihre Person betrifft, dann werde ich einen Strafantrag stellen im bewährungsfähigen Bereich. Ich kann und da muss ich aber auch gleich fairerweise immer dazu sagen, dass ich keine Garantie geben kann, ob das Gericht einem solchem Antrag folgt."

150 "Was können wir, was können wir nicht. Und ich habe die Erfahrung gemacht, dadurch dass man ehrlich ist und nicht versucht, Illusionen zu wecken, dass dadurch auch Grundvertrauen geschaffen werden kann."

vise their clients not to collaborate with them, which would make life as a prosecutor specializing in organized crime very difficult.

> "I represent the whole organized crime unit. And if I dishonor agreements, then our unit will be practically dead. Discredited. The whole process only functions if I honor the agreement, because the collaborator has taken a risk, a considerable personal risk. And not only physically, but also socially. They must leave the contacts, friends and relationships of past decades behind them. When the collaborator puts him or herself in such a position, the least I can do is to keep my promises" [6].[151]

The same is true for defence lawyers. If they dishonor an agreement, public prosecutors will not make deals with them in future cases, which will put their clients at a disadvantage (not only regarding possible collaboration but also concerning other agreements that a prosecutor and a defence lawyer can make). However, their position in the collaborators procedure is described as problematic because, even if the public prosecutors honor the agreement, they are left with uncertainty about the court's decision.

4.5.3.5 Conclusion

Based on the information obtained in the interviews, the police appears to be the initiating force in recruiting collaborators but does this in a somewhat cautious manner, i.e. during the instruction before the first interrogation. One of the main reasons for trying to recruit collaborators as soon as possible is because the German Criminal Code sets a deadline on the collaborators procedure. The collaborator must have disclosed the information regarding a third party before the start of the trial mainly because the statement can be verified and supporting evidence can be searched for in time. The court can then assess the reliability and value of the statement and conclude if the statement is false or suitable to lay the foundations for the successful prosecution of the third party.

One of the characteristic features of the collaborators procedure in German law is the uncertainty of the agreement. In the interviews, the 'agreement' made between the authorities and the collaborator is labeled a 'gentlemen's agreement' (which is honored most of the time). The public prosecutor cannot make any binding promises regarding the sentence (mitigation). It depends entirely on the application of the provision by the court, although courts appear to honor the agreement in most cases. The sentence mitigation is facultative and the court has wide discretion in choosing the sentence between

---

151 "Ich stehe dann ja auch für eine Abteilung. Und dann ist praktisch die Abteilung tot. Diskreditiert. [...] Aber das Ganze funktioniert nur, wenn ich honoriere, dass diese Leute ein Risiko, ein erhebliches persönliches Risiko eingehen. Nicht nur körperlicher Art, auch, ich sage mal, sozialer Art. Die müssen ihre gesamten jahrzehntelangen Bindungen möglicherweise aufgeben oder riskieren das zumindest und das muss man honorieren."

the minimum and maximum sentence prescribed. The courts have not sought to structure this discretion. This leaves the collaborator in the dark. He or she has to disclose information but has no idea of the benefit of doing so in regard to the sentence. A further disadvantage for the defence is that they have to commit themselves to a certain strategy at an early point in the investigation (while not knowing what the outcome will be).

4.5.4   Implementation and Scrutiny of the Undertakings

4.5.4.1   Undertakings Outside the Legal Framework of Section 46b and 49 StGB

The law on undertakings made to collaborators in the German Criminal Code is clear: the court can mitigate the sentence and, in exceptional cases, exempt from punishment. Although the law does not mention any other undertakings, in practice the picture is different. The topics discussed between the authorities and potential collaborators are: (a) immigration and right to residence; (b) pre-trial detention; (c) financial aspects; (d) decision not to prosecute and; (e) prison regime. What these undertakings have in common, is that the public prosecutor is the competent authority regarding these issues – whereas the court is the authority in deciding on the sentence mitigation – and he or she can therefore agree with a (potential) collaborator of justice to not file for pre-trial detention for example.

Both public prosecutors interviewed mentioned that immigration law is the most often discussed topic and is extremely important for many collaborators. According to them, the topic collaborators are most interested in is the right to residence in Germany. One public prosecutor [6] stated that in their experience in 95 percent of the organized crime cases the suspects have a (first or second) foreign nationality. The position of the public prosecutor in immigration law regarding collaborators is strong because Section 72 (4) of the Act on the Residence, Economic Activity and Integration of Foreigners in the Federal Territory (*Gesetz über den Aufenthalt, die Erwerbstätigkeit und die Integration von Ausländern im Bundesgebiet*, abbreviated: I) states that "a foreigner against whom legal proceedings are instituted by a public authority or preliminary investigations are instituted under criminal law may only be expelled or deported in consultation with the competent public prosecutor's office."[152] When the immigration service knows that the foreigner is subject to criminal investigation or is being prosecuted, they are required to consult with the public prosecutor about the right to reside.[153] The immigration service cannot reach a decision in such cases without consultation.

A second undertaking in which the public prosecutor has a strong position is pre-trial detention. As one of the public prosecutors [6] mentioned, when they still worked in

---

152 Translation <https://www.gesetze-im-internet.de/englisch_aufenthg/englisch_aufenthg.html>, last retrieved on 22 November 2016.
153 OLG Düsseldorf 21 December 1994 – 3 Wx 649/94, *NVwZ* 1995, 727.

'white collar' crime the first topic most suspects wanted to discuss was revocation of the pretrial detention decision.

> "When a suspect can prove that he poses no flight risk, then we can promise that deprivation of liberty will only start after the trial and that we will not demand pretrial detention. That is a promise we can make because we are not dependent on a third party concerning that decision. Therefore, we can talk about that with the collaborator as part of the deal."[154]

Further parts of the discussion include aspects of the imprisonment. For example, collaborators are interested in a (wholly or partially) conditional sentence. Furthermore, Section 456a StPO gives the public prosecutor's office as the competent authority (*Vollstredungsbehörde*) the possibility of dispensing with a prison sentence if the convicted person (*inter alia*) is removed from the territorial scope of the StPO. In some cases it may be of interest to the collaborator of justice to force this issue, and as a result this becomes part of the undertakings. Though the authorities have no direct influence on the penalty, they can offer the collaborator some benefits regarding his or her deprivation of liberty.

Financial aspects can also be part of the agreement. This can take many forms, including financial compensation, no confiscation of certain goods or repayment of social security benefits. According to one public prosecutor [6], the first of these two topics are those that collaborators most often ask about. The financial aspect is secondary, but may still be of interest to the collaborator as the two following quotes show:

> "What can hurt the collaborator, and is therefore also an important aspect of the discussion, is the confiscation of a car. For a lot of suspects their car is more important than one year more in prison. It sounds absurd, but it is true."[155]

Regarding this statement, one has to bear in mind that the confiscation of illegally obtained assets is mandatory if the prerequisites of Sections 73 StGB et seq. are met. Although Section 421 StPO allows for a waiver of confiscation under certain conditions, it is doubtful whether the prosecutorial authorities are allowed to make the aspect of confiscation subject to undertakings with the accused.[156]

---

154 "Wenn ein Beschuldigter glaubhaft machen kann, dass er keine Fluchtabsichten hat, kann man einem solchen Beschuldigten beispielsweise auch die Zusage erteilen, dass er den Haftantritt erst in der Vollstreck-ung haben wird und nicht in der Untersuchungshaft. Das ist etwas, das können wir zusagen, da sind wir nicht von Dritten abhängig und das ist etwas, wo man dann auch ohne Einschränkungen sagen kann, wenn das und das kommt, wird von uns kein Haftantrag gestellt. Und das ist etwas, worüber man dann tatsächlich umfassend reden kann."

155 "Also das sind Verhandlungen, die schmerzt teilweise die Wegnahme so eines Pkw mehr, als ob sie noch ein Jahr mehr oder so in Haft haben. Das hört sich jetzt absurd an, ist aber so."

156 For a detailed analysis see Ordner 2017, p. 50 et seq.

"It is an open secret. The authorities can say that the collaborator must pay back all the social security benefits received. 'We will pay you for collaborating, but you have to reimburse all the wrongly received benefits'. Do you know what the collaborator will say? He will say: 'try solving those crimes without my help'." [4].[157]

However, as mentioned by the leader of a witness protection team, a collaborator who is placed in the witness protection program will not receive more income than he or she received legally before being placed in the program.[158]

Furthermore, the public prosecutor can decide not to prosecute a criminal offence under certain circumstances, especially if the crime will not significantly add to the penalty in relation to other crimes for which the suspect will be prosecuted and when a decision may not be expected within a reasonable period of time (Section 154 (1) StPO). One public prosecutor [6] stated very clearly that not every offence has equal importance to the public prosecutor's office. Therefore in some cases it is possible to discuss the option of Section 154 StPO.

A further theme discussed during the negotiations is the prison regime in which the collaborator will be placed. It has a certain appeal to collaborators to be placed in a more open regime after a certain time or even from the beginning. Again, with regard to the latter aspect it should be noted that if the legal prerequisites for placement in an open institution or for leave from custody are met, these measures are, in principle, mandatory. Therefore, if the prosecutorial authorities were to make these measures subject to undertakings with potential collaborators, this would raise constitutional concerns.[159]

4.5.4.2   Scrutiny of the Undertakings

The defence lawyers mentioned their weak position after negotiating such undertakings. One defence lawyer [3] stated that they had three or four clients who complained afterwards that the authorities did not deliver all parts of the deal, for example, commitments made with respect to the right of residence. The position of the defence is weak because, as mentioned by a public prosecutor [6] in the next quote, not all the details will be documented (mostly because the documentation of certain aspects of the deal could

---

157 "Das ist ein offenes Geheimnis. Er könnte ja sagen, es stimmt nicht, ich muss die Sozialhilfe zurückzahlen. Aber Sie können ja mal dem ausländischen Dealer, der abgeschoben werden soll, dem können Sie ja mal sagen, wenn du das Geld jetzt kriegst, die Fangprämie, aber die Stütze, die du in der Zeit bekommen hast, die musst du jetzt schön zurückzahlen. Ja, wissen Sie, was der Ihnen sagt? Dann sagt der, macht euren Kram mal alleine."

158 "Es gibt einen Grundsatz im Zeugenschutz, dass eine Schutzperson durch die Aufnahme in den Zeugenschutz nicht bessergestellt werdend darf."

159 It would go beyond the scope of this article to discuss the general limitations for negotiated agreements in German Criminal Procedure in detail. For an in-depth discussion regarding white-collar-crime procedures see Lindemann 2012, p. 461 et seq.

also pose a risk to the collaborator's well-being). The deal is also not transparent because it depends on the circumstances of the case if the conversations with the collaborator form part of the case file.

> "There will be a document in any case. There are no conversations in my practice that take place completely off the record. It remains unclear however, where the documents are filed and I cannot answer that question in general. It could be that they are filed in the case file, we also have a personal 'file' on the case and, of course, there are also the barred documents under Section 96 StPO. It depends on the case, where the documents are filed. When I negotiated with a collaborator who is not prosecuted in the same case as the persons on whom he or she provided information but in a separate trial, then the conversation with the collaborator will not be filed in detail in the case of the other suspects".[160]

All three defence lawyers confirmed that these deals are non-transparent, especially the circumstances regarding financial aspects.

In summary, although the provisions of the StGB do not mention any other undertakings than sentence mitigation and exemption from punishment, a broader array of possible undertakings has developed in practice, i.e. (1) immigration and residence rights; (2) pretrial detention; (3) financial aspects; (4) decision not to prosecute and; (5) prison regime. Because not every detail is documented and it depends on the circumstances of the case where the document is filed, the undertakings are not transparent. This has led to problems for collaborators and/or defence lawyers. Firstly, a collaborator cannot prove his or her claim on certain undertakings because there is no detailed written agreement. Secondly, the defence lawyers do not know if promises have been made to the collaborator that could affect the reliability of the statements.

4.5.4.3   Scrutiny in General

One of the general problems regarding the application of the collaborators provisions is scrutiny of the agreement. This is no different in Germany. The judges, public prosecutors and defence lawyers all stated very clearly that not every detail will be documented. One defence lawyer [3] and one public prosecutor [6], respectively, described

---

160 "Also dokumentiert wird es auf jeden Fall. Es gibt, bei mir jetzt jedenfalls keine Gespräche, die in luftleerem Raum stattfinden. Die Frage ist nur, wo wird das dokumentiert und die kann man nicht pauschal beantworten letztlich. Es gibt die Verfahrensakten, es gibt die Handakten und es gibt natürlich gesperrte Vorgänge oder zu sperrende Vorgänge nach 96 StPO. Und das sind Einzelfallfragen, was wo rein kommt. Wenn ich einen Kronzeugen habe, der in einem Verfahren gegen mehrere Beschuldigte nicht selbst auf der Bank sitzen wird, sondern in einem anderen Verfahren, wird in dem Verfahren, in dem er Aussagen machen wird, nicht im Detail in der Akte stehen, was Gesprächsinhalt mit diesem Kronzeugen war."

more or less the same situation as an example of the absence of transparency and the possibility of scrutiny.

> "Sometimes the transcript of a conversation with a collaborator shows that it started at 13:05 and ended at 17:30, but it has only three pages of *verbatim* drawn up protocol. Then you ask yourself, what happened in there all that time"?[161]

> "The transcript shows that the conversation started at 9:00 and ended at 17:10 but it resulted in only one page".[162]

The public prosecutor [6] also stated that they will document that a conversation took place and that he or she will be available as a witness at trial. The other public prosecutor [7] stated that a *verbatim* protocol can put the collaborator in a dangerous position. Therefore, it is assumed to be necessary to exclude information.

As one defence lawyer [3] mentioned, it is not only the transparency of the agreement and the scrutiny of the information as such, that are problematic. Very often it will not be stated with whom the collaborator spoke and where. It will be impossible to determine whether the complete statement came about independently of another person's influence and what kind of undertakings were offered (which can also affect reliability).

> "Sometimes the collaborator is joined at the trial by five, six, seven armed agents of the *Bundeskriminalamt*. Of course, they talked with the chief judge about this team and the protection of the collaborator, but the defence was not informed of this meeting. Furthermore, sometimes the collaborator will be assisted by an attorney and they will both gather information. This results in a collaborator who is prepared by the authorities and his lawyer to make a statement at the trial but the defence does not know who this collaborator talked to, where he or she disclosed information and what he or she already knows about the case".[163]

---

161 "Manchmal ist der Beginn der Vernehmung, sagen wir, um 13.05 Uhr, Ende 17.30 Uhr und das Protokoll hat nur drei Seiten. Da fragen Sie sich natürlich, was ist eigentlich in der ganzen Zeit passiert?"

162 "Da stand drin, Beginn 9.00 Uhr morgens, Ende 17.10 Uhr und Sie hatten eine Seite Vernehmungsprotokoll."

163 "Dann kommt er in die Hauptverhandlung und hat zum Beispiel einen Zeugenschutz, der darin besteht, dass er von fünf, sechs, sieben bewaffneten BKA-Beamten begleitet wird, die vorher mit dem Vorsitzenden natürlich Gespräche geführt haben, über die wir nicht informiert werden. Der bekommt regelmäßig einen Zeugenbeistand beigeordnet, das macht das Gericht eigentlich schon von sich aus nach meinen Erfahrungen, ohne dass er das beantragen muss im Gegensatz zu anderen Zeugen. Der Zeugenbeistand verschafft sich Informationen, indem der Akteneinsicht beantragt. [...] Und dann ist es so, dass da ein vorbereiteter Zeuge kommt, von dem wir nicht wissen, mit wem der eigentlich schon überall gesprochen hat, wo der überall schon Aussagen gemacht hat, was der alles schon weiß. [...] Und wir sitzen alle da und wissen eigentlich gerade nicht, wie viel dieser konkrete Zeuge über seinen Zeugenbeistand über unser Verfahren schon weiß."

Even if the collaborator can be questioned at the trial, this does not mean that the defence (or the court) will get all the answers they are interested in, as was mentioned by a judge [1], a public prosecutor [6] and the defence lawyers. The collaborator must sign a contract of silence and needs permission to answer questions, and although this does not necessarily mean that his or her obligation to testify as a witness is suspended,[164] serious barriers to establishing the truth can arise if the court accepts the collaborator's refusal to testify. However, in the view of the leader of a witness protection unit, the courts tend to treat every witness equally and it is not the case that a witness from the protection program is treated differently.[165] The interviewee confirmed that the obligation to testify also applies to people who are part of a witness protection program.[166] In contrast, one defence lawyer [4] stated that the authorities will not allow the collaborator to answer any questions about tactical details of the procedure (and appear to succeed with this strategy in court).

> "A part of the trial will consist of answers by the collaborator in the sense of "I cannot answer that question because a truthful answer could lead to prosecution for violation of a duty of secrecy".[167]

To sum up, we may conclude from our data that there appears to be an unresolved conflict between the aim to keep the details of the witness protection program confidential and the jurisprudence of the Federal Court of Justice regarding the principal necessity for openness.[168] In our opinion, this aspect of the collaboration practice should be made the object of a future in-depth examination.

4.5.4.4   Conclusion

Based on the German Criminal Code, the only undertakings that may be made to collaborators are sentence mitigation and exemption from punishment. Although the law also provides for facultative mitigation grounds, the structure of the sentence framework is clear and explicitly applied in this way as shown by citations of court decisions.

---

164 See BGH 15 December 2005 – 3 StR 281/04, StV 2006, 171 which states that questions regarding the circumstances of intake into the witness protection program may not immediately be rejected, but that it is up to the court to decide on a case-by-case basis whether the information asked for is of any relevance to the case at hand. Additionally, permission to give evidence by the police authorities is not a general requirement for admissibility of the collaborator's statement.

165 "Also die Gerichte sind schon ziemlich genau. Der Zeuge im Zeugenschutz wird genauso behandelt wie jeder andere auch. Das Institut was wir haben, bewirkt nicht, dass er irgendwie in Watte gepackt wird."

166 "Die Aussageverpflichtung des Zeugen ist da und die ist auch nicht schön aber das erfährt man erst dann, wenn man vor Gericht gewesen ist."

167 "[E]in Teil unserer Hauptverhandlung hat dann damit zu tun, dass er immer sagte, ich kann, ich darf nichts sagen, weil ich mich strafbar machen würde, wenn ich hier wahrheitsgemäße Angaben machen würde, weil ich ja eben zur Geheimhaltung verpflichtet bin".

168 See footnote 164.

Although the framework, the range between minimum and maximum sentences, is clear, the court has wide discretion for mitigation within this framework.

Besides sentence mitigation, the authorities seem to use some other 'undertakings', which are mostly procedural decisions made (or influenced) by the prosecution and result in a benefit for the collaborator. For example, the collaborator will not be placed in pre-trial detention, goods will not be confiscated, the public prosecutor can instruct the immigration service that the suspect may not be deported and can decide not to prosecute some minor offences. As we have stated above, the inclusion of the issues at hand in the negotiations with a potential collaborator may give rise to criticism, given that the suspect may already have a legal right to such benefits. Additionally, these deals are usually part of a 'gentlemen's agreement'. Therefore, the collaborator cannot prove his or her claim if the authorities do not deliver (which they usually seem to do, though). Furthermore, the defence has no an idea about what contact there has been between the authorities and the collaborator or what kind of undertakings have been offered for the collaboration.

> "The procedure is in large parts closed. Sometimes something seeps through but I do not know if that is enough when information seeps through only sometimes, right?" [4].[169]

4.5.5 Relationship to Witness Protection

The relationship between the *Kronzeugen* provisions and the law on witness protection is a difficult one. As previously mentioned, most cases of collaboration with justice seem to take place at the lower impact levels of crimes and therefore many collaborators will have no need for witness protection. One of the defence lawyers [5] who also defended collaborators, stated that only two of their collaborating clients were placed in a witness protection program. However, certain collaborators, especially those who are part of a criminal organization, need some sort of witness protection. But it is by no means automatic that a collaborator will be placed in a witness protection program. Furthermore, not everyone in witness protection will be a criminal, although the leader of a witness protection team stated that most of the people in the program are charged suspects or convicted criminals.

The witness protection team is a specialist police unit. They are not involved in investigating crimes in any shape or form, because the possibility of a double role – investigator and protector – could easily come into conflict. This is also why they are completely independent of other police units and the justice department.[170] The

---

169 "Das ist weitestgehend verschlossen. Es sickert mal was durch, aber ich weiß nicht, ob es ausreicht, wenn mal was durchsickert, ja?"
170 See Heubrock et al. 2013, p. 60.

investigating police officers, the public prosecutor or the court cannot decide to place a witness in the program, but an assessment by the public prosecutor of the need for protection on the basis of the exclusive knowledge of the witness, is helpful according to the leader of a witness protection team [11].[171]

They further stated that the witness protection program pursues two goals: firstly, the team and the program aim to secure the criminal proceedings by keeping an important witness available, and, secondly, they protect and support the witness in the program. As the leader of a witness protection team [11] mentioned, their work (formally) stops at the door of the court room and from there it is the presiding judge who is responsible for the protection of the witness. However, normally the witness protection officers consult the court about the protection of the witness during the trial (such as the arrangement of the furniture, the seating for the public, the presence of witness protection officers during the trial, etc.). The court has no obligation to comply with the recommendations arising from the consultation.[172]

As mentioned above, the public prosecutor and the court do not have the competence to place a collaborator in the program. One judge [6] declared that they do not see anything about this in the case file nor hear anything about it during the trial.[173] Furthermore, the public prosecutor cannot make any promises in this sense (and the two prosecutors interviewed stated that they do not know much about the program).

> "I cannot say much about it. I do not take part in the placement in the program and I do not have any responsibilities in the program. The only thing that I must do is make an assessment of whether a collaborator needs protection. Everything beyond that is not my responsibility. I cannot make a binding promise to a collaborator that he or she will be placed in the program. The police have to check whether all the criteria for placement in the program are met." [7][174]

---

171 "Die Voraussetzungen für die Aufnahme in den Zeugenschutz stehen im § 1 ZSHG. Und eine Voraussetzung ist die nach einem gewissen Exklusivwissen. Wenn ich jetzt einen Staatsanwalt habe, der mit das so für sein Strafverfahren „bescheinigt"; dann ist das so und diese Voraussetzung für die Aufnahme in den Zeugenschutz wäre erfüllt."

172 "Und sie hören sich das auf jeden Fall an und entscheiden dann für ihren Gerichtssaal, das ist so ihr Wohnzimmer, ob sie bestimmte sitzungspolizeiliche Maßnahmen haben wollen oder nicht. Und wir geben nur die Hinweise, dass wir unsere Maßnahmen bis vor die Haustür, also bis zum Sitzungssaal so in einer bestimmten Art und Weise machen wollen. Wir sagen aber auch in dieser Beratung eindeutig, dass wir die Erwartungshaltung haben, dass wir unsere, unsere Schutzpersonen gerne entsprechend in den Gerichtssaal begleiten wollen."

173 "Aber wie gesagt, vom Zeugenschutz kriegen wir eigentlich überhaupt nichts natürlich mit, weil die ja auch nicht auftauchen und so weiter."

174 "Dazu kann ich Ihnen nur sehr wenig sagen […] Als Staatsanwalt habe ich da nur eine ganz kleine Funktion. Und zwar müssen wir als Staatsanwälte vor dem Einstieg in ein solches Programm natürlich eine Einschätzung abgeben, ob diese Person benötigt wird. Alles andere ist dann nicht mehr Aufgabe der Staatsanwaltschaft. […] jemand eine Zusage zu machen in ein Zeugenschutzprogramm aufgenommen zu werden. Eine solche Zusage kann durch die Justiz nie gemacht werden, weil die Aufnahme in ein Zeugenschutzpro-

"No, I do not play any role during the negotiations regarding witness protection. That is completely separate." [6][175]

On the one hand, it is clear that certain collaborators need some sort of protection, on the other hand, as has already been stated, the position of the collaborator remains uncertain because the public prosecutor cannot make any binding promises. It will be members of the special police unit who will decide whether someone is to be placed in the program. Furthermore, life in the program is really strict, witnesses in the program have to strictly adhere to the instructions of the police.[176]

This disconnection between the *Kronzeugen* provisions and the witness protection program and the nonexistent role of this topic during negotiation is criticized. According to one of the scholars [9], inclusion of the witness protection program in the negotiations could lead to more success in the recruitment of collaborators from criminal organizations. However, the intertwining of the issues in the course of the negotiations could be problematic too, in light of the risk that the decision about the inclusion in the witness protection program would no longer be taken solely on the basis of an assessment of the potential threat the witness is exposed to (which is what the ZSHG requires at this moment).

Furthermore, one defence lawyer [3] and one legal scholar [8] indicated that life in a witness protection program is not easy and many collaborators step out of the program.[177] A defence lawyer [3] referred to the inclusion of three of their clients in the program as a huge disappointment.[178] The leader of a witness protection team [11] and, as the following quote shows, another defence lawyer [5] confirmed this:

"Inclusion in the witness protection program places a substantial burden on the collaborator. He or she has to be very disciplined and to show complete obedience to the public officials of the *Landeskriminalamt*. Some collaborators do not want to lead such a restricted life. I have heard that from a lot of people. In one of

---

gramm voraussetzt, dass die Person Eignungskriterien erfüllt, die durch die Polizei eigenständig überprüft werden."

175 "{Haben Sie dann auch mit der Verhandlung über das Programm zu tun?} Nein. Also das ist ganz separat."

176 "Wir haben Menschen im Zeugenschutz, da werden die Maßnahmen beendet nach einem halben Jahr, weil die Zusammenarbeit nicht funktioniert hat, weil Absprachen nicht eingehalten wurden, weil einfach Voraussetzungen weggefallen sind. Aber wir haben auch, und da sind wir bei der Gefährdung, wenn man eine Gefährdung nicht minimieren kann, die dauerhaft vorhanden ist, dann bleibt im Grunde genommen schon das Instrument des Zeugenschutzes auch ein Leben lang."

177 Cf. also the examples at Heubrock et al. 2013, p. 64 et seq.

178 "Also in den drei Fällen, die ich jetzt konkret erinnere, waren das aber hinterher sehr sehr große Enttäuschungen. Die Betroffenen haben nur ganz kurze Zeit im Zeugenschutzprogramm ausgehalten, einmal ein halbes Jahr, einmal drei Monate. Also alles unter einem halben Jahr."

my cases in which I dealt with a collaborator, the collaborator was forced to leave the witness protection program. He or she did not stick to the conditions".[179]

4.5.6   Use of Evidence and Punishment

Section 46b StGB states that sentence mitigation or exemption from punishment can be granted to a collaborator who has substantially contributed to the discovery of a serious offence (falling under Section 100a (2) of the Code of Criminal Procedure) by voluntarily disclosing his or her knowledge. This contribution can take the form of information to start further investigation or that of a statement that can be used as evidence in a trial. Furthermore, as indicated above and stated by one public prosecutor [6] and the BKartA public official [10], collaboration can have two more beneficial effects, i.e. that it shortens the procedure because the cooperation of one suspect can persuade other suspects to collaborate, too. We will discuss these four options for using the collaborator's statement below. Thereafter, we will look at the reliability of the collaborator's statement as described by the interviewees. We will also describe the system of sentence mitigation in the context of the punishment of collaborators. Lastly, the difficulties at the trial created by the concurrent *Kronzeugen* provisions will be discussed.

4.5.6.1   Use of the Statements of the Collaborator of Justice

As one public prosecutor [7] stated, most courts are not thrilled when proof of evidence is based on a collaborator.

> "The court will know that when I use a collaborator, half the trial time will be consumed by a discussion of the reliability of the statements made by the collaborator. There will be lots of questions about the negotiations and requests about the process. The best way to use a collaborator is as supporting evidence at a later moment in the trial".[180]

---

179 "[A]ber da der Zeugenschutz ja mit auch erheblichen Auslagen für den betroffenen Zeugen verbunden ist und von ihm auch durchaus eine gewisse Disziplin verlangt und auch eine ziemlich rigorose Folgsamkeit im Hinblick über die Vorschriften, die einem da von den zuständigen Personen der Landeskriminalämter gemacht werden, die das nicht wollen, für die das einfach zu regeln ist. Das habe ich OFT schon gehört. Ich habe auch/ Jetzt gerade in einem Verfahren habe ich so von außen mitbekommen, da bin ich Verteidiger und da ist auch so ein großer wie der, für meinen Mandanten eigentlich nicht/ Also der hat nicht, das für den ein Problem wäre, also da waren viele Angeklagte da. Der ist halt irgendwann, ist er wieder aus dem Zeugenschutzprogramm rausgeflogen, weil er sich einfach nicht an die Auflagen gehalten hat."

180 "Wenn ich eine Anklage an einem Kronzeugen maßgeblich aufhänge, dann kann sich ein Tatrichter aus-rechnen, dass die halbe Verhandlung sich um die Glaubwürdigkeit dieses Kronzeugen drehen wird mit X Anträgen über die Vergangenheit dieses Kronzeugen und ähnliches mehr. [...] sondern ein Kronzeuge sollte im besten Falle lediglich ein die Beweisführung stützendes Element später sein."

As mentioned before, one public prosecutor [6] and the BKartA official [10] stated that one of the desired effects of collaborators' statements is that other suspects will also disclose information. As described below, the reliability of the statement will always be questionable. But when two or more suspects disclose information the evidence becomes much stronger. We have already mentioned a major case involving one of the interviewed public prosecutors. In that case brought against members of a criminal organization who were facing charges concerning weapons and drugs trafficking, extortion and violent crimes, someone in a top position in the organization collaborated. After the other suspects and their defence lawyers saw the wealth of information that the authorities had gathered, also through the statement of the collaborator, three more suspects disclosed information.

A second potential effect of the use of a collaborator's statement is that it can shorten the procedure (at least if there is no extensive debate about the reliability of the facts presented by the collaborator and other suspects following the example of the initial collaborator).

> "If we take this case (S.) as an example [this is the same case mentioned in the last section, ML & DvT], the total in prison sentences was about 60 years. That might have been much more difficult to achieve without the collaborator, at least in the same period of time" [6].[181]

The same public prosecutor [6] gave another example of a case where the suspects operated four large marihuana plantations and that case lasted for a year, in which the chamber concerned could not hear any other cases. The public prosecutor stated that they are definitely always interested in any opportunity to shorten trials. The domino effect itself also has a shortening effect. When more suspects acknowledge the charge, it is no longer necessary to put the collaborator on the stand for an examination. Furthermore, when several suspects collaborate, the reliability of those statements will not be as extensively questioned.

However, in most cases the collaborator has to take the stand mainly because there are always doubts about the reliability of his or her statements. But, as mentioned, during the examination it is very difficult to form an opinion about reliability because the collaborator may refer to his or her obligation to remain silent about the circumstances of his or her intake into the witness protection program, as mentioned by one of the defence lawyers [3]:

> "So, when we have evidence at trial about witness protection, then the protection agreement is something that is hidden from sight. I am really critical

---

181 "Wenn ich mir das hier anschaue, was jetzt zum Beispiel S. angeht, da sind jetzt Freiheitsstrafen von rund 60 Jahren rausgekommen, die ohne entsprechende Aussagen deutlich schwerer möglicherweise zu erreichen gewesen wären, jedenfalls, wenn man sich anschaut, in relativ kurzer Zeit."

about that. It is atypical for our criminal law system that a piece of evidence remains outside the defence's review. And when it is a collaborator who is placed in witness protection that is very very grievous in my opinion because nothing can be examined. We cannot review how great the collaborator's own interest is and some public official of the witness protection program becomes part of the proceedings but is officially not a participant in the trial, and the contact between collaborator and public official is non-transparent".[182]

One of the public prosecutors [7] mentioned the following tactic to demonstrate the reliability of a collaborator. They explained that they will use verifiable parts of the statement that have nothing to do with the charge.[183] An example they mentioned is where a collaborator states that one of the other people in his or her criminal organization receives visits from his or her sister-in-law in prison. This information can easily be verified with the prison visitors list.

Although the German Code of Criminal Procedure does not prescribe any rules of evidence, the courts are of course obliged to give reasons for their judgments, which, in the present context, includes the obligation to adress the reliability of the collaborator's statement. In this respect, the interview partners agreed that collaborators' statements are to be treated with caution. The Federal Court judge stated that in their view judges are well aware of the risks and use such statements with caution because they have no incentive to put an innocent person in jail.[184] This statement is in line with the case-

---

182 "Das ist ja eigentlich etwas, was das Beweismittel, was wir in der Hauptverhandlung haben, zu einem Teil der Überprüfung entzieht. Ich bin da sehr sehr kritisch, was das betrifft. [...] Aber den Zeugenschutz so, wie er von auch/ ich sage mal so vom Gesetzgeber immer ausgefeilt ist, ist aus meiner Sicht eigentlich ein bisschen systemfremd, man muss das Beweismittel ja in irgendeiner Form prüfen können. [...] Und wenn sich das miteinander verknüpft, dann, finde ich, ist das sehr sehr unheilvoll, weil man das nicht mehr kontrollieren kann. Man kann nicht mehr überprüfen, wie groß ist das eigene Interesse und da nimmt jemand Einfluss, der eigentlich nicht Verfahrensbeteiligter ist, auf den Ausgang des Verfahrens, ohne dass eine wirkliche Transparenz und Kontrolle da ist."

183 "Wenn ich dann aber Randwissen dieses Kronzeugen herausarbeite, das objektiv verifizierbar ist, dann ist das natürlich geeignet, die Glaubwürdigkeit des Kronzeugen auch im Kernbereich seiner Aussage zu stützen."

184 "Also dass man jetzt das Gefühl hat, da werden irgendwelche haltlosen Beschuldigungen von irgendwelchen Leuten, die sich sozusagen jetzt nur irgendwie so einen Strafmilderungsgrund verdienen wollen, einfach mal so geglaubt. Den Eindruck gewinnen wir jedenfalls erst mal nicht. [...] Also da hat keiner jetzt irgendwie ernsthaft Lust leichtfertig irgendeinem Dahergelaufenen, sage ich mal jetzt, irgendwas abzunehmen, um dann irgendeinen anderen irgendwie dafür lange irgendwie ins Gefängnis zu bringen. [...] aber in aller Regel ist es einem Richter ja eigentlich völlig egal, ob jetzt der Karl Müller irgendwie ins Gefängnis kommt oder nicht. Sondern der möchte nur, dass er ins Gefängnis kommt, wenn er die Tat begangen hatte und davon muss sich der Richter eben überzeugen und das will der, davon will der sich auch überzeugen, bevor er ihn ins Gefängnis bringt. Niemand hat irgendwie ein Interesse daran, einfach so Leute mal ins Gefängnis zu bringen."

law of the Federal Court of Justice, which also demands careful examination of a collaborator's statement.[185]

As is to be expected in light of their position, two defence lawyers ([3] and [4]) do not agree with the Federal Court judge's statement. In their opinion, the courts are not critical enough in their review of collaborators' statements.

> "My personal opinion is that the courts are not critical enough. They trust the collaborator in advance, when they are faced with him or her. The motto seems to be, he or she must have important information when he or she is treated as a collaborator by the authorities, and then he or she is actually a good guy or girl".[186]

Another defence lawyer [4] stated that in their view, judges tend to believe collaborators because they also make self-incriminating statements.

The assumption that courts tend to believe collaborators is confirmed by a statement made by a public prosecutor and another defence lawyer. The public prosecutor [6] claimed that they did not experience major problems with regard to reliability and application of the general provision of Section 46b StGB and the narcotics crime-specific

---

185 See for example BGH 8 June 2016 – 2 StR 539/15, StV 2016, 774, 775 (ECLI:DE:BGH:2016:080616 U2STR539.15.0): "Ein Zeuge vom Hörensagen ist zwar ein zulässiges Beweismittel, dessen Heranziehung und Bewertung nach den §§ 244 Abs. 2, 261 StPO zu beurteilen ist. Jedoch stellen die begrenzte Zuverlässigkeit dieses Zeugnisses und die Beschränkung der Nachprüfungsmöglichkeiten besondere Anforderungen an die Würdigung. Dies gilt nicht nur in Fällen, in denen die vom Gericht unmittelbar vernommenen Zeugen über Angaben einer anonymen Gewährsperson berichten (…). Dies muss erst recht gelten, wenn ein unmittelbarer Tatzeuge mit seinen Angaben, die einen anderen belasten, zugleich Vorteile i.S.v. § 31 S. 1 Nr. 1 BtMG oder § 46b StGB, einschließlich der Verschonung von U-Haft, erstrebt (…). Dann besteht eine erhöhte Gefahr dafür, dass dieser Belastungszeuge den Angekl. insgesamt zu Unrecht oder jedenfalls zu stark belastet haben könnte, ohne dass dies durch ergänzende Befragung in der Hauptverhandlung überprüft werden kann.
Allein durch sorgfältige Analyse des Aussageinhalts und Überprüfung der Aussagekonstanz kann in einer solchen Konstellation eine möglicherweise zu Unrecht erfolgende oder zu weit gehende Belastung eines anderen nicht ausreichend ausgeschlossen werden. Die allg. Glaubwürdigkeitskriterien erweisen sich in derartigen Fällen, etwa im Hinblick auf die Möglichkeit des »Kronzeugen«, nur die Person eines weiteren Beteiligten im Rahmen der Schilderung eines i.Ü. selbst erlebten Geschehens falsch zu bezeichnen, um dadurch seine eigene größere Tatbeteiligung oder die Beteiligung eines Dritten zu vertuschen, als unzureichend. Der Aufklärungsgehilfe kann in dieser Situation ein schlüssiges Gesamtbild auch dann erzeugen, wenn er nur einen Personentausch vornimmt (…).
Besteht in der Hauptverhandlung in einer solchen Situation auch keine Möglichkeit für das Gericht und die Verteidigung, durch Befragung des Tatzeugen, der erhebliche Eigeninteressen verfolgt, die Glaubhaftigkeit der Fremdbelastung zu überprüfen, ist die Verurteilung nur gerechtfertigt, wenn die belastenden Angaben durch weitere aussagekräftige Indizien unterstützt werden (…). Insoweit geht die Beweiswürdigung des LG von einem rechtlich zutreffenden Ansatz aus."
186 "Ich habe, das ist jetzt meine ganz persönliche Einstellung, aus meiner Sicht zu wenig kritisch. […] Ich glaube, das ist, wenn da jemand in dieser Rolle kommt, hat er einen enormen Vertrauensvorschuss. […]. Also das ist so nach dem Motto, wenn dem das schon angetragen wurde und wenn das schon so ist, dann hat er wichtige Informationen und dann ist das eigentlich auch ein Guter."

provision of Section 31 BtMG.[187] The defence lawyer [5] stated that in their 33 years of practice they did not ever experience a court which said: "we do not believe anything this collaborator is telling us".[188] Therefore, there appears to be a conflict, in theory at least. On the one hand, the use of a collaborator's statement can lead to extended litigation to establish the reliability of the collaborator's statement under the case-law of the Federal Court of Justice and, on the other hand, the interviewees stated that they never experienced problems regarding the court's assessment of the reliability of a collaborator.

To conclude, public prosecutors tend to try to use the collaborator's statement to find more evidence or to turn other suspects because the reliability of a collaborator is always an issue at the trial. According to the defence lawyers, it can be very difficult to assess the reliability of the collaborator at trial because he or she may refer to a contractual binding to remain silent (although this is not completely in line with the case-law of the Federal Court of Justice[189]). Despite all the questions that arise regarding the reliability of the collaborator, one public prosecutor and one defence lawyer stated that they never experienced that a court found the collaborator to be completely unreliable.

4.5.6.2   Punishment of the Collaborator of Justice

It has already been mentioned that the public prosecutor cannot make any binding promises regarding the sentence (mitigation). The trial judge holds sole authority and that puts the collaborator in a difficult position because he or she has to disclose his or her information but cannot be sure what the mitigation will be precisely. In comparison with the general rule of Section 46 StGB, which allows the judge to mitigate the sentence with regard to the offender's conduct after the offence, the collaborators provision offers a more clear-cut mitigation structure. As described above, if the requirements of Section 46b StGB have been met, the court can use a different range of sanctions. The following quotes will show this shift, as applied by a regional court in North Rhine-Westphalia in a case where one of the interview partners was the public prosecutor [6]:

"The court holds that it will use the facultative mitigation option of sections 46b and 49 StGB in favor of the accused U. Therefore, the possible punishment will shift from a minimum sentence of three months and a maximum sentence of five years to a minimum sentence of one month and a maximum sentence of three years and nine months imprisonment".[190]

---

187 "Aber in den klassischen Verfahren, wo dann wirklich der 46 b zur Anwendung gekommen ist, habe ich/ oder auch der 31 habe ich bis jetzt das nicht so als ganz großes Problem erlebt."

188 "[E]in Gericht dazu gebracht hat, also dem glauben wir gar nichts. Das habe ich persönlich so nicht erlebt."

189 See BGH *StV* 2006, 171 as cited above in footnote 152.

190 "Die Kammer hat zusätzlich zugunsten des Angeklagten U von der fakultativen Milderungsmöglichkeit nach §§ 46b Abs. 1 Nr. 1 StGB a.F., 49 Abs. 1 StGB Gebrauch gemacht, so dass sich der Strafrahmen von

"The court holds that it will use the facultative mitigation option of sections 46b and 49 StGB in favor of the accused K. Therefore, the possible punishment will shift from a minimum sentence of one year and a maximum sentence of fifteen years to a minimum sentence of one month and a maximum sentence of eleven years and three months imprisonment".[191]

On the one hand, sentence mitigation is still not automatic when a collaborator meets the requirements of Section 46b StGB, because it is a facultative decision of the court, while on the other hand, the mitigation range is clear if the court uses its discretion. According to several of the interviewees, including the legal scholars and the judges, this is an improvement in comparison with the general mitigation grounds of Section 46 StGB. Nevertheless, it has to be taken into account that the court still has considerable discretion between the minimum and maximum sentence and, as a consequence, the collaborator will not know the exact sentence.

As the next three quotes from a judge [2], a defence lawyer [5] and a public prosecutor [7] show, the courts usually apply their discretion and this results in considerable benefit for the collaborator.

"When a collaborator has met the requirements of the provision, the sentence decision and the mitigation is still a discretionary decision, but usually the court will apply the sentence mitigation principle for collaborators." [2][192]

"Six years and six months or seven years and three months is still a heavy penalty. But it is a great benefit when the imprisonment sentence would have been two-digits. That is a clear mitigation." [5][193]

"And the more he or she discloses and the more successes the authorities have in other investigations, the greater the mitigation expectation of the collaborator is.

---

drei Monaten bis zu fünf Jahren nochmals auf einen solchen von einem Monat bis zu drei Jahren neun Monaten Freiheitsstrafe reduziert hat."

191 "Die Kammer hat jedoch zugunsten des Angeklagten K von der fakultativen Milderungsmöglichkeit nach §§ 46b Abs. 1 Satz 1 Nr. 1 (a.F.), 49 Abs. 1 StGB Gebrauch gemacht, so dass sich der Strafrahmen insoweit von einem Jahr bis zu fünfzehn Jahren auf einen solchen von drei Monaten bis zu elf Jahren drei Monaten Freiheitsstrafe reduziert hat."

192 "Wenn ich jetzt weiß, ich habe das gemacht, ich habe die Voraussetzungen erfüllt, natürlich letztendlich ist natürlich der 46 b auch irgendwie eine Ermessensentscheidung und so weiter und das Gericht könnte davon absehen, aber das wird es halt in aller Regel nicht tun."

193 "[S]echs Jahre, sechs Monate oder später sieben Jahre, drei Monate hört sich immer noch heftig an [...] Aber es ist so, das was an sich verwirkt war und es wäre wahrscheinlich im zweistelligen Bereich ausgeurteilt worden, ist das natürlich ein deutlicher Strafabschlag."

That is the classic stereotype. And in my opinion the practice confirms that view. The court is inclined to apply a greater mitigation when the collaborator has disclosed a lot of information and took maybe four or five people with him or her." [7][194]

Although the sentence mitigation remains unclear till the judgment, one defence lawyer [5] declared that the collaborators provision still offers an important mitigation principle that can be used by the defence. The new provision, as mentioned by the defence lawyer, broadens the set of tactical instruments, especially in cases where the maximum penalties are high.

In comparison, the mitigation for the first company that discloses information about a cartel in anti-competitive cases is clearer and that is mentioned as an important factor to the success of the collaborators provision in that field of law. For the first company that discloses information which is not the initiator of the cartel or compelled other companies to take part in the cartel, the fine will be reduced by 100 percent.

"One of the main reasons that our system functions properly is that companies know exactly what the benefit is when they meet the requirements." [10][195]

As an example, the homepage of the BKartA lists a case in which ten companies collaborated with the BKartA after the first company disclosed information about a chocolate cartel:

"The company *Mars* will benefit from the bonus regulation and their fine will be reduced to zero. In the decision to fine the companies *Ritter, Nestlé, Kraft* and *Katjes*, the *Bundeskartellamt* will consider in favor of the companies that they collaborated with the *Bundeskartellamt*".[196]

4.5.6.3   Concurrent Provisions
What remains unclear in German practice is how the different options to mitigate the sentence are applied. Besides crime-specific provisions, the German Criminal Code offers

---

194 "Und je mehr er bringt und je mehr Erfolg die Ermittlungsbehörden aufgrund seiner Aussage haben, umso niedriger ist seine Straferwartung. Das ist so das klassische Bild. Und ich glaube, das entspricht auch der Praxis in der Strafverfolgung. Also ein Richter ist sehr geneigt, wenn ein Kronzeuge wirklich, wie man so schön sagt, die Hosen runtergelassen hat und wirklich noch vier oder fünf Leute ganz erheblich mitgenommen hat, dann größere Milde walten zu lassen, als wenn das nicht der Fall war."
195 "Die automatische Bußgeldimmunität ist ein wesentlicher Teil der Bonusregelung, sie schafft für Unternehmen, die kooperieren möchten, in einem sehr frühen Verfahrensstadium Rechtssicherheit."
196 http://www.bundeskartellamt.de/SharedDocs/Entscheidung/DE/Fallberichte/Kartellverbot/2013/B11-11-08.pdf?__blob=publicationFile&v=5, last retrieved on 22nd November 2016.

two possibilities for sentence mitigation. Section 46b StGB sets out multiple requirements for mitigation to be applied to collaborators and a structural framework for the mitigation (as described in § 4.4.3). Section 46 StGB is titled 'sentencing principles' and determines that "[w]hen sentencing the court shall weigh the circumstances in favor of and against the offender. Consideration shall in particular be given to (1) the motives and aims of the offender; (2) the attitude reflected in the offence and the degree of force of will involved in its commission; (3) the degree of the violation of the offender's duties; (4) the modus operandi and the consequences caused by the offence to the extent that the offender is to blame for them; (5) the offender's prior history, his personal and financial circumstances; (6) *his conduct after the offence, particularly his efforts to make restitution* and; (7) for the harm caused as well as the offender's efforts at reconciliation with the victim (numerical additions and Italic, ML & DvT)".[197]

Therefore, every disclosure of information about other criminal offences must be taken into account in the sentencing decision. As stated by several interviewees, including a judge [1], a public prosecutor [6] and a scholar [8], the courts will often use the general provision of Section 46 StGB to mitigate the sentence, even if the *Kronzeugen* provision could be applied. One of the scholars [8] stated that, in their opinion:

> "What can be learned about judgments is that the courts have difficulties in applying the criteria of Section 46b StGB. So instead they use the option to mitigate the sentence via Section 46 (2) StGB".[198]

This makes it difficult to make an assessment of the value of the *Kronzeugen* statements on the basis of written judgments.

4.5.6.4 Conclusion

To get around the possible difficulties and discussion of the reliability (or otherwise) of collaborator's statements, some of the interviewees mentioned that they tend to use the statement as a starting point or to turn other suspects to start a domino effect. If used as evidence, the collaborator is normally present at the trial and is examined and/or cross-examined. However, collaborators tend to refer to the contracts of confidentiality they had to sign (which is not fully accepted in the Federal Court of Justice's case-law[199]). Furthermore, although all the interviewees agreed that judges should be on the lookout for false statements, no interviewee reported a case where a collaborator's statement was regarded as wholly unreliable.

---

197 Translation www.gesetze-im-internet.de/englisch_stgb/, last retrieved on 5th December 2016.
198 "Was man feststellen kann ist ganz klar, dass die Gerichte sich noch schwer tun offenbar mit dieser Norm 46b und dass ganz oft dann doch irgendwie das über 46 II gelöst wird."
199 See BGH *StV* 2006, 171 as cited above in footnote 164.

The sentence mitigation of the *Kronzeugen* provision provides a clear-cut system whereby the range between the minimum and maximum sentence will shift. Courts will explicitly state this shift in their judgment. Difficulties in assessing the collaboration practice arise from the fact that Section 46 (2) StGB and Section 46b StGB are concurrent provisions. The courts that are uncertain about the application of the *Kronzeugen* provision may use the general mitigation argument to get around the requirements of Section 46b StGB.

4.6   Conclusion and Discussion

On the one hand, all the interviewees stated that collaborators of justice should be treated with the utmost care – because they remain persons suspected of a crime for their own interests and are not a part of the criminal investigation team.[200] On the other hand, most of the interviewees also see the necessity of the dealing with collaborators in certain areas of crime because they can provide information about the organizational structures of narcotics trafficking gangs, information that would otherwise be almost impossible to get.[201] This means there is a conflict between the trustworthiness and reliability of the collaborator and his or her statements and the value of the information disclosed for law enforcement. Therefore, there needs to be a balance between the two conflicting aspects of the collaborators provision and practice. In this section, we will draw conclusions about the results presented above. These conclusions are subdivided in two parts: (1) conclusions and discussion about the German legal provisions regarding collaborators of justice and; (2) conclusions and discussion about the German practice of dealing with collaborators of justice.

4.6.1   *Legal Provisions*

In general, the interviewees seemed to be satisfied with the provisions on collaborators of justice. A public prosecutor [7] stated that in his team (in one of the major cities of the country) the provision is not seen as problematic at all and, in their view, the provision of

---

200 "Also, was gefährlich ist aus meiner Sicht ist, das ist auch etwas, was ich von der Polizei dann einfordere, der Fehlvorstellung zu erliegen, ein Kronzeuge spielt in der eigenen Mannschaft, um es umgangssprachlich zu formulieren. Ein Kronzeuge ist eine sehr kriminelle Person und die ist mit äußerster Vorsicht zu genießen" [7].

201 "[A]lso für uns sind diese Regelungen extrem wichtig, weil die normalen Überwachungsmaßnahmen, die wir haben, also Telefonüberwachung zum Beispiel, die richtig Schlauen die benutzen verschlüsselte Kommunikation, WhatsApp, Skype und ich weiß nicht was. Da gibt es ja nun bestimmte Blackberry-Handys und ich weiß nicht was. Da kommt man (…) nur wenig dran. Oder die sind halt so schlau, dass sie sagen, okay, wir treffen uns. Punkt. [...] Mit der Konsequenz, dass wir auf Angaben von Informanten, Vertrauenspersonen und Kronzeugen oftmals angewiesen sind" [6].

the StGB offers an adequate range of possibilities.[202] The appellate judge [1] confirmed this. They see it as a win-win situation.[203] The provision leads to greater efficiency because it will shorten the procedure. Furthermore, the provision can lead to the prevention of very serious crimes. Besides, it also offers a benefit to the collaborator. The other interviewed public prosecutor [6] stated that the provision is "to a large extent, okay".[204] One of the defence lawyers [4] also stated that they understand and accept the necessity of the instrument.[205]

However, this does not mean that there is no discussion about specific aspects of the provisions. One aspect that is criticized or discussed is the requirement for connectivity. At least in theory, the requirement reduces the scope of the provision because a collaborator cannot benefit from disclosing information about any random crime in exchange for sentence mitigation. A judge [1] considered this requirement especially problematic with regard to the prevention of crimes. They stated that the prevention of serious crimes should always be possible in exchange for sentence mitigation.

Another aspect that is criticized, especially by defence lawyers, is that the disclosure has to take place before the opening of the trial in order to be eligible for the collaborators provision. Although they understand the necessity – especially the need to investigate the information given to see if it is reliable and can lead to the prosecution of another person – it demands that they choose a defence strategy early in the proceedings and, having decided to collaborate, they cannot change the strategy because the authorities already have the information.

Two other aspects are also criticized, both omissions, i.e. that the witness protection program is not an integral part of the discussions about becoming a collaborator, and that there are no strict rules regarding the collaboration procedure that results in a large

---

202 "Ich sehe das so, dass die Kronzeugenregelung aktuell überhaupt kein Diskussionsgegenstand im Haus ist. Null. […] Zumal die Handlungsmöglichkeiten, die man hat, ja völlig ausreichen. Also wenn man sich die Strafrahmen anschaut, die das StGB für die unterschiedlichen Straftaten gewährt, dann sind diese Strafrahmen ja unglaublich breit. […] Also im Prinzip sind die Fallgestaltungen, mit denen wir es jetzt zu tun haben ausreichend mit den gesetzlichen Instrumentalien zu bedienen. Und zwar sowohl nach oben wie auch nach unten."

203 "[S]tehe ich der Kronzeugenregelung positiv gegenüber, weil ich so wie sie gefasst ist, sozusagen eine Win-win-Situation sehe. Ich sehe einmal den Vorteil für die Strafverfolgungsbehörden, dass sie möglicherweise über diese Regelung eben leichter Straftaten aufklären können. Ich sehe Vorteile für, sage ich mal, im Bereich der Gefahrenabwehr, wenn/ der 46 b hat ja zwei Varianten, eben einmal die Verhinderungsvariante, also zukünftige Straftaten zu verhindern oder eben zur Aufklärung begangener Straftaten aufzuklären. Ich sehe also gerade auch bei Gefahrenabwehrvariante die Möglichkeit, eben zukünftige schwere Straftaten zu verhindern. Auf der anderen Seite ist dann die andere Gewinnsituation die, dass derjenige, der sich dann dazu bereit erklärt, sein Wissen zu offenbaren, eben auch die Chance hat, dass das entsprechend honoriert wird."

204 "[W]eitgehend ist es okay."

205 "Wir verstehen durchaus das Bedürfnis der Strafjustiz, sich eines Zeugen zu versichern, der eine Menge dazu sagen kann, zu dem, was also vorgeworfen wird, zu dem Anklagevorwurf oder zum Ermittlungsgegenstand. Und auch gerade deshalb, weil es natürlich repressive Strukturen gerade im Betäubungsmittelhandel gibt. Insofern ist das kriminalpolitische Bedürfnis zu verstehen, vielleicht auch zu akzeptieren."

degree of uncertainty for the collaborator. The witness protection program is completely independent of other police and justice departments, and operates independently in criminal cases, i.e. they cannot be given executive orders by the public prosecutor or a judge. This means that intake into the program is separate from the (gentlemen's) agreement about collaboration (and that placement in the program is not automatic for every collaborator). As we have stated above, the separation of the issues can also be beneficial for the potential collaborator, because the decision of the witness protection team to take him or her into the program will (at least in principle) be free of inappropriate considerations related to his or her compliance in the context of the collaborator's deal.

The second omission is the absence of procedural rules. The collaborators provision is part of the Criminal Code and therefore substantive law. If the collaborator fulfills certain requirements, he or she is eligible for sentence mitigation (or exemption from punishment). However, the law does not regulate the form of the discussions, the drafting of an agreement and the closing of the deal. The public prosecutor and collaborator can commit themselves to putting the collaboration before the trial judge in order to get sentence mitigation, but they are completely dependent on the judge's decision. So, there is a large degree of inequality: the collaborator has to disclose his or her information before the trial starts but does not know for certain whether he or she will receive a mitigated sentence, although the public prosecutor already has information that he or she can use to investigate and prosecute others.

4.6.2   Practice

The interviewees were largely satisfied with the legal provision concerning the collaborators instrument. They were also basically satisfied with the practice. One public prosecutor [6] stated that they considered the general provision (Section 46b StGB) and the crime-specific narcotics provision (Section 31 BtMG) to be practicable.[206] The Federal judge [2] explained that the risk of unreliable statements has decreased considerably since the requirement of connectivity and the deadline for the disclosure were introduced and that, in their opinion, judges act responsibly in regard to the reliability of the statements.[207]

The two defence lawyers ([3] and [5]) stated that the non-transparency creates the biggest practical challenge.[208] It can be difficult to find out where and to whom a collaborator

---

206 "Also ich halte die Regelung, sowohl von 46 b StGB als auch den 31 BtMG für in der Praxis praktikabel."
207 "Also in der jetzigen Ausprägung, also auch mit diesem Konnexitätserfordernis und eben mit dem, es muss halt frühzeitig gemacht werden und so weiter, [...] ist dieses Risiko deutlich geringer geworden und [...] auch der Umgang der Gerichte damit, durchaus verantwortungsvoll."
208 "[D]ass das Ganze eine große Intransparenz fördert und meines Erachtens der Wahrheitsfindung nicht oder nur sehr sehr wenig zuträglich ist. Und vom Anreiz für denjenigen, der das in Anspruch nimmt, zumindest einmal toll aussieht, aber vom Prinzip her ist eigentlich der Staat immer der Gewinner und die Strafrechts-

has disclosed information, what information he or she disclosed, and what he or she received for the collaboration. This is further underlined by the fact that a protected collaborator has to sign a contract of silence. Although the Federal Court of Justice decided that questions about the collaboration and the witness protection cannot be rejected *per se*, the Court leaves room for judges to decide on the contract of silence on a case-by-case basis (in light of the right of the defence to question a witness). Apparently, the uncertainty of the 'gentlemen's agreement' is an accepted part of the German collaboration practice because none of the interviewees mentioned this point when asked whether the law or practice concerning collaborators of justice instruments should be changed.

Another point of criticism challenged the witness protection program, especially the witness protection 'agreement' as a 'take it or leave it' deal. The witness has to adhere to the instructions of the witness protection team, otherwise he or she will be removed from the program. This rigorous change in lifestyle is difficult to manage and therefore the drop out rate is fairly high.

Lastly, we have seen from the interviews that, in practice, collaborators' agreements are not limited to sentence mitigation and exemption from punishment, but can also address issues such as immigration and the right to residence, pre-trial detention, financial aspects, the decision not to prosecute or questions regarding the prison regime. It would give rise to justified criticism if state authorities made the conferment of the aforementioned benefits subject to negotiation where the suspect already has a legal right to obtain them.

---

pflege, weil sie Ressourcen schont, aber nicht die betroffenen Leute" [3]; "Aber da war ich der Meinung, da sollte man zumindest versuchen, für mehr Transparenz zu sorgen" [5].

Appendix 1

Answers to the Research Questions

Legal Framework

1   *What types of undertakings are provided for?*

In Germany the instrument of undertakings to witnesses forms part of a sentencing instruction under substantive law. If the court rules that the witness has contributed to the investigation and prosecution of other criminal cases, this is taken into account in the sentencing of the witness in his own criminal case (Section 46b StGB (the German Criminal Code)). This can result in a sentence reduction, but under certain circumstances the sentencing may be omitted entirely. In practice other 'benefits' are also used which are not specified in the legislation (see also question 8). In practice agreements are made between the Public Prosecution Service and the witness before the judge applies the sentence reduction, but there is no formal framework for this, given that ultimately it is the court which implements the sentence reduction in exchange for a statement. The previous 'agreement' between the Public Prosecution Service and the witness is therefore not regulated by law and also does not depend on prior judicial scrutiny or any other formal requirements.

2   *In respect of which offences is it possible to use the instrument?*

The instrument in Section 46b StGB may only be used for an exhaustive list of crimes which can be found in Section 100a StPO (the German Code of Criminal Procedure). This is a list of crimes in respect of which a telephone tap may be used, and which in paragraph 2 is declared also to be applicable to the use of the above instrument. This list is difficult to summarise in general terms, given that it covers many different criminal offences from many different statutes. These include property crimes (e.g. fraud and money laundering), violent offences, homicide, tax offences and international crimes. The complete list is included as an annex to the country report for Germany.

3   *What is the legal basis for (using) the instrument?*

Section 46b StGB is the central provision in Germany for providing undertakings to witnesses and, as noted, this provision allows the judge to grant a sentence reduction or – under certain circumstances – to withhold punishment altogether. The degree to which sentence reduction may be granted is relatively complex, given that the German Criminal Code also provides for minimum sentences, and laid down in some detail (Section 49 StGB). Section 46b StGB clearly states that even in cases where the offence is subject to life imprisonment, sentence reduction in exchange for statements is permissible. In such cases however a prison sentence of at least ten years must be imposed.

Two features of the German legislation in particular stand out. The first of these is the statutory requirement that was introduced in 2013 of a substantive connection (*Zusammenhang*) between the offence about which the witness makes a statement and the offence of which he is suspected (Section 46b StGB). The legislature took the view that offering sentence reduction or exemption from punishment was not appropriate in cases where the witness makes statements about offences which are in no way related to the offences of which the witness himself is suspected. What the term substantive connection is understood to mean in this context, was left for the jurisprudence to decide, but in any event this may be said to be the case when the witness may be considered to be a co-accused of the person against whom he is testifying. In case of organised crime also, the requirement will usually be considered to have been met.

The second feature of the German legislation to stand out is that it includes a time limit or deadline: a witness who wishes to claim sentence reduction must present himself to the authorities before the court hearing starts (Section 46b paragraph 3 StGB). One of the reasons for this deadline is tactical in nature: the witness cannot delay his decision to collaborate until it becomes clear how strong or weak his position is in terms of his own criminal proceedings. A second reason lies in the fact that in this way the Public Prosecution Service has the opportunity to check the reliability and consider the usefulness of the information provided by the witness in good time. Finally, this approach will prevent the case against the witness himself from being delayed. However, this deadline is less strict than it appears. Even if the witness comes forward with relevant information about others during the court hearing, this may be taken into account in sentencing in the case of the witness himself, given that the judge is required to take all the relevant factors into account in the sentencing, including the cooperative attitude of the witness (Section 46 paragraph 2 StGB). Any sentence reduction based on this general principle however is otherwise unregulated, in contrast to any sentence reduction based on the aforementioned Section 46b StGB.

4   *How did the rules on collaboration with justice come about?*

Since 1982 the German counterpart of the Opium Act (*Betäubungsmittelgesetz*) has included a specific provision for undertakings to witnesses to combat organised drugs crime. This generated little debate in parliament at the time. In 1989 similar legislation was enacted for terrorism cases, this time however there was considerable debate in the literature and in parliament, in which the criticisms raised related mainly to the relationship with the applicable principle of legality (to be construed here as the duty to instigate a prosecution) and the matter of the reliability of the statements obtained in this way. The German legislation still includes several specific regulations on the use of undertakings to witnesses which to some degree deviate from the general provision currently in place.

The first general legislation on undertakings to witnesses was enacted in 2009 (as noted, while a number of special provisions which had previously been enacted remained in force). Since then Section 46b StGB has provided the statutory basis for granting sentence reduction in exchange for information on criminal offences either committed in the past or about to be committed. This legislation also encountered serious criticism mainly from members of the judiciary and the criminal defence bar, but this criticism did not prevent the legislation from being enacted. Initially, the new legislation was applied to all unsolved criminal offences on which a witness made a statement, but in 2013 the legislation was amended in such a way that the instrument of undertakings to witnesses could only be applied to a narrowly defined list of criminal offences (Section 100a paragraph 2 StPO). In 2013 the requirement previously mentioned of a substantive connection was also introduced to prevent the legislation being too widely interpreted. See the response to question 3 for further details of both these aspects.

5   *Who holds authority to make use of the instrument and where does the responsibility lie in this regard?*

Given that the instrument of undertakings to witnesses is interpreted in Germany as a sentencing instruction, the judge has been cast in the leading role. Ultimately it is he who decides whether the witness has made a significant contribution (*wesentlicher Beitrag*) to the investigation and prosecution of other criminal offences and, for that reason, is eligible for a sentence reduction. The responsibility of the public prosecutor is limited to the possibility of promising the witness that he will not be prosecuted for certain criminal offences (Sections 153-154 StPO) and – should there be cause to do so – to urging that the witness be included in a witness protection programme by the authority responsible for that. The public prosecutor cannot make any binding agreements with the witness about the sentencing, given that this forms part of the exclusive competence of the judge. The only commitment that the public prosecutor may make to the witness is that he will make every effort to inform the judge about the cooperation provided by witness in the investigation and prosecution of other criminal offences and that he will make a mitigated sentencing demand as a result.

6   *How does the instrument relate to other measures whereby private individuals provide information for the purposes of criminal investigation and/or prosecution?*

A distinction has to be made between the witness to whom undertakings are made – referred to in the German literature as *Kronzeuge* or *Aufklärungsgehilfe* – and those termed *informers* and *confidants. Informers* are persons who provide the authorities with information about a single criminal offence, while generally they themselves are not the object of a criminal investigation. *Confidants* are individuals who provide information on multiple criminal offences on a more regular basis and who are paid for this. An important distinction between *Kronzeugen* on the one hand and *informers* and *confidants* on the other is that the latter are under the control of the authorities while they gather information, while *Kronzeugen* provide information after the fact – while they themselves are already considered suspects – which they have obtained in the past. This means therefore that *Kronzeugen* are not actively approached by the authorities, other than when during their interrogation as a suspect the possibility arises that in exchange for a sentence reduction they could cooperate with the investigation and prosecution of other criminal offences. Another difference is that *Kronzeugen* are by definition also suspected or convicted persons, while that does not have to be the case with *informers* and *confidants.*

7   *How does the instrument relate to the phenomenon of witness protection?*

The protection of witnesses is laid down in the *Zeugenschutz-Harmonisierungsgesetz* (ZSHG). This legislation provides the basis for a witness protection programme that is open to all witnesses who – as a result of their role as a witness – are at risk and is therefore more widely used than just for witnesses to whom undertakings have been made while, conversely, not all witnesses to whom undertakings are made will be included in a witness protection programme. Any protection which is provided to a witness to whom undertakings are made is separate from his collaboration, in the sense that such measures will be taken if and insofar as there is a need for them in view of the danger which the witness is exposed to, but do not depend on the matter of whether or not the witness meets his 'obligation' to cooperate. These are separate procedures. If the public prosecutor believes that the witness should receive protection, he can put the witness forward to the police department authorised to do so (*Zeugenschutzdienstelle*). The police unit concerned decides on whether or not he will be included in the programme.

Practice

8   *What types of undertaking are used in practice?*

The legislation itself provides for the possibility of sentence reduction or the wholesale exemption of punishment. In practice other 'benefits' are also used, which fall under the discretionary powers of the public prosecutor. The undertaking most commonly requested by witnesses concerns residence rights. An individual who is the subject of a criminal investigation can only be deported with the consent of the Public Prosecution Service. Furthermore, the public prosecutor can prevent the witness from being put in pre-trial detention, by not ordering it. During the talks between the public prosecutor and the witness, financial aspects (in the widest sense) may also be covered (although this fact is not widely broadcasted), which could cover the seizure of goods, not claiming the repayment of illicitly received social security benefits, and the payment of a sum of money. Other possibilities include the option of not prosecuting more minor offences and arranging for a milder penitentiary regime.

9   *How often and on the basis of which considerations is the instrument used or not used?*

It is not possible to draw any reliable conclusions about the number of witnesses to whom undertakings have been made, not from the literature and published case law, nor from official case law sources and the ministry, or the interviews. The most common use of the instrument is with the co-accused of an offence of a less serious nature, such as theft and other property-related crimes. The instrument is also applied in cases of organised crime, but this happens much less often.

The 'typical' usage of the instrument can be put down to pragmatism. Every perpetrator who makes a confession and at the same time makes a statement about one or more other co-perpetrators is eligible for the benefits offered by the law. The instrument is used for organised crime because it would be almost impossible to solve, prosecute and convict the criminal offences that are perpetrated in this context without insider information. See also question 12.

10   *What have the positive and negative experiences been in practice with the instrument and the legal framework in this regard?*

On the whole, public prosecutors, defence lawyers, judges and the police are satisfied with the various options provided for by the legislation. The two biggest drawbacks of the German legislation are: 1) the lack of a formal framework within which agreements on undertakings may be made; and 2) the complete dissociation of the instrument of undertakings to witnesses from the witness protection procedure. The lack of a formal framework within which agreements can be made, which can lead to uncertainty about the application of the instrument, seems to be less of a problem in practice however given that public prosecutors generally honour their verbal agreements and the judges generally abide by the procedure. With regard to the second problem, it would appear that the argument is that disconnecting the two aspects, in which witness protection in its entirety forms no part of the instrument of undertakings to witnesses, means that witnesses may be less inclined to cooperate with the authorities. The fact that the witness protection programme is extremely rigid is also said to have a detrimental effect on the willingness of a witness to collaborate. Finally, defence lawyers commented that the deadline for providing information means that they have to commit to a defence strategy at a very early stage, while at that point in time it is by no means yet clear what form the collaboration will ultimately take (which in turn is related to the lack of formal guidelines on making the agreements).

11   *What results have been achieved by use of the instrument in individual cases?*

On the one hand there is no reliable quantitative data about the use of the instrument, including what type of undertakings and how many have been made. On the other hand, the respondents reported no negative experiences with regard to the assessment of the reliability of the statement made by the witness. The latter implies that when the instrument is used, it is also used successfully in the sense that it contributes to the investigation, prosecution or conviction of other suspects (assuming that the statement actually made a real contribution to this; see question 13). In this context it should be noted that it will often remain unclear what undertakings – besides sentence reduction – have been made, which may influence the reliability of the statement made (see further questions 8 and 15). It should also be noted here that from the interviews it appears that the undertaking most requested related to the residence status of the witness; as indicated, decisions on such matters fall under the discretionary powers of the public prosecutor.

12   *Which factors contribute to the successful use of the instrument and which*
    form obstacles in this regard?

Trust is the key in the context of the German legislation on undertakings to witnesses, because there is no formal framework of any kind. The agreements made are not committed to paper and the honouring of verbal agreements takes place on a basis of mutual trust. Public prosecutors are well aware of this and therefore must take care not to lose the trust placed in them, otherwise no one will 'do business' with them in the future. This would cause major problems in future cases, particularly for the public prosecutors responsible for the investigation and prosecution of organised crime. Where defence lawyers abuse the trust placed in them, public prosecutors will not speak with them again about the possible use of the instrument in the future. Trust is also a crucial factor for the witnesses themselves. A witness has to reveal information during the criminal investigation, but only gets to hear in the judgment whether he has received a sentence reduction.

13   *In general, do the rules on collaboration with justice achieve their objective?*

Although there has been no official analysis of the effectiveness of the legislation (as with all statistical data on the instrument), the present study provided an opportunity to reflect on the question of whether the German legislation has achieved its goal. It should be noted here that the law requires that the statement of the witness to whom undertakings are made must make a real contribution to the investigation, prosecution or conviction of other suspects. Only then can the sentence of the witness be reduced. Given that none of the respondents had experienced any negative assessments of the reliability of the witness, it would appear that it is reasonable to conclude that the instrument is to some extent effective. This goes for the prosecutorial authorities as well as the judiciary – cases are solved and tried more quickly (in which regard it should be noted that in Germany improved efficiency is important, given that court hearings take considerably longer there than in the Netherlands, for example) – as well as for the defence, in that the witness will benefit from the sentence reduction. To describe it from the perspective of the authorities: the legislation itself incorporates a measure for effectiveness in the application criteria, because the sentence reduction can only be granted if the input provided by the witness actually contributed to the investigation, prosecution or conviction of another accused.

SCRUTINY, TRANSPARENCY AND DEBATE

14   *To what extent is the use of the instrument subject to scrutiny by a judicial or other authority?*

The criminal court is the only competent authority which may apply sentence reduction or decide to withhold punishment. For other undertakings which fall under the discretionary powers of the public prosecutor (see question 8) and which cannot specifically be connected with the witness (because unlike sentence reduction and the exemption from punishment they are not awarded in the context of the trial against them), such as not making a demand for pre-trial detention, there is no scrutiny by another authority. The witness protection dossier is also not examined by judges, because it is a separate process over which the public prosecutors have no authority. Accordingly, in this context also there is a lack of scrutiny by another body, other than that performed by the police department competent to make decisions on such matters.

15   *In how far is the instrument itself and the use thereof in individual cases publicly transparent?*

The granting of sentence reduction to a witness or withholding punishment altogether in exchange for a statement takes place in an entirely transparent manner, because the judgment makes specific reference to the sentencing framework. The other undertakings however are not transparent. Moreover, in practice there is no formal framework for the agreements made in advance by the Public Prosecution Service and the witness, and a record of any agreement made is not always included in the case file.

16   *To what extent is there debate or discussion regarding the use of the instrument? On which aspects of the instrument is the debate focused?*

The risk concerning the reliability of the statements is generally always referred to as a theoretical danger inherent to the instrument of undertakings to witnesses but – as previously mentioned – in practice the statements are almost always deemed to be reliable. There has also long been discussion (for decades) about the matter of whether or not the application of sentence reduction in exchange for witness statements contravenes the principle of equal treatment, for example, because different sentences are handed down to those perpetrating the same criminal offences. It seems however that most lawyers, and certainly the respondents, now generally consider the instrument of undertakings to witnesses as a necessary instrument that (in principle) is not contrary to any principle of law.

Regarding the statutory provision currently in place, there is some discussion on the provision's scope and the time limit referred to above. The application of the instrument is now limited to cases in which there is a substantive connection between the offence about which the witness makes a statement and the offence of which he is suspected. The witness is also required to reveal what he knows before the start of the trial (for further details of both requirements, see also question 3). The first requirement prevents the instrument from being used for statements about random criminal offences about which the witness has some coincidental knowledge. Since 2013 the legislature has taken the view that the legislation on undertakings to witnesses is not intended for that purpose. The second requirement limits tactical manoeuvring by the defence because it is necessary to commit to a defence strategy at an early stage of the proceedings. Other obstacles with respect to the German instrument also previously mentioned include the lack of a formal framework within which agreements between the public prosecutor and the witness may be made, and its detachment from witness protection, although these obstacles were also played down (see also question 10).

17   *In how far and in what regard has scrutiny, transparency and debate led to changes in the regulation of the instrument?*

The aforementioned limitation on the scope of the legislation to cases in which there is a substantive connection (see question 3) arose due to criticism of the wide-ranging application of the legislation in force at the time to random offences. The legislation has not been further amended since then (2013).

Appendix 2

List of Respondents of the Interviews

1. Court of appeals judge
2. A Federal Court of Justice judge
3. A defence lawyer specializing in crimes against the State and terrorism
4. A defence lawyer with a general criminal law practice
5. A defence lawyer with a general criminal law practice
6. Prosecutor, focused on organized crime in a large municipality
7. Prosecutor, focused on organized crime in a large municipality
8. Legal scholar
9. Legal scholar
10. A member of the National Cartel
11. A leader of a witness protection team

Appendix 3

Section 100a Code of Criminal Procedure [Conditions Regarding Interception of Telecommunications]

(1) Telecommunications may be intercepted and recorded also without the knowledge of the persons concerned if

1. certain facts give rise to the suspicion that a person, either as perpetrator or as inciter or accessory, has committed a serious criminal offence referred to in subsection (2) or, in cases where there is criminal liability for attempt, has attempted to commit such an offence or has prepared such an offence by committing a criminal offence; and
2. the offence is one of particular gravity in the individual case as well; and
3. other means of establishing the facts or determining the accused's whereabouts would be much more difficult or offer no prospect of success.

(2) Serious criminal offences for the purposes of subsection (1), number 1, shall be:

1. *"pursuant to the Criminal Code:*
   a. *crimes against peace, high treason, endangering the democratic state based on the rule of law, treason and endangering external security pursuant to sections 80 to 82, 84 to 86, 87 to 89a and 94 to 100a;*
   b. *taking of bribes by, and offering of bribes to, mandate holders pursuant to section 108e;*
   c. *crimes against the national defence pursuant to sections 109d to 109h;*
   d. *crimes against public order pursuant to sections 129 to 130;*
   e. *counterfeiting money and official stamps pursuant to sections 146 and 151, in each case also in conjunction with section 152, as well as section 152a subsection (3) and section 152b subsections (1) to (4);*
   f. *crimes against sexual self-determination in the cases referred to in sections 176a, 176b, 177 subsection (2), number 2, and section 179 subsection (5), number 2;*
   g. *dissemination, purchase and possession of pornographic writings involving children and involving juveniles, pursuant to section 184b subsections (1) to (3), section 184c subsection (3);*
   h. *murder and manslaughter pursuant to sections 211 and 212;*
   i. *crimes against personal liberty pursuant to sections 232 to 233a, 234, 234a, 239a and 239b;*

j. gang theft pursuant to section 244 subsection (1), number 2, and aggravated gang theft pursuant to section 244a;

k. crimes of robbery or extortion pursuant to sections 249 to 255;

l. commercial handling of stolen goods, gang handling of stolen goods and commercial gang handling of stolen goods pursuant to sections 260 and 260a;

m. money laundering or concealment of unlawfully acquired assets pursuant to section 261 subsections (1), (2) and (4);

n. fraud and computer fraud subject to the conditions set out in section 263 subsection (3), second sentence, and in the case of section 263 subsection (5), each also in conjunction with section 263a subsection (2);

o. subsidy fraud subject to the conditions set out in section 264 subsection (2), second sentence, and in the case of section 264 subsection (3), in conjunction with section 263 subsection (5);

p. criminal offences involving falsification of documents under the conditions set out in section 267 subsection (3), second sentence, and in the case of section 267 sub-section (4), in each case also in conjunction with section 268 subsection (5) or section 269 subsection (3), as well as pursuant to sections 275 subsection (2) and section 276 subsection (2);

q. bankruptcy subject to the conditions set out in section 283a, second sentence;

r. crimes against competition pursuant to section 298 and, subject to the conditions set out in section 300, second sentence, pursuant to section 299;

s. crimes endangering public safety in the cases referred to in sections 306 to 306c, section 307 subsections (1) to (3), section 308 subsections (1) to (3), section 309 subsections (1) to (4), section 310 subsection (1), sections 313, 314, 315 subsection (3), section 315b subsection (3), as well as sections 316a and 316c;

t. taking and offering a bribe pursuant to sections 332 and 334;

2. pursuant to the Fiscal Code:

a. tax evasion under the conditions set out in section 370 subsection (3), second sentence, number 5;

b. commercial, violent and gang smuggling pursuant to section 373;

c. handling tax-evaded property as defined in section 374 subsection (2);

3. pursuant to the Anti-Doping Act:

criminal offences pursuant to section 4 (4) number 2 (b);

4. pursuant to the Asylum Procedure Act:

a. inducing an abusive application for asylum pursuant to section 84 subsection (3);

b. commercial and gang inducement to make an abusive application for asylum pursuant to section 84a;

5. pursuant to the Residence Act:

a. smuggling of aliens pursuant to section 96 subsection (2);

   b. *smuggling resulting in death and commercial and gang smuggling pursuant to
       section 97;*

6. *pursuant to the Foreign Trade and Payments Act:*
    *wilful criminal offences pursuant to sections 17 and 18 of the Foreign Trade and
    Payments Act;*

7. *pursuant to the Narcotics Act:*

    a. *criminal offences pursuant to one of the provisions referred to in section 29 sub-
        section (3), second sentence, number 1, subject to the conditions set out therein;*

    b. *criminal offences pursuant to section 29a, section 30 subsection (1), numbers 1, 2
        and 4, as well as sections 30a and 30b;*

8. *pursuant to the Precursors Control Act:*
    *criminal offences pursuant to section 19 subsection (1), subject to the conditions set out
    in section 19 subsection (3), second sentence;*

9. *pursuant to the War Weapons Control Act:*

    a. *criminal offences pursuant to section 19 subsections (1) to (3) and section 20 sub-
        sections (1) and (2), as well as section 20a subsections (1) to (3), each also in con-
        junction with section 21;*

    b. *criminal offences pursuant to section 22a subsections (1) to (3);*

10. *pursuant to the Code of Crimes against International Law:*

    a. *genocide pursuant to section 6;*

    b. *crimes against humanity pursuant to section 7;*

    c. *war crimes pursuant to sections 8 to 12;*

11. *pursuant to the Weapons Act:*

    a. *criminal offences pursuant to section 51 subsections (1) to (3);*

    b. *criminal offences pursuant to section 52 subsection (1), number 1 and number 2,
        letters c and d, as well as section 52 subsections (5) and (6)."*[209]

---

209 Translation www.gesetze-im-internet.de/englisch_stpo/, last retrieved on 28 July 2016.

5   COLLABORATION WITH JUSTICE IN ITALY

M.L. Ferioli & M. Caianiello

5.1   INTRODUCTION

5.1.1   The Italian Criminal Justice System

In order to facilitate an understanding of the Italian legal framework on collaboration with justice, a brief introduction to the basic features of the Italian criminal justice system is in order. The Italian legal system is that of a civil law State, based on a written constitution. In 1988, Italy abandoned the inquisitorial model – in which it was the task of investigating judges to collect all the evidence and issue a verdict – and adopted a hybrid system with features inspired by the adversarial Anglo-American tradition. The reform introduced a clear distinction between the investigative and the trial phase of proceedings. Investigating judges were replaced by public prosecutors – responsible for the collection of evidence – and judges with adjudicating functions. Together, public prosecutors and judges form the judiciary, which is granted full independence and autonomy from the legislative and executive powers (Article 104 of the Constitution). Prosecutors and judges are seen as the expression of the same power and they are both referred to as 'the judicial authority'. They are selected through the same competitive process of examinations and they are both classified as 'magistrates'.[1] As such, they can switch functions at their request.

The prosecutor is in charge of the investigation. To this end, he directs and supervises the investigative police (*polizia giudiziaria*).[2] In every Prosecution Office (*Procura della Repubblica*) there is a unit of the investigative police composed of members of different police forces.[3] Investigative police officers are 'functionally dependent' on the prosecutor in that they must follow his directions and report to him on every crime without delay,[4] so as to allow the prosecutor to immediately take charge of the investigation.[5] However, they are organizationally dependent on their hierarchical superiors within the police and

---

1   It has rightly been observed that '[t]he inclusion of prosecutors within the same constitutional category as judges conceptualizes the prosecutorial function as judicial, or at least quasi-judicial', Caianiello 2012, p. 250.
2   Under Article 109 of the Constitution, 'judicial authorities directly avail themselves of the investigative police'. See also Articles 56 and 58 of the Code of Criminal Procedure (hereinafter 'c.c.p.').
3   Article 58 c.c.p.
4   Article 347 c.c.p.
5   Gialuz 2014, p. 26.

thus, ultimately, on the Executive.[6] In practice, the degree of autonomy of the police varies depending on the complexity of the investigation.[7] In investigations concerning organized crime and terrorism (the only crimes in respect of which collaboration is possible) the prosecutor is always fully in charge. In each of the 26 District Courts of Appeal (located in the district's main city), a specialized Prosecution Office and police force have been established with exclusive competence over organised crime and terrorism investigations (*Direzione Distrettuale Antimafia* – DDA and *Direzione Investigativa Antimafia* – DIA, respectively). DDAs and DIAs are coordinated at the national level by the Anti-mafia National Bureau (*Direzione Nazionale Antimafia*-DNA), located in Rome and headed by the National Anti-mafia Prosecutor.

The judge for preliminary investigations (*Giudice per le indagini preliminari* – GIP) supervises the pre-trial phase, intervening only at the request of the parties (mainly the prosecutor) for specific purposes foreseen by the law. It would be incorrect to say that the GIP supervises the investigation; rather, he has a guarantee function towards the suspect. For example, he decides on the application of measures restricting personal liberty and freezing orders, he authorizes interception of communications and decides on the prosecutor's request to dismiss the case.

If, at the end of the investigation, the prosecutor decides to press a formal charge against an individual, he summons the person before the judge for the preliminary hearing (*Giudice dell'udienza preliminare* – GUP) who decides whether to commit the person to trial. The trial is held before a different judge (*Giudice del dibattimento*). During the trial, the prosecution acts as a party, introducing evidence against the accused in support of his conviction. In the current system, the information gathered during the investigation cannot in principle form the basis of the judge's decision.[8] Only the evidence presented orally in court and challenged through cross-examination may be used at trial. The separation between the investigative and the trial phase is ensured through the mechanism of the 'double dossier', aimed at ensuring that the trial judge does not have access to the materials gathered during the investigation.[9] During the investigation, all records of evidence are collected in the prosecutor's dossier. After the preliminary hearing, the contents of this dossier are split. The trial judge is given a new trial-dossier that contains only the evidence that is objectively impossible to reproduce in court (*corpus delicti*, wiretappings, records of searches performed by the police, records of prior convictions of the accused). The trial-dossier is then supplemented with the records of the evidence taken orally at trial.[10] After the preli-

---

6   Montana 2009, p. 13-14; Illuminati & Caianiello 2007, p. 133-134.
7   Caianiello 2010, p. 373-423.
8   Illuminati 2005, p. 572. There are, however, exceptions to this principle. For example, under Article 431(2) c.c.p., the parties may agree to include investigative activities in the trial dossier. Moreover, the Code envisages a number of simplified proceedings, such as the 'abbreviated trial', whereby the judge's decision is based on the investigative dossier. See also § 5.4.5 of this report.
9   Panzavolta 2005, p. 586ss.
10   Panzavolta 2005, p. 587-588.

minary hearing, the records of the investigation (for example, statements given by a witness to the police or the prosecutor) are available only to the parties, who can use them to prepare for trial or to challenge witnesses' credibility during their testimony in court.

The Italian legal framework on collaborators with justice must be understood in light of two fundamental features of the criminal justice system. First, the principle of mandatory prosecution enshrined in Article 112 of the Constitution, according to which the prosecutor must commence an investigation whenever a crime is brought to his attention by the police or a private person. The principle of mandatory prosecution forbids any kind of agreement or bargaining between the prosecutor and defendants over possible immunity from prosecution in exchange for collaboration. As will be seen, both the content of the collaboration and the benefits provided in exchange for the collaboration are exhaustively regulated by the law, with no margin for negotiation between the parties.

The second fundamental feature of the Italian system against which the Italian legal framework on collaboration with justice must be understood is its sentencing regime. By providing minimum and maximum penalties, aggravating and mitigating circumstances, and lists of factors making for greater severity or leniency, the law leaves little room for discretion to prosecutors in requesting a certain punishment, and to judges in deciding upon the prosecutors' requests. For example, the crime of participation in a mafia-type association is punished with a minimum term of 10 years and a maximum of 15 years of imprisonment.[11] The punishment for the leaders is harsher: from 12 to 18 years.[12] In case of particular aggravating circumstances (i.e., the use of firearms) it can increase to up to 20 years for 'simple' members and 26 years for organizers and leaders.[13] As will be seen, the law equally dictates the margins of discount that judges may grant to offenders who collaborate with justice. It is worth emphasizing at the outset that the Italian law pursues a precise strategy intended to incentivize collaborations. By providing for a so-called 'double-track' regime, the law makes sure that defendants who decide to cooperate with the authorities will receive a much more lenient sentence and penitentiary treatment than those who do not.

5.1.2   Structure

After defining the concept of 'collaborator' (§ 5.2), the present report provides an excursus on the Italian legislation on the institute of collaboration with justice, starting from the motives that prompted its introduction in 1991 and the reasons for its amendment in 2001 (§ 5.3). Subsequently, the report moves on to consider the legal framework. It will

---

11   Article 416-*bis* of the Criminal Code (hereinafter 'c.c.'), which punishes the simple participation in a mafia-type association. Each one of the specific crimes (extortions, murders, etc.) committed as part of the association's program is punished separately. See Turone 2007, p. 53.

12   Article 416-*bis* (2) c.c.

13   Article 416-*bis* (4) c.c.

first focus on the 'judicial/courtroom aspects', that is, the powers and responsibilities that prosecutors and judges have towards collaborators, and the benefits that the latter may be granted as a reward for the information provided to the judicial authority (§ 5.4). Secondly, the report addresses the system of protection (including the economic assistance) of collaborators, managed by the Central Commission and the Central Protection Service within the police (§ 5.5). The final section of the report (§ 5.6) focuses on the practice. It contains the most recent data on the phenomenon of collaboration with justice as well as the perspective of several practitioners (judges, prosecutors, defence counsels, police officials and sociologists) on selected issues concerning the application of the law.

5.2 CONCEPTUALIZATION, TERMINOLOGY AND RELATIONSHIP TO OTHER INFORMATION PROVIDERS

5.2.1 Police Informants

The category of collaborators with justice must be distinguished from other information providers who play a very different role and have a very different *status* in the course of proceedings. The police informant (*confidenti*) is neither defined nor regulated by law. The only definition of 'police informants' can be found in the case law. In particular, the Court of Cassation has described them as 'persons who, occasionally but systematically, reveal confidential information relating to a crime to the police in exchange for monetary compensation or other advantages.'[14] Of course, these are persons who belong to a criminal circle. The police informant is an indispensable instrument in the hands of the police for infiltrating criminal organizations in order to conduct investigations and report the commission of crimes back to the prosecutor.[15] The use and purpose of police informants is limited to the investigation and the information revealed by them is not intended for use at trial. For this reason, the law bestows the police with the privilege of keeping their sources confidential, even from the judicial authorities. Under Article 203 c.c.p., police and security service officers who testify at trial cannot be compelled by the judge to reveal the name of their informants. In such case, however, their testimony cannot be used as evidence at trial. This provision is in line with the general principle by which anonymous testimony is forbidden. Under Article 195(7) c.c.p., in fact, if a witness cannot or does not want to reveal the source of his/her knowledge (i.e.: the identity of the person who revealed certain information to him/her), the testimony of that witness cannot be taken into consideration by the judge.

---

14 Court of Cassation, sent. n. 36720 of 12 June 2001; Court of Cassation, sent. n. 46023 of 7 November 2007.
15 Auricchio, Panico & Pini 2009, p. 3.

It must be emphasised that the 'appointment' and management of confidential informants is the exclusive competence of the police, with no interference or oversight from the prosecutor. There is no way of knowing what the 'advantages' that informants might gain in exchange for their help with the investigation are. It cannot be excluded that, sometimes, they may consist of favourable treatment when it comes to the investigation of crimes committed by the informant. This is a grey area that appears to be left to the judgment and ethics of police officers. It bears noting, however, that the norms of the Italian criminal code on aiding and abetting and neglect of duty would be applicable in these circumstances.[16]

5.2.2 Witnesses of Justice

Collaborators of justice must also be distinguished from 'witnesses of justice' (testimoni di giustizia). Both figures are regulated by Law n. 82 of 15 March 1991, as amended by Law n. 45 of 13 February 2001 (hereinafter 'the Law'), which will be discussed extensively in the following paragraphs. The difference between collaborators and witnesses is as follows. Whereas the former are members of a criminal organization who decide to dissociate themselves therefrom and cooperate with the authorities, the latter are persons who have never belonged to a criminal circle. Collaborators are criminals who, seemingly for reasons of convenience, break the bonds with their organization. As a consequence, they sign an 'agreement'[17] with the State by which, in exchange for vital information on the structure and the activities of their organization, they are given sentence discounts, penitentiary benefits, protection or economic support for themselves and their families.[18]

The situation could not be more different for witnesses of justice. Usually, they are victims of mafia activities (for example, extortions), who decide to come forward and denounce the abuses they are subject to; other times they are simple citizens who happened to witness the commission of a crime and report it to the authorities, thereby putting their lives at risk.[19] It is worth noting that the contribution that witnesses of justice can make to the investigation is usually much more limited than that of collaborators. Unlike collaborators, witnesses of justice are able to narrate only single, unrelated criminal events. They do not have an overview of the entire structure and dynamics of the organization. Conversely, collaborators are capable of providing an invaluable (and frequently indispensible) insight into the strategies and the goals

---

16 Ibid., 9.
17 It is worth re-stating that this agreement is regulated by the law in all its parts, with no margins of discretion or room for negotiation between collaborators and prosecutors. See further at § 5.4.2.
18 Webpage of the Anti-mafia Commission of the Parliament: http://www.camera.it/_bicamerali/leg15/comm-bicantimafia/documentazionetematica/25/schedabase.asp. See also Article 9(2)(3) of the Law.
19 Ibid. See also Article 16-bis (1) of the Law.

pursued by the organization. Despite these significant differences, there are similarities between collaborators and witnesses.

First of all, they are both called to testify at trial. In substance, therefore, they appear in court as witnesses, with the crucial difference that collaborators are also a party to the proceedings and they thus have an interest in the outcome of the trial.[20] Collaborators, in fact, are often co-defendants of the persons that they accuse in the same or in a separate/ connected proceeding. In the latter case, there are two or more trials, often in different cities, where the issues to prove are substantially connected; collaborators, thus, may be called to testify in each other's trial. In addition, collaborators may be already convicted and called to testify against their former associates. As self-confessed accused, co-accused or convicted persons, their testimony will cover both the criminal activity perpetrated by them, and that perpetrated by their former associates (*chiamata in correità*).[21]

Second, both collaborators and witnesses (and their respective families) are in grave danger because of their testimony and therefore need protection. In 2001, the Law was amended in order to extend the measures of protection and assistance available to collaborators and witnesses of justice and their families.[22] Although the present report focuses on collaborators, it is worth addressing briefly the main differences in the regulation of these two categories. First, whereas the collaboration of offenders may relate only to the most serious crimes, the collaboration of witnesses may refer to crimes of any gravity and, for the purpose of the application of the measures of protection, the only requirement is that the testimony be reliable.[23] Conversely, the information provided by collaborators must not only be reliable, but also complete and must bring new knowledge to the investigation. Second, the assistance measures envisaged for witnesses are more extensive, in that they must guarantee the same living standard that the witness enjoyed prior to the decision to collaborate.[24] This requirement is not envisaged for the measures of assistance to collaborators. Finally, only witnesses are entitled to receive a refund to compensate for their loss of earnings in case they had to quit their job in relation to their testimony.[25]

5.3   DEVELOPMENT OF (LEGAL) RULES

From the late '60s to the early '80s, Italy was in a state of socio-political turmoil, characterised by the 'armed fight' between right-wing and left-wing movements. These years have been marked by numerous attacks on and kidnapping of high-profile public

---

20 Ruggiero 2012, p. 1-2.
21 Ruggiero 2012, p. 1-2.
22 Article 16-*ter* of the Law.
23 Article 16-*bis* (2) of the Law.
24 Article 16-*ter* (1) (b) of the Law.
25 Article 16-*ter* (1) (e) of the Law.

figures (such as judges, journalists and businessmen), and by indiscriminately targeting bombs at the general public, in order to force a change of government (black terrorism) and/or public policies (red terrorism).[26]

The first legislation containing incentives for collaboration dates back to the anti-terrorism legislation of the 1980s. A number of special laws were issued which, on the one hand, provided for harsher penalties for the perpetrators and, on the other hand, for mitigating circumstances for those who dissociated themselves from their accomplices and collaborated with the authorities.[27] At the time, the legislator did not deem it necessary to provide for a system of physical protection of collaborators, nor for a comprehensive intervention on the subject, due to the belief that terrorism was an exceptional phenomenon, limited in time, that could be addressed with *ad hoc* emergency legislation.[28]

Rewarding collaboration proved to be extremely effective in the fight against terrorism. However, it was not until the beginning of the 1990s that similar legislation was introduced with respect to other kinds of organised crime, i.e. drug trafficking, association for the purpose of drug trafficking and the mafia-type crimes. With respect to the former two, Law n. 309 of 9 October 1990 on Narcotics introduced sentence discounts (from a half to two thirds of the penalties envisaged therein) for those who cooperate with the authorities. With respect to the mafia-type crimes, the debate surrounding the legislation on collaboration enacted in those years was particularly heated. It bears observing that mafia-type crimes constitute a very particular kind of organised criminal activity. The mafia has deep roots in certain parts of society, and its defeat is not foreseeable in the immediate future.[29] Many people believed that, unlike terrorists – who could 'repent' due to a crisis of conscience or a loss of faith in their ideology – *mafiosi* could not do so, owing to the different characteristics, aims and methods of their criminal activities.[30] Accordingly, many concerns were raised regarding the trustworthiness and reliability of mafia collaborators.

The insight and knowledge of collaborators (the so called '*pentiti*'), however, proved to be crucial in the maxi-trial against the Sicilian Mafia held in Palermo between 1986 and 1987, with its 475 defendants. The testimony of collaborators such as Tommaso Buscetta and Salvatore Contorno was crucial to secure the conviction of many top-level *mafiosi* and gave the authorities an insight into the internal dynamics of a criminal system that was mostly unknown at the time. In the wake of the maxi-trial, the influence and proposals of judge Giovanni Falcone[31] were determinant in the decision to extend the

---

26 Transcrime 2007.
27 See, in particular, Law Decree n. 625 of 15 December 1979 discussed further at § 5.4.7.1, and Law n. 304 of 29 May 1982, also called 'law on collaborators of justice' (now abrogated). D'Ambrosio 2002, p. 10. See also Vigna 2005, p. 1.
28 Ruggiero 2012, p. 96.
29 Ibid.
30 D'Ambrosio 2002, p. 15; Vigna 2005, p. 2.
31 Giovanni Falcone was a prosecuting magistrate of the investigative pool of Palermo, leader in the fight against the Sicilian Mafia. He was killed by a car bomb in May 1992, together with his wife, Francesca Morvillo, and his bodyguards Vito Schifani, Rocco Dicillo and Antonio Montinaro.

norms on collaborators of justice to mafia-type crimes. One of the first incentives to collaboration with respect to these crimes was introduced by Law n. 152 of 12 May 1991, which, at Article 8, envisages a special mitigating circumstance for those who distance themselves from the organization and help the authorities in establishing the facts or in locating and capturing other offenders.[32]

With respect to mafia, however, it soon became clear that the incentive of sentence discounts through mitigating circumstances was not sufficient. These had to be complemented by a series of post conviction benefits[33] and, very importantly, by an articulated system of physical protection and assistance for collaborators and their families. The first comprehensive regulation on these subjects was introduced in 1991, through Law n. 82/1991, which capitalized on the experience of the anti-mafia maxi trials of the 80s. It bears emphasizing that, before 1991, the protection of collaborators was left to the initiative of the prosecutor who took their statements, together with the local police. In the absence of a comprehensive legal framework, there was great uncertainty as to the situations and conditions under which protection could be granted, as well as a lack of clarity regarding the degree of protection to be afforded in a given situation.[34] The law of 1991 introduces a clear set of prerequisites for the granting of protection and establishes an *ad hoc* centralized body attached to the Ministry of the Interior, the Central Commission, responsible for establishing a 'special protection program' for collaborators upon the request of the prosecutor. As will be seen, this system is still in place with some relevant modifications having been introduced in 2001. It is worth listing the most relevant drawbacks of Law n. 82, so as to be able to understand the reasons for its amendment in 2001 and, by extension, the guiding principles behind the current legal framework.

5.3.1   The Shortcomings of Law N. 82/1991

The most problematic aspects of the 1991 regime can be summarized as follows: i) collaborators were too easily admitted to the special protection program and, as a result, the system became 'clogged' with an excessive number of protected collaborators and family members, whose management became very difficult; ii) the regime did not have sufficient safeguards in place against unreliable collaborators. These two aspects are connected and inter-related. For the sake of clarity, however, they will be examined separately.

---

32 See § 5.4.7.1 of this report.
33 In the course of this Report the terms 'prison benefits', 'post conviction benefits' and 'penitentiary benefits' are used interchangeably.
34 Vigna 1992, p. 133; see also Ruggiero 2012, p. 96-97, describing the symbiotic relationship between prosecutor and collaborator that this system favoured.

5.3.1.1   The 'Clogging' of the System

The main cause for the clogging of the system lay in a combination of factors. First, Law n. 82/1991 envisioned a link between the possibility of being granted sentence discounts/post-conviction benefits and the admission to the measures of protection. In order for the former to be granted by the judge, the collaborator must have been admitted to the special program of protection by the Central Commission. Therefore, the decision of the judicial authority on the provision of post-conviction benefits depended on the decision of the administrative authority to admit the person to the protection program.[35] By linking two moments, this norm created excessive rigidity in the system, whereby prosecutors were also 'obliged' to request protection for persons who were not in serious danger in order to ensure the availability of post conviction benefits and, by so doing, secure their collaboration.

Second, such rigidity was especially problematic in light of the excessively favourable treatment regarding prison and post conviction benefits. In particular, convicted collaborators were eligible for parole and other benefits in the absence of a minimum time of sentence served and pre-trial detention could be revoked or replaced as an automatic reward for collaboration. The prospect of benefitting from such a convenient treatment made the choice of collaboration very appealing and led to an immediate growth in the number of collaborations. Under this regime, many dangerous *mafiosi* admitted to the protection program were automatically released and, in some instances, did not spend a day in prison.[36] Understandably, this scandalised public opinion, sparking huge controversy and negative media attention. In addition, many collaborators provided false or altered information in order to 'impress' the prosecutor and appear indispensable for the progression of the investigation,[37] so as to be immediately liberated. Above all, the link between measures of protection and prison-benefits, combined with an excessively favourable penitentiary treatment, resulted in a vicious circle. It was not infrequent that collaborators would threaten to withdraw their statements or remain silent at trial if they were not admitted to the protection program.[38] As a consequence, prosecutors would be inclined to overestimate the danger to which collaborators were subject, so as to obtain the admission to the protection program by the Central Commission and, by so doing, secure as many collaborations as possible.[39]

Another problematic aspect of Law n. 82/1991 is that it did not envisage a graduated system of protection. Under its regime, collaborators could be granted either the usual/ordinary protection by law enforcement authorities, or they could be admitted to the special protection program by the Central Commission. The ordinary measures of

---

35   D'Ambrosio 2002, p. 60.
36   D'Ambrosio 2002, p. 62.
37   Ruggiero 2012, p. 127-128.
38   D'Ambrosio 2002, p. 62.
39   Ruggiero 2012, p. 127-128.

protection,[40] which pre-existed the Law, were usually greatly insufficient to ensure a meaningful safeguard of mafia-crimes collaborators.[41] Conversely, the special program adopted by the Central Commission envisaged a thorough scheme of protection – involving, *inter alia*, the transfer of the person to a protected place or the issuing of cover documents – that, due to its costs, should have been applied only in the most serious cases. The absence of a middle ground of protection between the ordinary measures and special program, resulted in an excessive use of the latter, with a huge waste of resources as a result.

Finally, the special measures of protection were applicable to investigations concerning a wide variety of crimes, i.e., all the crimes for which Article 380 c.c.p. prescribes mandatory arrest *in flagrante delicto* (among which, for example, some kinds of theft, robbery and nearly all crimes relating to fire-arms and narcotics).[42] This category was too wide and also allowed for measures of protection to be granted to collaborators who were not under a serious risk of retaliation from a criminal organization.

5.3.1.2   Unreliable Collaborators

The second problematic aspect of Law n. 82 related to the insufficiency of the safeguards against unreliable collaborators. Law n. 82 did not envisage a deadline by which collaborators would have to share their knowledge with the authorities. *De facto*, this gave collaborators the capacity to dictate the timing of their revelations. It was not unusual for collaborators to deliberately withhold pieces of information in the initial interrogatories, only to reveal them subsequently at their convenience (this phenomenon came to be named '*dichiarazioni a rate*', that literally means 'declarations in instalments'). Of course, this behaviour raised serious concerns regarding the reliability of these collaborators. Moreover, there was the problem of abuses in the use of *colloqui investigativi* of detained collaborators (i.e., 'investigative interviews' conducted in jail). Under Article 18-*bis* (1) of Law n. 354/1974 regulating the Penitentiary System, the judicial police[43] may interview the detainees in prison 'for investigative purposes, in order to obtain information useful to prevent and repress the commission of crimes by criminal organizations'.[44] *Colloqui investigativi* are not investigative acts in a formal sense; their

---

40 They consisted in ordinary means of surveillance or in assigning collaborators to certain penitentiary institutions and not to others. Ruggiero 2012, p. 100, footnote 8.

41 Franco Roberti, 'Nella netta distinzione tra premio e tutela, un contributo al superamento delle distorsioni', in Guida al Diritto, Il Sole 24 Ore, 24 March 2001, p. 45, footnote 1.

42 D'Ambrosio 2002, p. 113, footnote 1.

43 Namely, the personnel of the DIAs (Investigative Anti-mafia Directorates), the police officials of the central and provincial services of the judicial police, and the police officers delegated by them. Pursuant to Article 18-*bis* (2) of Law n. 354/1974, *colloqui investigativi* by police officials and officers must be authorised by the prosecutor conducting the investigation or the Ministry of Justice.

44 Under Article 18-*bis* (5) of Law n. 354/1974, *colloqui investigativi* may also be conducted by the National Anti-mafia Prosecutor as part of his coordinating functions (in this case, no authorization is required).

function is merely that of prompting further investigations. As such, their nature is confidential, they are not put officially on record,[45] and they are not used at trial. Typically, through the *colloqui investigativi*, the authorities also assess whether the margin for collaboration. It can safely be said that one of the purposes of *colloqui investigativi* is that of prompting collaborations of detained defendants.[46] In the past, many individuals started to collaborate with the authorities after these investigative interviews, and continue to do so nowadays. In the past, however, police officials have pressured detainees and directed their statements towards a specific version of the facts, useful for the investigation.[47] Clearly, stronger safeguards had to be put in place in order to prevent these abuses and, more generally, to ensure the reliability of collaborators.

5.3.2   The Amendments of Law N. 45/2001

Law n. 82/1991 was amended ten years later, by Law n. 45/2001. Law n. 45 does not replace Law n. 82, but rather, intervenes on it in order to remedy the shortcomings caused by that law. Since the amended text of Law n. 82/1991 is the current legal framework on the institute of collaboration with justice, this section gives only a brief account of the major changes brought forward by Law n. 45/2001. A detailed analysis of the integrated text is conducted in § 5.4 of this report. The goal of Law n. 45/2001 is twofold. On the one hand, it seeks to ensure a more rigorous selection of collaborators; on the other hand, it is aimed at guaranteeing a higher degree of reliability of their declarations.[48]

5.3.2.1   A More Rigorous Selection of Collaborators

Law n. 45 severs the link between physical protection and sentence discounts/post-conviction benefits. The latter is now completely independent from protection measures. Since 2001, prosecutors can propose, and judges can grant, mitigating circumstances and post-conviction benefits to collaborators, irrespective of the decision of the Central Commission regarding their protection. In addition, Law n. 45 introduces a graduated system of physical protection by envisaging a 'middle ground' between ordinary measures and special protection programme. In particular, Law n. 45 introduces a set of 'special protection measures' applicable to collaborators for whom ordinary measures would be insufficient, but whose situation is not so serious as to require admission into the special protection program. At the same time, Law n. 45 envisages a more rigorous application of penitentiary benefits: collaboration does not automatically determine the

---

45 However, Article 18-*bis* (3) of Law n. 354/1974 mandates that the date, time and duration of the interview are annotated in a confidential roster by the Director of the prison.
46 D' Ambrosio 2002, p. 154. See also, § 5.6.3 of this report.
47 Ibid.
48 Parrini 2007.

revocation/substitution of pre-trial detention and, in order to be eligible for post-conviction benefits, the person must have served at least one-fourth of the sentence. By making collaboration less appealing and ensuring that protection be granted only where strictly necessary, these amendments successfully put an end to the 'vicious circle' described in the previous paragraph.

Finally, Law n. 45 limits the range of crimes for which a reward can be granted for collaboration. Protection and benefits are now limited to collaboration in relation to the most serious crimes (terrorism, subversion and mafia-type crimes under Article 51(3-*bis*) c.c.p.).

5.3.2.2   Ensuring the Reliability of Collaborators

Law n. 45 introduces a number of safeguards aimed at preventing unreliable collaborations. First, it establishes a time limit of six months for the collaborator to reveal *everything* that he knows to the authorities. The underlying rationale of the 180-day deadline is preservation of the 'genuineness' of the contribution and avoiding the risk that, with the passing of time, the collaborator be subject to external influences or pressures to modify/adjust his statements. Moreover, it is also aimed at stopping the phenomenon described in the previous paragraph, by which collaborators would 'save' important information during the initial interrogations and disclose it at their convenience at a later stage. Second, Law n. 45 introduces a number of provisions aimed at avoiding contacts between collaborators in jail, and communications between them and their families or other persons at liberty. In the same logic, it introduces a prohibition for the authorities to conduct *colloqui investigativi* during the time in which the declarations of the collaborator are put on record. Another crucial novelty of Law n. 45 is the provision that obliges collaborators to disclose all the information concerning their properties, liabilities and financial status. Having a full knowledge of collaborators' financial situation is essential in order to assess their credibility, and for a better understanding of the extent and nature of their ties to the criminal organisation. Finally, Law n. 45 introduces specific sanctions aimed at punishing collaborators who provided false or altered declarations. Specifically, it envisages the revocation of the measures of economic assistance and protection, as well as the retrial of the collaborator. It is now time to examine all these provisions in detail in describing the current legal framework.

5.4   LEGAL FRAMEWORK

As has been seen, Law n. 82 of 15 March 1991,[49] as amended by Law n. 45 of 13 February 2001[50] ('the Law') comprehensively regulates the institute of collaboration with justice. The Law must be read in conjunction with the Decrees of the Minister of the Interior for its implementation.[51] The following analysis will focus on the 'judicial/courtroom aspects' of the legal framework. It addresses the scope of the Law, the procedure by which collaborators' declarations must be recorded by the prosecutor and the specific rules for their evaluation by the judge at trial. Moreover, it illustrates the sentence discounts and penitentiary benefits that collaborators may be awarded.

5.4.1   Regarding Which Offences?

Under Article 9(2) of the Law, the benefits envisaged therein can be granted to defendants who collaborate in the investigation/prosecution of the crimes of subversion, terrorism, and the mafia-type crimes referred to in Article 51(3-bis) c.c.p. These are: mafia-type association (Article 416-bis c.c.), association for the purpose of trafficking in drugs (Article 74 of Law n. 309/1990), association for the purpose of smuggling tobacco products (Article 291-quater of Law n. 43/1973), association for the purpose of kidnapping to extort ransom money (Article 630 c.c.), crimes committed through the 'mafia method'[52] or perpetrated with the aim of assisting the activities of mafia-type associations, association for the purpose of enslavement (Article 600 c.c.), association for the purpose of child prostitution, child pornography, sex tourism (Article 600-bis, ter and quarter c.c.), association for the purpose of human trafficking (Article 601 c.c.), and for the purpose of slave trade (Article 602 c.c.).

5.4.2   The Responsibility for Providing Undertakings

The prosecutor is the authority in charge of the investigation and, as such, is also primarily responsible of managing the relationship with collaborators in the phase of

---

49 Law n. 82/1991 introduces 'New norms on kidnapping for ransom, the protection of witnesses of justice and the protection and the sanctioning of offenders who cooperate with justice'.

50 Law n. 45/2001 introduces 'Amendments to the framework on the protection and the sanctioning of offenders who cooperate with justice, and new dispositions on witnesses of justice'.

51 Ministerial Decree n. 263 of 24 July 2003 on the transfer of assets and other properties owned by collaborators; Ministerial Decree n. 161 of 23 April 2004, envisaging procedures for the implementation of the special protection measures; Ministerial Decree n. 138 of 13 May 2005, envisaging measures for the social reintegration of persons under protection; Ministerial Decree n. 144 of 7 February 2006, dictating specific rules for the detention of collaborators.

52 See further at § 5.4.7.1.

the investigation. Once an offender reaches the decision to collaborate, he requests a *colloquio* (a meeting) with the prosecutor. From this moment on, the Law regulates every aspect of the relationship between collaborators and the judicial authority (i.e., prosecutors and judges), including the benefits to which collaborators are entitled and the obligations to which they are subject.

Under Article 16-*quater* (1) of the Law, within 180-days from the manifestation of the willingness to collaborate, the collaborator must reveal: a) all the information in his possession regarding the facts about which he is interrogated by the prosecutor; b) all other information in his possession regarding facts of major gravity and social alarm; c) all the information that is necessary to locate, seize and confiscate the money or assets in his ownership or in the ownership of other members of the organization (both directly and through a dummy).

As discussed in the following sub-paragraph, all of the above information must be given in the form of a statement that is put on record (*verbale illustrativo della collaborazione*). Pursuant to Article 16-*quater* (4), the collaborator must also formally declare that he is not in possession of further information, even unrelated to the episodes that he has narrated, regarding facts of serious gravity or social alarm. Accordingly, the collaborator must disclose his entire knowledge to the investigative authority; there is nothing that he can withdraw from the prosecutor. The benefits that the collaborator will gain in exchange for the information provided are those (and only those) foreseen by the Law. The prosecutor does not make any 'promise' to the collaborator; he and defence counsel merely inform the latter of the existence of such benefits and on how they apply in the specific situation. Under Article 9(3) of the Law, the information provided by the collaborator must be *intrinsically reliable, complete*, and must bring *new knowledge* to the investigation, or it must appear important for the trial or the advancement of the investigation concerning the organizational structure, the equipment, the domestic and international relationships and the purposes of the criminal organization. The assessment of these requirements lies within the full discretion of the prosecutor.[53] By interrogating the person on the facts that are most relevant to the investigation, the prosecutor will form an opinion on the utility of the contribution and the reliability of the person. Based on this evaluation, the prosecutor may also choose between various 'aspiring' collaborators. For example, if several defendants approach the prosecutor expressing their willingness to reveal information regarding the same criminal pattern, the prosecutor has the discretion to decide whose revelations fulfil the requirements of reliability, completeness and novelty foreseen by the Law (also in light of the knowledge acquired by the authorities by that time through other means of investigation such as the interception of communication).[54]

---

53 De Lucia 2016.
54 Ibid.

5.4.3   Procedure to be Followed and Deadline

Pursuant to Article 16-*quater* (1)(3) of the Law, the collaboration must be given in the form of a statement that must be put on record (*verbale illustrativo della collaborazione*) within 180 days from the manifestation of the willingness to cooperate.[55]

The *verbale illustrativo* represents the first crucial moment of evaluation and control of the 'genuineness' of the collaboration.[56] Moreover, as will be seen in the following sub-section, it is also a requirement for obtaining the sentence discounts and penitentiary benefits and, very importantly, for the admission to the protection measures. It is due to the crucial importance of this document that the Law imposes a deadline for its completion as well as particular forms and modalities for its recording.[57] When the collaborator is detained, the *verbale illustrativo* must be fully recorded through the use of audio and video recording equipment.[58] There is no such obligation when the person is not detained. The Law does not expressly require that the *verable illustrativo* be made in the presence of defence counsel, but in practice the collaborator's attorney is always present.

There is another important rule that applies when the collaborator is detained, aimed at safeguarding the 'genuineness' of the collaboration. Under Article 13(14) of the Law, until the *verbale illustrativo* is completed, the collaborator is kept in 'isolation' from the other detainees – especially those who have also expressed a willingness to collaborate – and from his family (phone calls and letters are forbidden).[59] What must be avoided is that collaborators detained in the same facility agree on a 'strategy' or provide so-called *dichiarazioni concertate* (concerted declarations), as well as that they are negatively influenced or discouraged by their family in sticking with their choice. In the same logic, *colloqui investigativi* with the police (and the prosecutors of the National Anti-mafia Bureau) are forbidden during the six months, in order to avoid pressure by the investigative authorities.[60] If the above rules are violated, the statements made after the commission of the violation cannot be used at trial.[61]

5.4.4   Failure to Meet the 180-Day Deadline

The 180-day deadline binds both the collaborator and the prosecutor. Failure to complete the *verbale illustrativo* within six months from the manifestation of the willingness to collaborate entails very serious consequences for both; the collaborator cannot be granted

---

55 For the rationale of this deadline see *supra* at § 5.3.2.2.
56 D'Ambrosio 2002, p. 119.
57 Ibid.
58 Article 16-*quater* (3) of the Law and Article 141-*bis* c.c.p.
59 See also Article 3 of the Ministerial Decree n. 144 of 2006.
60 Article 13(14) and (15) of the Law.
61 Article 13(15) of the Law.

the benefits envisaged by the Law (sentence discounts, penitentiary benefits, protection and economic assistance) or the latter are revoked;[62] and the statements given after the six-month term cannot be used as evidence. This is the legal sanction of the so-called *inutilizzabilità*, which literally means: 'forbidden use'.[63]

Given the importance of the consequences that derive from the failure to respect this deadline, it is striking that the Law does not specify the modalities through which the 'manifestation of the willingness to cooperate' must be formalized.[64] The Court of Cassation has intervened on this matter several times, clarifying that the willingness to cooperate 'cannot be manifested in a generic way', but must be recorded by the prosecutor in a formal act, from whose date the 180 days shall be counted.[65] In practice, since it is often impossible to collect the entire content of the collaboration in only one session (certain collaborators have decades of criminal activity to narrate), the prosecutor meets with the collaborator several times in order to finalize the *verbale illustrativo* under Article 16*quater* (1)(3). The latter, therefore, is composed by a number of *verbali illustrativi* that the prosecutor forms in the span of 180 days, elapsing from the completion of the first one.

With respect to the content of the *verbale illustrativo*, the latter must set the 'perimeter' of the collaboration.[66] The Court of Cassation has constantly held that 'the sanction of the *inutilizzabilità* for the declarations given after the 180-day deadline applies only to the statements concerning new facts or the responsibility of new persons, and does not concern the clarifications or integrations aimed at better explaining what the collaborator has previously revealed'.[67]

Therefore, what the prosecutor is required to do within the 180 days is to ensure that all the *essential passages* of the collaborator's story are listed in the *verbale illustrativo*. As long as the 'backbone' of the collaboration is included in the *verbale*, the details can be expanded upon at trial. It would be infeasible and unrealistic, in fact, to expect from collaborators a photographic memory of events dating back from several decades. In other words, the 180-day deadline concerns the so-called 'unforgettable facts', that is, the events that – due to their social or psychological relevance – cannot be erased by the mind of an average person.[68]

---

62 Article 16-*quater* (7) of the Law and Article 16-*quarter* (1) of the Law.
63 Under Article 16-*quarter* (9) of the Law: 'any statement given by the person to the prosecutor or the police after six months from the manifestation of the willingness to collaborate cannot be used as evidence against others' (i.e., the statements can be used only against the collaborator himself).
64 Laudati 2003, p. 33.
65 Court of Cassation, Sez. VI penale, sent. n. 15556 of 25 March 2011; Court of Cassation, Sez. I penale, sent. n. 47513 of 29 November 2007, Schiavone et al.; Court of Cassation, Sez. I penale, sent. n. 41028 of 13 November 2002, Fiore. See also De Lucia 2016.
66 De Lucia 2016.
67 Court of Cassation, Sez. V penale, sent. n. 506 of 25 September 2006; Court of Cassation, Sez. I penale, sent. n. 13697 of 8 March 2007.
68 Court of Cassation, Sez. V penale, sent. n. 1746 of 20 November 2007; see also De Lucia 2016.

Finally, it is important to mention another crucial jurisprudential intervention that has considerably narrowed the scope and the consequences of the sanction imposed by Article 16-*quater* (9) of the Law. As mentioned, this norm provides that 'any statement given by the person to the prosecutor or the police after six months from the manifestation of the willingness to collaborate cannot be used as evidence against others'. The Court of Cassation, however, has considerably narrowed the scope of this sanction, stating that the latter must be intended as relative and not absolute (*inutilizzabilità relativa*).[69] Pursuant to the interpretation of the Court, it is now established that the only forbidden use of the late declarations of collaborators is that of the so-called *contestazioni* under Article 500 c.c.p. This means that the parties cannot challenge or support the testimony of the collaborator at trial by using those declarations.[70] This implies that if the collaborator repeats the content of the late declarations before the judge on his own initiative, the latter may take them into account for the purpose of the decision.[71] Finally, the late declarations may (and must) prompt an investigation by the prosecutor into the new facts (in accordance with the principle of mandatory prosecution); they may form the evidentiary basis of the prosecutor's request for coercive measures to the judge of the preliminary investigation, and they may be used as evidence in the 'simplified proceedings' where the judge issues a decision based on the investigative dossier.[72]

5.4.5 The Use of the Declarations at Trial

Under Article 16-*quater* (3) of the Law, the *verbale illustrativo* is inserted in its entirety in a file kept by the prosecutor who recorded it. However, the excerpts of the *verbale* that relate to other investigations are transmitted to the competent Prosecutor's Offices across the country, and are included in their investigative-dossiers. Collaborators usually report on several criminal episodes/acts committed by members of their criminal organization. As a consequence, a number of proceedings against various persons may be opened simultaneously, following their declarations. This also means that the same collaborator may be (and most often is) called to testify in more than one trial.[73]

The nature of the *verbale illustrativo* is certainly that of an investigative act.[74] Therefore, it follows the rules concerning the use of investigative acts at trial. As was seen in the introduction to this report, the statements provided by witnesses to the Prosecution during the investigation are not included in the trial-dossier and, thus, are not accessible to

---

69 Court of Cassation, S.U, sent n. 1149 of 25 September 2008, Magistris.
70 For a more detailed explanation of the concept of '*contestazione*' see the following paragraph.
71 Court of Cassation (n. 69), Magistris.
72 The Code of Criminal Procedure envisages a number of 'alternative' or 'simplified' proceedings. For example, the 'abbreviated trial' under Article 438ss c.c.p.
73 D' Ambrosio 2002, p. 54.
74 Article 12(2) of the Law; Giordano 2001, p. 56.

the judge, but only to the parties.[75] Under Article 500 c.c.p., witness statements contained in the prosecutor's file can be used by the parties to challenge the testimony of the witness at trial. As such, they can be evaluated by the judge only for the purpose of assessing the credibility of the witness (and only if the parties bring them to his/her attention), but not as a proof of the facts narrated therein. In practice, this means that, after the collaborator has testified in court, defence counsel of the persons that the collaborator has accused may cross-examine him, highlighting possible contradictions or discrepancies in what he has previously declared in the *verbale illustrativo*. Based on this confrontation, the judge may draw conclusions as to the reliability of the collaborator. However, he cannot, *per se*, consider as 'proved' either of the two different versions of the facts narrated by the collaborator. This is the general rule that governs the use of declarations of witnesses (including collaborators) at trial.

It bears reminding, however, that under Article 438ss c.c.p., defendants may choose the so-called 'abbreviated trial'. With the abbreviated trial, the defendant accepts to be sentenced based on the materials contained in the investigative dossier (including witness/collaborators' statements), in exchange for a sentence discount of one-third.

5.4.6   The Judicial Scrutiny of the Declarations

At the outset, it is important to clarify that, ultimately, it is the judge who decides whether the collaborators presented at trial by the prosecutor are reliable. Simply put, it is the judge (and not the prosecutor) who decides who is a collaborator and who is not. The judge is called to evaluate the statements made by collaborators in two moments: 1) in the pre-trial phase/investigation phase, if the prosecutor requests the judge for the preliminary investigation (GIP) the issuance of a coercive measure (es. pre-trial detention) against persons accused by the collaborator. In this case, the GIP evaluates the collaborators' statements (together with the rest of the investigative material presented by the prosecutor) in order to decide whether to issue the measure; 2) at trial, in order to decide on the guilt or innocence of the defendants accused by the collaborator, as well as on the sentence discounts and the benefits for the collaborator himself. If the collaborator and the person he accuses are co-defendant in the same trial, these issues will be decided jointly (i.e., in the same sentence). Conversely, if the collaborator is a defendant in a separate/connected trial (see supra at § 5.2.2) the issues will be decided separately before the respective competent judges. It goes without saying that deciding on the 'guilt' of the collaborator means deciding on the sentence discounts and the penitentiary benefits to which he is entitled by the Law. A collaborator, in fact, will always be found 'guilty', in that

---

75 Despite the terminological distinction between 'witnesses' and 'collaborators' adopted by the Law, the procedural nature of the declarations contained in the *verbale illustrativo* is that of witnesses' statements.

he is a self-confessed defendant. However, unlike the other defendants who have decided not to collaborate, he will be rewarded with sentence discounts and penitentiary benefits.

Article 273(1*bis*) c.c.p. demands that the statements of collaborators be evaluated according to the same criteria in both the pre-trial and the trial phase. In this respect, the Code of Criminal Procedure dictates a specific rule that binds the udge. Pursuant to Article 192(3) c.c.p., the statements made by collaborators shall be corroborated by other evidence confirming their reliability.[76] By limiting the freedom of the judge to select and weigh evidence – which is the general principle regulating the evaluation of evidence in the Italian system – Article 192(3) demonstrates a certain degree of scepticism towards the probative value of the declarations of collaborators. This is understandable, as collaborators constitute a very specific kind of witness, with an interest in the outcome of the proceedings. They provide a testimony following an 'agreement' with the State, and in exchange for a number of benefits. As such, their statements must be evaluated with particular caution. Article 192(3) c.c.p., thus, is primarily aimed at avoiding that convictions are based solely on the declarations of collaborators of justice, in the absence of additional elements confirming the responsibility of the accused.[77]

This provision does not specify what may constitute valid 'corroborating evidence'. The Court of Cassation has ruled several times on the correct interpretation of Article 192 (3) c.c.p.[78] It has clarified that the evaluation of the declarations of collaborators must be carried out in accordance with a three-prong test and in the following order: a) First, the credibility of the collaborator must be established. To this end, the judge must consider the collaborator's personality, his social and economic status, his personal criminal record, his relations with the accused and the reasons that have prompted him to collaborate with the authorities. It is of course the job of the prosecutor to provide the judge with all the relevant information in these respects. b) Second, the intrinsic credibility of the statements must be assessed. To this end, the judge must evaluate their coherence, precision, consistency and spontaneity. c) Third, the judge shall verify the existence of external elements of corroborations (*riscontri esterni*). Such elements must consist of objective facts that are external and independent from the declarations of the collaborator. For example, if the collaborator narrates that he, together with accused X, committed a murder and buried the body in a certain location, the external element of corroboration will be the discovery of the corpse in that precise location. The *riscontri esterni* must confirm every segment of the collaborator's narration. This means that, if the collaborator reports a number of criminal episodes with the participation of several co-defendants, it is not sufficient that the *riscontro* confirms the occurrence of only one of the episodes (or the participation of one co-defendant) in order for the entire narration

---

76 Literally: 'statements made by persons co-accused of the same crime or by persons accused in related proceedings or of a related crime shall be evaluated next to other evidence that confirms their reliability'.
77 Ruggiero 2012, p. 48.
78 Court of Cassation, S. U., sent. n. 1653 of 22 February 1993, Marino.

to be deemed reliable. To the contrary, every crime and the participation of every single person will have to be verified. In this respect, it must be noted that the *riscontri* must be '*individualizzanti*', that is, they must unequivocally link the commission of the narrated crime to the accused. Therefore, in the above-stated example, the prosecutor will have to gather additional external evidence that confirms that the murder was committed in cooperation with accused X, and not with accused Y or someone else.[79]

The *riscontro esterno* may consist of any type of evidence, including declarations of other collaborators or witnesses that confirm the version of events provided by the first collaborator.[80] In such cases, however, the judge must verify that the statements of the various collaborators had not been agreed on beforehand, or, in any case, that collaborators did not – even inadvertently – influence each other.[81]

Finally, it is important to stress the role of the judge in attributing what in the legal community is referred to as a 'credibility license' to collaborators. This means that, if a collaborator has been deemed reliable in a final sentence, the latter may be used as evidence in the other trials in which the collaborator is called to testify.[82] As a consequence, the first step of the aforementioned three-pronged test for the assessment of the credibility of the collaborator will not have to be repeated by the judge in other trials.

5.4.7   Nature of the Undertakings

The benefits that may be provided collaborators fall into two categories: 1) judicial benefits, accorded by a judge; 2) protection/assistance benefits, accorded by the administrative authority. This paragraph is concerned with the first category. Within this group, a distinction can be drawn between sentence discounts deriving from the application of mitigating circumstances by the trial judge, and benefits related to the penitentiary treatment in the pre-trial and post-conviction phase. The following sub-paragraphs will examine them separately. Here, it is worth recalling that Article 16-*quinquies* (1) and 16*nonies* (4) of the Law prescribe that judicial benefits may be granted only to defendants whose statements have been recorded in the *verbale illustrativo* within the 180 days.[83]

---

79 Court of Cassation, Sez. I penale, 8 November 2000, Cannella et al., quoted by Ruggiero 2012, p. 67.
80 Court of Cassation, Sez. I penale, 13 April 1992, Tommaselli; Court of Cassation, S.U., 13 February 1990, Belli; Court of Cassation, S.U., 6 December 1991, Scala; Court of Cassation, Sez. I penale, 24 July 1992, Procopio; Court of Cassation, Sez. I penale, 24 July 1992, Bono; See Ruggiero 2012, p. 67.
81 Court of Cassation, S.U., sent. n. 20804 of 29 November 2012.
82 Pursuant to Article 238-*bis* c.c.p., judgments that have become final may be used as evidence for the facts established therein, subject to the above-stated evaluation criteria dictated by Article 192 (3) c.c.p. (that is, together with other elements that confirm their reliability).
83 See *supra* at § 5.4.2, § 5.4.3 and § 5.4.4.

5.4.7.1   Sentence Discounts

With respect to sentence discounts, the Law contains a mere reference to the mitigating circumstances listed in the special legislation[84] and in the Criminal Code (hereinafter 'c.p.').[85] In this respect, the Italian legal framework envisages a so-called 'double track' regime[86] to differentiate the position of offenders who cooperate with justice from those who do not. The latter are subject to a much harsher treatment.[87] For example, with respect to the crimes of terrorism and subversion, Law Decree n. 625/1979 – entitled 'Urgent Measures for the Protection of the Democratic Order and Public Safety'[88] – introduces the crime of 'association for the purpose of terrorism'[89] in the Criminal Code, and provides that the penalties envisaged by the Code for terrorism-related activities always be increased by one-half.[90] At the same time, it envisages a special mitigating circumstance for offenders who, 'dissociating themselves from the group, help the police or the judicial authorities in gathering elements that are decisive for reconstructing the events or prosecuting other members of the group'. In such cases, a sentence of life imprisonment is replaced by a sentence of 12 to 20 years, and the other penalties (i.e., imprisonment) are reduced by one-third to one-half.[91]

The anti-mafia legislation was inspired by this provision. Article 7 of the Law Decree n. 152/1991 – introducing 'Urgent Measures for the Fight against Organized Crime'[92] – envisages a special aggravating circumstance applicable to all the crimes committed by the use of the 'mafia method',[93] or aimed at facilitating the activities of a mafia-type association. Pursuant to this special aggravating circumstance, the penalty is increased by one-third to one-half. Conversely, Article 8 of the same Law Decree envisages a much more lenient treatment for offenders who cooperate with justice, who enjoy the same sentence discounts as collaborative terrorists (life imprisonment is replaced by 12 to 20-year sentence, reduction of other penalties by one-third to one-half).

Along the same line, Article 74(7) of the Law n. 309/1990 on Narcotics establishes a specific mitigating circumstance for collaboration in relation to the crime of association for trafficking in drugs. According to that provision, the penalty established by the same

---

84 See *supra* at § 5.3.
85 Under Article 62 and 62-*bis* c.p., mitigating circumstances may be considered by judges, in particular, where the alleged offender has paid compensation or attempted to minimize or remove the consequences of the offence, before the trial proceedings. In such cases, the sentence may be reduced up to one third.
86 D' Ambrosio 2002, p. 28.
87 The same is true for the provisions relating to the post-conviction treatment that will be examined below at § 5.4.7.2. Article 16-*quater*.
88 Converted with Law n. 15/1980. See also Articles 1-3 of Law n. 304/1982, and Article 1 of Law n. 34/1987.
89 Article 270-*bis* c.c.
90 Article 1 of Law Decree n. 625/1979.
91 Article 4 of Law Decree n. 625/1979.
92 Converted with Law n. 203/1991.
93 Under Article 416-*bis* (3) c.c., the key elements of the 'mafia method' are: a) the intimidatory power deriving from the strength of the associative bond; b) the state of subjection and c) *omertà* (i.e., code of silence) that result from the above-stated power.

article shall be reduced by one-half to two-thirds for the accused who 'effectively endea-voured to secure the evidence of the crime or deprive the association of decisive resources for the perpetration of offences'.

It is important to stress that judges are absolutely independent in deciding: i) whether to grant the sentence discounts envisaged by the Law; ii) in case of positive decision, whether to follow the request of the prosecutor. In other words, it is the judge (and not the prosecutor) who ultimately decides who is a collaborator and who is not (i.e., it is the udge who decides whether the person presented by the prosecutor as a collaborator is reliable, and whether his contribution is of sufficient 'weight' to justify the granting of the benefits).

5.4.7.2   Penitentiary Benefits

Law n. 354/1975 on the prison system (*ordinamento penitenziario*) regulates the penitentiary treatment of convicted persons. This law enshrines the general rule by which persons con-victed of terrorism and mafia-type crimes cannot be granted the penitentiary benefits envi-saged therein,[94] to which persons convicted of other crimes are entitled. This norm is another clear expression of the 'double track' regime, aimed at stronger repression of organised crime. In the same logic, the law on the prison system envisages an exception for persons convicted of terrorism and mafia-type crimes who decide to collaborate with the authorities. Under Article 58-*ter* of the above-mentioned law, collaborators of justice may be granted the benefits of *semilibertà* (day-release),[95] *permessi premio* (good behaviour license)[96] and *lavoro all'esterno* (work outside the correction facility),[97] even before the expiration of the ordinary time limits. Article 16-*nonies* of the Law integrates this legal framework. It provides that convicted collaborators may also be granted the benefits of parole (*liberazione condizionale*)[98] and dom-iciliary detention (*detenzione domiciliare*)[99] in derogation of the ordinary time limits, pro-vided, however, that the person has served at least 1/4 of the sentence, or at least 10 years in cases in which the person has been sentenced to '*ergastolo*' (30 years of imprisonment).

These benefits are granted by the Surveillance Court (*Tribunale di Sorveglianza*) or the Surveillance Magistrate (*Magistrato di Sorveglianza*)[100] upon the request of the Chief Prosecutor before the Appeals Court, or of the National Anti-mafia Prosecutor.[101] They may be revoked on the same conditions that determine the revocation of the protection measures.[102]

---

94 Article 4-*bis* of Law n. 354/1975. The only exception is the concession of 'anticipated liberation' under Article 54 of the same law, which can also be granted to detainees convicted for mafia-type crimes.
95 Article 48 and 50 of Law n. 354/1975.
96 Article 30-*ter* (4) of Law n. 354/1975.
97 Article 21(1) of Law n. 354/1975.
98 Article 176 c.c.
99 Under Article 47-*ter* of Law n. 354/1975.
100 The judges called to supervise the execution of the sentence in the Italian system.
101 Article 16-*nonies* (1) of the Law.
102 Article 16-*nonies* (7). See further at § 5.4.8 and § 5.5.2.

Finally, the treatment concerning detention prior to conviction must be mentioned. With regard to precautionary measures against defendants charged with a mafia-type crime, the Code of Criminal Procedure enshrines the presumption that the only adequate measure is pre-trial detention in jail. Less afflictive measures, such as domiciliary detention, are not applicable to these defendants.[103] Before the reform of 2001, the Law envisaged an exception for detained defendants who decided to collaborate. The latter could be automatically released, and would spend the time before their trial in domiciliary detention. This provision allowed for the immediate liberation of many collaborators who had committed serious crimes, and whose reliability was still very dubious. Law n. 45/2001 thus intervened on this point. Under the current regime, custody pending trial cannot be automatically revoked or replaced for the sole reason that the defendant has started to cooperate with the authorities.[104] In principle, then, during the investigation custody is also the rule for collaborators. Nevertheless, pre-trial detention may be revoked or re-placed with a less coercive measure when the pre-trial judge deems that the person in question has relinquished all connections with the criminal organization and, in case that person has been subject to special protection measures, he has met the obligations undertook pursuant to Article 12 of the Law (see further at § 5.5).

5.4.8   Sanctions for False or Reticent Declarations

Further investigations or declarations of new collaborators might reveal that the collaborator had provided false statements or has omitted relevant information in his possession. If this becomes apparent after the collaborator has been convicted, Article 16-*septies* of the Law mandates that the prosecutor request a retrial to the competent judge, under Articles 629ss c.c.p. The same sanction applies if – within 10 years after a final judgment has been rendered – the collaborator commits a crime indicating that he still belongs to a criminal organization.[105] Naturally, in these cases, the penitentiary benefits will also be revoked.[106]

If the falseness or incompleteness of the collaborator's statements is discovered before a definitive judgment has been rendered, the prosecutor may request an extension of the time-limit for appealing the sentence.[107]

In addition, false or reticent declarations may integrate the crime of calumny under Article 368 c.c. The Law provides that, in such cases, the penalty envisaged in the c.c. is increased by one-third to one-half and, if the collaborator had been granted the benefits

---

103 Article 275(3) c.c.p.
104 Article 16-*octies* of the Law.
105 Article 16-*septies* (1) and (2); the crime must be one of those listed in Article 380 c.c.p. (i.e., a crime for which the arrest *in flagrante delicto* is mandatory).
106 Article 16-*septies* (3) and 16-*nonies* (7) of the Law.
107 Article 16-*septies* (6) of the Law.

envisaged by the Law, the penalty is increased by one-half to two-thirds.[108] As will be seen below, in case of false or reticent declarations, the measures of protection may also be revoked.

5.5   The Protection of Collaborators

Offenders who collaborate with justice are exposed to the risk of retaliation from the criminal group to which they belonged. It is therefore necessary to protect them and their families from the serious danger that collaboration with justice often entails. Before delving into the content of the measures of protection, it bears emphasizing that, pursuant to Article 12 of the Law, in order for the measures to be granted, the person must sign a 'Memorandum of Understanding' regulating the obligations that he undertakes.[109] It is the prosecutor who, before making a proposal of protection to the Central Commission (see further at § 5.5.2), is required to explain to the collaborator what obligations he is under. Those are: a) complying with the security measures that are put in place and actively cooperating in their implementation; b) being questioned during the investigation and at trial; c) complying with the obligations envisaged by the Law and the obligations that he is under; d) not sharing the information with anyone (except for police authorities, judicial authorities and his lawyers), and avoiding any contact with persons belonging to a criminal organization and with other collaborators; e) providing full disclosure of all the goods/properties/assets that he owns or controls (directly or through a third party) and, after the protection measures are put in place, handing over the money originating from illicit activities. The judicial authorities are required to seize the aforementioned goods and money immediately. As will be seen, under Article 13-*quarter* (2) of the Law, failure to fulfil the obligations under b) and e) results in the immediate revocation of the protection.

Finally, the collaborator must sign a *declaration* in which he provides full details of his family status and financial situation, any existing debts and any criminal, civil and administrative proceedings pending against him, as well as his diplomas, professional qualifications or titles, commercial licenses and any other permits in his possession.[110] The prosecutor shall attach this declaration to his request for protection.

---

108 Article 16-*septies* (7) of the Law.
109 Article 9 of the Ministerial Decree n. 161/2004; Cauduro & Di Nicola 2005, p. 83.
110 Article 12 (1) of the Law. It bears noting that this information is used solely for the purpose of granting the protection measures. It does not go to trial if it is not related to the facts that must be proven therein.

5.5.1   The Measures of Protection

The Law is inspired by the principle of graduated protection measures.[111] Depending on how great the risk is, collaborators can benefit from ordinary or special protection. In particular, the Law distinguishes between: a) ordinary protection measures; b) special protection measures; and c) a special protection program.

Ordinary protection measures are adopted by the police authorities, or, when the person is in custody, by the Department of the Penitentiary Administration of the Ministry of Justice.[112] They existed prior to the entry into force of the Law. Special protection measures will be taken when the ordinary measures are insufficient, but the danger is not so grave as to require the transfer of the person to a protected locality.[113] Collaborators subject to these measures thus remain in their hometown, but special surveillance is put in place to protect them, their families, their properties and their goods. They are not granted financial assistance, except for exceptional contributions aimed at social reintegration. These measures can be extended to cover people living on a permanent basis with the collaborator and, in specific situations, to people found to be exposed to a serious and concrete danger because of their relation with the collaborator. The special protection measures may consist of: 1) surveillance and protection measures by local police; 2) technical security arrangements for the person's home and properties (for example, video surveillance cameras or remote alarms); 3) measures necessary for temporary transfers to localities other than the place of residence; 4) for collaborators in detention, special custody arrangements, transfers and guarding; 5) measures aimed at the social rehabilitation, including financial support; 6) any other necessary measure.

In cases where the special protection measures would be inadequate given the seriousness and concrete nature of the danger facing the collaborator, the special protection measures are adopted through a special protection program.[114] The program entails the transfer of the collaborator and his family to a secret and protected locality. Collaborators admitted to the special protection program and their family, thus, are 'relocated' to a different region. In practice, this means that they are transferred to Central and Northern Italy, since the mafia organizations are rooted in the south of the country, where relocations are not possible.

In addition to the surveillance measures, the special protection program involves a modification of the registers and forms of economic assistance. As such, the program provides for additional measures to the ones already indicated, for example: 1) transfer of persons (that are not in custody) to a secret and protected location; 2) cover documents; 3) change of identity (governed by Decree-Law n. 119 of 29/3/1993, but only in

---

111 Vigna 2005, p. 3.
112 Article 9(2) of the Law and Article 3(1)(i) of the Ministerial Decree n. 161/2004.
113 Article 13(4) of the Law and Article 7(4) of the Ministerial Decree n. 161/2004.
114 Article 13(5)-(11) of the Law and Article 8(4) of the Ministerial Decree n. 161/2004.

very exceptional circumstances);[115] 4) special modalities of managing the documents in the file; 5) measures to encourage the social rehabilitation of the collaborator and other people given protection; 6) measures of personal and economic assistance. The final measure may comprise: i) accommodation, ii) medical expenses, iii) legal fees, iv) living expenses (through a monthly allowance), in case it is impossible for the collaborator to work. The amount of the allowance varies depending on the number of the family members of the collaborator.[116]

As will be seen in the following paragraph, all of the above measures of protection are granted by a Central Commission within the Ministry of the Interior and implemented by a Central Protection Service within the police. It also bears noting that this is the only kind of protection that collaborators can be admitted to. The economic assistance that collaborators receive should not be mistaken for a disguised reward for their testimony. To the contrary, it is aimed at sustaining the collaborator and his family during the time that they spend under the protection of the State. As will be seen, in fact, it is often impossible for them to work during these years due to the restrictions that the life under protection entails (see further at § 5.6.6.2). The economic assistance provided by the State, thus, is always proportionate to the needs of the collaborator and his family, and never amounts to an undue profit.

5.5.2   The Admission to Protection and Its Revocation

The admission to the special protection measures and the special protection program is decided by a Central Commission, attached to the Ministry of the Interior.[117] The Commission is chaired by an Under-secretary of State of the Ministry of the Interior and is composed of two magistrates and five State officials.[118] The Central Commission has exclusive competence to decide on whether to grant protection measures, without any further scrutiny. However, it adopts the measures on the request/recommendation of the prosecutor in charge of the investigation or the Chief of Police-Director General of Public

---

115 The difference between covert documents and change of identity must be highlighted. Every person in the protection program is given covert documents (ID card, health insurance card etc.) as a temporary measure, lasting until the end of the program. These provisional documents do not attribute a new identity to the person but are only meant to be used in the protected location. No official legal act can be carried out through these fake documents (their use for this purpose constitutes an offence). Conversely, the change of identity is a permanent measure by which the person is given a new identity in all the Official Registries. It is granted only in the most exceptional circumstances, upon the authorization of the Central Commission and a joint-decree of the Minister of the Interior and the Minster of Justice.

116 The minimum amount of the allowance is € 900 per month, see interview of the Director of the Central Protection Service on La Stampa.it (further at n. 143).

117 Article 10 (2) of the Law.

118 Article 10 (2-*bis*) of the Law. The members of the Commission are experts in the field of organized crime but they are not working on the case concerned and are not otherwise involved in the prosecution of terrorism or Mafia-type crimes.

Security (who must consult with the prosecutor).[119] The proposal is formulated in conjunction with the other Prosecutor's Offices involved in the investigation and with the National Anti-mafia Bureau. The information provided by and viewpoint of the Prosecutor's Offices and the National Anti-mafia Bureau are crucial for the Commission's decision. Usually, the Commission follows the request/recommendation of the prosecutors. However, it is not bound by it, and it can autonomously (i.e., through the Central Protection Service) conduct inquiries to assess the risk to which collaborators are subject to.

In the most urgent and serious cases, the Commission may also put into place a provisional protection plan without formalities, based on the brief allegations of the prosecutor (or Chief of Police). The provisional plan ceases to have effects if, after 180 days, the competent authority has not formulated a formal proposal of admission to the special protection measures or program.[120]

The Commission sets a duration for the special measures and the protection program, within the limits prescribed by the Ministerial Decree (from 6 months to 5 years).[121] However, the situation of collaborators is periodically reviewed and, should the danger persist (or decrease), the duration of the measures may be extended and/or the measures may be modified accordingly. In the same logic, the measures of protection might also be revoked. As has been seen, the measures are automatically revoked if the collaborator does not comply with the obligations under Article 12(2) (b) and (c) of the Law (i.e., responding to questioning by the authorities and disclosing all his properties and financial situation). Moreover, they are automatically revoked if the collaborator commits a crime that indicates that he is 'falling back into' a criminal circle. In case the collaborator breaches any of the other commitments undertaken pursuant to Article 12(2), the Central Commission may revoke the protection on a case-by-case basis, depending on the circumstances.[122]

5.5.3   The Implementation of the Protection

Since the special protection measures do not entail the transfer of the collaborator to a protected place, they are set up and implemented by the Prefect[123] of the place of residence of the collaborator, and are executed by the local police. Conversely, the special protection program is implemented by a centralized body, the Central Protection Service.[124] The Central Protection Service belongs to the Department of Public Security under the Central Directorate of the Criminal Police; it is staffed with personnel

---

119 Article 11(1)(3) of the Law.
120 Article 13(1) of the Law.
121 Article 13-*quater* (3) of the Law and Article 10 (7) and (8) of the Ministerial Decree n. 161/2004.
122 Article 13-*quater* (2) of the Law.
123 The head of the local government administration.
124 Article 14 of the Law and Article 8 (1) of the Ministerial Decree n. 161/2004.

from the various branches of the police, such as *Carabinieri* and the Financial Guard (*Guardia di Finanza*), and the Civil Administration of the Minister of the Interior. It is divided into two autonomous divisions (one for collaborators of justice and the other for witnesses of justice), which are assisted by an accounting department and a general management department. The Service has its headquarters in Rome, but it has peripheral units all over the country (*Nuclei Operativi di Protezione*- NOP), which are tasked with the local management of protected collaborators relocated across the country.[125] In particular, the NOPs are responsible for the logistics, the material assistance to collaborators and their 'camouflaging' in a new environment (for example, with regard to accommodation, job-search, healthcare, enrolment of children to a new school etc.).[126] The NOPs are crucial actors in the management of collaborators, in that they are the authorities with whom the latter turn to for every aspect of their daily life. At the same time, the NOPs are also tasked with monitoring the collaborators. They assess whether collaborators respect the security measures put in place and report the breaches to the Central Protection Service. More generally, they monitor collaborators' overall behaviour and how they are coping with life under protection.[127] Conversely, the local police are tasked with the aspects concerning the security of collaborators (i.e., surveillance, escorting collaborators to court hearings to testify, transfers to a new location for security reasons etc.).

5.5.4 The Exit from the Protection

Besides the cases of 'pathological' revocation (i.e., revocation determined by the collaborator's breaches of his obligations), there is also a natural ending to the measures of protection. The latter occurs when the collaborator has given his testimony in all the trials that he was required to, or when, for whatever reason, the danger ceases to exist.[128] The Central Protection Service has not been endowed with the competence to create job opportunities for collaborators after leaving the protection programme. However, it does help collaborators in assessing the work-related projects (including the bureaucratic aspects) that they have managed to find autonomously. Upon exit from the protection circuit, collaborators are awarded a *capitalizzazione*, that is, the payment of a lump sum consisting of their monthly allowance for a maximum of five years.[129] The *capitalizzazione* is granted by the Central Commission upon the collaborator's request, and with the approval of the prosecutor. The goal of this

---

125 NOPs are located in every region's main town. They are composed by a number of police officers that varies from 13 to 41 persons. See Report of the Working group (further n. 137), p. 44.
126 D' Ambrosio 2002, p. 110.
127 Montanaro & Silvestri 2005, p. 120-125.
128 Article 11 (1) of the Ministerial Decree n. 161/2004.
129 Article 10 (14) of the Ministerial Decree n. 161/2004.

measure is to facilitate the social reintegration of the person. In order to obtain it, the collaborator must provide documentation explaining how he intends to invest the requested sum (the purchase of a property for starting of a business etc.).[130]

Other measures aimed at facilitating social reintegration are provided for in the Ministerial Decree n. 138/2005. According to that degree, collaborators who are public or private employees are entitled to retain their job after they exit the protection system (unpaid leave).

5.6   Practice

5.6.1   Methodology

The present report benefits from the perspective and insights of several practitioners with decades of experience on collaboration with justice. Interviews were conducted with three judges operating in areas with a high level of organised crime,[131] three prosecutors with experience in the DDA, the National Anti-mafia Bureau and the Central Commission,[132] two police officials of the Central Protection Service[133] and three defence counsels. Among the latter, two represent collaborators of justice and one represents defendants accused by collaborators of justice.[134] In their respective capacities, all the interviewees have worked on the most important organised crime trials of the country and have dealt with the most crucial and 'famous' collaborators.[135]

Their main area of expertise relates to the Sicilian Mafia, the organisation among whose ranks the phenomenon of collaboration arose. Some of them, however, have also extensive experience with collaborators that formerly belonged to Camorra and 'Ndrangheta. In addition, this report benefits from the contribution of two of the most prominent researchers on the phenomenon of organized crime and collaboration with justice in Italy: Stefania Pellegrini, Professor of sociology of law at the University of Bologna,[136] and Giovanna Montanaro, sociologist and researcher, former consultant for the Anti-mafia Commission of the Parliament and member of the Working Group on the measures of protection for collaborators and witnesses of justice established in 2014 by the Ministry of the Interior.[137]

---

130 Article 10 (15) of the Ministerial Decree n. 161/2004.
131 Interviewees n. 1, 2 and 3.
132 Interviewees n. 4, 5 and 6.
133 Interviewees n. 7 and 8.
134 Interviewees n. 9, 10 and 11.
135 One of the interviewed defence counsels, for example, represents collaborator Gaspare Spatuzza, see further at § 5.6.5.
136 Professor Pellegrini (interviewee n. 12) teaches the course of 'Mafie and Antimafia' at the University of Bologna and is director of the Master on the 'Management and Reutilization of the Assets and Goods Confiscated from Mafie. Pio La Torre' of the same University.
137 Interviewee n. 13. The results of the working group were published in 2015 in a Report of the Working Group on the measures of protection for collaborators and witnesses of justice, chaired by the Vice Minister

Montanaro is the only researcher in Italy who has been authorized to interview collaborators with justice in protected locations, and could thus gain an inside-outlook on the complex, diversified and 'closed' world of collaborators from a scholarly perspective.[138]

Except for two conducted on the phone, the interviews were carried out in person by the author of this report (no one else was present besides the interviewer and the interviewee). The same open-ended questions were asked to all interviewees so that their answers could be more easily analysed and compared. The answers were written down by the interviewer in the course of the meeting. Subsequently, the relevant paragraphs of the report were sent to each interviewee for confirmation and approval.

As will be seen in the course of this section – with the important exception of the defence counsel representing persons accused by collaborators – judges, prosecutors, police officials and defence counsels of collaborators tend to share the same views on the legal framework and the practical application of the law on collaboration with justice. In this respect, it bears noting that the interests of defence counsels representing collaborators are, inevitably, mostly in line with those of the prosecutors. As a result, the perspective included in this report is mainly that of the authorities devoted to the prosecution/adjudication of crimes and the enforcement of the law.

5.6.2   *Application: Frequency and Results*

The most recent data on collaborators with justice is contained in the latest Report of the Ministry of the Interior on 'The Special Measures of Protection, their Effectiveness and the Modalities of their Practical Application' to the Parliament, dated 30 June 2016.[139] According to the Report, there is a total of 6.525 protected persons, among which 1.277 are collaborators of justice, 4.915 are relatives of collaborators of justice, 78 are witnesses of justice and 255 are relatives of witnesses of justice.[140] These numbers are impressive for a

---

of the Interior Filippo Bubbico: 'Per una Nuova Frontiera della Protezione di Testimoni e Collaboratori di Giustizia: Bilanci e Prospettive dell' Applicazione del Decreto Legge n. 8 del 1991 e s.m.i.', 2015.

138 See Montanaro & Silvestri 2005, containing 18 interviews with collaborators belonging to the different types of criminal organizations operating in the country; see also Montanaro 2013, containing the interview with the collaborator Gaspare Spatuzza; and Mareso & Pepino 2013, headings: 'Collaboratori di Giustizia' and 'Protezione e Sicurezza'.

139 These ministerial reports have been issued since 1994 and they contain the only official data on collaborators and witnesses of justice.

140 Ministry of the Interior, 'Report on the Special Measures of Protection, their Effectiveness and the Modalities of their Practical Application', II semester 2015 – I semester 2016, p. 21-24. Unfortunately, there is no data available on how often judicial benefits are provided, and on the types of penitentiary benefits and the amount of sentence discounts that are granted. From the interviews with practitioners, however, it has emerged that sentence discounts and penitentiary benefits are granted very often, and judges tend to follow the requests of the prosecutors. The general perception is that prosecutors are competent and professional. As such: i) they are able to select only the most reliable collaborators, ii) they are able to present solid

relatively small country like Italy,[141] and similar to those in the U.S. and Russia. Moreover, the trends show that they are increasing. Collaborators have almost doubled since 2006[142] and they have now reached an historical peak. This data has given rise to controversy and discontent among the general public, and has received negative attention in the press.[143]

The criminal organization with the greatest number of collaborators is the 'Camorra' from the region of Campania (557 collaborators), followed by the Sicilian 'Cosa Nostra' (310 collaborators) and the Calabrese ''Ndrangheta' (171 collaborators).[144] The fact that the vast majority of collaborators were former affiliates of Camorra can be explained by the characteristics of that organization. Unlike the Sicilian Cosa Nostra – with its very hierarchical structure, strong ideology, and strict selection of affiliates – Camorra is more 'horizontal', less ideological, and open to the recruitment of even petty criminals. Camorra's affiliates, thus, are more likely to 'betray' the organization. Equally, the few collaborators from 'Ndrangheta can be explained by the fact that its recruitment method is based on family bonds. As a result, 'Ndrangeta's organizational structure rests on family clans that are extremely cohesive and united. The family relationship is a major deterrent to collaborations, in that collaborating would entail denouncing the next of kin (parents, siblings, cousins etc.) to the authorities.[145]

According to the Director of the Central Protection Service, "we are now in a different phase from that of the mid- 1990s, when 'the big' of the Sicilian Mafia (such as Tommaso Buscetta, Gaspare Mutolo or Pino Marchese) started to collaborate. Nowadays, we are dealing with mid-level foot soldiers who mostly belong to Camorra (45%), who turn themselves in because they have no other choice".[146] According to the Chief of the *Squadra Mobile* (State Police) of Naples, these collaborators "are very young, their criminal affiliation is 'improvised' and unstructured, they are more violent and less authoritative, and they do not last long: either they are killed or they are given a life-sentence within a couple of years".[147] The 'weight' and importance of the contribution of these mid-level offenders to the investigations is increasingly put into question by the press, and even by some insiders.[148]

---

corroborating evidence of collaborators' statements at trial. Judges, therefore, tend to believe collaborators and, consequently, grant them all the benefits envisaged by the law (within the limitations provided therein).

141 Italy has a population of nearly 63 million people, see: http://www.italiaora.org.

142 See the previous Report of the Ministry of the Interior (I semester 2015, 30 June 2015), which, at p. 9, shows that in 2006 collaborators were 790. For an overview of the distinguishing traits of the mafia-type organizations operating in the country see: Europol 2013.

143 Bernardo Fanti, 'Il record dei pentiti', in LaVerità of 4 January 2017; Marco Grasso and Matteo Indice, 'E' Record di pentiti ma le loro rivelazioni contano meno', in La Stampa.it on 28 November 2016.

144 Latest Report of the Ministry of the Interior (n. 140), p. 22.

145 Interview with Giovanna Montanaro (interviewee n. 13).

146 This quote has been translated from the article on La Stampa.it (n. 143).

147 This quote has been translated from the article on La Stampa.it (n. 143).

148 See anonymous source from the Carabinieri Corps of the Police quoted in the article on La Stampa.it (n. 143) and the article on LaVerità (n. 143).

Only 63 collaborators are women. Conversely, women form the majority among the protected family members (of the 4.915 relatives of collaborators, 2.877 are women).[149] Women make up a large number of witnesses of justice (26 out of 78).[150] Many of them are wives of *mafiosi* who decide to denounce their husbands in order to give their children a better future. Protected collaborators are mainly adults of working age: 15 of them are between 19 and 25 years old, 418 between 26 and 40 years old, 750 between 41 and 60 years old, and 94 are over 60 years old. Conversely, among the family members, the majority are minors (2.036).[151] With respect to the legal status of collaborators, the previous Ministry's report reveals that, as of June 2015, 484 collaborators are at liberty, 295 are detained in a penitentiary institution and 456 have been granted alternative measures to detention.[152]

With respect to the costs of the system of protection, for the year 2015, the total expenditure effected by the Central Protection Service for collaborators and witnesses was € 85.572.716,1.[153] The biggest expenses were made for the costs of renting the protected locations (€ 34.886.651,7), followed by the monthly allowances (€ 29.951.864,3). For the *capitalizzazioni*, the Service spent € 7.391.721,39.

5.6.2.1   The Scope of the Law

According to all the interviewed practitioners, the institute of collaboration should be limited to organised crime (i.e., to crimes with a systemic character). In this respect, the Law envisages collaboration in relation to a sufficient number of offences. Some interviewees, however, suggested that it would be useful to extend rewarding mechanisms also to large-scale corruption and some forms of widespread economic criminality, which are often closely linked to mafia activities.[154] One of the principal characteristics of the Italian mafia-type associations, in fact, is that they do not limit their operations to the conventional illicit businesses; they 'pollute' the public sector by accessing the official economic markets and political spheres.[155] One judge noted that, in the past thirty years, the mafia has become less violent and more 'business-minded'. The traditional brutal methods have progressively been replaced with more 'civilized' criminal practices. Lately, investigations have shown that, in many cases, the 'core business' of mafia organizations is corruption, rather than extortions.[156] It also bears noting that, like mafia, endemic corruption is a social and cultural phenomenon,[157] which may be very

---

149 Ibid., p. 28.
150 Ibid., p. 26.
151 Ibid., p. 23-24.
152 Previous report of the Ministry of the Interior (n. 142), p. 19-20.
153 Ibid., p. 21 and Latest Report of the Ministry of the Interior, (n. 140), p. 56.
154 Interviewees n. 1, 2, 6 and 9.
155 Gounev & Bezlov 2010, p. 162-167.
156 Interviewee n. 1.
157 Ibid., p. 163: '[c]orruption in Italy does not reveal the direct participation of organised crime such as, for example, the mafia. Rather, it shows the spreading of a "mafia method" in conducting business and doing

difficult to prove in a criminal trial. As another judge and a prosecutor noted, the Italian law criminalizes both the briber and the public official who accepts the bribe. Both of them, thus, have an interest in maintaining the deal secret. Introducing sentence discounts for the partner who denounces the agreement would create a 'conflict of interests' between corruptor and corrupted, helping to break the bond between the two.[158] As a result, this would facilitate the authorities in discovering widespread corrupt practices.

5.6.2.2   The 180-Day Deadline

As has been seen, the Law mandates that collaborators disclose their entire knowledge to the authorities within 180 days. All the interviewed judges and prosecutors agree in considering this, *per se*, as a necessary and adequate deadline. Prosecutors noted that it allows for an assessment of the seriousness and reliability of the collaborator in a relatively short time, and provides an adequate time frame for the investigative authorities to search for the corroboration that will be used at trial. Most importantly, it prevents crucial information from being revealed later on, at the collaborator's will. The latter aspect was also stressed by two of the interviewed judges.[159] According to them, 'this deadline is important and necessary. Under the previous legislation, where no such limit was envisaged, collaborators would reveal at trial crucial information that should (and could) have been disclosed years earlier to the investigative authorities. In many cases, the newly revealed facts were so striking and important that collaborators could not have forgotten them. Their omission, thus, was due to a deliberate choice of collaborators based on their personal interests and calculations. This practice had to be stopped.'

With respect to the adequacy of the deadline, prosecutors noted that six months are enough to obtain the essential information from collaborators, including those who have several decades of criminal activity to narrate. A slightly different view, however, was taken by defence counsels of collaborators.[160] According to them, some collaborators would need more time (preferably one year) to remember events that happened in a remote past. Interestingly, they also noted that keeping collaborators isolated[161] is sometimes counterproductive, in that their morale and capacity to remember is negatively affected by this condition.[162] In practice, however, the 180-day deadline does not seem to represent an in-

---

politics. [..] Public representatives assimilate elements of the mafia culture [...] The "mafia method" is becoming the prevailing method inspiring the crimes of the powerful and [...] it affects market freedom and the democratic system as a whole'.

158 Interviewees n. 2 and 6.

159 Interviewees n. 2 and 3.

160 Interviewees n. 9 and 10.

161 See *supra* at § 5.4.3.

162 All the interviewed prosecutors, however, stressed the importance of 'isolating' of the collaborator throughout the compilation of the *verbale illustrativo*. This is essential both for safety reasons (in that the beginning

surmountable problem. As has been seen, according to the Court of Cassation, what is crucial is that the *verbale illustrativo* contains the 'backbone' of the collaboration.[163] In the situations where six months appear not to be enough to record all the collaborator's information, defence counsel and the prosecutor assist the person in drawing a list of *all* the macro-topics that form the object of the collaboration. The prosecutor will then delve into and question the collaborator only on the most important ones;[164] as a consequence, the *verbale illustrativo* will be detailed on some topics and more concise on others. According to prosecutors and defence counsels of collaborators, this practice represents a viable way to respect the deadline envisaged by the Law while at the same time including in the *verbale* all the necessary information. A very different view was taken by defence counsel representing defendants accused by collaborators. In his opinion, the *verbale illustrativo* is often too generic. This makes it difficult to prepare an adequate defence for the accused.[165]

From an investigative/judicial perspective, what is problematic is the consequence attached to the failure to meet this deadline. The Law does not only 'punish' the reticent collaborator by stating that he will lose the benefits, but also the investigative and judicial authorities by prescribing that the late declarations cannot be used as evidence. By now, however, 'this is issue is more theoretical than practical'.[166] As has been seen, in fact, the impact of this rule has been very limited by the Court of Cassation, which has considerably reduced the scope of the sanction (see *supra* at § 5.4.4).

5.6.3   The Process of Becoming a Collaborator of Justice

By now, the mechanism of collaboration is so well established (it has been in place for over 25 years) that many people belonging to criminal circles are perfectly aware of its rules and functioning, including the benefits to which they are entitled to. This is especially true for offenders belonging to the Sicilian mafia, with its long history of collaborations. In these cases, it is not the prosecutor or the police who approach defendants to persuade them to collaborate, but the other way around.[167] It has also been seen that, often, detained persons decide to collaborate following a *colloquio investigativo* with police authorities (or the prosecutors of the National Anti-mafia Bureau).[168] This is especially the case of low-level

---

of a collaboration is the most delicate and risky phase of the whole process), and for ensuring the truthfulness of the declarations.

163 See *supra* at § 5.4.4.

164 Naturally, the importance is determined by the prosecutor based on the strategy that he intends to pursue at trial.

165 Interviewee n. 11.

166 Interviewee n. 1.

167 Interviewees n. 5 and 6.

168 Interviewees n. 4, 5 and 6.

criminals who are not familiar with the system. The latter mostly belong to Camorra, which is the organization with the greatest number of collaborators at the moment.[169]

Typically, the information that collaborators are requested to provide is the following: (i) personal criminal record; ii) internal organizational and hierarchical structure of the organization they belong to (leaders, mid-level and low-level members); iii) mid-terms objectives and strategies of the organization, what crimes it has committed so far and by whom exactly, and what crimes are planned for the future; iv) connections between the organization and external actors such as businessmen and politicians.[170] All the interviewed prosecutors stressed the importance that collaborators truthfully disclose their financial situation and the properties/assets that they own, (including through intermediaries).

From the interviews with prosecutors and defence counsels of collaborators, it has emerged that the motives that prompt an offender to come forward are generally very similar. In many cases, they do not want to face a life-sentence (*ergastolo*). Therefore, they may start to collaborate during the investigation if – upon consultation with their lawyer on the gravity of the charges and the seriousness of their criminal record – they realise that in all likelihood they will be sentenced to a lifetime in prison; or they may start to collaborate after the conviction so as to be entitled to early release. A second reason why offenders approach the authorities has to do with the internal dynamics of their criminal association. For example, they might have 'fallen from grace' within the organization (for reasons of betrayal, internal fights etc.) and thus they are afraid of retaliations. In this case, they turn to the State in order to receive protection for themselves and their families (in addition, of course, to sentence discounts and penitentiary benefits).[171] Finally, the practice has shown that, sometimes, an incentive to collaborate may also come from the relatives of the offender. Many of them are married or partnered to women who do not belong to criminal circles and, with the passing of time, they find themselves incapable of managing the risks that a criminal lifestyle entails for them and their children.

As one prosecutor explained, 'the motives that determine the initiation of a collaboration must be distinguished from the motives that sustain the person throughout the collaborating process'.[172] At the beginning, collaborations are almost always prompted by a mere assessment of costs and benefits. However, practice has shown that, sometimes, collaborators gradually come to a true repentance. Offenders who genuinely repent are by no means in the majority, but they do exist.[173] One of the most famous cases is that of collaborator Gaspare Spatuzza, whose revelations were essential to the reconstruction of the events concerning the bombing campaign launched by the Sicilian mafia between 1992 and 1994. By now, it is widely acknowledged and believed that Spatuzza' s decision to

---

169 Interviewees n. 5 and 6.
170 Interviewees n. 4, 5 and 6 and Webpage of the Anti-mafia Commission of the Parliament:
    http://www.camera.it/_bicamerali/leg15/commbicantimafia/documentazionetematica/25/schedabase.asp.
171 Interviewee n. 4.
172 Interviewee n. 6.
173 Interviewees n. 6, 9 and 10.

collaborate was prompted by a true repentance, due to a religious conversion that he came to while in jail.[174] Authorities agree in defining the revelations of Spatuzza as 'revolution-ary' and completely reliable (see further at § 5.6.5).[175]

5.6.4 Factors Determining the Success of a Collaboration

In the practitioners' view,[176] two factors in particular determine the success of a collaboration[177] in a given case. First, the personal situation of the collaborator and, in partic-ular, the support that he enjoys from his family in making this choice and maintaining it throughout the process. The decision to collaborate entails a complete life-change, not only for the collaborator, but also for his family. Whereas the former will generally be detained (at least at the beginning), the latter will be relocated to a different region, under fake identities, and will have to comply with all of the security measures put in place by the authorities. Naturally, living undercover and far away from the place of origin, entails a great deal of restriction to personal freedom and great psychological stress. Not every family is willing to accept this.[178]

A second factor that is crucial for a fruitful collaboration is the professional compe-tence of the magistrates involved.[179] Dealing with collaborators with justice (and with mafia-related crimes in general) requires very specific skills. This is especially true for the prosecutor, in that it is the latter who makes the first assessment of the reliability of the collaborator. Such specific competences can be categorized as follows:

a   The Ability to Interrogate
In order to 'get the most' out of collaborators, the prosecutor (but also the judge) must have a lot of experience in the examination of this particular kind of defendant, in that they use a particular language and have the mind-set of the *mafioso*, which follows a precise logic and adheres to a specific set of criminal 'values'.[180] In addition, the prosecutor must be capable of reordering the great amount of information provided by collaborators. The latter is often confused, in the sense that it does not follow a precise

---

174 See Montanaro 2013; see further at § 5.6.5.
175 See interviews by Giovanna Montanaro with prosecutors Giuseppe Quattrocchi (Chief of the *Procura* of Florence), Sergio Lari (Chief of the *Procura* of Caltanissetta) and Francesco Messineo (Chief of the *Procura* of Palermo), in Montanaro 2013, p. 119ss, 193ss and 247ss.
176 Interviews with prosecutors, judges and defence counsels of collaborators.
177 By 'success' of a collaboration it is meant that: i) the person sticks to his choice of collaborating and main-tains a collaborative attitude throughout the proceedings (i.e., complies with the security measures, truth-fully discloses all his properties and financial situation etc.); ii) the collaborator's testimony at trial confirms the prosecutor's case; iii) the judge deems the collaborator reliable.
178 See further at § 5.6.6.1.
179 Interviewees n. 3, 4, 5 and 6.
180 Bolzoni 2008.

chronological order. The collaborator will start by narrating what he thinks it is important, but this does not always match with what the prosecutor needs to know for the purpose of the investigation.[181] It is essential, thus, that the prosecutor puts an order to the collaborator's narration in coherence with the requirements for the content of the collaboration envisaged by the Law (novelty, completeness, importance for the purpose of the investigation).

b   The Importance of the 180 Days

The 180 days is the time period in which the prosecutor and the police will search for the external evidence to corroborate the collaborator's statements. For this purpose, it is very important that no time is wasted and that the prosecutor builds as solid a case as possible, in order to bring only the most 'verified' collaborators to trial, so that they will success-fully withstand cross-examination before the judge.[182] In this respect, it bears emphasiz-ing that, since the Law was introduced, many things have changed. When the phenom-enon of collaboration started in the early 1990s, collaborators would reveal the existence of criminal structures that were mostly unknown to the authorities. Indeed, it was they who shed the first light on criminal episodes that marked the history of the country. At that time, the process of verifying the statements and searching for corroborating evidence was very lengthy and complex, an obscure path full of obstacles.[183] Today the situation is very different. Since (and thanks to) the first collaborations, the authorities have progressively obtained more and more insight into the activities and methods of the various criminal organizations of the country. Any declaration made by collaborators today is evaluated against this solid wealth of knowledge, developed in the course of the years. This makes it easier to assess whether the collaborator is telling the truth or not. In addition, investigative techniques have also changed. In this respect, prosecutors stressed the importance of the interception of communications. Much of what is revealed by collaborators nowadays can easily be challenged and/or corroborated by intercepted con-versations that are already in the possession of the authorities.[184]

In conclusion, it is worth stressing that, since the channels of protection and judicial benefits have been separated (i.e., since the entry into force of the amendments of Law n. 45/2001), the degree and quality of protection afforded to collaborators is not a factor that conditions the management of collaborators at trial anymore. Until 2001, there would be cases in which collaborators would refuse to speak at trial because they were unsatisfied with some of the logistical aspects of their life under protection (for example, the characteristics of the house in which they had been relocated).[185] This does not hap-

---

181 De Lucia 2016.
182 Interviewee n. 3.
183 Interviewee n. 5.
184 Ibid.
185 Interviews with prosecutors, judges, defence counsels of collaborators and police officials.

pen anymore. Today, there is no point in bringing these sorts of complaints before a prosecutor or a judge.[186] One police official noted that sometimes collaborators threaten to withdraw their testimony but in practice it never happens. Collaborators are aware that prosecutors or judges have no power to improve their living conditions, as the relevant decisions are taken by the Central Commission independently; any complaints regarding the restrictions of the life under protection are addressed by the Central Protection Service (mainly by the NOPs).

Finally, it bears noting that the failure to respond to the questions of the judicial authority constitutes a major breach of the commitments undertaken under Article 12 of the Law (see *supra* at § 5.5). As has been seen, such breach determines the immediate revocation of the protection measures, and this is a risk that collaborators cannot afford.

5.6.5   Reliability of Collaborators

In the experience of judges, prosecutors and defence counsels of collaborators, the latter are generally reliable. As was seen in the previous paragraph, collaborators are 'filtered' by the prosecutor so that, normally, only the most 'solid' collaborators are presented at trial.[187] Judges in particular noted that prosecutors are generally highly trained and specialised in dealing with collaborators of justice and, thus, it is rare that the latter's testimony at trial is not backed up by solid corroborating evidence.[188] As a consequence, judges tend to grant the sentence discounts and the penitentiary benefits requested by prosecutors.[189] In other words, these practitioners believe that the Law contains enough and adequate provisions that make it inconvenient for collaborators to lie (first and foremost, the revocation of protection). Moreover, it gives adequate tools to the judicial authority to assess whether they are telling the truth. They all manifested great trust in the criteria under article 192(3) c.c.p. (see *supra* at § 5.4.6), and, in particular, in how the judges have interpreted them. Since such criteria are quite strict, they believe they are fair to the defendants accused by collaborators.

This conviction, however, is not shared by defence lawyers operating on the opposite front. In the view of a counsel representing defendants who are accused by collaborators, the latter often misrepresent the facts or even openly lie. This is because the interests of collaborators and those of the judicial authority (i.e., prosecutors and judges) are somewhat in line. On the one hand, collaborators know that with the choice of collaborating they lose the protection of their criminal organisation and become dependent from the State for protection and sustenance; as a consequence, they are inclined to 'please' the

---

186 Ibid.
187 Interviewees n. 1, 2 and 3.
188 Interviewees n. 2 and 3.
189 Interviewees n. 1, 2 and 3.

judicial authorities by providing all the information that they expect, so as to be granted protection. On the other hand, the judicial authorities – whose aim is discovering the truth – feel greatly facilitated in their task by collaborators, and thus have a tendency to believe their stories at the cost of stretching reality.[190]

To a certain extent, divergent views by practitioners operating on opposite fronts are inevitable. Without taking any side in this dispute, it is worth spending a few words on one of the most serious miscarriages of justice occurred in the country after the murder of the anti-mafia judge Paolo Borsellino. The latter was killed – together with his body-guards Agostino Catalano, Emanuela Loi, Vincenzo Li Muli, Walter Eddie Cosina and Claudio Traina – by a car bomb in Palermo on 19 July 1992.[191]

By 2003, the responsibilities connected with the Borsellino's murder had been established at three stages of proceedings (first instance, appeals, Court of Cassation), and many persons had been convicted in relation to that murder. In 2008, however, the investigations were re-opened due to the revelations of Gaspare Spatuzza, a former killer on the payroll of the Graviano family, a mafia clan in Palermo. Spatuzza was arrested in 1997 and was convicted for a series of bomb attacks and for his participation in nearly forty homicides,[192] for which he received several life-sentences. In 2008, he started his collaboration with the prosecutors of three different Procure (Caltanissetta, Florence and Palermo), after spending 11 years on a very strict detention regime. Spatuzza revealed that it had been him who had stolen the car used for the attack that killed the judge, thereby disproving the version of events provided by several collaborators who had falsely incriminated themselves, allegedly under the pressure of some police officials. Under-standably, at the beginning the new revelations of Spatuzza were met with great scepti-cism. However, the accuracy and precision of his narration prompted new investigations. The investigative authorities carefully verified every statement made by Spatuzza and, in the end, were able to gather evidence that not only confirmed Spatuzza's story in its entirety, but also clarified many inconsistencies and contradictions that had been left unresolved. After several months, the authorities accepted that Spatuzza was telling the truth. Following the revelations of Spatuzza, the Court of Appeals of Catania suspended the execution of the sentence against eight persons who had been convicted for the mur-der of judge Borsellino (seven of them had been sentenced to life-imprisonment).[193] In total, eleven people had been falsely accused and wrongfully convicted pursuant to the declarations of the false collaborators.[194] The latter were put on trial under calumny

---

190 Interviewee n. 11.
191 The attack against judge Borsellino came nearly two months after the assassination of his friend and fellow judge Giovanni Falcone, who was killed by a car bomb on 23 May 1992, on the motorway near the town of Capaci, close to Palermo, Sicily.
192 Montanaro 2013, p. 8.
193 Six persons were immediately liberated, other two remained in jail in relation to other crimes.
194 Montanaro 2013, p. 147.

charges.[195] Equally, criminal charges were filed against three police officials for mislead-
ing the investigations (now archived).[196] An investigation against other six police officers
is currently underway.[197]

This story is a reminder that every system is fallible, even in case of the most developed legislation. The impression is, however, that the grave episodes of the Borsellino
trial are due to the negligence and errors of the authorities involved (at best), rather than
to inherent flaws of the Law.

5.6.6   The System of Protection

With respect to protection, practitioners agree that the system is very effective. No
collaborators under protection have been murdered or harmed since 1991. Ensuring the
physical safety of the protected population is of course the primary function of the system, and the success achieved in this respect is cause of pride for the Italian institutions.[198] As judge Giovanni Falcone rightly foresaw, being able to guarantee the safety
of mafia collaborators and their families is indispensable in order for them to be willing to
testify at trial.

Besides the capacity to achieve its paramount goal, however, the effectiveness of a
system of protection may be assessed under (at least) other two perspectives. The first
one relates to the well being of the protected persons throughout the time the measures
are in place. Physical safety alone is not enough. The psychological condition of
collaborators is also a crucial factor that impacts on their behaviour in courtroom. The
second key aspect has to do with the mechanisms that the system puts in place in order to
ensure that collaborators are reintegrated into society upon the exit from the protection
program. The following subsections will address these two issues separately.

5.6.6.1   Psychological Assistance

Entry into the protection program is a traumatic moment not only for collaborators, but
also, and above all, for their families. In addition to the rigid code of conduct to which
they are subject,[199] collaborators' wives and children suffer the disruption of being

---

195 Aaron Pettinari, 'Borsellino quarter, tra falsi pentiti e silenzi istituzionali', Antimafiaduemila, 12 December
    2016.
196 These cases, however, were archived on 8 January 2016: see 'Via d' Amelio: archiviata l'indagine su poliziotti
    accusati di avere depistato inchiesta', Repubblica.it Palermo, 8 January 2016.
197 Giuseppe Pipitone, 'Borsellino, altri quattro poliziotti indagati per la strage di via d'Amelio', on Il Fatto
    Quotidiano.it of 2 March 2016.
198 Interviewees n. 4, 5, 7 and 8.
199 Protected persons must obtain the authorization of the Central Protection Service for carrying out the most
    basic activities: phone calls to their relatives in their hometown, job searches, family trips, medical appoint-
    ments etc. More generally, in their relationships with others, they must be very careful not to reveal their
    identity and their protected status. See Montanaro & Silvestri 2005, p. 134ss.

uprooted from their cities in the south of the country, and having to adapt to a new and unfamiliar surroundings in the centre or the north.[200] Minors are most affected by life under protection.[201] Moreover, it is not unusual for protected persons be transferred to other regions when new safety concerns arise, which only adds to the feeling of isolation and stress.[202]

The psychological assistance to collaborators and their families is an issue to which greater attention should be paid. There are only three State Police psychologists at the Central Protection Service. Clearly, they are not supposed to treat the entire protected population. Whenever a protected person requests psychological assistance (or whenever the NOPs note a situation of psychological distress), the Service's psychologists make a preliminary assessment of the situation and direct the person to one of the accredited structures of the public healthcare system,[203] usually, the closest to the person's place of residence.[204] The psychologists are briefed on the particular status of their patient beforehand, but are not given any details about the person's criminal past or true identity, and that person is not supposed to disclose it either.[205] In the view of Montanaro, 'selecting the psychologists of the public healthcare system based on the mere criterion of proximity to the protected location is not the ideal solution'.[206]

Many psychological conditions in protected persons arise precisely because of the abrupt change of identity, life-style and social status that protection entails, as well as the restrictions to their liberties imposed by the security measures. One of the biggest causes of distress among protected persons is the fear that their identity will be revealed.[207] This fear leads them to isolation and makes them reluctant to seek psychological help. According to Montanaro, the most qualified psychologists and psychotherapists should be selected and trained by the Central Protection Service, which should acquaint them with the specificities and functioning of the protection system. Therapists, in fact, should be familiar with the system in order to provide the best treatment to protected patients.[208]

The Working Group on the measures of protection for witnesses and collaborators noted the 'absolute necessity' that professionals entrusted with the psychological assistance of collaborators be part of the Central Protection Service.[209] To this end, the group proposed that *ad hoc* agreements between the Service and the National Boards of Psy-

---

200 Interviewees n. 7 and 8. See also, latest Report of the Ministry of the Interior (n. 140), p. 40ss.
201 Montanaro & Silvestri 2005, p. 145; latest Report of the Ministry of the Interior (n. 140), p. 42.
202 Interviewees n. 7 and 8.
203 Montanaro & Silvestri 2005, p. 148.
204 Interview with Giovanna Montanaro (interviewee n. 13).
205 See ibid., interview by Montanaro with the then director of the Service' s Division for collaborators, p. 149.
206 Interview with Giovanna Montanaro (interviewee n. 13). See also Report of the Working Group (n. 137), p. 49.
207 Interview with Giovanna Montanaro (interviewee n. 13).
208 Ibid.
209 Report of the Working Group (n. 137), p. 49.

chologists and Psychotherapists be established, setting forth specific criteria regarding the required experience of and training for the therapists. In addition, the working group proposed that the personnel of every NOP include a psychologist.[210] Finally and very importantly, the working group highlighted the necessity of providing psychological assistance to protected persons not only upon request (as it is now), but from the first moment of contact between the collaborator and the judicial authority.[211] At the moment at which the collaborator undertakes the commitments under Article 12 of the Law, the presence of a psychologist would be useful. The latter, in fact, could assess the person's situation and provide the authorities with an accurate overview of his general psychological state, fears and expectations. This would also limit the risks of misunderstandings or unrealistic expectations on the part of collaborators regarding the characteristics of the life under protection.[212]

5.6.6.2 Social Reintegration

The most problematic aspect of the Italian system of protection relates to the lack of sufficient mechanisms to ensure the effective social reintegration of collaborators upon exiting the protection system. In this respect, it bears emphasizing that it is very difficult for collaborators to work while they are under protection. There are several reasons for this. First, many collaborators have a low level of education and scarce professional skills; moreover, unlike witnesses of justice, they cannot benefit from preferred channels of employment.[213] Second, collaborators are usually very busy with their 'courtroom commitments'. They must travel to various parts of the country in order to testify at the (often many) trials in which their collaboration is required.[214] Finally and most importantly, carrying out a professional activity is often incompatible with the safety measures to which they are subject. This is true not only for collaborators, but also for their families. It bears recalling that the great majority of protected persons are given fake identities through cover documents. The latter, however, cannot be used in legal acts vis-à-vis third parties. This means that protected persons cannot open a bank account, obtain a licence to start a business and so on.[215] According to the Report of the Ministry of the Interior, between January and June 2016, only 49 collaborators managed to find a job.[216]

The experts of the working group noted the 'tendency among protected persons to develop forms of dependency and habituation to the measures of protection, especially

---

210 Ibid., p. 49.
211 Ibid., p. 47-48.
212 Ibid., p. 47-48.
213 Previous Report of the Ministry of the Interior (n. 142), p. 28.
214 In some cases, collaborators may be required to attend court hearings up to four days a week. See Montanaro & Silvestri 2005, p. 149. It must be highlighted, however, that since 1998, collaborators of justice may attend the trial through a video-conference pursuant to Law n. 11/1998.
215 Montanaro & Silvestri 2005, p. 135.
216 Latest Report of the Ministry of the Interior (n. 140), p. 46.

when the latter are disposed for a long period of time'.[217] The exit from protection is thus a critical phase. Persons who have been maintained by the State for years are suddenly faced with the difficulties of finding a lawful occupation and reinserting themselves into society. Upon exiting the system of protection, many collaborators are close to the retirement age and have been outside of the job market for many years.[218] Some of them have never had a lawful occupation in their lives.

The experience has shown that, in many cases, the *capitalizzazioni* have not been put to a good use. In the absence of monitoring mechanisms, many collaborators have wasted this sum of money and, after a while, found themselves in a state of poverty and abandonment. There is therefore a risk that the system of *capitalizzazioni* – rather than equipping collaborators with the necessary tools for reinserting themselves into society – amounts to a form of 'passive welfarism'.[219] In these circumstances, it is not uncommon for collaborators to fall back into the criminal circles.[220] According to Giovanna Montanaro (interviewee n. 13), 'this is a major defeat. Collaborators give a great contribution to the State, but also represent a great cost. It is essential that, once their contribution is over, they are put in the condition of becoming autonomous and economically independent'.[221] In her view, the current system could be improved in the following ways. First, the Central Protection Service should conduct a prior assessment of the feasibility of the work-related projects that collaborators present in order to obtain the *capitalizzazione*. This assessment has not always been carried out as thoroughly as it should have, with collaborators remaining solely responsible for the success or failure of their projects. Second, specific monitoring mechanisms should be put in place in order to verify how collaborators spend the money awarded with the *capitalizzazioni*. More generally, the Central Protection Service should be endowed with the necessary resources and competences to play a more active role in the social-reintegration phase. Reinserting collaborators into society is certainly not an easy task, given the crisis that Italy's economy is facing and the understandable reservations of employers towards persons with a criminal record. However, agreements could be put in place with trade and professional associations in order to develop employment plans for collaborators or, at least, the members of their families (especially their children, who often have education levels and qualifications higher than those of their fathers).[222]

---

217 Report of the Working Group (n. 137), p. 54.
218 Previous Report of the Ministry of the Interior, (n. 142), p. 35; interviewees n. 7 and 8.
219 Ibid., p. 35-36.
220 Ibid., p. 35-36.
221 Interview with Giovanna Montanaro (interviewee n. 13).
222 Report of the Working Group (n. 137), p. 86.

5.7 Conclusion

Nowadays, the key instruments in the fight against organized crime are the interception of communications and collaboration with justice. Whereas the former provide the authorities with fragmentary 'snapshots' of the activities of the organization, the latter equip the investigators with the codes for interpreting those snapshots. Collaborators let the authorities 'inside' the organization, in that they are capable of explaining in an organic manner its 'logic', its internal dynamics and objectives for the future.[223] Interestingly, an affirmation recurred in every interview that this author conducted: "without collaborators of justice, the most important mafia-trials of the Country would not have been possible". Prosecutors, in particular, stressed the importance that collaborators' contributions continue to have for their investigations nowadays.

The importance of collaboration, however, is not limited to the investigative value. Collaborators also have a crucial cultural and historical importance. The presence of collaborators is a great source of weakness for the organization's power, in that they disintegrate its traditional cohesion, break the silence around it and challenge the traditional idea of impunity from which its strength derives. Collaborators do not only break the organization from within, but also from the outside. When the first collaborators started to narrate the appalling criminal acts committed by some of their affiliates at the beginning of the 1980s, the idea of a 'romantic' mafia, dispensing justice in the absence of the State, began to shatter. In other words, collaborators played a decisive role in debunking the mythology of the 'men of honour' in Italy, and changed the way in which the public opinion conceived the various types of mafia operating in the country.[224] Finally, the wealth of knowledge disclosed by collaborators is also of crucial importance for sociologists, historians and criminologists in their studies on the phenomenon of organized crime.[225] Despite the opinion of the insiders, however, collaborators are often met with mistrust and scepticism by the general public, due to the 'interest' that they have in the proceedings and to the benefits that they gain in exchange for their information.

The Italian system regulating rewards and protection for collaborators with justice is, taken as a whole, functional and efficient. As has been seen, over the course of 25 years the legal framework of Law n. 82/1991 has been reformed, so as to remedy to the most serious shortcomings of the previous regime. In addition, the Court of Cassation has intervened with a corrective interpretation on the aspects that remained problematic. As a result, the institute of collaboration with justice is now well established, and does not constitute an object of debate or contention nowadays.

There are, however, problematic aspects that relate to the management of collaborators by the Central Protection Service. Based on the findings of the Working

---

223 De Lucia 2016.
224 Interview with Giovanna Montanaro (interviewee n. 13).
225 Ibid.

Group on the measures of protection for collaborators and witnesses of justice established by the Ministry of the Interior in 2014, this report identified two areas that require improvement: the psychological assistance to protected persons and the mechanisms to facilitate the reintegration of collaborators into society upon exiting the protection program. Both of these aspects are crucial to achieve the broader goal of the system: ensuring that, through the 'journey' of collaboration, offenders who have helped the State in the repression and prevention of crimes, return to abide by the rules of social coexistence with the support of the institutions.

APPENDIX 1

ANSWERS TO THE RESEARCH QUESTIONS

LEGAL FRAMEWORK

1   *What types of undertakings are provided for?*

The benefits that may be provided to collaborators of justice are those (and *only* those) foreseen by law (that is, Law n. 82/1991, as amended by Law n. 45/2001, hereafter 'the Law'), and fall into two categories: 1) judicial benefits, accorded by a judge; 2) protection/assistance benefits, accorded by an administrative authority. In light of the fact that the Italian criminal justice system is governed by the principle of mandatory prosecution (as opposed to the principle of prosecutorial discretion), it is not possible to grant immunity to collaborators.

The first category comprises: i) sentence discounts deriving from the application of mitigating circumstances by the trial judge, and ii) benefits related to the penitentiary treatment in the pre-trial and post-conviction phase. With respect to both, the Italian legal framework envisages a so-called 'double track' regime to distinguish the position of offenders who cooperate with justice from those who do not. The latter are subject to much harsher treatment. In this regard it should be noted that the Italian sentencing regime is governed by a system of minimum and maximum penalties, aggravating and mitigating circumstances, and lists of factors making for greater severity or leniency. Accordingly, in Italy there is very little room for discretion to prosecutors in requesting a certain punishment, and to judges in deciding upon the prosecutors' requests. Equally, Italian law dictates the margins of discount that judges can and must grant to offenders who collaborate with justice. See also the answer to question 8.

As to the second category of benefits, depending on how great the risk of retaliation is, collaborators can benefit from ordinary or special protection. Special protection measures include surveillance and protection measures by local police; technical security arrangements for the person's home and properties; measures necessary for transfers to localities other than the place of residence; for collaborators in detention, special custody arrangements, transfers and guarding; and measures aimed at the social rehabilitation, including financial support. In cases where the special protection measures would be inadequate given the seriousness and concrete nature of the danger facing the collaborator, the special protection measures are adopted through a special protection program, entailing the transfer of the collaborator and his family to a secret and protected locality. In addition to the surveillance measures, the special protection program involves a modification of the registers and forms of economic assistance, whereby the latter may comprise accommodation, medical expenses, legal fees and living expenses (through a monthly allowance) in case it is impossible for the collaborator to work. The amount of the allowance varies depending on the number of the family members of the collaborator.

2   *In respect of which offences is it possible to use the instrument?*

Under the Law, the instrument of collaboration with justice is available in respect of a limited number of (serious) crimes: the crimes of subversion and terrorism, and Mafia-type crimes (Mafia-type association, association for the purpose of trafficking in drugs, association for the purpose of smuggling tobacco products, association for the purpose of kidnapping to extort ransom money, crimes committed through the 'mafia method' or perpetrated with the aim of assisting the activities of mafia-type associations, association for the purpose of enslavement, association for the purpose of child prostitution, child pornography, sex tourism, association for the purpose of human trafficking, and for the purpose of slave trade).

3   *What is the legal basis for (using) the instrument?*

The basis for providing undertakings is a comprehensive, formal law: Law n. 82/1991, as amended by Law n. 45/2001. This law regulates the undertakings that may be provided by the authorities, i.e. the 'benefits' set out above, the undertakings by the collaborator (the provision of a statement, whereby the collaborator must also formally declare that he is not in possession of further information, even unrelated to the episodes that he has narrated, regarding facts of serious gravity or social alarm), the offences in respect of which the instrument may be used (see under question 2), the responsibilities of the prosecutor in this regard, the procedure to be followed including the 180-day period within which the collaborator must provide a statement (from the moment of manifestation of the willingness to collaborate) and the consequences of not meeting this deadline (the statement cannot be used as evidence and the collaborator cannot receive the benefits referred to under question 1 or they are revoked).

In addition, the Italian Supreme Court has clarified some aspects of the legislative framework, including what the collaborator must disclose within the 180-day deadline (according to the Supreme Court, the collaborator need to only disclose the essential elements of his narration, which may then be elaborated on at trial) and the consequences of failure to meet the 180-day deadline (according to the Supreme Court, the consequences are not absolute so far as the use of the statement is concerned), as well as how to test the reliability of statements at the deliberation stage (although the judge is free to select and weigh evidence, in respect of the testimony of collaborators of justice the judge must carry out a three-pronged test to evaluate the testimony: first, the credibility of the collaborator must be established; second, the intrinsic credibility of the statements must be assessed; and third, the judge must verify the existence of external elements of corroborations.

4   *How did the rules on collaboration with justice come about?*

The comprehensive legislation referred to under the previous question came about in the wake of the first maxi-trials against the Sicilian mafia in the late 1980s (Law n. 82/1991). However, the first legislation on the use of collaborators of justice dates back to the anti-terrorism legislation of the 1980s, which was not comprehensive in nature (the legislator did not consider comprehensive regulation to be necessary in light of the belief that terrorism was an exceptional phenomenon) and did not provide for the physical protection of collaborators. The first comprehensive legislation of the use of undertakings Law n. 82/1991 was amended in 2001, in light of perceived shortcomings of the existing legislation: collaborators were too easily admitted to the special protection program and, as a result, the system became 'clogged' with an excessive number of pro-tected collaborators and family members, whose management became very difficult; and the regime did not have sufficient safeguards in place against unreliable collaborators. This last shortcoming led to the introduction of the 180-day deadline referred to under the previous question (of which the purpose is twofold: one the one hand, it is meant to prevent collaborators from disclosing only partial information based on their personal convenience, on the other hand, it is meant to avoid the risk that, with the passing of time, the collaborator is subjected to external influences or pressures to modify/adjust his statements).

5   *Who holds authority to make use of the instrument and where does the*
         responsibility lie in this regard?

The Public Prosecutor is the authority in charge of the investigation and as such is also primarily responsible for managing the relationship with collaborators. Once an offender reaches the decision to collaborate, he requests a meeting with the prosecutor. From this moment on, the Law (that is, the comprehensive legal framework referred to under ques-tions 3 and 4) regulates every aspect of the relationship between collaborators and the judicial authorities (i.e. prosecutors and judges), as well as every benefit to which collaborators are entitled. Under the Law, the information provided by the collaborator must be intrinsically reliable, complete, and must bring new knowledge to the investigation, or it must appear important for the trial or the advancement of the investigation concerning the organizational structure, the equipment, the domestic and international relationships and the purposes of the criminal organization. The assessment of these requirements lies within the full discretion of the prosecutor. By interrogating the person on the facts that are most relevant to the investigation, the prosecutor will form an opinion on the utility of the contribution and the reliability of the person, and whether to present them at trial. Nevertheless, it is important to note that, ultimately, it is the judge who decides whether the collaborators presented at trial by the prosecutor are reliable. Simply put, it is the judge (and not the prosecutor) who decides who is a collaborator and who is not.

The admission to the special protection measures and the special protection program is decided by a Central Commission, attached to the Ministry of the Interior. The Commission is chaired by an Under-secretary of State of the Ministry of the Interior and is composed of two magistrates and five State officials. The Central Commission has exclusive competence to decide on whether to grant protection measures. It does so on the basis of the proposal/recommendation of the Public Prosecutor in charge of the investigation or the Chief of Police-Director General of Public Security (who must consult with the Public Prosecutor). The proposal is formulated in conjunction with the other Prosecutor's Offices involved in the investigation and with the National Anti-Mafia Bureau. See also the answer to question 8.

6   *How does the instrument relate to other measures whereby private individuals provide information for the purposes of criminal investigation and/or prosecution?*

In Italy, a distinction is drawn between collaborators of justice on the one hand and police informants and 'witnesses of justice' on the other. The police informant is neither defined nor regulated by law. The only definition of 'police informants' can be found in the case law: 'persons who, occasionally but systematically, reveal confidential information relating to a crime to the police in exchange for monetary compensation or other advantages.' Of course, these are persons who belong to a criminal circle. The use and purpose of police informants is limited to the investigation and the information revealed by them is not intended for use at trial. For this reason, the law bestows the police with the privilege of keeping their sources confidential, even from the judicial authorities. The management of confidential informants is the exclusive competence of the police, with no interference or oversight from the prosecutor. There is no way of knowing what the 'advantages' that informants might gain in exchange for their help with the investigation are.

Collaborators of justice must also be distinguished from 'witnesses of justice'. Whereas the former are members of a criminal organization who decide to dissociate themselves therefrom and cooperate with the authorities, the latter are usually victims of mafia activities (for example, extortions), who decide to come forward and denounce the abuses they are subject to; other times they are citizens who happened to witness the commission of a crime and report it to the authorities, thereby putting their lives at risk. The contribution that witnesses of justice can make to the investigation is usually much more limited than that of collaborators. Unlike collaborators, witnesses of justice are able to narrate only single, unrelated criminal events. They do not have an overview of the entire structure and dynamics of the organization. Nevertheless, there are similarities between collaborators and witnesses. First, they are both called to testify at trial, with the crucial difference that collaborators are also a party to the proceedings and they thus have an interest in the outcome of the trial. As self-confessed accused or co-accused, their testimony will cover both the criminal activity perpetrated by them and that perpetrated by their former associates. Second, both collaborators and witnesses are both in grave danger because of their testimony and therefore need protection, which Italian law provides for. It is worth addressing briefly the main differences in the *regulation* of the two categories. First, whereas the collaboration of offenders may relate only to the most serious crimes, the collaboration of witnesses may concern crimes of any gravity and, for the purpose of the application of the measures of protection, the only requirement is that the testimony be reliable. Conversely, the information provided by collaborators must not only be reliable, but also complete and must bring new knowledge to the investigation. Second, the assistance measures envisaged for witnesses are more extensive, in that they must guarantee the same living standard that the witness enjoyed prior to the decision to collaborate. This requirement is not envisaged for the measures of assistance to collaborators. Finally, only witnesses are entitled to receive a refund to compensate for their loss of earnings in case they had to quit their job in relation to their testimony.

7   *How does the instrument relate to the phenomenon of witness protection?*

There is a clear distinction in both law and practice between the rules on undertakings on the one hand, and the phenomenon of witness protection on the other. See further the answers to questions 1 and 5.

PRACTICE

8   *What types of undertaking are used in practice?*

As stated, Law n. 82/1991, as amended by Law n. 45/2001, regulates the institute of collaboration with justice in relation to a limited number of crimes (these are the most serious offences committed by criminal organizations, such as mafia-type and terrorism crimes), and envisages the following benefits as a reward for collaboration: i) sentence discounts, ii) penitentiary benefits, iii) the admission to protection measures. All of these benefits are applied in practice, as they are an 'automatic' consequence of collaboration under the terms of the Law. In the Italian system, suspects/defendants who decide to collaborate acquire the status of 'collaborators', from which the benefits envisaged by the Law follow automatically. Of course, the Prosecutor has the discretion to decide whose collaboration is worthy of consideration (see also the answer to question 9), and the degree of the benefits will be calibrated depending on the circumstances (but always within the boundaries established by the Law). For example, when a defendant collaborates in relation to a mafia-type crime, the sentence discount must 'always' be granted: life imprisonment is replaced by 12 to 20-year sentence, the other penalties are reduced by 1/3 to 1/2. The judge has the discretion to decide the actual amount of sentence discount (the Prosecutor will formulate a request in this respect, but the judge is not bound by it). It bears emphasizing, however, that if the judge is not convinced of the reliability of the collaborator, he will not grant the sentence discount at all. The same is true for penitentiary benefits. Usually (but not always), judges stick to the request of the Prosecutor. As to protection measures, they are not granted by the judicial authority, but by a Central Commission attached to the Ministry of the Interior upon the request and recommendation of the Prosecutor. Usually, the Central Commission follows the indication of the Prosecutor with respect to protection, although it is not bound by it.

9   *How often and on the basis of which considerations is the instrument used or not used?*

The most recent data on collaborators with justice is contained in the latest Report of the Ministry of the Interior on 'The Special Measures of Protection, their Effectiveness and the Modalities of their Practical Application' to the Parliament, dated 30 June 2016. According to the Report, there is a total of 6.525 protected persons, among which 1.277 are collaborators of justice.

The instrument is used every time a defendant decides to collaborate in relation to a crime foreseen by the Law, provided that the information revealed presents the characteristics required by the Law (it must bring new knowledge to the investigation, it must be complete and reliable). The Prosecutor has the discretion to decide who fulfils these requirements, based on a careful assessment of the personal history of the person, a thorough verification of the information provided, and the importance of the latter for the overall investigation/Prosecution's strategy. If an aspiring collaborator is willing to provide information that the Prosecutor already has, for example, the person will not be considered a collaborator.

10   *What have the positive and negative experiences been in practice with the instrument and the legal framework in this regard?*

The positive experiences outweigh the negative ones. The interviewed practitioners agree in considering collaboration with justice an indispensable instrument in the fight against organized crime (see also the answer to question 11). They were also positive about the legal framework in place, which clearly states which benefits can be granted and in what circumstances. In this regard it should be noted that practitioners took issue with the very word 'undertaking'. Prosecutors in particular were keen to emphasize that they do not make any promise to collaborators. They just explain what the Law foresees, what benefits are envisaged for them if they provide reliable information.

Nevertheless, problems have been encountered in practice, especially in the early years. In this regard it should be noted that the first contact between the Prosecutor and the collaborator is a very delicate moment. Prosecutors must be careful not to raise unrealistic expectations in collaborators. They must emphasize that it is ultimately the judge who decides to believe them or not and, therefore, to grant the sentence discount or the penitentiary benefits. Equally, they must explain very clearly the limitations and the shortcomings of a life under protection. The interviewed prosecutors reported that some aspiring collaborators (usually, those who are inexperienced and do not have a long criminal record) believe that the State will take care of them, that they will be given a lot of money and that the choice for collaboration will entail a very convenient deal for them. Prosecutors must be very clear in reducing these expectations, they must explain what collaboration really entails, based on the circumstances of the case. Some prosecutors and defense counsel stated that this has not always happened (especially in the 90s, in the first years of the application of the Law).

Another problem encountered in the early years was the insufficiency of the safeguards against unreliable collaborators. To this end, in 2001 a number of safeguards were introduced aimed at preventing unreliable collaborations. These are: 1) a time-limit of six months by which collaborators must reveal everything that they know to the Prosecutor, so that they cannot withdraw information and reveal it later at their convenience; 2) a number of provisions aimed at avoiding contacts between collaborators in jail (so that they cannot agree on a strategy or influence each other), and communications between them and their families or other persons at liberty; 3) specific sanctions aimed at punishing collaborators who provided false or altered declarations (specifically, the revocation of the benefits and the protection, as well as the retrial of the collaborator). The practitioners interviewed stated that these safeguards are very effective. They also stated that, in the majority of the cases, collaborators are reliable, which they attribute to the fact that over the course of 25 years, prosecutors and judges have acquired sufficient experience and skills to understand who is reliable and who is not.

Further problems relate to the management of collaborators by the Central Protection Service. Based on the findings of the Working Group on the measures of protection for collaborators and witnesses of justice established by the Ministry of the Interior in 2014, this report identified two areas that require improvement: the psychological assistance to protected persons and the mechanisms to facilitate the reintegration of collaborators into society upon exiting the protection program. Both of these aspects are crucial to achieve the broader goal of the system: ensuring that, through the 'journey' of collaboration, offenders who have helped the State in the repression and prevention of crimes, return to abide by the rules of social coexistence with the support of the institutions.

11   *What results have been achieved by use of the instrument in individual cases?*

Collaborators let the authorities 'inside' the organization, in that they are capable of explaining in an organic manner its 'logic', its internal dynamics and objectives for the future. The value of collaborators for investigative purposes is immense. All the practitioners underlined the fact that the biggest trials against mafia in Italy would not have been possible without the information provided by collaborators.

12   *Which factors contribute to the successful use of the instrument and which form obstacles in this regard?*

Two factors in particular are worthy of note here: 1) The experience and skills of prosecutors and judges in interrogating collaborators and in interpreting their answers; and 2) The support that the collaborator has from his family in his decision to collaborate. Turning first to the former, collaborators who formerly belonged to mafia, in fact, use a particular language and have the mind-set of the *Mafioso*, which follows a precise logic and adheres to a specific set of criminal 'values'. Prosecutors and judges must be familiar with the collaborators' frames of reference. As to the latter, the decision to collaborate entails a complete life-change, not only for the collaborator, but also for his family. Whereas the former will generally be detained (at least at the beginning), the latter will be relocated to a different region, under fake identities, and will have to comply with all of the security measures put in place by the authorities. Naturally, living undercover and far away from the place of origin, entails a great deal of restriction to personal freedom and great psychological stress. Not every family is willing to accept this.

13   *In general, do the rules on collaboration with justice achieve their objective?*

As stated, all the practitioners interviewed for the purposes of this report underlined the fact that the biggest trials against mafia in Italy would not have been possible without the information provided by collaborators of justice. Indeed, generally speaking, the effectiveness/necessity of an institutionalized system of reward and protection for collaborators of justice is not a contentious issue anymore among insiders. The interviewees mainly agree that the system is effective and fair.

This conviction, however, is not shared by defence lawyers operating on the opposite front. In the view of a counsel representing defendants who are accused by collaborators, the latter often misrepresent the facts or even openly lie. This is because the interests of collaborators and those of the judicial authority (i.e., prosecutors and judges) are somewhat in line. On the one hand, collaborators know that with the choice of collaborating they lose the protection of their criminal organisation and become dependent from the State for protection and sustenance; as a consequence, they are inclined to 'please' the judicial authorities by providing all the information that they expect, so as to be granted protection. On the other hand, the judicial authorities feel greatly facilitated in their task by collaborators, and thus have a tendency to believe their stories at the cost of stretching reality.

Scrutiny, Transparency and Debate

14   *To what extent is the use of the instrument subject to scrutiny by a judicial or other authority?*

In Italy, there is no automatic scrutiny by a third party of the initial phase of the process by which an individual becomes a collaborator of justice, i.e. the talks between the individual in question and the public prosecutor. During the investigation, the prosecutor is the only authority involved and responsible for the selection and management of collaborators. It is the prosecutor who decides whether to present a person as a 'collaborator' at trial. The prosecutor collects the declarations in the statement within 180 days and searches for all the necessary corroboration of the information revealed by the collaborator. The Prosecutor also proposes the measures of protection to be adopted by the Central Commission.

Nevertheless, the reliability of the statements provided by an aspiring collaborator is a matter subject to judicial scrutiny at trial, in order to decide on the guilt or innocence of the defendants accused by the collaborator, as well as on the sentence and benefits for the collaborators himself (collaborators are always convicted in that they are self-confessed defendants). Regarding the judicial scrutiny at trial, it should be noted that, under the ordinary procedure, pre-trial witness statements (including statements provided by collaborators) are not included in the trial-dossier and thus are not accessible to the judge, but only to the parties. Under Italian law, witness statements contained in the Prosecutor's file can be used by the parties to challenge the testimony of the witness at trial. As such, they can be evaluated by the judge only for the purpose of assessing the credibility of the witness, but not as a proof of the facts narrated therein. In practice, this means that, after the collaborator has testified in court, defense counsel of the persons that the collaborator has accused may cross-examine him, highlighting possible contra-dictions or discrepancies in what he has previously declared in the pre-trial statement. Based on this confrontation, the judge may draw conclusions as to the reliability of the collaborator. However, he or she cannot, per se, consider as proven either of the two different versions of the facts narrated by the collaborator. This is the general rule that governs the use of declarations of witnesses (including collaborators) at trial.

15   *In how far is the instrument itself and the use thereof in individual cases publicly transparent?*

Since the Law regulates every aspect of the institution of collaboration with justice, it may be said to be publicly transparent.

16   *To what extent is there debate or discussion regarding the use of the instrument? On which aspects of the instrument is the debate focused?*

There is almost no debate on collaboration with justice nowadays. As has been seen, over the course of 25 years the legal framework of Law n. 82/1991 has been reformed, so as to remedy to the most serious shortcomings of the previous regime. In addition, the Court of Cassation has intervened with a corrective interpretation on the aspects that remained problematic. As a result, the institute of collaboration with justice is now well established, and nowadays does not constitute an object of debate or contention. Nevertheless, it bears noting that recently the system of collaboration with justice received some negative atten-tion by the press, concerning the excessive costs of the protection system due to the fact that there are too many 'petty' collaborators (i.e. mid-level foot soldiers, whose revelations are not so crucial for the progress of the investigation) admitted to protection measures. The 'weight' and importance of the contribution of these mid-level offenders to the investigations is increasingly put into question by the press, and even by some insiders.

17   *In how far and in what regard has scrutiny, transparency and debate led to changes in the regulation of the instrument?*

As mentioned under question 16 there is almost no debate on collaboration with justice nowadays. In 2001 the Law was amended so as to overcome the major shortcomings of the previous system (i.e. the clogging of the system of protection, and the lack of sufficient safeguards against unreliable collaborators) and, since then, the debate stopped.

Appendix 2

List of Respondents of the Interviews

1. Former judge at the Court of Assize of Caltanissetta, currently General Prosecutor at the Court of Cassation
2. Judge for the preliminary investigations at the Tribunal of Palermo, currently seconded at the European Court of Human Rights
3. Judge for the preliminary investigations at the Tribunal of Palermo
4. General Prosecutor at the Court of Appeal of Milan, former prosecutor at the National Anti-mafia Bureau
5. Prosecutor at the National Anti-mafia Bureau and member of the Central Commission, former prosecutor at the DDA of Palermo
6. Prosecutor at the DDA of Rome, former prosecutor at the DDA of Palermo and Reggio Calabria
7. Police official of the Central Protection Service
8. Police official of the Central Protection Service
9. Defence counsel of collaborators, bar of Rome
10. Defence counsel of collaborators, bar of Naples
11. Defence counsel of defendants accused by collaborators, bar of Rome
12. Stefania Pellegrini, Professor of sociology of law at the University of Bologna
13. Giovanna Montanaro, sociologist and researcher, former consultant for the Anti-mafia Commisson of the Parliament and member of the Working Group on the measures of protection for collaborators and witnesses of justice

6 COLLABORATION WITH JUSTICE IN CANADA

N. Kovalev

6.1 INTRODUCTION

In order to facilitate an understanding of the Canadian approach to the institution of collaboration with justice, a brief introduction to the basic features of the Canadian criminal justice system seems appropriate. Essential elements of the Canadian criminal justice system were inherited from England in the form of the common law tradition of an independent judiciary, adversarial trial by jury, a strong criminal bar and a system of law based primarily on judicial decisions. However, unlike many common law jurisdictions, Canada also codified substantive criminal law and criminal procedure in one single statute – the Criminal Code of Canada.

Canada is a federal state consisting of ten provinces[1] and three territories[2] and governmental powers are divided between federal and provincial authorities.[3] While the federal government has exclusive jurisdiction over the criminal law and procedure,[4] the administration of justice in the provinces, including the constitution, maintenance, and organization of provincial criminal courts is within the jurisdiction of the provinces.[5] This means that each province and territory develops its own policies and practices in relation to the prosecution of criminal cases, including policies regarding the use of undertakings.

In 1982, Canada amended its Constitution to include the *Charter of Rights and Freedoms*, which had a profound impact on the development of the criminal justice system.[6] It provided for new safeguards of the rights of accused at the pre-trial and trial stage of criminal proceedings. In addition, it changed the role of judges in that they became more active in forming criminal justice policies and ruling on the constitutionality of legislation.[7] In particular, the Charter gave judges powers to exclude illegally obtained

---

1   Alberta, British Columbia, Manitoba, Ontario, Prince Edward Island, Quebec, New Brunswick, Newfoundland and Labrador, Nova Scotia, and Saskatchewan.
2   Nunavut, Northwest Territories, and Yukon.
3   See for more about the distribution of governmental power between the federal and provincial authorities, Hogg 2012.
4   Section 91(27) of the Constitution Act, 1867.
5   Section 92(14) of the Constitution Act, 1867.
6   Constitution Act, 1982.
7   See for more about the impact of the Charter of Rights and Freedoms (hereinafter the Charter) on the judiciary and criminal process in Canada, Cameron 1996; Cameron & Stribopoulos 2008; Berger & Stribopoulos 2012; Stuart 2014.

evidence[8] and to grant other remedies to rectify the violation of the constitutional rights of defendants.[9]

The Canadian system of criminal courts consists of the nine-member Supreme Court of Canada, which is the highest judicial authority; the Courts of Appeal of the provinces and territories, which hear appeals from the Superior and Provincial courts; Superior courts,[10] which adjudicate the most serious crimes, such as murder, with or without juries, and sometimes hear appeals from provincial courts; and provincial (inferior) courts, which try the vast majority of criminal offences[11] and do not hear any appeals.

Policing in Canada is administered at the provincial, territorial and municipal level. The federal police service, the Royal Canadian Mounted Police (RCMP), is responsible for enforcing federal statutes in each province and territory. The RCMP also provides provincial/territorial policing and municipal policing services in all provinces and territories, with the exception of Quebec and Ontario. These two provinces have their own provincial police services: Sûreté du Québec and the Ontario Provincial Police.[12]

Similarly, there are two types of prosecution office in Canada: federal and provincial. Upon admission to the Bar, lawyers can join the Crown Attorneys' Office in a province and become Crown attorneys (prosecutors) responsible for prosecuting the vast majority of criminal offences in provincial and superior courts; or they can join the Public Prosecution Service of Canada (PPSC), which is responsible for prosecuting offences under more than forty federal statutes, including those dealing with drugs, organized crime, terrorism, tax law, money laundering and proceeds of crime, crimes against humanity and war crimes, Criminal Code offences in the territories, and a large number of federal regulatory offences.[13] Unlike some jurisdictions where prosecutors oversee the pre-trial investigation, Canadian prosecutors are less involved in the investigation of crime. However, prosecutors do work closely with the investigators and often give legal advice to the police during criminal investigations.

The Canadian criminal process system is based on the adversarial procedural model. Among other things, this means that the prosecution bears the burden of proof beyond a reasonable doubt that the accused is guilty of the offence with which he is charged. At the same time, it should be noted that, unlike defence lawyers 'who are ethically mandated to be zealous advocates for their clients', a prosecutor's 'paramount duty is to ensure that justice is done'.[14]

---

8   See Section 24(2) of the Charter.
9   Sharpe & Roach 2013.
10 In the legal and constitutional doctrine of Canada, these courts are called courts of 'inherent jurisdiction', which means that they are not dependent on a particular statute for their authority and hence in theory can try any criminal matter. Section 468 of the Criminal Code confirms this by stating that superior courts have jurisdiction to try any indictable offence. In practice, however, they usually try the most serious crimes such as murder and any other crime if the defendant elects trial by judge and jury.
11 See Section. 553 of the Criminal Code of Canada.
12 Roberts & Grossman 2008.
13 See generally the Public Prosecution Service of Canada Deskbook (hereinafter the PPSC Deskbook), 2014.
14 Penney, Rondinelli & Stribopoulos 2011.

One of the key principles of the adversarial model of criminal procedure is that Canadian prosecutors enjoy independence from the police and have wide *prosecutorial discretion*. In Canada, prosecutorial discretion means that prosecutors can make the ultimate decisions as to whether a prosecution should be brought, continued or ceased, and what the prosecution ought to be for.[15] The fundamental importance of prosecutorial discretion is justified by the necessity of enabling 'prosecutors to make discretionary decisions in fulfilment of their professional obligations without fear of judicial and political interference.'[16] Although in most provinces the authority to charge any person with a criminal offence belongs to the police, the ultimate decision of whether to proceed with or terminate the prosecution – the 'screening process' – is the sole jurisdiction of Crown counsel.[17] However, prosecutorial discretion is not absolute. The decision to prosecute or terminate a prosecution may not be arbitrary and should be based on several factors, including: (1) whether there is a reasonable prospect of conviction; (2) whether it is in the public interest to discontinue a prosecution even if there is a reasonable prospect of conviction; (3) whether the proper charge has been laid; (4) whether the investigation is complete; and (5) whether an offer of diversion should be made to the accused.[18] The Public Prosecution Service of Canada Deskbook states that to ensure public confidence in its administration, prosecutorial discretion must be exercised in a manner that is objective, fair, transparent and consistent.[19] It also contains a similar test for initiating a prosecution. When deciding whether to initiate and conduct a prosecution on behalf of the federal Crown, Crown counsel must consider two issues: (1) is there a reasonable prospect of conviction based on evidence that is likely to be available at trial?; and, if there is, (2) would a prosecution best serve the public interest?[20]

The principle of independence of the Attorney General or Crown office is another fundamental principle of the organization of the prosecution services. Barristers employed as in-house prosecutors and private sector advocates, who are retained as prosecutors are called Crown counsel. At the federal level Crown counsel exercise their independence as representatives of the Director of Public Prosecution (DPP). Crown counsel are obliged to make decisions in accordance with the directives of the Attorney General and the guidelines of the DPP. Crown counsel act under the direction of Chief Federal Prosecutors (CFP), who in turn are answerable to the DPP and his or her Deputy DPPs. At the same time, Crown counsel retain a degree of discretion in individual cases, unless the law or guidelines require an approval or consultation with senior officials in the office. The principles of independence and prosecutorial discretion together form the

---

15 *Krieger v. Law Society of Alberta*, 2002 SCC 65, [2002] 3 S.C.R. 372 at para. 47.
16 *Miazga v. Kvello Estate*, 2009 SCC 51, [2009] 3 S.C.R. 339 at para. 47.
17 Roberts & Grossman 2008 at 39.
18 Ontario Ministry of Attorney General, Crown Policy, 2005 at https://www.attorneygeneral.jus.gov.on.ca/english/crim/cpm/2005/ChargeScreening.pdf
19 PPSC Deskbook, n. 13.
20 Ibid. at 3.

legal basis for immunity agreements and providing other benefits to persons in exchange for their cooperation and testimony in court.

As in other countries where the adversarial procedural model is used, only a small proportion of cases go to trial in Canada because the vast majority of criminal defendants plead guilty. There are various reasons why an accused may plead guilty to a criminal offence, including 'genuine remorse, a desire to be released from custody or an agreement with the prosecutor to plead guilty in exchange for a charging or sentencing benefit'.[21] As the Supreme Court of Canada explained in one of its judgements, a guilty plea 'carries an admission that the accused so pleading has committed the crime charged and a consent to a conviction being entered without any trial'.[22] The same judgement also observed that in pleading guilty, the accused 'relieves the Crown of the burden to prove guilt beyond a reasonable doubt, abandons his non-compellability as a witness and his right to remain silent and surrenders his right to offer full answer and defence to a charge'.[23] According to some criminologists and legal scholars, up to ninety percent of criminal cases are resolved through guilty pleas.[24] Another practice which is closely connected to guilty pleas, is the so-called practice of plea bargaining, or, as it is officially called, 'resolution discussions'.[25] A guilty plea often, but not always, is the result of plea bargaining between a prosecutor and the accused or his or her defence lawyers. As will be shown in this report, a guilty plea is often required as a part of the partial immunity granted to accused who are willing to testify against their co-accused. The plea bargaining or resolution discussions between Crown counsel and defence counsel 'may engage in conduct that ranges from simple discussions – through to negotiations – [...] to concrete agreements, all of which are perceived to be binding' on the two parties.[26] There are two types of resolution discussions or conferences: (1) the crown pre-trial conference (CPT) and the judicial pre-trial conference (JPT). If during the CPT counsel reach a resolution, and the defendant agrees to plead guilty, parties submit their joint statement on sentencing to the judge. If, however, parties fail to reach an agreement, then the matter will proceed to a JPT, where parties meet with a judge either in his or her chamber or in open court to consider the matters that will 'promote a fair and expeditious hearing'.[27] Judicial pre-trial conferences are mandatory in cases to be tried with a jury, but can be conducted in any other case on application by a prosecutor or defence lawyer or on the court's own motion.[28] There is no uniform approach towards the role of the judge

---

21   Ibid. at 629-630.
22   R. v. Adgey [1975] 2 S.C.R. 426 (1973).
23   Ibid.
24   Seifman & Freidberg 2001.
25   According to a research paper of the Canadian Department of Justice (authored by Milica Potrebic Piccinato), in Canada there was a movement away from the use of the term 'plea bargaining' and toward more neutral expressions such as 'plea discussions', 'resolution discussions', 'plea negotiations' and 'plea agreements'. See Potrebic Piccinato 2004, at 1; see also Brook et al. 2016, at 1157.
26   Roberts & Grossman 2008, at 129.
27   Section 625.1 of the Criminal Code of Canada.
28   Section 625.1 of the Criminal Code of Canada.

during the JPT. Some judges play an active role and express their opinion regarding the strength of the case.[29]

Although agreements between the parties are binding, any promises by Crown counsel in relation to a specific sentence may be declined by the sentencing judge.[30] At the sentencing stage, both prosecuting and defence counsel usually present the result of their resolution discussion in the form of joint submissions. Sentencing judges may refuse to accept such joint submissions and impose either a more lenient or severe sentence than is suggested by the prosecutor. The law stipulates that the judge may accept the guilty plea only if he or she is satisfied that the defendant is making it voluntarily and understands: (1) that the plea is an admission of the essential elements of the offence; (2) the nature and consequences of the plea; and (3) that the court is not bound by any agreement made between the defendant and the prosecutor.[31] It also stipulates that, 'if the court is satisfied that the proposed sentence is disproportionately lenient, or would 'bring the administration of justice into disrepute' it is entitled to 'jump' a joint submission, imposing a higher sentence than that endorsed by counsel'.[32] In other cases, judges are not authorised to decline the terms and conditions of the plea or immunity agreement between the parties.

A distinctive feature of the Canadian criminal justice system is the use of jurors in criminal trials. A trial by jury of twelve lay citizens is guaranteed by the Canadian Charter of Rights and Freedoms in all criminal cases punishable by five years of imprisonment or a more severe punishment.[33] This means that, in cases in which an accused pleads not guilty to a charge, he or she can elect a trial by jury or judge sitting alone. There are no concrete statistics on the number of jury trials in Canada. As will be further explained below, a trial by jury has some important implications for the proceedings involving witness-offenders who are testifying against others.[34]

Another important feature of the Canadian criminal justice system is that in cases where an offender is willing to testify against another accused in exchange for a lenient sentence (not full immunity[35]), their trials are usually severed. This means that the case against an offender who testifies as a witness for the prosecution would usually be resolved through a guilty plea and a sentence following his or her testimony in court in the trial against another.

Upon a guilty plea or a guilty verdict, the trial judge may sentence a convicted person to one of the following: an absolute or conditional discharge, probation, a fine of up to

---

29   Brook et al. 2016, at 1158.
30   In practice, however, judges almost always defer to the agreement reached between the parties.
31   Section 606(1.1) of the Criminal Code of Canada.
32   Brook et al. 2016, at 1159.
33   The Charter, s. 11(f).
34   See § 6.6.5 of this report.
35   Here it bears observing that in case of full immunity, the person is not brought to trial as an accused.

$5,000 for individuals and an unlimited amount for corporations, imprisonment for a fixed term of up to twenty years or life imprisonment with a possibility of parole.

6.2   Methodology

This report is based on desk research and interviews with seven Canadian criminal justice practitioners. The collection of empirical data was a challenging task due to several factors, including a reluctance on the part of some practitioners to participate in the project for various reasons, such as a lack of experience with the use of undertakings, a lack of time to participate, an inability to obtain approval from their superiors or a lack of interest. After months of discussions involving numerous phone calls and email exchanges with various departments in provincial (Ontario) and federal law enforcement organizations and private defence offices, consent was obtained to interview seven practitioners in three different Canadian cities: Montreal, Ottawa and Toronto. In this regard it should be noted that although criminal procedure law does not differ in Quebec and Ontario, each jurisdiction in Canada may differ slightly in terms of their practice and culture in the office. However, such differences should not have a great impact on (the outcome of) cases involving undertakings.

For the purpose of this research, seven interviews were conducted. In Toronto, interviews were conducted with a defence counsel (interviewee [1]), a former senior official and prosecutor from the Ontario Ministry of the Attorney General (interviewee [2]) and a judge (interviewee [3]). In Ottawa, interviews were conducted with two RCMP officers (interviewees [4] and [5]) and a senior federal prosecutor from the PPSC's office (interviewee [6]). In Montreal, a senior federal prosecutor from the PPSC's office was interviewed (interviewee [7]). All interviews were conducted in the period between 29 November 2016 and 20 February 2017. Four interviews were audiotaped and transcribed. Three interviews were conducted without audio recording, but notes were taken during the interview. Each interview lasted from an hour and a half to two hours.

6.3   Conceptualization, Terminology and Relationship to Other
         Information Providers

Official and unofficial agreements between Canadian criminal justice authorities on the one hand and persons involved in criminal activity on the other hand are reached every day on the street, at police stations, or the office of the prosecutor. There are various types of agreement, but they usually involve promises by the criminal justice officials to provide certain benefits to persons engaged in criminal activity or associated with the criminal underworld in exchange for information, which can help the police and prosecutors to investigate, prosecute and resolve criminal matters. All agreements between criminal justice officials and citizens can be divided into two categories: (1) street or practical agreements; and (2) official or technical agreements. As will be explained in the practical part of this report, the first type of agreement is not regulated by legal rules and guidelines and are used by the police officers in their everyday work, in particular, in their work with confidential informants. The second type of agreement is regulated by legal rules, including statutory and common law and ministerial guidelines. Examples of the second type of agreement are plea bargaining or resolution agreements and immunity agreements.

The legal concepts of prosecutorial discretion, plea bargaining and the granting of full or partial immunity in exchange for testimony against a co-accused are closely connected to each other. As stated above, prosecutorial discretion is the main basis for granting a person involved in criminal activity immunity from prosecution. Often partial immunity, such as reducing the charge, is made in exchange for pleading guilty to a lesser charge.

In Canada, criminal procedure is regulated by federal legislation and case law. As mentioned above, the main statute regulating both substantive criminal law and criminal procedure is the Criminal Code of Canada.[36] The Criminal Code does not contain any express provisions regulating immunity from prosecution or other undertakings to offenders who are willing to give evidence in the prosecution of others. However, Canadian courts have recognized that the Crown has legal authority to grant immunity from prosecution.[37] Immunity from prosecution, like many other procedural matters that are not provided for in the legislation, is regulated by guidelines and directives issued by the prosecution agencies. At the federal level, employees of the PPSC and its private-sector agents have to follow the guidelines compiled in the PPSC Deskbook. The PPSC Deskbook is issued by the Director of Public Prosecutions and the Attorney General of Canada.[38] Similar manuals and guidelines were issued by the Ministry of Justice and Solicitor General of Alberta,[39] the Ministry of Justice of British Columbia,[40] the Office of the Attorney General of New Brunswick,[41] and the Nova Scotia Public Prosecution Service.[42]

---

36   There is no separate procedural code in Canada. Criminal procedure legislation is the exclusive jurisdiction of the federal government.
37   *R. v. Edward D.* (1990), 73 OR (2d) 758 (ON CA); *Bourrée v. Parsons* (1987), 29 CCC (3d) 126 (Ont Dist Ct); *R. v. Betesh* (1975), 30 CCC (2d) 233 (Ont Co Ct).
38   PPSC Deskbook, n. 13.
39   Ministry of Justice and Solicitor General of Alberta, Crown Prosecutors' Manual, Immunity from Prosecution and other Consideration for Witnesses and Informants, May 20, 2008.
40   Ministry of Justice of British Columbia, Crown Counsel Policy Manual, Immunity From Prosecution – Witness & Informants, April 13, 2015.
41   Office of Attorney General of New Brunswick, Public Prosecution Operational Manual, Policy No. 34, September 1, 2015, available at http://www2.gnb.ca/content/dam/gnb/Departments/ag-pg/PDF/en/Public-ProsecutionOperationalManual/Policies/CrownImmunityandPublicInterestAgreements.pdf.
42   Nova Scotia Public Prosecution Service, Immunity From Prosecution Policy, November 23, 2015, available at http://www.novascotia.ca/pps/publications/ca_manual/prosecutionpolicies/immunity_from_prosecution.pdf.

During the pre-trial investigation, the police may receive information from various sources. As will be discussed below, not every source of information will be presented in court as a witness.

Confidential Informants (Informers)

Confidential informers provide information to the police on the condition of anonymity in order to protect their identity. Such informers do not testify in court as a witness, because they are granted Crown (police informer) privilege.[43] However, their information can and is frequently used by the police to obtain a search warrant. The police do not disclose the identity of their informers to others. Even in their application to obtain a search warrant, the police office refers to the informer as an unnamed confidential informer or by an assigned informant number.[44] In some cases, however, the informant may waive the police informer privilege if they decide to become an agent or a witness and testify in court.

In-Custody Informer

Unlike confidential informants, in-custody or jailhouse informers may be called as a witness in judicial proceedings. An in-custody informer is defined as 'someone who: (a) allegedly receives one or more statements from an accused, (b) while both are in-custody, (c) where the statements relate to offences that occurred outside of the custodial institution'.[45] This type of informant does not include persons who are intentionally placed in proximity to the accused by the authorities, for the specific purpose of acquiring evidence (such persons are known as agents, about which more is said below).[46] The legal practitioners interviewed for the purposes of this project stated that jailhouse informers are a very restricted category. According to a senior federal prosecutor, there are only around ten cases per year across Canada where jailhouse informers are used as witnesses. The same prosecutor observed that the Canadian authorities are currently very careful in accepting jailhouse informers' statements as evidence and do so only if the prosecutor believes that the informer is reliable. One of the problems with jailhouse informers is that they are often aggressive in asking questions to and manipulating the accused.

Even though in-custody informers have been identified as a significant contributing factor in cases of wrongful conviction,[47] Canadian courts still allow for the use of their

---

43 Van Allen 2012, p. 213. See also the special guideline of the Director of Public Prosecution of Canada regulating informer's privilege, Section 3.1 of the PPSC Deskbook, n. 13.
44 Van Allen 2009, p. 205.
45 Department of Justice of Canada, Report on the Prevention of Miscarriages of Justice, 2004, p. 75, at http://canada.justice.gc.ca/eng/rp-pr/cj-jp/ccr-rc/pmj-pej/pmj-pej.pdf.
46 Ibid. at 75.
47 See, e.g. the Kaufman Report, which states that: 'Jailhouse informant is intrinsically, though not invariably, unreliable and many of us have failed in the past to appreciate the full extent of this unreliability. It follows that prosecutors must be particularly vigilant in recognizing the true detracting from, or supporting, [their]

testimony in criminal trials. However, the prosecutorial guidelines warn Crown counsel to pay special attention to issues of credibility when dealing with jailhouse informers.[48] In particular, the federal prosecutorial guideline stipulates that 'at a minimum, Crown counsel should subjectively assess the jailhouse informer's proposed testimony and examine the details of the evidence, possible motives for lying, and the possibility of collusion, where the is more than one in-custody informer'.[49] Moreover, in addition to the general factors that prosecutors should consider in determining whether immunity may be appropriate (about which more is said below),[50] Crown counsel should consider the following factors when dealing with in-custody informers:

1. The jailhouse informer's background, including: his or her psychological and psychiatric profiles; any prior claims of having received in-custody statements; the reliability of any previous information; any prior testimony; any convictions for offences involving dishonesty;

2. The circumstances of the informer's incarceration, including the placement of the informer within the prison facility and access to information about the crime in question;

3. The relationship between the informer and the police and the circumstances surrounding the giving of the 'confession', including: when, where and how the statement was made; Whether the police solicited the evidence; whether there was any prior association between the in-custody informer and the police officer involved in the investigation; whether the police approached the informer prior to 'receiving' the 'confession'; whether the police provided information to the informer prior to the making of the statement; and whether the police asked leading questions;

4. The circumstances surrounding the disclosure of the alleged statement to the Crown;

5. The benefits sought or received in return for the information;

6. Whether tests were used to ensure reliability; and the extent to which the statement is corroborated by other evidence;

7. The specificity of the statement.[51]

Agents

Informants may be distinguished from agents. Thus, '[u]nlike the informant, who assumes the passive role of an observer, an agent plays an active role in the investigation. Agents are used to make evidence purchases, to introduce and vouch for undercover police officers, to

---

reliability'. Canada, *Report of the Kaufman Commission on Proceedings Involving Guy Paul Morin*, vol 1 (Toronto: Queen's Printer, 1998) at 487.

48 See Section 3.3 of the PPSC Deskbook, n. 13.
49 Section 3.3 of the PPSC Deskbook, n. 13 at para. 7.1.
50 See Section 3.3. of the PPSC Deskbook, n. 13 at paras. 5.1-5.6.
51 Section 3.3. of the PPSC Deskbook at para. 7.1.

'befriend' criminals and infiltrate criminal organizations, to gather evidence and even to become involved in providing justifiable opportunities to induce individuals to commit crimes.'[52] Informer privilege does not apply to 'police agents' or the 'agent provocateur.'[53]

There are two types of agents: undercover police officers and civilians who are recruited by the police. While confidential informers can become agents by waiving their confidential status, agents cannot become confidential informants. In the case law, the distinction between an informer and an agent is explained as follows:

> 'In general terms, the distinction between an informer and an agent is that an informer merely furnishes information to the police and an agent acts on the direction of the police and goes 'into the field' to participate in the illegal transaction in some way. The identity of an informer is protected by a strong privilege and, accordingly, is not disclosable, subject to the innocence at stake exception. The identity of an agent is disclosable.'[54]

There is no special legislative framework regulating the status of informers or police agents. Their status is governed by ministerial guidelines[55] and common law.

6.4 DEVELOPMENT OF THE (LEGAL) RULES

In a working paper published in 1992, the Law Reform Commission of Canada (LRCC) observed that granting immunity in Canada 'appears to be related to the former English practice of offering pardons to accomplices, and thereby allowing them to avoid being indicted for offences in respect of which their testimony was sought.'[56] One of the first reported Canadian cases to recognize the prosecutorial discretion to grant immunity from prosecution was *R. v. Betesh* (1975). In that case, Judge Graburn wrote that, 'notwithstanding the lack of any express provision in the Criminal Code allowing a grant of immunity by the Attorney-General for Canada, I am satisfied he possesses such a power and that with rare exceptions he be trusted to exercise it in accordance with the highest traditions of the administration of justice.'[57] It appears that prior to the 1990s, Canadian prosecutors did not have specific policies regulating the prosecutorial discretion to grant immunity.

---

52 Van Allen 2012, p. 228.
53 See the special guideline of the Director of Public Prosecution of Canada regulating informer's privilege, Section 3.1 of the PPSC Deskbook, n. 13.
54 *R. v. Babes* (2002), 146 CCC (3d)
55 E.g. the PPSC Deskbook.
56 Law Reform Commission of Canada, Immunity from Prosecution (LRCC), Working Paper No. 64, 1992, Ottawa, p. 3.
57 *R. v. Betesh*, n. 37, para. 36.

The LRCC's Working Paper is considered to be one of the most comprehensive reviews of the use of immunity agreements in Canada. The LRCC proposed a new legal framework for regulating immunity agreements. Specifically, the LRCC recommended sixteen rules to be adopted either in the form of legislation or uniform guidelines.[58] To date, the Canadian government has not adopted any legislation regulating the granting of immunity from prosecution. It is not clear why the federal government did not adopt a specific legislative act in this regard, although it should be noted that the Canadian legislator is usually reluctant to impose rules which operate to restrict prosecutorial discretion. One of the federal prosecutors interviewed for the purposes of this project (interviewee [6]) provided another explanation for the lack of a legislative framework. In his opinion, the Canadian Criminal Code usually does not regulate the pre-trial stage of the criminal proceedings:

'Some of that is inertia and some of that [...] is [...] a view that, and I think it still prevails today, the Criminal Code is very much about the criminal procedure in court and substantive criminal law [...]'

'[E]ven with the UK and the common law tradition that we adopted, we take a starkly different approach in modern times with things like police powers. We codify almost nothing and rely on the common law. The UK codifies most of it. And the best example is the idea [...] of police ability to do what is necessary in carrying out their duty, to use as much force as is necessary [...] or anything that is reasonable in the context. Our Supreme Court [...] essentially said under the common law the police can do within reason whatever they need to do. And that comes from the UK and [the Supreme Court judges] have never followed that line of cases. There is one case from 1969. [The Supreme Court] decided it and forgot about it. And it is the basis of all of our police powers from sniffer dogs to search upon arrest. So, even from the UK we have this unique divergence.'

Indeed, Canada never developed a separate criminal procedure code and almost all the procedural provisions in the Criminal Code refer to trial proceedings (the judicial stage of criminal proceedings).[59]

Instead of a legislative framework, as stated above, the PPSC and provincial Ministries of Justice adopted some of the LRCC recommendations in the form of guidelines. These guidelines are not binding on the prosecution, although if individual prosecutors do not follow the guidelines, they can be the subject of labour and/or disciplinary actions. The

---

58 LRCC Working Paper No. 64, n. 56, pp. 45-77.
59 See Sections 493-670 of the Criminal Code of Canada.

point is that violations of the guidelines do not automatically nullify the proceedings. In other words, a breach by an individual prosecutor of the policies and guidelines does not lead to the automatic exclusion of the evidence obtained thereby; rather the issue of admissibility is decided on a case-by-case basis.

Another important factor in adopting policy guidelines in some of the Canadian provinces, in particular Ontario, was the controversial case of Karla Homolka, with whom the Crown office entered into a plea agreement and a partial immunity agreement. Karla Homolka and her ex-husband, Paul Bernardo, participated in sexual assault resulting in the killings of three teenage girls, including Homolka's younger sister. According to the plea agreement, Homolka received a lower charge of manslaughter and a twelve-year sentence in exchange for her testimony against her husband, who was convicted for double-murder and sentenced to life imprisonment without the possibility of parole for at least twenty-five years. Shortly after the trial of Paul Bernardo, during which a more active and willing role of Homolka in the death of the victims came to light, which was not known to the Crown at the time of the conclusion of the agreement with Homolka, the Attorney General of Ontario appointed Patrick Galligan, a retired judge of the Court of Appeal for Ontario, to inquire into and report on certain matters relating to, inter alia, the plea arrangement with Karla Homolka.[60] In his report, Justice Galligan denied that Karla Homolka had been given 'preferential treatment'.[61] In particular, Justice Galligan concluded that:

> 'The first decision, to agree to a twelve-year sentence, was driven by sheer necessity and not by a desire to treat Karla Homolka differently than any other criminal. I have no doubt that the Crown would have preferred that Karla Homolka appear in the prisoner's dock with Paul Bernardo facing first degree murder charges. However, without her evidence, at the time the decision was made, the police did not have evidence to charge Paul Bernardo with the offences arising out of the deaths of Leslie Mahaffy and Kristen French, much less convict him of them.'

> 'Distasteful as it is, the practice which has existed for over three hundred years of giving immunity or a "discount" to an accomplice to obtain her evidence against a co-perpetrator is sometimes a necessary one and it is a legal one. Regrettably, the investigation and prosecution of crime is rarely easy and often requires the taking of steps which are unpleasant.'[62]

60　In particular, the Ministry of the Attorney General of Ontario asked Justice Galligan to consider, inter alia, two issues: (1) whether the plea arrangement entered into by Crown counsel with Karla Homolka was appropriate in all the circumstances; (2) whether in all the circumstances, it is appropriate or feasible to take further proceedings against Karla Homolka for her part in the deaths of the victims. The Honourable Patrick T. Galligan, Report on Certain Matters Relating to Karla Homolka, 1996.

61　Ibid. at 215.

62　Ibid. at 216.

It appears that this case had a significant impact on the policies developed by the Ministries of the Attorney General at both the federal and provincial levels. After this case, many provinces adopted policies and guidelines regulating immunity issues. The federal Ministry of the Attorney General and the Ministries of the Attorney General of the majority of provinces made their policies regarding immunities and other undertakings available to the public. In Ontario, by contrast, the Crown policy manual, at least the part of the manual which is not considered to be privileged,[63] does not contain many provisions or principles regarding immunity agreements and other undertakings.

6.5   LEGAL FRAMEWORK

This report predominantly relies on the PPSC Deskbook, which contains directives of the Attorney General of Canada and guidelines of the Director of Public Prosecution. The decision to use the *federal* framework for the purposes of setting out the legal framework regulating undertakings in Canada was made for the following reasons. First, the Criminal Code does not regulate immunity agreements and the PPSC's Deskbook is currently the most developed compilation of Crown directives and policy guidelines, which is available to the public. Second, most of the practitioners interviewed for the purposes of this report were criminal justice officials representing federal agencies, specifically, the PPSC and RCMP. Third, the federal legal framework is used in respect of a variety of serious criminal offences, including white-collar crime and drug offences; as will be seen below, it is in such cases (rather than regular street crime) that the use of immunities and other forms of undertakings is most common.

6.5.1   *Responsibility for Providing Undertakings*

At the federal level, immunity from prosecution in exchange for testimony is regulated by Section 3.3 of the PPSC Deskbook, which contains the Guideline of the Director issued under Section 3(3)(c) of the Director of Public Prosecutions Act.[64] According to this guideline, the term 'immunity agreement' means any agreement by the Crown to refrain from prosecuting someone for a crime or to terminate a prosecution, in return for providing testimony or other valuable information, cooperation or assistance.[65] The guideline also states that only the DPP acting through Crown counsel, and not the investigative agency, is entitled to confer immunity from prosecution. However, the same guideline recognizes that investigative agen-

---

63 The Attorney General for Ontario's Crown Policy Manual consists of three parts: policies; practice memoranda and confidential legal memoranda. The third part is privileged and confidential. See https://www.-attorneygeneral.jus.gov.on.ca/english/crim/cpm/2005/CPMAccessStructure.pdf.
64 See the PPSC Deskbook, n. 13.
65 Ibid. at 3.3: 4.

cies have the discretion to exercise a form of immunity by deciding not to lay charges in the first place.[66] In determining whether immunity from prosecution may be granted, Crown counsel is required to weigh several important factors, including: (1) the seriousness of the offence; (2) the reliability of the person; (3) the reliability of the anticipated evidence; (4) whether the information-provider has made full and candid disclosure; (5) the importance of the person's testimony or co-operation; (6) the nature and extent of the person's involvement in the offence; (7) whether other, lesser forms of reward or benefit would be appropriate; (8) the person's history of co-operation; and (9) the public interest.

The decision to grant immunity to an information-provider is not made by a single person or department of the PPSC. Crown counsel is required to consult with senior officials within the organization. The federal guideline stipulates that Crown counsel must consult with the CFP before entering into an immunity agreement.[67] Moreover, in cases of significant public interest,[68] the CFP should consult the appropriate Deputy Director of Public Prosecutions (DPP) before finalizing an arrangement.

Although as stated above, only Crown counsel may enter into immunity agreements with information-providers, the federal guideline recognizes the important role of the police in reaching immunity agreements. The guideline states that:

'In most cases, the immunity process begins with discussions between the information-provider and the case investigators without prior consultation with Crown counsel. Following these discussions, investigators usually approach the prosecutor. Crown counsel rely on these investigating agency's input in weighing the relevant public interest criteria. Crown counsel should be satisfied that the agency's lead investigator responsible for overseeing such agreements has reviewed and approved the proposed agreement. The investigating agency makes a recommendation to Crown counsel. However, Crown counsel bears the ultimate responsibility for deciding who is prosecuted and who is called as a witness.'

Thus, the police can influence the prosecutor's decision of whether to provide immunity or another type of undertaking if they believe it can assist the investigation in collecting evidence and strengthening their case against other suspects or accused.

As to the terms and conditions of the witness protection program, at the federal level these matters are discussed and offered by the police, not prosecuting counsel. The federal prosecutors who were interviewed for the purposes of this project provided a number of explanations as to why the witness protection program is administered by the police and

---

66 Ibid. at 3.3: 6.
67 Ibid. at 3.3: 11.
68 Section 3.3 of the PPSC Deskbook does not clarify when a case may be considered to be of 'significant public interest', however these cases usually include high-profile cases, which generate significant media coverage in Canada and abroad.

not the prosecutor's office. For example, one prosecutor (interviewee [6]) stated: 'witness protection program is an operational issue to the police. This program includes some innocent people. They are related, but separate tracks. We [PPSC] don't have special expertise'. Another federal prosecutor (interviewee [7]) also observed: 'The Canadian Government decided that it [witness protection program] should be responsibility of the Public Security Department. The role of prosecutor in Canada is different at the federal level. The investigative responsibility is within the sole responsibility of the RCMP. Federal prosecutors are not actively involved. We are not responsible for investigation. There should be some distance from the investigative body to be more independent'.

6.5.2   Regarding Which Offences?

Neither the law, including the case law, nor the policy guideline restricts the types of offence in respect of which undertakings may be provided. Nevertheless, it is clear from guideline that the use of undertakings is considered an important tool in the battle against organized crime.

However, in relation to full immunity, the guideline states that, generally, it should be considered only when the information provided relates to the commission of a serious offence, or when the prosecution of a case is otherwise important in achieving effective enforcement of the law. It also stipulates that, as a rule, the immunity should not be considered in relatively minor cases.

There are reported cases where immunity and witness protection were granted to Crown witnesses in murder cases in exchange for assistance in the police investigation and testimony in court.[69] In the province of Ontario, full immunity tends to be used in the most serious cases. As a former senior prosecutor interviewed for this project (interviewee [2]) observed: 'It is really about very serious crime like murder or gang related crime, which might put you [witness] in a dangerous situation. The general rule is that the witness evidence has to be important. It has to be a serious case and important piece of evidence'.

Similarly, immunity has been granted to witnesses in fraud cases[70] and drug importation cases.[71] As one federal prosecutor interviewed for this project (interviewee [6]) explained, immunity may be offered in any type of (federal) case. Another federal prosecutor (interviewee [7]) observed that immunity has been offered in the context of various types of crime, including organized crime, major fraud, corruption and murder. The only type of case in which it has never been used is terrorism.

---

69 *R. v. Smith*, [2009] 1 S.C.R. 146; *R. v. Illes*, [2008] 3 S.C.R. 134; *R. v. Hamilton*, [2011] O.J. No. 2306, 2011 ONCA 399; *R. v. Yumnu*, [2010] O.J. No. 4163, 2010 ONCA 637; *R. v. Thompson*, [2008] O.J. No. 3914, 2008 ONCA 693; *R. v. Brown*, [2005] O.J. No. 1952.
70 *R. v. Drabinsky*, [2011] S.C.C.A. No. 491; *R. v. Bisram*, [2011] O.J. No. 3048.
71 *R. v. Deol*, [2017] O.J. No. 1462 (C.A.).

6.5.3　Nature of the Undertakings

The PPSC stipulates different mechanisms by which the Crown can confer immunity: (1) a stay of proceedings;[72] (2) immunity from future prosecutions; and (3) 'use immunity' investigative assistance agreements. The main difference between immunity agreements and 'use immunity' agreements is that the latter focuses on the uses that may be made of the information provided, rather than acts which will not be prosecuted. For instance, under the 'use immunity' agreement, the person who is willing to give details of their knowledge of criminal activity in audiotaped or videotaped interviews, may receive assurances that the information provided during these interviews will not be used directly against them for investigative purposes.[73]

Within the framework of full or partial immunity agreements, federal prosecutors can promise a range of terms and conditions to the cooperative witnesses. The federal guideline stipulates a non-exhaustive list of terms and conditions or undertakings, which can be included in a immunity agreement: (1) dropping charges; (2) reducing charges; (3) dropping or reducing the charges of others, such as family members or friends; (4) agreeing to a lesser sentence; (5) the timing of dealing with outstanding charges; (6) the resolution of pending applications for the return of offence-related property or proceeds of crime; (7) reward money.[74] The list does not include witness protection measures, such as relocation, new identity, assistance in securing employment, and special privileges while in jail, which may arise during negotiations between the investigator and the information-provider, since this falls within the remit of the police. Nevertheless, the Crown should be (made) aware of these matters. As discussed below (in Section 6.6.4 of this report), the terms and conditions of the witness protection program are discussed and negotiated between the police and the witness, not the Crown and the witness.

6.5.4　Procedure to Be Followed and (Interim) Scrutiny

As stated above, the process usually starts with a discussion between the police investigator and the potential information-provider, and involves consultations with Crown counsel supervising the investigation and other senior officials of the PPSC. The

---

72　Federal prosecutors may enter a stay of proceedings under Section 579.1 of the Criminal Code. The Code empowers the prosecutor to end the proceedings at any time after the charge and before judgement. Since the decision to enter a stay is administrative and not judicial, it does not require the court's approval. Penney, Rondinelli & Stribopoulos 2011, p. 454.

73　See the PPSC Deskbook, n. 13 at 3.3: 5.

74　Ibid. at 3.3: 10-11. As explained by one of the practitioners interviewed for this project (interviewee [2]), in Canada, the general rule is that the prosecutors do not use reward money. 'The police tend to offer these only in cases where there are no leads – so called 'cold cases'. Money is offered in relation to information to get started. Often the police make a condition of payment of money in case of successful prosecution'.

PPSC's guideline stipulates the responsibilities of Crown counsel in this regard. In particular, Crown counsel should:

1. strongly encourage the immunity seeker to obtain the assistance of legal counsel before entering into any immunity agreement and negotiate through this lawyer;

2. whenever possible, limit his or her meetings with the person and deal primarily with the other lawyer until the agreement is finalized and ready for signature;[75]

3. never meet the immunity-seeker alone (i.e. the investigating officer should always be in attendance);[76]

4. maintain detailed records of all negotiations with the immunity-seeker and his or her lawyer leading up to the agreement;

5. be diligent not to expose the immunity-seeker to facts or evidence about the prosecution to which his or her testimony, information, assistance or cooperation will apply;

6. canvass the areas usually explored in cross-examination before deciding whether to conclude the agreement;

7. be fully aware of the circumstances, such as who approached whom, the numbers of interviews and the parties attending, whether the interviews were recorded;[77]

8. explore whether, during the debriefing process, the information-provider consciously or unconsciously may have absorbed facts previously unknown to him or her, that investigators had obtained from other sources;

9. make it clear that he or she does not have unfettered discretion to approve any immunity agreement that is negotiated; rather any such agreement must be approved in accordance with the procedures outlined in the guideline (see above);

10. be familiar with other guidelines, including the one on resolution discussions;

11. reduce in writing any immunity agreement that is negotiated and ensure that the written agreement is signed by the immunity-seeker and, if applicable, his or her lawyer;

---

75 The main reason behind this requirement is the need to ensure the fairness of the proceedings. The prosecutor should be viewed as a neutral official in this process. One of the concerns here is that a prosecutor can take unfair or improper advantage of the circumstances. Also, general rules of ethics require counsel not to approach or communicate with a person who is represented by another lawyer. For example, Rule 7.2-6 of the Law Society of Upper Canada Code of Professional Conduct states that: 'if a person is represented by a legal practitioner in respect of a matter, a lawyer shall not, except through or with the consent of the legal practioner (a) approach or communicate or deal with the person on the matter; or (b) attempt to negotiate or compromise the matter directly with the person.' This ethical obligation is applicable to all prosecutors also, because in Canada all Crown counsel are members of the Law Society in the province where they practice law as prosecutors.

76 The Rules of Professional Conduct usually require that counsel should not communicate with an unrepresented person alone and it is prudent to have a witness present. See e.g. Commentary to Rule 5.1-2 of the LSUC Rules of Professional Conduct.

77 This is an important consideration because during the cross-examination of the cooperating witness, the defence will ask these questions and Crown counsel should be aware of the circumstances of the negotiation process.

12. avoid agreeing to grant complete immunity from criminal responsibility unless it is absolutely necessary in order to obtain the required testimony, information, assistance or cooperation. The granting of a limited form of immunity is generally preferred.

An immunity agreement in Canada is not usually subject to judicial scrutiny. At the same time, as will be discussed below, copies of the immunity agreement are filed in court and provided to counsel defending the accused against whom the information-provider intends to testify in court as part of the disclosure package.[78]

6.5.5   Relationship to Witness Protection

A person who is granted immunity and whose safety is at risk because he or she cooperated with the police and agreed to provide information, including testimony in court, may be protected through the witness protection program. The federal Witness Protection Program (WPP) is administered by the RCMP. Similar programs exist in some provinces, such as Ontario. Unlike the issue of immunity, which is not regulated by federal law, but rather by a PPSC guideline, the witness protection program is regulated by a special statute, i.e. the Witness Protection Program Act. Protectees (protected witnesses) enter into a protection agreement with the RCMP. In order to prevent a conflict of interest, the officers providing services to protectees are completely independent from the officers involved in the investigation of crime.[79] Unlike officers who are involved in the investigation of crime, the officers providing services to witnesses do not have any interest in the outcome of the criminal case.

---

78 Crown counsel has a duty to make disclosure in accordance with the law. The duty of disclosure is a fundamental principle of the Canadian criminal process. This duty was recognized by the Canadian Supreme Court in the case of *R. v. Stinchcombe*, [1991] 3 S.C.R. 326. According to this decision, the Crown is under a duty at common law to disclose to the defence all material evidence, whether favourable to the accused or not. Transgression with respect to this duty constitutes a very serious breach of legal ethics. The Crown also has a duty to make reasonable inquiries regarding the disclosure of police misconduct information. See *R. v. McNeil*, 2009 SCC 3, [2009] 1 S.C.R. 66. See also Section 2.5 of the PPSC Deskbook. The disclosure should be made in a timely manner during the pre-trial investigation. It is a continuous obligation. The copy of the immunity agreement should be filed before the trial starts. This obligation is also stipulated in Section 3.3 of the PPSC Deskbook at para. 10.
79 Witness Protection Program, available at http://www.rcmp-grc.gc.ca/fwpp-pfpt/qa-qr-eng.htm.

6.6   PRACTICE

6.6.1   Application: Frequency and Results

At neither the federal nor the provisional level do the Canadian police or prosecutors' offices collect data on how often and what types of undertakings are used in practice. The main reasons for the lack of data are as follows: (1) as mentioned above, the power of prosecutors, and in some cases, of the police, to provide undertakings is discretionary and often informal; and (2) there is no legal requirement to collect such data because the process is not regulated by any statute.

   As stated, generally speaking, undertakings and the various types of deals between the police and persons allegedly involved in criminal activity are frequent on the informal level. As a former prosecutor from Ontario (interviewee [2]) observed in his interview:

> 'When you speak of undertakings here, you are speaking of considerations given to the accused persons in terms of some sort of favour or assistance for something that they are [providing] in return. So, the first thing to note is that while there are various rules in place for a prosecution service [...] there is a large open window. And the large open window refers to what happens before the prosecutor [approaches] or is involved. For example, if a police officer makes an agreement on the street that the evidence will not be used against someone, [...] then the dye is probably cast. It has nothing to do with the prosecution. It may be [...] a poor deal for the state. But there is always a soft spot for police officers to exercise their judgement, make good or bad agreements right on the street. And those agreements are, in general terms, binding [also on the prosecutor]. There is one exception. They cannot say that you will never be prosecuted. [...] there is a huge underbelly that goes on notwithstanding the Attorney General and the machinery of justice. I am not saying that it is hugely prevalent, but it is there and it has to be taken into account when you are designing a system or making changes to rules.'

The practice of informal dealings and undertakings between the police and offenders was also touched upon by the defence counsel interviewed for the purposes of this project (interviewee [1]):

> 'Everybody who is on the streets knows that the police are always interested in making a deal and, in fact, much of that is police work. [...] there are two levels [...] in drug investigations. [T]here is the street crime level; [.....] the user will tell them [the police] where they got it from. Somebody in possession will say: 'I

got my coke from that guy over there'. And they [the police] may say: 'You tell us who it is and we will let you go and not charge you with possession'. Then they use that intelligence to go to the dealer […] and then pinch him for seeing a buy […]. They bring him in and say to him: 'Off the record, if you help us we will help you. We want to know where you get your stuff from'. And 9 times out of 10 […] they rat the next guy out and the next thing you know they are only being charged with possession [instead of trafficking].'

An important consideration in deciding whether to use undertakings is the tradition of using plea agreements in cases where either the prosecution case is weak or the Office of the Prosecutor is understaffed. Another practical consideration is the inability to prosecute tens or hundreds of defendants at once (arrested as a result of a massive police anti-organized crime operation). A former prosecutor from Ontario (interviewee [2]) provides the following example:

'In 2005 there was sort of a shift, an important event that galvanized public attention in Ontario. It is called the Boxing Day shootings. […] on Yonge Street, a young person is going out to purchase sneakers on Boxing Day. [He] happened to be caught in a crossfire of gangs shooting at each other. And this is the busiest street on the busiest shopping day in Canada. […] That caused […] a review of how we are doing in terms of gangs. And the truth is that they [gangs] have been growing and taking over neighbourhoods and the use of guns has been increasing. So, that generated a massive expenditure in Ontario of 55 million dollars. […] There was a great amount of money put into specialized police hires and prosecution hires and intelligence abilities and cameras on street corners. And as a result of that, there was a targeted [approach] as opposed to being reactive, which mostly the police are in Canada. […] and in the next number of years there was a risk analysis done, neighbourhoods were identified, gangs were gone after. [Police used various means] including […] undertakings […] to try to build some cases. […] […] the result of that was that over the next number of years there were groups of 50, 100, 120 people charged. And the truth is you can't prosecute 120 people in the […] Canadian system and hope to succeed. […] the only way you can make a dent is to use undertakings and take plea agreements and have attractive deals, and also look for people, to the extent that you can find them, who might be willing to assist your case and put them in witness protection […]. If you are going to get at […] [serious crimes], you have to make […] use of undertakings and the related tools […]. […] It is hard enough to bring 4-8 people before a jury and make it all make sense. You could not do that with 100 or 50 or 120. So, you have got to make choices about who is going to be put forward, who is not. [You try to determine if] anybody could help you, and [if there are] 'at-tractive' arrangements [in] that people are getting less than they deserve […].'

One of the federal prosecutors (interviewee [6]) confirmed that at the federal level, all types of undertaking mentioned in the PPSC Deskbook are used in practice. The use of a particular type of undertaking depends on the type of offence and particular circum-stances of the case:

> 'We use a gamut from full immunity to a favourable sentence. Maybe, the person is facing a mandatory minimum and we can have discretion [in relation to] what is charged, maybe the police withdrew the original charge and charged them with something covered by the same activity but [it] is not subject to a mandatory minimum. Maybe, they are on their second conviction and have certain factors that would add up to a custodial sentence but we would enter a joint submission based on their cooperation to mitigate that would result in not having a custodial sentence based on the offence.'

All seven interviewees agreed that full or complete immunity is not frequently granted either at the federal or provincial (Ontario) level. This practice reflects the policies established in the federal and provincial prosecutors' offices, which state that immunity should be the exception rather than the norm.[80] As stated above, neither the RCMP nor the PPSC collect statistics on the use of undertakings or formal immunity agreements in criminal cases, and this data is not available through (other) public sources. At the same time, there is information available on the use of the Witness Protection Program. For instance, in the period between 1 April 2016 and 31 March 2017, the total expenditures for the federal witness protection program was more than 11.6 million Canadian dollars; the total number of cases assessed for the witness protection program was sixty-four and only fourteen protectees were admitted to the witness protection program, with thirteen secure identity changes and forty-two refusals of protection by witnesses.[81] Comparable expenditures were made in previous years, however, the number of protectees admitted to the WPP fluctuated from year to year. According to the annual reports published by the federal department of Public Safety Canada, these fluctuations are largely due to: (1) law enforcement activities during the fiscal year; (2) single protectees, rather than those with dependants, being admitted to the WPP; and (3) variables outside the admission of the program.[82]

---

80 See the PPSC Deskbook, n. 13 at 3.3: 6.
81 Witness Protection Program Act – Annual report: 2016-2017, available at https://www.publicsafety.gc.ca/cnt/rsrcs/pblctns/wtnss-prtctn-rprt-2016-17/index-en.aspx.
82 Ibid.

At the federal level, immunity is used more frequently in so-called 'victimless crimes'. As one federal prosecutor (interviewee [6]) stated:

> 'In our federal prosecution we do not use immunity agreements a great deal. But they do come up more often [...] in certain areas. One of the areas that we use them quite frequently [...] is in relation to drug prosecutions. Maybe, we have an informant that is a lower level in an organization that is dealing drugs that comes forward or, maybe, they are caught up in the system and offer up assistance in order to mitigate their liability. [...] There are other areas where it [immunity agreement] doesn't come up at all. But in the anti-corruption area it has come up frequently in proportion to the number of cases but we do not have a high number of [such] cases.'

Another federal prosecutor (interviewee [7]) similarly explained the need to use immunity in the context of 'consensual crimes':

> '[G]etting testimony from a person implicated in an offence is often very useful in *consensual crime*. Corruption is a consensual crime. Drugs is a consensual crime. It is the type of criminality that you can only find out if you try to seek it. [...] these are 'victimless crimes'; there is no one who goes to police to denounce the fact that an offence has happened.'

For the police, the use of immunity and other forms of undertaking can be essential for collecting and explaining evidence. It is especially relevant in cases involving white-collar crime, where financial documents and other types of evidence can be too complex to assess and explain before the court. One of the RCMP officers interviewed for this project (interviewee [4]) provided an explanation as to why an immunity agreement is often a crucial tool to prove the required elements of a criminal offence:

> 'There are two types of investigations: (1) relying on documents and (2) relying on witnesses. The second is the trickiest part. [...] [In a fraud case involving senior accounting executives] a dozen of people were recruited [as controllers who were] tools in committing the crimes. [...]. The job of corporate controllers was to enter numbers [and they were told] to change numbers by the CFO on behalf of the CEO. For us to prove *mens rea* [of the senior executives] we needed people to tell the story, to explain the documents. We understood that corporate controllers committed a crime. We could charge them, but we decided not to do so. We knew and thought that the only reason they committed those crimes was because they were instructed by the senior officers and they did not want to lose their jobs. [...] We sat together with the Crown officer

to discuss the question of immunity [for the controllers, who would testify against the senior executive officers].'

Most of the legal practitioners interviewed for the purposes of this project, with the exception of the defence lawyer, expressed generally positive views regarding the use of immunity agreements and undertakings. Nevertheless, it should be noted that the RCMP and prosecutors do not always achieve the results they initially aim to achieve by using immunity agreements. The interviewees mentioned several factors which can affect the negotiation process. For example, one of the RCMP officers (interviewee [4]) said:

'There are number of challenges with witnesses [...] [for example, in civil litigation]. [For example], the company was being sued by shareholders. The company was very guarded to allow their employees to talk to the police or anybody else. The RCMP cannot compel witnesses to provide a statement. The only chance to do so is to subpoena a witness [during the trial], but we need it earlier before the trial [starts]. This is a huge impediment for us. We look how to mitigate that. Many people are afraid that they lose their jobs. [One option is] s. 425.1 [of the Criminal Code] – the whistle-blower provision.[83] People are reassured that they will not lose their job. Accountants can be afraid of losing their professional designation if they testify and disclose the fact of wrongdoing.'

The issue of civil liability for the economic damage caused by their criminal activity also came up in the interview with the other RCMP officer (interviewee [5]):

'Civil litigation is a huge issue. We avoid the topic of civil litigation [during the discussions with potential witnesses]. [...] It is a concern for many cases. It is in the back of their [witnesses'] mind. We feel some of the witnesses are afraid of civil litigation.'

One of the federal prosecutors interviewed for this project (interviewee [6]) confirmed the issue of (the threat of) civil litigation, but stated that this issue is unique to white-collar crime:

---

83 Section 425.1 of the Criminal Code, which was introduced in 2004, created a form of whistle-blower protection: 'The section makes it an offence for an employer or anyone acting on behalf of an employer to take or threaten to take disciplinary or other measures such as termination against an employee with the intent to compel the employee not to provide information to persons whose duties include enforcement of federal or provincial law respecting an offence that the employee believes has been or is being committed by the employer, an officer or employee of the employer or directors of a corporation.' Marie Henein, 2017 Martin's Annual Criminal Code, 2016, at 799.

'Witnesses are reluctant [...]. [...] That is [concern with civil litigation] something we do not see at all in the drug street crime world [but] see quite regularity in economic crimes [...]. [...] [In drug crimes] they [witnesses] do not come forward [without] worries, but [civil litigation is not one of these worries] [...]. [...] [The issue of civil litigation] [...] came up in the context of RCMP's integrated market teams looking at insider trading etc. that were established in the early 2000's. And those [integrated market teams] were reviewed because they were considered unsuccessful with the lack of prosecutions resulting. [...] one of the things that came out of the review was a recommendation that the federal government [should] consider some form of compelled questioning for witnesses with the idea being that many witnesses in the white-collar area are reluctant to testify or cooperate based on worries about civil liability but also damage to their careers and their reputations [...]. [...] if they had the cover [...] of being compelled through a court order to cooperate and received immunity [they would cooperate]. [...] [But] I cannot imagine indemnifying people from civil liability.'

Another factor important to the successful negotiation of an immunity agreement is the involvement of the defence lawyer representing the potential information-provider. One of the RCMP officers (interviewee [5]) provided two different examples of where defence counsel played a critical role in this regard:

'In [...] case we approached two people, but one refused to participate. [...] I think that the lawyer did not advise his client and I wish we could contact the witness directly, because he was not the operating mind.'

'In the [...] case he [the information provider] hired a U.S. lawyer. The witness contacted the investigator and said that he had some information. Then a lawyer offered a proffer.'

These two examples demonstrate that if the defence attorney fails to understand the process of negotiation or for various reasons is reluctant to participate therein, it can directly impact on potential immunity agreements.

Some interviewees indicated that there is a difference between a (defence) counsel working predominantly in the field of corporate law who is not very familiar with criminal law practice and a counsel who is experienced in criminal law. When it comes to the negotiation process over immunity agreements, the participation of lawyers who are not familiar with criminal law practice can be challenging for the negotiation process. As one of the federal prosecutors (interviewee [6]) explained:

'[I]n my work on corruption I find that the companies [have] corporate counsel and their Bay Street [a street in Toronto, where most of the big corporate law firms are located] counsel who are not criminal lawyers but […] help them [the companies] with [mergers] and [may] detect this [corruption problem]. Many of those same lawyers work in the area of competition law so they expect it to work the same way. […] I will often even send them the Deskbook [PPSC] chapter to say that this is how we view this […]. So, if [their] client is clearly implicated from the beginning as a directing mind in the criminal conspiracy […] etc., they are not going to get immunity just for putting up their hand. And the other thing that will come up is they may believe that the offence has been undetected. They [counsel] may think they are coming forward saying [that they] have information that [PPSC] otherwise [does not] have. And they [counsel] always seem to be convinced that we will never find out about it but for them coming forward. And if the police are already engaged in an investigation it gets tricky because we are not going to tell them [counsel] [about an ongoing investigation].'

Another factor which can affect the outcome of an immunity agreement negotiation is the assessment of the truthfulness of the witness by the prosecutor and the police. The decision not to provide immunity can be made any time before the agreement is signed. One of the federal prosecutors (interviewee [7]) provided the following example:

'To me a failure would be for the prosecution to give immunity to a witness who outright lies. In one case I did not get to that point because based on the proffer that the witness was providing, we looked at it and found out that the witness was not truthful. So, it failed in a sense that we ended it, but it did not fail from the public interest perspective.'

From the interviews it appears that the immunity agreement process usually works very well in the area of white-collar crime, but can sometimes fail in other contexts, mostly due to a high risk of violence against the witnesses in some types of case. As one of the federal prosecutors (interviewee [6]) pointed out:

'It has worked well for us in the economic crime area. […] Where it would fail is other areas, […] [for example], in the drug and organized crime area. In particular, it [happens when] […] the person gets cold feet. They get scared. They take off and we cannot find them at the time of the trial. […] They may have been threatened and taken off. […] Depending on the circumstances and the timing we may reinstitute the original charges against that person and they would be facing a warrant for their arrest. Or, we may charge them with something else, with obstruction, if there is evidence for it. But most likely if they take off we would reinstitute the charges that were stayed and they would be facing a warrant that follows them until they are found.'

6.6.2 The Process Becoming a Collaborator of Justice

There are different ways for an offender to become a cooperating witness. In all types of case at both the federal and provincial level, usually, but not always, the process of negotiation over the immunity agreement is initiated by defence counsel for the information-provider. As the defence counsel from Ontario (interviewee [1]) put it:

'[W]hat would traditionally happen is you would have a multiple target investigation when one of the targets either before or after arrest, usually through [defence] counsel but not always. Sometimes the police go to the weakest link and give them an offer. Sometimes the weakest link goes to the police and [asks what he or she can negotiate] [...]. But a lot of time it is [done] through the counsel. [...]'

One of the federal prosecutors (interviewee [6]) acknowledged that the defence usually initiates the process:

'[I]t is the vast majority [of cases] where they would approach us. And we, as the prosecution service, [...] would almost never approach an information provider directly. [...] In the drug context the police officer is going to [do it].'

The former senior prosecutor from Ontario (interviewee [2]) also stated that the initiative to negotiate often comes from the defence:

'[F]rom a prosecutor's point of view, it is always best if the defence counsel approaches you. You do not want to look too desperate, but it does not always work that way. And sometimes there will be discussions between counsel about that. For example, three or four people are charged and there are people at the lower end who are wanting to extract themselves and it does not have to be a particularly violent crime, it can be a fraud with a fair amount of paper and effort. So, you are having a plea discussion with one of the lower accused's counsel and the issue is what is the least penalty that they can get. And the answer will differ [depending on] if they are prepared to assist. [...] Assist[ance] can mean [...] giving some help [with] what paperwork means or having a good interview, but the best kind of assistance is if they are prepared to testify, which they only would be if they felt that there would be no repercussions to their reputation or their safety. And sometimes that happens. So, you have this discussion with the defence counsel that [their client will get X, but if they testify, they will get less].'

At the same time, several interviewees acknowledged that they had been involved in cases in which the police had initiated contact. In this regard one of the RCMP officers interviewed for this project (interviewee [5]) explained that:

'If the police want to contact a prospective cooperative witness, they contact the Crown office and explain why they want cooperation of a particular person. Next step [takes place] if the advising Crown counsel believes that the person can be a potential information provider. [The Crown counsel] would [then] contact the defence counsel representing the person (at that point the person would be aware of the potential investigation against him or her).'

Nevertheless, as was mentioned earlier, some of these contacts fail to produce immunity agreements.

It should be noted that according to the general rules on lawyers' ethics in Canada, counsel, including prosecuting counsel, should never contact a person directly if he or she is represented by a lawyer. Another RCMP officer (interviewee [4]) said that in one case, he personally participated in the discussions with defence counsel regarding potential cooperation.

No matter which party initiates the process of negotiation, from the witnesses' point of view, the aim is to get the best deal, preferably full immunity from prosecution. As indicated by the legal professionals interviewed for this project, there is always room for negotiation. The authorities may accommodate various requests and conditions, for example paying the debt owed by a witness' relative or moving a person to a particular location in Canada. Some conditions, however, are not negotiable, as a former senior prosecutor interviewed for this project (interviewee [2]) observed: witnesses must tell the truth, they must show up in court and they must not commit other crimes. The process of negotiation, reaching the final immunity agreement and the testimony in court may involve several steps and can last weeks, months or even years depending on the complexity of the case, the stage of the process, the number of suspects involved, the culture within a particular province and the other factors mentioned above, such as the contribution of defence counsel. As one of the federal prosecutors (interviewee [6]) stated:

'[…] that is very much going to depend on the separate trial process but even on a […] witness approaching to an agreement being signed. [..] it is not going to be a quick process. Unless there is some reason for moving really quickly, it is going to take weeks, in some cases months, where there is not something driving that witness to come forward. [...] If it is going to be strictly about the person's testimony in a trial it [...] is not going to be the same reason to move quickly. If it is going to be about the person providing investigative assistance as the police continue to investigate and to move forward and no one is been charged, there may be more of a motivation on behalf of the police to move it quickly because it is going to unlock further investigative steps. But again, all the steps set out in the Deskbook [PPSC] need to be followed. [...] these things take time in terms of vetting the information. There is going to be some investigation that goes into verifying the person's story [...], their background. If someone is sort of a serial co-operator, they are much less likely going to get immunity than somebody [...] who has never had any criminal record or involvement in the criminal justice system. [...] We have had other immunity agreements in foreign corruption cases [...] where the witness has been oversees. And it has taken [...] months to arrange things and to go back and forth and to do all the vetting [...]. That is entirely a matter of how quickly the matter is moving before the courts and we are talking at that point, frankly, years.'

As indicated in the section describing the legal framework which regulates immunity agreements,[84] before an official agreement is signed between the Crown and the information-provider, the police and the Crown need to follow several steps. According to one of the RCMP officers interviewed (interviewee [4]), the police need to explain to the Crown that (1) they fully understand the role of the potential witness in the criminal act committed, for instance, that the witness is not a guiding mind behind the scheme; (2) they know what type of evidence the witness can provide; and (3) whether this evidence supports the elements of the crime.

One of the frequent and formal ways to start the process with a potential cooperative witness prior to signing the immunity agreement is the system of proffer. Here is how one of the interviewed RCMP officers (interviewee [4]) described the process:

'A defence lawyer offers a proffer. Now the Crown attorney and lawyers meet without a client. During the meeting the [defence] lawyer says what the client could give us in exchange of immunity. [...] If we agree with the offer, then we draft the agreement. One of the conditions of the agreement is that the witness must be completely truthful. If they [witness] are not [...] then it can be used against them. That is our 'insurance policy'. The people [witnesses] should also accept their wrongdoings, explain that they understood that what they were doing was wrong.'

---

84 See § 6.5 in this report.

The system of proffer was also commended by one of the federal Crown counsel (interviewee [7]):

'The proper procedure that I like to follow is pretty much the same as what the Americans do. [...] I agree with the American practice of proffers, which is before we even start discussing with the witness we should have an idea of what the witness could say. So, I think it is an optimal practice to ask the counsel on behalf of the witness to give some form of proffer statement to the Crown advising the type of evidence that will be provided. Once that is done, then the police and the Crown attorney can [...] evaluate and see if [...] we are facing a witness that is candid and truthful. And then the next step should always be to get an investigative assistance agreement [...] – an agreement where the witness will provide a statement with the proper promises and the proper safeguards saying that the evidence will not be used against the witness, except in cases of perjury, for example, for these types of offences. I think that should always be done [and] only after that, depending on the reliability of what the witness said and how he performed during the providing of the statement [...] we can start discussing whether we want to provide immunity: complete or partial.'

To summarize, the usual process of immunity agreement negotiation at the federal level includes four steps: (1) proffer; (2) an investigative assistance agreement; (3) a video statement; and (4) the signing of the immunity agreement.

6.6.3   Execution and Scrutiny of the Undertakings

As described above, undertakings which result in signed agreements between the Crown office and the information-provider should be approved by senior officials including the chief prosecutors and, often, the deputy Attorney General of Canada.

As stated above, courts do not usually scrutinize immunity agreements. However, as indicated by several interviewees, in cases in which either the police or the prosecutor repudiate the agreement reached between the parties and decide to prosecute the potential witness, the latter can claim prosecutorial misconduct or abuse of process. In that case, the court will review the alleged misconduct by the prosecutor. In this regard, a federal prosecutor (interviewee [6]) observed that:

'If we were to exercise our discretion to stay a charge under the [Criminal] Code and something went wrong with the agreement and we want to reinstitute and the person argues abuse, the court is going to decide that. [...] We do not have that kind of system, but I can see a jurisdiction in another country or where we had codified it whether a judge would have to bless an immunity agreement.'

Even an informal promise provided by the police or the prosecutor who did not sign any official immunity agreement with the witness may be subject to judicial review on the grounds of abuse of process. However, the abuse of process argument will not always succeed. As a former Ontario prosecutor (interviewee [2]) explained:

'[I]f you use the example of 'if you give me this information or this testimony [...], we will not prosecute against you', you can try to prosecute, but instantly, you will have an abuse of process [argument], which may or may not be successful depending on how egregious the deal was. [F]or example, because only the Attorney General can grant immunity from prosecution [...] if the police officer made a poor deal on the street without consulting the prosecution system and the crime was extremely serious, [...] the prosecutors [...] will say [that they] are going [...] to push that through the court because the use of an informal deal was not in the public's interests.'

A serious concern regarding the effective execution of the immunity agreement as identified by one of the prosecutors interviewed is the limitation period for reinstituting charges against a witness who failed to testify during the trial in exchange for a stay of charges. In Canada, a Crown office has only a one year limitation period for reinstituting the charges after they were stayed by the prosecution. Sometimes, the process can go beyond the one year limitation period and witnesses could no longer have any inducements to testify. As one of the federal Crown counsel (interviewee [6]) stated:

'The only area for us where [...] it is [...] less than ideal [...] would be the one year limit that we have on reinstituting charges. [...] a year is an arbitrary time frame and one that runs up against in some of our provincial jurisdictions the realities of how long it will take to have something brought before the courts. [...] I am not saying that we have had concrete cases where we have had a witness that has failed to follow through in their agreement and we have run into the fact that we cannot do it. I am just saying [...] we are looking at a year to 18 months to schedule a prelim in [some provinces] as the fastest we can get it done. If we enter into an agreement in the investigative stage, [as the Crown we have] automatically lost that as a leverage.'

6.6.4   Relationship to Witness Protection

In their work, the police rely on various information-providers, including confidential informants, who are never brought into court to testify. As discussed above, the Witness Protection Program (WPP) is separate from immunity agreements and is administered by the police, not the Crown office. At the same time, these programs are obviously connected and sometimes used in combination in relation to cooperative witnesses. Witness protection measures are used in organized crime and drug offences. They are not used in white-collar crimes. In fact, as one of the RCMP officers (intervie-wee [5]) explained, there was only one case where they had a witness protection concern because the witness' family lived in a foreign country. The same officer stated: 'I don't think we could get the approval for WPP in a financial case'.

There are cases in which cooperating witnesses need protection and the decision of whether to place the witness in the Witness Protection Program should be made as early as possible in the process of granting immunity, because, in some cases, a witness will not qualify for the Witness Protection Program. As one federal prosecutor (interviewee [7]) explained:

'Certain witnesses will need protection. I have one case where I do have a witness that is under protection. That in our system is taken care of by the RCMP. [...] Certain witnesses once they have become witnesses may find themselves in a situation of a need of protection. [T]he ideal situation is to address [this] before any immunity is provided or at the very least before any use of the witness [...]. It makes no sense to get evidence from a witness and provide immunity to a witness, if later that witness will not be able to testify because he needs police protection. The police have to evaluate whether the witness will be someone who is eligible to the program [WPP] and they can move forward with that. And we have had cases where that became proble-matic because they were looking at a particular witness to use and then found out that they could not because the witness could not go into witness protection because he was divorced and had to exercise visiting rights to his children. That type of thing became a problem. [These were situations] where we did not get to the immunity agreement but that was resolved at the outset. Police found a problem and then we did not go forward. [...] But you can imagine if all of that was ignored and nothing was said and promises of [participation in WPP were made]. And then you arrive at the end of the process, you have got people charged, you have got immunity provided and then you look at the witness and [when the witness protection is explained] the witness says [that he or she is not interested or does not qualify]. [They can compromise] the whole system. [...] It could be also that it may be not just the protection of the witness, it may be required to give protections to [...] family members. Sometimes [...] these family members may not all live in Canada, so that raises another issue. [...] You really need to evaluate whether you can provide that protection and whether you will provide that protection before anything else is done.'

As stated above, the Witness Protection Program is coordinated by police officers who are not involved in the investigation process and prosecutors rely on them to ensure the witness' appearance in court to give testimony. As one federal prosecutor (interviewee [7]) observed:

'There are very practical issues [for example, where the prosecutors could prepare the witness]. In [one] case in particular, we met the witness out of province; neither the prosecutors nor the investigators knew where the witness was. [Another practical issue is testimony in court] and working with the courthouse to make sure that all the arrangements are [made] for the witness to be able to appear in court and [not to] come from the main door.'

Separate witness protection programs exist at the provincial level in Ontario and at the federal level. Witness protection programs are very costly, but they were not created for the purposes of unfairly enriching witnesses for their testimony. The main purpose of these programs is to protect witnesses who are at risk because of their cooperation with the prosecution. However, in some cases the authorities can have serious problems with certain witnesses, as explained by a former Ontario prosecutor (interviewee [2]):

'[T]he reason [we] came up with this idea of having witness protection in Ontario was because of the taint of if you do well in testimony, we will give you a big wad of cash. The courts have generally disapproved of that. So, what is the cleanest thing you could do? [...] you could come up with a safe, somewhat generous system of preserving their [witnesses'] lifestyle. It does not mean that someone who was a mechanic can suddenly have the life of an international playboy. It has to be somewhat corresponding to what it was. The difficult one is when you have the international playboy. Does it really look nice to pay them truckloads of money to keep up with the lifestyle that nobody approves of? That does not happen often, but [these cases are] a little more challenging.'

6.6.5   Use of Evidence and Punishment

As mentioned above, the fact that the witness was promised leniency or immunity, as well as the actual copy of immunity agreement, is subject to disclosure to the defence. As one of the federal prosecutors (interviewee [6]) observed:

> '[W]hen we enter into that type of immunity agreement we are going to dis-close it to the others involved, the defence for the other accused and we are going to file it with the court. [...] We have got it all out in the open. So that acts for us as a buffer for arguments against an abuse of process because if it is an agreement with the person testifying and they refuse, it is not hard for us to establish that we are reinstituting the charges because they did not live up to their end of the agreement.'

Since the information is disclosed to the other accused, the defence lawyer can and usual-ly does use this information to attack the credibility of the cooperating witness during the trial. Moreover, the trial judges instruct jurors (if there is a jury) or themselves that they should treat the evidence of unsavoury[85] witnesses with caution. In Canada this type of instruction is called a *Vetrovec* warning.[86] An Ontario judge interviewed for this project (interviewee [3]) mentioned that there are several types of these instructions. One of them is the warning written by the Honourable Mr. Justice David Watt, who is a judge of the Ontario Court of Appeal. The following excerpt is taken from the Watt's Manual of Criminal Jury Instructions:

Witnesses of Unsavoury Character
(Vetrovec Warning)

[1] (Name of the witness, NOW) testified for the Crown. You have heard that (specify briefly reasons why evidence should be treated with caution).
[2] Common sense tells you that there is good reason to look at (NOW)'s evidence with the greatest care and caution. You should look for some confir-mation of (NOW)'s evidence from somebody or something other than (NOW) before you rely upon it in deciding whether Crown counsel has proven the case against (Name of the Accused, NOA) (or, the persons charged), beyond a rea-sonable doubt.
[3] (NOW) and the circumstances in which (s/he) testified might well make

---

85   An unsavoury witness is defined as one of 'demonstrated moral lack'. See *R. v. Vetrovec*, [1982] 1. S.C.R. 811, 67 C.C.C. (2d) 1.
86   The name comes from the case *R. v. Vetrovec*, [1982] 1. S.C.R. 811, 67 C.C.C. (2d) 1.

you wish that somebody or something else confirmed what (NOW) said. You may believe (NOW)'s testimony, however, if you find it trustworthy, even if no one or nothing else confirms it. When you consider it, however, keep in mind who gave the evidence and the circumstances under which (NOW) testified.

[4] You may find that there is some evidence in this case that confirms or supports some parts of (NOW)'s testimony. It is for you to say whether this or any evidence confirms or supports his/her testimony and how that affects whether or how much you will believe of or rely upon (his/her) testimony in deciding this case.

The evidence to which I am about to refer illustrates the kind of evidence that you may find confirms or supports (NOW)'s testimony. It may help you. It may not. It is for you to say.

(Illustrate potentially confirmatory evidence.)[87]

When the judge tries a case alone, he or she can find the witness untrustworthy and reject the testimony. However, if there is a jury trial, the judge would provide this instruction or other version of the *Vetrovec* warning and leave it to the jury to decide whether they want to accept the evidence of the cooperating witness. As the Supreme Court of Canada has explained, trial judges can craft their own *Vetrovec* warnings, but all warnings should contain four elements: (1) drawing the attention of the jury to the testimonial evidence requiring special scrutiny; (2) explaining why this evidence is subject to special scrutiny; (3) cautioning the jury that it is dangerous to convict on unconfirmed evidence of this sort, though the jury is entitled to do so if satisfied that the evidence is true; and (4) that the jury, in determining the veracity of the suspect evidence, should look for evidence from another source tending to show that the untrustworthy witness is telling the truth as to the guilt of the accused.[88]

As mentioned above, if the witness violates the terms of the immunity agreement, the Crown can reinstitute the charges against the witness. The witness can provide a false statement or false testimony in court. There are various reasons why witnesses are not completely honest with the police, the Crown or the court. Some of them were discussed above in relation to civil liability, the loss of professional credentials, an interest in playing down their own involvement and/or exaggerating the involvement of other accused. There are some other factors that may affect the truthfulness of the witness, as described by a federal prosecutor (interviewee [7]):

---

87 Watt 2003, p. 163-164.
88 *R. v. Khela*, [2009] S.C.J. No. 4, 1 S.C.R. 104.

'[E]ither in a white-collar crime case or in an organized crime case it may be difficult for the witness to be truthful. It may be more painful for the witness to be truthful against everyone. So there are sometimes witness[es] [who] will gladly provide evidence in regards to target A, but will be reluctant to provide evidence against target B. [...] It could be personal friendships. It could be the fact that that person is at the same level or even a below level [in a criminal organization structure]. It can be all sorts of situations.'

Problems can arise when the person provides a false statement, but detailed immunity agreements help to mitigate those problems. The following observations were made by a federal prosecutor (interviewee [6]):

'In terms of the person giving false testimony that is a bit trickier in terms of proving that [...]. And that could be something that we would reinitiate the original charges but that could also be where the police would charge them with obstruction if somebody was in that sort of a classic situation of 'I will testify against these individuals and here is what I will say.' And that is set out in the agreement. [...] If they get to court and they said they were going to testify 'black' and then they testify 'white', [this becomes] a true case of a false testimony. We could have perjury, we could have obstruction depending on what they do in terms of the investigation. There are avenues to be followed and that is a risk. But what we do to mitigate that is these agreements are extremely detailed in terms of what cooperation they are expected to give and how it will manifest itself.'

It can be argued, however, that the fact that a witness has recanted their statement in court does not always mean a true case of a false testimony. There could be various factors why a witness might change their story in court. For example, during the pre-trial investigation the witness may have been motivated by his or her own interest not to be prosecuted and to blame an innocent party; in court he or she may nevertheless choose to tell the truth under cross-examination by the defence. Indeed, it could be argued that if a witness has falsely accused a defendant at an earlier stage he or she would be more likely provide false testimony in court in order to avoid charges for perjury or obstruction of justice.

6.7   FINAL OBSERVATIONS

This report considers the legal framework and practice with respect to the use of undertakings and immunity agreements in Canada at the federal level, with reference to the practice in the province of Ontario. Several general observations may be made about the system of undertakings in Canada. Firstly, Canada does not have a developed legislative framework regulating undertakings. Instead, Canadian authorities, including prosecution offices, rely on internal policies created by the Ministry of the Attorney General. Secondly, undertakings are used on a regular basis, but complete immunity is very rare. Thirdly, there is no publicly available data regarding the use of either undertakings or even immunity agreements in Canada. Fourthly, currently there is no public debate on how the system of undertakings should be reformed in the future. In Canada, there have not been any cases in recent years, with the exception of Karla Homolka's affair, in which prosecutors have been criticized for providing immunity to someone. The PPSC Deskbook at the federal level and policies at the provincial level are public. Canadian prosecutors have been successful in applying these policies without provoking public outcry. To date, there has not been any reported case of a miscarriage of justice concerning a person who was convicted mainly or solely on the basis of false testimony of a cooperative witness. There is a forum for debate, and that is the trial itself, because all prosecution witnesses are cross-examined by the defence. Finally, the prosecution enjoys wide discretion in selecting witnesses for immunity agreements and there is no general judicial oversight beyond a general abuse of process approach.

Appendix 1

Answers to the Research Questions

Legal Framework

1   *What types of undertakings are provided for?*

In Canada, undertakings may be provided within the context of an 'immunity agree-ment', i.e. an agreement by the Public Prosecution Service to refrain from prosecuting someone for a crime or to terminate a prosecution, in return for providing testimony or other valuable information, cooperation or assistance. There are four different mechanisms by which immunity can be conferred: (1) a stay of proceedings; (2) immunity from future prosecutions; (3) 'use immunity' investigative assistance agree-ments; and (4) guarantees of immunity for Competition Act offences. The main differ-ence between immunity agreements and 'use immunity' agreements is that the latter focuses on the uses that may be made of the information provided, rather than acts which will not be prosecuted.

   In Canada, then, it is possible to grant full or complete immunity from prosecution. In determining whether immunity may be granted, prosecution counsel is required to weigh several factors, including: (1) the seriousness of the offence; (2) the reliability of the person; (3) the reliability of the anticipated evidence; (4) whether the information-provi-der has made full and candid disclosure; (5) the importance of the person's testimony or co-operation; (6) the nature and extent of the person's involvement in the offence; (7) whether other, lesser forms of reward or benefit would be appropriate; (8) the person's history of co-operation; and (9) the public interest. Nevertheless, the granting of a limited form of immunity is generally preferred over (full or complete) immunity from prosecution. Indeed, the PPSC Deskbook states that full immunity should be the exception rather than the norm, that it should be considered only when the information provided relates to the commission of a serious offence or when the prosecution of a case is otherwise important in achieving effective enforcement of the law, and that, as a rule, it should not be considered in relatively minor cases. As to lesser forms of reward or benefit, the Deskbook sets out a non-exhaustive list of terms and conditions, or undertakings, that may be included in an immunity agreement: (1) drop-ping charges; (2) reducing charges; (3) dropping or reducing charges of others, such as family members or friends; (4) agreeing to a lesser sentence; (5) the timing of dealing with outstanding charges; (6) the resolution of pending applications for the return of offence-related property or proceeds of crime; and (7) reward money. It does not include the provision of protective measures; the terms and conditions of witness protection do not fall within the remit of the PPSC, but are rather a matter for the federal police, i.e. the Royal Canadian Mounted Police (RCMP).

2   *In respect of which offences is it possible to use the instrument?*

The PPSC Deskbook does not restrict the type of offence in respect of which undertakings may be provided. However, the type of offence (i.e. of the offence under investigation) is a factor relevant to the determination of which undertaking to provide (for example, full immunity should only be considered in the more serious cases). More-over, it is clear from the Canadian rules that the instrument is considered an important tool in the battle against organized crime.

3   *What is the legal basis for (using) the instrument?*

To date, the Canadian government has not adopted any legislation regulating the instrument of collaboration with justice. At the federal level the instrument is regulated by uniform guidelines, specifically by Section 3.3 of the PPSC Deskbook, entitled 'Immu-nity Agreements', which contains the Guideline of the Director issued under Section 3(3) (c) of the Director of Public Prosecutions Act. At the provincial level also, the instrument is regulated by guidelines.

4   *How did the rules on collaboration with justice come about?*

In 1992, the Law Reform Commission of Canada (LRCC) published a working paper in which it proposed a new legal framework for regulating immunity agreements in Canada, having established that the use of immunity agreements has long been recognized in the case law (since 1975 at least). Specifically, the LRCC recommended sixteen rules to be adopted either in the form of legislation or uniform guidelines. As stated above, to date, the Canadian government has not adopted any legislation regulating the instrument of collaboration with justice. While it is not clear why the federal government has not adopted a specific legislative act, an explanation may be sought in the general reluctance on the part of the Canadian legislator to adopt rules that operate to restrict prosecutorial discretion. Instead of a legislative framework, the PPSC and provincial Ministries of Justice adopted some of the LRCC recommendations in the form of guidelines. Both the federal and the provincial guidelines are available to the public.

5   *Who holds authority to make use of the instrument and where does the*
           responsibility lie in this regard?

According to the (federal) guideline contained in the PPSC, only the Director of Public Prosecution through prosecution counsel (whereby prosecution counsel is required to consult with senior officials within the organization), and not the investigative agency, is entitled to confer immunity from prosecution. However, the same guideline recognizes that investigative agencies have the discretion to exercise *a form of* immunity by deciding not to lay charges in the first place.

Although only prosecution counsel can enter into immunity agreements with information-providers, the federal guideline recognizes the important role of the police in reaching immunity agreements between information providers and authorities. The guideline states that in most cases, the immunity process begins with discussions between the information-provider and the case investigators without prior consultation with prosecution counsel. Following these discussions, investigators usually approach the prosecutor. Prosecution counsel rely on the investigating agency's input in weighing the relevant public interest criteria, and should be satisfied that the agency's lead investigator responsible for overseeing such agreements has reviewed and approved the proposed agreement. The investigating agency makes a recommendation to prosecution counsel, however, prosecution counsel bears the ultimate responsibility for deciding who is prosecuted and who is called as a witness.

6   *How does the instrument relate to other measures whereby private*
           individuals provide information for the purposes of criminal investigation
           and/or prosecution?

Information-providers with whom immunity agreements are made can be distinguished from other individuals who provide information for the purposes of criminal investigation and/or prosecution, such as confidential informants and police agents.

7   *How does the instrument relate to the phenomenon of witness protection?*

There is a clear distinction between immunity agreements on the one hand and witness protection on the other. While the responsibility for the former lies with the prosecutor, the responsibility for the latter lies with the RCMP, whereby the officers involved are completely independent from those involved in the investigation of crime (so as to prevent a conflict of interests). Indeed, the terms and conditions of witness protection are discussed and offered by the police, not the prosecutor, and the provision of witness protection does not constitute an undertaking within the meaning of the federal guideline. Nevertheless, the matter of witness protection may well arise in the initial stages of the immunity agreement negotiations, and the rules stipulate that the prosecutor should be (made) aware of this.

Practice

8   *What types of undertaking are used in practice?*

The full range of undertakings is used in practice, although full immunity is granted only rarely.

9   *How often and on the basis of which considerations is the instrument used or not used?*

Quantitative data on the use of undertakings is lacking in Canada and it was not possible to obtain this information in other ways. Accordingly, it is impossible to draw reliable conclusions as to the frequency with which the instrument is used. An important consideration in determining whether or not to use the instrument is the nature of the crime being prosecuted. Practitioners state that the instrument is most often used in respect of so-called 'victimless' crimes, for example, drug-related crime, white-collar crime and corruption.

10   *What have the positive and negative experiences been in practice with the instrument and the legal framework in this regard?*

See the answer to question 12. Otherwise it is not possible to provide a reliable answer to this question on the basis of the empirical research conducted.

11   *What results have been achieved by use of the instrument in individual cases?*

According to some of the practitioners interviewed for the purposes of this project, the instrument allowed them to obtain convictions in several cases. However, there is no data in how many cases the instrument was the decisive factor for achieving conviction.

12   *Which factors contribute to the successful use of the instrument and which form obstacles in this regard?*

Several factors can affect the negotiation process. In cases involving white-collar crime in particular, a particular obstacle is the threat of civil litigation, which makes witnesses reluctant to cooperate or testify. Another factor is the involvement and professionalism of defence counsel of the information-provider; participation of (experienced) defence counsel is key to a successful negotiation process.

13   *In general, do the rules on collaboration with justice achieve their objective?*

It is not possible to provide a reliable answer to this question on the basis of the empirical research conducted.

Scrutiny, Transparency and Debate

14   *To what extent is the use of the instrument subject to scrutiny by a judicial or other authority?*

An immunity agreement in Canada is not usually subject to judicial scrutiny. At the same time, copies of the immunity agreement are filed in court and provided to counsel defending the accused against whom the information-provider intends to testify in court. The fact that the witness was promised leniency or immunity in exchange of his or her testimony is therefore subject to disclosure to the defence, which the defence can and usually does use to attack the credibility of the cooperating witness at trial. Moreover, whenever a witness' credibility or reliability is seriously in doubt (as it may be when the witness has been promised benefits in exchange for his or her testimony), special scrutiny is required. In jury trials the trial judge is required to instruct the jury to treat the evidence of the cooperating witnesses with caution.

   Although the immunity agreement is not subject to scrutiny by a third party, in a situation in which the prosecution decides to prosecute a person who was earlier promised immunity from prosecution in exchange for their testimony, that person can seek a judicial stay of proceedings for abuse of process. A decision on the merits of such an application would involve scrutiny of the agreement between prosecuting counsel and the individual in question.

15   *In how far is the instrument itself and the use thereof in individual cases publicly transparent?*

Both the federal guidelines and the provincial guidelines on the provision of undertakings to offenders in exchange for their testimony in the prosecution of others are available to the public. Further, copies of immunity agreements are filed in court and provided to counsel defending the accused against whom information providers intend to testify in court.

16   *To what extent is there debate or discussion regarding the use of the instrument? On which aspects of the instrument is the debate focused?*

17   *In how far and in what regard has scrutiny, transparency and debate led to changes in the regulation of the instrument?*

An important factor in the adoption of policy guidelines regarding the use of immunity agreements at both the federal and provincial level was the case of Paul Bernardo and Karla Homolka. Since that case, however, there has been little to no public debate on the use of the instrument and how the use of immunity agreements should be reformed in the future.

Appendix 2

List of Respondents

1. A defence counsel in Toronto, Ontario
2. A former senior official and prosecutor from the Ontario Ministry of the Attorney General
3. A judge in Toronto, Ontario
4. An RCMP officer in Ottowa, Ontario
5. An RCMP officer in Ottowa, Ontario
6. A senior federal prosecutor from the PPSC office in Ottowa, Ontario
7. A senior federal prosecutor from the PPSC office in Montreal, Quebec

7   COMPARATIVE ANALYSIS

J.H. Crijns, M.J. Dubelaar, K.M. Pitcher & D.A.G. van Toor

7.1   INTRODUCTION

With the law and practice with respect to the institution of collaboration with justice having now been set out for the four jurisdictions under examination in this report – the Netherlands, Germany, Italy and Canada – and having answered sub-questions 1 to 17 of the research project for each of these jurisdictions,[1] it is time to turn to the penultimate sub-question, namely:

> 18   *In which respects do the law and practice in Germany, Italy and Canada correspond to that in the Netherlands, and in which respects do they differ?*

The purpose of this chapter, then, is to compare the Dutch law and practice in this regard with that of Germany, Italy and Canada, ultimately with a view to drawing lessons from the comparative exercise for the Dutch law and practice in particular. The question of which lessons can be drawn from the comparative exercise for Dutch law and practice – the final sub-question of this research[2] –, however, is addressed in the following chapter.

   The comparative exercise that lies at the heart of this chapter will be conducted within a framework of themes, rather than on the basis of individual sub-questions. In this regard it may be recalled that the sub-questions of this research project are divided into three categories, namely 'legal framework', 'practice', and 'scrutiny, transparency and debate',[3] and that in dividing the sub-questions into such categories, it was accepted at the outset that there would likely be a degree of overlap in the answers thereto. It is precisely this overlap that prompted a 'thematic' approach to the comparative exercise in this chapter,[4] and the desire to provide a *comprehensive* analysis of the institution of collaboration with justice, insofar as possible combining legal and empirical research and thereby illustrating how the law works, or does *not* work, in practice. That said, it is worth emphasizing that the answers to sub-questions 1 through 17, as addressed in each of the four country reports, form the

---

1   For the sub-questions themselves, see § 1.1.
2   Sub-question no. 19.
3   See n. 1.
4   While the thematic approach of this chapter was to a large extent inspired by the desire to avoid overlap, it has not been possible to avoid it altogether, given the interwovenness of the themes under discussion. Where there is overlap, this is indicated in the text itself or in a footnote.

basis for the current chapter. For the sake of convenience, mention is made in a footnote at the beginning of each section of the sub-question(s) being addressed.[5]

Finally, it should be noted that the themes making up the framework of this chapter were identified not only on the basis of what from a *Dutch* perspective warrants particular attention (an approach warranted by the ultimate aim of this research, i.e. to draw lessons from the comparative exercise for Dutch law and practice), but also on the basis of what was found to constitute 'common ground' between the four countries, in terms of the issues raised by the instrument.

7.2 The Instrument of Collaboration with Justice: General Observations[6]

It is clear from the various country reports that in each of the four jurisdictions under consideration, collaboration with justice is considered a legitimate and necessary instrument in the investigation and/or prosecution of (serious) crime, although there are differences between them in this regard (as apparent from, among other things, the scope of application of the instrument, about which more is said below) and also the extent to which the legal framework in place can be depicted as an 'instrument' at all. Turning to the latter point first, in the Netherlands, Canada and Italy it certainly seems appropriate to speak of an instrument in this regard; in each of these countries, the authorities actively and consciously make use of undertakings in order to combat certain types of serious crime (and organized crime, in particular). Moreover, in the Netherlands in particular, there is an extensive legal framework in place which regulates significant parts of the process by which undertakings are made and agreements are reached in the first place. In Germany, by contrast, the general picture to emerge is not necessarily that of a targeted instrument that may be deployed in only the most serious cases, but of a (sentencing) provision that is applied afterwards by the judge, as soon as he or she is satisfied that the witness has made a significant contribution to the investigation and prosecution of another (or others), and regardless of any agreement made between the public prosecutor[7] and the individual concerned. This is not to say that the legal framework in place may not be construed as an instrument by which to persuade otherwise unwilling 'offender witnesses' to cooperate with the authorities (by pointing to the benefits on offer), or that German practitioners do not view it as such.[8] The point is that, even in the absence of any prior agreement or contact

---

5 Most sections combine sub-questions in the 'legal framework' and 'practice' categories, while some sub-questions are addressed in their own section (such questions warranting separate attention in our view). Other sub-questions still, owing to their general nature, do not form the focus of a particular section, but are rather dealt with over various sections; see, in particular, sub-question 10.
6 In this section, sub-questions 3, 4, 5 and 6 are addressed.
7 More will be said about the authorities responsible for organizing the cooperation aimed at securing the individual offender's testimony below, in § 7.5.
8 For this reason and also for the sake of convenience, throughout this chapter reference will (continue to) be made to the 'instrument of collaboration with justice' in the German context also.

between the prosecuting authorities and the witness, sentence reduction may be granted as a reward for cooperation.

Further differences between the jurisdictions concern the manner in which the instrument is legally embedded. In the Netherlands, Germany and Italy, the instrument of collaboration with justice is set forth in one way or another in statute,[9] whereas in Canada it is not, but rather forms the subject matter of an internal guideline of the Public Prosecution Service. In those (European) jurisdictions in which it *is* provided for in statutory law, there are differences as regard the manner in which they have done so. Thus, whereas in Germany the instrument is a matter of substantive criminal law, i.e. is regulated in the German Criminal Code only, specifically, the section thereof pertaining to sentencing, in the Netherlands and Italy it is largely a matter of procedural law (supplemented by sentencing provisions in the Criminal Code). This goes some way to explaining why, in Germany, it may not be entirely accurate to speak of an instrument, whereas in the Netherlands (and Italy), it is.

A related issue (and one which was touched upon above) concerns the question of whether and to what extent formal agreements are made regarding the provision of a witness statement in exchange for some benefit, and whether and to what extent such agreements are preceded by a process of negotiation between the authorities and the potential witness. Whereas in the Netherlands and Canada this certainly appears to be the case (in the Netherlands, for instance, the process by which such – formal, bilateral – agreements are made is set out in considerable detail in the rules and the agreement has independent legal meaning), in Germany, any agreement made between the public prosecutor and the individual in question is best viewed as a 'gentlemen's agreement'. This means that, in Germany, the public prosecutor can do no more than commit him- or herself to bring the fact of the cooperation to the court's attention, in the hope that the court will grant the benefit in question (although, again, whether the court does so would not appear to be dependent on the existence of an agreement between the public prosecutor and the witness). In other words, in Germany, any agreement made lacks independent legal meaning; no agreement in a formal sense comes about. In the context of the Italian instrument on collaboration with justice also, it may be inappropriate to speak of a process of negotiation, promises or undertakings, or a *bilateral* agreement between the authorities and the potential witness. Rather, in Italy, it appears that the role of the public prosecutor – the authority responsible for organizing the cooperation aimed at securing the individual's testimony[10] – is best viewed as being limited to informing the individual in question of the law and drawing his or her attention to the benefits available thereunder and explaining how they apply in a specific situation.

---

9   In the Netherlands, it is governed by the Instructions on Undertakings to Witnesses in Criminal Cases (hereafter: 'the Instructions'), also, a set of policy rules laid down by the Board of Procurators General – the Public Prosecution Service's highest authority – in consultation with the Minister of Justice and Security.

10   See n. 7.

There are also differences between the jurisdictions as regards the questions of who may be considered a collaborator of justice and how collaborators relate to other private individuals who provide information for the purposes of criminal investigation and/or prosecution and, by extension, of establishing the truth in criminal cases. While in the Netherlands and Italy, the cooperation required in order to be considered a collaborator of justice (and to be granted benefits) is limited to the provision of a statement and giving evidence at trial, in Canada and Germany, the instrument is less strictly defined in this regard. Thus, in Canada, an immunity agreement[11] may not only be made with a person who assists the authorities by giving evidence at trial, but also a person who provides other valuable information, assistance to or cooperation with the Public Prosecution Service and/or investigative agency (in exchange for benefits). In Germany, the official legal term is *Aufklärungsgehilfe*, which literally means 'clarification helper'. There, a collaborator of justice is a person who assists the justice department in discovering the truth in criminal cases prior to the commencement of trial. Provided the individual concerned has provided valuable information to the authorities in a timely fashion, the trial judge may apply the collaborators' provision and grant the benefits listed therein. Accordingly, while in all four jurisdictions under examination in this report collaboration with justice is a distinct instrument, in that in each jurisdiction, it can be distinguished from other instruments whereby private individuals provide information for the purposes of criminal investigation and/or prosecution (for example, the informer or the infiltrator), in some jurisdictions it is more distinct than in others, in theory at least.

Finally (and as mentioned above), there are differences between the four jurisdictions as regards the scope of application of the instrument in terms of the offences in respect of which it is available, including in the first place the offences in respect of which the witness' testimony is sought.[12] In the Netherlands, the instrument is viewed as a measure of last resort aimed at investigating and/or prosecuting serious (organized) crime and, more specifically, as a useful tool for penetrating the higher echelons of a criminal organization. This is apparent not only from the fact that the instrument is available in respect of certain (serious) offences only, but also from the express requirements of proportionality and subsidiarity. In Italy also, the instrument of collaboration with justice is viewed as a measure aimed at combatting serious, organized crime. In Germany and Canada, the instrument appears to be wider in its scope of application than in the Netherlands and Italy; for Germany, this is apparent from the extensive list of offences in respect of which it is available (although the law does stipulate that the offence(s) about which the collaborator proposes to testify must in some way be connected to the offence that they have committed) and its application in practice (about which more will be said

---

11 As was seen in Chapter 6, in Canada it is in the context of immunity agreements that the topic under consideration in this report arises and undertakings may be made to 'offender witnesses'.

12 More is said about the offences in respect of which the instrument is available in each of the jurisdictions below, in § 7.3.

below[13]), and for Canada, from the fact that there, the instrument is not limited to certain offences (although it is clear that the Canadian instrument is considered an important tool in the battle against organized crime).

In conclusion, the various manifestations of the instrument in the four jurisdictions under examination in this report are clearly comparable, entailing as they do the granting of benefits in exchange for testimony in the prosecution of others, but there are note-worthy differences between them as regards the extent to which the legal framework in place can be depicted as an 'instrument', how the instrument is legally embedded, who may be considered a collaborator of justice and the availability of the instrument. In the sections below, further similarities and differences between the four jurisdictions as regards the instrument and its application in practice will be set out according to a num-ber of themes.

7.3   TYPES OF OFFENCES[14]

As stated in the previous section, there are differences between the jurisdictions under examination in this report as regards the offences in respect of which the instrument is available, including in the first place the offences in respect of which the witness' testimony is sought. In short, the German and Canadian instruments on collaboration with justice appear to be broader in their scope of application than their Dutch and Italian counterparts.

Under Dutch law,[15] undertakings may be provided in the context of a criminal investigation into (1) offences in respect of which pre-trial detention may be lawfully ordered,[16] which were committed in the context of organized crime and which give rise to severe public disorder on account of their nature or connection to other criminal offences; and (2) offences punishable by eight years' imprisonment or more. Accordingly, in the Netherlands, the availability of the instrument of collaboration with justice is not limited to organized crime. Nevertheless, the need to effectively combat organized crime appears to have been a key consideration in introducing the instrument into the Code of Criminal Procedure in 2006 and since then, this is the con-text in which the instrument has been applied in practice. In the three cases in which the instrument has been used, the underlying facts concerned (attempted) murder, among other things. In the Netherlands, suggestions to broaden the scope of application of the instrument in terms of the offences in respect of which it may be used have been met with limited enthusiasm in practice. The general sentiment is that the current range of offences

---

13   See § 7.3 and 7.8.
14   In this section sub-question 2 is addressed.
15   Specifically, Article 226g(1) of the Dutch Code of Criminal Procedure.
16   According to Article 67(1) of the Dutch Code of Criminal Procedure.

in respect of which the instrument may be used is already quite broad and, in any case, unproblematic in practice (given also that the instrument is intended to be a measure of last resort).

Under Italian law[17] the instrument may be employed in the context of a criminal investigation into the crimes of subversion, terrorism, or the mafia-type crimes referred to in Article 51(3-bis) of the Italian Code of Criminal Procedure. While the practitioners interviewed for the purpose of the Italian country report were of the view that the instrument of collaboration with justice is available in respect of a sufficient number of offences, some suggested it should be extended to large-scale corruption, which, they observed, is closely linked to organized (mafia) crime. In this regard one interviewee, a judge, observed that over the decades, the mafia has become less violent and more business-like in their criminal activities. In the Netherlands and Italy, then, the instrument of collaboration with justice is available in respect of the most serious offences only, although the Dutch instrument appears to be (slightly) broader in its scope of application than its Italian counterpart; in the Netherlands, it should be recalled, the availability of the instrument is not limited to organized crime, but extends to offences punishable by eight years' imprisonment or more, also.

According to the German Criminal Code, undertakings may only be provided in the context of a criminal investigation into the crimes listed in Section 100(2) thereof. This exhaustive catalogue of offences lists – from the perspective of the German legislator – all grave crimes. It is difficult to provide an overview of the catalogue because it includes specific offences from several statutes (such as the German Criminal Code, the Weapon Control Act, the Tax Law, the Anti-Doping Law and the Asylum Law).[18] While the German list does not appear to be limited to organized crime, the law stipulates that the offence(s) about which the collaborator proposes to testify must in some way be connected to the offence that they have committed,[19] whereby clear examples of 'connected offences' are those committed by a group of criminals, or members of such a group. Despite this requirement, however, the German instrument appears to be broader in its scope of application than its Dutch and Italian counterparts, the requirement of connected offences not being limited to organized crime in the strictest sense of the term, as apparent from the practice, also. Although the German Criminal Code provides for an extensive (and exhaustive) list of offences, according to practitioners and scholars, in practice, it is in cases involving moderate property crimes, when suspects disclose information about their co-offenders, that the general collaborators' provision is most often applied,[20] which may be contrasted with the Dutch and Italian law and practice in particular.

---

17 Specifically, Article 9(2) of Law n. 82 of 15 March 1991, as amended by Law n. 45 of 13 February 2001.
18 The complete German catalogue can be found in Appendix 1 of the German country report, in Chapter 4.
19 Section 46b of the German Criminal Code.
20 See also § 7.8 below.

As to Canada, there the rules do not set any limitations as regards the offences in respect of which the instrument is available, although the type of offence is a factor relevant to the determination of which undertaking to provide. At the same time, it is clear from the preamble to the rules (as set out in the Public Prosecutor Service of Canada Deskbook) that the instrument is considered an important tool in the battle against organized crime.

A further point regarding the offences in respect of which the instrument is available, is that in the three jurisdictions to limit the scope of application of the instrument to certain offences only – the Netherlands, Italy and Germany – there are differences regarding the manner of limitation. Whereas in the Netherlands, the application of the instrument is determined by a *general* limitation, in Germany and Italy, the relevant legislation exhaustively lists the specific crimes in respect of which the instrument is available (although it bears observing that the German catalogue is a lot longer than the Italian one). In Canada, it should be recalled, the type of offence is a factor relevant to the determination of which undertaking to provide. In this regard it should be noted that according to the rules, full immunity should only be provided when the collaborator's statement contains information relating to the commission of a serious offence and that, as a rule, it should not be considered in relatively minor cases.

Thus far the comparison has focused on the offences in respect of which the witness' testimony is sought. However, there are also differences between the jurisdictions as regards the availability of the instrument in terms of the offence(s) (allegedly) committed by the witness. Whereas in the Netherlands it is not possible to grant the sentence reduction envisaged by the law where there is a genuine prospect that the information-provider will in his or her own case be sentenced to life imprisonment, in Germany, Italy and Canada, there appear to be no limitations in this regard (although in Germany, where the law expressly distinguishes between the offence in respect of which the testimony is sought (the *Katalogtat*) and the offence (allegedly) committed by the witness (the *Anlasstat*), the instrument is not available where the latter concerns a minor offence, i.e. an offence punishable only by the standard minimum sentence of one month's imprisonment or a fine).

In conclusion, the scope of application of the instrument of collaboration with justice differs as between the jurisdictions, both in terms of the offence in respect of which the testimony is sought and the offence (allegedly) committed by the witness. In terms of the former, in the Netherlands and Italy, the instrument appears to be narrower in its scope of application than in Germany and Canada, i.e. limited to the most serious offences. In terms of the latter, the Dutch instrument is (slightly) narrower than its German, Italian and Canadian counterparts.

7.4   Nature of the Undertakings[21]

This section is concerned with the undertakings that the (prosecuting) authorities may provide to witnesses in exchange for their testimony, or the benefits on offer in this regard.[22] The provision of witness protection and the 'undertakings' provided by the information-provider are dealt with elsewhere in this report.[23] First the range of undertakings on offer in each jurisdiction will be addressed, followed by a comparison of certain undertakings, namely sentence reduction, immunity from prosecution and financial compensation. Before doing so, however, it is worth noting that while in Italy, the (statutory) law *exhaustively* regulates the benefits that may be granted, in the Netherlands and Germany it does not, in that the law itself appears to allow for other undertakings to be provided or that other ('unofficial') undertakings are provided in practice, while in Canada, the (non-statutory) rules provide for a *non-exhaustive* list of undertakings. A related point is that while in the Netherlands, there is an ongoing discussion as to whether or not the (statutory) provisions of the Code of Criminal Procedure should be considered a closed system for providing undertakings to witnesses, i.e. whether and to what extent there is still room to provide other undertakings than those explicitly mentioned therein,[24] in the other jurisdictions, there is little to no discussion as to the lawfulness of certain undertakings. Regarding the provision of 'unofficial' undertakings, the issue in Germany is not so much that undertakings are being made that are not provided for by law, but rather that the individual concerned may, in the circumstances, already have a legal right to the benefit in question, and also that such undertakings do not always make it to the case file.[25] More is said about such undertakings below.

As to the range of undertakings that may be made or the benefits on offer, in Canada, the range of undertakings that the authorities may provide appears to be broader than in the other jurisdictions. There, the Public Prosecutor Service of Canada Deskbook sets out a *non-exhaustive* list of benefits that may be included in the immunity agreement, including full immunity from prosecution, dropping or reducing the charges (against the collaborator and/or family members or friends), agreeing to a lesser sentence, return of confiscated goods and reward money. According to one of the federal prosecutors interviewed for the purposes of this report, the full range of undertakings is used in practice. While at first glance sentence reduction and 'small courtesies' would appear to

---

21 In this section sub-questions 1 and 8 are addressed.
22 Here it should be recalled that, in Italy, the notion of providing undertakings or making promises to witnesses in the context of the institution of collaboration with justice is not self-evident. See § 7.2 above.
23 For the provision of witness protection, see § 7.6 below, for the undertakings provided by the information-provider, see in particular § 7.5.
24 More concretely, the question is whether the Instructions are contrary to the statutory system as regards the undertakings that may be provided. See also n. 9.
25 Regarding this last point, see § 7.7.1 and § 7.9.

be the only benefits on offer in the Netherlands (examples of 'small courtesies' are the expedited return of confiscated goods and seeking a milder penitentiary regime for the individual in question; they fall within the remit of the public prosecutor, not the court[26]), both the law itself (the (statutory) provisions of the Dutch Code of Criminal Procedure) and the fact that Dutch criminal procedure is governed by the principle of prosecutorial discretion appear to allow for *other* benefits to be granted.[27] According to the Public Prosecution Service (based on its interpretation of the legislative history and on the (appellate) case law) and pursuant to the Instructions on Undertakings to Witnesses in Criminal Cases (hereafter: 'the Instructions'), these include reduction of the confiscation of unlawfully obtained advantage sought by a maximum of fifty percent and withdrawal of a request for extradition.[28] However, there continues to be some discussion as to whether these two benefits may be promised, owing to the more general (and ongoing) discussion referred to above.[29] Also worth noting here is that in the Netherlands, the Instructions also stipulate a number of *prohibited* undertakings (again, drawing on the legislative history and the appellate case law). These include dropping the charges, reducing the charges (for example, from murder to manslaughter), granting immunity where this would conflict with prevailing prosecutorial policy, granting reward money and the adoption of protective measures. While in Germany the law itself recognizes only two benefits, i.e. sentence mitigation or exemption from punishment, other benefits are provided in practice, including assistance in obtaining the right to residence in Germany (the benefit most frequently sought), financial compensation, the return of confiscated goods and penitentiary benefits. What these 'unofficial' undertakings have in common is that it is the public prosecutor who is the competent authority in this regard, whereas for sentence reduction, it is the court. In Italy, the only benefits that may be granted to collaborators are sentence discounts and penitentiary benefits.

In all four jurisdictions, then, sentence reduction is a form of reward, while in three of the four jurisdictions – the Netherlands, Germany and Italy – it appears to be the *main* benefit on offer. While in Canada also, the prosecuting authorities may undertake to assist a collaborator in obtaining a reduced sentence, it is unclear whether this is the main undertaking in this regard. Under Dutch law,[30] the trial judge may, upon the request of the public prosecutor pursuant to an agreement between the public prosecutor and the

---

26 See Section 8 of the Instructions.
27 Nevertheless, it is important to note here that, pursuant to the Instructions, an undertaking which comprises no more than what the public prosecutor would have decided under normal circumstances based on existing policy is not an undertaking within the meaning thereof.
28 See Section 4 of the Instructions.
29 For an overview of this discussion, see § 3.3.4 and § 3.4.3.3 of the Dutch country report. Nevertheless, it bears emphasizing that in the *Passage* case, both the Amsterdam District Court and the Amsterdam Court of Appeal largely followed the Public Prosecution Service's line of reasoning regarding the availability of benefits other than sentence reduction and 'small courtesies'.
30 Specifically, Article 226g of the Dutch Code of Criminal Procedure and Article 44a of the Dutch Criminal Code.

collaborator, reduce the punishment that he or she was originally going to impose, whether in the form of imprisonment, community service or a fine, by a maximum of fifty percent.[31] In considering whether to do so, the judge is required to take into account the fact that, in providing a statement, the individual in question will have made, or may be making, an important contribution to the investigation or prosecution of criminal offences.[32] In case of collaboration with an individual who has already been convicted, the benefit on offer is cooperation on the part of the public prosecutor with a request for clemency, in the form of a recommendation that the sentence imposed should be reduced by a maximum of fifty percent.[33] According to numerous practitioners interviewed for the purposes of this report, the sentence reduction envisaged by the law – a maximum of fifty percent – may be insufficient to secure the cooperation of potential collaborators; they cite this as a reason why so many of the procedures initiated eventually come to nothing.[34] As to Germany (where the sentencing framework provides for maximum *and* minimum sentences), there, Article 49(1) of the German Criminal Code allows the court to, in case of an offence punishable by a determinate period of imprisonment, reduce the maximum penalty envisaged by the law by up to one-quarter, and additionally provides for reduced minimum sentences. Furthermore, in Germany, a life sentence may be converted to a determinate period of imprisonment of no less than ten years. In Italy (where, as in Germany, the sentencing framework provides for maximum *and* minimum sentences), the sentencing framework provides for a so-called 'double-track' regime, aimed at incentivizing collaboration by ensuring that those who opt to collaborate with the authorities are punished less severely (and/or are subject to a more lenient penitentiary regime), than those who do not. In respect of the crimes of terrorism and subversion, and of mafia-type crimes, Italian law allows the court to convert a life sentence to a determinate period of imprisonment of twelve to twenty years, and, in case of an offence punishable by a determinate period of imprisonment, to reduce the penalty that it was going to impose by anything between one-third to one-half. In respect of narcotics-related crimes, the punishment may be reduced from one-half to two-thirds. On the basis of the foregoing it may be concluded that the maximum amount of sentence reduction that may be granted differs as between the jurisdictions; in the Netherlands it is fifty percent, in Germany it is twenty-five percent (and in minor cases, one hundred percent[35]), in Italy it is anything between one-third to one-half or one-half to two-thirds, while in Canada there appears to be no limit in this regard. Also worth noting here is that there are differ-

---

31 Alternatively, the trial judge may convert up to fifty percent of the unconditional part of a punishment (again, whether in the form of imprisonment, community service or a fine) to a conditional punishment, or replace up to a third of the imprisonment imposed by community service or a fine.

32 More is said about this requirement below, in § 7.7.1.

33 Article 226k of the Dutch Code of Criminal Procedure.

34 See further § 7.8.2.

35 In Germany, it should be recalled, exemption from punishment is an undertaking (although, as will be seen below, only in minor cases).

ences between the jurisdictions as regards the point of departure for determining the discount. Thus, whereas in Germany it is the maximum penalty envisaged by the law, in Italy and the Netherlands it is the punishment that the trial judge was originally going to impose (within the parameters set by the law, and taking into account the public prosecutor's demand in this regard).

By contrast, immunity from prosecution is a reward in only one of the jurisdictions under examination: Canada. Nevertheless, according to the (federal) guideline contained in the Public Prosecution Service of Canada Deskbook, full or complete immunity should only be granted when the collaborator's statement contains information relating to the commission of a serious offence and should not be considered in relatively minor cases. According to all seven practitioners interviewed for the purposes of this report, full or complete immunity is rarely granted in practice. In the Netherlands (where, as in Canada, criminal procedure is governed by the principle of prosecutorial discretion), it should be recalled, there is a (principled) prohibition on granting immunity as a reward. At the same time, the prosecutorial authorities are not precluded from granting immunity *in accordance with prevailing prosecutorial policy* (and later calling that person as a witness). A person granted immunity on the latter basis would not, however, be considered a collaborator of justice within the meaning of the law.[36] Accordingly, the question of whether a person may be granted immunity in exchange for their testimony in the prosecution of others is something of a grey area in the Netherlands, albeit one that does not appear to be overly problematic in practice, in that there is nothing to suggest that immunity on the latter basis is being granted on a wide scale (also in light of the fact that, pursuant to the Instructions, an undertaking which comprises no more than what the public prosecutor would have decided under normal circumstances based on existing policy is not an undertaking within the meaning thereof). In Germany and Italy, it is not possible to grant immunity from prosecution at all, owing to the fact that there, criminal procedure is governed by the principle of mandatory prosecution. Nevertheless, in Germany, courts can withhold punishment altogether in minor cases (where the offence in question is punishable by a determinate period of imprisonment and the offender would, in the circumstances, not be sentenced to a term exceeding three years), and the public prosecutor can decide not to prosecute a criminal offence where prosecution for that offence would not significantly add to the penalty to be imposed in respect of the other offences for which the individual in question will be prosecuted (and when a decision may not be expected within a reasonable period of time). Regarding the immunity that may be granted in Canada and the exemption from punishment that may be granted in Germany, it is worth noting that while in the current context, such benefits are in a general sense comparable, in Canada, the question of whether immunity is appropriate is dependent on the seriousness of the offence in respect of which the

---

36   Within the meaning of Article 226g of the Dutch Code of Criminal Procedure, that is.

collaborator's testimony is sought, whereas in Germany, the question of whether the collaborator may be exempted from punishment is dependent on the seriousness of the case against the collaborator, i.e. the sentence likely to be imposed upon conviction.

Turning now to financial compensation or reward money, as stated above, in the Netherlands, there is a (principled) prohibition on granting reward money in the context of collaboration with justice. Moreover, this is considered by some to be a reason not to allow the authorities to promise the reduction of the confiscation of unlawfully obtained advantage, such a promise being considered tantamount to a promise of financial reward. In Canada and Germany, however, financial compensation or reward money is a benefit on offer. Moreover, in Germany, the authorities may undertake not to confiscate certain goods or seek repayment of social security benefits. While in Canada the granting of reward money does appear in the (non-exhaustive) list of undertakings that prosecution counsel may make in the context of an immunity agreement, there may be some reluctance on the part of prosecution counsel to make a promise of financial reward to collaborators.[37] In Italy, financial compensation is not a form of reward in the context of collaboration with justice.

In conclusion, while Italian law exhaustively regulates the benefits that may be granted, the Dutch and German law does not, while in Canada the rules provide for a non-exhaustive list of undertakings. In Canada, it seems, the authorities may provide a broader range of undertakings to cooperating information providers than in the other jurisdictions. In three of the four jurisdictions examined for the purposes of this report – the Netherlands, Germany and Italy – sentence reduction is the main benefit on offer, and while in Canada also, the prosecuting authorities may undertake to assist a collaborator in obtaining a reduced sentence, it is unclear whether this is the main undertaking in this regard. Regarding sentence reduction, in each country, the judge is afforded a margin of discretion in determining the sentence to be imposed on the collaborator. While at first glance the maximum amount of sentence reduction that may be granted in each jurisdiction would appear to be comparable, it is difficult to draw a meaningful comparison in this regard. Whereas in Canada, the prosecuting authorities may grant full immunity in exchange for testimony, in the three other jurisdictions, this is not possible. In the Netherlands, this is forbidden as a matter of principle in the specific context of collaboration with justice, while in Germany and Italy, this is because, there, criminal procedure is governed by the principle of mandatory prosecution (whereas in Canada and the Netherlands, it is governed by the principle of prosecutorial discretion). Nevertheless, in Germany, a court may (in minor cases) exempt a convicted collaborator from punishment altogether. Finally, financial compensation is a form of reward in only two of the four jurisdictions: Canada and Germany.

---

37 See Chapter 6, n. 74.

7.5   THE PROCESS OF BECOMING A COLLABORATOR OF JUSTICE[38]

With the availability of the instrument and the nature of the undertakings that may be provided (or benefits on offer) having now been set out, it is time to turn to the process by which an individual becomes a collaborator of justice more generally, and the similarities and differences between the four jurisdictions examined for the purposes of this report in this regard. In short, the most significant similarities are that in all four jurisdictions, the initiative to collaborate comes, in most cases, from the individual or their lawyer, and that while in all four jurisdictions the police have an important role to play in the aforementioned process (particularly the initial stages thereof), it is the public prosecutor who is the competent authority to negotiate the agreement or, as the case may be, manage the relationship with the aspiring collaborator.[39] Moreover, in all four jurisdictions, the collaborator's statement should contain important information for, and/or contribute in a significant way to, the investigation and/or prosecution of a third party, and the collaborator is in principle required to testify at trial. Differences as regards the process by which an individual becomes a collaborator of justice concern what is required by way of disclosure on the part of the information-provider, the 'output' of the talks between the individual in question and the authorities and the nature of any agreement reached in this regard, the review mechanisms in place in respect of the decision to enter into an agreement in the first place, and the safeguards in place against false or otherwise unreliable statements (other than those at the trial and deliberation phase of proceedings[40]). In the paragraphs below, the aforementioned similarities and differences are discussed in more detail.[41] Finally, it should be noted that in all four jurisdictions, the process by which protective measures are adopted does not form part of the process by which an individual becomes a collaborator of justice; accordingly, the former process is not addressed in this section.[42]

7.5.1   The Initiative to Collaborate and Responsibility for Negotiating the Agreement

Although the Dutch rules do address the procedure for entering into agreements with witnesses in some detail, they are somewhat vague as regards the very initial stages of the process. According to the members of the Dutch police and Public Prosecution Service

---

38 In this section sub-questions 3 and 5 are addressed.

39 Here it should be recalled that, in Italy, it may be inappropriate to speak of a process of negotiation (or a bilateral agreement) between the authorities and the potential witness. See § 7.2.

40 These are dealt with elsewhere in this chapter, in § 7.7.2 below.

41 With the exception of the point regarding 'output' and the nature of any agreement reached; this issue is addressed above, in § 7.2.

42 The process by which protective measures are adopted is dealt with in § 7.6.

interviewed for the purposes of this report, in most cases the initiative to collaborate comes from the aspiring collaborator of justice or his lawyer. Moreover, according to the interviewees, it is the police that conduct preliminary talks with the potential collaborator, in which the police try to gain insight into what the collaborator can declare and inform the witness about the various possibilities and the consequences of making a statement (although the public prosecutor is also involved at this stage and must give permission for these talks). The statements made during this phase cannot be used in any way until a formal agreement has been made and has been approved by the investigative judge (although even in the absence of such an agreement, the witness may yet give permission for such statements to be used). In the Netherlands, only the public prosecutor may enter into an agreement with the witness.

In Italy also, it is the individual or his lawyer who takes the initiative to collaborate, not the public prosecutor or the police, which may be attributed to the fact that the instrument of collaboration with justice is by now so well-established that persons belonging to criminal circles are well aware of the rules and their functioning. Once an individual decides to collaborate, they request a meeting with the public prosecutor. However, unlike in the Netherlands, in Italy, this initial phase of the process by which an individual becomes a collaborator of justice is strictly regulated by law, whereby the legal framework imposes on the individual a number of obligations, some of which are addressed below in setting out the differences between the four jurisdictions as regards the safeguards in place against false or otherwise unreliable statements.

In Germany, it should be recalled, the instrument is a matter of substantive criminal law, which goes some way to explaining why, there, the process is not formally regulated. Nevertheless, the process by which an individual becomes a collaborator of justice in Germany is comparable to that in the Netherlands and Italy, in that, there, also, the police and the public prosecutor play an essential role in the initial phase of the process. There, the police will mention the possibility of collaborating during the interrogation of a suspect. When a suspect is interested in becoming a collaborator of justice, the public prosecutor will take over the interrogation in order to assess the information in the suspect's possession, and to go over the requirements in this regard. Although the process is not formally regulated, which was cited by German practitioners as a disadvantage, most were nevertheless satisfied with the procedure, mainly because, in practice, the public prosecutor and the collaborator of justice will honour the verbal agreement, and in most cases the trial judge will apply the collaborators' provision, i.e. grant the benefits provided for therein.

As in Germany, in Canada, the rules do not provide for a set procedure for entering into immunity agreements (although it does set out the responsibilities of Crown (prosecuting) counsel in negotiating such agreements and also what may be required by way of internal consultation in this regard). According to the Canadian practitioners interviewed, it is usually a defence lawyer who initiates the process of negotiation with Crown counsel, although in most cases, the overall process begins with discussions between the potential collaborator and the police. However, only the Public Prosecution Service (acting through Crown counsel) is entitled to negotiate an immunity agreement. In all four jurisdictions, then, it is the public prosecutor who is the competent authority to negotiate the agreement or, as the case may be, manage the relationship with the aspiring collaborator (although the police have an important role to play in the initial stages of the forementioned process).

7.5.2   The Collaborator's Statement

A further similarity between the jurisdictions is that the collaborator's statement should contain important information for, and/or contribute in a significant way to, the investigation and/or prosecution of a third party. In the Netherlands, the collaborator's statement must make an *important* contribution to the investigation or prosecution of criminal offences, while in Italy, the information provided by the collaborator must bring *new knowledge* to the investigation, or it must appear important for the trial or the advancement of the investigation concerning the organizational structure, the equipment, the domestic and international relationships and the purposes of the criminal organization. In Germany, the collaborator is required to provide information either on an offence already committed, in which case the statement should make a *substantial* contribution to the investigation or prosecution of the crime (although it is not a requirement that the information actually leads to a conviction or is used as evidence; the trial judge need only be convinced that the statement provides a reliable foundation for a successful prosecution), or one that has not yet been committed, in which case the information provided should make it possible for the authorities to prevent the crime (meaning that it should be provided in a timely manner). Finally, in Canada, the importance of the collaborator's testimony or cooperation is a factor relevant to the determination of which undertaking to provide. Another similarity between the four jurisdictions is that the collaborator is, in principle, required to give evidence at trial.

As to what is required by way of disclosure on the part of the information-provider, as stated at the beginning of the section, there are differences between the jurisdictions in this regard. At first glance, the scope of disclosure required in the Netherlands is narrower than that in Italy. In Italy, collaborators are required to disclose not only all information in their possession regarding the facts about which they are being questioned by the public prosecutor, but also all other information in their possession regarding facts of major gravity and social alarm, and all information necessary to locate, seize and confiscate the money or assets in their ownership or in the ownership of other members of the organization. In the Netherlands, the collaborator is required to give full information and transparency on the offences in respect of which they are willing to give evidence, including any share they have had therein. Accordingly, and as confirmed by the members of the Public Prosecution Service and police interviewed for the purposes of this report, the collaborator is not required to disclose any information in their possession regarding *other* offences that are not (yet) known to the authorities. Nevertheless, the same interviewees observed that it is in the Public Prosecution Service's interests that they do so, in order to decide whether to enter into an agreement with the person concerned in the first place, and also in order to avoid being put in a difficult position later on in the process, upon any such information becoming known to the defence. In Germany, the law itself is unclear as to whether the collaborator is required to disclose all information in their possession regarding known criminal offences; at least one of the prosecutors interviewed for the purposes of this report took a pragmatic view in this regard, seemingly viewing 'selective' disclosure as par for the course. In Canada, 'full and candid' disclosure on the part of the collaborator regarding their involvement in criminal activity in general and of all information pertaining to the activity in question or likely to affect their credibility is a factor relevant to the determination of which undertaking to provide.

7.5.3   Review of the Decision to Collaborate

Furthermore, there are differences between the four jurisdictions as regards the review mechanisms in place in respect of the decision to enter into an agreement in the first place. In the Netherlands, an extensive internal *and* external review procedure must be conducted before the agreement may be considered to be established (about which more is said below[43]). In other words, in the Netherlands, the public prosecutor does not have the authority to finalize the agreement; there, the agreement will only be considered to be final where the Board of Procurators General (the Public Prosecution Service's highest authority) has provided permission for it, and the investigating judge has ruled favourably on the lawfulness thereof. In Canada, the agreement is signed by the Crown and the collaborator, and, if applicable, his lawyer. The normal procedure is that the collaborator's lawyer offers a proffer, and, after it has been accepted, the Crown and the lawyer will sign the agreement. The decision to enter into an immunity agreement is not made by Crown counsel alone; he or she must consult senior officials of the Public Prosecution Service before doing so. As in the Netherlands, then, in Canada, there are internal mechanisms in place in respect of the decision to enter into an agreement, although these mechanisms appear to be less strict than those in the Netherlands in the sense that they 'merely' require consultation. By contrast, in Italy and Germany, there appear to be no formal internal mechanisms in place. More is said about this issue below,

---

43 See § 7.7.1.

in addressing the matter of scrutiny of the process by which an individual becomes a collaborator of justice.

7.5.4   *Safeguards Against False or Otherwise Unreliable Statements*

Further differences between the four jurisdictions as regards the process by which an individual becomes a collaborator of justice concern the safeguards in place against false or otherwise unreliable statements (again, other than those at the trial and deliberation phase of proceedings, which are dealt with below). While in all four jurisdictions ensuring the reliability of the statements made is an important aspect of the process by which an individual becomes a collaborator of justice, the mechanisms or practices aimed at doing so differ in each. Italian and German law both prescribe a deadline by which the aspiring collaborator must provide the information sought. In Italy, the collaborator's statement must be made within 180 days of the first manifestation of the willingness to collaborate, in order to prevent collaborators from 'declaring in instalments' and thereby ensure the 'genuineness' or sincerity of the contribution (whereby the underlying idea is that someone who provides only certain information but withholds other details, cannot be trusted), and to prevent or minimize the risk that, with the passing of time, the collaborator be subject to external influences or pressures to adjust or modify their statements.[44] The Italian prosecutors and judges interviewed for the purposes of this report consider this deadline to be necessary and adequate. In Italy, a further safeguard against false or otherwise unreliable statements concerns the contents of the collaborator's statement; as stated above, it must include: all information in their possession regarding the facts about which they are being questioned by the public prosecutor; all other information in their possession regarding facts of major gravity and social alarm; and all information that is necessary to locate, seize and confiscate the money or assets in their ownership or in the ownership of other members of the organization. According to the prosecutors interviewed, the information regarding the collaborator's financial situation is essential to establish the credibility of the information and genuineness of the collaboration. In Germany, the collaborator must disclose the information in his possession prior to the commencement of the trial proceedings. The main purpose of this deadline is to allow the authorities to assess the reliability of the statement before the start of the trial phase. In the Netherlands also, there are safeguards in place to prevent or minimize the risk of false or otherwise unreliable statements, the most notable being the scrutiny provided by the investigating judge at the pre-trial stage of proceedings, which not only entails an assessment of the lawfulness of the (proposed) agreement, but also of the reliability of the statement(s) provided.[45] While in Canada, there is no

---

44 Regarding this risk, a further safeguard is that where the collaborator is being detained, they are kept in 'isolation' from the other detainees.

45 However, as will be explained below in § 7.7.1, this scrutiny does not apply to (provisional) agreements in which the public prosecutor has undertaken to grant 'small courtesies'.

external scrutiny of the initial phase of the process by which an individual becomes a collaborator of justice, there are internal, consultation, mechanisms in place, the primary concern of which appears to be preventing or minimizing the risk of false or otherwise unreliable statements. More is said about the matter of scrutiny below.[46]

In conclusion, overall, the process by which an individual becomes a collaborator of justice in each jurisdiction is comparable: the roles of the information-provider, police and the public prosecutor in the initial phase of the process are similar in each, as is what is required from the information-provider in terms of contribution to the investigation and/or prosecution of a third party. Moreover, in each jurisdiction, ensuring the reliability of the information provided – the statement – is an important aspect of the process. However, there are also noteworthy differences between the jurisdictions as regards the process by which an individual becomes a collaborator of justice, concerning the extent to which it is formally regulated[47] (whereby it is worth noting that in the jurisdictions with the strictest rules in this regard – the Netherlands and Italy –, the scope of application of the instrument is narrower than that in the jurisdictions in which a formal procedure is more or less lacking[48]), the information to be disclosed by the information-provider, the review mechanisms in place in respect of the decision to enter into an agreement and the safeguards against false or otherwise unreliable statements.

7.6   Relationship to Witness Protection[49]

In agreeing to give evidence in the prosecution of other offenders, witnesses may be exposing themselves and/or their families to physical danger. This is particularly so where the subject matter of the evidence to be given concerns the activities of a criminal organization. Due to this danger, the witness and/or his family may be in need of physical protection. The fact that a willingness to give evidence in the prosecution of other offenders may give rise to the need for witness protection raises questions as to the relationship between the cooperation of the individual offender and the authorities for the purposes of securing the individual's testimony in the prosecution of others on the one hand, and the provision of witness protection on the other. One such question is whether the fact that the individual in question is prepared to give evidence in the prosecution of others *entitles* them to witness protection (provided they are in physical danger), with all that this entails, or, put differently, whether the provision of witness protection is a decisive or pertinent factor in securing the cooperation of the individual

---

46   See § 7.7.
47   See in this regard also § 7.2.
48   Regarding the scope of application of the instrument in the various jurisdictions, see § 7.3 and also § 7.2.
49   In this section sub-question 7 is addressed.

in question. In this regard it may be observed that in each of the jurisdictions examined for the purposes of this report, the cooperation between the individual in question and the authorities for the purpose of securing the individual's testimony and the provision of protective measures are considered to be separate matters, as reflected in, for example, the fact that the responsibility for organizing each lies with a different authority. The fact that they are considered to be separate matters suggests that for each of these jurisdictions, the aforementioned question may be answered in the negative. Whether this is so is examined below, in considering the similarities and differences between the four juris-dictions as regards the degree of separation between the two matters.

In the Netherlands, the separation of the aforementioned matters is reflected in the fact that witness protection is not considered to constitute an undertaking as such, i.e. an undertaking aimed at securing the testimony of the individual concerned (which has to do with the fact that the authorities have a stand-alone duty to protect witnesses from physical harm, deriving from the positive obligations flowing from the ECHR, specifically Articles 2 and 8 thereof), that they are regulated in separate (written) agreements (such that witness protection does not form part of the agreement on the cooperation between the individual offender and the authorities for the purposes of securing their testimony), and that the procedure to be followed in respect of each is separate, involving different authorities. Thus, while organization of the cooperation falls under the remit of the 'Crim-inal Intelligence Team' (*TCI*), a specialist police unit at the regional level whose task it is to gather and analyse criminal intelligence relating to serious and/or organized crime, and the public prosecutor responsible for the gathering and use of criminal intelligence by the police (*CI-officier*), the matter of witness protection falls under the responsibility of the 'Witness Protection Team' (*TGB*), another specialist police unit (at the national level), and the public prosecutor responsible for witness protection (*TGB-officier*).

While in the Netherlands the two matters – cooperation between the individual offender and the authorities for the purposes of securing the individual's testimony in the prosecution of others and witness protection – are in principle separate, in practice the two issues are more entwined. Thus, Dutch practitioners refer to instances in which the individual offender has refused to enter into an agreement with the authorities in the first place, or has suspended or threatened to suspend cooperation with the authorities, due to discontent over the protection on offer or the protection being provided, and observe that this has the potential to cause, and has in fact caused, significant delay and uncertainty in the proceedings. They observe that while the two issues are in principle distinct, witnesses tend not to see it that way; to witnesses, physical protection *does* form part of the agreement on the cooperation aimed at securing their testimony in the prosecution of others, i.e. is not separate from the cooperation, a view apparently held by some of the interviewees also. Moreover, as one interviewee observed, witnesses 'see' only one police force, i.e. they do not distinguish between different police units (or, pre-sumably, different public prosecutors), and as yet another practitioner pointed out, because witness protection is only minimally regulated in the Netherlands (in that while the law recognizes a general duty to protect witnesses from physical harm, a concrete framework setting out the measures that may be adopted in this regard, the duration thereof and the costs that may be incurred, is lacking), witnesses see that there is room to negotiate the terms of their protection. In this regard it may be observed that in some cases, dissatisfaction over the protection on offer has indeed had an effect on the witness' willingness to cooperate, i.e. provide a statement. Dutch practitioners have suggested a number of solutions to the problems caused by a witness' refusal to cooperate in the first place and/or suspension of cooperation with the authorities, including clearer and stricter regulation of witness protection, whereby there is less to no room for negotiation; that any agreement between the authorities and the individual in question regarding the provision of witness protection be formalized in writing (so as to avoid any misunderstandings in this regard); and that witnesses are only brought to trial once the talks on witness protection have been concluded.

In Germany, Italy and Canada also, cooperation between the individual offender and the authorities for the purposes of securing the individual's testimony in the prosecution of others and witness protection are considered to be separate matters. In Germany, this is reflected in the fact that the procedure to be followed in respect of each is separate, involving different authorities. Thus, while the responsibility for organizing the cooperation lies with the public prosecutor, entry into the witness protection programme is organized and supervised by a specialist police unit, the witness protection bureau (*Zeugenschutzdienststelle*), which is not in any way involved in investigating crime, and which is therefore completely independent of other police units, as well as the Ministry of Justice and of the public prosecutor's office. Regarding entry into the programme, the public prosecutor's role is limited to providing an assessment of the need for physical protection, i.e. to making recommendations in this regard, but the public prosecutor cannot decide to place a witness in the programme (or make any promises in this regard); this is the exclusive competence of the witness protection bureau. Thus, witness protection does not form an integral part of the negotiations between the individual and the public prosecutor aimed at securing the individual's testimony in the prosecution of others; in the context of such negotiations, witness protection is a take-it-or-leave-it matter. The take-it-or-leave-it nature of witness protection in Germany is a cause for concern among practitioners and scholars. In this regard suggestions have been made to integrate the question of witness protection into the negotiations between the individual and the public prosecutor aimed at securing the individual's testimony, with a view to incentivizing cooperation. In the Netherlands, such suggestions have been met with limited enthusiasm among practitioners; they cite the need to guarantee the safety of the witness (which might be compromised if details concerning the protective measures to be adopted were to become known to a wider audience) and to remove any pressure on, or temptation on the part of, the public prosecutor to make far-reaching promises regarding witness protection in order to further the case as reasons for maintaining the separation between the two matters.

In Italy also, the separation of the two matters is reflected in the fact that the procedure to be followed in respect of each is separate, involving altogether different authorities. While the responsibility for organizing the cooperation aimed at securing the individual offender's testimony lies with the public prosecutor, witness protection falls within the remit of a commission attached to the Ministry of the Interior, chaired by an under-secretary of state of the Ministry of the Interior and composed of two magistrates and five state officials (the 'Central Commission'). The protective measures themselves are implemented by the local government administration of the place of residence of the collaborator, or a centralized police body known as the Central Protection Service. Accordingly, it is not the public prosecutor who decides on whether to grant protective measures, but the Central Commission. Nevertheless, the public prosecutor has an important role to play in this regard, since the Central Commission may only adopt protective measures at the request of the prosecutor in charge of the investigation. While the Central Commission is not bound by the prosecutor's proposal and can conduct its own inquiries in this regard, a member of the Central Commission interviewed for the purposes of this report observed that the Commission usually follows the prosecutor's proposal. The fact that the decision of whether to grant protective measures is taken not by the public prosecutor but by an altogether different body – an administrative authority – goes some way to explaining why, nowadays, collaborators rarely suspend or threaten to suspend cooperation with the authorities, by refusing to give evidence at trial due to discontent over protective measures, as does the fact that the availability of sentence discounts and post-conviction, penitentiary benefits is no longer dependent on the individual having been admitted to the witness protection programme. Whereas previously – prior to the legislative amendments of 2001 – it was not unusual for collaborators to threaten to withdraw their statements or remain silent at trial if they were not admitted to the protection programme (by which they could become eligible for sentence reduction or post-conviction benefits), resulting in the tendency of prosecutors to overestimate the dangers to which the collaborator was subject so as to ensure admission into the protection programme (and by doing so, securing as many collaborations as possible), nowadays, Italian practitioners observe, there is no point in bringing such complaints before a prosecutor or judge. Nowadays, it is not necessary to provide witness protection in order to be able to incentivize cooperation through the prospect of sentence reduction and/or post-conviction benefits. Also worth noting in this regard is the fact that the Italian legislation provides for a concrete framework setting out the protective measures that may be adopted and that the same legislation stipulates that failure to respond to questions at trial will result in immediate revocation of any protective measures put in place.

Finally, in Canada also, the separation of the two matters is reflected in the fact that they are regulated in separate agreements and that the procedure to be followed in respect of each is separate, involving altogether different authorities. While the responsibility for organizing the cooperation aimed at securing the individual offenders testimony lies with the prosecutor (although in most cases the immunity process begins with discussions between the individual and the case investigators, following which the investigators usually approach the prosecutor), witness protection falls within the remit of the federal police, i.e. the Royal Canadian Mounted Police (RCMP), whereby the officers involved are completely independent from those involved in the investigation of crime (so as to prevent a conflict of interests). Thus, in Canada the terms and conditions of the witness protection are discussed and negotiated between the police and the witness, not the prosecutor and the witness. Nevertheless, the matter of witness protection may well arise in the initial stages of the immunity agreement negotiations (between the individual and the case investigators), and the rules stipulate that the prosecutor should be (made) aware of this.

In conclusion, while in each of the jurisdictions examined for the purposes of the present research, the cooperation between the individual in question and the authorities for the purpose of securing the individual's testimony in the prosecution of others, and the provision of protective measures are considered to be separate matters, the degree of separation differs between them, as reflected in the margin for collaborators to negotiate the terms of their protection in each jurisdiction in particular. In Germany and Italy, for example, there seems to be little to no room for negotiation in this regard, while in the Netherlands, there seems to be more margin for doing so (although it bears emphasizing here that, in the Netherlands, the instrument of providing undertakings has been deployed in only a handful of cases, which warrants caution in drawing general conclusions in this regard). In this regard it may be observed that in Germany and Italy, the question of witness protection is the responsibility of an altogether different authority than the one responsible for organizing the cooperation aimed at securing the individual offender's testimony, whereas in the Netherlands, the responsibility for each of these matters lies with *a* public prosecutor. Although the role played by each public prosecutor – the *CI-officier* and the *TGB-officier* – is different, they are both public prosecutors employed by the Public Prosecution Service. While this may not be tantamount to placing the responsibility for both matters on a single authority, it is not difficult to see how this feature of the Dutch system might give rise to the perception among witnesses that there is room to negotiate and that suspending cooperation may well be worth their while, particularly in combination with the fact that, in the Netherlands, witness protection is only minimally regulated (whereby it may be observed that the level of regulation of the matter of witness protection also differs between the four jurisdictions). Of course, a witness' *perception* that there is room to negotiate need not actually thwart the criminal proceedings in which they propose to give evidence; whether a perceived margin for negotiation on the part of the witness will (actually) thwart the proceedings is dependent on other factors also, such as how important the testimony is to the case in question (which, in turn, is likely to depend on how much information the prosecutor (already) possesses on the criminal organization in question, among other things) and, more generally, how prepared the authorities are to see the case fail as a result of the suspension of cooperation due to discontent over protective measures (which, in turn, is likely to depend on the seriousness of the case and the stage of the proceedings at which the witness is threatening to suspend cooperation, among other things). This issue is addressed further in the final chapter of this report, in which lessons are drawn for Dutch law and practice.

7.7   SCRUTINY[50]

The fact that the institution of collaboration with justice entails the promise of certain benefits to persons who themselves are suspected of, or who have been found guilty of, committing a criminal offence, in exchange for their testimony in the prosecution of others, raises questions as to the nature and extent of the benefits that may be provided to such persons, and to the reliability of any statement provided by such a person. In turn, such questions would appear to give rise to the need for *transparency* as regards the process by which the cooperation between the individual in question and the authorities for the purposes of securing the individual's testimony is set up, and, by extension, for *scrutiny* thereof, as well as of the reliability of any statement provided in this regard. It is this latter topic that forms the focus of the current section.[51] In each of the jurisdictions examined for the purposes of this report, there is some form of scrutiny of one or more of the aforementioned issues, and from the law and practice of such jurisdictions it is apparent that scrutiny can take a variety of forms; it may be internal or external in nature, or may entail something in between or a combination of the two. The most significant similarities and differences between the four jurisdictions in this regard are set out below, first in relation to the process by which an individual becomes a collaborator of justice,[52] thereafter in relation to the reliability of the statements provided.[53]

7.7.1   *Scrutiny of the Process By Which an Individual Becomes a Collaborator of Justice*

There are significant differences between the four jurisdictions examined for the purposes of this research as regards the matter of scrutiny of the process by which an individual

---

50   In this section sub-question 14 is addressed.
51   Transparency forming the subject matter of § 7.9, below.
52   See § 7.7.1.
53   See § 7.7.2.

becomes a collaborator of justice, i.e. the talks between the individual in question and the authorities, as well as any agreement reached in this regard. While the Dutch rules provide for an extensive system of *automatic* internal and external, judicial, review of the process by which the cooperation between the individual offender and the authorities is set up and of the (provisional) agreement (where the benefit being promised is sentence reduction, at least[54]), whereby judicial review is carried out at both the investigative stage (by the investigating judge) and the trial stage (by the trial judge, in the case in which the individual in question has given evidence, as well as in the case against that individual), in the other jurisdictions, the scrutiny appears to be less extensive.

In Germany, the process is subject to judicial scrutiny at the trial stage only, by the trial court in the case against the individual in question, in order to determine whether the requirements stipulated by the law have been satisfied (in respect of the benefits recognized by the law, i.e. sentence mitigation and exemption from punishment), for example, that the information was provided voluntarily and that there is a connection between the offence committed by the collaborator and the offence regarding which they are giving evidence, which appears to be standard practice. In Germany, then, there is no (automatic) scrutiny in the *investigative phase* of the proceedings of the process by which an individual becomes a collaborator of justice – the talks between the individual in question and the public prosecutor, and the ensuing 'agreement'. Regarding the lack of scrutiny in this phase, it should be recalled that in Germany, the institution of collaboration with justice is a matter of substantive criminal law. Moreover, there, any agreement reached between the individual in possession of information and the public prosecutor constitutes a 'gentlemen's agreement', with all that this entails.[55] Accordingly, in Germany, it is the trial judge who determines who is a collaborator of justice and who is not (within the meaning of Section 46b of the German Criminal Code – the central provision in Germany on collaboration with justice – at least), not the public prosecutor. Indeed, the determination of whether to *reduce the sentence* or *exempt from punishment* is within the full discretion of the court. This goes some way to explaining the lack of (automatic) scrutiny in the investigative phase of the proceedings of the initial phase of the process by which an individual becomes a collaborator of justice. However, the lack of scrutiny in Germany is not limited to the undertakings envisaged by the law. In Germany, it should be recalled, 'other' undertakings are provided in practice over which the public prosecutor does have (more) control or the ultimate decision on which does not depend on the court, whereby the concern appears to be that such undertakings may not come to light in the proceedings against the third party, at least. In this regard, numerous practitioners interviewed for the purposes of this report observed that not every detail of the initial phase of the process by which an individual becomes a collaborator of justice is documented and most of the time, a verbatim protocol is not made. Moreover, the talks

---

54 See in this regard n. 62 and accompanying text.
55 See in this regard § 7.2.

between the individual in question and the public prosecutor will not always end up in the case file. According to the defence counsel interviewed, this impacts on the ability of the court to, in the case in which the individual in question has given evidence, assess the reliability of the witness. More will be said about this issue below, in addressing the matter of scrutiny of the reliability of the statements provided.[56]

In Italy, there is no automatic scrutiny by a third party of the initial phase of the process by which an individual becomes a collaborator of justice, i.e. the talks between the individual in question and the public prosecutor (although the reliability of the statements provided by such persons is a matter subject to judicial scrutiny). In this regard it should be recalled that, in Italy, the role of the public prosecutor appears to be limited to informing the individual in question of the law and drawing his attention to the benefits available thereunder and explaining how they apply in a specific situation, it then being up to the trial judge to decide who is a collaborator of justice and who is not, with all that this entails for the granting of benefits. In both Germany and Italy, then, the determination of who is a collaborator of justice and who is not (within the meaning of the law, at least) is within the full discretion of the trial judge. In the Netherlands this appears to be more complex; while on the face of it this determination is within the full discretion of the trial judge, there the law itself[57] suggests that the trial judge may not set aside the agreement between the collaborator and the prosecuting authorities without good reason. In the literature there is support for the view that the trial judge's 'room to manoeuvre' in this regard is limited. The lack of scrutiny in Italy may, moreover, be explained by the fact that Italian law *exhaustively* lists the benefits that may be granted to collaborators,[58] which are, moreover, granted by the judicial authorities. In Italy, the law does not allow for *other* undertakings to be provided, in order to incentivize otherwise unwilling individuals. By contrast, in the Netherlands the central provision on collaboration with justice[59] does not purport to exhaustively list the undertakings that may be provided to witnesses (although, as will be explained below, the system of review in place in the Netherlands does not apply to 'small courtesies').[60]

In Canada, as in Italy, there is no automatic scrutiny by a third party of the initial phase of the process by which an individual becomes a collaborator of justice, i.e. the talks between the individual in question and the public prosecutor and the ensuing agreement. Here it bears observing that in Canada, there is no (principled) restriction of the undertakings that may be provided to witnesses, or an exhaustive list of undertakings in this regard. Regarding the *internal* mechanisms in place (whereby Crown (prosecuting) counsel is required to *consult* senior officials of the Public Prosecution Service of Canada before

---

56 See § 7.7.2.
57 See Article 44a(1) of the Dutch Criminal Code.
58 See in this regard § 7.4.
59 Article 226g of the Dutch Code of Criminal Procedure.
60 See in this regard § 7.4.

entering into an immunity agreement[61]), the concern appears to be not so much that pro-mises are being made that should not be, but rather that the making of promises has the potential to affect the reliability of the testimony. Although there is no *automatic* scrutiny of the process by which an immunity agreement is reached as such, several practitioners inter-viewed for the purposes of this report observed that, in a situation in which the prosecution decides to prosecute a person who was earlier promised immunity from prosecution in exchange for their testimony, that person can seek a judicial stay of proceedings for abuse of process. A decision on the merits of such an application would involve scrutiny of the agreement between prosecuting counsel and the individual in question.

In none of the jurisdictions examined for the purposes of this report is the process by which protective measures are adopted, or the protective measures ultimately adopted, transparent, due to security considerations. In the Netherlands, this is something of a contentious issue. There, it should be recalled, the provision of a financial reward for testimony is strictly prohibited, while witness protection is only minimally regulated and the rules on witness protection allow for the payment of a lump-sum to witnesses in order to organize their own protection (which does happen in practice, though only where the witness cannot be admitted to the full protection programme). The payment of a (large) sum of money to witnesses for such purposes is considered by some to be tantamount to the provision of a financial reward for testimony, such that any promise on the part of the authorities in this regard should be considered an unlawful undertaking (the ultimate decision on which, moreover, does not depend on the court). Such promises, however, are not subject to the system of scrutiny referred to at the beginning of the section; witness protection, it should be recalled, is within the discretion of a specialist police unit and the public prosecutor responsible for witness protection. In this regard suggestions have been made (in the case law and in the literature) to subject this process to some form of external scrutiny, in order to prevent the process by which protective measures are adopted from being utilized to provide otherwise unlawful undertakings, i.e. promises of financial rewards, to witnesses. Such suggestions were well received by the prosecuting authorities interviewed for the purposes of this report, as well as by other practitioners.

Finally, while in the Netherlands there is an extensive system of *automatic* internal and external, judicial, review in place of the process by which the cooperation between the individual offender and the authorities for the purposes of securing the individual's testimony is set up and of the (provisional) agreement, more extensive than in the other jurisdictions, that system of scrutiny may be less extensive and/or robust than the rules suggest. To begin with, according to the Dutch Code of Criminal Procedure, the system of review referred to at the beginning of the present section only applies to (provisional) agree-ments in which the public prosecutor has undertaken to seek sentence reduction or, as the case may be, cooperate with a request for clemency; it does not apply to (provisional) agree-

---

61 See in this regard § 7.5.

ments in which the public prosecutor has undertaken to grant 'small courtesies', such as actively cooperating with a request to suspend pre-trial detention (although any such agreement must be added to the case file[62]). Moreover, it is questionable whether it applies to the undertakings concerning the reduction of the confiscation of unlawfully obtained advantage or the withdrawal of a request for extradition (i.e. the undertakings provided for in the Instructions but not the Code of Criminal Procedure,[63] and over which, it may be observed, the public prosecutor has more control).[64] Regarding the undertakings in respect of which scrutiny must be provided, a point of concern in practice is the (external) review carried out by the investigating judge of the lawfulness of the agreement between the individual in question and the authorities. Thus, some practitioners interviewed for the purposes of this report expressed the view that the investigating judge is involved at too late a stage in the process to be able to conduct a meaningful review of the lawfulness of the agreement, and at short notice. For the same reason, practitioners expressed doubts as to the ability of the investigating judge to scrutinize the reliability of the statements provided. More will be said about this in the following section.

In conclusion, there are significant differences between the four jurisdictions examined for the purposes of this research as regards the matter of scrutiny of the process by which an individual becomes a collaborator of justice. While the Dutch rules provide for an extensive system of internal and external, judicial, review of the process by which the cooperation between the individual offender and the authorities for the purposes of securing the individual's testimony is set up and of the (provisional) agreement, in the other jurisdictions, the scrutiny is (significantly) less extensive. In Germany, the process is subject to scrutiny by the trial court in the case against the individual in question, in order to determine whether the legal requirements have been met (where the undertakings provided are those provided under Section 46b of the German Criminal Code, at least), which appears to be standard practice, while in Canada and Italy there is no automatic or standard scrutiny of the aforementioned process. Regarding such differing approaches to the matter of scrutiny, the following observations may be made. First, in the Netherlands and Germany there is a (perceived) lack of clarity and/or transparency as regards the undertakings that may be provided to witnesses,[65] whereas in Italy, this does not seem to be an issue at all. Second, whereas in the Netherlands there is a (principled) restriction of the undertakings that may be provided to witnesses, in Canada

---

62 Article 226g(4) of the Dutch Code of Criminal Procedure.

63 See in this regard n. 28 and accompanying text.

64 Nevertheless, it is worth noting that, according to the Instructions, it also applies to undertakings concerning the reduction of the confiscation of unlawfully obtained advantage and the withdrawal of a request for extradition.

65 It bears recalling here that in the Netherlands, the law, i.e. the relevant provisions of the Code of Criminal Procedure, does not purport to exhaustively list all of the undertakings that may be provided to witnesses while there continues to be discussion as to the lawfulness of certain undertakings, while in Germany, the 'other' undertakings provided in practice and which are not set out in Section 46b of the German Criminal Code, will not always make it to the case file.

there is no restriction in this regard. Third, whereas in Germany and Italy the determination of who is a collaborator of justice and who is not is within the full discretion of the trial judge, in the Netherlands this appears to be more complex; there the law itself implies that the trial judge may not set aside the agreement between the collaborator and the prosecuting authorities without good reason. The aforementioned goes some way to explaining the differing approaches to the matter of scrutiny of the process by which an individual becomes a collaborator of justice. Thus, a (perceived) lack of clarity and/or transparency as regards the undertakings that may be provided to witnesses or the benefits on offer would appear to call for a higher degree of scrutiny of that process. A (principled) restriction of the undertakings that may be provided would also appear to call for a higher degree of scrutiny, particularly where the restriction is not backed up by clear and cohesive legislation in this regard. Further, the more involved the prosecution is in the determination of who is a collaborator of justice and who is not (as may be apparent from the importance attached to the existence of a formal agreement between the prosecuting authorities and the individual in question, also), the more scrutiny would appear to be required. Of course, the need for scrutiny is not dependent on the aforementioned considerations alone. For one thing, the confidence of other actors (and of the general public) in the prosecuting authorities is likely to have a bearing on this issue. These issues are addressed further in the final chapter of this report, in which lessons are drawn for Dutch law and practice.

7.7.2   Scrutiny of the Reliability of the Statements Provided

As stated above, the fact that the institution of collaboration with justice entails the provision of certain benefits to persons who themselves are suspected of, or who have been found guilty of, committing a criminal offence, in exchange for their testimony in the prosecution of others, would appear to give rise to the need for scrutiny of the reliability of any statement provided in this regard. For the purposes of this section, scrutiny of the reliability of the statement does not encompass the process by which the law enforcement and/or prosecuting authorities verify or falsify the information provided or otherwise assess the reliability thereof with a view to determining whether it is worth proceeding with the individual in question,[66] but rather the assessment carried out by an external authority, i.e. the judicial authorities.

In all of the jurisdictions examined for the purposes of this report, the very nature of the institution of collaboration with justice is a reason to treat the collaborator's testimony with caution, i.e. to subject it to (special) scrutiny. Dutch and Italian law both prescribe special rules of corroboration in this regard. Thus, the Dutch Code of Criminal Procedure provides for a rule stipulating that a conviction may not be based

---

66   Nor is this section concerned with features of the procedure aimed at preserving the reliability of the statement provided; such features are dealt with in § 7.5.

on the statement(s) of a collaborator of justice alone.[67] Moreover, in light of such concerns, the trial judge is required, upon use of such statements, to provide reasoning in this regard.[68] Regarding the rule on the need for corroboration, a judge interviewed for the purposes of this report observed that the rule is somewhat ambiguous as to the extent of the corroboration required, i.e. as to whether *all* aspects of the statement pertaining to the participation of the accused require corroboration by an independent source, in derogation of the normal rule pursuant to which confirmation is required in a more general sense. The same judge argued that any broadening of the instrument that would make collaboration with the authorities more attractive should be accompanied by a tightening of the rule on corroboration.

In Italy, the judge is bound by Article 192(3) of the Italian Code of Criminal Procedure,[69] pursuant to which the statements of collaborators must be corroborated. In Italy, therefore, a conviction may not be based on the statement(s) of a collaborator of justice, i.e. the collaborator's evidence at trial,[70] alone. While the provision itself does not specify what, exactly, is required by way of corroboration, the Supreme Court of Cassation has determined that the assessment of the statements is to be carried out in accordance with a three-pronged test, whereby the judge is required to assess (1) the collaborator's credibility (by considering, among other things, the collaborator's social and economic status, criminal record, relationship to the accused and the reasons that prompted the collaboration[71]); (2) the intrinsic credibility of the statement (by considering its coherence, precision, consistency and spontaneity); and (3) whether the statement is corroborated by 'external elements', i.e. evidence (of any type) from an independent source. Regarding the last prong of the test, it should be noted that *every* segment of the collaborator's narration needs to be confirmed by external elements, in that every crime and the participation of every person will have to be corroborated by an independent source. None of the practitioners interviewed for the purposes of this report took issue with (the stringency of) this aspect of the test, seemingly on the basis that it is a matter of fairness towards the accused.

While in Germany judges are expected to treat collaborators' statements with caution, German law prescribes no special rule of corroboration in this regard (although, there,

---

67   Article 344a(4) of the Dutch Code of Criminal Procedure.
68   Article 360(2) of the Dutch Code of Criminal Procedure.
69   In Italy, the reliability of a collaborator's statement(s) is subject to judicial scrutiny at two moments: (1) in the investigative phase of proceedings, in the context of a request by the public prosecutor for the investigating judge to order certain coercive measures (for example, pre-trial detention); and (2) in the trial phase, in the case in which the individual in question has given evidence as well as in the case against that individual. While different evidentiary thresholds apply in respect of each, in both contexts the judge is bound by Article 192(3) of the Italian Code of Criminal Procedure, pursuant to which the statements of collaborators must be corroborated.
70   In Italy, it should be recalled, only evidence presented orally in court and challenged through cross-examination may be used at trial.
71   Such information is presented at trial, by the prosecutor.

courts are obliged to give reasons for their judgments, and, in the context of collaboration with justice, address the reliability of the collaborator's statement). Nor is corroboration a requirement in Canada, in that the jury is entitled to convict on unconfirmed evidence if it is satisfied that the evidence is true. Nevertheless, whenever there are serious reasons to be concerned about the credibility or reliability of an important witness, a jury is strongly encouraged to seek confirmation in this regard (although in order to be considered confirmatory, evidence does not have to implicate the accused). In Canada, whenever there are serious reasons to be concerned about such matters the trial judge is required to issue a warning to the jury. According to the Supreme Court of Canada, the trial judge should, in issuing such a warning, (1) draw the attention of the jury to the testimonial evidence requiring special scrutiny; (2) explain *why* this evidence is subject to special scrutiny; (3) caution the jury that it is dangerous to convict on unconfirmed evidence of this sort, though the jury is entitled to do so if satisfied that the evidence is true; and (4) instruct the jury to, in its determination of the veracity of the suspect evidence, look for evidence from another source tending to show that the untrustworthy witness is telling the truth as to the guilt of the accused.[72] Accordingly, in Canada, where a witness' credibility or reliability is seriously in doubt, special scrutiny is required, and this applies no less in cases in which the judge tries the case alone, i.e. without a jury.

In the Netherlands and Germany in particular, the practitioners interviewed for the purposes of this report expressed concerns as to the ability of the judicial authorities to assess the reliability of the statements provided. Turning first to the Netherlands, as stated above, a point of concern in practice is that the investigating judge is often involved at too late a stage in the process to be able to properly assess the reliability of the statements provided. As to the scrutiny in the trial phase, once the investigating judge has deemed the agreement to be lawful, it is up to the trial judge to, in the case in which the individual in question has given evidence as well as in the case against that individual, assess the reliability of the statement provided (as well as the lawfulness of the agreement).[73] Here it bears recalling that, in principle, the collaborator is required to give evidence at trial and that the defence has a right of confrontation in this regard. From the interviews conducted with Dutch practitioners, it is clear that there are divergent views on the matter of reliability. One prosecutor was keen to emphasize that the fact that an individual has been promised certain benefits need not mean that the statement provided is not truthful. According to the interviewee, while the judge should be aware of any agreement between the prosecuting authorities and the witness, the reliability of the statement should be determined on the basis of the other evidence before the court and of the questioning conducted at trial. Further, while the (Dutch) prosecutors and judges

---

72 *R v. Khela*, [2009] 1 SCR 104, 2009 SCC 4 (CanLII) [37], http://canlii.ca/t/2260t, accessed 10 May 2017.

73 And in the case against that individual, to assess the contribution of his testimony to the prosecution of others, for the purposes of determining whether to enforce the undertaking provided by the public prosecutor, i.e. whether to reduce the sentence.

interviewed for the purposes of this report acknowledged that the assessment of the reliability of statements provided by collaborators of justice presents challenges, they also observed that this is true for the statements of other types of witness also. The defence lawyers interviewed for the purposes of this report were more critical in this regard. While one acknowledged that the fact that an individual has an 'improper' motive to testify need not mean that the evidence given is not truthful, they were nevertheless of the view that the promise of benefits to persons – criminals – who are out to protect their own interests is conducive to false testimony.

As to German practice, as stated above, there practitioners – defence counsel – have expressed doubts as to the ability of the court to properly assess the reliability of any statement provided, among other things, due to a lack of transparency as regards the initial phase of the process by which an individual becomes a collaborator of justice. This is problematic in light of the fact that the undertakings that may be provided to witnesses in exchange for their testimony are not limited to those set out in Section 46b of the German Criminal Code; indeed, the public prosecutor may provide *other* undertakings to witnesses than those provided for by law, over which they do have (more) control, or the ultimate decision on which does not depend on the court, and which may cast doubt on the reliability of the information provided. A further point of concern as regards the ability of the court to assess the reliability of the testimony is the fact that, in Germany, a collaborator who is under protection is required to sign a con-tract of silence regarding the circumstances surrounding his or her entry into the witness protection programme. While this does not mean that the defence is precluded from questioning a protected witness on such circumstances, the trial court is free to accept any refusal on the part of the witness to answer such questions on this basis. More generally, defence lawyers are critical of the tendency of the courts to believe collaborators. *That* courts tend to believe collaborators does not appear to be contested (one of the prosecutors interviewed for the purposes of this report confirmed this); however, whereas the defence lawyers interviewed put this down to the courts not being critical enough, one prosecutor suggested that this is because reliability is less of a con-cern in practice than it is in theory, in that the testimony of a collaborator need not be unreliable. In Italy also, a defence lawyer representing persons who are accused by collaborators was critical in this regard, arguing that, in light of what is at stake, collaborators are inclined to 'please' the judicial authorities by providing certain information, while the judicial authorities, feeling greatly facilitated in their truth-finding endeavour, tend to believe such information.

In conclusion, while in all four jurisdictions the fact that the institution of collaboration with justice entails the provision of certain benefits to persons who them-selves are suspected of, or who have been found guilty of, committing a criminal offence, in exchange for their testimony in the prosecution of others, is a reason to treat such testimony with caution, the measures adopted in this regard differ as between them. In particular, whereas Dutch and Italian law prescribe special rules of corroboration in this regard, in Germany and Canada there is no such rule. At the same time, while potential unreliability is a reason to treat collaborators' statements with caution, it is clear from the interviews conducted in the various jurisdictions that minds differ as to the issue of reliability and how problematic such statements are in practice.

7.8   Frequency and Success

7.8.1   Frequency[74]

For none of the jurisdictions under examination in this report is it possible to draw reliable conclusions as to the frequency with which the instrument of collaboration with justice is used. Reliable and up-to-date quantitative data regarding the use of the instrument is lacking in all jurisdictions, while it was not possible to obtain such information in other ways, for example, from the literature, case law or the interviews conducted for the purposes of this report. Nevertheless, it is possible to say *something* about the frequency with which the instrument is used in each jurisdiction on the basis of the country reports, and to make a comparison in this regard. Thus, the general picture to emerge from the German country report is that of an instrument that is deployed on a frequent basis, as apparent from the fact that it is in cases involving moderate property crimes, when suspects disclose information about their co-offenders (whereby it may be recalled that the requirement of 'connected offences' is not limited to organized crime in the strictest sense of the term), that the general collaborators' provision is most often applied. It also bears recalling here that in Germany, the instrument is available in respect of a wide range of offences.[75] The overall impression to arise from the Italian country report is also that of an instrument that has been applied frequently, as apparent from, among other things, the quantitative data available on persons subject to protective measures as a result of their collaboration with the authorities within the meaning of this report. It is more difficult to piece together a picture of the Canadian practice in this regard, although it bears recalling here that in Canada, the instrument is not limited to certain offences. A very different picture emerges from the Dutch country report; in the Netherlands the instrument has been applied in a handful of cases only (although it bears observing that quantitative data regarding failed processes, i.e. procedures initiated that eventually come to nothing, is lacking also).

The difference in frequency between Germany and Italy on the one hand and the Netherlands on the other cannot be explained by reference to the scope of application

---

74   In this section sub-question 9 is addressed.
75   See § 7.3.

of the instrument alone; while the German instrument appears to be broader in its scope of application than that in the Netherlands in terms of the offences in respect of which it is available, the Italian instrument is comparable to the Dutch instrument in this regard, i.e. is limited to the most serious offences (although, as stated above, the Dutch instrument appears to be (slightly) broader in its scope of application than its Italian counterpart).[76] An explanation for the difference in frequency between the Netherlands and Italy may, however, be sought in other factors, such as the stringency of the procedure for setting up the cooperation and experience with the instrument more generally. In this regard it bears recalling that whereas in the Netherlands that procedure is quite stringent in that it entails an extensive system of automatic internal and external, judicial, review of the process by which the cooperation between the individual offender and the authorities is set up, as well as the ensuing agreement, in Italy, there is no automatic scrutiny of that process.[77] In general, it is fair to assume that the more stringent the procedure, the less the instrument will be applied. It is also fair to assume that the more experience is gained with the instrument, the more readily it will be applied. Italy has extensive experience with the instrument, whereas the Netherlands does not (where the instrument is also relatively 'young'), while the nature of the organized crime (and, correspondingly, the urgency to address it) also differs as between the two countries.

In conclusion, while in the absence of quantitative data on the frequency with which the instrument of providing undertakings to witnesses is used it is impossible to draw reliable conclusions as to how the jurisdictions compare in this regard, it is possible to piece together a picture thereof on the basis of the country reports. In short, in Germany, it seems, the frequency is highest, followed by Italy, while in the Netherlands it is lowest, and while it is more difficult to piece together a picture of the Canadian practice in this regard, the Canadian instrument certainly appears to have been used more frequently than its Dutch counterpart.

7.8.2   Success[78]

The absence of quantitative data regarding the use of the instrument makes it impossible to draw reliable conclusions as to other issues also, such as the results achieved by the use of the instrument in individual cases and more generally, and the factors contributing to or diminishing its successful use.[79] Moreover, for none of the four jurisdictions was it possible to identify measurable goals for the instrument, making it difficult to draw

---

76   Ibid.
77   See § 7.7.1, in particular.
78   In this section sub-questions 11, 12 and 13 are addressed.
79   For a discussion of when the instrument may be considered to be a success, see § 2.5. There it was argued that success is more than the securing of convictions alone.

reliable conclusions as to whether, in general, the instrument achieves its objectives. Nevertheless, on the basis of the country reports and the views of practitioners set out therein in particular, it is possible to say *something* about the results achieved by (using) the instrument and the relative success of doing so for each of the jurisdictions, and also to make a comparison in this regard.

In terms of results achieved, the general picture to emerge from the foregoing chapters is that in all four jurisdictions, use of the instrument in individual cases has made it possible to obtain convictions that otherwise would not have been obtained. Further, German practitioners cite the ability of the instrument to shorten proceedings, thereby allowing for more efficient prosecutions (which in Germany is a matter of some importance in light of the fact that there, criminal procedure is governed by the principle of mandatory prosecution, and also in light of the length of trial proceedings), in this regard, while in Italy (use of) the instrument has made it possible to gain insight into the internal dynamics and objectives of criminal organizations, and 'to put the mafia on trial', so to speak. In both Germany and Italy, it should be noted, overall, practitioners appear to be satisfied with the possibilities afforded by the statutory framework in place, among other things in terms of the scope of application of the instrument and the undertakings that may be provided or the benefits on offer. In those jurisdictions, it may be said that, overall, the instrument is considered by practitioners, and prosecutors and judges in particular, to be a success in terms of contribution to the investigation and prosecution of (serious) crime, whereby the positive experiences with the statutory framework in place outweigh the negative experiences and/or risks. A somewhat different picture emerges from the Dutch context; numerous (though, not all) practitioners interviewed for the purposes of this report consider the particular legal framework in place to be too restrictive, thereby pointing to the fact that most processes initiated thereunder eventually come to nothing.

If contribution to the investigation and/or prosecution of serious crime is indeed the primary marker of success of the instrument,[80] and the perception of success differs as between the jurisdictions under consideration, the question arises as to what factors are considered to contribute to or to diminish the success thereof. One factor identified in the German country report as key to the success of the instrument is mutual trust between the public prosecutor and the collaborator, and also an awareness of the importance of trust, especially on the part of the public prosecutor, whereby it should be recalled that in Germany, no formal agreement comes about, the process by which the cooperation is set up is largely unregulated and the determination of who is a collaborator of justice and who is not is within the full discretion of the trial judge.[81] In the Netherlands also, the ability of the collaborator to trust the prosecutorial authorities was identified as an important factor in this regard. In the Italian country report, the professionalism of the

---

80 See n. 79.
81 See § 7.2, § 7.5 and § 7.9.

public prosecutor (and the judge) was cited as a factor key to the success of the instrument, in terms of experience and skills in dealing with potential collaborators, who, as (former) members of a criminal organization, have a certain mind-set. In the context of the Dutch instrument in particular, the undertakings that may be provided were identified as an important factor, whereby the suggestion was that the current range of undertakings (which, it bears observing, is comparable to that in Italy and to a lesser extent to that Germany) may be insufficient in this regard.

In conclusion, although the absence of quantitative data regarding the use of the instrument makes it impossible to draw reliable conclusions as to results achieved, on the basis of the country reports it is fair to say that an important result achieved in all jurisdictions is that use of the instrument has led to convictions that otherwise would not have been possible, but that perceptions of success of the particular legal framework in place differs as between them, whereby German and Italian practitioners appear to be more positive than their Dutch counterparts in this regard. Further, there is some overlap between the jurisdictions as regards the factors that are considered key to success of the instrument, the professionalism of the public prosecutor seemingly being crucial in all jurisdictions.

7.9   TRANSPARENCY AND DEBATE[82]

As observed above,[83] the very nature of the institution of collaboration with justice would appear to give rise to the need for *transparency* as regards the benefits that may be granted and the process by which the cooperation between the individual in question and the authorities for the purposes of securing the individual's testimony is set up. Transparency is important not only to the parties to proceedings, but also to the 'outside world', i.e. to the general public. Whether the institution of collaboration with justice may be said to be transparent in a given jurisdiction would appear to be dependent not only on the existence of a general set of rules or legal framework in this regard, but also on the conduct of proceedings in individual cases. Regarding the other issue under consideration in this section, it is not difficult to see how the aforementioned questions might give rise to or fuel ongoing *debate* on the political, scholarly and popular level regarding the use of the instrument of collaboration with justice, entailing as it does the promise of certain benefits to persons who themselves are suspected of, or who have been found guilty of, committing a criminal offence. In the paragraphs below, the similarities and differences between the four jurisdictions as regard the issues of transparency and debate are discussed in more detail.

Turning first to the issue of transparency, while in all four jurisdictions there are formal and publicly accessible rules in place for the institution of collaboration with justice, there are significant differences between them as regards the degree and clarity

---

82   In this section sub-questions 15, 16 and 17 are addressed.
83   See § 7.7.

thereof. Regarding the undertakings that may be provided or the benefits on offer,[84] for example, while in Italy, it should be recalled, the law *exhaustively* lists the benefits that may be granted to aspiring collaborators of justice, in that the law does not allow for other benefits to be provided than sentence reduction and penitentiary benefits, in the Netherlands, the relevant provision of the Dutch Code of Criminal Procedure does not purport to exhaustively list the undertakings that may be provided and there is some discussion in practice (and in the scholarship) as to the lawfulness of certain undertakings, despite such undertakings being listed as lawful undertakings in the Instructions.[85] Similarly, while in Germany the law itself recognizes only two benefits, i.e. sentence mitigation or exemption from punishment, other benefits are provided in practice. In Canada, it should be recalled, the Public Prosecution Service of Canada Deskbook sets out a *non-exhaustive* list of benefits that may be included in the immunity agreement. In the Netherlands, Germany and Canada, therefore, the rules on which undertakings may be provided are less transparent than the Italian rules on the benefits that may be offered. In the Netherlands the (perceived) lack of clarity and/or transparency in this regard[86] is exacerbated by fact that the (principled) restriction of the undertakings that may be provided is not backed up by a clear and cohesive legal framework. There, it should be recalled, the provision of a financial reward for testimony is strictly forbidden, while witness protection is only minimally regulated and the rules on witness protection allow for the payment of a lump-sum to witnesses in order to organize their own protection (which does sometimes happen in practice[87]). Similarly, while the granting of immunity in exchange for testimony is prohibited, the law does not preclude the Public Prosecution Service from granting immunity in accordance with prevailing prosecutorial policy (and later calling that person as a witness).[88]

There are significant differences between the four jurisdictions as regards the regulation (and, by extension, transparency) of the process by which the cooperation between the individual in question and the authorities for the purposes of securing the individual's testimony is set up, also. In the Netherlands and Italy, for example, the written rules governing the institution of collaboration with justice regulate significant aspects and/or parts of the aforementioned process (although there are differences between the two jurisdictions in this regard), whereas in Germany, there is no procedural framework in place, i.e. the process is not formally regulated.[89] In the Netherlands and Italy, therefore, the process by which the cooperation between the individual in question and the authorities for the purposes of securing the individual's testimony is set up is

---

84 See generally § 7.4.
85 See in this regard § 7.4 and also § 7.7.1.
86 See in this regard § 7.7.1.
87 See in this regard § 7.7.1.
88 See § 7.4 in this regard.
89 See in this regard § 7.5. In this regard it should be recalled that, in Germany, the institution of collaboration with justice is a matter of substantive criminal law. See in this regard § 7.2 and § 7.7.1.

more transparent than in Germany. In Germany, the lack of transparency as regards this process is exacerbated by the fact that not every detail thereof is documented and that the talks between the individual in question and the public prosecutor will not always end up in the case file, a fact lamented by the defence counsel interviewed for the purposes of this report in particular. Disclosure, then, is an important mechanism by which to ensure transparency of the process by which an individual becomes a collaborator of justice in individual cases, as is the ability of the defence to question the collaborator at trial. Here it bears observing that in all four jurisdictions, the fact of a witness' collaboration is a matter subject to disclosure (although beyond this fact, the extent of the disclosure differs as between them), and, as stated above, the collaborator of justice is, in principle, required to give evidence at trial. Also worth noting here is that the fact that the process by which protective measures are adopted, and the protective measures ultimately adopted, are not transparent (due to security considerations) has the ability to impact on the extent of disclosure and questioning at trial and, by extension, on the transparency of the afore-mentioned process more generally.[90]

Turning now to the issue of debate, while in none of the jurisdictions does there currently appear to be any political debate regarding the institution of collaboration with justice as such, in the lead up to the adoption of the legislation or rules in each jurisdiction, critical questions were asked and concerns raised. In all four jurisdictions, a particular point of concern was that the promise of benefits may be conducive to false testimony.[91] In Italy, this concern led the legislator to amend the law in 2001 to incorpo-rate measures aimed at filtering out disingenuous *mafiosi* and thereby preventing or minimizing the risk of such testimony. In the Netherlands, it led to the adoption of a special rule of corroboration in respect of the statement(s) of a collaborator of justice, and a requirement that, upon use of such statements, the trial judge provide reasoning in this regard. In Canada, the potential unreliability of the collaborator and their statements is something of a central theme throughout the Public Prosecution Service of Canada's guideline on the use of immunity agreements, whereby Crown (prosecuting) counsel are reminded to be vigilant in this regard. In Italy and Germany, ongoing political debate has led to the introduction of *restrictions* in respect of the instrument. Thus, in 2001 the Italian legislator narrowed the scope of application of the instrument, set restrictions on the penitentiary benefits that may be granted and introduced (procedural) measures aimed at preventing unreliable testimony, in the form of a deadline within which the collaborator had to disclose all information, while in Germany, the restriction was sub-stantive in nature; in 2013, the availability of the instrument was limited to instances in which the crime in respect of which the collaborator proposed to give evidence was in some way connected to the crime committed by the collaborator. By contrast, in the Netherlands, where the legal framework is considered by some Dutch policy makers,

---

90   See § 7.7.1 and § 7.7.2.
91   See in this regard also § 7.7.2.

prosecutors and law enforcement officials to be too restrictive and the instrument has been used in only a handful of cases, the Minister of Justice and Security is proposing to *expand* the instrument in terms of the undertakings that the authorities may provide in exchange for testimony and of the offences in respect of which the instrument is available, in the hope that it will contribute to its success from a law enforcement perspective.[92]

More generally, it may be observed that in none of the jurisdictions examined for the purposes of this report does there currently appear to be any debate as to the legitimacy of the instrument as such.[93] However, while in the Netherlands the debate among scholars and practitioners is (still) focused on the instrument itself, in Italy, the debate appears to have moved on; there, the primary concern now appears to be the fate of the collaborators themselves, specifically, 'protected' collaborators of justice, in terms of their psychological well-being and reintegration into society. In this regard it is worth noting that in Italy, the legal framework for collaboration with justice has been in place for longer and appears to be stricter and clearer than that in the Netherlands (particularly as regards the benefits on offer[94]), and, more generally, that, in Italy, the institution of collaboration with justice appears to be more established than in the Netherlands.

In conclusion, overall, the Italian legal (statutory) framework on collaboration with justice appears to offer the most transparency, in that it exhaustively lists the benefits on offer and regulates important aspects of the process by which the cooperation between the individual in question and the authorities for the purposes of securing the individual's testimony is set up. Regarding the issue of debate, it is noticeable that in all four jurisdictions a particular concern has been the risk of false testimony, and that in one jurisdiction – Italy – the debate appears to have moved on from the familiar epistemic and non-epistemic concerns surrounding the instrument, to the welfare of the collaborators of justice subject to protective measures.

7.10   Concluding Remarks

The purpose of this chapter was to compare the Dutch law and practice with that of Germany, Italy and Canada, with a view to being able to draw lessons from the comparative exercise for the Dutch law and practice. To this end, the law and practice of the different countries were compared within a framework of themes, which were identified not only on the basis of what from a Dutch perspective warrants particular attention, but also on the basis of what was found to constitute 'common ground' between the four countries, in terms of the issues raised by the instrument. It was seen that there are similarities and differences between the countries as regards both the sub-

---

92 See for this proposal § 1.1.
93 See in this regard also § 7.2.
94 See in this regard § 7.4 and § 7.7.1.

stantive and procedural aspects of the instrument. Thus, there are similarities and differences as regards the scope of the instrument itself, the (types of) offences in respect of which it is available and the benefits on offer in this regard, but also as regards the degree and nature of the regulation of the instrument (and the extent to which the legal framework in place can be depicted as an instrument at all), including the procedural aspects thereof, such as the degree of scrutiny to which the process by which an individual becomes a collaborator of justice and the reliability of the statements provided is subject. The question that now needs to be answered is which lessons can be drawn from the comparative exercise for Dutch law and practice (sub-question 19). That question is addressed in the following chapter, in which the findings from the Dutch practice and the comparative law analysis are brought together in an attempt to provide input for the determination of whether or not to introduce a new statutory provision or to refine the existing framework in the Netherlands.

8   Concluding Observations

J.H. Crijns, M.J. Dubelaar & K.M. Pitcher

8.1   Introduction

The preceding chapters described the legislation surrounding the instrument of collaboration with justice and its application in practice in four different jurisdictions. Thereafter a number of relevant aspects of the law and practice in those four countries were compared. In this chapter the final research question of this study is addressed:

19   *Which lessons can be drawn from the comparative exercise for the Dutch regulation of, and practice with respect to, the instrument of collaboration with justice?[1]*

Accordingly, the comparative law analysis from the previous chapter provides the starting point for the concluding observations made here: what stands out when the Dutch legislation and practice are viewed in the light of the law and practice in the various comparison countries and to what extent can the Netherlands benefit from this? The comparative law analysis was however not the only source for the observations in this chapter, given that at certain points reference will be made to the observations made concerning the Dutch legal framework and practice as set out in Chapter 3. As will become apparent from what follows, the findings from the comparative law analysis and from the Dutch empirical study do not always point in the same direction.

     First, a few remarks will be made about the instrument itself. In this regard the general differences with respect to the nature of the instrument and the manner in which it has been legally embedded will then be considered, along with attitudes towards the instrument in the Netherlands compared with the other countries and how successfully the instrument is used in practice. Next, based on the findings from the comparative law analysis, a number of aspects of the Dutch legal framework and practice will be more specifically considered. To be clear, not all of the topics previously discussed in Chapters 3 and 7 will be addressed again here. This chapter will only consider those themes which may be relevant for the legislature in the context of any amendments that may be made to the legal framework. The chapter will conclude with a few brief comments concerning the

---

1   See § 1.2.

possible implications of the foregoing observations for the future of the Dutch legal framework and practice concerning undertakings to witnesses.

8.2   General Reflection on the Instrument Based on the Comparative Law Analysis

The comparative law analysis shows that the instrument of undertakings to witnesses is regulated in one way or another in each of the countries included in this study. There are, however, major differences between the countries in terms of how the instrument is regulated.

Many of these differences can be traced back to a fundamental difference in approach to the phenomenon of undertakings to witnesses as such. While the use of undertakings to witnesses implies that a particular procedure must be followed in the Netherlands and Italy, rewarding a cooperative approach to the proceedings by assisting with the investigation and prosecution of others in Germany, for example, is not limited to situations in which agreements are made with the witness before a statement is made. This is reflected not only in the much more frequent use of the instrument, for example, but also explains the lack of a formal procedure that must be followed in advance of any 'use of the instrument' and the lack of scrutiny in the phase prior to this 'use'.[2] In other words, there is a clear connection between the way in which the instrument is embedded and the basic attitude with regard to that instrument, on the one hand, and how often it is used and the procedure to be followed, on the other.

In terms of the basic attitude, the picture that emerges from the different country reports and the comparative law analysis is that in the comparison countries people appear to be more at ease with the instrument of collaboration with justice than they are in the Netherlands.[3] Even though the risks and objections to the use of undertakings to witnesses also appear to be fully recognised in Germany, Italy and Canada, it would appear that these are not considered to be so momentous that they constitute a material obstacle to the use of the instrument.[4] At the same time this does not mean that there is no criticism of the use of the instrument in the various comparison countries. In both Germany and Italy, for example, at a certain point in time the legislation was restrictively amended; in Germany through the introduction of the requirement of *Konnexität* (about which more will be said below), and in Italy through the introduction of a deadline and by limiting the scope of the legislation and the benefits on offer.[5] Moreover, respondents in both countries, particularly defence lawyers, voiced criticisms of the instrument and the way in which it is used in practice. Nevertheless,

---

2   See § 7.2, § 7.5, § 7.7.1 and § 7.8.1 for further details.
3   See § 7.9.
4   Which is not to say that the instrument is used with the same frequency everywhere. See § 7.8 and § 8.2.2.
5   For further details see § 4.3 and § 5.3.

none of the reports for the comparison countries presents a picture in which the use of undertakings to witnesses as such is (still) considered to be a controversial instrument.

Furthermore – and in line with the foregoing – it is clear from the comparative law analysis that the Dutch instrument of undertakings to witnesses is more extensively regulated than its German, Italian and Canadian counterparts in terms of the procedure to be followed and the matter of scrutiny.[6] Although there may be good reasons why the Dutch legislation is so detailed,[7] at the same time it would seem that compared with the other countries, in the Netherlands there is the most debate about the legal framework and how it should be interpreted and applied.[8] To some extent this would appear to be linked to the fact that in Germany and Italy criminal procedure is governed by the principle of legality, i.e. mandatory prosecution, while in the Netherlands it is governed by the principle of prosecutorial discretion, which raises questions as to whether or not the statutory provisions of the Dutch Code of Criminal Procedure should be considered a closed system for providing undertakings to witnesses.[9] Another explanation for this might be the fact that the legal framework currently in place in the Netherlands is still relatively young and little used, which means that there is still not much jurisprudence to hand by which the legislation can be further interpreted. Nevertheless, this all constitutes something of a paradox.[10]

Although no hard quantitative data could be obtained from any of the countries surveyed, the comparative law analysis also showed that in the comparison countries the instrument of collaboration with justice was used to a greater extent than in the Netherlands.[11] In Germany, in particular, it appears that the scheme is applied on a relatively large scale, which may be due (or, at least, to some extent due) to the way in which the instrument has been embedded. Furthermore, in Germany any accused who provides information about certain offences listed in the law, is entitled to claim sentence reduction under the legislation, even if there has been no previous contact whatsoever with the Public Prosecution Service. While the Italian instrument is less widely available than its German counterpart, there too, it would appear that considerably more use of the instrument is made than in the Netherlands, most particularly in the context of the investigation and prosecution of organised crime. For Canada too, also in view of the wider scope of the legislation, it may be assumed that the instrument is being applied

---

6   To a certain extent this can possibly be explained by the fact that – more than in other countries – the agreement between the witness and the Public Prosecution Service has independent legal meaning, which makes it all the more important that the content and conclusion of such should be regulated in some detail. See § 7.7.1.

7   As previously concluded in this study, this has to do with the long-drawn-out process of enacting the statutory provision and the events preceding it, in particular the IRT scandal and its aftermath. See § 3.3 and § 3.7 for further details.

8   See also § 3.7 and § 7.9.

9   See § 8.4.1 for further details.

10   Melai's quote is apt here: "the more the law regulates, the more it leaves unregulated".

11   See § 7.8.1 for further details.

on a larger scale than in the Netherlands. While the impact of those cases in which the instrument has thus far been used (three)[12] has been significant in more ways than one, the frequency with which the Dutch instrument has been used stands in sharp contrast with that in the comparison countries.

At the same time it should not readily be concluded that the legal framework currently in place in the Netherlands is therefore inadequate or has not been successful. Here it bears observing that the legislation was based on the notion that it would be used with the utmost caution, a notion which – also in view of its aforementioned turbulent history – endures even today among the police and the prosecutorial authorities. Moreover, the statutory provision only entered into force in 2006, making it a relatively young provision compared with its counterparts in the other countries surveyed and also in the light of the subject matter. Added to which, almost immediately after its entry into force the legislation was applied to a very large case (the *Passage* case), which took up most of the capacity of the divisions of the police and the Public Prosecution Service directly involved. Finally, the empirical study conducted in the Netherlands brought to light certain practical problems surrounding the application of the legislation, which are related more to the experience and capacity of the police and the Public Prosecution Service than the soundness of the current legal framework.[13] This is not to say that the study of the Dutch legal framework and its practical application did not reveal any needs and problems which call for further reflection based on the results of the comparative law analysis. The following will therefore consider a number of aspects of the legal framework of potential relevance to any determination to be made of whether or not to introduce a new statutory provision on collaboration with justice or to refine the existing one.

8.3   Scope of the Legal Framework

8.3.1   Types of Offences

The comparative law analysis showed that the scope of application of the German and Canadian instruments is much wider than the Italian and Dutch instruments. In Canada there are no limitations on the types of offences for which the instrument may be used, although it is fair to assume that in practice the instrument will not be used for commonplace crime given that in the preamble to the relevant guideline it is described as an important tool for combatting organised crime. Germany has a limitative list of criminal offences in respect of which the instrument may be used, but this list is fairly extensive and not limited to organised crime; it is, however, a requirement that there

---

12 See § 3.5.2.3 for further details.
13 See § 3.7 for further details concerning the matter of the degree to which the Dutch law and practice concerning undertakings to witnesses may be deemed a success.

should be some inherent connection between the offence on which the witness makes a statement and the offence of which he is accused.[14] From the practice also it is apparent that the German legal framework is applicable in respect of less serious offences also, although it is not clear whether in cases involving such offences formal or informal agreements had been made in advance with the Public Prosecution Service or it was simply a matter of applying the relevant sentencing provision 'afterwards'. The scope in Italy – limited to narrowly defined categories of offences that are generally committed in an organised context[15] – appears to be largely similar to that in the Netherlands, although the scope of the Dutch legal framework is even slightly wider, given that it may also be applied to offences punishable by eight years' imprisonment or more without the need for an 'organised' connection.[16]

This raises the question of whether arguments can be derived from the comparative law analysis for or against widening the scope of application of the Dutch instrument. Here it bears recalling that in his letter to the Lower House in 2013, the then Minister of Security and Justice expressed the wish for the instrument of undertakings to witnesses to also be available in respect of "a different category of offences than those which are currently eligible for undertakings".[17] In this context certain forms of anti-competitive financial and economic crime and corruption were mentioned as more specific examples.[18] Based on the findings of the empirical study in the Netherlands it can be seen that respondents' opinions differ concerning the need for such a widening. Some respondents emphasised that the present legal limits offer sufficient room and that the existing possibilities have so far not been fully utilised, also due to a capacity shortage and lack of the right mind-set among the relevant officials in this context. According to senior

---

14 See § 4.4 and § 8.3.2 for further details.
15 See § 5.4.1 for the precise scope of the Italian legislation.
16 See § 7.3 for further details.
17 See Parliamentary Papers II 2012/13, 29 911 no. 83, p. 6 ff.
18 With regard to introducing the possibility of using the instrument in the investigation and prosecution of corruption, it should be noted that when the Minister suggested this in 2013, the maximum sentences for the various forms of bribery had not yet been increased. This has happened in the meantime, with the result that the applicable penalty for active and passive bribery of a public official (Section 177 and Section 363 CC) has been increased from four to six years and the applicable penalty for the various forms of bribery of non-public officials (Section 328ter CC) is now four years. See the Extending Measures to Combat Financial and Economic Crimes Act *(Wet verruiming mogelijkheden bestrijding financieel-economische criminaliteit)* of 14 November 2014, Bulletin of Acts and Decrees 2014, 445, that entered into force on 1 January 2015. As a consequence, the various forms of corruption potentially all fall within the scope of the present legislation on undertakings to witnesses, although only insofar as they were committed in an organised context and they meet the additional criterion that the offences in question give rise to severe public disorder on account of their nature or connection to other criminal offences (see Section 226g paragraph 1 CCP). Regarding the use of the instrument in the context of corruption, it should be noted that Article 37 of the United Nations Convention against Corruption requires Member States to 'consider providing for the possibility, in appropriate cases' of reducing the sentence or granting immunity from prosecution to witnesses who provide substantial cooperation in the investigation or prosecution of an offence established in accordance with the Convention.

figures at the Public Prosecution Service, however, there may well be situations where it would be desirable to use the instrument, while currently this is not possible under the legislation.[19] There is some truth to both these claims. While the instrument thus far has mainly been used in the Netherlands for the investigation and prosecution of homicides in the context of organised crime, a wider application would certainly be possible under the statutory provision. The close connotation between the legislation and combatting organised crime[20] in particular, appears to obscure the fact that undertakings to witnesses could be used in other more serious cases provided that the offence in question is punishable by eight years' imprisonment or more. This could include armed robbery, aggravated assault and manslaughter or attempted manslaughter. In those cases in which the applicability of the legislation does depend upon the existence of an 'organised connection', i.e. in case of offences punishable by four years' imprisonment or more, as things currently stand in the relevant jurisprudence, the organised connection can be relatively easily assumed. However there is a category of more serious offences which currently fall outside the scope of this legislation. Examples were mentioned during the interviews such as the theft of a Rembrandt painting or corruption outside of an organised context. In Canada or Germany the instrument of collaboration with justice may be used for the purpose of investigating and prosecuting such offences.[21]

Finally, it is clear from the comparative law analysis that none of the countries compared set any limitations in absolute terms with regard to the seriousness of the offence(s) the witness is accused of, in the sense of an upper limit.[22] Accordingly, in all four countries, it is possible to make undertakings to witnesses who themselves are accused of (very) serious criminal offences, such as homicide and/or other offences which are subject to life imprisonment.[23] The Netherlands is the only country to have drawn a boundary in this regard; as apparent from the legislative history, making agreements with witnesses who themselves run the genuine risk of being sentenced to life imprisonment was considered unacceptable by the Minister.[24] Otherwise the determination of whether undertakings may be made to witnesses who are (also) accused of serious offences is to be made on a case-by-case basis, in the context of the assessment of proportionality and subsidiarity. Nevertheless, the question arises as to how hard the aforementioned boundary is, given that under Dutch law, offences punishable by life imprisonment are punishable by a determinate sentence of imprisonment of up to 30 years also, and that, in the absence of minimum sentences, public prosecutors have wide discretion in making

---

19 See § 3.6.2.1.
20 Given the purpose of the legislation insofar as it can be derived from the parliamentary history, this connotation can easily be understood. See § 3.3.
21 In Italy, however, this is not possible. See § 7.3.
22 In Germany, however, the law does set a lower limit in this regard. For further details see § 7.3.
23 In Italy and Germany the law expressly provides for the conversion of a sentence of life imprisonment to a determinate sentence of imprisonment, also setting lower limits in this regard. See § 4.4 and § 5.4.7.1.
24 See § 3.4.2.

their sentencing demands. In principle, therefore, agreements within the meaning of Section 226g CCP may be made with any witness, i.e. regardless of the seriousness of the offence(s) the witness is accused of, so long as the choice not to demand life imprisonment in case of an offence in respect of which this would be possible is not unreasonable. The limited experience thus far in the Netherlands shows that in practice, undertakings have been made to witnesses who themselves are accused of very serious offences; indeed, both witnesses in the Passage case were accused of and later prosecuted for multiple homicides.[25] Regarding the witness Fred R. it may be added that in the first instance proceedings, the Public Prosecution Service demanded life imprisonment.[26] Had the district court sentenced him to life imprisonment, it is questionable in light of the aforementioned prohibition whether the Public Prosecution Service would have made an agreement with him in the appeal proceedings that followed. In the end, however, the district court sentenced him to 30 years' imprisonment (for more or less the same facts that the Public Prosecution Service based its initial sentencing demand of life imprisonment on), in so doing seemingly creating scope for an agreement to be made in the appeal proceedings.[27] In this regard, the question may be raised as to whether the current, somewhat implicit, prohibition on making undertakings to witnesses who themselves run the genuine risk of being sentenced to life imprisonment has much practical meaning.

A further point is that it is not entirely clear whether this prohibition extends to agreements with witnesses who in their own cases have definitively been sentenced to life imprisonment, given that – in contrast to the provision of Section 44a CC in conjunction with Section 226g CCP – Section 226k CCP does not restrict the undertaking envisaged therein to determinate sentences of imprisonment. Equally unclear is whether it applies to undertakings other than sentence reduction, for example, the small inducement envisaged under Section 226g paragraph 4 CCP.[28] In light of the foregoing, it would seem appropriate for the legislature to once again consider the compatibility of the instrument of undertakings to witnesses with instances in which the witness has already been, or runs the risk of being, sentenced to life imprisonment. In doing so, consideration could be given not only to the developments of the past decades in terms of the number of life sentences imposed,[29] but also the fact that – contrary to its original purpose – the existing scheme appears to be particularly attractive to witnesses who themselves are also accused of serious offences.[30] Regardless of the outcome of this reconsideration, the foregoing calls for a clearer articulation in the legal framework of the position adopted in this regard.

---

25 See § 3.5.2.3.
26 In the end, the district court sentenced him to 30 years' imprisonment. See Amsterdam District Court 29 January 2013, ECLI:NL:RBAMS:2013:1294.
27 See Amsterdam Court of Appeal 29 June 2017, ECLI:NL:GHAMS:2017:2495.
28 See § 3.4.2.
29 For further details see § 3.4.2.
30 See § 3.7 and § 8.4.2.

8.3.2 Requirement of a Substantive Connection

Since 2013 the German legislation has required that there should some substantive connection between the offence which the witness himself is accused of, and the offence on
which he makes a statement. By introducing the requirement of *Konnexität* the German
legislature has to some extent attempted to limit the broad scope of the existing
legislation.[31] At the same time the German jurisprudence does not set particularly high
standards for this requirement, which means that it has rarely prevented the instrument
from being used due to a lack of substantive connection.[32]

A similar matter was raised at the time of the parliamentary treatment of the Dutch
legislation, i.e. the question of and to what extent the legislation should include a
requirement that the witness should be part of the organised network about which he is
making a statement. At the time it was also deliberately decided not to include this as it
was considered to be unnecessarily limiting.[33] No arguments were put forward during the
present study that might warrant the inclusion of a requirement of a substantive connection in the legislation. In practice there will often be such a connection, but this is not to
say that in cases where there is none it should not be possible to use the instrument. Were
such a requirement to be introduced, the hypothetical situation of a detainee more or less
accidentally hearing incriminating information about another prisoner, which he then
offers to the authorities in exchange for a reduction in sentence that may or may not
have already been imposed, would no longer be covered by the legislation. Beyond the
general objections to the use of undertakings to witnesses, in the Dutch context there are
no reasonable arguments conceivable for why such a situation should not be covered by
the legislation. In other words, there would appear to be no reason to amend the law in
relation to this point. The use by an accused or convicted person of information about an
altogether different criminal case as leverage in his own case is not something that would
immediately be seen as a problem in the Netherlands.[34]

8.4 Nature of the Undertakings

8.4.1 Open or Closed System?

With regard to the nature of the undertakings that may be made to the witness, what
stands out from the comparative law analysis is that there appears to be little or no

---

31 See § 4.3 for further details of the reasons why the German legislature decided to introduce this requirement.
32 See § 4.4 for further details.
33 See § 3.2.1.
34 The German legislature thought differently about this when the substantive connection requirement was
introduced. See § 4.3 for further details.

discussion in the comparison countries about the matter of what undertakings may law-fully be made to the witness.[35] As apparent from the Dutch country report, even today, in the Netherlands, there is discussion in this regard, on account of differing opinions as to the nature of the relationship between the statutory provisions of Section 226g ff. CCP and the principle of prosecutorial discretion, and whether or not this legislation for pro-viding undertakings to witnesses should be considered as a closed system.[36] Partly as a result of the long-drawn-out parliamentary treatment of the bills which led to the present statutory provision, there is an ongoing discussion in the legal practice regarding this matter, in the context of which the parliamentary and legislative history leaves room for both viewpoints. That such a debate does not appear to be happening in the comparison countries may well be explained for Germany and Italy by the fact that both systems of law are, as mentioned, based on the principle of mandatory prosecution, and also that the legislation in each country has been in force for some time. Be that as it may, the current uncertainty in the Netherlands may well be detrimen-tal to the legitimacy of instrument and, from that perspective, therefore there is much to be said for the legislature reaching a clear decision on this matter, ideally in the text of the legislation itself in the form of an amendment to the present statutory provision or other-wise – insofar as such a clarification would be considered problematic in light of the principle of prosecutorial discretion – by setting out in plain terms during the parliamen-tary debate of any proposed legislation whether the statutory provision should be inter-preted as open or closed.

8.4.2   Amount of the Sentence Reduction

With regard to the amount of any sentence reduction to be granted the comparative law analysis showed that the percentages vary between the comparison countries.[37] It appears that Canada has no restrictions on the amount of the sentence reduction to be granted. In Germany, a sentence reduction of twenty-five percent is the starting point but this can run to a hundred percent for less serious offences.[38] In Italy – where the instrument is reserved for more serious offences – the sentence reduction may amount to two-thirds of the sentence that the court would have imposed without the cooperation of the witness. Schemes like those in Germany and Italy, in which the degree of sentence reduction is made dependent of the severity of the offence of which the witness himself is accused,[39] make it possible to differentiate (more) between individual cases in terms of what the

---

35   See § 7.7.1 and § 7.9.
36   See § 3.3.4, § 3.4.3.3 and § 3.7.
37   See § 7.4.
38   The maximum reduction is reserved for offences where under normal circumstances the court would not impose a prison sentence of more than three years. See § 4.4.3 and § 8.4.3.
39   In the sense that the law applies different 'rates' which are linked to different types of offences.

authorities can offer the witness. Strictly speaking, this is possible in the Netherlands also, but in practice it appears that the maximum amount of sentence reduction – fifty percent – is applied more or less automatically, because the legislation is considered fairly minimal in this regard.[40] It also appears that the effect of the legislation has been somewhat paradoxical, in the sense that – contrary to the legislation's original purpose – it is mainly those accused of more serious offences who appear to have benefited from it.[41] Indeed, it is in cases in which the accused finds himself facing a long prison sentence that the sentence reduction of fifty percent will be most attractive. Viewed in this light, a higher level of sentence reduction could be considered in cases where the witness himself is accused of a relatively less serious criminal offence.

In 2013 the former Minister of Security and Justice expressed his intention to widen the legislation by making it possible in certain (otherwise not further specified) 'exceptions' to allow a sentence reduction of more than half.[42] Whether the comparative law analysis provides support for such a step is unclear. While in contrast to the Netherlands, Germany and Canada allow for punishment to be withheld altogether in exceptional cases,[43] in terms of the amount of sentence reduction on offer, the Netherlands, where the sentence may be reduced by a maximum of fifty percent, does not appear to be out of step with Germany or Italy. This is all the more so given that in the Netherlands – and in contrast to Germany, for example – the point of departure for determining the discount is the public prosecutor's sentencing demand in the case at hand, rather than the (abstract) maximum penalty envisaged by the law, which gives the Dutch public prosecutor much more room to manoeuvre in this regard. The fact that there are significant differences between the countries in terms of the maximum (and, as the case may be, minimum) penalties that may be imposed for the various offences and in terms of the approach to the concurrence of offences, only compounds the difficulty of drawing a meaningful comparison regarding the amount of sentence reduction that may be offered.[44] Nevertheless, it is worth trying to tease out the issue by considering the possibilities in cases in which the witness is accused of an offence (also) punishable by life imprisonment. In Germany, it bears observing, a sentence of life imprisonment may be converted to a determinate sentence of no less than ten years' imprisonment, while in Italy, such a sentence may be converted to a determinate sentence of anything between twelve and twenty years' imprisonment (where the facts in question are so serious as to warrant the imposition of a life sentence, at least). Regarding the most serious offences,

---

40 This impression is based not only on the three cases to date in which the instrument has been used, but also on what respondents have said in this regard, whereby it is fair to assume that such comments are based on procedures to have run aground, also. See § 3.5.2.3 and § 3.6.2.1.

41 See e.g. § 3.7.

42 See the letter from the Minister of Security and Justice to the Lower House dated 5 July 2013 (Parliamentary Papers II 2012/13, 29 911 no. 83, p. 6 ff.

43 See § 8.4.3.

44 See also § 7.4.

therefore, the Dutch legal framework is not out of step with its German and Italian counterparts. In the Netherlands, it should be recalled, offences which are punishable by life imprisonment are also punishable by a determinate sentence of imprisonment of up to 30 years, while in the absence of minimum sentences, public prosecutors have wide discretion in making their sentencing demands. Conceivably, this could – in cases in which the instrument of undertakings to witnesses is being used – result in a sentencing demand that falls below the German and Italian thresholds set out above.[45] In light of the foregoing, the conclusion that the Dutch legal framework is 'lagging behind' its counterparts in the countries compared in terms of the amount of sentence reduction on offer may therefore not be entirely justified, so far as the most serious cases are concerned at least.[46]

If the intention to widen the legislation by making it possible to allow a sentence reduction of more than half were to be followed through on, this then raises the question as to the types of offences for which this should apply and how that could be done in the legal framework. There are two conceivable options in this context. The first is a differentiated model along the above lines, in which the amount of the sentence reduction is made dependent on the seriousness of the criminal offence of which the witness is accused, as is the case also in Italy and Germany. The second is a generic increase in the present maximum sentence reduction where it would be left to those involved in the practical application of this to determine what degree of sentence reduction should be granted in an individual case, in line with the existing Dutch model. The advantage of the first option is that the legislature could determine the maximum amount of sentence reduction appropriate in each case. Here it bears observing that the experience in the Netherlands thus far tends to suggest that if the legislature were to set no limit, in practice the inclination would be to award the maximum sentence reduction permitted (even if only because the witness and his defence lawyer will strive for that).[47]

8.4.3   Immunity and Withholding Punishment

Further to the foregoing what the comparative law analysis revealed was that an important difference between the four jurisdictions in terms of the undertakings on offer

---

45 Thus, the witnesses to whom undertakings were made in the Passage case, Peter la S. and Fred R., were in their own cases sentenced to eight and fourteen years' imprisonment, respectively, for their role in various offences punishable by life imprisonment or a determinate sentence of up 30 years' imprisonment. See Amsterdam Court of Appeal 29 June 2017, ECLI:NL:GHAMS:2017:2494 (Peter la S.) and Amsterdam Court of Appeal 29 June 2017, ECLI:NL:GHAMS:2017:2495 (Fred R.).

46 On the understanding that the aforementioned prohibition on making undertakings to witnesses who themselves run the genuine risk of being sentenced to life imprisonment applies. In other words, the more prospect there is of a sentence of life imprisonment being imposed, the less room there is to promise sentence reduction. See § 8.3.1.

47 See what has already been said about this above. See also § 3.5.2.3 and § 3.6.2.1.

concerns the matter of whether or not it is permitted to grant immunity from prosecution or to withhold punishment altogether. In the Netherlands and Italy this is expressly not permitted, while in Canada and Germany it is possible.[48] This raises the question of whether such far-reaching undertakings should also be made possible in the Netherlands. The problem, however, is that it is unclear in the Canadian and German situations in how many and what types of cases undertakings are made not to prosecute or impose a sentence. It is clear from the legal framework in both countries however that such far-reaching undertakings are subject to certain restrictions. The permissibility of imposing no sentence in Germany depends on the penalty that the witness is faced with (i.e. only in case of less serious criminal offences), while in Canada the permissibility of offering immunity from prosecution depends on the seriousness of the criminal offence that will be cleared up with the aid of the witness statements (i.e. only in the event of serious criminal offences).[49]

It was mentioned in the focus group in the Netherlands that when considering whether and to what extent the possibility of immunity from prosecution or not imposing any sentence at all should be introduced, consideration should also be given to how the sentence reduction currently envisaged actually works in practice. In this context reference was also made to the relatively light sentencing regime in the Netherlands in which a substantial group of accused are sentenced to relatively short prison sentences of no more than a few years.[50] As previously pointed out, the current possibilities for sentence reduction are less favourable for this group of people.[51] As mentioned, when viewed from this perspective, specifically in cases where the witness himself is accused of a relatively minor criminal offence, being able to offer a greater amount of sentence reduction or even omit sentencing altogether, could provide a solution.

Should the legislature come to the conclusion that it should be possible on the basis of the Dutch legal framework to offer more sentence reduction, to the extent that in certain cases, punishment could be withheld altogether, then there are two ways to achieve this result: 1) the possibility of making an undertaking not to prosecute the offences of which the witness is accused at all; 2) the possibility of providing an undertaking that a sentence reduction of 100% will be demanded in the context of the criminal prosecution of the witness himself. The witness himself will naturally be inclined to prefer the first of these two options. This is because in this scenario he would not only be spared the inconve-

---

48 See § 7.4. As previously noted, the prosecution phase in Germany and Italy is based on the principle of mandatory prosecution, while in the Netherlands the decision to prosecute is governed by the principle of prosecutorial discretion. On this basis it would be expected that immunity could be granted in the Netherlands and not in Germany. In both countries the legislature saw cause to make an exception to the point of departure in question (although for Germany, strictly speaking, this is not immunity as such but the wholesale exemption from punishment).

49 See § 7.4.

50 See § 3.6.1.1.

51 See § 3.7 and § 8.4.2.

nience of a criminal prosecution but also – and perhaps more importantly – he will be assured in advance that the undertaking will likely be honoured given that the decision to do so lies in the hands of the same authorities to have made the undertaking in the first place. In the event of an undertaking that no sentence at all will be demanded the witness is still dependent on the court's cooperation for this to happen – as is presently the case in respect of an undertaking on sentence reduction. This second alternative would however be preferable in terms of public perceptions, as well as the transparency and legitimacy of the instrument, if only because this would then safeguard the court's independence and impartiality to pass judgment in the matter of what the witness himself is accused of. Moreover, in that scenario it would be for the judge to decide whether or not the witness can claim the ultimate reward of exemption from punishment in exchange for his cooperation, which in view of the far-reaching nature of this form of reward, would appear to be the appropriate way forward.

8.4.4   Financial Compensation

There is a clear desire within the Public Prosecution Service in the Netherlands to be able to offer financial compensation to witnesses who lend their cooperation.[52] This would be not only an allowance for the expenses incurred by the witness for the purpose of his protection, but also compensation for the loss he suffers as a result of making a statement. In the legislative history the undertaking to provide financial compensation in exchange for a statement is expressly ruled out, based on the idea that a witness statement may not be 'bought'.[53] We will not pursue the question here of whether providing financial compensation would be to the detriment of the reliability of the statement, as is generally assumed.[54] At the moment a witness can only claim financial compensation if at some time in advance (i.e. before the witness presents himself) a reward has been offered further to the Ministerial Circular on Special Payments for Investigation Purposes. Nevertheless, in practice some friction is felt here, not least because TCI informants can be paid for the information they provide to the authorities.[55] Moreover, in the Instructions on Undertaking to Witnesses in Criminal Cases and the case law it has thus far been assumed that it is also possible to reduce a confiscation order by half,[56] which means that the witness then receives a financial benefit from making a statement. Therefore financial incentives have not been banned entirely from the Dutch system of

---

52 See § 3.6.2.1.
53 See § 3.4.3.4. This ban is also expressly laid down in the Instructions on Undertakings to Witnesses in Criminal Cases, Government Gazette 2012, 26860 (entered into force on 1 January 2013), although what is stated there is that an undertaking to provide a financial reward is banned.
54 For further details of the discussion surrounding reliability, see § 3.5.6.1.
55 See § 3.6.2.1. For further details of the Circular referred to and the relationship between informants and witnesses to whom undertakings are made, see also § 3.2.2.3.
56 See § 3.4.3.3.

undertakings to witnesses.[57] It could also be asked what the difference is in principle between a financial incentive and an incentive that is based on a sentence reduction. In both cases these are essentially tools that are intended to persuade someone to make a statement that he would not otherwise be willing to do.

What is clear in any event is that providing a reward or financial compensation is a sensitive matter, not only in the Netherlands. In Italy, for example, it is said in this context that the economic support which these witnesses receive in the context of witness protection should not be seen as a "disguised reward for their testimony". Conversely, in Canada the possibility of providing a financial reward is explicitly recognised in the present legislation, but it is not clear from the analysis to what extent this actually happens. This option is also available in Germany, although it is not expressed as such in the *Kronzeugenreglung*.[58] For the sake of completeness it should be noted that in the comparison countries it appears possible to provide the witness with a certain sum of money in the context of his protection,[59] which – as the present study showed – also takes place in the Netherlands under certain circumstances. These will also be funds that have been earmarked for this purpose.[60]

8.5 PROCEDURE AND SCRUTINY

The comparative law analysis showed that the Dutch procedure surrounding the use of the instrument of undertakings to witnesses is very detailed relative to the various comparison countries – certainly in terms of the scrutiny of the proposed agreement – and that the Netherlands is also the only country which has prior judicial involvement concerning the instrument.[61] The detailed procedure together with the judicial involvement clearly arose from the fairly reticent attitude in political circles (and in academia) towards the instrument when the legislation was enacted, and there are thus clear reasons for that.[62] From the empirical study carried out it was clear that most of the Dutch respondents did not hold a negative view of the present procedure surrounding providing undertakings. No arguments were put forward for major changes to be made in the procedure itself.[63] However the study itself has raised a number of issues in this regard, some of which arose in the comparative law analysis, and some in the study conducted in the Netherlands which looked at how the procedure is applied, interpreted and regarded in the Netherlands. The next section will consider the following: 1) the possibility of setting a

---

57 See also § 3.4.3.4 for further details.
58 See § 7.4.
59 For example, regarding Italy, see § 5.5.1. Regarding Germany and Canada, see Korten 2015, p. 178 and p. 208.
60 See § 3.5.5.1. For further details of the Witness Protection Team, see § 8.6.
61 See § 7.5 and § 7.7.1.
62 See § 3.3.
63 See § 3.5.3.7.

deadline on the potential witness concerning his collaboration; 2) how the multiple levels of judicial scrutiny in the Netherlands work in practice; 3) whether there could be more differentiation in the procedures; 4) the position of the witness to whom undertakings are made; and 5) the requirements with respect to the evidence.

8.5.1   Deadline for the Potential Witness

An aspect that stands out in the comparative law analysis is the fact that two of the comparison counties, i.e. Germany and Italy, have some sort of deadline when it comes to witness collaboration. If an accused wishes to be eligible for undertakings on the part of the Public Prosecution Service in exchange for his statements as a witness, then he will have to express this intention before a certain point in the proceedings and then make his statements within a certain time frame. The aim of such a deadline is to prevent witnesses waiting for a suitable moment when, for strategic reasons, they consider it opportune to cooperate with the police and the prosecutorial authorities, something which in those countries is considered to be undesirable partly in connection with the reliability of the statements to be made.[64] That such situations can also arise in the Netherlands is clear from the example of the second witness to whom undertakings were made in the Passage case. This concerned the witness Fred R. who only presented himself to the Public Prosecution Service as a witness after he had been sentenced by the court in the first instance proceedings – where he had consistently maintained his right to remain silent – to thirty years' imprisonment.[65] Such a situation could be prevented by introducing a requirement that a witness must have presented himself to the Public Prosecution Service no later than before the start of the trial in his own criminal case, for example. Such an option was not specifically addressed during the interviews, as a result of which nothing can be said about whether and to what extent there would be support among the respondents for such a deadline. It was however discussed in the focus group. The members of the focus group however did not see this as an attractive option in the Dutch situation, not least because it would mean that potentially interesting information would be ruled out in advance. People also had reservations about setting a hard cut-off date: why should a potential witness be excluded simply because a certain period of time had elapsed? To put this in perspective, it should also be noted that in Italy, the deadline is less strict in practice.[66] In any event, the findings from the Dutch empirical study did not directly suggest that it would be desirable to introduce a deadline for potential witnesses should they wish to be eligible for undertakings by the Public Prosecution Service.

---

64 See also § 4.4, § 5.4.3 and § 7.5.4.
65 See § 3.5.2.3.
66 See § 5.4.4.

To nevertheless persuade witnesses to come forward as early as possible in the proceedings, it could instead be considered to make use of the avenues currently offered by the statutory provision in a regressive manner, in the sense that potential witnesses who present themselves to the Public Prosecution Service at an early stage or as the first such witness would be eligible for a higher level of sentence reduction than those who only come forward at a later stage or as the second or third witness for example. In this context inspiration could be drawn from the clemency scheme for cartel practices as applied by the Netherlands Authority for Consumers & Markets. This scheme makes a distinction between 'penalty immunity' (*boete-immuniteit*) and 'penalty reduction' (*boetereductie*) in which penalty reduction is then subdivided into three categories, i.e. 30-50%, 20-30% and 0-20%. The question of which category a clemency request then falls into depends on whether the Authority for Consumers & Markets has not already begun an independent investigation of the cartel in question, and whether and to what extent others have gone before the applicant in requesting clemency, as well as whether and to what extent the new applicant provides new information in addition to what is already available.[67] In terms of the instrument of collaboration with justice the basis for such a regressive system could fairly easily be found in the requirements of proportionality and subsidiarity that already apply, following which this could be made more explicit or expanded upon in the Instructions on Undertakings to Witnesses in Criminal Cases, if so required.

8.5.2   Multiple Levels of Judicial Scrutiny

As briefly touched upon above, unlike in the comparison countries, in the Netherlands express provision is made for the scrutiny of the intended agreement by a judge before it becomes final. In this respect the Netherlands is the only country with judicial involvement in the preliminary phase.[68] The fact that such scrutiny does not take place in other countries raises the question of why the Dutch legislation differs so noticeably in this respect. The Dutch country report sets out the background to the enactment of the present statutory provision and the role of the investigating judge in the procedure. From which it is apparent that the prior judicial scrutiny by the investigating judge was a deliberate choice on the part of the legislature and is intended as an additional safeguard to ensure the cautious and lawful use of the instrument.[69] Based on the comparative law analysis, it may be added that there may also be a greater need for prior scrutiny of the agreements in the Netherlands than in the comparison countries. Firstly, the independent legal meaning of the agreement between the Public Prosecution Service and the witness, in relation to the

---

67 See the Policy Regulation on Clemency dated 4 July 2014, Government Gazette 2014, 19745, which entered into force on 1 August 2014.
68 See § 7.7.1.
69 See § 3.3.2 and § 3.4.4.3.

task and position of the trial judge with regard to the instrument of undertakings to witnesses, is greater in the Netherlands than in the comparison countries.[70] Secondly, the Dutch legislation specifically rules out certain undertakings on principle (such as immunity from prosecution). Thirdly, however, the legislation is not entirely conclusive concerning the matter of whether or not certain other undertakings are permissible.[71] As was previously argued in the comparative law analysis, these three aspects mean that there may well be more need in the Netherlands than in the comparison countries for an additional prior (judicial) scrutiny of the intended agreement.[72]

Nevertheless, based on the study carried out in the Netherlands, it may also be asked whether the prior judicial scrutiny of the proposed agreement is sufficiently effective. As apparent from the empirical study, in practice the scrutiny by the investigating judge, by necessity, entails an assessment of the reasonableness of the agreement only. The investigating judge has too little time and too few means available to be able to properly assess the intended agreement in any depth.[73] This need not be problematic, however, given that under the statutory system the trial judge may also assess the lawfulness of the agreement. The Amsterdam Court of Appeal in the Passage case however assumed that primary responsibility for the scrutiny of the lawfulness of the agreements rests with the investigating judge and that, in principle, the trial judge only acts if defence arguments are put forward on the matter, following which the judge will consider such arguments in the context of Section 359a CCP.[74] In this sense it would appear that what is expected in terms of the task to be performed by the investigating judge in scrutinising the lawfulness of the agreement, does not fully correspond with what he can actually do in practice. When the trial judge, mindful of this expectation, then only assesses the lawfulness of the proposed agreement when it is raised by the defence (and by making an assessment of the reasonableness of the proposed agreement), the danger is that at no stage – either pre-trial or trial – will the proposed agreement have been subject to proper, de novo scrutiny, which is not what was intended by the legislature.

The investigating judge only examines the intended agreement within the meaning of Section 226g CCP, but has no overview of what has been agreed concerning witness protection. This can put the judge in a difficult position when the witness invokes agreements made in that context or refuses to lend further cooperation because he is dissatisfied with the protection procedure.[75] Despite the problems and questions which arise with respect to the scrutiny by the investigating judge, practitioners are not in favour of dropping such scrutiny. On the contrary, most of the respondents argued that his task should be extended by also giving him a role in the scrutiny of the witness protection

---

70   See § 7.2 and § 8.2.
71   See § 3.4.3.3, § 3.4.3.4 and § 8.4.1.
72   See § 7.7.1.
73   See § 3.5.4.2 and § 3.7.
74   See also § 3.4.4.4.
75   See § 3.5.4.2.

procedure.[76] If the legislature should decide to amend the legislation concerning this aspect, it would be helpful to indicate precisely what is expected of the investigating judge with regard to the scrutiny of the intended agreements and to provide him with clear guidelines in that context.[77] In addition to this, the working procedures should then be set up in such a way to allow the investigating judge to properly perform the role as it has been assigned to him.

8.5.3 Differentiation in the Procedures to Be Followed

As stated above, the procedure in the Netherlands for using the instrument of collaboration of justice is more stringent than those in the other countries examined. As also discussed above, there are good reasons for this and the present procedure is also widely supported by the respondents who took part in the study.[78] That there is such support should however be seen in the light of the types of cases for which this instrument has so far been used and the types of witness with whom agreements have been made (who themselves were accused of very serious offences). It may reasonably be assumed that there is a certain connection between how an instrument is viewed within a legal system, the scope of the instrument that was determined on this basis, and the way in which the procedure and the use of this instrument is set up. For example, it is clear that the wider scope of the frameworks in place in Germany and Canada is linked to a less stringent procedure, while the more narrow frameworks in place in Italy and the Netherlands, where the instrument was created for the most serious offences, are associated with a much stricter procedure.[79]

Along these lines it could be argued that any changes to the scope of the Dutch legislation – for example, in terms of the type of offences in respect of which the instrument may be used or the nature of the undertakings on offer – could be accompanied by changes to the aforementioned procedure. That there is some room to differentiate into the procedure to be followed is already apparent from the framework currently in place in the Netherlands, given that the stringent procedure was drawn up for the undertakings related to sentence reduction,[80] but that a much lighter regime applies to the 'inducement' within the meaning of Section 226g paragraph 4 CCP. These are decisions that will ultimately have to be made by the legislature, although it bears emphasis-

---

76 See § 8.6 for further details.

77 In that case, consideration should also be given to the question of how to protect confidential information in the remainder of the proceedings. See § 8.6.

78 See § 8.5.

79 See § 7.5.

80 According to the Instructions on Undertakings to Witnesses in Criminal Cases, Government Gazette 2012, 26860 (entered into force on 1 January 2013), this stringent procedure is also to be followed for undertakings relating to the confiscation of unlawfully obtained gains or the withdrawal of a request for extradition or a European Arrest Warrant for the purpose of conducting a criminal prosecution.

ing that the comparative law analysis clearly shows that the scope of the instrument and the procedure for its use should be in alignment.

8.5.4   The Position of the Witness

The country report on the situation in Italy showed that considerable attention is now being given there to the position and welfare of the witness, as well as his re-integration into society.[81] It is increasingly recognised that as a result of his collaboration with the authorities and the strict protection measures associated with that, the witness finds himself in a difficult position which can have a major impact on his psychological well-being.[82] For these reasons, more than in the past, in Italy today more effort is being put into providing long-term psychological support to cooperative witnesses.[83] More attention is also being given to the re-integration of the witness into society when it is no longer necessary to continue the protection measures.[84] Given that the viewpoint of the witnesses themselves was not an important element in this study, not least given the essentially impossible task of asking these people about their experiences, the study provided little comparative material in this context. Nevertheless, one of the Dutch respondents who has personal experience of providing legal assistance to a witness to whom undertakings had been made, specifically mentioned that consideration should be given to the pressure on the witness. He was also in favour of further regulation of the legal position of the witness and better practical facilities for the witness, for example, for the communication with his defence lawyer.[85] Given that most of the respondents were not specifically asked about this matter, little can be said on the basis of the current study about the practice in the Netherlands on this point, whether in absolute or relative terms. Nevertheless, whatever the reasons may be for someone to decide to collaborate with justice, the position of the witness should be properly provided for, both legally and practically, not only in terms of the witness' own interests, but also to serve the interests of the criminal investigation, by ensuring that even after a certain period of time the witness will still be willing to cooperate with the authorities.

8.5.5   Requirements with Respect to the Evidence

The comparative law analysis showed that the reliability of the statement made by the witness to whom undertakings are made is an important consideration in all the

---

81   See § 5.6.6 and § 7.9.
82   Regarding the matter of witness protection, see § 8.6.
83   See § 5.6.6.1.
84   See § 5.6.6.2.
85   See § 3.5.4.3.

comparison countries, but that the standards that apply to the use of the statement as evidence differ.[86] In the Netherlands and Italy the law requires that there must also be supporting evidence before the court can use the statement of the witness. This requirement does not exist as such in Germany and Canada, with the proviso that where there are serious doubts about the credibility of the witness to whom undertakings have been made, the jury in Canada will be urged to look at whether there is support for the contested statement (although it is not required that the available supporting evidence directly points to the accused). The empirical study in the Netherlands showed that the evidence minimum requirements currently provided for in the legislation (in Sections 342 paragraph 2 and 344a paragraph 4 CCP) can be interpreted in various ways, given that it is not clear to what extent 'double coverage' of the accused's participation in the offence is required before it may be concluded that the charges have been proven.[87] This lack of clarity is likely to be removed in the future, given that in the context of the legislative process for modernising the Dutch Code of Criminal Procedure, the legislature has indicated that it intends to scrap the special[88] evidence minimum laid down in Section 344a paragraph 4 CCP, which means that only the general evidence minimum requirement for the use of witness statements in the present Section 342 paragraph 2 CCP will remain.[89] Based on the current jurisprudence of the Supreme Court of the Netherlands this means that double coverage for perpetration will not be required; an substantive connection between the witness statement and the other evidence will be sufficient.[90] Based on the quality of the statement and the character of the witness it will then be up to the court to decide whether in the particular circumstances of the case additional evidence is required. In other words, in future the judge will have the same degree of freedom to make an evaluation in this regard as he or she currently has in other cases in which the witness' statement is decisive. This would appear to be different in a country like Italy, where the requirement of supporting evidence is interpreted in such a way that all aspects of the statement pertaining to the accused's participation in the offence must be corroborated by an independent source.[91] The fact that in Italy higher standards are set for the use of statements obtained by the use of undertakings, does not

---

86 See § 7.7.2.

87 See § 3.5.6.1.

88 In the sense that the evidence minimum requirement is specifically concerned with the statements of witnesses to whom undertaking have been made. See § 3.4.4.4 for further details.

89 See § 4.3.2.4 of the Draft bill adopting Book 4 of the new Code of Criminal Procedure (Trial) and § 5.1.5 and § 5.1.8 of the associated Draft Explanatory Memoranda. Both documents can be consulted at www.rijksoverheid.nl. The formal consultation is still in progress and will run until 1 August 2018, and may yet lead to amendments in the proposal.

90 The Supreme Court of the Netherlands states that a witness statement may not stand alone and must be sufficiently supported by evidentiary material from another source (cf. e.g. SC 6 March 2012, NJ 2012/252 with commentary by Sch.), but does not require that this supporting evidence confirms the direct involvement of the accused (which may also be derived from SC 22 April 2012, NJ 2014/328 with commentary by Rozemond).

91 See § 5.4.6.

necessarily mean that this should also be the case in the Netherlands, particularly given that the requirements in Germany and Canada appear to be less strict. However, it is important that the standards set by the law with regard to the use of the evidence are viewed in relation to how the instrument is used and is legally embedded. Should the legislature decide to widen the scope of the legislation and/or amend the procedure concerning the instrument of collaboration with justice, it would be worth taking another close look at the requirements which apply to the supporting evidence and/or to the giving of reasons for the decision to use the statement of the witness as evidence.[92]

8.6   RELATIONSHIP TO WITNESS PROTECTION

It emerged from the empirical study in the Netherlands that the relationship between the instrument of undertakings to witnesses and the witness protection procedure is sometimes perceived as problematic. While formally separate, in practice the procedures cannot be viewed as separate from one another, not least because the way in which the protection of a witness can or will be provided can affect the witness' willingness to cooperate (or continue to cooperate) with the authorities.[93] The comparative law analysis showed that the processes are separate in the comparison countries too.[94] The Netherlands therefore does not differ in that respect. It does appear however that the authorities responsible for witness protection in the comparison countries are further removed from the authorities responsible for the process by which undertakings are made. The lesson that may therefore be drawn from the comparative law analysis is that both procedures – particularly from the perspective of the outside world – need to be better separated by placing the Witness Protection Team further away from the Public Prosecution Service and to remove responsibility for the witness protection from the latter body.[95] Placing the witness protection at a greater distance however will not necessarily quash the suggestions in practice that the witness protection agreement may well contain elements that would be unlawful in the context of the agreement under Section 226g paragraph 1 or Section 226k.[96]

Given the present situation in which both procedures ultimately fall under the auspices of the Public Prosecution Service, some form of external scrutiny of the witness protection agreement could also be considered. This should mainly be seen in the light of the lack of

---

92 See also the comment made about this by a respondent from the judiciary in § 3.5.6.1.
93 See § 3.4.5, § 3.5.5 and § 3.7.
94 The degree to which and the way in which both procedures are separate from one another differs from one country to another. See § 7.7.
95 It would of course also be possible for the actual implementation of the measures to protect the witness to be placed with another body, but there are clear drawbacks to this given the available expertise in the Witness Protection Team of the police. In the comparison countries also responsibility for the actual protection lies primarily with the police. The police are also responsible for the implementation of the general Surveillance and Protection System. See § 3.4.5 for further details.
96 See § 3.4.5 and § 3.5.5.3 for further details.

transparency surrounding the agreements made (which is unavoidable given the nature of such) and the room for negotiation that there appears to be in this regard in the Netherlands. There would also appear to be widespread support among the Dutch respondents for some form of external (judicial) scrutiny of the witness protection agreement. There is some debate however about how this should be done. Those in the field mentioned that a form of scrutiny such as this would only be useful if it also included some clear means or measures by which a court (or some other body) can assess the agreement and it is clear what must be done if, on the basis of this framework, the assessment is negative.[97] As previously discussed, at present there is no clear legal framework to provide guidance for the agreements which may be made in the context of the witness protection procedure.[98] The lack of clear guidelines also creates room for negotiation. Important to note in this regard is that witnesses are not always included in a witness protection programme (in the sense that they become subject to the whole package of measures), but in certain cases it is made possible for them to arrange their own protection.[99] A further point is that although none of the countries compared provide for external scrutiny of the protective measures to be adopted, there are differences between them as regards the nature of the regulation of witness protection; in particular, witness protection in the Netherlands appears to be less strictly regulated than in the other countries.[100]

In brief, two options were revealed by the study: either more clearly separating responsibilities or setting up some form of independent scrutiny of the agreements relating to witness protection together with a clear assessment framework. A combination of the options is not necessarily the solution, particularly where this would entail the external scrutiny envisaged being carried out by a judge or investigating judge. This is because, in line with the distribution of tasks and responsibilities within the Dutch criminal justice system, it would then be up to the Public Prosecution Service to order the scrutiny of the witness protection agreement made by the judge or investigating judge, and the Public Prosecution Service that would be accountable in this regard. Were the responsibility to be removed from the Public Prosecution Service, however, this could be combined with some form of external scrutiny by an independent body created specifically for the purpose of scrutinizing the protective measures to be adopted. Given the many forms such an approach may take, however, it is difficult to gauge in advance what problems might lie ahead in this regard.

---

97 See § 3.6.2.2 for further details. In this context, consideration should also be given to the question of how and under which circumstances confidential information may be protected for the remainder of the proceedings.

98 See § 3.5.5.1.

99 See § 3.5.5.4.

100 See § 7.6. Regarding the legal frameworks in place in Germany and Canada, see Korten 2015.

8.7 To Conclude

At the end of the third chapter it was concluded in relation to the Dutch law and practice that, although in the recent past some significant results have been achieved in individual cases with the aid of the instrument, both the legal and more practical obstacles to the use of the instrument are relatively high. It was also concluded that the Dutch legislation has been applied differently in practice than was originally intended by the legislature and that – despite the high degree of detail in some areas – in practice, it still leaves certain, often important, questions unanswered.[101] In this regard this study demonstrates that it may be worthwhile to consider amending the existing legislation (or parts thereof).

To answer the question of which points and in what areas the existing legislation should be amended, inspiration may be drawn from the law and practice on collaboration with justice in Germany, Italy and Canada. In this chapter, consideration was given to those aspects of the Dutch law and practice in respect of which lessons may be drawn from the comparison with these three countries. The more general picture to emerge from the comparative law study is that in terms of its scope and what is possible the Dutch legal framework is more restrictive and presents greater obstacles than the legal frameworks in place in the various comparison countries. It should be borne in mind however that the country selection in this study was made on the basis of the prior impression that the legislation in the countries concerned is more flexible and more widely applicable.[102] While this impression was largely confirmed in this study, this is not to say that the Netherlands is lagging behind in this regard. Nor does it imply that the Dutch legislation *should* be widened.[103] In this context it bears recalling that in the past, Germany and Italy have amended their legislation to make it more restrictive, because the legislation in place was perceived to be 'too attractive'.[104] In this context it should also be noted that the present study has provided only a limited view of the matter of how successful the various schemes have been in practice; it would therefore being going too far to conclude that the legislation in the various other countries is more successful than the Dutch legislation, simply because they appear to be wider in scope. The question of whether or not the Dutch statutory framework should be widened ultimately requires a political legal assessment which looks not only at the available options for a wider provision, but also at the nature of criminality in the Netherlands, the criminal law system in place and the risks associated with and objections to the instrument (especially one that is widely applicable).[105] Finally, it should be noted that the actual use and success of the instrument of collaboration with justice is determined only to a certain extent by the

---

101 See § 3.7.
102 See § 1.4.
103 See § 1.3 for the nature and limitations of comparative law analysis.
104 See § 8.2 and the references provided there.
105 See § 2.4 for further details.

statutory framework (and its scope); the sentencing regime more generally and the 'supply' of cooperative witnesses from criminal circles, the capacity, expertise and experience within the police and the prosecutorial authorities and how the available opportunities are used, are equally significant.[106]

---

106 See also § 3.7.

Summary

One of the more far-reaching investigative tools in criminal cases is the instrument of collaboration with justice, the measure by which undertakings are made to otherwise unwilling 'offender witnesses', i.e. witnesses who themselves are suspected or who have been found guilty of committing a criminal offence, in order to persuade them to cooperate with the authorities, by giving (incriminating) evidence in the prosecution of others. While the instrument is generally viewed as a useful tool for penetrating the higher echelons of a criminal organization, it is not uncontroversial, entailing as it does the promise of 'benefits' to persons who themselves are suspected of, or who have been found guilty of, committing a criminal offence, thereby posing a risk to the reliability of the testimony as well as to the integrity of the proceedings and the criminal justice system more generally. This study aims to gain insight into the legal avenues available for making undertakings to witnesses in exchange for their evidence in several countries – the Netherlands, Germany, Italy and Canada –, ultimately with a view to drawing lessons from the comparative exercise for the Netherlands in particular.

The Netherlands has had a statutory provision since 2006 on collaboration with justice. In July 2013 the then (Dutch) Minister of Security and Justice sent a letter to the Lower House of Parliament in which he indicated that in the context of effectively combatting organized crime, he considered it necessary 'to widen the scope for working with members of the civilian population who themselves are – or have been – active in groups which are subject to investigation, or who are in some way closely related to members of such groups'. The statutory framework which currently applies to the instrument of collaboration with justice was felt to be too restrictive, in the minister's view. For these reasons he announced that a bill would be prepared 'that provides for a widening of the Public Prosecution Service's [...] room to negotiate in order, in exceptional situations, to be able to make greater undertakings than are now possible.' As an example the minister referred to undertakings to reduce sentences by *more* than half, i.e. more than may currently be granted, without this amounting to an undertaking of complete immunity from prosecution, or providing financial compensation, which is currently forbidden. The minister also indicated that he wanted to make the instrument of collaboration with justice available for more offences than is currently possible under the statutory provisions. As part of the current legislative process for modernising the Dutch Code of Criminal Procedure, this topic is once again up for consideration by the Dutch legislator. In drawing lessons from the comparative exercise for the Netherlands, then, the more specific aim of this study is to provide input for the purpose of the determination of whether or not to introduce a new statutory provision on collaboration with justice or to refine the existing one. Given that the bill promised by the minister in 2013 aims to widen the scope for using the instrument of collaboration with justice, in selecting countries for the purpose of the comparative exercise, the logical solution was to consider countries where the possibility of making undertakings to witnesses appears at first glance to be greater than in the Netherlands. This is the case in all three of the countries selected.

In examining each of the four countries, it has been considered how the instrument has been legally framed, along with how it is applied in practice, and what kinds of problems and public debate that has engendered. Accordingly, this study is not only concerned with 'the law in the books', but also 'the law in action', and this is reflected in the research questions. Thus, the main questions that have been answered in this study are as follows:

a. How is the instrument of collaboration with justice (hereafter: 'the instrument') regulated in each of the countries under examination?
b. How is the instrument applied in practice in each of the countries under examination, and what are the experiences and results achieved in this regard?
c. How does the relevant law and practice in Germany, Italy and Canada compare to that in the Netherlands?

These main questions are subdivided into nineteen more concrete research questions, which fall into three main categories, reflecting the aforementioned 'law and practice' approach. The first category of questions concern the legal framework. In this regard the researchers looked at the legal basis and history of the instrument; the types of undertakings provided for; the types of offences in respect of which the instrument may be used; the responsibility for using the instrument; the relationship with other measures whereby private individuals provide information for the purposes of investigation and prosecution; and the relationship with the phenomenon of witness protection. The second category of questions addresses the functioning of the instrument in practice by asking what types of undertakings are actually used in practice; how often and on the basis of which considerations the instrument is used or not used; what the positive and negative experiences have been in practice with the instrument and the legal framework in this regard; what results have been achieved in individual cases by use of the instrument; which factors contribute to the successful use of the instrument and which factors form obstacles in this regard; and whether the rules on collaboration with justice achieve their objective in general. The third category of questions addresses the matters of scrutiny, transparency and debate by asking to what extent the use of the instrument is subject to (judicial) scrutiny; in how far the (use of the) instrument is publicly transparent; to what extent there is debate regarding the use of the instrument; and in how far and in what regard scrutiny, transparency and debate has led to changes in the regulation of the instrument. All of these questions have been answered for each of the four countries, eventually leading to the answers to the final two sub-questions: in which respect do the law and practice in Germany, Italy and Canada correspond to that in the Netherlands, and in which respect do they differ (sub-question 18); and which lessons can be drawn from the comparative exercise for the Dutch regulation of, and practice with respect to, the instrument (sub-question 19)?

To determine the legal framework and how it was arrived at, an analysis was carried out in the form of desk research of the relevant legislation and regulations, the case law, the literature on the topic and the policy documents and parliamentary documentation available for each of the countries included in the study. It was also attempted – insofar as possible – to gain insight into how often the instrument is used and what variations there may be in the undertakings given. Further, in all the countries concerned semi-structured interviews were conducted with various practitioners in the field including public prosecutors, police officers, judges and defence lawyers. These interviews focused on: 1) determining the common methods in practice insofar as these are not clearly described in public or other documents; 2) providing insight into how often the instrument is used; 3) highlighting the problems encountered and successes achieved, and; 4) creating an inventory of the views held and perceived needs in the practice with regard to the use of the instrument. For the Netherlands a focus group was also organized in which representatives of the various professional groups were brought together to reflect on the results of the study in the Netherlands and the countries compared. This offered an opportunity, on the one hand, to validate and probe more deeply into the perceptions surrounding the instrument of collaboration with justice in Dutch practice and, on the other hand, to examine how representatives of various professional groups view the legislation and the methods used in the countries compared.

The report comprises an introduction (Chapter 1), a more detailed consideration of the instrument of collaboration with justice as such (Chapter 2), four country reports (Chapters 3 to 6), a comparative law analysis (Chapter 7) and a concluding analysis in which the findings from the Dutch practice and the comparative law analysis are brought together, in an attempt to provide input for the determination of whether or not to introduce a new statutory provision or to refine the existing framework in the Netherlands (Chapter 8).

Following the introduction to the research project and its exact scope and methodology in Chapter 1, Chapter 2 looks more closely in general terms at the subject of this comparative law study by describing in more detail the instrument of undertakings to witnesses and its aims. The risks and objections associated with the use of this instrument are also discussed and the question of when the use of the instrument may be deemed a success was also considered, along with the perspectives which need to be taken into account when answering this question. This paved the way for the country reports in which the legislation and the practical implementation of the instrument of undertakings to witnesses are set out for each of the four countries included in this study. Finally, brief consideration is given to the jurisprudence of the ECtHR in this regard, in terms of the right to a fair trial (Article 6 ECHR).

The country reports in Chapters 3 to 6 – in which the aforementioned sub-questions are addressed for each of the four countries involved in this research – are largely structured in the same way although the emphasis may be placed in different areas and the problems which arise in practice may differ. Each of the country reports first considers the development of the legal framework. Various aspects of the scheme are then further examined, followed by an examination of the practice. The individual country reports make no comparison with the Netherlands. In other words, the law and practice in the various countries were described entirely independently, without reference to the Dutch situation. In light of the richness of the various country reports it is impossible to summarize them all here, but the answers to the research questions in the annexes to the country reports provide a good first insight into the findings relating to each country. Regarding the Netherlands (Chapter 3) it was concluded that since the introduction of the current legislation in 2006, the use of the instrument has been limited. Nevertheless some satisfying results appear to have been achieved in individual cases with the aid of this instrument. At the same time, it became apparent that there are significant legal and practical obstacles to the (successful) use of the instrument. Among other things, this is reflected in the fact, as shown by the empirical research, that while exploratory talks with potential witnesses for the purpose of determining whether or not an agreement could be reached have taken place much more often in recent years, the majority of these talks produced no result. It also appears that the scheme is most favourable to those accused of more serious crimes, who find themselves facing a long (or very long) prison sentence, while originally the scheme was intended mainly for witnesses who are accused of relatively less serious crimes. It also appears that several questions and problems which arise in practice cannot be adequately resolved by reference to the legislation. Examples of this include the ongoing discussion regarding the permissibility of certain undertakings, the sometimes unclear relationship in practice with the agreements concerning witness protection, and the lack of clarity concerning the scope of the scrutiny of the proposed agreement by the investigating judge.

In Chapter 7 the Dutch law and practice is compared to that of Germany, Italy and Canada, with a view to being able to draw lessons from the comparative exercise for the Dutch law and practice. To this end, the law and practice of the different countries were compared within a framework of themes. It was seen that there are similarities and differences between the countries as regards the scope of the instrument itself, the (types of) offences in respect of which it is available and the benefits on offer in this regard, but also as regards the degree and nature of the regulation of the instrument (and the extent to which the legal framework in place can be depicted as an instrument at all), including the procedural aspects thereof, such as the degree of scrutiny to which the process by which an individual becomes a collaborator of justice and the reliability of the statements provided is subject. There were also significant differences between the countries with regard to the use of the instrument in practice, for instance in terms of frequency. While the general picture to emerge from the German, Italian and Canadian country reports is that of an instrument that is deployed on a (fairly) frequent basis, in the Netherlands the instrument has been applied in a handful of cases only since the introduction of the current legislation in 2006. And in terms of the basic attitude, the picture is that in the other countries the legal community appears to be more at ease with the instrument of undertakings to witnesses than it is in the Netherlands.

Chapter 8 addresses the question of which lessons can be drawn from the comparative exercise for Dutch law and practice, in an attempt to provide input for the determination of whether or not to introduce a new statutory provision or to refine the existing framework in the Netherlands. The more general picture presented by the comparative law study is that in terms of its scope and what is possible the Dutch legislation is more restrictive and gives rise to greater obstacles than the legislation in the various other countries. From this perspective, the comparative law analysis combined with the findings on the Dutch law and practice in Chapter 3 gives cause for reconsideration of several aspects of the Dutch scheme, for instance with regard to: the types of offences in respect of which the instrument is available; the ability to make agreements with witnesses who themselves run the genuine risk of being sentenced to life imprisonment or who have already been convicted thereto; the open or closed character of the scheme with regard to the nature of the undertakings that may be provided; and the ability to make undertakings entailing full immunity from prosecution or total exemption from punishment. Further, this research gives cause to reconsider some procedural aspects of the current framework as well as the relationship between the instrument of undertakings to witnesses and the protection of witnesses and the responsibilities in this regard. However, the foregoing does not mean that the Dutch scheme is more restrictive than its German, Italian and Canadian counterparts in all respects. For instance, with regard to the amount of sentence reduction that may be granted, the Dutch scheme seems to be fairly in line with its Italian and German counterparts (at least in cases in which the collaborator himself is accused of more severe crimes). In conclusion, on the basis of the findings of the legal and empirical research set out in the Dutch country report in Chapter 3 and the comparative analysis in Chapter 7, Chapter 8 identifies aspects of the Dutch law and practice on collaboration with justice that give cause for reconsideration.

In reconsidering the Dutch scheme it should be borne in mind however that the selection of countries for the purposes of the comparative exercise was made on the basis of the impression that the legislation in these countries is more flexible and more widely applicable. While this impression was largely confirmed in this study, this is not to say that the Netherlands is lagging behind in this regard. Nor does it imply that the Dutch legislation *should* be widened. In this context it should be noted that in the past, Germany and Italy have amended their legislation to make it more restrictive, because the legislation in place was perceived to be 'too attractive'. In this context it should also be noted that the present study has provided only a limited view of the matter of how successful the various schemes have been in practice; it would therefore being going too far to conclude that the legislation in the various other countries is more successful than the Dutch legislation, simply because they appear to be wider in scope. The question of whether or not the Dutch statutory framework should be widened ultimately requires a political legal assessment which looks not only at the available options for widening the scheme, but also at the risks and objections to the instrument (and its wider application). Finally, the actual use and success of the instrument of collaboration with justice is determined only to a certain extent by the statutory framework (and its scope); the sentencing regime more generally and the 'supply' of cooperative witnesses from criminal circles, the capacity, expertise and experience within the police and the prosecutorial authorities and how the available opportunities are used, are equally significant.

REFERENCES

Abels 2005
I.M. Abels, 'Toezeggingen aan getuigen in strafzaken of toch deals met criminelen', *Ars Aequi* 2005, p. 861-864.

Achenbach 2015
H. Achenbach, 'Die Bußgeldtatbestände des GWB', in: H. Achenbach, A. Ransiek & T. Rönnau (eds.), *Handbuch Wirtschaftsstrafrecht*, 4th edition, Heidelberg: C.F. Müller 2015, p. 442-444.

Allgeier 2012
S. Allgeier, 'Die Kronzeugenregelung – eine kritische Anmerkung', in: *Abschied von der Wahrheitssuche. 35. Strafverteidigerstag*, Berlin: Schriftenreihe der Strafverteidigungvereinigungen 2012.

D'Ambrosio 2002
L. D'Ambrosio, *Testimoni e Collaboratori di Giustizia*, Cedam 2012.

Auricchio, Panico & Pini 2009
A. Auricchio, D. Panico & S. Pini, *I Profili Giuridici dell' Informatore di Polizia Giudiziaria*, 4 Rassegna dell'Arma 2009.

Van der Bel, Van Hoorn & Pieters 2013
D. van der Bel, A.M. van Hoorn & J.J.T.M. Pieters, *Informatie en Opsporing. Handboek informatieverwerving, -verwerking en -verstrekking ten behoeve van de opsporingspraktijk*, Zeist: Uitgeverij Kerckebosch 2013.

Berger & Stribopoulos 2012
B.L. Berger & J. Stribopoulos, *Unsettled Legacy: Thirty Years of Criminal Justice under the Charter*, LexisNexis 2012.

Beulke 2016
W. Beulke, *Strafprozessrecht*, 13th edition, Heidelberg: C.F. Müller 2016.

Beune en Giebels 2012

K. Beune en E. Giebels, *The management of protected witnesses: a behavioural perspective*, Enschede: University of Twente 2012.

Bleichrodt 2010

F.W. Bleichrodt, *Over burgers en opsporing* (oratie Rotterdam), Deventer: Kluwer 2010.

Bleichrodt en Korten 2012

F.W. Bleichrodt en M.C.P. Korten, 'Het onontgonnen terrein van getuigenbescherming', *NJB* 2012, p. 1564-1571.

Bohlander 2012

M. Bohlander, *Principles of German Criminal Procedure*, Oxford: Hart Publishing 2012.

Bokhorst 2012

R.J. Bokhorst, *De Wet afgeschermde getuigen in de praktijk*, Memorandum 2012-3, Den Haag: WODC 2012 (available at: www.wodc.nl).

Bolzoni 2008

A. Bolzoni, *Parole d' Onore*, Biblioteca universale Rizzoli 2008.

Van Boom en Van Gestel 2015

W. van Boom en R. van Gestel, 'Rechtswetenschappelijk onderzoek. Uitkomsten van een landelijke enquête', *NJB* 2015, p. 1336-1347.

Brinkhoff 2014

S. Brinkhoff, *Startinformatie in het strafproces* (diss. Nijmegen), Deventer: Kluwer 2014.

Brook et al. 2016

C.A. Brook, B. Fiannaca, D. Harvey, P. Marcus, J. McEwan & R. Pomerance, 'A Comparative Look at Plea Bargaining in Australia, Canada, England, New Zealand, and the United States', 57 *William & Mary Law Review* 2016, 1147.

Buruma 2004

Y. Buruma, 'Deals met criminelen. Antwoord aan een bedreigde officier', *Trema* 2004, p. 197-200.

Caianiello 2010
M. Caianiello, 'Chapter 9: Italy', in: *Effective Criminal Defence in Europe*, Intersentia 2010.

Caianiello 2012
M. Caianiello, 'The Italian Public Prosecutor: An Inquisitorial Figure in Adversarial Proceedings?', in: E. Luna & M.L. Wade (eds.), *The Prosecutor in Transnational Perspective*, Oxford: Oxford University Press 2012.

Cameron 1996
J. Cameron, *The Charter's Impact on the Criminal Justice System*, Carswell 1996.

Cameron & Stribopoulos 2008
J. Cameron & J. Stribopoulos (eds.), *The Charter and Criminal Justice. Twenty-five years later*, LexisNexis 2008.

Cauduro & Di Nicola 2005
A. Cauduro & A. Di Nicola, 'Comparative Study: Italy', in: G. Vermeulen (ed.), *EU Standards in Witness Protection and Collaboration with Justice*, 2005.

Christoph 2014
S. Christoph, 'Die nicht mehr ganz so große Kronzeugenreglung', *KritV* 2014, 1.

Crijns 2004
J.H. Crijns, 'Een pleidooi voor een wettelijke regeling inzake toezeggingen aan getuigen', *NJB* 2004, p. 1172-1173.

Crijns 2010
J.H. Crijns, *De strafrechtelijke overeenkomst. De rechtsbetrekking met het Openbaar Ministerie op het grensvlak van publiek- en privaatrecht* (diss. Leiden), Deventer: Kluwer 2010.

Dannecker 2015
G. Dannecker, 'Nationales Kartellrecht', in: T. Rotsch (ed.), *Criminal Compliance*, Baden-Baden: Nomos 2015, p. 499-502.

Dubelaar 2014
M.J. Dubelaar, *Betrouwbaar getuigenbewijs. Totstandkoming en waardering van strafrechtelijke getuigenverklaringen in perspectief* (diss. Leiden), Deventer: Kluwer 2014.

Eisenberg 2008
U. Eisenberg, 'Zeugenschutzprogramme und Wahrheitsermittlung im Strafprozess', in: E. Weßlau & W. Wohlers (eds.), *Festschrift für Gerhard Fezer*, Berlin: De Gruyter 2008.

Enquêtecommissie opsporingsmethoden 1996
Enquêtecommissie opsporingsmethoden, *Inzake opsporing*, Den Haag: Sdu uitgevers 1996.

Europol 2013
Europol, *Threat Assessment: Italian Organised Crime*, Europol: The Hague, 2013.

Forum Levenslang 2011
Forum Levenslang, *Factsheet feitelijke gegevens over de levenslange gevangenisstraf*, 2011 (available at: www.forumlevenslang.nl).

Frahm 2014
L.N. Frahm, *Die allgemeine Kronzeugenregelung. Dogmatische Probleme und Rechtspraxis des § 46b StGB*, Berlin: Duncker & Humblot 2014.

Fyfe & Sheptycki 2005
N. Fyfe & J. Sheptycki, *Facilitating witness co-operation in organised crime cases: an international review*, Home Office Online Report 27/05, London: Home Office Publications 2005.

Gialuz 2014
M. Gialuz, 'The Italian Code of Criminal Procedure: A Reading Guide', in: M. Gialuz, L. Lupària & F. Scarpa (eds.), *The Italian Code of Criminal Procedure: Critical Essays and English Translation*, CEDAM 2014.

Giordano 2001
P. Giordano, 'Il verbale illustrativo a garanzia del rapporto', in: *Guida al Diritto* 2001.

Gounev & Bezlov 2010
P. Gounev and T. Bezlov, *Examining the Links Between Organised Crime and Corruption*, Sofia: Publication of the Centre for the Study of Democracy 2010.

Hardinghaus 2015

A. Hardinghaus, *Strafzumessung bei Aufklärungs- und Präventionshilfe. Der Kronzeuge im deutschen Strafrecht unter besonderer Berücksichtigung von § 46b StGB*, München: Herben UTZ Verlag 2015.

Heubrock et al. 2013

D. Heubrock et al., *Umgang mit bedrohten Zeugen. Empfehlungen zur Vernehmung und zum Zeugenschutz*, Frankfurt: Verlag für Polizeiwissenschaft 2013.

Hogg 2012

P.W. Hogg, *Constitutional Law of Canada*, Carswell, 2012.

Van Hoorn 1996

A.M. van Hoorn, *De Wet getuigenbescherming. Een uitzonderlijke regeling*, Leiden: Rijksuniversiteit Leiden 1996 (available at: via www.wodc.nl).

Hoyer 1994

A. Hoyer, 'Die Figur des Kronzeugen', *JZ* 1994.

Illuminati 2005

G. Illuminati, 'The Frustrated Turn to Adversarial Procedure in Italy (Italian Criminal Procedure Code of 1988)', *4 Washington University Global Studies Law Review*, 3, 2005.

Illuminati & Caianiello 2007

G. Illuminati and Michele Caianiello, 'The Investigative Stage of the Criminal Process in Italy', in: E. Cape, J. Hodgson, T. Prakken, T. Spronken (eds.), *Suspects in Europe: Procedural Rights at the Investigative Stage of the Criminal Process in the European Union*, Mortsel: Intersentia 2007.

Janssen 2013

S.L.J. Janssen, *De kroongetuige in het Nederlandse strafproces. Vertrouwen is goed, controle is beter* (diss. Leiden), Den Haag: Boom Juridische uitgevers 2013.

Jeßberger 2015

F. Jeßberger, '*Nulla poena quamvis in culpa*. Anmerkungen zum Kronzeugenregelung § 46b StGB', in: H. Satzger, C. Fahl, S. Swoboda & E. Müller (eds.), *Festschrift für Werner Beulke*, Heidelberg: C.F. Müller 2015.

Kaspar & Christoph 2016a
J. Kaspar & S. Christoph, 'Kronzeugenregelung und Strafverteidigung', *StV* 2016, 5.

Kaspar & Christoph 2016b
J. Kaspar & S. Christoph, 'Die Kronzeugenregelung in der Rechtswirklichkeit – erste empirische Erkenntnisse aus einem Forschungsprojekt zur Aufklärungs- und Präventionshilfe gemäß § 46b StGB', in: F. Neubacher, N. Bögelein (eds.), *Krise, Kriminalität, Kriminologie*, Mönchengladbach: Forum Verlag Godesberg 2016.

Kneba 2011
N. Kneba, *Die Kronzeugenregelung des § 46b StGB*, Berlin: Duncker & Humblot 2011.

König 2009
S. König, 'Wieder da: Die große Kronzeugenregelung', *NJW* 2009, 34.

Korten 2015
M.C.P. Korten, *Getuigenbescherming in Nederland* (diss. Rotterdam), 2015 [in-house publication].

Labs 2016
K. Labs, *Die strafrechtliche Kronzeugenregelung. Legitimation einer rechtlichen Grauzone?*, Marburg: Tectum Verlag 2016.

Laudati 2003
A. Laudati, 'La Collaborazione con la Giustizia ed il Verbale Illustrativo dei Contenuti. Un Oggetto Misterioso Introdotto dalla Legge 45/2001', in: 3 *Diritto e Giustizia*, 2003.

Lindemann 2012
M. Lindemann, *Voraussetzungen und Grenzen legitimen Wirtschaftsstrafrechts*, Tübingen: Mohr Siebeck 2012.

Lorenz 2016
M. Lorenz, 'Die Zulässigkeit der Vertraulichkeitszusage gegenüber Vertrauenspersonen und Informanten sowie deren Auswirkung auf das Strafverfahren', *StraFo* 2016, 316.

De Lucia 2016
M. De Lucia, 'I Collaboratori e i Testimoni di Giustizia', presented at the Conference: *Il Processo di Mafia Trent' Anni Dopo*, Court of Cassation, 14 October 2016 (forthcoming publication).

Malek 2010

K. Malek, 'Die neue Kronzeugenregelung und ihre Auswirkungen auf die Praxis der Strafverteidigung', *StV* 2010, 4.

Mareso & Pepino 2013

M. Mareso & L. Pepino, *Dizionario Enciclopedico di Mafie e Antimafia*, Torino: Gruppo Abele Edizioni 2013.

Mayring 2015

P. Mayring, *Qualitative Inhaltsanalyse. Grundlagen und Techniken*, 12th edition, Weinheim: Beltz 2015.

Mehrens 2001

S. Mehrens, *Die Kronzeugenregelung als Instrument zur Bekämpfung organisierter Kriminalität. Ein Beitrag zur deutsch-italienischen Strafprozeßrechtsvergleichung*, Freiburg i. Br.: Edition Iuscrim 2001.

Mellinghof 2014

R. Mellinghoff, 'Strafgleichheit', in: D. Heid et al. (eds), *Festschrift für Manfred A. Dauses*, Verlag C.H. Beck 2014.

Menza 1999

A.J. Menza, 'Witness immunity: unconstitutional, unfair, unconscionable', *Seton Hall Constitutional Law Journal* 1999, vol. 9, p. 505-547.

Mischkewitz 2014

A. Mischkewitz, *Das staatliche Zeugenschutzprogramm in Deutschland. Übersicht, Analyse der Rechtslage und Problemfelder des polizeilichen Zeugenschutzes*, Holzkirchen: Felix-Verlag 2014.

Montana 2009

R. Montana, 'Paradigms of judicial supervision and co-ordination between police and prosecutors: the Italian case in a comparative perspective', *European Journal of Crime, Criminal Law and Criminal Justice* 2009, Vol. 17(4), p. 309–333.

Montanaro 2013

G. Montanoro, *La Verità del Pentito. Le Rivelazioni di Gaspare Spatuzza sulle Stragi Mafiose*, Sperling & Kupfer 2013.

Montanaro & Silvestri 2005
G. Montanaro & F. Silvestri, *Dalla Mafia allo Stato. I Pentiti: Analisi e Storie*, Torino: Gruppo Abele Edizioni 2005.

Mühlhoff & Mehrens 1999
U. Mühlhoff & S. Mehrens, *Das Kronzeugengesetz im Urteil der Praxis*, Baden-Baden: Nomos 1999.

Nijboer 1994
J.F. Nijboer, *Een verkenning in het vergelijkend straf- en strafprocesrecht*, Arnhem: Gouda Quint 1994.

Oderkerk 2001
M. Oderkerk, 'The Importance of Context: Selecting Legal Systems in Comparative Legal Research', *NILR* 48:293 et seq.

Ordner 2017
J. Ordner, 'Die Verständigungseignung von vermögensabschöpfenden Rechtsfolgen', *wistra* 2017, Vol. 36(2), p. 50-57.

Panzavolta 2005
M. Panzavolta, 'Reforms and Counter-Reforms in the Italian Struggle for an Accusatorial Criminal Law System', *North Carolina Journal of International Law and Commercial Regulation* 2005, Vol. 30(3), p. 577-624.

Parrini 2007
D. Parrini, *Collaboratori e Testimoni di Giustizia: Aspetti Giuridici e Sociologici*, 2007 (available at: http://www.altrodiritto.unifi.it/ricerche/law-ways/parrini/).

Peglau 2013
J. Peglau, 'Neues zur Kronzeugenregelung – Beschränkung auf Zusammenhangstaten', *NJW* 2013, 27, p. 1910-1913.

Penney, Rondinelli & Stribopoulos 2011
S. Penney, V. Rondinelli & J. Stribopoulos, *Criminal Procedure in Canada*, LexisNexis, 2011.

Plooy 2004

J. Plooy, 'Toezeggingen aan getuigen in strafzaken – de rechtsstaat in het geding?', *Trema* 2004, p. 185-196.

Pluimer 2015

O.S. Pluimer, *Criminele burgerinfiltratie. Een onderzoek naar de herintroductie van de criminele burgerinfiltrant in het Nederlandse strafproces*, Amersfoort: Celsus Juridische Uitgeverij 2015.

Potrebic Piccinato 2004

M. Potrebic Piccinato, *Plea Bargaining*, Department of Justice of Canada 2004 (available at http://www.justice.gc.ca/eng/rp-pr/csj-sjc/ilp-pji/pb-rpc/pb-rpc.pdf).

Roberts & Grossman 2008

J. Roberts & M. Grossman, *Criminal Justice in Canada: A Reader*, 2008.

De Roos 2006

Th.A. de Roos, 'Bewijs met bijzondere getuigen', *Strafblad* 2006, p. 5-13.

Roxin 2015

C. Roxin, *Täterschaft und Tatherrschaft*, 9th edition, Berlin: De Gruyter 2015.

Ruggiero 2012

R.A. Ruggiero, *L' Attendibilità delle Dichiarazioni dei Collaboratori di Giustizia nella Chiamata in: Correità*, Torino: Giappichelli 2012.

Schuyt 2009

P.M. Schuyt, *Verantwoorde straftoemeting* (diss. Nijmegen), Deventer: Kluwer 2009.

Seifman & Freidberg 2001

R. Seifman & A. Freidberg, 'Plea bargaining in Victoria: The role of counsel', *Criminal Law Journal* 2001, vol. 25, p. 64-74.

Sharpe & Roach 2013

R.J. Sharpe & K. Roach, *The Charter of Rights and Freedoms*, Irwin, 2013.

Siems 2014

M. Siems, *Comparative law*, Cambridge: Cambridge University Press 2014.

Stuart 2014

D. Stuart, *Charter Justice in Canadian Criminal Law*, Carswell, 2014.

Tak 1997

P.J.P. Tak, 'Deals with Criminals: Supergrasses, Crown Witnesses and Pentiti', *European Journal of Crime, Criminal Law and Criminal Justice* 1997, Vol. 5(1), p. 2-26.

Tak 2000

P.J.P. Tak, *Heimelijke opsporing in de Europese Unie. De normering van bijzondere opsporingsmethoden in de landen van de Europese Unie*, Antwerpen/Groningen: Intersentia Rechtswetenschappen 2000.

Transcrime 2007

Transcrime, *Terrorism and Counterterrorism in Italy from the 1970's to date: A Review*, Università degli Studi di Trento 2007 (available at: http://www.transcrime.it/wp-content/uploads/2013/11/14_Terrorism_and_Counterterrorism_in_Italy1.pdf).

Turone 2007

G. Turone, *Legal Frameworks and Investigative Tools For Combating Organized Transnational Crime In the Italian Experience*, 134th International Training Course Visiting Experts' Papers, Tokyo: UNAFEI 2007, p. 48-64.

Van Allen 2009

B. Van Allen, *Police Powers: Law, Order and Accountability*, Pearson, 2009.

Van Allen 2012

B. Van Allen, *Criminal Investigation: In Search of the Truth*, Pearson, 2012.

Vasiliev et al. 2013

S. Vasiliev et al., 'Introduction', in: G. Sluiter et al. (eds.), *International Criminal Procedure. Principles and Rules*, Oxford: Oxford University Press, p. 1-37.

Vigna 1992

P.L. Vigna, 'La Gestione Giudiziaria del Pentito: Problemi Deontologici, Tecnici e Psicologici', in: A.A.V.V., *Chiamata in Correità e Psicologia del Pentitismo nel Nuovo Codice di Procedura Penale*, Padova 1992.

Vigna 2005

P.L. Vigna, *Report on the Protection of Witnesses and Collaborators of Justice in the Fight against Terrorism and Organized Crime: the Italian Experience*, 3rd High-level Multilateral Meeting of the Ministries of the Interior, Poland 2005.

Watt 2003

D. Watt, *Ontario Specimen Jury Instructions (Criminal)*, Carswell 2003.